All For Jesus

ALL FOR JESUS

A CELEBRATION OF
THE 50TH ANNIVERSARY OF
COVENANT THEOLOGICAL SEMINARY

EDITORS: ROBERT A. PETERSON & SEAN MICHAEL LUCAS

MENTOR

© 2006 Covenant Theological Seminary
www.covenantseminary.edu

ISBN 1-84550-139-X
ISBN 978-1-84550-139-X

10 9 8 7 6 5 4 3 2 1

Published in 2006
in the
Mentor Imprint
by
Christian Focus Publications, Ltd.
Geanies House, Fearn, Tain,
Ross-shire, IV20 1TW, Great Britain.

www.christianfocus.com

Cover Design by Moose77.com

Printed and bound by
Bercker, Germany

TABLE OF CONTENTS

PREFACE

ifty years ago, a small, brand-new Christian college relocated to a twenty-acre parcel of land in the countryside of west St. Louis County, Missouri. The founder of the college was a man of great vision, passion, and determination. When he led the college to this new location, migrating from Pasadena, California, he decided that he would start a seminary as well. After all, his fledgling denomination, newly formed that year, would need ministers. But his vision for that new seminary included not merely the production of ministers and missionaries for the church. Rather, his desire was that everything that the seminary would teach and do would be for Jesus' glory. This determination was expressed in the selection of the seminary hymn, sung at every convocation and commencement since 1956: "All for Jesus." And so, Robert G. Rayburn helped to found Covenant Theological Seminary, along with Covenant College, to train ministers for the (then) Bible Presbyterian Church, Columbus Synod.

A lot has changed since that founding year. The college moved from its St. Louis location to a former resort hotel property near Chattanooga, Tennessee, in 1964. The denomination that the seminary served would change its name (to the Evangelical Presbyterian Church), merge with another denomination (to form the Reformed Presbyterian Church, Evangelical Synod), and then join and be received by still another denomination (the Presbyterian Church in America). Dr. Rayburn stepped down as president in 1977 and has been succeeded by three other men. And yet, with all that has changed, two things have remained at the center of what Covenant Seminary is about: we train gospel ministers for the church, and we seek to do it "all for Jesus."

The primary purpose for this collection of essays is to celebrate the fifty-year anniversary of Covenant Theological Seminary. However, the faculty did not desire simply to highlight current research areas, press certain ideological perspectives, or stir the pot on the latest theological fancies. Rather, we especially wanted to highlight the *Christ-centered* focus of our mission and callings at Covenant Seminary. This does not mean that some of these essays are not challenging; indeed, several of them stimulate serious thoughtful reflection. Nor does this mean that other essays do not seek to advance theological or exegetical discussion. What it does mean is that the majority of these essays seek to set forward a common understanding of the Seminary's mission as we seek "to train servants of the Triune God to walk with God, to interpret and communicate God's Word, and to lead God's people." And that common understanding is summed up in the words *Christ-centered.*

Therefore, the essays in this book shine the light on what it means to be Christ-centered from a variety of perspectives stemming from our colleagues' unique disciplines. For some, to be Christ-centered means having a grace-shaped approach to Scripture that enables Bible students and Christian preachers to read all of Scripture as teaching us something about the human predicament and the divine character. For others, to be Christ-centered represents a rallying-cry for entering into disciplines that have become profoundly secular – such as psychology, communication theory, the arts, or education – in order to bring the Christian gospel to bear. For still others, to be Christ-centered calls us to deal sensitively with distant cultures or forgotten pasts, seeking to understand that which is foreign to us with great sensitivity and graciousness in order to learn what God's calling to our contemporary age might be. And yet, each of these essays reveals a great desire and determination that what we do and think and write would be "all for Jesus."

There is another purpose, though, for these essays. Unbeknownst to three of our colleagues, these essays represent a kind of *Festschrift* for them as well. For, in the two-year period between 2006 and 2008, Lord willing, Robert I. Vasholz, David Clyde Jones, and David B. Calhoun will be celebrating significant anniversaries as well: in 2006, Vasholz turns seventy years old and will have served the seminary for over thirty years as an administrator and faculty member; in 2007, Jones will celebrate his seventieth birthday and forty years of teaching at the seminary; in 2008, having celebrated his seventieth birthday the year before, Calhoun will have maintained over forty-five years of association with the seminary, first as a student and then as a faculty member for over thirty years. We cannot imagine Covenant Seminary without these three men; they represent exactly what we mean when we talk about being Christ-centered. We join our voices to honor our fathers and brothers for their lifetime of service to the seminary and the church.

Dr. Robert I. Vasholz, professor of Old Testament, was born on September 27, 1936, in Kansas City, Missouri, to Jewish parents, Mr. and

Mrs. Frank Vasholz. Through the witness of neighbors, the Vasholz family turned to Jesus as God's Messiah and began attending Bible chapels in the Kansas City area. When it came time for college, Vasholz decided to attend Bob Jones University in Greenville, South Carolina. While at college, he met a Louisiana girl, Julia Martin; they were married on June 15, 1963, and they later had a daughter, Rachel Kay. Vasholz stayed at the university and received the Bachelor of Arts, Master of Arts, and Bachelor of Divinity degrees. After leaving Bob Jones, the Vasholz family came to St. Louis so that Bob could study at Covenant Seminary; in 1967, he received the Master of Theology degree for his thesis, "The Quotations and Allusions to the Pentateuch in the Old Testament." In 1972, he came back to the seminary to serve as director of admissions, assistant dean of students, and instructor of Hebrew. After being appointed to the faculty in 1975, he received a Master of Arts degree from St. Louis University and a Doctor of Theology degree from the University of Stellenbosch (South Africa) the following year. He has written a number of books, including *Hebrew Exercises: A Programmed Approach* (1981); *Data for the Sigla of the BHS* (1983); *The Old Testament Canon in the Old Testament Church* (1990); *Pillars of the Kingdom* (1997); and a forthcoming commentary on Leviticus.

Dr. David Clyde Jones, professor of systematic theology and ethics, was born on July 26, 1937, to Mr. and Mrs. J. Clyde Jones in Greenville, South Carolina. After graduating from Bryan College with his Bachelor of Arts degree in 1959, he attended Westminster Theological Seminary in Philadelphia. There he came under the influence of John Murray; generations of Covenant Seminary students have learned to love Murray through Jones' teaching ministry. He received his Bachelor of Divinity degree in 1962 and stayed on for two more years of study, graduating with the Master of Theology degree in 1964. Certainly, those two years of study were made more bearable because he married the former Sue Ellen Bilderback on June 17, 1962; the Joneses would have two sons, Mark David and Keith Andrew. After two years of pastoral ministry in the West Indies, the Joneses came to St. Louis so that David could join the faculty of Covenant Seminary in 1967. During his tenure at the seminary, he not only taught systematic theology and ethics to generations of students, but also received his Th.D. degree from Concordia Theological Seminary in St. Louis in 1970, served as dean of faculty at Covenant from 1978 to 1988, and authored a widely praised textbook on ethics, *Biblical Christian Ethics* (1994). In addition, Jones has been a churchman: he served as moderator of the General Synod for the Reformed Presbyterian Church, Evangelical Synod in 1978; served on a number of General Assembly study committees on ethical issues; and continues to serve his church through a wide-ranging preaching ministry and presbytery involvement.

Dr. David B. Calhoun, professor of church history, was born to Mr. and Mrs. David H. Calhoun in Flat Rock, Kentucky, on November 9, 1937. His father was a part-time pastor, serving churches throughout South Carolina. When it was time for college, Calhoun's choice was between Bob Jones University and Columbia Bible College; he decided to attend Columbia in 1955. He graduated with the Bachelor of Arts degree in 1959 and then decided to attend Covenant Theological Seminary that same year. After graduating from the Seminary, he decided to stay to pursue a Master of Theology degree, which he received in 1963 for his thesis, "The Ceremonial Law in the Psalms." He taught for four years at Columbia Bible College, and then served as principal at Jamaica Bible College for another four years. In 1972, he received a Master of Theology degree in New Testament from Princeton Theological Seminary, after which he served for four years as the coordinator for Ministries in Action (MIA), also in Jamaica. While there, he helped to co-author MIA's plan for church growth and also helped to develop a number of the early training materials for the PCA's Mission to the World agency. After receiving his Ph.D. degree in church history at Princeton Theological Seminary, Calhoun came back to his alma mater to teach in 1978. He has written a number of books, including a two-volume history of Princeton Seminary (1994, 1996); major local church histories for First Presbyterian Church, Columbia, South Carolina (1995), First Presbyterian Church, Augusta, Georgia (2004), and Independent Presbyterian Church, Savannah, Georgia (2005); and *Grace Abounding: The Life, Books, and Influence of John Bunyan* (2005).

It is our prayer that these essays will serve to honor our three fathers and brothers, as well as to celebrate this momentous anniversary in the life of Covenant Theological Seminary.[1] Above all, it is our prayer that this effort will be received by our Triune God as having been "all for Jesus." This project would not have been brought to completion without a number of people working together with a high degree of commitment and competence. In particular, we would like to thank our faculty colleagues, all of whom participated in and supported this project with their encouragement, prayers, and attention to deadlines. The real burden of the project was borne by our outstanding copyeditors, Beth Ann Patton, Rebecca Rine, Jim Pakala, and especially, Rick Matt. Rick's careful attention to detail, ready service, and yeoman's effort greatly improved every single essay. We are grateful as well for the support of the seminary's administration, especially Bryan Chapell and David Wicker. We are thankful to Willie MacKenzie and Christian Focus Publications for their gracious willingness to work with us on this project. And above all, we are grateful to all of the faculty, trustees, and supporters of Covenant Seminary throughout its fifty-year history: for they have helped us to fulfill our mission of living, thinking, writing, and teaching "all for Jesus."

Robert A. Peterson and Sean Michael Lucas

---

1. See Appendix A for complete bibliographies of Professors Vasholz, Jones, and Calhoun.

PART ONE:

CHRIST-CENTERED STORIES

1

HERE WE STAND:

Rooted in Grace for Reformation and Transformation

BRYAN CHAPELL
Professor of Practical Theology
President

My conscience is captive to the Word of God ... Here I stand.
I can do no other. God help me. Amen.

These legendary words of Martin Luther's undaunted defense of biblical teaching before a church court that was commanding him to recant or die stir our hearts even today. Courage rising from biblical conviction led Luther to stand on Reformation principles we yet affirm: Scripture is the sole authority for life and doctrine (*sola Scriptura*), faith is the sole instrument of our union with Christ (*sola fide*), and grace is the sole ground of our justification before God (*sola gratia*). These *solas* were the foundation of a clear and convincing stand that not only led many in Luther's church back to the Bible, but also led future generations into biblical faithfulness that transformed the world. When we see what God can do with a faithful stand, then we at Covenant Theological Seminary are compelled to ask, "Where do we stand and what transformations do we pray to see?" This question is especially appropriate as the seminary prepares to celebrate its Jubilee Year in 2006.

The current program of Covenant Seminary primarily derives from three historical distinctives and one contemporary development. The historical distinctives are: faithfulness to Scripture, commitment to a covenantal view of our Reformed heritage, and a priority on pastoral training. A renewed focus on the grace that is at the heart of Reformed theology and is the Bible's central message is the contemporary distinctive yet developing.

FAITHFULNESS TO SCRIPTURE

Scripture is the foundation of all we believe, teach, and do. Because all Scripture is inspired by God, it reflects his perfect, trustworthy, pure, sure, and altogether righteous character (cf. Ps. 19). Where the Bible speaks, God speaks. Thus, the Bible is our only infallible rule of faith and practice. By his providential provision of his enduring Word in our midst, the Lord provides all that we need for life and godliness (2 Peter 1:3). This gracious provision of divine truth demands that we both study to discern its meaning and bow before its truths. In these tasks we confess that we may err, but we remain confident that the Word of God properly interpreted and received is entirely true.

This commitment to biblical inerrancy is not merely the bedrock of our faith commitments but also the only rational basis of hope in a fallen world. For, if we have nothing but human opinion and preference to determine our way in this darkness, then the only voice that would return to us when we cry for help would be our own. God's transcendent truth in his revealed Word is our trustworthy and sufficient guide. We praise God for the unwavering commitment and constant zeal of Covenant Seminary's founding fathers to the truth of God's Word and by the grace of God commit ourselves to the same.

REFORMED AND COVENANTAL HERITAGE

Our understanding of the dependability of Scripture fuels our devotion to what it teaches. We sincerely receive and adopt the Westminster Confession of Faith and Catechisms as containing the system of doctrine taught in the Holy Scripture. We also affirm with our Confession that the final arbiter of all truth can be nothing but that which is revealed by the Holy Spirit in the Scriptures (WCF I.9–10). As the national seminary of the Presbyterian Church in America, we have promised to be true to the Holy Spirit's call to communicate the significance of his Word consistent with the principles of our heritage and the needs of our generation (*Semper Reformata, Semper Reformanda* – always Reformed, always being Reformed).

Consciousness of our constant dependence upon God's provision for every dimension of faithfulness drives us to a covenantal perspective of our Reformation distinctives. This covenantal perspective reveals the glory of God's initiating and maintaining his sovereign rule and redemptive plan over the whole of life. Out of his great power and love, he provides all creation around us and all aspects of his new creation for us. This confidence of his sovereign provision for every aspect of our salvation makes every sphere of life, family, church, and society subject to his rule and the legitimate concern of the citizens of his kingdom. Because the Bible declares that the earth is the Lord's and everything in it, we echo Abraham Kuyper's affirmation that there is not one square inch of the world over which the God of our creation and covenant does not stand and declare, "This is mine."

PASTORAL TRAINING PRIORITY

God's covenantal claims upon all of life motivate us to serve him by preparing those who will proclaim his salvation through Jesus Christ to all the world. Since its inception, Covenant Seminary has made training for pastoral ministry its primary focus. We believe the Lord has given us a special calling to give the highest quality academic and practical preparation to those who will serve as local church leaders. Consistent with this ministry, but secondary to it, has been our willingness to use the teaching resources concentrated at the seminary to prepare lay leaders more effectively to serve Christ in their churches and vocations. Our commitment to preparing church leadership rises from the biblical teaching that the church is the primary instrument of world transformation (Eph. 1:22-23). We are committed to preparing leaders who will transform the church that will transform the world in God's timing and for Christ's glory.

As a leader seminary for pastoral preparation, we have placed priorities on: expository preaching; teaching the Bible and systematic theology in the original languages of Scripture (i.e. an exegetical systematic); hiring faculty with pastoral experience as well as academic credentials; integrating church service with academic preparation; and creating a worshiping community that will provide students with a model of godliness, humility, forgiveness, and mutual love on which to base their future church leadership. We are committed to being more than a divinity school that credentials persons to be literate in the philosophical developments and historic debates of the church. We have seen the damage to the church caused by leaders trained merely polemically to do theology in the attack mode. We are committed to providing models of piety and learning because we believe that the health of the church depends upon leaders who can understand the gospel in terms of covenant relationships. Thus, we prioritize the relationships of students and professors as much as we do the content of classroom instruction. Our prayer is that we would not merely prepare the pastor's intellect but also serve the church by preparing well-trained pastors whose prayers echo John Calvin's: "My heart I offer you, O Lord, promptly and sincerely."

ROOTED IN GRACE

A grace (i.e. Christ-centered, or redemptive) focus has more recently risen from our historic distinctives as we have sought to address unhealthy responses made by the contemporary church to the erosion of biblical orthodoxy and the rise of cultural secularism. Alarm over the encroachments of secularism, while understandable, has led some too quickly to equate biblical spirituality with legalistic observance of Christian disciplines, cultural conservatism, or creedal compulsion. At the same time, concerns to boost the gospel's impact have too often led to an unreflective promotion of worldly satisfaction or success as evidence of God's blessing (demonstrated in churches promoting themselves through consumer strategies indistinguishable from secular appeals).

As contrary as these legalistic and consumer approaches to faith may seem, they actually spring from the same source – the error of attempting to establish one's standing before God on the basis of human achievement or acceptance. We believe the corrective for such deviations from biblical values is not new standards but rather a return to the heart center of our historic faith – the message of *sola gratia*. By reminding ourselves and others that grace alone is the source and sustenance of our salvation, we turn the heart to Christ for initial justification, continued sanctification, and ultimate glorification. Self-serving and performance-driven spiritualities die when we preach the gospel to ourselves each day. Such practice reminds us that we daily live and move and have our being only by the mercy of God and the provision of his Son. Knowing Jesus Christ personally, not merely academically, is the highest calling of every minister. This makes Christ's provision the central message of Scripture and the central truth of our lives that must continually humble us even as it eternally secures us. We will have failed in our ministry if our students do not know Jesus better when they leave this seminary than when they entered.

The more that we learn to see that all Scripture is Christ-centered, the more we will apply the Bible to our lives as the Savior intended. After his resurrection, on the road to Emmaus, Jesus revealed how all the Scriptures spoke of him (Luke 24:27). Similarly, the apostle Paul said that everything that was written aforetime was written to give us hope, and that he devoted his own ministry to knowing nothing but Jesus Christ and him crucified (Rom. 15:4; 1 Cor. 2:2). Such statements should not be simplistically interpreted as commanding nothing but a basic evangelism plan in every sermon and conversation. The Savior's and the apostles' teachings were far more than repetitious rehearsals of what happened on Calvary. We will not properly interpret Scripture by forcing every text into some mysterious or allegorical reference to Jesus. Not all texts mention Jesus, but all have a role in preparing us more fully to understand his person and work. The biblical words chosen by our founders from Colossians 1:18 for the crest of Covenant Seminary were: "In All Things Christ Preeminent." More and more, we are discovering the wisdom and glory of these words.

God's provision of saving, sustaining, and glorifying grace is the golden thread uniting all Christian Scripture and enabling all Christian faithfulness. Consistent adulation of the mercy of God most fully revealed in Christ motivates love for him and his service. Jesus said, "If you love me, you will obey what I command" (John 14:15). This means all works honoring God – including our personal sanctification, our love for neighbors and enemies, our zeal for world mission, our free offer of the gospel, our warnings of judgment, our promises of eternity, our mercy toward the poor and oppressed, our stewardship of God's world, our battles against Satan, our prayer for God's blessing, and our work toward Christ's coming – all find proper motivation and enablement in love for Christ. The wonder and joy of these truths for those preparing for church leadership comes with the understanding that God is not calling them to ministries of guilt-manipulation, arm twisting, and doctrinal haranguing.

As Christ's ministers emphasize grace, they are not compromising holiness but rather are promoting the power of the gospel for all endeavor that is truly Christian. Though the world may interpret grace as the license to do as it pleases, the Bible reminds us that grace teaches us to say no to ungodliness and worldly passions because it binds the human heart to the heart of the Savior (Titus 2:11-12). Of course, the secular and rebellious will use grace to excuse sin, but the principles of grace revealed in all of Scripture are the fuel of personal holiness and spiritual revival for those led by the Spirit.

REVIVED FOR THE GOSPEL

We acknowledge that Christ-centered instruction can be merely a reaction to various manifestations of legalism and false definitions of spirituality that have taken root in much of the evangelical world, including our own church. Yet, as we have carefully articulated what the Bible says about the role of grace in motivating and enabling holiness, we have dared to dream that the Lord might use us for a larger and more enduring purpose. Already we have seen many students experience a life-renewing understanding of the gospel (and we ourselves have been renewed) through a Christ-centered view of Scripture and life. This renewal comes when those who have long lived as though their justification is based on their sanctification (by making the indicatives of our union with Christ conditional on the satisfactory performance of his imperatives) understand that they are eternally held solely by the grace of God.

Resting on God's grace alone causes all of our and our students' perspectives and relationships to change. We learn to see ourselves as he sees us in Christ. We learn to treat others as he has treated us through Christ. As a consequence, the joy that is our strength floods into our lives to drive us to greater levels of Christian humility, love, and commitment. Thus, presenting the doctrines of grace in a warm and winsome way is not the converse of holy boldness; rather, courageous compassion is the compulsion of humbled and grateful hearts that have bowed before the wonders of God's sovereign mercy and now yearn to extend the blessings of his everlasting covenant to all he loves from every tribe, language, people, and nation. As the kindness of God has led to repentance and renewal among us, we are committed to a manner and ministry that reflects his grace (cf. Rom. 2:4; 1 Peter 3:15).

Our dream is that the personal revivals we see on campus would be a germinating force for a greater revival in our church, our country, and the whole world. We must be on guard not to grow so to prize the beauty of the grace message that God has brought to us (or our particular expression of it) that the gospel becomes a jewel that we admire and adore for the joy it brings us rather than for the hope it offers the world. We pray that the precious truths of grace God has allowed us to embrace will spark gospel proclamation rather than personal pride or institutional protectionism.

Finite creatures cannot make spiritual revival happen. The Spirit blows where he wills. However, if the Lord should choose to deepen and expand the spiritual awakening on our campus, then we should count ourselves doubly blessed as those chosen both to know grace and to share in the joys of its propagation. In recent years, we have been given reason to believe that the Lord may be preparing us to participate in such revival. As of this writing, the Lord has brought us seventeen consecutive years of record enrollments. He has blessed us with quality students and blessed those desiring to work in ministry with places in which to minister. The Lord has given us the shoulders of giants on which to stand in the form of faithful founding professors and long-term trustees who have loved the Gospel well and sacrificed to maintain its purity. Now we have a new generation of professors and seminary leaders who are equipping students so well for life in ministry that their retention rate is four times the average for all seminaries in North America. These students' love for the church and zeal for the Lord is so expansive that one in four will plant a new church within eight years of graduation.

Through the work of this seminary and others faithful to the gospel, God is preparing an army of ministers who love their Lord and his bride. The results cannot be predicted with certainty, but our calling *is* certain: we must provide the instruction that will prepare this army for the great purposes of their Savior, and then leave the timing of his victory to him.

CALLED FOR FUTURE FAITHFULNESS

There are those who say that nothing can come from seminaries but the inevitable corruption of gospel truths. These are the voices of the cynical selectively citing the history that supports the story they want to tell. But there is another story. I have had the privilege of visiting the actual classrooms of some of the great theologians of our heritage: Martin Luther, John Calvin, and Charles Hodge. None of their classrooms were as large as those that we now provide for our students on this campus. Yet, in the days when these godly instructors taught, students crowded by the scores into those small classrooms as the vanguard of great movements of the Spirit of God. Yes, it is true that sometimes error has sprung from seminaries; but it is also true that the greatest movements of revival and renewal have sprung from the classrooms of those who were faithful to Scripture. We should not prejudge how the Lord will use the work of our time. Ours is only to believe that God's Word does not return to him void. When we are faithful to him, he will use us beyond our fathoming for the furtherance of his kingdom.

At the convocation of the first Presbyterian seminary in America, three students gathered with one professor, Samuel Miller. To his fledgling student body, Dr. Miller gave this auspicious encouragement:

> From us blessings will flow to millions.
> The eyes of the church are upon us,
> The eyes of the angels are upon us,
> And, above all, the eyes of King Jesus are upon us.[1]

The words may have appeared presumptuous, even foolish, to those who viewed the few students gathered for pastoral preparation. Still, for those who looked with the eyes of faith, the words reflected neither presumption nor vanity. Those who know that God always blesses the faithful proclamation of his Word as he knows is best recognize that the reverberations of gospel truth will always echo beyond human limitations. If onlookers then saw in faith that millions could ultimately be touched by the ministries of three students, our hope should know no bounds as we consider the potential ministries of over a thousand who now gather each year to study at Covenant Theological seminary. It is not too great a thing to believe that the Lord could use this Seminary in his plans for renewal and revival. As we remain faithful to his gospel, he will use us as he knows is best. Glory for the gospel uncompromised is the promise of the Heavenly Father, and it is our hope for this generation and many more as we humble ourselves before the grace and truth of his Word.

1. Adapted from David B. Calhoun, *Princeton Seminary*, vol. 1: *Faith and Learning, 1812–1868* (Edinburgh: The Banner of Truth Trust, 1994), 33–4.

2

BY HIS GRACE, FOR HIS GLORY:
The Story of Covenant Theological Seminary

DAVID B. CALHOUN
Professor of Church History

---

n 1956, Covenant Theological Seminary was founded a few miles from the great river that divides the United States into the East and the West, at just about the place where the North becomes the South and the South becomes the North. For the little school that, in fifty years, would draw students from all fifty states and from many foreign countries, this strategic location near the nation's population center was providential. By 2006, Covenant Seminary is among the largest seminaries in North America, with a student body of more than a thousand.

AN AUDACIOUS ACT OF FAITH: THE EARLY YEARS

When it began, Covenant was the theological seminary for the Bible Presbyterian Church, one part of the small movement in the 1930s to preserve historic Reformed Christianity in American Presbyterianism. The roots of the Bible Presbyterian Church reached back to the first American Presbytery of 1706, and the seminary in St. Louis stood in the tradition of the first theological schools of the American Presbyterian church – the Log College at Neshaminy, Pennsylvania, and the college and seminary at Princeton.

It was an audacious decision (or an act of great faith) for 9,000 Bible Presbyterians to attempt to create and support a college and a seminary. Controversy in the Bible Presbyterian Church (centering on the program and methods of Carl McIntire, one of the denomination's most prominent and influential leaders) led to the creaton of two Bible Presbyterian denominations – Collingswood Synod and Columbus Synod – in 1955. As a result of this rift,

Robert G. Rayburn, the president of Highland College, a small independent college in Pasadena, California, and most of the faculty and students of that institution, left Highland to begin a new college under the control of the Bible Presbyterian Church (Columbus Synod). Twenty-three students were enrolled during the school's first year.

The college was named "Covenant" – an expression used almost 300 times in the Bible to set forth God's grace to his people and his people's God-given response to that grace. It was also a word that commemorated the heroic struggle of Scottish Presbyterians to found and maintain a church for "Christ's crown and covenant" against the claims and pretensions of popes, bishops, and kings. Signs of Scottish tradition abounded at Covenant College – the symbol of the thistle on banners and publications, *Bagpipe* and *Tartan* as names for the student newspaper and yearbook, and a snack shop called the "Blink," an allusion to the brief period of respite for the persecuted Covenanters.

In 1956, Covenant College moved from Pasadena to Creve Coeur in St. Louis County, Missouri. Near the center of the greater St. Louis area today, in 1956 Creve Coeur was thought to be "way out in the country" by St. Louis residents. The new campus comprised twenty-one acres of hilly, wooded land, with a solidly built house of concrete and steel, a log cabin, and a few small buildings and sheds. Originally a private estate, the property had for some years been leased by the Roman Catholic Passionist Fathers for a retreat center. It seemed perfect for Covenant College, but initially beyond the financial reach of the trustees and the Bible Presbyterian denomination, until money from a charitable trust managed by Mr. Albert N. Edwards, a partner of the brokerage firm of A. G. Edwards and Sons, made the purchase possible. The cost for the house and property was $160,000. A president's home was built on the campus and faculty homes (which also provided offices and classrooms for the Seminary) were put up along Conway Road – appropriately named for a Kentuckian who was one of the first Presbyterian elders in the territory of Missouri.

Over the summer of 1956, several faculty and students moved from California to St. Louis, while others came from the East Coast. Covenant had little money, so the professors, with pioneering spirit, rented trucks and drove themselves and their possessions to St. Louis. Dr. J. Oliver Buswell, Jr., outstanding scholar and former college president, amused his colleagues with the story of how, dressed in overalls and driving a truck, he pulled into a motel to stop for the night, only to be told by the clerk that the motel did not accept truck drivers!

During its first year, Covenant Seminary enrolled eleven students. One came as a transfer student from another seminary because, he said, he wanted to be taught "by the godly scholars who had gathered to start the new school." "They were men of vision," he remembered many years later, "and that vision was contagious. They knew the Bible and how to teach it. The spiritual atmosphere was dynamic. God was at work."[2] Another student wrote that "the faculty opened their hearts, homes and minds to the students with a great blend of scholarship and piety."[3]

Professors and their families (most of whom lived on the campus), along with the college and seminary students, formed a close, caring community. The students enjoyed playing with Max, Dr. Rayburn's boxer, who had the unusual habit of chewing on rocks. Members of First Bible Presbyterian Church, which in 1954 had moved from the city to its new building on Ballas Road not far from the campus, welcomed students and faculty. Women from the church harvested apples from the campus trees and made applesauce to enhance the cafeteria meals. First Bible Presbyterian Church (in 1961, it became The Covenant Presbyterian Church of St. Louis) became the church home for many students and faculty. For a time, the Seminary held chapel services and some classes at the church, as the growing enrollment of both the college and the seminary strained campus facilities. On the occasion of the church's fiftieth anniversary in 1989, Seminary president Paul Kooistra wrote to the congregation, "Covenant Seminary would not exist without the leadership and support of Covenant Church. The first meetings of the seminary board were held in the pastor's office of Covenant Church."[4] The pastor of Covenant Church was the Reverend Donald MacNair, who in 1964 became director of National Presbyterian Missions, the denomination's home missions agency. Through the years, until his death on March 3, 2001, Dr. MacNair was a valued adjunct professor of practical theology at Covenant Seminary.

Covenant Seminary announced its doctrinal standards as "first, the Bible as the infallible Word of God, and, second, the Westminster Confession and Catechisms as setting forth the system of doctrine taught in the Bible."[5] Throughout its history, Covenant Seminary has required each member of the faculty and board of trustees to subscribe to the Westminster Confession of Faith and Catechisms annually in writing.

The Seminary organized its curriculum "around the study of the Bible itself, interpreted with the use of the original languages." A third of the substantial curriculum was in Old Testament studies, and Hebrew and Greek were prerequisites for all the upper level courses. In addition to beginning and intermediate Hebrew, the Seminary's first catalogue listed courses in advanced Hebrew grammar and syntax, elementary Syriac, elementary Arabic, and elements of Babylonian! "Auxiliary courses" – such as those in Bible introduction, apologetics, and church history – complemented Bible study, the catalogue stated, and "a synthesis and an application" were made in systematic and practical theology.[6]

The original seminary faculty was a godly, gifted, and colorful group of men. Robert G. Rayburn was the first president of the college and seminary. The Kansas-born Rayburn attended Wheaton College, Omaha Presbyterian

Theological Seminary, and Dallas Theological Seminary, where he earned the Doctor of Theology degree. His earliest ambition was to become a concert pianist, but during his sophomore year at Wheaton, to the great joy of his parents, he felt that God was calling him to the ministry. Rayburn served Presbyterian churches in Nebraska and Texas, then became a military chaplain in Europe and later in Korea with the 187th Airborne. His book *Fight the Good Fight* applies his experiences in the Korean War to living the Christian life.[7] Rayburn was deposed from the ministry by the Presbyterian Church in the United States of America (PCUSA) on the suspicion that he was not loyal to the denomination's program. He served the non-denominational College Church of Wheaton, Illinois, for three years, and then was called to be president of Highland College in Pasadena, California.

In addition to serving as president of Covenant College and Seminary, Dr. Rayburn taught the seminary's courses in practical theology and homiletics. Rayburn's commitment to producing able expositors and preachers of the Bible has marked Covenant Seminary's entire history. Rayburn taught a class in biblical worship that led to his highly respected book, *O Come, Let Us Worship*.[8]

In every sense of the word, Dr. Rayburn was the leader of the two schools. His example and teaching became "law" for many students, who feared doing anything that would displease Dr. Rayburn – although the college students were a little more daring than the seminary students!

James Oliver Buswell, Jr., became dean of Covenant Seminary and taught theology and church history. Buswell grew up in Wisconsin, where his father was a missionary among the loggers of the North Woods. Buswell graduated from the University of Minnesota, studied for the ministry at McCormick Theological Seminary, served as a chaplain during World War I (he was wounded in the leg by shrapnel), pastored congregations of the Presbyterian and Reformed Church in America, and in 1926 was elected the third president of Wheaton College. At thirty-one years of age, he was the youngest college president in the United States. During his tenure at Wheaton, Buswell led the college to full academic accreditation, recruited a strong faculty, and brought national recognition for Wheaton as an outstanding Christian liberal arts college. Despite his accomplishments, Dr. Buswell was asked by the Wheaton trustees to resign because they felt that the college president should not be involved in denominational controversies such as the one taking place in the PCUSA. In 1936, Buswell was deposed by his presbytery (an act upheld by the General Assembly of the PCUSA) for his role in founding and supporting the Independent Board for Presbyterian Foreign Missions.

Covenant Seminary students were impressed with Buswell's knowledge (he learned by memory large parts of the Greek New Testament), his vigorous wood-chopping for exercise, and his love of teaching (which, he said, he would continue to do in heaven, but the angels would take the roll and grade the papers). One of those students, William S. Barker, wrote:

A crackling fire would warm the early morning winter class in the basement office/classroom of Dr. Buswell on the campus of Covenant Seminary in the late 1950s. The firewood had been chopped by the professor himself. The warmth of the fire might have a soporific effect on those students who had stayed up too long over the books the night before, but this would generally be overcome by the personal warmth of the teacher, whose wood-chopping energy carried over into the classroom.[9]

When Dr. Buswell's two-volume *Systematic Theology of the Christian Religion* came out in 1962 and 1963, F. F. Bruce found a "welcome freshness" in Buswell's organization, style, and language and praised the work as "so thoroughly biblical." "It is based," Bruce wrote, "from first to last on an intelligent belief in the authority of Holy Scripture."[10] In the 1976 commemorative issue of *Presbyterion* (Covenant Seminary's journal) honoring Buswell on his retirement from the Seminary, Kenneth Kantzer wrote: "Among the Evangelical theologians of his own day ... he looms rather as a giant figure with few peers and none who stood taller."[11] Carl F. H. Henry wrote that Buswell did what was given him to do "with fidelity and dignity." Many of Buswell's students and associates, he added, retain "some unpaid and unpayable debt to J. Oliver Buswell, Jr."[12]

Buswell loved his denomination, the Bible Presbyterian Church, but did not idealize it. He recognized its many problems. John W. Sanderson, Jr., who in 1976 became professor of biblical theology at Covenant Seminary, remembered a conversation with Buswell in which the young Sanderson unburdened his heart about the conditions of the denomination and his expectations for it. Buswell listened thoughtfully and replied, "It is a mess. But it's the best mess there is."[13]

Robert Laird Harris taught Old Testament at Covenant Seminary. Intending to pursue a career in engineering, Harris came to Washington University in St. Louis for graduate study. At Memorial Presbyterian Church, near the Washington University campus, Harris received God's call to the ministry. Also at Memorial, he met J. Gresham Machen, who came to the church for a Bible conference. Harris studied at Westminster Theological Seminary in Philadelphia, earned a doctorate from Dropsie University, and taught at Faith Theological Seminary in Wilmington, Delaware, before joining the faculty at Covenant Seminary in 1956.

Just before retiring from teaching at Covenant Seminary in 1981, Dr. Harris wrote to prospective students, stating his own life commitment as well as summarizing the passion and purpose of Covenant Seminary:

> I was called to the ministry myself forty-seven years ago out of graduate study in chemistry, and I have always praised the Lord for giving me this call and opportunity. The needs of the world for the gospel are so great and the command of Christ is so explicit and his promises so wonderful that we are thankful indeed to see you also moved to take part in this ministry with

us. We at Covenant believe that basic to all these fields of service is, first, a wholesouled commitment to Christ and his work and, second, a thorough grounding in the content, background, and exegesis of the Word of God. The world is full of conflicting voices and a large section of protestant Christianity is given over to a powerless gospel that is not the gospel. All of us at Covenant believe in the Bible's truth and its power to save and bless the souls of men. You ought to settle for nothing less than a theological education from this historic Christian perspective.[14]

Elmer Smick, pastor and scholar (his Ph.D. was from Dropsie University), taught Hebrew and Old Testament. Wilber Wallis (also a Ph.D. from Dropsie University) taught Greek and New Testament. An early student remembered that the kindly Dr. Wallis "could almost make you feel smart as he gave a right application to your wrong answer."[15] William A. Sanderson taught a variety of courses in both the college and seminary (as indeed did all the faculty). Peter Stam was dean of students. Rudolph Schmidt was registrar.

John W. Sanderson, Jr., taught philosophy and apologetics for a year, and then, for several years, came to give Bible lectures for the entire student body. Sanderson had studied at Wheaton College and Faith Seminary, and served as the first pastor of the First Bible Presbyterian Church of St. Louis (from 1940 to 1943). He taught at Faith Seminary and later at Westminster Seminary. From 1963 to 1969 Sanderson was dean of faculty at Covenant College. In 1976, he returned to the resident faculty of the Seminary. William S. Barker describes Sanderson's "masterful teaching style, characterized by particularly apt illustrations that helped to clarify complex subjects, and a preaching style that could cause chapel listeners to ponder God's truth during what became known as the 'Sandersonian pause.'"[16]

Francis A. Schaeffer had a close connection with Covenant Seminary from its beginning. Schaeffer, a friend of Rayburn and the other Covenant faculty, had served as pastor of the First Bible Presbyterian Church of St. Louis from 1943 to 1947, when he and his wife, Edith, moved to Switzerland to minister to children. (The Schaeffers had founded an organization called Children for Christ in 1945.) In 1955, they began L'Abri Fellowship, a ministry to college students and others with intellectual questions about the Christian faith. Schaeffer lectured regularly, usually every other year, at Covenant Seminary. For those several weeks he was an exotic figure on campus. "Typically dressed in a turtle-neck sweater and knickers with knee-sox, with long hair and a goatee," writes William Barker, "he spoke with passion about the contemporary currents of culture and the need for communicating biblical truth and Christian love into the world."[17]

Schaeffer appreciated Covenant Seminary. He wrote:

Covenant Theological Seminary means a great deal to me personally. I am thankful for its existence in this day of such confusion. Above everything else

I am glad that it has stood completely firm concerning the Scriptures and holds without compromise or "waffling" the fact that the Bible is without error, not only when it speaks of religious things but when it speaks of history and those things which touch upon science. It also holds that the Bible gives us absolutes concerning right and wrong in the area of human behavior. At the same time I am glad for the scholarship of the faculty at Covenant Seminary, and I am thankful that its teaching is not isolated from the needs of the twentieth-century world but takes into account the specific needs of our own generation.[18]

Pastor-scholar W. Harold Mare (his Ph.D. was from the University of Pennsylvania) joined the Covenant faculty in 1963, after ten years of pastoral ministry. Dr. Mare developed the W. Harold Mare Institute for Biblical and Archaeological Studies at the Seminary with a collection of hundreds of ancient artifacts, many of them discovered by Mare himself and his teams of Covenant students during their excavations at the ancient city of Abila of the Decapolis in Jordan.

Covenant Seminary's founders were battle-scarred veterans of the "fundamentalist–modernist" controversy of the early twentieth century. At great personal cost, they had taken their stand for historic Christianity against a modern version of the Christian faith that, they believed, compromised and undermined the faith "once delivered to the saints." They stood for the "fundamentals" – the virgin birth of Christ, the miracles, the blood atonement, and the bodily resurrection of Christ – and the doctrine that undergirded these and other doctrines of true Christianity: the inerrancy of Scripture. Like their admired predecessors – the men of "Old Princeton," such as J. Gresham Machen and Robert Dick Wilson – they taught and defended these doctrines with all the learning and scholarship at their disposal. Kenneth Kantzer's description of J. Oliver Buswell could be applied aptly to each of the original Covenant faculty: "Here was a Fundamentalist with a wide-open creative mind."[19]

There was a breadth of view at Covenant Seminary toward Bible-believing Christians of different theological persuasions. The Reformed faith was upheld as the most biblical system of doctrine, but those who saw the Bible differently, such as dispensationalists and charismatics, were accepted as true Christians – even while they were gently corrected for their errors. The one group that fell outside the Covenant faculty's generosity were those theological conservatives who chose to remain within the mainline denominations to attempt to bring about reform from within. These people, especially those who remained in the PCUSA, were seen as compromisers and came in for criticism. Years later, Francis Schaeffer, reflecting on the division in the PCUSA, deplored the fact that "true brethren" who did not "feel led by the Lord" to leave the PCUSA were not treated by their seceding brethren with dignity and Christian love.[20]

With all its strengths – scholarly teaching; warm, evangelical piety; and solid emphasis on the inerrancy of the Bible – there were nonetheless some areas of weakness at Covenant Seminary. The fear of liberalism tended to set the agenda for the school, limiting courses such as church history from offering a wider perspective. The history of struggles within the Bible Presbyterian Church, and the ongoing legacy of those struggles, resulted in much energy being expended on unedifying squabbles. The importance of minor doctrines, such as premillennialism, was exaggerated, and certain views of Christian living – especially total abstinence from alcoholic beverages – became absolutes. Biblical theology and covenant theology were neglected. Calvin was honored but not read.

During Covenant's early years, financial support came mostly from donors making small contributions. The seminary appealed to its little denomination and people responded, many sending one dollar a month in an envelope supplied for that purpose. Sometimes salaries were not paid on time, occasionally falling as much as three months behind. Faculty wives sought employment, and some professors found additional part-time work. Looking back to these early years, a later president of the seminary commented:

> No one thought that Covenant Seminary would amount to anything. What we see before us is God's free grace as he has seen fit to bless this ministry. How humbling it is for all of us when we look back at the sacrifice others have made to realize that we are nothing but instruments, and all that we see that is good and pure and worth talking about comes because of the gracious and mighty hand of our God.[21]

GREAT GAINS AND GROWING PAINS:
FACING THE CHALLENGES OF THE 1960S AND 1970S

The main building on the Covenant campus was named Edwards Hall in appreciation for the generous support of the Edwards family – Albert N. Edwards, who had provided the money to ensure the purchase of the property, and his nephew Presley W. Edwards, a trustee of Covenant College and Seminary and the main source of financial support of the seminary in its early years.

In 1961, a large two-story house on the grounds of nearby St. John's Mercy Hospital was donated by the Sisters of Mercy and moved down Conway Road to be remodeled and expanded as the administration building for the college and seminary. Through the years, this building would also house the library for a time and serve temporarily as a residence for male students. Today, in 2006, the building is still the home of the seminary's administrative offices.

The little campus was no longer adequate for the needs of two growing institutions. Covenant College had grown to almost 150 students and the seminary to 50. A nationwide search led to the purchase of an ideal campus on

Lookout Mountain, Georgia, near Chattanooga, Tennessee. Some observers thought that both the seminary and the college should move to Lookout Mountain, but the board decided that the seminary should remain in St. Louis, where good facilities for theological research were available.

In 1964, the college students made the move to the new college campus. College Dean of Faculty John Sanderson, who had taught at both the college and the seminary, believed that the move would be good for both institutions. Not only would there now be room to grow for both college and seminary, but, Sanderson believed, the seminary would be forced to "stand more on its own." Sanderson's thoughts on the subject were summarized by a writer for *The Evangelical Presbyterian Reporter* in a 1964 interview: "Although vital in its ministry, the seminary has sometimes taken a back seat to the more colorful world of collegiate activities."[22]

For a year, Dr. Rayburn continued to serve as president of both institutions, commuting weekly between St. Louis and Chattanooga. He rode an evening train from St. Louis, sleeping in a Pullman car, before doing two days of teaching and administrative work at the college and returning to St. Louis for similar tasks at the seminary. After a year with this arrangement, the board of trustees of the two schools decided that Rayburn should continue as president of Covenant Seminary, and Dr. Marion D. Barnes came to the college as its president.

In 1962, the Bible Presbyterian Church (Columbus Synod), the supporting denomination of Covenant College and Seminary, changed its name to the Evangelical Presbyterian Church (EPC). In 1965, the EPC united with the smaller Reformed Presbyterian Church – a denomination with roots reaching back to the days of the Covenanters of Scotland – and became the Reformed Presbyterian Church, Evangelical Synod.

J. Oliver Buswell, Jr., retired in 1970 at the age of seventy-five. He brought the commencement address that year, delivered without notes, on the subject of "The Christian's Attitude Toward the Passage of Time." In introducing Dr. Buswell, President Rayburn said, "Covenant Theological Seminary itself will always through the years ahead be a monument to the wisdom and dedication of this great man."[23]

In 1967, David C. Jones joined the Covenant Seminary faculty to teach in the area of theology. He was the first of a new generation of faculty who would consolidate the work of the founders.[24] In 1972, William S. Barker accepted a call to be academic dean and professor of church history at the Seminary. He was the first graduate of the institution to serve on its faculty.

In 1975, *Presbyterion: Covenant Seminary Review* was launched as "an extension of the seminary's calling and task." The introductory editorial stated that "we will be writing for working ministers, ruling elders and informed laymen."[25]

Upon Dr. Rayburn's retirement, Dr. Barker became the second president of Covenant Theological Seminary in 1977. His inaugural address from Matthew 28:16-20 was entitled "The Lordship of Jesus and the Preparation of His Servants." Barker told the Seminary audience:

> As I meditated upon my calling, I was reminded by one of the trustees yesterday of Joshua. Another one reminded me of the Abrahamic promises. "God will be our God and we shall be his people" is echoed all the way through the Bible. I have been reflecting also upon Moses as he said to the Lord, "If thy presence does not go with us, do not lead us up from here." We dare not go unless the Spirit of Christ fills us, goes with us, and leads us.[26]

A St. Louis native and part of the Edwards family that had so generously supported the seminary in its early years, Will Barker graduated from Country Day School, Princeton University (with high honors and elected to Phi Beta Kappa), Cornell (where he earned a Master of Arts degree in history), and Covenant Seminary. Barker served as pastor of the Hazelwood Reformed Presbyterian Church. In 1964, he went with Covenant College to Lookout Mountain, where he was professor of history (and dean of faculty for three years). He completed his Ph.D. in church history at the Divinity School of Vanderbilt University in 1967. Barker's doctoral dissertation was "The Writings of John Bradford: An Example of English Reformation Piety."

During a year-long sabbatical following his retirement from the presidency, Dr. Rayburn taught at the China Graduate School of Theology in Hong Kong and the Presbyterian Theological Seminary in India. He returned to Covenant Seminary as chairman of the Practical Theology Department.

During these years, the seminary was experiencing some "growing pains." Facilities were crowded because of increased enrollment, and new buildings were added to the campus. On May 18, 1979, the Robert G. Rayburn Chapel was dedicated. (The J. L. Mabee Foundation of Tulsa, Oklahoma, provided substantial financial support for the chapel, as it did also for the J. Oliver Buswell, Jr., Library that was completed in 1975). A 114-year-old tracker pipe organ was moved from Cincinnati (where it had served a Jewish temple and then a Roman Catholic church) to St. Louis and installed in the new chapel.

In July 1979, Covenant Seminary was deeply saddened by the death of Professor J. Barton Payne, when he fell while climbing Mount Fuji in Japan. The noted Old Testament scholar had joined the Covenant faculty in 1972.

Dr. Rayburn had been diagnosed with cancer in February 1976. After radiation treatment in March, he was pronounced cancer-free in June. Early in 1981, Dr. Rayburn shocked the seminary community when he announced in chapel one morning that the cancer had returned. After a short, frank, moving account of his situation and what, according to his doctor, lay ahead of him, he concluded by asking the seminary congregation to join him in singing the hymn,

Whate'er my God ordains is right: his holy will abideth;
I will be still whate'er he doth, and follow where he guideth.
He is my God; though dark my road, he holds me that I shall not fall:
Wherefore to him I leave it all.[27]

For the seminary's twenty-fifth anniversary in 1981, Francis Schaeffer gave the baccalaureate sermon and R. C. Sproul the commencement address. Laird Harris retired, honored by a tribute from the board of trustees that read: "In your knowledge, your kindness, your extraordinary humility, your patience, your practical realism and your delightful humor, we join your students – 'You have been our teacher.'"[28]

Dr. Barker said at the seminary's twenty-fifth anniversary that "the passage of twenty-five years marks a generation .... A major part of one generation's responsibility is to pass on to the next generation the knowledge of what God has done."[29] As Covenant Seminary moved into its second generation, the administration and faculty attempted to keep alive and strengthen the vision of the founders. While maintaining its concern for "the purity of the visible church," the seminary, however, cautiously moved away from its strict separatist position in several important areas. A seminary catalogue contained the statement: "Study at Covenant Theological Seminary is not preparation for a restricted ministry tied to traditions of a past generation, but the building of a vital foundation for those who take seriously the Saviour's commission and are determined to be qualified for effective witness in the contemporary age."[30]

In its early years, Covenant's leaders had resisted seeking accreditation out of fear of worldly entanglements and theological compromise. Those doubts were eventually resolved, and Dr. Barker and Dr. David Jones, who became academic dean in 1977, led the seminary into full accreditation with the North Central Association of Colleges and Schools (NCA) and the Association of Theological Schools (ATS) by June 1983. Regional accreditation (NCA) demonstrated that the seminary's work met the general academic standards for graduate education. Professional accreditation (ATS) expanded the seminary's influence. In time, Covenant personnel would take leadership roles in the accrediting agencies.

Covenant also joined the St. Louis Theological Consortium, organized to promote cooperation and dialogue among various theological traditions.[31] Covenant's faculty members expanded their conference participation beyond the Evangelical Theological Society to include the American Academy of Religion/Society of Biblical Literature.

David Jones summed up Covenant's "second generation" "as being less parochial, less defensive, more involved in broader theological culture, and, theologically, more appreciative of standing in the Reformed tradition."[32]

During the 1980s, tensions developed in the Covenant Seminary faculty over a number of issues: the precise definition of the Reformed faith, the meaning of subscription to the Westminster Confession of Faith, the trial of a local minister by the presbytery, and the training of women students at the seminary. The seminary struggled to maintain "the unity of the Spirit in the bond of peace" (Eph. 4:3), but it was a difficult time for the Covenant family.

In 1982, a "Joining and Receiving" brought together the Reformed Presbyterian Church, Evangelical Synod (RPCES), and the Presbyterian Church in America (PCA) – uniting many Bible-believing Presbyterians of the North and the South. This unusual and historic church union, orchestrated by a number of people – including Donald MacNair, a long-time adjunct professor at Covenant Seminary – was furthered by Dr. Barker and supported by the Covenant faculty. The PCA did not have a college and seminary of its own until 1982, when Covenant College and Covenant Seminary became part of the enlarged denomination. Of this, Dr. Rayburn wrote:

> The joining of the Reformed Presbyterian Church, Evangelical Synod, with the Presbyterian Church in America was accomplished with a firm agreement that both of the educational institutions would remain permanently under the control of the General Assembly of the combined church rather than being changed to independent institutions as some suggested at the time. That there should be direct accountability to the courts of the church on the part of these two educational institutions has been a firmly held conviction of those who founded the schools, because the college and seminary are directly involved in the progress and spiritual growth of the church.[33]

Covenant Seminary was now the national seminary of the PCA – the only seminary whose board of trustees was elected by and responsible to that denomination.

FROM JERUSALEM TO THE ENDS OF THE EARTH:
EXPANDING INFLUENCE IN THE 1980s

Dr. Barker, whose tenure was marked by spirituality, scholarship, and humility, resigned as president of Covenant Seminary in 1984. He felt that, after seven years, he had contributed what he could to the seminary and that it was time for new leadership. Dr. Barker became the editor of the *Presbyterian Journal*, in which capacity he helped with the further development of the PCA. In 1987, he went to Westminster Theological Seminary in Philadelphia as professor of church history. In 1991, he became academic dean at Westminster. Dr. Barker retired in 2000 and returned to St. Louis, where he once again teaches at Covenant Seminary as adjunct professor of church history. Covenant Seminary professor Robert A. Peterson, commenting on *Word to the World: The Collected Writings of William S. Barker*, aptly summarized the life and ministry of Covenant Seminary's second president as "a combination of forthrightness and fairness, prudence and much wise counsel, a reverent, even worshipful, tone, and, above all, the fruit of a mind and heart devoted to the Bible."[34]

Minnesota native Paul Kooistra (his grandparents had come from the Netherlands to America) became Covenant Seminary's third president in 1985. A graduate of the University of Minnesota, Columbia Theological Seminary, and the University of Alabama, Kooistra brought to the Seminary experience in pastoral ministry and teaching at Belhaven College and Reformed Theological Seminary. Dr. Kooistra was excited to come to Covenant Seminary for two reasons:

> First, it is the denominational seminary of the PCA. I believe the denominational seminary will help to build an identity for the PCA, which the denomination critically needs. Second, we're at a particularly exciting time in the life of conservative and Reformed seminaries. There is a great need for creative growth and development to realize our full potential.[35]

Dr. Kooistra emphasized that Covenant Seminary must be faithful to the teaching of the Bible and "hold tenaciously to our understanding of what it means to be Reformed." We must, however, be Reformed "in a warm and winsome way," not "believing that we must do battle with believers who differ. If we are going to build a Reformed movement in America we must see Satan as the enemy, not those with divergent views in non-essentials. Simply put, faith which is not expressed in love is not biblical faith, and therefore is not Reformed."[36] Kooistra set out to build a faculty "deeply committed to the Lord Jesus Christ and to the Reformed faith, who have pastoral hearts, and who can communicate with students."[37] He often reminded the faculty and students that "a seminary education is successful only if, at its end, the student knows Jesus Christ more intimately than at its beginning."[38]

Covenant continued to move out of its ecclesiastical isolation and reach out to evangelical students in St. Louis and beyond. The beginning of two PCA churches in St. Louis City, Grace and Peace Fellowship in 1969 and New City Fellowship in 1992, awakened the seminary's students to the possibility of urban ministry. An Urban Ministry Initiative was begun in 2001 to serve the city and prepare students for ministry in the world's urban areas.

African-American students from the St. Louis area began to enroll at Covenant Seminary, and African-American graduates led a movement within their churches to teach and promote the Reformed faith in St. Louis. The Sovereign Grace Conferences featured speakers such as John Piper and Bryan Chapell. Michael Campbell, 1994 Master of Divinity graduate of Covenant Seminary and a respected pastor and leader in the PCA, has expressed well what is the conviction and goal of Covenant: "Christ has made us black, white, Hispanic, American, Caribbean, Latin American, and He has made us one. We are to be about recognizing what Christ has done and living it out."[39]

Philip Douglass came to Covenant Seminary to teach in the area of practical theology in 1986, after fourteen years in pastoral ministry in the Washington, D.C., area, where he planted three churches. Dr. Douglass' experience and enthusiasm for church planting led to many Covenant students being called into this work. Over half of the seminary's Master of Divinity graduates from 1987 to 2004 have planted churches![40]

Presbyterian Mission International (PMI) was founded in 1988 and operated by Covenant Seminary faculty, staff, and area pastors and church leaders to enable international graduates of the seminary to return to their homelands as full-time Christian workers. The first PMI missionary was Khen Tombing (from Manipur, India); by 2006, over thirty outstanding Covenant-trained nationals were receiving support through PMI for graduate study, evangelism, and church-planting ministries on four continents.

In 1989, the Francis A. Schaeffer Institute (FSI) was established at Covenant Seminary. Jerram Barrs came from England to lead the work of FSI, serving as its Resident Scholar, as well as professor of Christian studies and contemporary culture for the seminary. Barrs, who was converted to Christ while a student at the University of Manchester, had studied with Francis Schaeffer at L'Abri in Switzerland (where Jerram met his wife, Vicki). On Dr. Schaeffer's advice, Barrs came to Covenant Seminary to study in the fall of 1968. After graduating, Jerram and Vicki went to England, where they served at the English L'Abri for sixteen years. Jerram, with several others, also pastored a congregation of the International Presbyterian Church.

Jerram Barrs explained that FSI sought "to take those biblical emphases central to the life and work of Francis and Edith Schaeffer that God so richly used and make them part of the purpose and ministry of Covenant Theological Seminary." Barrs listed seven ways in which this would be done.

1) Devotion to Christ and a reality of prayer as we live in daily dependence upon the Lord.
2) Confidence in biblical truth.
3) Commitment to genuine humanness expressed in servanthood and love, and displayed in supernaturally restored relationships.
4) Commitment to apply God's truth to the whole of life and to encourage Christians to make a contribution to the wider culture.
5) The appreciation of God's gifts in all of life.
6) The need to understand the culture we live in and communicate to it.
7) The preparedness to give honest answers to honest questions in such a way that the unbeliever may be faced with the truth claims of Christianity.[41]

The Schaeffer Institute mission statement sums up the purpose of FSI as the training of "God's servants to demonstrate compassionately and defend reasonably the claims of Christ upon the whole of life."[42] Twice-yearly lectureships by leading Christian thinkers in many fields (the Francis A.

Schaeffer Lectures), and other FSI ministries such as Apologetics on Saturday, Art at the Institute, and Friday Nights at the Institute, focused the Covenant Seminary community on the need to understand modern culture and respectfully communicate the gospel to modern people. Former FSI Director Wade Bradshaw moved the Friday Nights at the Institute series from campus to off-campus secular bookstores in order to reach more non-Christians with a Christian interpretation of life and the arts. Later Director Luke Bobo comments: "Our day and age is not unlike the apostle Paul's day – people are interested in ideas. People come to bookstores ready to engage with new ideas – and for some, Christianity is a new idea."[43]

Robert G. Rayburn, Covenant's founding president, died on January 5, 1990. The funeral was conducted on January 13 in Rayburn Chapel on the Covenant Seminary campus. From the J. S. Bach prelude to the choral benediction, the impressive service carefully followed Dr. Rayburn's own teaching on worship. Dr. Rayburn's son, Dr. Robert S. Rayburn (a 1975 Covenant Seminary graduate and the pastor of Faith Presbyterian Church in Tacoma, Washington), preached the sermon, "The Christian's Greatest Means of Grace," from Philippians 1:18-26.[44]

Between 1989 and 1991, forty-eight student apartments were built on campus, greatly enhancing Covenant's commitment to maintain a sense of community life – a feature of the seminary that went back to its earliest days. Heidi Lewis, wife of student André, spoke for many when she said: "I have never lived in a community quite like this. We share burdens, prayers, and responsibilities. It's not perfect, but our time with people at Covenant has taught me more of living together in Christian community."[45]

Recognizing the overwhelming need for competent Christian counselors to help pastors in the work of ministry to people suffering from abusive experiences, depression, and a host of mental and psychological problems, Covenant Seminary inaugurated the Master of Arts in Counseling degree in the fall of 1993. Richard Winter, a qualified clinical physician with a specialty in psychiatry, an elder-pastor of the International Presbyterian Church, and a member of the staff of L'Abri for thirteen years, came from England to head Covenant's new counseling department.

GRACE AT THE CENTER: RENEWAL AND REVITALIZATION IN THE 1990S

After serving as Covenant Seminary's president for ten years, Dr. Kooistra resigned in 1994. The seminary had made dramatic progress under his leadership. Kooistra became coordinator of the PCA's Mission to the World, the largest Presbyterian mission force in the world. Kooistra said about his new position, "God gives us jobs bigger than we are to stretch our faith."[46]

Vice President and Dean of Faculty Bryan Chapell was chosen as Covenant Seminary's new president. Dr. Hudson Armerding, Covenant Seminary trustee and former president of Wheaton College, announced Dr. Chapell's appointment to a gathering of students, staff, and professors amid a standing ovation and cheers. Board of Trustees Chairman Lanny Moore described the new president as a man endowed by God "with great preaching and teaching gifts, and with extraordinary gifts of vision, wisdom, administration, discernment and leadership."[47]

After graduation from Northwestern University, Chapell attended Covenant Seminary while pastoring a Presbyterian church in Illinois. There, he met and married musician Kathleen Gabriel. Bryan worked for the seminary's development office, headed the admissions office, and directed student services. For six years, he was pastor at Bethel Reformed Presbyterian Church in Sparta, Illinois. In 1983, he became visiting lecturer in preaching at the seminary and two years later, assistant professor of practical theology. He earned the Ph.D. degree from Southern Illinois University in 1987. He became dean of faculty in 1988 and executive vice president in 1993.

Dr. Chapell became president in 1994. The inaugural vows were administered to the new president at the General Assembly of the Presbyterian Church in America (meeting in Dallas, Texas, the following year) by long-time seminary trustee James B. Orders. Dr. Chapell preached from Isaiah 6 on the holiness of God – a holiness not only majestically transcendent but also graciously transferred to sinful people. He said of the preacher's task, "We have not finished when we have convicted of sin; we must also convince of grace."[48] In his first report to the General Assembly, Chapell characterized Covenant Seminary as "a learning community united in the quest for world transformation through the proclamation of what God has committed to us to hold dear, defend, and deliver to the world."[49]

The new president reiterated "three historical distinctives" of the seminary: "faithfulness to an inerrant view of Scripture, commitment to a covenantal approach to the Reformed faith, and a focus on training for pastoral ministry." Chapell called for "a renewed focus on grace ... a return to the heart center of our historic doctrinal statements – the message of *Sola Gratia,* a dynamic concentration on the centrality of the Cross as the motive and enablement for all truly Christian endeavor."[50]

Daniel Doriani, who joined the Covenant Seminary faculty in 1991, became academic dean in 1995, after Dr. David Jones had returned to the office of dean for an interim year at Dr. Chapell's request. A popular teacher and preacher, Dr. Doriani led the faculty in selection of new professors and creative strategies for achieving the seminary's goals. (Dr. Doriani returned to full-time pastoral ministry in 2003, while continuing to teach as an adjunct professor at the seminary.)

Bryan Chapell's *Christ-Centered Preaching* – named 1994 Book of the Year by *Preaching Magazine* – quickly became the standard text for homiletics classes in many seminaries in the United States and abroad.[51] Its theme influenced the entire work of the seminary, as the various departments began to consider more deeply what it means to follow a Christ-centered approach to the specific activities and disciplines of the theological curriculum.

As the primary point of the Bible – both the Old Testament and the New – and the main emphasis of the Protestant Reformation, the doctrine of grace was, from the beginning, an important part of Covenant Seminary's heritage. Dr. Kooistra had led the seminary in a conscious and comprehensive emphasis on grace, not only in its doctrinal descriptions but also in its practical implications for every class and activity at Covenant Seminary, and, indeed, for all of life. The grace emphasis was continued by Dr. Chapell, who, in the acknowledgments in his *Christ-Centered Preaching*, wrote: "I am especially grateful to Paul Kooistra, who preceded me in the presidency of Covenant Seminary and whose encouragement, ministry, and many hours of conversation along our jogging path about the role of grace in preaching sharpened and strengthened my thought."[52]

Dr. Chapell described grace as capturing "the fullness, beauty, and inestimable blessing of God's redeeming work in Jesus Christ."[53] "Cultivating transformed lives through appreciation of the grace of God provided through no merit of our own is a distinctive of Covenant Seminary," he asserted.[54] In his preaching, teaching, and writing (as in his *Holiness by Grace: Delighting in the Joy that is Our Strength*),[55] Dr. Chapell emphasized the role of God's grace in sanctification as well as in justification. The 1997 seminary catalogue stated that "it is by grace we are saved, and by grace alone we live the Christian life."[56]

Of this grace emphasis, former student Anthony Bradley (a 1998 Master of Divinity graduate who, in 2005, joined the Covenant Seminary faculty) wrote:

> One of the reasons I came to Covenant was this school's commitment to the doctrine of grace. In fact, in one of the first classes I took here, we spent half the semester on grace! I learned I had really taken grace for granted. Yes, I could tell you it is God's unmerited favor, but seeing how it applies to my life and how it is manifested every day in the life of the church and the world was really a challenge and an encouragement to me.[57]

The seminary's 2005–6 catalogue states that Covenant Seminary believes "that the foundation for all that we do must be the Gospel of grace – our absolute confidence in God's acceptance provided through His redemptive work as the supreme motivation and enablement for love and holiness."[58]

The seminary's faculty today is an outstanding group of pastor-scholars. Trained at many prestigious universities in America and abroad, they are experts in their fields; they are also dedicated to caring for and ministering to students. Twenty-two faculty members were appointed between 1984 and 2005, nineteen of whom are still serving at the seminary.[59]

One of these, C. John ("Jack") Collins, joined the faculty in 1993. With two degrees from Massachusetts Institute of Technology and the Ph.D. degree from the University of Liverpool (England), Collins brought an expertise in science (demonstrated in his books *The God of Miracles: An Exegetical Examination of God's Action in the World* and *Science and Faith: Friends or Foes?*)[60] and in the biblical languages. Dr. Collins served as chair of the Old Testament Translation Committee for the English Standard Version of the Bible, published in 2001. (R. Laird Harris was chairman of the Committee on Bible Translation for the New International Version, completed and published in 1978.)

Hans F. Bayer, a native of Germany and a graduate of Aberdeen University with a Ph.D. in New Testament studies, came to Covenant Seminary in 1994. The seminary catalogue states that Dr. Bayer is "an outstanding model of the 'pastor-scholar,' and his strong personal interest in world missions adds a rich multicultural dimension" to his teaching.[61]

Covenant's interest in overseas missions was greatly strengthened by a very active Student Missions Fellowship in the mid-1990s and by the appointment in 1999 of J. Nelson Jennings (for twelve years a missionary in Japan) as professor of missions. Jennings, who studied for his Ph.D. degree with the acclaimed missiologist Andrew Walls at the University of Edinburgh, focused the seminary community's vision on global Christianity and challenged students to consider cross-cultural ministry.

In 1997, theologian Robert A. Peterson, who had joined the Covenant Seminary faculty in 1990, became editor of *Presbyterion: Covenant Seminary Review.* He succeeded Old Testament professor V. Philips Long, who served as editor for eight years. Peterson, a prolific author of books on hell and eternal punishment, the atonement, and adoption, among others, has helped to make the journal a useful and respected publication.

Through the seminary's "The Jewel of Grace, Fire for Ministry" capital campaign that commenced in 1998, faithful trustees and donors provided over $14 million for the support of the seminary. The campaign funded the renovation and expansion of the J. Oliver Buswell, Jr., Library, as well as more scholarships for students. It also enabled the seminary to enhance its ministry of teaching and preparing leaders for the church by the funding of five faculty chairs. Money from the campaign and from the 1999 PCA Women in the Church Love Gift created the Uniting Hearts in Ministry Scholarship, an endowment that enables spouses of full-time students to take seminary classes without cost. "The spousal scholarship program literally does unite hearts in ministry as it grounds couples in God's Word and gives them a unified vision to serve God's people," explained Seminary President Bryan Chapell.[62]

Through the years, the Lord has furthered the progress of the seminary through capable administrators and staff. Dear to the Covenant family and to generations of students are names such as Monicia Clayton, Betty Porter, Edwina Aven, June Dare, Eunice Lanz, Zin Graham, Bob Thomas, Wallace Anderson, Diane Preston, Gordon Shaw, Floyd Simmons, Wayne Copeland,

Allen Duble, Bob Palmer, John Prentis, Ben Homan, Marvin Fornwalt, Jim Hatch, Kathy Woodard, Dave Wicker, and Mark Dalbey.

The remodeled J. Oliver Buswell, Jr., Library, was triple the size of the original building, and included faculty and staff offices. The building was dedicated on April 27, 2001. Church history professor David Calhoun gave the dedicatory address. He said:

> We thank God today for this magnificent building that houses over 80,000 volumes and other treasures. We thank Him for many friends whose gifts made this building a reality. We thank God for Library Director James Pakala and his staff who serve us in it.
>
> We watched with amazement and then with delight as we saw the old library transformed before our eyes – from a rather plain building into this beautiful place, from a dark and crowded library into one of light and space. This very building is a parable of the transformation that God is, day by day, working in our lives. And part of that transformation will happen in the library.[63]

The library contains the PCA Historical Center that, in the words of its director, Wayne Sparkman, preserves and makes known "a record of God's continuing faithfulness in our midst."[64]

In recent years, Covenant Seminary has expanded its mission to include young people not yet in seminary and those who have completed seminary and are now serving in youth ministry. In 1999, Lilly Endowment, Inc., awarded the seminary $1.2 million for the creation of a Youth in Ministry Institute (affectionately known as "YIMI"). The institute enhances the training of youth ministers, produces youth ministry resources, and ministers to high school students by presenting teaching in theology and Bible.

Only 6.8 percent of Covenant Seminary graduates leave ministry within the first five years. (The average of all seminaries nationwide is 30 percent.) To maintain and improve that record, Covenant inaugurated the Center for Ministry Leadership in 2004. The center is under the direction of Robert Burns, a churchman with thirty-four years of experience in pastoral ministry and a doctoral degree in education from the University of Georgia. Initially supported by a $2 million grant from Lilly Endowment, Inc., the Center for Ministry Leadership promotes excellence in ministry by creating lifelong learning and renewal opportunities for pastors. The center has four primary objectives. First, the Pastors Summit is a joint effort between Covenant Seminary, Reformed Theological Seminary, and Westminster Theological Seminary[65] that brings together (at each institution) groups of ten pastors who meet six times over the course of two years for teaching, fellowship, discussion, and reflection. Second, Intersect is a forum for church and business leaders that offers interaction concerning biblical leadership in the church and the workplace. Ten pastors and ten ruling elders (each of whom operates a family business) met at the first Intersect in April 2005. Third, the Pastor in Residence program brings experienced pastors to the Covenant Seminary campus for periods of two weeks up to a full semester for mutually beneficial interaction with students and faculty. Fourth, the *Connect* Conference promotes pastoral excellence and renewal in ministry through an annual gathering of pastors and other Christian leaders.

Donald C. Guthrie came to Covenant Seminary in 1998. Guthrie, who holds the Doctor of Education degree from the University of Georgia, developed a field education component for Covenant's Master of Divinity students, as well as programs in Christian education (leading to a new Master of Arts in Educational Ministries [M.A.E.M.] degree) and youth ministry. Guthrie, who became vice president for academics in 1999, led the successful effort to attract major foundation grants for new seminary programs.

For years, Covenant experimented with methods of delivering seminary training to off-campus students. This led to the seminary's popular distance learning program called *Access,* a Web-enhanced, video- or audio-based format. *Access* students receive guidance from on-campus, faculty-approved mentors as they work through course materials. In February 2001, Covenant Seminary was approved to offer a fully accredited Master of Arts in Theological Studies (M.A.T.S.) degree through *Access*. Covenant's *Access* program, under the capable supervision of Dr. Brad Hough (whose Vanderbilt doctoral dissertation dealt with using the Internet to enhance community during the learning process), also enables students to begin a program of seminary studies to be completed on campus, or enrich life and ministry through seminary studies.

Covenant Seminary has experienced "a growing ministry to the evangelical church at large," while enthusiastically embracing "its commitment, loyalty, and submission" to the PCA.[66] As a denominational seminary, Covenant has taken seriously its role of leadership for the Church and service to it. Dr. Rayburn was a respected leader in the Reformed Presbyterian Church, Evangelical Synod, and its predecessor denominations. Dr. Barker was active in that denomination and the PCA. He was elected moderator of the RPCES in 1973 and of the PCA in 1994. Dr. Kooistra went from Covenant Seminary to become coordinator of the PCA's Mission to the World. Dr. Chapell has served on many denominational committees and represents the PCA nationally in his preaching. Covenant Seminary faculty members are active in presbyteries and at General Assembly, preach and teach in PCA churches (as well as churches of other denominations), and pray for and support the church as a whole. As the denominational seminary, Covenant recognizes its responsibility to provide leadership when difficult or controversial issues face the PCA. "Our unchanging task is to ask, 'What does the Bible say?'" explains President Chapell. "Then we must speak with clarity, charity, and courage."[67] Dr. Chapell joined with other denominational leaders in organizing the

Presbyterian Pastoral Leadership Network to work for unity, peace, and renewal in the PCA.

At the heart of Covenant Seminary's mission, as it has been since the beginning, is the preparation of students in the Master of Divinity program to be faithful and effective ministers. The four traditional disciplines of biblical study – exegetical, theological, historical, and practical – govern the curriculum. Eleven different concentrations allow students to develop a measure of specialization in areas such as: biblical studies; bioethics; Christian education; Christianity and contemporary culture; church growth, planting, and renewal; counseling; music and worship; theology; urban ministry; world mission; and youth ministry.

"One of the distinctives of Covenant Seminary – in the past and certainly in the present – is that of pastors training pastors," said church history professor David Calhoun. "With God's help we do it by teaching, by example, by friendship, and by prayer."[68] Covenant Groups, where students and faculty meet together in small group settings for prayer and discipleship, and ministry lunches, with faculty and guest speakers presenting a variety of ministry-related topics, develop faculty-student friendships, encourage spiritual growth, and promote ministry skills. In Covenant Groups, which are part of the academic curriculum for every incoming Master of Divinity student, first-year students meet with peers and professors weekly to discuss how their studies are informing and affecting their lives. During the second year, local pastors and church leaders meet with the students and professors to discover how seminary studies apply to ministry in the church. "Our goal is to connect classroom, community, and church into a comprehensive educational program that truly serves the church by academically, practically, and spiritually preparing the next generation of her leaders," President Chapell told the 31st General Assembly of the PCA in 2003.[69]

MISSION TO THE FUTURE: THE YEAR OF JUBILEE – AND BEYOND

By its fiftieth year, Covenant Seminary had built on its twenty-one acres in nearly every direction. Classrooms, office space, and offsite student apartments had more than doubled in the previous decade to serve a student body that had almost tripled during the same time. The purchase of land adjacent to the campus – described as "a once in a lifetime" opportunity – was approved by the trustees. Expanding the campus by more than 50 percent, the new property offers space for more student housing, provides a retreat center for pastors, and increases green space. A more park-like atmosphere for the campus was realized in 2005, when campus roads were relocated to create a pleasant and beautiful pedestrian center between the Rayburn Chapel, Buswell Library, and Edwards Hall.

The "By His Grace, For His Glory" capital campaign was launched in 2005 to celebrate Covenant's fiftieth year and to enable the seminary to continue to "shape our church and culture with gifted leaders who will be faithful to the Scriptures, true to our Confession, and rooted in grace for a lifetime of ministry."[70] The seminary looked to the Lord and to his people to provide 12.5 million dollars to be used for the construction of a new academic building, the expansion of the faculty, an enhanced community life center, and campus beautification.

For fifty years, Covenant Theological Seminary has trained "servants of the triune God to walk with God, to interpret and communicate God's Word, and to lead God's people." Thousands of Covenant graduates are serving God today in churches and ministries in the United States and around the world. Since 1987, the placement rate for Covenant's Master of Divinity graduates seeking full-time ministry positions through the placement office has been 97 percent; since 1995, when the first class of Master of Arts in Counseling candidates graduated, 97 percent of these students also have been placed. Currently, one in four Covenant graduates will plant a church within eight years of graduation. A large number of graduates have become campus ministers with Reformed University Fellowship (RUF), the PCA's impressive ministry to university students. An increasing number of Covenant graduates are seeking to serve God in overseas missions.

The story of the first fifty years of Covenant Seminary is, above all, the story of God's abundant grace poured out upon a small band of faithful men and a few students – and upon the teachers and over a thousand students today – to the end that the men and women of Covenant Seminary will, throughout their lives and ministries, "glorify God and enjoy Him,"[71] and lead others to do the same. As we celebrate Covenant Seminary's jubilee, may these words from Holy Scripture remain uppermost in our minds and hearts: "Not unto us, O Lord, not unto us, but unto thy name give glory, for thy mercy, and for thy truth's sake" (Ps. 115:1 KJV).

1. For their help with this short history of Covenant Seminary, I would like to thank William Barker, David Jones, Robert S. Rayburn, Bryan Chapell, and especially, Wayne Sparkman. And with great esteem for them, I dedicate this chapter to the Seminary's two remaining original faculty members – R. Laird Harris and Wilber B. Wallis.

2. Theodore W. Martin, *In Covenant* 11, no. 5 (October/November 1996): 15.

3. Cal Frett, *In Covenant* 11, no. 5 (October/November 1996): 15.

4. Paul D. Kooistra to the congregation of The Covenant Presbyterian Church, November 1, 1988, in *Covenant at Fifty* (St. Louis, Mo.: The Covenant Presbyterian Church of Saint Louis, 1989), 17.

5. *Bulletin of Covenant Theological Seminary*, Catalogue Issue 10 (April 1965): 13.

6. Ibid., 27–34.

7. Robert G. Rayburn, *Fight the Good Fight: Lessons from the Korean War* (Lookout Mountain, Tenn.: Covenant College Press, 1956). This book was reprinted in 2003.

8. Robert G. Rayburn, *O Come, Let Us Worship: Corporate Worship in the Evangelical Church* (Grand Rapids, Mich.: Baker Book House, 1980).

9. William S. Barker, "An Appreciation of Dr. J. Oliver Buswell, Jr.," *Presbyterion: Covenant Seminary Review* 2, no. 1–2 (Spring/Fall 1976): 142.

10. F. F. Bruce, quoted in W. Harold Mare, "Buswell as Educator," *Presbyterion: Covenant Seminary Review* 2, no. 1–2 (Spring/Fall 1976): 33.

11. Kenneth Kantzer, "Buswell as Theologian," *Presbyterion: Covenant Seminary Review* 2, no. 1–2 (Spring/Fall 1976): 67.

12. Carl F. H. Henry, "The Silent Dignity of a Devout Spirit," *Presbyterion: Covenant Seminary* 2, no. 1–2 (Spring/Fall 1976): 135.

13. John W. Sanderson, Jr., "Buswell as Churchman," *Presbyterion: Covenant Seminary Review* 2, no. 1–2 (Spring/Fall 1976): 109.

14. R. Laird Harris, quoted in John W. Sanderson, Jr., "Biographical Introduction," *Presbyterion: Covenant Seminary Review* 7, no. 1–2 (Spring/Fall 1981): 3–4.

15. Robert Scott in "Letters from Covenant Seminary's Entering Class," ed. Bob Thomas, *In Covenant* 11, no. 5 (October/November 1996): 16.

16. William S. Barker, *"In All Things...": The Preeminence of Jesus Christ in the History of Covenant College, 1955–2005* (Chattanooga, Tenn.: Covenant College Foundation, 2005), 32.

17. Barker, *"In All Things..."*, 42.

18. Francis A. Schaeffer quoted in untitled Covenant Theological Seminary academic catalogue for 1977–79, 16 (Summer 1977): back cover.

19. Kantzer, "Buswell as Theologian," 69.

20. Francis A. Schaeffer, "A Step Forward," *The Presbyterian Journal* 32, no. 45 (March 6, 1974): 7. Schaeffer was calling the newly formed National Presbyterian Church (later the Presbyterian Church in America) to exhibit and practice "God's love toward all true Christians in whatever groups they are" (8).

21. Paul D. Kooistra to the congregation of The Covenant Presbyterian Church, November 1, 1988, in *Covenant at Fifty* (St. Louis, Mo.: The Covenant Presbyterian Church of Saint Louis, 1989), 17.

22. "There Are Some Real Problems. A Few Answers," interview with John Sanderson in *The Evangelical Presbyterian Reporter* 9, no. 2 (February 1964): 10.

23. Robert G. Rayburn quoted in "Dr. Buswell Retires," *Covenant Seminary Newsletter* 2, no. 3 (Summer 1970): 4.

24. Fifteen faculty members were appointed between 1967 and 1980. Five of those fifteen did their Master of Divinity study at Covenant Seminary (and one other studied for one year at Covenant). Four of those five are still connected with the seminary – David C. Jones, Robert I. Vasholz, and David B. Calhoun as full-time professors, and William S. Barker as adjunct professor. See Appendix B, "Succession of Presidents, Faculty, and Trustees."

25. Editorial, *Presbyterion: Covenant Seminary Review* 1, no. 2 (Fall 1975): 65.

26. William S. Barker, *Word to the World: The Collected Writings of William S. Barker* (Fearn, Ross-shire, Scotland: Christian Focus Publications, 2005), 16.

27. "Whate'er My God Ordains Is Right," hymn by Samuel Rodigast (1675), translated by Catherine Winkworth (1863). Founding Old Testament Professor R. Laird Harris also asked the student body to sing this hymn when he announced the terminal illness of his first wife to the Seminary community.

28. Text of tributary plaque, quoted in *Threshold* (Winter 1981–82): 5.

29. William S. Barker, "From the President," *Threshold* (Winter 1981–82): 1.

30. *Covenant Theological Seminary academic catalogue for 1971–73* 13 (June 1971): 25.

31. The St. Louis Theological Consortium broke down with the formation of Concordia Seminary in Exile.

32. David C. Jones, e-mail to author, August 29, 2005.

33. Robert G. Rayburn, "Covenant College and Covenant Theological Seminary," unpublished paper, Presbyterian Church in America Historical Center, St. Louis, Missouri.

34. Robert A. Peterson, e-mail to author, August 4, 2005.

35. Paul D. Kooistra, "Covenant President Leads Seminary as Team Ministry to PCA," interview, *Covenant Seminary '86* 1, no. 1 (Spring 1986): 1.

36. Paul D. Kooistra, "The Why and the How of the Reformed Faith," *Covenant Seminary '88* 3, no. 2 (Spring 1988): 3.

37. Kooistra, "Covenant President Leads Seminary as Team Ministry to PCA," 1.

38. *Covenant Theological Seminary 2005–6 Catalogue*, 82.

39. Michael Campbell, quoted in an untitled Covenant Theological Seminary Admissions department promotional brochure, circa 2002–4.

40. Almost 30 percent of Covenant Seminary's Master of Divinity graduates who are presently serving in the Presbyterian Church in America have planted churches in the United States or overseas during the last fifty years.

41. Jerram Barrs, quoted in *Covenant Theological Seminary 1990–91 Catalogue*, 54.

42. "What is the Francis A. Schaeffer Institute?" *Covenant* 19, no. 2 (Summer 2004): 23.

43. Luke Bobo, quoted in "Just Browsing? Francis A. Schaeffer Institute Shares Truth in the Marketplace," *Covenant* 16, no. 2 (April/May 2001): 18.

44. Robert S. Rayburn, "The Christian's Greatest Means of Grace," *Presbyterion: Covenant Seminary Review* 16, no. 1 (Spring 1990).

45. Heidi Lewis, quoted in "What is Covenant Community?" *Covenant* 18, no. 4 (Winter 2003–4): 11.

46. Paul D. Kooistra, quoted in "Kooistra Heads Mission to the World," *In Covenant* 10, no. 1 (Winter 1995): 10.

47. Lanny Moore, quoted in "Announcing Bryan Chapell – Covenant Seminary's Fourth President," *In Covenant* 10, no. 1 (Winter 1995): 4.

48. Bryan Chapell, quoted in "The PCA General Assembly Witnesses the Making of a President," *In Covenant* 11, no. 1 (Fall 1995): 8.

49. Ibid.

50. Bryan Chapell, "An Interview with President Chapell," *In Covenant* 10, no. 1 (Winter 1995): 5.

51. Bryan Chapell, *Christ-Centered Preaching: Redeeming the Expository Sermon* (Grand Rapids, Mich.: Baker Academic, 1994).

52. Bryan Chapell, *Christ-Centered Preaching: Redeeming the Expository Sermon*, 2nd ed., (Grand Rapids, Mich.: Baker Academic, 2005), 21.

53. Bryan Chapell, "Our Time in History," in *By His Grace, For His Glory: Covenant Theological Seminary Capital Campaign* (Covenant Theological Seminary: St. Louis, Mo., 2005), 1.

54. Bryan Chapell, "From the President," *Covenant Theological Seminary 2005–2006 Catalogue*, 1.

55. Bryan Chapell, *Holiness by Grace: Delighting in the Joy that is Our Strength* (Wheaton, Ill.: Crossway Books, 2001).

56. *Covenant Theological Seminary 1997 Catalogue*, 4.

57. Anthony Bradley, quoted in *Covenant Theological Seminary 1997 Catalogue*, 4.

58. *Covenant Theological Seminary 2005–6 Catalogue*, 82.

59. See Appendix B, "Succession of Presidents, Faculty, and Trustees."

60. C. John Collins, *The God of Miracles: An Exegetical Examination of God's Action in the World* (Wheaton, Ill.: Crossway Books, 2000); *Science and Faith: Friends or Foes?* (Wheaton, Ill.: Crossway Books, 2003).

61. *Covenant Theological Seminary 1997 Catalogue*, 28.

62. Bryan Chapell, quoted in "Uniting Hearts in Ministry," *The Campaign for Covenant: Jewel of Grace, Fire for Ministry* 4, no. 1 (Spring 1999), 4.

63. David B. Calhoun, "The Book, the Books, and the Building," address for the dedication of the renovated J. Oliver Buswell, Jr., Library at Covenant Theological Seminary, April 27, 2001.

64. Wayne Sparkman, "Report of the PCA Historical Center to the Twenty-Seventh General Assembly of the Presbyterian Church in America," in *Minutes of the Twenty-Seventh General Assembly of the Presbyterian Church in America* (Atlanta, Ga.: Presbyterian Church in America, 1999), 243.

65. In Dr. Chapell's report to the 32nd General Assembly of the PCA (2004), he said, "Covenant Theological Seminary, Reformed Theological Seminary, and Westminster Seminary have great appreciation for each other and recognize together the great calling God is jointly giving us to prepare an even greater generation of ordinary people with an extraordinary hope" (*Covenant* 19, no. 3 [Fall 2004]: 26).

66. *Covenant Theological Seminary 1997 Catalogue*, 4.

67. Bryan Chapell, "Regarding the New Perspective," *Covenant* 20, no. 2 (Summer 2005): 29.

68. David Calhoun, quoted in an untitled Covenant Theological Seminary Admissions department promotional brochure, circa 2002–4.

69. Bryan Chapell, "Stronger When We Are Connected," *Covenant* 18, no. 3 (Fall 2003): 15.

70. *By His Grace, For His Glory: Covenant Theological Seminary Capital Campaign* (St. Louis, Mo.: Covenant Theological Seminary, 2005), 3.

71. *Westminster Shorter Catechism*, answer 1.

PART TWO:

CHRIST-CENTERED GOSPEL

3

THE NECESSITY OF PREACHING GRACE
for Progress in Sanctification

BRYAN CHAPELL
Professor of Practical Theology
President

---

y concern for the role of grace in sanctification had an intensely
personal beginning. The inadequacies of my preaching were
torturing me, and I wondered whether I should leave the ministry.
I could not figure out what was wrong. Church members complimented
my preaching, but their own lives were consistently plagued by depression,
addictions, and anger with each other. I had to question, "If I am such a
good preacher, then why are the people I serve doing so badly?" Ultimately, I
determined that a central reason for their despair, their escapist compulsions,
and their judgmental impatience with one another was a pattern of thought
that I was unintentionally encouraging.

PREACHING THAT UNDERMINES HOLINESS

The pattern of thought that I reinforced was not immediately apparent to me
because I believed that my preaching was faithful to the commands of God's
inerrant Word. The same Bible that attests to my Savior's virgin birth, sinless
life, substitutionary atonement, physical resurrection, Great Commission,
and sovereign rule also calls God's people to holiness. I knew that I could
not embrace all that is dear to me in God's Word without also embracing its
commands. So, I preached the whole counsel of God as I understood it.

Week after week, I told the imperfect people in my church to "do better."
But this drumbeat for improvement, devoid of the encouragements and
empowerments of grace, actually undermined the holiness that I was seeking
to exhort. When God's people hear only the imperatives of the Word, they are

forced to conclude that their righteousness is a product of their efforts. There are only two possible reactions to such preaching: Some will reason, "I will never meet God's requirements," leading them to despair; others will assert, "I have measured up to what God requires – at least, compared to other people," leading to spiritual pride that manifests itself in the body of Christ as arrogance and/or intolerance.

Preaching the Redemptive Context

I recognized that these reactions were symptoms of spiritual maladies. What I needed to learn was that the cure was not preaching less of Scripture, but more. In particular, I needed to learn to preach each text in its redemptive context. Paul writes in Romans, "For whatever was written in earlier times was written for our instruction, so that through perseverance and the encouragement of the Scriptures we might have hope" (Rom. 15:4).[1] Scanning the scope of the law and the prophets, the apostle is able to say that all was intended to give us hope. All Scripture has a redemptive purpose. None of the Scriptures are so limited in purpose as to give us only moral instruction or lifestyle correction. Paul says that even the law itself functions as our "schoolmaster to lead us to Christ" (Gal. 3:24 KJV). Jesus also says, "All the law and the prophets testify of me" (cf. Luke 24:27; John 5:39).

Yet, we will call into question the accuracy of Paul and Jesus on this point if we think of messianic revelation only in terms of explicit mention of the person of Christ. Vast portions of both the Old and New Testaments make no explicit mention of Christ. Even the prophetic books that predict the coming Messiah contain much material that does not have Jesus as the direct subject. Christ surely knew this when Luke records of the Savior's post-resurrection teaching, " ... beginning with Moses and all the Prophets, he explained to them what was said in all the Scriptures concerning himself" (Luke 24:27). How can Jesus offer such exposition, and by corollary require such exposition from us, if the text does not make direct reference to him?[2]

In his discussions of the law, Paul helps us understand the varying dimensions of the Bible's redemptive hope. Though Paul never denies the efficacy of obedience, he explains that, through the law, he died to the law. The righteous requirements of the holiness of God that were always beyond his grasp signaled the death of hope in human achievement for spiritual life. The moral instruction of a holy God revealed that no one was capable of holiness by his own efforts. Our best works are judged but filthy rags in the Old Testament (Isa. 64:6), and the Savior echoes, "So you also, when you have done everything you were told to do, should say, 'We are unworthy servants; we have only done our duty.'" (Luke 17:10).

The same law that reveals the requirements of God's holiness also reveals the inescapable reality of our unholiness. Because of the great disproportion between our best works and God's righteousness, we are always and forever incapable of the righteousness that would reconcile us to a holy God. This hardly seems a redemptive message. It would not be were it not for the alternative it demands.

By revealing the holy nature of the God who provides redemption and the finite nature of humanity that requires redemption, the law points to the necessity of a Redeemer and prepares the human heart to seek him. The law, however, is only one aspect of Scripture that may help flesh out the person and work of Christ without making explicit mention of him.

Christ-centered exposition of Scripture does not require us to unveil depictions of Jesus by mysterious alchemies of allegory or typology; rather, it identifies how every text functions in furthering our understanding of who Christ is, what the Father sent him to do, and why. The goal is not to make a specific reference to Jesus magically appear from every camel track of Hebrew narrative or every metaphor of Hebrew poetry (leading to allegorical errors), but rather to show where every text stands in relation to the person and/or work of Christ, whose grace alone achieves our salvation.

Such an interpretive approach will always take the preacher to the heart of covenantal and Reformed theology by requiring discernment of the progressive and ever-present revelation of God's sovereign grace through Scripture. Discerning the gracious character of God in his revelation also rescues Reformed theology from its tendencies to narrow faith to abstract principles and points of debate. By consistently preaching of the God who traverses the universe he created to redeem his creatures by his blood, we become relationally bound to the reality of a living and loving Lord.[3] Our listeners become so bound as well – truly linked to God in heart rather than being proud of thoughts or practices that they feel distinguish them from others who are less informed or less good.

APPROACHES TO DISCERNING REDEMPTIVE CONTEXT

A primary approach to discerning the redemptive nature of a biblical text is identifying how the passage *predicts, prepares for, reflects,* or *results from* the person and/or work of Christ.[4] This approach includes what is known as the redemptive/historical method, which seeks to identify how the passage furthers the progress or understanding of what Christ has done or will do in redemptive history. Prophecies obviously *predict* Christ and explain much of what he will do. The temple sacrifices predict what Christ will do, but also typologically *prepare* the people of God to understand the nature of the atoning work of the Savior. The relationship of Hosea and Gomer not only prepares the covenant people to understand how God will love Israel despite her sin, but also *reflects* the need and nature of God's pardoning mercy in all ages. Our ability to seek that pardoning mercy at the throne of grace is a *result* of our great High Priest going before us to prepare the way and to make petitions in our behalf.

Dead Ends and Bridges

The preceding four categories of redemptive/historical explanation are not, and should not be, rigidly segregated. Instead, preachers bear the greatest expository fruit when they understand that what they are seeking to expose to the view of God's people are the gospel truths that presage and apply God's work of redemption in Christ. Entire epochs and genres of Scripture serve special purposes in revealing the dimensions of grace that will ultimately be accomplished and applied in Christ.[5] For example, the period of the judges not only reveals the power of divine aid, it also demonstrates the folly of seeking to do what each person finds acceptable in his own eyes to maintain a covenant people. The kingship of Israel similarly demonstrates the folly of depending on human leaders to establish a righteous rule for the covenant people. The Old Testament takes us down many such redemptive *dead ends* for the purpose of turning us from human to divine dependence.[6]

By way of contrast, some aspects of Scripture function as redemptive *bridges* that allow the covenant people to progress in their understanding of redeeming grace. The Lord's calling and preservation of the diminutive nation of Israel serves as a perpetual statement that God's mercy is not extended only to the strong, capable, and deserving (Deut. 7:7). The provision of the manna in the wilderness, as well as of the prophets of the Word, helps all subsequent generations remain confident in God's provision of living bread – his Word (John 6:35; 1 Cor. 10:3, 16). Again, these categories should not be rigidly maintained. The temple sacrifices are at one level a dead end, in that they demonstrate that the blood of bulls and goats could never fully atone for sin. Yet, at another level the sacrificial system is also a bridge to the understanding of what God would do for the nations through the Lamb of God.

Other classifications also function well in relating the many varieties of Scripture passages to the person and work of Christ.[7] The goal is not to determine a master metaphor that will provide a proper niche for all passages. Such pigeonholing of texts typically limits the implications of the Bible's own rich variety of metaphors that are used to relate redemptive truth (e.g. kingdom, family, Sabbath, tree). What we should not lose sight of among the infinite possibilities for redemptive interpretation is the necessity of exposing the truths of grace that all Scripture is designed to help us see.[8]

Lenses for Macro- and Micro-Interpretations

We should always observe the text through spectacles whose lenses are these questions: (1) How is the Holy Spirit here revealing the nature of God that provides redemption? and/or, (2) How is the Holy Spirit here revealing the nature of humanity that requires redemption? As long as we use these lenses to observe the text, we will interpret as Christ did when he showed his disciples how all Scripture spoke of him.

Asking these two questions (i.e. using these two lenses) maintains faithful exposition and demonstrates that redemptive interpretation does not require the preacher to run from Genesis to Revelation in every sermon to expound a text's redemptive truths. While there is nothing wrong with such macro-interpretations, it is also possible – and often more fruitful – to identify in the immediate text the doctrinal statements or relational interactions that reveal some dimension of God's grace. The relational interactions in such micro-interpretations can include how God acts toward his people (e.g. providing strength for weakness, pardon for sin, provision in want, faithfulness in response to unfaithfulness) or how an individual representing God provides for others (e.g. David's care for Mephibosheth, Solomon's wisdom recorded for others less wise).[9]

Fallen Condition/Divine Solution Focus

In essence, redemptive exposition requires that we identify an aspect of our fallen condition that is addressed by the Holy Spirit in each passage which he inspired for our edification, and then show God's way out of the human dilemma.[10] Such a pattern not only exposes the human predicament that requires God's relief, but also forces the preacher to focus on a divine solution. Our salvation rests in his provision. God's glory is always the apex purpose of the sermon. The vaunting of human ability and puffing of human pride vanish in such preaching not because imperatives of the law of God are minimized, but because God is always the hero of the text.[11] He enables our righteousness, pardons our unrighteousness, and provides for our weakness.

REDEMPTIVE PREACHING FOR SANCTIFICATION

This consistent preaching of the dimensions of God's grace does not render superfluous the commands of the law, but rather honors their authority by providing the biblical motivation and enablement necessary for our obedience. The fear that the regular preaching of grace will lead to antinomianism is sometimes justified. The human heart is more than capable of abusing grace to excuse sin. Those who come from a legalistic background often overcompensate for their gospel-weak past by launching into law-deaf pastimes. Still, despite this danger, there is no alternative to preaching the grace that underlies all biblical testimony. Such preaching does not define grace as the world does – a license to do as I please – but rather as the Bible teaches: a mercy so overwhelming that it compels me to do what pleases God.[12]

Grace-based preaching does not eliminate the moral obligations of the law. The Bible's standards reflect the character of God and are provided for our good and his glory. The preaching of grace should not negate the law but provide an antidote for pride in its performance and an incentive for conscientiousness in its observance.[13]

Motivating Holiness by Grace

The motivating power of grace is evident in Christ's words, "If you love me you will obey what I command" (John 14:15). Because the redemptive interpretation of Scripture leads to sermons marked by consistent adulation of the mercy of God in Christ, hearts in which the Spirit dwells are being continually stoked with more cause to love God.[14] This love becomes the primary motivation for Christian obedience as hearts in which the Spirit dwells respond with love for their Savior.[15] For the believer, there is no greater spiritual motivation than grace-stimulated love – not fear, or guilt, or gain (though each of these can have secondary roles in God's motivation hierarchy if they are not separated from love).[16] And, as our love results in discipleship that demonstrates the beauty and blessing of walking with God, greater love for him grows and stimulates even more desire for obedience.

The Bible recognizes no definition of grace that excuses sin or encourages moral license. The burning love for God fueled by the consistent preaching of grace makes those in whom the Spirit dwells want to walk with God and follow the commands that please him. This is why the apostle Paul could say that the grace of God teaches us to say no to ungodliness and worldly passions (see Titus 2:12). When grace is properly perceived, the law is not trashed; it is treasured. Because we love God, we want to honor the standards that honor him.

In grace-based preaching, the rules do not change; the reasons do.[17] We serve God *because* we love him, not *in order* to make him love us. After all, how could production of more filthy rags make God love us? He releases us from the performance treadmill that (falsely) promises to provide holiness through human effort, but the effect on the heart is love that is more constrained to please him. God's overwhelming and unconditional mercy ensures that there is now no condemnation for those who are in Christ Jesus (Rom. 8:1), but rather than promoting license this kindness leads to repentance (Rom. 2:4). We *want* to turn from the sin that grieves the One we love (Eph. 4:30).

Motivating Holiness by the Cross

The primary message that stimulates such love is the cross. Contemporary theologians sometimes wince at such statements because they seem to slight the resurrection, second coming, and other key redemptive events. It is certainly true that, without the resurrection, the Cross would have signaled nothing but a gory death on a distant hill. The victory over sin accomplished by the resurrection, and the vindication of righteousness promised in the Consummation, are vital truths for perseverance in Christian faithfulness. Still, when Paul wrote to the Corinthians that he resolved to preach nothing among them but Christ crucified, he reflected a profound understanding of humanity (1 Cor. 2:2). The Father's gift of his Son stirs the heart at its deepest level to make it tender toward God, receptive of his Word, and zealous for his will.

The old preaching imperative, "make much of the blood," reflects great wisdom about human motivation. The Cross stimulates love for God, the resurrection zeal for his purposes, and the second coming perseverance in his cause. All are necessary, but God's mercy toward the undeserving – as it unfolds through Scripture and culminates in the Cross – is still the message that programs the heart to receive and employ all the other truths of the gospel.

The primary reason we must preach the grace of God from all the Scriptures is not so that we will master an interpretive skill, or even produce correct exegesis. Biblical theology practiced merely as a science of interpretation encourages theological debate and spiritual pride as we strive to find and promote the master metaphor that will unite all Scripture (e.g. kingdom, covenant, creation-fall-redemption, family). These are helpful lenses through which to see the structure of Scripture; but the true goal of redemptive preaching is to expound the ways in which God progressively and consistently shows dimensions of his mercy in all ages so that we will understand Christ's sacrifice more fully and, consequently, love him more.[18] Any practice of biblical theology that does not have this relational aim[19] is misdirected.

We should study the Scriptures so that we may glorify God and enjoy him (WSC.1). Without a profound love for him, we can do neither. Love for him leads us to seek him, serve him, repent to him, and return to him. All the requirements of love for God find their impulse at the Cross. From there radiate many implications and imperatives, but still the Cross is the center for the heart seeking God.

Enabling Holiness by Union with Christ

Christ's victory on the Cross provides freedom from both the guilt and power of sin. The apostle Paul reminds us that, because Jesus resides in us, we possess the resurrection power that raised Jesus from the dead (Gal. 2:20; Eph. 1:18-23). John adds, "Greater is he that is in you than he that is in the world (1 John 4:4 KJV). This is more than a promise that Jesus will add to our strength or aid our resolve. Because we are in union with Christ, all of the merits of his righteousness have become ours, and his Spirit now enables us to resist the sin that he reveals to us.[20] In the terms of classic theology, once we were not able not to sin (*non posse non peccare*), but now we are able not to sin (*posse non peccare*).[21] Enough of the influence of our sin nature persists that we will not perfectly perform his will until we are with Jesus in eternal glory (*non posse peccare*), but even now we are freed from Satan's lie that we cannot change. Sin has no more dominion over us (Rom. 6:14-18). We can make progress against the besetting sins of our lives because we are alive in Christ – whose resurrection power indwells us.

The release of sin's guilt *and* the reception of Christ's benefits are the more complete gospel of grace. Sometimes preachers preach only a partial gospel, indicating that the debt of our sin has been paid by the suffering of Christ (i.e. his passive righteousness). This is a glorious and precious truth for all Christians who know their need of forgiveness. Yet, even if our debt has been paid, it is still possible to live with a sense of inadequacy and humiliation because of our sin. It is as though we recognize that our debt has been paid, but, though we are grateful, our spiritual math still indicates that we have only a zero-sum balance: Christ's death in our behalf makes us feel guilty and small rather than free of debt.

To counter such feelings, we need the full benefits of the gospel. We have not only been freed of our debt, we have also been supplied with Christ's righteousness (resulting from his active and passive righteousness). Before God, we are already accounted as heirs of heaven, co-heirs with Christ, and children of God (Rom. 8:16-17). This adoption signals our worth and preciousness to God prior to our entry into heaven. So sure is our status and so rich is our righteousness that our Heavenly Father already considers us holy and pleasing to him (Rom. 12:1) and has already seated us in heavenly places (Eph. 2:6). Because we are in union with Christ, his status is ours (Gal. 2:20; 1 Cor. 1:30; 2 Cor. 5:21). Though we are striving with the power of Christ's Spirit to overcome sinful thoughts and acts in our lives, God has already reckoned us holy by his grace embraced through our faith. Our positional sanctification gives us the foundation for our progressive sanctification.[22] In an intentional turn of words, it is because our feet are firmly planted in heaven that we have the foundation to resist the assaults of Satan.

Enabling Holiness by Indicatives of the Gospel

Future grace awaits us in glory, but we already possess its status through the certainty of the promises of God and the guarantee of the Spirit in us (2 Cor. 5:5). The mark of that Spirit is not the absence of sin in our lives, but the presence of new desires and new power to overcome temptation (Rom. 8:5-15). When we weep over our sin, we may question if the power of the Spirit is real in us. But, in a wonderful confirmation of our status as new creatures in Christ, the grief we feel for sin is the assurance of our salvation.[23] Before the Spirit filled us, our hearts were – and only could be – hostile to God. But now when we sin, we hate it. The hatred of sin and godly sorrow for its expression are the evidence of the Spirit in us and heaven before us. Were not the Spirit in us there could be no sorrow for sin (other than the sorrow of consequences). But when we truly grieve that our sin has grieved the Spirit, trampled on the blood of our Savior, and offended our Heavenly Father, then we evidence a heart renewed by the Spirit and secured for eternity.

Hatred of sin, freedom from past guilt, possession of Christ's righteousness and power, and assurance of future grace combine to equip Christians for the holy race God calls us to run. However, it is important to remember that all of these truths rest on the person and work of Jesus Christ. There will be no progress in the Christian life without the past, present, and future grace of our Lord. Jesus said, "Apart from me, you can do nothing" (John 15:5). No sentence in Scripture more underscores the need for Christ-centered preaching. The grace of God that is ultimately revealed in Christ frees us from our guilt and enables us to obey. Preaching that seeks to issue imperatives (what to do) from a biblical text without identifying the indicatives of the gospel (who we are by grace alone) to which the text points robs listeners of their only source of power to do what God requires.[24]

Most preachers approach the text with only one question in mind: What does this text instruct me to tell my people to do? But if we only tell people what to do without leading them to understand their dependence on the Savior to obey, then they will either be led to despair (I cannot do this) or false pride (If I work hard enough, I can do this). No one can serve God apart from Christ. A message full of imperatives (e.g. Be like ... a commendable Bible character; Be good ... by adopting these moral behaviors; Be disciplined ... by diligence in these practices) but devoid of grace is antithetical to the gospel. These "be messages" are not wrong *in* themselves, but *by* themselves they are spiritually deadly because they imply that our path to God is made by our works.[25]

When we preach a biblical imperative in isolation from grace, we take what should be a blessing and make it as deadly for the soul as an untreated cashew nut is for the body. Africans love the sweetness and nourishment of the cashew nut, but they know that the nut in its natural form can be deadly. Unless heat is added, cyanide contained in the nut will poison those who ingest it. Similarly, the imperatives of the law are good and nourishing for the Christian life – unless the warmth of the gospel is lacking. When no explanations of grace accompany the preaching of the law, it also becomes spiritually deadly, creating despair for those who honestly realize that they cannot fully meet the law's requirements or stimulating pride in those who wrongly imagine that they can.[26]

Without a foundation of grace, striving for holiness only sinks the soul in a quagmire of human inadequacy. We must remember that even our best works deserve God's reproof unless they are sanctified by Christ (WCF XVI.5). God delights in our good works only when they are presented in Christ (WCF XVI.6). This means that, even if we do not mention Jesus by name in the explanation of a text, we must show where the text stands in relation to his grace in order to provide hope that the obligations of the text will be fulfilled.[27] Just as the necessity of a Christ-focus in all preaching is indicated by Jesus' words, "Apart from me you can do nothing," so also the power of such a focus is indicated in Paul's words, "I can do all things through Christ who strengthens me" (Phil. 4:13 NJKV).

PREACHING THE WALK OF FAITH

How does this strengthening actually occur? All pastors recognize that people are constantly asking how they can access the power that God promises through Christ. This is a difficult question for preachers – and perhaps the difficulty explains why the question is so often ignored or simply relegated to the category of those things which are the fruit of more human endeavor. Though most sermons focus on telling people what to do, the imperatives are rarely new or unknown. What remains hidden for most people is knowing how to do what they know they should do but fail repeatedly to do. Until the preacher answers the how question, people remain in a spiritual quandary, regardless of the correctness of the imperatives preached.[28] For example, preachers may assure people that, if they pray harder, longer, and with greater faith, then they will gain the power of God. This instruction is indeed true, but it ignores the paradox that the power we seek *in* our prayer is required *for* our prayer. We cannot pray (or obey any other command of God) adequately apart from the enabling power of God.

Believing the Shepherd of Grace

The power that enables true obedience is from God, and we access it through a walk of faith. We walk with God by leaning on his strength, resting in the goodness of his providence, and believing his Word. This trust relationship is ultimately the source of our strength.[29] We act with the strength that comes from the simple faith that the Good Shepherd will be true to his Word and will accomplish what is right for us as we obey him.

The power of this faith does not reside in the strength or degree of our spiritual expression, but rather resides in the power and goodness of the One in whom we trust.[30] As an elevator is effective not on the basis of the strength of the person who walks in, but on the basis of the strength of the cable and motors that power it, so also our blessing depends not so much on any strength in us, as in relying on the power of God. Obedience is a result of faith in the grace of God and is not a means to produce his grace. Blessings flow from obedience – but even these are the product of the grace in which we trust.

The power that results from this grace initially comes from the belief that what God's Word says is true. The Bible says that those who place their faith in Christ are new creatures who have the power to resist sin (2 Cor. 5:17). If we do not believe this, then we have no power to combat the sin. We cannot obey if we do not believe we can. Yet, if we believe that God has already provided the assurance and resources for victory – no matter how great the opposition – then we will act and we will overcome. If we do not believe that God has forgiven our past, then there will be no reason to risk failure or deny our lusts now or in the future. Yet, if we believe that our past is forgiven, our present is blessed, and our future is secure, we will repent of sin and return to our walk with him.[31]

Engaging the Disciplines of Grace

The reason that we engage in the Christian disciplines of prayer, Bible reading, Christian worship, and fellowship is not to bribe God to act in accord with his nature, but to feed our faith in his unchanging nature so that we will consistently act in accord with his Word. Too many Christians practice the disciplines of the Christian life with the intention of turning God's face toward them and inclining his heart to favor them. They forget that God has loved them with an eternal and infinite love. He turned his face from our sin when he placed it on his dying Son, but now he never looks away from us and his heart never ebbs in affection for us. Every act of providence is for our eternal good from infinite love. Communing with God in prayer, understanding his ways through his Word, and embracing his glory and goodness through Christian fellowship and worship are means by which enabling grace fills our lives. These disciplines of grace are nourishments of the faith that we need to act in accord with God's purposes. They do not force or leverage God's hand, but enable us to see it, grasp it, and receive the blessings it provides. The Christian disciplines do not earn blessings, but guide us into the paths where God's grace has planted his blessings.

If God's blessings depended upon the adequacy of our performance of his requirements, then we would know no blessings and would eventually turn from him. We do not practice the disciplines of the Christian life with the expectation that they would ever be sufficient in quality or duration to merit God's favor, but with the expectation that they will help us better to know, love, and trust him.[32] The disciplines defeat this purpose if they are preached as payment to a god with an insatiable appetite for human sweat and tears.

The Christian disciplines can be compared to the nourishment that parents encourage their children to eat. If parents promise their love only on the condition that children will eat, then the children may very well clean their plates, but they will grow up hating the food that nourishes them – and, ultimately, hating the parents who made their love subject to a child's abilities. By contrast, the parents who promise unconditional love may still struggle with the eating habits of their children, but as the children mature they will naturally love that which nourishes them and the hands that provide it. In a similar way, preaching of the Christian disciplines helps God's people mature and cherish these aids to faith when they perceive that such practices nourish their growth in grace rather than purchase it.[33]

Confidence in the mercy of the Father purchased solely by the blood of his Son, belief in our new nature and secure future provided entirely by our union with Christ, and trust in God's paths and providence consistently nurtured by the disciplines of grace – all these combine to constitute the walk of faith that the Spirit uses to stimulate repentance and empower faithfulness. The first lesson of this walk of faith for preachers is that, while we must convict of sin, we are not finished preaching until we have also convinced of grace. Full application of the Word requires us to expound grace that not only teaches God's people *what* and *whom* to follow, but *why* to follow (out of love for him) and *how* (in dependence upon him). The second lesson is equally vital: without love there is no faith to empower obedience. Faith is the confidence that God is present, sovereign, and good (Heb. 11:1, 6). We will put no faith in one we do not love. The faith that empowers the Christian life requires love for God.

PREACHING THE POWER OF THE WHY

Christian preaching must consistently proclaim the grace of God because in helping God's people to love him we enable them to serve him. The *why* is the *how*; motive and enablement unite in holiness.[34] Great love for God is great power for obedience. This is not only because love is necessary for true faith, but also because love is power. We will only do, and can only do, what we love most to do. We cannot long and well do a job that we hate doing. Though we may persist for a while, ultimately our loss of enthusiasm will lead to a loss of quality in our work. Even if our work remains good, it will not be as good as it could have been had we served with our whole heart. Even if we do well a task that we find distasteful, it is only because we have a compelling love for the fruit of our labors or an ideal that is fulfilled by our work. [35]

We ultimately only do that which produces or honors what we most love. Persons who sin but claim that they still love God may not think that they are lying, but in the moment that they sinned, the individuals loved the sin more than they loved God. Such persons are no different than an adulterer who says to his wife, "The other woman meant nothing to me; I still love you." The man may still love his wife, but in the moment of the sin, he loved the other person – or, at least, the passion – more than he loved his wife.

Preaching the Christ-focus of all Scripture is not simply an interpretive scheme or an exegetical device; it is regular exposure of the heart of God to ignite love for him in the hearts of believers. We preach grace to fan into flame zeal for the Savior. Our goal is not merely academic, but relational and spiritual. We consistently expound the gospel truths that pervade Scripture to fill the hearts of believers with love for God that drives out love for the world. The reason is simple: people are not tempted by what they have no desire to do.

When love for Christ dominates our affections, sin loses its allure and, consequently, loses its power. Love for Christ is the power of obedience.[36] Preaching that floods the heart with affection for the Savior simultaneously loosens the hold of false idols on our hearts, chokes the appeal of sin, and nourishes the desire for holiness. When love for Christ is preeminent, doing his will is our greatest compulsion and joy. Thus, the joy of the Lord is our strength (Neh. 8:10), and helping to produce this joy is the great privilege of Christ-centered preaching.

Preaching remains a joy when pastors discern that their task is not to harangue or guilt parishioners into servile duty, but rather to fill them up with love for God by extolling the wonders of his grace. Too many preachers leave ministry or become ineffective in it because they perceive their lot in life to be whipping recalcitrant parishioners into more diligent service. Of course, preaching must condemn sin and challenge the slothful, but without the context of love such ministry becomes a burden to all – including the minister. There is a better way to preach.

The better way always connects Scripture's commands with the motives and enablement of grace. Imperatives do not disappear from such preaching because the commands of God are an expression of his nature and of his care for us. Still, the imperatives are always founded on the redemptive indicatives that give people confidence in God's faithfulness even in the face of their failures. We discourage people from basing their justification on their sanctification (i.e. determining if they are right with God based on the quality or quantity of their religious performance), and instead encourage them to live in the assurance of the completed work of Christ on their behalf.[37]

When our people perceive the present value of the blood of Christ, then they serve God with growing confidence of his blessing rather than with increasing dread of, or callousness to, his frown. Those who know that their forgiven status and family position are not jeopardized by the weaknesses of their present humanity live in loving service to Christ, rather than in self-justifying competition and judgment of each other.[38]

PREACHING THE JOY THAT DISTINGUISHES

Consistent preaching of the gospel's assurances drives despair and pride from the Christian life. As a consequence, congregations find that spiritual fatigue, competitiveness, and insensitivity wane; in their place flow new joy in Christ, desire to make him Lord over the whole of life, understanding of the weak, care for the hurting, forgiveness for those who offend, and, even, love for the lost. In short, the Christian community becomes an instrument of grace because God's love becomes the substance of the church's soul. In such contexts, ministers thrive and their ministries become a blessing to all (including themselves and their families) rather than a burden. Without question, there will also be challenges and disappointments, but even these will not destroy the joy that God builds on a foundation of grace.

The necessity of grace for preaching that is true to the gospel leads to a basic question that all must answer in order to affirm that they are preaching the Christianity of the Bible: "Do I preach grace?" Would your sermons be perfectly acceptable in a synagogue or mosque because you are only encouraging better moral behavior that any major religion would find acceptable? [39] If this is so, the path to a better, more Christian message is not through preaching any less of Scripture, but rather through preaching more. Do not stop preaching until Christ has found his place in your sermon and his grace has found its way into the heart of your message. In this way, the people to whom you preach will walk with him, and his joy will be their strength to do his will.

1. Unless otherwise indicated, the author's Bible references are quoted from the New International Version (NIV).

2. See the author's *Christ-centered Preaching: Redeeming the Expository Sermon*, 2nd ed. (Grand Rapids, Mich.: Baker, 2005), 275–6.

3. Sidney Greidanus, *Preaching Christ from the Old Testament* (Grand Rapids, Mich.: Eerdmans, 1999), 54.

4. Chapell, *Christ-centered Preaching*, 282–8.

5. Sidney Greidanus, *The Modern Preacher and the Ancient Text: Interpreting and Preaching Biblical Literature* (Grand Rapids, Mich.: Eerdmans, 1988), 166.

6. Chapell, *Christ-centered Preaching*, 305–6.

7. Edmund Clowney, *The Unfolding Mystery: Discovering Christ in the Old Testament* (Phillipsburg, N.J.: P&R Publishing, 1988), 9–16.

8. Jonathan Edwards proposes such an approach in his "Letter to the Trustees of the College of New Jersey" saying, " ... [T]he whole of it [Christian theology], in each part, stands in reference to the great work of redemption by Jesus Christ" as the "summum and ultimum of all divine operations and decrees." See Clarence H. Faust and Thomas H. Johnson, eds., *Jonathan Edwards* (New York: American Book, 1935), 411–12.

9. Chapell, *Christ-centered Preaching*, 306–8.

10. Ibid., 48–52 and 299–305.

11. Ibid., 289–95.

12. J. I. Packer, *Rediscovering Holiness* (Ann Arbor, Mich.: Servant Press, 1992), 75.

13. Westminster Shorter Catechism, question 1; Westminster Larger Catechism, questions 32, 97, 168, 174, 178; Heidelberg Catechism, questions 1, 2, 32, 86; Westminster Confession of Faith, 16.2; 19.6, 7; 20.1; 22.6.

14. See the author's *Holiness by Grace* (Wheaton, Ill.: Crossway, 2001), 154; and *Christ-centered Preaching*, 321.

15. Thomas Chalmers, "The Expulsive Power of a New Affection" in *Sermons and Discourses*, vol. 2 (New York: Carter, 1846), 271. See also Walter Marshall, *The Gospel Mystery of Sanctification* (1692; reprint, Grand Rapids, Mich.: Reformation Heritage, 1999).

16. Chapell, *Holiness by Grace*, 29–31; and *Christ-centered Preaching*, 320–3.

17. Chapell, *Christ-centered Preaching*, 312.

18. Geerhardus Vos, "The Idea of Biblical Theology," a pamphlet form of Vos's inaugural address upon assuming the new chair of biblical theology at Princeton Seminary (Covenant Theological Seminary Library, n.d.; 1895 probable), 16. This address in elaborated form became the introduction of Vos' *Biblical Theology* (1948; reprint, Grand Rapids, Mich.: Eerdmans, 1975).

19. Graeme Goldsworthy, *Preaching the Whole Bible as Christian Scripture* (Grand Rapids, Mich./Cambridge, UK: Eerdmans, 2000), 92–6.

20. Chapell, *Holiness by Grace*, 52–63 and 140–3.

21. John Murray, *Principles of Conduct* (Grand Rapids, Mich.: Eerdmans, 1957), 216–21.

22. See the author's *In the Grip of Grace* (Grand Rapids, Mich.: Baker, 1992), 54–8; and Jerry Bridges, *The Discipline of Grace: God's Role and Our Role in the Pursuit of Holiness* (Colorado Springs, Colo.: NavPress, 1994), 108.

23. Chapell, *In the Grip of Grace*, 32–7.

24. H. Ridderbos, *Paul: An Outline of His Theology* (Grand Rapids, Mich.: Eerdmans, 1975), 253.

25. Chapell, *Christ-centered Preaching*, 289–95.

26. John Calvin, *Institutes of the Christian Religion*, II.7.i–iii and ix.

27. Chapell, *Christ-centered Preaching*, 303.

28. Ibid., 323–7.

29. Chapell, *Holiness by Grace*, 52–62, 85–8, and 107.

30. Ibid., 193–203.

31. Ibid., 141–3.

32. John Murray, *The Collected Writings of John Murray*, vol. 4, ed. Iain H. Murray (Carlisle, Pa. Banner of Truth, 1982), 233; Thomas Manton, *A Treatise of the Life of Faith* (reprint, Ross-shire, Great Britain: Christian Focus, 1997), 65; C. S. Lewis, *Mere Christianity*, II.4 (New York: MacMillan, rev. 1952), 59–61; and Bridges, *Discipline of Grace*, 13–19 and 78–9.

33. Chapell, *Holiness by Grace*, 56–7.

34. Chapell, *Christ-centered Preaching*, 326.

35. Murray, *Principles of Conduct*, 226.

36. Chapell, *Holiness by Grace*, 107–9; and *Christ-centered Preaching*, 326.

37. Richard Lovelace, *Dynamics of Spiritual Life* (Downers Grove, Ill.: InterVarsity, 1979), 101.

38. Francis Schaeffer, *True Spirituality* in *The Complete Works of Francis Schaeffer*, vol. 3 (Wheaton, Ill.: Crossway, 1982), 200; and *The God Who Is There* (Downers Grove, Ill.: InterVarsity, 1968), 134.

39. Jay Adams, *Preaching with Purpose: A Comprehensive Textbook on Biblical Preaching* (Grand Rapids, Mich.: Baker, 1982), 152.

4

THE GREATNESS OF GOD'S GRACE

ROBERT A. PETERSON
Professor of Systematic Theology

Grace, grace, God's grace, grace that will pardon and cleanse within;
Grace, grace, God's grace, grace that is greater than all our sin.
Refrain: *"Marvelous Grace of Our Loving Lord"*
Julia H. Johnston (1910)

Wonderful the matchless grace of Jesus, deeper than the mighty rolling sea;
Wonderful grace, all sufficient for me, for even me.
Broader than the scope of my transgressions, greater far than all my sin and shame;
O magnify the precious name of Jesus, praise his name!
Refrain: *"Wonderful Grace of Jesus"*
Haldor Lillenas (1918)

Christians love to sing of God's grace – and rightly so, because all we have and are in Christ is due to grace. The refrains to the two familiar songs quoted above illustrate this fact. They also illustrate something else – the difficulty of measuring grace. According to these two songs, grace is great, matchless, deep, wonderful, sufficient, broad, and again, great. Songwriters strain to express the immensity of grace. This fact suggests an important question for Christian theology: How well have our formulations captured the greatness of grace?

The thesis of this essay is that the grace of God that brings salvation is far greater than most of us assume. We have some correct ideas concerning grace, but the Bible's portrayal of grace is much larger than our ideas. We have truncated the rich scriptural presentation of grace. We are feasting on true delicacies, but there is a side of the banquet table that we have not even visited.

This essay will not treat what in the Reformed tradition has been called common grace. Better called creational grace, common grace is the goodness of God, deriving from creation, whereby he preserves his creatures in spite of sin, restrains evil, and bestows good to believers and unbelievers alike – in fact, to all of his creatures. Three things distinguish creational grace (common grace) and saving grace. First, creational grace belongs to the order of creation while saving grace belongs to the order of redemption. Second, creational grace is therefore universal while saving grace is particular. Third, creational grace therefore does not save while saving grace does; that is why it is called saving grace. In this essay, we will deal with saving grace, not common (creational) grace.

Too often Christians have conceived of God's saving grace only as the past love of God revealed in the New Testament that puts us into a right relation with God. Every part of this description is biblical and therefore correct. Our mistake is not in what we include under the heading "the grace of God"; rather, we err in what we omit. God's grace *is* past, but it is *also* present and future. It does concern God's love, but it also concerns his power. It abounds in the New Testament, but is first revealed in the Old Testament. It puts us into a right relation with God, but it also keeps us saved until the end. Outlined below is an attempt to expand our conception and enjoyment of saving grace. The points are not mutually exclusive. Certainly they are not jointly exhaustive of the saving grace of God. The rest of this essay will examine each of these points in some detail.

- Grace is present in the Old Testament and abounds in the New.
- Grace is God's love and power.
- Grace is past, present, and future.
- Grace includes saving grace and preserving grace.

GRACE IS PRESENT IN THE OLD TESTAMENT AND ABOUNDS IN THE NEW

Ironically, we begin to demonstrate this point not with an Old Testament passage, but rather with John 1:17: "For the law was given through Moses; grace and truth came through Jesus Christ."[1] This is ironic because of the views of many Christians, epitomized in the note of the original *Scofield Reference Bible* on John 1:17, that:

> Law is connected with Moses and works; grace with Christ and faith. ... As a dispensation, grace begins with the death and resurrection of Christ. ... The point of testing is no longer legal obedience as the condition of salvation, but acceptance or rejection of Christ, with good works as a fruit of salvation.[2]

The amazing thing is, however, that "grace and truth" as referred to in John 1:17 (and 1:14) is an Old Testament concept![3] It appears in many Old Testament passages, but I will quote only a few:

> The LORD passed before him and proclaimed, "The LORD, the LORD, a God merciful and gracious, slow to anger, and abounding in steadfast love and faithfulness. ..." (Ex. 34:6)

> For your steadfast love is great above the heavens; your faithfulness reaches to the clouds. (Ps. 108:4)

> For great is his steadfast love toward us, and the faithfulness of the LORD endures forever. Praise the LORD! (Ps. 117:2)

At least twenty-five times, the Old Testament speaks of God's "love and faithfulness" together.[4] So, John 1:17 could not possibly mean that God's "grace and truth" were absent in the Old Testament and only revealed in Jesus Christ. Rather, John's point is that, compared to the abundant revelation of God's grace and truth in Christ, the Old Testament appears legal by comparison. Scofield missed John's use of hyperbole – his habit of stating comparisons in bald terms. The classic example is found in John 15:22-24:

> If I had not come and spoken to them, they would not have been guilty of sin, but now they have no excuse for their sin ... If I had not done among them the works that no one else did, they would not be guilty of sin, but now they have seen and hated both me and my Father.

If one missed John's hyperbole, one could conclude that Jesus was denying original sin: His hearers were not sinners until they rejected him! Of course, Jesus is doing nothing of the kind. Instead, he makes a comparison without using comparative language. He means that the guilt of the Jewish leaders in rejecting his words and deeds is so great that their prior guilt (which is, of course, considerable) is as no guilt in comparison.

Thus, far from denying the existence of God's love and faithfulness in the Old Testament, John 1:17 uses these Old Testament concepts to accentuate the gigantic outpouring of God's grace in the ministry of Jesus Christ. John's point is not: *OT=no grace/NT=grace*. Instead, it is: *OT=much grace/NT=immeasurable grace*.

GRACE IS GOD'S LOVE AND POWER

Customarily, we define God's grace as his unmerited favor or love. And so it is in passages such as Ephesians 2. Paul digs a deep pit for us: before salvation we were spiritually dead, worldly, under Satan's influence, driven by sinful passions, and deserving of God's wrath (Eph. 2:1-3). Grace means that God climbed down into the pit, threw us over his shoulder, and carried us out.

> But God, being rich in *mercy*, because of the great *love* with which he loved us, even when we were dead in our trespasses, made us alive together with Christ – by *grace* you have been saved – and raised us up with him and seated us with him in the heavenly places in Christ Jesus, so that in the coming ages he might show the immeasurable riches of his *grace* in *kindness* toward us in Christ Jesus. For by *grace* you have been saved through faith. And this is not your own doing; it is the gift of God, not a result of works, so that no one may boast. (Eph. 2:4-9; emphasis added)

In this passage, Paul speaks of God's "grace" three times and uses as near synonyms for grace the words "mercy," "love," and "kindness." The initial saving grace of God is, therefore, akin to his mercy, love, and kindness. But notice that this love is not merely unmerited favor; it is favor *against* merit. We deserve divine wrath and receive divine mercy. We sow sin and reap eternal life. We merit judgment and obtain forgiveness. We deserve hell and get heaven. *That* is grace!

Astonishingly, grace is also *more* than that. It is more than God's saving love that makes us Christians in the first place. It is also God's power that enables us to live for him each day. In the famous "resurrection chapter" of 1 Corinthians, Paul, when he lists persons to whom the risen Christ appeared, puts himself last. The apostle explains:

> Last of all, as to one untimely born, he appeared also to me. For I am the least of the apostles, unworthy to be called an apostle, because I persecuted the church of God. But by the grace of God I am what I am, and his grace toward me was not in vain. On the contrary, I worked harder than any of them, though it was not I, but the grace of God that is with me. (1 Cor. 15:8-10)

Although he was a persecutor, Paul tasted the initial grace of God, that is, his divine compassion: "by the grace of God I am what I am" (1 Cor. 15:10). But not only so! God's initial saving compassion was truly received by Paul, and as a result, he worked harder than any of the other apostles. (Paul's frankness here is shocking to us moderns; we consider ourselves far too "spiritual" to say anything like this!) Paul's work ethic outstrips that of his fellows, but he qualifies his statement: "I worked harder than any of them, though it was not I, but the grace of God that is with me" (v. 10).

Here God's grace is not chiefly his favor against merit, but his divine enablement – his power – that strengthens Paul to work very hard. Theologians have sometimes labeled this "enabling grace" to distinguish it from initial "saving grace." God not only loves the unlovely and makes them members of his family by saving grace, he also equips those so loved by granting them enabling grace day by day, that they may live lives that are fruitful and pleasing to him.

In 2 Corinthians 12:1-10, Paul also testifies that God's grace is his power as well as his love. Here the apostle recounts the story of a man who "was caught up to the third heaven," to paradise, to the very presence of God (2 Cor. 12:2). The man turns out to be Paul himself, who saw and heard ineffable revelations from God, things that could easily puff up Paul beyond measure.

> So to keep me from being too elated by the surpassing greatness of the revelations, a thorn was given me in the flesh, a messenger of Satan to harass me, to keep me from being too elated. Three times I pleaded with the Lord about this, that it should leave me. But he said to me, "My grace is sufficient for you, for my power is made perfect in weakness." Therefore I will boast all the more gladly of my weaknesses, so that the power of Christ may rest upon me. For the sake of Christ, then, I am content with weaknesses, insults, hardships, persecutions, and calamities. For when I am weak, then I am strong. (2 Cor. 12:7-10)

To prevent Paul from being conceited, God gave him a physical malady – perhaps bad eyesight (cf. Gal. 4:13-15) – to humble him. Although Paul asked God three times to take away the problem, God refused. Instead, he told Paul: "My *grace* is sufficient for you, for my *power* is made perfect in weakness" (v. 9; emphasis added). The parallelism between God's grace and his power is unmistakable. Here grace is God's power that enables believers like Paul to live for God in spite of great difficulties.

Generally, believers have underestimated the importance of God's grace for the Christian life. Grace is not only initial, instantaneous, and saving; it is also ongoing, progressive, and enabling. We are not only justified by grace through faith in Christ; we are also progressively sanctified the same way – by grace through faith in Christ.[5] We can no more successfully live the Christian life in our own strength than we can make ourselves Christians in our own strength. *Living the Christian life requires as much dependence on the supernatural grace of God as does becoming a Christian in the first place.* We become the children of God our Father due to his matchless love and power; we live in the Father's family by relying on his love and power too.[6]

And yet, God's grace is still greater.

GRACE IS PAST, PRESENT, AND FUTURE

It is common for Christians to speak of God's grace in the past tense. Testimonies recount the ways in which God brought people to know grace in times past. But we give little attention to our present need for grace, and most of our testimonies have little to say about future grace. Here again the Scriptures expand our conception of grace, for the Bible speaks of grace in three tenses: past, present, and future.

Past Grace

It is correct to speak of grace as past. Recall this familiar text, which was discussed above: "For by grace you *have been saved* through faith" (Eph. 2:8; emphasis added). Now let us consider a less familiar one:

> I thank him who has given me strength, Christ Jesus our Lord, because he judged me faithful, appointing me to his service, though formerly I was a blasphemer, persecutor, and insolent opponent. But *I received mercy* because I had acted ignorantly in unbelief, and *the grace of our Lord overflowed for me* with the faith and love that are in Christ Jesus. The saying is trustworthy and deserving of full acceptance, that Christ Jesus came into the world to save sinners, of whom I am the foremost. But *I received mercy* for this reason, that in me, as the foremost, Jesus Christ might display his perfect patience as an example to those who were to believe in him for eternal life. To the King of ages, immortal, invisible, the only God, be honor and glory forever and ever. (1 Tim. 1:12-17; emphasis added)

In recounting his transformation from a persecutor to a propagator of the gospel, Paul knows to whom the glory belongs – to "the King of ages ... the only God." Notice the apostle's use of the past tense to depict his reception of grace: "I received mercy," "the grace of our Lord overflowed for me," and again, "I received mercy" (vv. 13, 14, 16). Plainly, here the accent is on grace in the past tense. But it is incorrect to limit the grace of God to the past. It also is present and future.

Present Grace

God's grace overflows in the lives of Christians in the present too. Hebrews extols the incomparable high priesthood of Jesus Christ.

> Since then we have a great high priest who has passed through the heavens, Jesus, the Son of God, let us hold fast our confession. For we do not have a high priest who is unable to sympathize with our weaknesses, but one who in every respect has been tempted as we are, yet without sin. Let us then with confidence draw near to the throne of grace, that we may receive mercy and find grace to help in time of need. (Heb. 4:14-16)

The readers of the epistle to the Hebrews are to persevere despite persecution for their faith because Christ is the unique divine human high priest. Christ is divine: he, unlike all the Old Testament priests, has returned to the Father in heaven, and is designated by the divine title, "Son of God" (v. 14). But he is also God become man: he can empathize with us because he was tempted as we are and yet never sinned (v. 15). Consequently, believers are summoned to come to the exalted Christ in prayer to receive his aid.

Note the awesome way in which the throne of God is described. It is not called "the throne of the divine majesty," "the throne of God's justice," or "the throne of exalted holiness," all of which are accurate descriptions of God's heavenly throne. Instead, because of the work of our great High Priest, the throne of God has become for us "the throne of grace" (Heb. 4:16)! And from that throne, the ascended Son of God grants mercy and grace to those who approach confidently (v. 16). Here is grace in the present tense – "grace to help," given by Christ to his people who call upon him in time of need.

How can we limit God's grace to the past when Christ bids us come and ask for it now? The apostle Paul did not so limit it, for he begins and ends his epistles with salutations and benedictions that speak of present, enabling grace. One example of this will suffice. In the salutation of 1 Corinthians, Paul writes, "Grace to you and peace from God our Father and the Lord Jesus Christ;" and in the closing, "The grace of the Lord Jesus be with you" (1 Cor. 1:3; 16:23). Is the grace with which Paul begins and ends his epistles initial saving grace? Is he asking the Father and Son to save those to whom he writes? The answer to both questions is negative. Paul writes to believers: "to the church of God that is in Corinth, to those sanctified in Christ Jesus, called to be saints ..." (1 Cor. 1:2). He, therefore, does not begin and end his letters by mentioning past saving grace already received by his readers; rather, he prays that they currently will receive grace that will enable them to live for Christ. The salutations and closings of Paul's letters contain references to present grace, a fact that ought to enable us to pray better. Perhaps we too should pray that God would grant present enabling grace to those whom he places on our hearts as we wait before him.

Peter also speaks of grace in the present tense. After addressing the elders among his readers, he says:

> Likewise, you who are younger, be subject to the elders. Clothe yourselves, all of you, with humility toward one another, for "God opposes the proud but gives grace to the humble." (1 Peter 5:5)

Peter exhorts the young men to humility and then cites Proverbs 3:34 (LXX) as an incentive. Those who exalt themselves over others in the church set themselves against God, but those who humble themselves before their fellow believers put themselves in a position to receive grace from God. This is present enabling grace.

Peter concludes his second epistle by exhorting his readers to grow in Christ's grace: "But grow in the grace and knowledge of our Lord and Savior Jesus Christ. To him be the glory both now and to the day of eternity. Amen" (2 Peter 3:18). The apostle wants his readers to make progress in their Savior's grace and in the knowledge of him. Once more, this grace is not the initial saving grace that made them Christians. Rather, it is ongoing, strengthening grace that enables them to live as befits the people of God.

Future Grace

God's marvelous grace is past, present, and also future. His grace made children of God out of children of the devil. His grace empowers his children to live for him. His grace also will be poured out upon them at the second coming of Christ. Perhaps this is seen most clearly in the following passage:

> Therefore, preparing your minds for action, and being sober-minded, set your hope fully on the grace that will be brought to you at the revelation of Jesus Christ. As obedient children, do not be conformed to the passions of your former ignorance, but as he who called you is holy, you also be holy in all your conduct, since it is written, "You shall be holy, for I am holy." And if you call on him as Father who judges impartially according to each one's deeds, conduct yourselves with fear throughout the time of your exile... (1 Peter 1:13-17)

Peter urges his readers to live as the obedient and holy children of a holy Father, serving him in the fear of honor, a fear compatible with love for him. Before doing so, however, the apostle exhorts them to readiness and seriousness and tells them to put their hope of future salvation entirely "on the grace that will be brought to you at the revelation of Jesus Christ" (1 Peter 1:13). This is future grace – grace to be brought by our Savior at his return.

I have taught adult Sunday school for many years. At times, class members have opened up and shared their mixed emotions concerning the second coming. On the one hand, they know that they are to love the Lord's appearing (2 Tim 4:8). But on the other hand, they are made uneasy at the prospect of being ashamed before him at his return (1 John 2:28). They are troubled at the prospect of bringing sins into his presence. In short, they are conflicted concerning a major tenet of the Christian faith – the return of Christ.

I ask the class members to think of one special friend, an older Christian who loves them more than any other human being. Their thoughts alight on a parent, pastor, or trusted friend. I then ask them what their response would be if it suddenly came to their attention that they had wronged this one who loves them so. Invariably, their response is to make contact – to phone or e-mail as soon as possible – in order to set things right. They are so secure in their relationship with their special friend that their disquiet over their offense is dwarfed by the immensity of their friend's unconditional love for them. I then remind them that all believers have a Special Friend indeed, compared to whose love any mere human being's love fades to insignificance. We need not fear the second coming, even if it means confessing some sins to our Savior. We need not fear as we set our "hope fully on the grace that will be brought to" us "at the revelation of Jesus Christ" (1 Peter 1:13). Praise God that his grace is past, present, *and* future!

GRACE INCLUDES SAVING GRACE AND PRESERVING GRACE

Frequently, we conceive of grace as the love of God that brings us into a saving relationship with Christ. Although it is correct to do so, God's grace is much larger than that. Grace not only brings us into union with Christ, it also sustains that union. Grace not only saves us, it also keeps us. Grace is not only saving grace, it also is preserving grace. There is no better place in Scripture to see this than in the classic text for God's preservation of his saints – Romans 8:28-39:

> And we know that for those who love God all things work together for good, for those who are called according to his purpose. For those whom he foreknew he also predestined to be conformed to the image of his Son, in order that he might be the firstborn among many brothers. And those whom he predestined he also called, and those whom he called he also justified, and those whom he justified he also glorified.
>
> What then shall we say to these things? If God is for us, who can be against us? He who did not spare his own Son but gave him up for us all, how will he not also with him graciously give us all things? Who shall bring any charge against God's elect? It is God who justifies. Who is to condemn? Christ Jesus is the one who died – more than that, who was raised – who is at the right hand of God, who indeed is interceding for us. Who shall separate us from the love of Christ? Shall tribulation, or distress, or persecution, or famine, or nakedness, or danger, or sword? As it is written, "For your sake we are being killed all the day long; we are regarded as sheep to be slaughtered." No, in all these things we are more than conquerors through him who loved us. For I am sure that neither death nor life, nor angels nor rulers, nor things present nor things to come, nor powers, nor height nor depth, nor anything else in all creation, will be able to separate us from the love of God in Christ Jesus our Lord.

In this passage Paul offers four arguments for our safety in Christ.

God's Plan (Rom. 8:28-30)

Romans 8:28 is one of the most famous verses in all of Scripture: "And we know that for those who love God all things work together for good, for those who are called according to his purpose." Here God promises to make all things, even sufferings and groaning (vv. 18, 23), contribute to the ultimate benefit of those who love him, those whom he has brought to Christ. Believers' confidence is strengthened by the message of the next two verses: the people whom God fore-loved,[7] he also predestined to share the moral likeness of their older Brother Jesus, and these he called to be saved, justified, and glorified. Paul uses five verbs in the simple past tense to teach that the work of salvation is God's work from the beginning (fore-loving his people before creation) to the end (glorifying them in his presence). God foreknew, predestined, called, justified, and glorified his people. Remarkably, their future glorification is put in the past tense. This is Paul's way of underscoring the fact that they are safe in God's invincible grace.

God's Power (Rom. 8:31-32)

Another argument that Paul uses to show that God's grace keeps his people for final salvation concerns God's power: "What then shall we say to these things? If God is for us, who can be against us?" (v. 31). As is often his custom, Paul uses a rhetorical question to teach. He means that, if God the Father Almighty, Maker of heaven and earth, is on our side, who can successfully oppose us? Of course, the answer is: No one, for God is all-powerful. The only question is: How can we be certain that Almighty God is indeed on our side? Paul anticipates the objection and replies: "He who did not spare his own Son but gave him up for us all, how will he not also with him graciously give us all things?" (v. 32). The supreme demonstration that God is *Deus pro nobis* – "God for us," as the Reformers liked to say – is that he sent his Son to be our Savior. He who freely gave his Son will not withhold any good thing, including final salvation, from those who know and love his Son. God's powerful grace preserves us to the end.

God's Justice (Rom. 8:33-34)

God's preserving grace is also based on his justice. Paul writes: "Who shall bring any charge against God's elect? It is God who justifies" (v. 33). Here again the apostle employs a rhetorical question as a teaching device. He asks, Who will bring a legal accusation against God's chosen ones and make it stick? His response indicates that the answer to this question is: No one, no one at all. He reminds his readers: "It is God who justifies" (v. 33). Our case has gone to the world's highest court – the court of heaven – and has been heard by the supreme Judge – God himself. And the God of justice, who knows our sinfulness better than we ever will, has declared righteous all who believe in his Son. There is no higher court of appeal. Our enemies are silenced. God has pronounced us guiltless and no one will henceforth condemn.

Paul continues his legal argument for preservation: "Who is to condemn?" (v. 34). The Bible's answer is that the Last Judgment will be presided over by the Father and the Son. Here Paul mentions the Son, but not as his people's judge; rather, he is their Redeemer: "Christ Jesus is the one who died – more than that, who was raised – who is at the right hand of God, who indeed is interceding for us" (v. 34). The Judge of all the earth will not condemn us. Indeed, he died, was raised, ascended to God's right hand – from whence he presents his perfect sacrifice on our behalf – and prays for us. Christ will not condemn us because he has taken extreme measures to rescue us and to keep us saved. Once more Paul emphasizes the fact that God's loved ones are safe in his preserving grace.

God's Love (Rom. 8:35-39)

Believers are kept safe by God's preserving grace according to his plan (Rom. 8:28-30), his power (vv. 31-32), his justice (vv. 33-34), and, especially, according to his love. After all, his preserving grace *is* his love! Again, Paul begins with a rhetorical question: "Who shall separate us from the love of Christ?" (v. 35). He then lists seven terrible things that threaten to tear us from God's love, shows by Old Testament quotation that it is customary for God's children to suffer, and then concludes, "No, in all these things we are more than conquerors through him who loved us" (vv. 35-37). Nothing at all can separate God's people from Christ, their Lover – not even death, which Paul includes under the symbol "sword" in his list, as well as in the mention of God's people being "killed all day long" and "slaughtered" in the quotation of Psalm 44:22 (vv. 35, 36).

Paul more emphatically protests that nothing will ever sever those whom God loves from his love: "For I am sure that neither death nor life, nor angels nor rulers, nor things present nor things to come, nor powers, nor height nor depth, nor anything else in all creation, will be able to separate us from the love of God in Christ Jesus our Lord" (Rom. 8:38-39). The apostle's language is comprehensive, for what is *not* included in our life and death, or in things present and things to come (he has already pronounced us justified from past sins and more, v. 33)?

After saying that evil personalities and powers will not be able to disconnect us from God's love, Paul asserts that nothing "else in all creation" will be able to do so either. All that exists belongs to one of two categories: Creator or creature. Paul has repeatedly affirmed the Creator's intention to keep us (vv. 30, 31-32, 33-34, 35, 37). Now he says that no creature will defeat God's love and damn us. Some people protest, "But we can separate *ourselves* from his love by unbelief." Such reasoning is unsound because we are creatures and therefore included in the words, "nor *anything else* in all creation, will be able to separate us from the love of God in Christ Jesus our Lord" (v. 39; emphasis added). I do not see how Paul could have proclaimed more comprehensively or more clearly that God's love not only saves but keeps the people of God for final salvation.

CONCLUSION

Christians have significantly underestimated the grace of God. Although grace abounds beyond measure in the New Testament, we have seen that it is also present in the Old Testament in large measure. Grace accurately describes God's love that saves us; it also depicts God's power that equips us and enables us to live lives worthy of our high calling.[8] We are not only justified by grace; we are also progressively sanctified in the same way – a truth that we neglect to our peril. We have correctly defined God's grace as his past love for us, but have incorrectly neglected present and future aspects of grace that encourage us in our struggles and give us bright hope for the future. Our accent has been upon saving grace, while at the same time we have deemphasized preserving grace; yet both are worthy of our attention.

Having used the terminology of systematic theology to describe grace as present in both Testaments – as saving and enabling; as past, present, and future; as initial and progressive; as justifying and sanctifying; and as saving and preserving – it is high time for me to make a confession. Such theological categories are somewhat helpful if they expand our appreciation for the dimensions of God's grace. But, lest we take ourselves and our theologizing too seriously, we are forced to admit that these categories are frail human attempts to describe the one overarching grace of God. Categories have their place, but let us not confuse them with the grace of God itself as revealed in Scripture. In Scripture, God's grace is a seamless garment, certainly encompassing everything that these categories partially convey, but including more – *much* more! – as well.

We began this study with quotations from two hymns – human attempts to capture in poetic language the essence and beauty of God's all-encompassing grace. Yet, good as these hymns are, they – like our limited theological categories – are ultimately incomplete expressions of that grace. Let us close, therefore, with an inspired prayer from Holy Writ itself, a prayer that transcends all theological categories and all merely human attempts to celebrate God's matchless, wonderful, and exceedingly great grace:

> For this reason I bow my knees before the Father, from whom every family in heaven and on earth is named, that according to the riches of his glory he may grant you to be strengthened with power through his Spirit in your inner being, so that Christ may dwell in your hearts through faith – that you, being rooted and grounded in love, may have strength to comprehend with all the saints what is the breadth and length and height and depth, and to know the love of Christ that surpasses knowledge, that you may be filled with all the fullness of God. (Eph. 3:14-19)

1. Unless otherwise indicated, the author's Bible references are quoted from the English Standard Version (ESV).

2. *The Scofield Reference Bible*, ed. C. I. Scofield (New York: Oxford University Press, 1909, 1917), 1115.

3. Lester J. Kuyper, "Grace and Truth: An Old Testament Description of God, and Its Use in the Johannine Gospel," *Interpretation* 18 (1964): 3–19.

4. The tally is that of R. Laird Harris in *Theological Workbook of the Old Testament*, ed. R. Laird Harris (Chicago: Moody Press, 1980), 307. See also Psalm 36:5; 57:10; 86:15.

5. This is the theme of Bryan Chapell's edifying book *Holiness by Grace* (Wheaton, Ill.: Crossway, 2001) and plays a prominent place in my *Adopted by God: From Wayward Sinners to Cherished Children* (Phillipsburg, NJ: P&R Publishing, 2001).

6. Enabling grace is also seen in 2 Timothy 2:1: "You then, my child, be strengthened by the grace that is in Christ Jesus."

7. For the argument that "foreknew" here means "fore-loved," see Robert A. Peterson and Michael D. Williams, *Why I Am Not an Arminian* (Downers Grove, Ill.: IVP, 2004), 54–6.

8. Space prohibits me from discussing 1 Peter 4:10-11, which indicates that spiritual gifts are particular manifestations of God's grace given to members of Christ's body for mutual edification.

5

"BUT WHERE SIN ABOUNDED, GRACE DID MUCH MORE ABOUND":

Lessons from the Book of Genesis

ROBERT I. VASHOLZ
Professor of Old Testament

The title of this essay represents a classic expression from Romans 5:20b (KJV). In this brief clause, the apostle Paul makes a profound utterance as he exults in the divine superseding of sin by God's grace, an enabling grace that makes sin impotent. God's grace more than matches the intensification of sin revealed in the law. Though sin reigns by an awareness of God's law, grace overrules.[1] It is the grace of God that depletes the vigor of sin that leads to judgment; it is this same grace that was displayed in the treatment of defectors from God's law who fell under judgment.

How often was God willing to restrain the exercise of his judgment so that his people might enjoy his generosity? How often did the Old Testament prophets proclaim God's willingness to forgive Israel in spite of the people's blatant rebellion? The prophet Micah summarizes it all in 7:18: "Who is a God like you, who pardons iniquity and passes over the rebellious act of the remnant of his possession?" (NASB). To state it in the vernacular, sin is big, but, by all accounts, God's grace is bigger.

But is it only the Old Testament prophets and the New Testament writings that project this message? Are there not also intimations of this same motif – God's compassionate response to human failing – at the very beginning of Holy Scripture, namely, in Genesis? I suggest that the quintessence of this grace is demonstrated in instances when God mitigated the severity of his judgments all the way back in the earliest chapters of the Bible.

GRACE FOR A CURSE

God's grace is so abundant and the examples of its presence are so numerous that one hardly knows where to begin. Let us therefore limit this study mainly to instances that might be somewhat unclear in English translations. The first example in which God mitigates his judgment appears in Genesis 3:16: "To the woman he said, 'I will greatly increase your pains in childbearing; with pain you will give birth to children. Your desire will be for your husband, and *he* will rule over you'"(NIV; emphasis added).[2] There is no dispute that these words were pronounced by God as a curse on the woman, and, through her as the queen of her gender, on all females in creation. Because she was deceived by the serpent, ate of the tree of the knowledge of good and evil, and enticed her husband to eat too, she came under sanctions. Unlike before her sin, she would now experience great pain when bearing children. Such was the curse pronounced on the woman. An interesting additional aspect of the curse, though, is that the man is given "to rule" over the woman.

The Hebrew word for "rule" (מֹשֵׁל) is first used in Genesis 1:18. This verb can denote authority, as it does in Genesis 45:8, where Joseph tells his brothers that God made him ruler (מֹשֵׁל) over all the land of Egypt. The word is used approximately eighty times in the Old Testament and has a wide semantic range. Its various usages principally mean that it must be translated in regard to its context. In Genesis 1:18 the sun, moon, and stars are ordered "to rule" (מֹשֵׁל) the day and the night. Obviously, in this instance the sense of the word is not the same as that used to describe Joseph's rule over Egypt! The rule of these celestial bodies pertains to their light overcoming the darkness (Gen. 1:17-18; cf. Jer. 31:35). "Ruling" here means "overcoming." Creation brings glory to God by overcoming adverse circumstances – such as birds overcoming the adversity of gravity in flight, fish overcoming the adverse environment of water to thrive in it, and the luminaries overcoming darkness with their light.[3] This, I suggest, is the way one must understand "to rule" (מֹשֵׁל) in Genesis 3:16.

But even more important, from my viewpoint, is the fact that the clause usually translated "*he* will rule over you" should be translated not "*he*" but "*that* will rule over you." The antecedent of "he" is not the "husband," as it is so commonly translated, but rather, "your desire." "Your desire" refers to the woman's affection for her husband. Because of her affection toward him, she will be willing to endure the great suffering that childbearing will now bring. Her desire toward her husband will afford her the strength to prevail, to overcome, and to be willing to provide him with sons and daughters. The curse, then, should read, "To the woman he said, 'I will greatly multiply your pain in childbirth; in pain you will bring forth children; but your desire will be to your husband, and *that* [desire] will rule you."

How has this verse come to be so misunderstood? Ironically, the reason seems to be a "gender issue" arising from the gender of the noun translated "desire." In the Hebrew text, this noun appears to be feminine in form; if that is indeed the case, it does not agree in gender with the following masculine pronoun (or demonstrative adjective) translated "he" (הוּא). However, in the Pentateuch, it is not uncommon for masculine pronouns – and particularly this one – to have a feminine antecedent.[4] But is it even necessary to consider this grammatical fine point? In Genesis 4:7, where the same word – "desire" (תְּשׁוּקָה) – is used, a masculine pronominal suffix refers to this feminine noun: תִּמְשָׁל־בּוֹ.[5] In other words, the Hebrew text of Genesis views the word "desire" as a masculine noun.

The suggested translation of Genesis 3:16 has several advantages. First, it rightly ties into the preceding clause with its emphasis on "pains in childbearing." It is natural and likely that what follows should be related to the immediate subject of suffering in childbearing. Second, this understanding of the passage serves to mitigate the judgment on the woman, even as the Lord God will soon do for Cain in Genesis 4:15. The Lord here graciously provides the woman strength to endure. This text ultimately portrays the woman as triumphant over the curse, though her triumph will not occur without some measure of suffering. In spite of the curse, she will prevail; her capacity for love and her affection for her husband will triumph over the prospect of suffering.

Grace in Exile

The next example in which God tempers his judgment by his grace is Genesis 3:24: "After he drove the man out, he placed on the east side of the Garden of Eden cherubim and a flaming sword flashing back and forth to *guard* the way to the tree of life" (NIV; emphasis added). The state of affairs depicted here is appalling. The greatest tragedy in the history of mankind had just occurred: Adam had sinned and brought all of his posterity down with him. It is impossible to exaggerate the seriousness of this situation. Not only did all of mankind fall with Adam – the race's federal head – but the entire creation that man was commissioned to rule came under a curse as well. In addition, Adam forfeited the privilege of partaking of the tree of life in Eden, a privilege that had been promised to "overcomers."[6] Abundant life would have been his reward for obeying God.[7] Now mankind was in *double trouble*. Not only had Adam sinned, but he had also failed to obtain abundant life.

We can only ponder the nature of the transformation Adam would have experienced had he been able to eat of the tree of life. In concert with Adam's transformation, the whole creation would have experienced a glorious rejuvenation, becoming fully energized by the life of God. (Instead, this miraculous transformation would have to wait for another Adam to come along.) Thus, by Adam's disobedience, all mankind forfeited the opportunity to eat from the tree of life, and the man and his wife were both driven out of Eden. As C. John Collins aptly expresses it, "they may not stay in the garden."[8]

We can hardly fathom the enormity of that simple statement. Adam fell and brought down all of his progeny with him. He must have been indescribably disheartened. What would now become of the human race? And on top of that, to keep man from returning to Eden in his present fallen state, the angels of God were placed at the gates of the Garden to *guard* the way back to the tree of life. How apparently hopeless was mankind's situation! But in the midst of such grave despair, the Lord once again mitigated his judgment, as we will now see.

It must be noted that the verb in Genesis 3:24 that is translated "to guard" (שמר) has another meaning as well. On the one hand, it can mean "to guard," in the sense of a sentry assigned to protect something from any harmful intrusion. Such was the responsibility of the priests who were assigned to guard the tent sanctuary in the wilderness by preventing any impurity from entering its environs. However, the predominant use of this verb in Genesis is "to keep" in the sense of caring and preserving. (The priests, by guarding the sanctuary, not only protected it from harm, but also *kept* it open and accessible to worshipers.) The NIV translates this verb "to keep" four times.[9] In the chapter immediately prior to the one we have been considering, at Genesis 2:15, we read that "the Lord God took the man and put him in the garden ... *to take care* (שמר) of it" (NIV; emphasis added). In Genesis 28:15, 20 and 30:31 the verb is translated "watch over" (cf. Gen. 41:35). The crux of the matter is that God not only placed his angels at Eden to *guard* the way to the Tree of Life, but to *maintain* it as well.[10] When man was at his lowest, overwhelmed by discouragement, the Lord provided hope. The way to Life was not closed forever. Indeed, how can it be in light of Revelation 2:7b: "To him who overcomes, I will give the right to eat from the tree of life, which is in the paradise of God" (NIV)? In spite of man's dismal showing, the Lord lifts his spirit by assuring him that all has not been forever lost. The way to life is being preserved for him and his posterity in anticipation of another who will achieve the goal that the first Adam failed to reach.

GRACE FOR A WANDERER

God's grace is even more apparent in our next example. Cain killed his brother Abel (cf. Gen. 4:8). Murder is the first of the "You shall nots" in the Ten Commandments that addresses conduct between people. Its placement as first of these commandments suggests its precedence and gravity.[11] Cain made an offering to God that did not please him. Consequently, Cain was admonished by God concerning the significance of his failure to bring an offering worthy of his Creator: "If you do what is right, will you not be accepted? But if you do not do what is right, sin is crouching at your door; it desires to have you, but you must master it" (Gen. 4:7 NIV). In the Old Testament, the verb root (רבץ) of the normalized participle "crouching" commonly means "to lie down." It is used mainly to describe animals at rest.[12] Obviously, it does not mean that in Genesis 4:7. The context suggests not that sin is lying *down* but that sin is lying *in wait*, i.e. *is lurking*. This meaning finds support from a cognate root.[13] This root is used as a noun in extra-biblical sources to depict demons lurking at a door; could this suggest, perhaps, that "sin" in Genesis 4:7 is a metonym for "demon"?[14] Whatever the case, the Lord was here graciously warning Cain that his un-Abel-like attitude made him vulnerable to sin's power.

Cain gave no heed to this warning. The rejection of his offering by God – or rather, his own rejection of God – led Cain to commit violence toward his brother Abel: "... and while they were in the field, he slew him." The shedding of Abel's blood is a prime example of the disharmonies among brothers that came about as a result of the Fall. Stigers remarks that the phrase "in the field" indicates a place known to both Cain and Abel. Here indeed was a place so affected by the curse that it seemed to be beyond rescue. "Thus there is here the history of the first *premeditated* murder. Cain is now of the 'seed of the Serpent' (cf. 1 John 3:12). Here is the first attempt to prevent the incarnation-resurrection work of God in man."[15] The judgment God pronounced on Cain was that the ground Cain was farming would no longer be productive: "... it will no longer yield its crops for you" (Gen. 4:12 NIV). Cain is thus stripped of his vocation – a punishment that harkens back to that of his father Adam and that would drive him, like his father, away from the presence of God (cf. Gen. 3:24; 4:14-16). Cain's judgment is that he will be a vagabond, a wanderer on earth.

This, of course, raises the issue of capital punishment. Subsequently, in the law of Moses, capital punishment for murder is unequivocally required. The idea that Cain's sentence is worse than death (Cain probably thought so) has always found some advocates. The absoluteness of the dictum of death for premeditated murder in the Mosaic law suggests that Cain's situation must not be taken as normative. In any case, the penalty that God pronounced upon Cain for his sin was just. Administering justice, however, does not exclude the possibility of showing mercy.

Cain's response to God's judgment was, "My punishment is more than I can bear." Cain feared that he would have to live the rest of his life looking over his shoulder. He surmised that he would be the object of vengeance, or that he would be killed out of fear that he might repeat his crime, or both. He would always be on the run, so to speak, living in constant terror of retribution. He could never again lie down at night feeling safe. He could never settle down. This, he cried out, was too much to bear (Gen. 4:13).

Did this cry of despair mark a change in Cain's attitude? Was he who seemed so arrogant at last humbled? The Lord God responded by mitigating Cain's sentence. He provided a mark "so that no one finding him would slay him" (Gen. 4:15b NASB). The Lord himself would be Cain's fierce avenger against anyone who violated God's warning. And what was the *mark* put on

Cain? The speculations about this are legion when one takes into account both Jewish and Christian sources. Assuming that it was a visible mark placed on Cain's body, the proposed possibilities include: a bright-colored coat, leprosy, a horn, or the last letter of the Hebrew alphabet placed on Cain's forehead.[16] Even a phylactery has been suggested.[17] The Bible does not explain what the mark was. That it was a mark on Cain's body is, however, questionable. Genesis 4:15b can and should be read as, "He placed a sign *on behalf of* Cain so that any who would encounter him would not smite him."[18] This amazing grace to Cain, who murdered one of God's elect, alleviated to some degree Cain's fear of reprisal and his dread of always living on the move. In fact, Cain eventually was able to settle down in the land of Nod (Gen. 4:16).

GRACE FOR THE GENERATIONS

Another remarkable instance of God's grace abounding by way of his moderating a sentence is in Genesis 9:19-25. This pertains to the curse on Canaan, Ham's son, for Ham's impropriety: "Noah, a man of the soil, proceeded to plant a vineyard. When he drank some of its wine, he became drunk and lay uncovered inside this tent. Ham, the father of Canaan, saw his father's nakedness and told his two brothers outside" (Gen. 9:20-22 NIV).

One man viewing another man while he is unclothed may not appear to be an egregious act to us moderns, but in the world of the Old Testament a man who showed himself naked – or even beardless – was humiliated. This was the case when Hanun, king of the Ammonites, humiliated David's envoys by shaving off half of each of the envoys' beards and cutting off their garments in the middle as far as their hips, exposing them. David therefore advised the envoys to stay out of the public eye until their beards grew back (1 Sam. 10:1-5).[19] Ham, by viewing his father when he lay drunk and uncovered, committed not only a serious breach of ancient etiquette, but also an act of great disrespect.[20] His action brought on a curse which, though given by Noah and not directly by God, is generally considered to have divine authority. In delivering the curse, though, Noah has apparently learned from the Lord's previous dealings with men to temper judgment with grace, for he curses Ham's son Canaan instead of Ham himself. This is a conundrum that has baffled commentators for centuries. Why was Canaan cursed for the sin of his father? And, in the context of our present discussion, how does this reflect God's grace?

Countless answers to the first question have been proposed. These include: (1) Canaan was a child of incest, being the son of Ham and Noah's wife; (2) Canaan was another name for Ham; (3) Ham was Noah's youngest son, so Noah cursed Ham's youngest; (4) Canaan was the instigator of the objectionable deed, or, at least, a participant in it; (5) the curse is an etiology that explains why the Canaanites practiced aberrant sexual behavior; (6) Noah had previously blessed Ham and so could not revoke his blessing (cf. Gen. 9:1).[21]

Interesting as these proposals are, all of them have shortcomings. Is there room for yet another interpretation? I think so. Genesis 9 already provides a background of mitigating judgment as an illustration that grace can supersede a curse brought on by sin (see above). We can add to this several more examples that are quite apparent. The first curse was allayed when God himself provided clothing for Adam and Eve in lieu of their own efforts: "The Lord God made garments of skin for Adam and his wife, and clothed them" (Gen. 3:21 NIV; cf. 3:7). Later, judgment was more than moderated for mankind when Noah and his family were spared from perishing in the Flood (Gen. 6:17-18; here is a precursor to the remnant motif that emerges so prominently among the Old Testament prophets).[22] Judgment was subsequently assuaged at Babel with the confusion of tongues that spared mankind from another worldwide catastrophe (Gen. 11:1-8). The cursing of Ham once again shows God's gracious mitigation of his judgment.

In Genesis 9:18 we are told that Noah had three sons who survived the Flood: "Now the sons of Noah ... were Shem and Ham and Japheth; and Ham was the father of Canaan" (NASB). (It seems clear from this verse that Canaan was not another name for Ham, as one interpretation suggests.) The Scriptures also provide an extensive list of the progeny of each of these sons in Genesis 10, including the sons of Ham and their progeny: "The sons of Ham were Cush and Mizraim and Put and Canaan" (Gen. 10:6 NASB). Whether or not Noah's curse also extended to Canaan's children is debatable, but not inconceivable. Whatever the case, had Noah cursed Ham directly, he would have cursed all four of Ham's sons. Instead, the curse was confined to just one son, with the result that not all of Ham's posterity "shall be a servant of servants to his brothers." Though this was indeed an act of judgment on Ham, it was judgment restrained by grace. Though this solution to the dilemma still does not answer the question as to why Canaan was cursed and not one of his brothers, it does explain why Ham was not.

GRACE, NOT VENGEANCE

Finally, a most surprising mitigation of deserved retribution is exemplified in the grace shown by Joseph to his brothers. His brothers' profound jealousy, triggered by their father Jacob's favoritism, incited their murderous proclivity.[23] That proclivity was already apparent when two sons of Jacob, Simeon and Levi – both sons of Leah – murdered the Hivites, including Hamor and Shechem. While they were angry because Shechem had violated their sister Dinah, their ensuing actions were devious: they covenanted peace with the Hivites and insisted on using as the sign of that covenant the same sign that was given as a sign between Abraham and God – circumcision.[24] The Hivites assented, and while they were thus incapacitated, the sons of Leah killed them. These actions were particularly odious, and their motives were further revealed to be suspect when Jacob's sons plundered the Hivites (Gen. 34:26-29).[25]

This murderous spirit attended other brothers as well, for when the group of them later saw Joseph, they said to one another, "Come now, let's kill him and throw him into one of these cisterns and say that a ferocious animal devoured him" (Gen. 37:20 NIV). It could be argued that the murder of Shechem had some justification – "because they had defiled their sister" – and because there is no expressed disapproval of this action in Scripture. Nevertheless, Jacob's comment on the matter reveals that his sons' chicanery would be viewed by the inhabitants of the region with great disdain: "Jacob said to Simeon and Levi, 'You have brought trouble on me by making me a stench to the Canaanites and Perrizites, the people living in this land. We are few in number, and if they join forces against me and attack me, I and my household will be destroyed'" (Gen. 34:30 NIV). One could hardly have expected anything less from a society that saw in its midst a family that behaved so abominably.

Graciously, God responded to Jacob's fear, though it is doubtful that Jacob's sons deserved it. God told Jacob to go to Bethel, where he had appeared to him before and had ministered to Jacob in the day of his distress (cf. Gen. 35:3). Jacob and his sons discarded their idols, purified themselves, and put on new garments – that is, showed signs of repentance. As they journeyed to Bethel, God placed a great terror on the nearby cities that would be expected to seek reprisals. Once at Bethel, Jacob built an altar to God. Considering the whole picture, God's protection of Jacob and his sons is exceedingly gracious – a mitigation by divine intervention that prevented serious retaliation.

It is not possible to determine exactly how much this example of grace extended to Jacob influenced his son Joseph. It seems reasonable to assume that the memory and the effects of this event must have filtered down to the rest of the family. There can be no question, however, that Joseph himself exhibited abounding grace in his mercy toward his brothers, who had so cruelly sinned against him. That Joseph did not misinterpret his brothers' intent toward him and saw it for the wickedness it was is obvious from the text. After Jacob died, the brothers feared that Joseph would then seek revenge. And certainly Joseph had good cause to desire retaliation, for as he himself said, "As for you, you meant evil against me ..." (Gen. 50:20 NASB). He does not gloss over their evil design that led to his misery.[26] Joseph was also in the perfect position to wreak retribution on his brothers, had he desired to do so, both by virtue of the authority he wielded and as justification for their past deeds.

And yet, just the opposite reaction was the case. The whole incident is extraordinary, especially in light of the many ancient oriental despots who were infamous for seizing every opportunity to inflict misery on those who had wronged them. But instead of repaying evil with evil, Joseph rendered good for evil. In this respect, Joseph anticipated the words – and the deeds – of Jesus, Paul, and Peter:

You have heard that it was said, "An eye for an eye, and a tooth for a tooth." But I say to you, do not resist an evil person; but whoever slaps you on your right cheek, turn the other to him also. If anyone wants to sue you and take your shirt, let him have your coat also. Whoever forces you to go one mile, go with him two (Matt. 5:38-41 NASB).

Bless those who persecute you; bless and do not curse. ... Never pay back evil for evil to anyone (Rom. 12:14-17 NASB).

Do not repay evil with evil or insult with insult, but with blessing, because to this you were called so that you may inherit a blessing (1 Peter 3:9 NIV).

What is even more remarkable here is that Joseph did not simply forgive his undeserving brothers for their murderous actions, but also provided more than amply for their future welfare: "So, therefore, do not be afraid; I will provide for you and your little ones.' So he comforted them and spoke kindly to them" (Gen. 50:19-21 NASB; cf. 47:11-12). Without a doubt, it was "grace that taught [their] heart[s] to fear and grace [their] fears relieved," as the great hymn "Amazing Grace" so beautifully expresses.

The mitigating of the severity of judgment in cases such as those we have been examining is indubitably gracious. This, in fact, is the very nature of grace: It intervenes where it is undeserved and unexpected. In the world of the Old Testament, where more often than not treachery, vengeance, reprisals, duplicity, brutality, and barbarity reigned, where people often delighted in inflicting punishment on one another, and where charity toward others was atypical to say the least, the tempering of a harsh response to wrongdoing is remarkable. That is how such acts would have been viewed by a society that reveled in extracting its pound of flesh. Indeed, that is how they are often viewed today, even in our supposedly more enlightened times. Such acts of grace displayed to the ancient world – as they do to ours – that there is a wideness in God's mercy that extends even to the most undeserving, and they provide a glorious anticipation of the unfolding magnanimity of God that is fully revealed in Jesus Christ.

---

1. The word "abounds" in Greek is *huperperisseuō*. It means, "to be plentiful beyond measure." The apostle uses the word only one more time, in 2 Cor. 7:4: "I am overflowing with joy in all our affliction" (NASB). Paul does not mean that grace is a license to sin so that grace might abound (Rom. 6:15). That is a misinterpretation of grace. Rather, grace is greater than sin and prevails over its archrival, the power of sin. A seminary student I know has portrayed it this way: If sin is a breeze, then grace is a tsunami!

2. There is very little variance among the English translations of this passage. Cf., for example, NASB, NIV, KJV, RSV, ESV, ASV.

3. Overcoming as a motif appears at the very beginning of creation. Creation emerges out of formlessness and emptiness, existence out of non-existence, light from darkness (Gen. 1:2). Creation is portrayed as an overcoming of nothingness.

4. For a limited number of instances of this in Genesis alone, see 3:20; 4:22; 7:22; 14:17; 19:20, 38; 20:35; 22:24; 23:2, 15, 19; 24:44; 25:21; 26:9; 27:38; 29:25; 34:14; 35:6, 19, 20, 27; 37:2; 38:14, 16; 43:32; 47:6; 48:7. In addition, see B. K. Waltke and M. O'Connor, *An Introduction to Biblical Hebrew Syntax* (Winona Lake, Ind.: Eisenbrauns, 1990), 302: "The masculine pronoun is often used for a feminine antecedent."

5. It is noteworthy that the noun "sin" (חַטָּאָה), commonly treated as feminine in the Old Testament, is treated in both 3:16 and 4:7 as masculine! These are the only two places in the Old Testament where this occurs.

6. The tree of life is promised to those who overcome: "To him who overcomes, I will grant to eat of the tree of life which is in the Paradise of God" (Rev. 2:7b [NASB]; cf. 2:11, 17, 26; 3:5, 12, 21; 21:7). In Jeremiah 17:13, the Tree of Life is called the "fountain of living waters."

7. That Adam was mortal explains the need for the tree of life. This is evident for several reasons: (1) Food was provided for man to survive before the Fall (Gen. 1:29-30). Who can deny the necessity of food for sustaining physical life? (2) Death was already present. In Genesis 1:30, the Lord said, "I give every green plant for food" (NIV). Everything that is eaten must first die, even vegetation. (3) Adam was mortal. If he had already possessed eternal life, then what purpose did this tree serve? Most probably it was a reward for Adam's "overcoming," that he might eat of it and thus live forever (cf. Gen. 3:22). The point is that Adam did not fall from immortality; rather, he never achieved it. (4) Is it possible that, if Adam had not eaten of the tree of the knowledge of good and evil, he would still be alive? I think not. Rather, Adam's mortality meant that his probationary period had temporal limitations. This explains how the serpent could be the great deceiver. The serpent said to the woman, "You surely will not die" – implying that God meant physical death when he had told Adam, "in the day that you eat from it you will surely die" (NASB). But God meant spiritual death, not immediate physical death. The evil one misled the woman by using the same words but filling them with different meaning.

8. C. John Collins, *Science and Faith: Friends or Foes?* (Wheaton, Ill.: Crossway, 2003), 144.

9. Gen. 17:9, 10; 18:19; and 41:35. "To keep" is an expression used in regard to preserving the covenant bond between Abraham and God.

10. The Hebrew Bible is replete with wordplay. A classic example is in Mal. 1:9: "Now implore God to be gracious to us. With such offerings from your hands, will he accept you?" (NIV). The verb translated "implore" (חלה) may have a different root, though even with a different root it would be written the same way in this Hebrew text. That different root means "to profane" (חלל). In other words, Malachi is suggesting that the priests curse the Lord in order to make him act benevolently towards them: "But now curse God so that he might be gracious to us ..." (author's translation). What irony! This sentiment fits well with that expressed in Mal. 1:8, where the prophet suggests offering sick cattle to the governor as a way of pleasing him. Indeed, that is exactly what the priests have been doing to the Lord (cf. Mal. 1:6-8)!

11. Capital punishment for premeditated murder under the Mosaic law is absolute; it is accompanied with the expression "show no pity" (Deut. 19:11-13). Other sentences where the expression "show no pity" occurs refer to apostasy, false testimony in court, and an indecent act (cf. Deut. 13:8; 19:21; 25:12). The expression, though absolute in these cases, infers that justice allows for the weighing of circumstances before a sentence is pronounced. In all fairness, one must consider mitigating circumstances. There is a wideness in the Mosaic law that curbs the use of justice to prevent it from creating injustices. "Justice, and only justice, you shall pursue. ..." (Deut. 16:20 [NASB]; cf. Deut. 22:23-27).

12. G. Botterweck, Helmer Ringgren, and Heinz-Joseph Fabry, eds. *Theological Dictionary of the Old Testament*, vol. 13 (Grand Rapids, Mich.: Eerdmans, 2004), 298–303. Hereafter referred to as Botterweck, Ringgren, Fabry.

13. In Akkadian the root is rabatsu. The word is used in the context of beasts of prey lying in wait. See *The Assyrian Dictionary*, vol. 14 (Chicago: University of Chicago Press, 1956–99), 12.

14. Botterweck, Ringgren, Fabry, 303.

15. Harold Stigers, *A Commentary on Genesis* (Grand Rapids, Mich.: Zondervan Publishing House, 1976), 89.

16. Old Hebrew script shaped the last letter of the alphabet like an X.

17. A phylactery is a small leather case containing Scripture that fervent Orthodox Jews fasten to their arms or foreheads with leather thongs when praying (cf. Ex. 13:9; Deut. 6:8; 11:18).

18. The preposition used here for "on behalf of" is what is called a dativus commodi. See T. Muraoka, *A Grammar of Biblical Hebrew* (Roma: Editrice Pontificio Istituto Biblico, 1996), 133d. Cf. "... the Lord appointed a sign for Cain " (NASB).

19. Other examples that demonstrate sensitivity to exposure are Gen. 3:7; Ex. 20:26; Jer. 13:26; and Hosea 3:3 [E]. The husband's right to expose his adulterous wife seems to correspond with ancient Near Eastern law.

20. That the offense was looking upon his father naked is explicit. "But Shem and Japheth took a garment and laid it upon both their shoulders and walked backward and covered the nakedness of their father; and their faces were turned away, so that they did not see their father's nakedness" (Gen. 9:23 NIV).

21. E. A. Speiser, Genesis, in *Anchor Bible* (Garden City: Doubleday and Co., Inc., 1964), 62; Nahum M. Sarna, Genesis, in *JPS Torah Commentary* (Philadelphia: The Jewish Publication Society, 1989), 66 ; Gordon J. Wenham, Genesis 1–15, in *Word Biblical Commentary* (Waco, Tex.: Word, 1987), 201; Herman Gunkel, *Genesis*, trans. by Mark E. Biddie (Macon, Ga.: Mercer University), 83–84; David H. Aaron, "Early Rabbinic Exegesis on Noah's Son Ham and the so-called 'Hamitic Myth,' "*Journal of the American Academy of Religion*

63 (1995): 721–59; F. W. Basset, "Noah's Nakedness and the Curse of Caanan: A Case of Incest?" *Vetus Testamentum* 21 (1971): 311–14. Cf. also, Victor P. Hamilton, *Handbook of the Pentateuch* (Grand Rapids, Mich.: Baker Book House, 1982), 77–80.

22. The preservation of a remnant is a recurring theme among the eighth-century prophets.

23. Jacob's preference for his wife Rachel over his wife Leah extended even to their children (Gen. 29:30-31). In addition, Jacob's other sons were children of concubines. One's social status in the world of polygamy more often than not depended on the status of one's mother. Nevertheless, while parental favoritism is usually quite destructive (see, for example, King Lear), there is no question that Jacob loved all of his sons (cf. Gen. 42:36; 49).

24. In the patriarchal era, the protocol, particularly among nomads, for establishing one's integrity was through covenants. Respect for keeping covenant in a society where there was no law was paramount in order to maintain some form of civility among nomadic peoples. "Brethren, I speak in terms of human relations: even though it is only a man's covenant, yet when it has been ratified, no one sets it aside or adds conditions to it" (Gal. 3:15 NASB). It should be highlighted that the Lord reproaches those who make covenants – social contracts – and break them (Mal. 2:14). Integrity via covenant-making is revered and underscored.

25. Deut. 13:12-18 offers a corrective to an improper motive for destroying an apostate city. If an Israelite city served other gods than Yahweh, a thorough and complete investigation had to be done. If apostasy was the case, the inhabitants of that city were to be destroyed. In addition, everything in that city had to be destroyed and that city could not be rebuilt. Nothing was to be left. This ensured that the motivation for annihilating a city was a proper one and not simply a desire for material gain! Ironically, it was avarice that saved Joseph: "Judah said to his brothers, 'What will we gain if we kill our brother and cover up his blood? Come, let's sell him to the Ishmaelites and not lay our hands on him; after all, he is our brother, our own flesh and blood.' His brothers agreed. So when the Midianite merchants came by, his brothers pulled Joseph up out of the cistern and sold him for twenty shekels of silver to the Ishmaelites, who took him to Egypt" (Gen. 37:26-28 NIV).

26. While there is very little that explicitly describes Joseph's suffering, it does come through in his response to Pharaoh's chief baker. After Joseph interprets the baker's dream favorably and notes that the baker will return to serve Pharaoh, Joseph's plea to him demonstrates Joseph's pain: "Only keep me in mind when it goes well with you, and please do me a kindness by mentioning me to Pharaoh and get me out of this house ... I have done nothing that they should have put me into the dungeon" (Gen. 40:14-15 NASB). One might add to that the suffering that comes from being falsely accused (Gen. 39:11-20).

6

THE GREAT COMMISSION
AS THE CONCLUSION OF MATTHEW'S GOSPEL

DAVID W. CHAPMAN
Assistant Professor of New Testament and Biblical Archaeology

---

But the eleven disciples proceeded to Galilee, to the mountain which Jesus had designated. When they saw Him, they worshiped Him; but some were doubtful. And Jesus came up and spoke to them, saying, "All authority has been given to Me in heaven and on earth. Go therefore and make disciples of all the nations, baptizing them in the name of the Father and the Son and the Holy Spirit, teaching them to observe all that I commanded you; and lo, I am with you always, even to the end of the age." (Matt. 28:16-20)[1]

The Great Commission has long held a prominent place in the hearts and minds of Christians around the world. This short text (Matt. 28:16-20) has launched mission movements and motivated Christians for centuries. For many, it is one of the first portions of Holy Scripture that they memorized. Yet, as is frequently the case with well-known verses, the familiarity of this passage can too easily lead us to view it as a contextless utterance of Jesus without reference to its import in the Gospel of Matthew.

However, in the context of Matthew, the report of the Great Commission constitutes the conclusion of the Gospel. In New Testament narrative, the conclusion was an opportunity to drive home the author's main points.[2] It should be no surprise then that Matthew, who shows great skill in forming his Gospel, would have been quite conscious of the import of his concluding words.

This essay beckons the reader to look again at the Great Commission with an eye to observing how it draws together themes found throughout the Gospel of Matthew.[3] The importance of this passage in Matthew then enables the careful reader to better understand many of Matthew's special emphases in his Gospel; and these emphases also facilitate more careful exegesis of the Great Commission itself. This essay does not attempt a full commentary on the passage.[4] Rather, it purposes primarily to observe a few thematic connections in the Gospel's conclusion in order to consider their import for reading Matthew and for understanding the Commission.[5]

Here we are assuming that Matthew worked carefully in the crafting of his Gospel. Christians have long recognized the truth of John 21:25 that there were "… many other things which Jesus did, which if they were written in detail, I suppose that even the world itself would not contain the books which were written." The Gospel authors were constrained by space, and also by their responsibility as communicators of the good news, to select carefully what to narrate from Jesus' ministry. New Testament scholarship has increasingly admired the ability of these authors to convey through narrative their theological understanding of Jesus. While many scholars have gone so far as to question the historical accuracy of the Gospels, in affirming the authors to be excellent craftsmen we need not assume that the Gospels depart from Jesus' *ipsissima vox* (i.e. his intended meaning). Rather, each author has particular theological and historical emphases that he sought to convey to his audience.[6] We can reasonably affirm that these emphases are both rooted in the ministry of Jesus himself and grounded in the experience of each Gospel author, who then mediated to his own audience the story of Jesus' ministry. In this way, the conclusion of Matthew's Gospel can be understood as a God-inspired ending, which draws together many of the emphases that God intended Matthew to convey to his audience.

WORSHIP

Other than Jesus' immediate family, the first people to encounter Jesus in the book of Matthew are the magi. Significantly, in that narrative the word "worship" (προσκυνέω) appears repeatedly.[7] The magi arrive in order to worship the child king (Matt. 2:2). While seeking information from the magi, Herod claims the same worshipful purpose (2:8), though with the actual intent of murdering Jesus. And, upon viewing Jesus, the magi immediately respond by falling down in worship (2:11). This threefold repetition of προσκυνέω in the pericope conveys to the reader the sense that Jesus, though a mere child, was rightly to be worshiped. Even Herod, as a clear foil to the magi, knew this to be proper.

It is striking that the last encounters with Jesus in Matthew's Gospel echo strongly this first experience. When Jesus' followers see their risen Lord, they immediately react by falling down in worship. This occurs as the women are departing the empty tomb and meet the risen Jesus (28:9). The same response also begins the pericope of the Great Commission (28:17): "And when they saw Him, they *worshiped* Him …."[8]

The worship theme is evident elsewhere in the Gospel, though its import is often obscured in modern translations.[9] Those in need of miracles often first do obeisance to Jesus by falling down in worship (8:2; 9:18; 15:25 – all employing προσκυνέω). Even in the midst of her improper request, the mother of the sons of Zebedee recognizes such obeisance to be the proper approach to Jesus when she wishes to appeal for special eschatological privileges for her sons (20:20). When Jesus walks on the water toward his disciples and calms the sea, the disciples react by worshiping Jesus and by acknowledging that "you truly are the Son of God" (14:33). The worship response to Jesus thus often forms an act of confession as to Jesus' power and authority.

Such worship can have royal overtones. Hence, aside from Jesus, the only other person to be so "worshiped" in Matthew is a king in one of Jesus' parables (18:26, cf. 18:23); this king clearly represents God himself. The magi approach Jesus as a king. And the mother of Zebedee's sons refers to Jesus' coming "kingdom" (20:21). However, the theme goes beyond mere human royalty with the proclamation of Jesus as the "Son of God" (14:33), who is sovereign over creation itself.

Perhaps the height of what it means to "worship" Jesus in Matthew can best be measured by Jesus' encounter with Satan. Satan entices Jesus to worship him (4:9), but Jesus' own response is to affirm the Deuteronomic command: "'You shall worship the Lord your God, and serve Him only'" (4:10; cf. Deut. 6:13).[10] This statement, occurring a couple of chapters after the magi's response to Jesus and appearing before the multiple examples of Jesus accepting worship later in the Gospel, heightens the latent claim to deity represented by the worship theme in Matthew.[11]

Therefore, in the conclusion to Matthew's Gospel, even before the Great Commission is pronounced, our skillful narrator has drawn out a theme – a theme inaugurated by the first encounter with the child Jesus and culminating in the disciples' response to the risen Lord. Jesus is to be worshiped.

DOUBT

Given the importance of worship in Matthew, it is all the more striking how Matthew 28:17 continues: "And when they saw Him, they worshiped Him; *but some were doubtful.*" Commentators grapple over this acknowledgment of doubt about the risen Jesus.[12] Certainly, despite some scholarly skepticism, it adds a touch of further realism to the scene.[13] Scholarly debates here often focus on whether the eleven disciples are among the doubtful.[14] Also, the text is frequently compared with doubting responses to the resurrected Jesus in other Gospels (such as Thomas in John 20; see also Luke 24:41) – responses that then are changed into glorious belief. However, few commentators fully study the theme of doubt in the Gospel of Matthew.

To begin, this is not the first time doubt and worship appear in the same context. Above, we noted the worshipful response Jesus received after he walked on water toward his disciples (Matt. 14:33). Yet, in that passage, worship is preceded first by the disciples' fear, and then by Peter's inability to walk on water to his Lord. Peter is rebuked by Jesus in verse 31: "O you of little faith, why did you doubt?" This is the same word for doubt (διστάζω) found in Matthew 28:17. Noticeable here is the juxtaposition of faith and doubt. Doubt consists of "little faith."

A related opposition of faith to doubt can be found in Jesus' response to the disciples in Matthew 21:21: "Truly I say to you, if you have faith, and do not doubt, you shall not only do what was done to the fig tree, but even if you say to this mountain, 'Be taken up and cast into the sea,' it shall happen." Faith constitutes a lack of doubt (here represented by διακρίνω).[15]

Although the specific Greek words for doubt are rare in Matthew, the author often conveys the concept of "little faith." He even has a particular term for this – ὀλιγόπιστοςςς. It has been observed that the disciples are frequently rebuked for having little faith (e.g. 6:30; 8:26; 14:31; 16:8; 17:20), while other characters only briefly associated with Jesus exhibit great faith (e.g. 8:10; 9:2, 22, 29; 15:28; also cf. 8:13). "Little faith" is evidenced by an anxiety for one's life (6:30), a fear of impending doom despite the very presence of Jesus (8:26; 14:31), a misunderstanding of the Lord's teaching (16:8), and an inability to accomplish miracles through prayer (17:20). The disciples often exhibit "little faith," though occasionally they can even be accused of being among the "faithless" generation (17:17, using ἄπιστος) – terminology normally reserved for the opponents of Jesus (Matt. 13:58; 21:25, 32; also cf. 27:42).

Hence, in Matthew the disciples are repeatedly called to exhibit faith. Simultaneously, a major aspect of discipleship failure issues from the "little faith" and the "doubt" of the disciples.[16] Surprisingly, Matthew does not concern himself with demonstrating that all those who followed Jesus (even those deemed "disciples") eventually exhibited a fully confident faith. On the contrary, it appears likely that these passages about doubt and "little faith" appear throughout Matthew in order to call readers to examine themselves as to their own faith stance toward the Christ. For this reason, one must be careful not to too quickly comfort moderns with the notion that doubt is normal and acceptable in discipleship, as is done by some commentators.[17] Certainly Jesus, while rebuking his followers for little faith, did not reject them, but graciously kept on instructing them even to the end of the Gospel.[18] Nevertheless, Matthew is determined to move followers of Jesus away from "little faith." Therefore, in his conclusion Matthew again presents his readers an opportunity to side with those who doubt or with those who believe and worship.

AUTHORITY

Jesus announces that "all authority on heaven and earth has been given to me" (Matt. 28:18). This is by no means the first time that Matthew associates Jesus with "authority" in his Gospel. The crowds observe that Jesus teaches with an authority unlike the scribes (7:29), and he explicitly claims the authority to forgive sins (9:2, 6). The crowd recognizes such authority (9:8), though the scribes accuse Jesus of blasphemy.

Jesus' authority is also frequently displayed in his miraculous control over nature and disease. The healing miracles, beginning in chapter four, exhibit command over a variety of diseases and even over the demonic. The authoritative significance of this is brought out in the series of longer miracle accounts in chapter eight. Here the centurion, in a manner praised by Jesus, associates the ability of Jesus to heal with the kind of military authority that allows one to command assent (8:9). This provides a paradigm for understanding Jesus' authority, even as shortly afterwards the narrative represents Jesus' explicit verbal commands given over a vanquished multitude of demons (8:28-34). It is not from worshiping Satan that Jesus has such authority (4:9-10; 12:24-29; cf. 10:25); rather, Jesus has the capacity to refute the temptations of the devil and the authority to subject Beelzebub's demonic hosts.

Other evidences of Jesus' authority abound.[19] The Father has handed over all things to Jesus, and he alone makes the Father known (11:27). Jesus proclaims himself (the Son of Man) to be the Lord of the Sabbath (12:8). His walking on water invites worship (14:22-33). He claims the right to eschatological judgment (13:40-43; 16:27). His authority is manifest in the transfiguration where he appears alongside Moses, the giver of the law, and the great prophet Elijah (17:1-8). And in the transfiguration God himself instructs Jesus' followers to listen to him (17:5). Indeed, much of the Gospel appears designed to convince the reader that Jesus is truly God's Son (cf. 3:17; 17:5), with all the Christological and authoritative import that title bears.

The authoritative Jesus also grants authority to his disciples, even giving them the keys to the kingdom of heaven (16:19; cf. 18:18). Significantly, the disciples' first major mission starts with Jesus announcing his gift to them of the "authority" to heal diseases and cast out demons (10:1). Thus, in the missional context of the Great Commission, it is important that Jesus' commissioning of his disciples is preceded by the great and final announcement of his own authority to deliver such a decree.

However, in the Gospel of Matthew Jesus' authority does not go unchallenged. The opposition to Jesus from the chief priests, elders, and scribes is represented fundamentally in the question: "By what authority are you doing these things, and who gave you this authority?" (21:23). The Jewish leaders' querying of Jesus' authority does not even merit a direct response from him (21:27). However, this interaction continues to prove that the leaders do not recognize the true origin of Jesus' power (cf. 12:24ff.). Such opposition culminates in the hearing of Jesus before Caiaphas the high priest (26:57ff.). There the question put to Jesus concerns whether he assumes the authoritative claim to be the Son of God (26:63). Jesus' firm response calls forth Caiaphas' proclamation that Jesus is a blasphemer. This is similar to the only other time that Jesus is directly charged with blasphemy in Matthew, namely, when he claims the authority to forgive sins (9:3, 6). Indeed, a strong case can be made that Caiaphas' charge of blasphemy is particularly rooted in Jesus' claim to have the authority of the Son of Man who sits on the right hand of God himself (26:64-65).[20] Thus, Jesus' death is the direct result of his claim to authority and the rejection of that claim by the Jewish leaders.[21]

In light of this discussion, Jesus' pronouncement of his authority in the Great Commission takes on a fuller import. The resurrection of Jesus has proven his claims to authority. Despite being spurned by his own people and crucified by the Gentiles, Jesus truly is the king of the Jews and even Lord of heaven and earth.[22] Therefore, the reader can trust that all things are under the Messiah's rule. Despite Caiaphas' rejection of Jesus' claim, Jesus does indeed now sit at God's right hand. His kingdom has indeed been inaugurated. His authority, glimpsed earlier in his miraculous deeds, culminates in his resurrection glory and his heavenly rule. His teaching, now proven, bears full authority, even as the Father earlier directed the reader to listen to Jesus' words. Jesus can truly forgive sins. And Jesus has the right to dispense his authority to his disciples in their missionary calling.

Going

When we understand that the Great Commission forms the conclusion to Matthew's Gospel, this allows the careful exegete to compare syntactical forms of expression in the Commission with the rest of the book. One of the great syntactical debates in the Great Commission involves the use of the string of participles in verses 19-20. Although often obscured for practical reasons in English translations, the verbs "going ... baptizing ... and teaching" are all participles in Greek. The only true imperatival form in the Commission is the command to "make disciples." The result in Greek is that the three participles bear some subsidiary relationship to the imperative. This can be represented in the following simplified syntactical diagram:

> going
> make disciples of all the nations
> baptizing them in the Name ...
> teaching them to observe ...

The central issue concerns the proper participial usage in these verses. There are some complexities involved in this discussion, but let us start with the simple observation that one participle ("going") precedes the imperative while the other two ("baptizing ... teaching") follow it. The first participle thus possibly plays a different role than the others.

What then are the possible functions of the participle "going"? Because it is subordinate to an imperative, it could take on that imperative force as well (thus being translated as "go, make disciples ...").[23] Or it could represent the means of accomplishing the command ("by going, make disciples ..."). Or it could have a temporal reference ("while you go, make disciples ..." or "as you go, make disciples ... ").[24] Some authors suggest that it is best designated as an "attendant circumstance" participle, which bears some imperatival flavor, though with the greater emphasis residing on the actual imperative itself.[25] This last category holds the most promise, although I would argue that here we can say even more than the grammarians often do.

Upon studying participles that precede imperatives in Matthew, a common pattern appears. Often, Matthew presents a participial verb of motion prior to a specific command. The following are literal word-for-word translations of Greek participles preceding imperatives in Matthew:[26]

- Going, make a careful search for the child ... (2:8)
- Arising, take the child and his mother ... (2:13,20)
- And then coming, present your offering ... (5:24)
- And shutting your door, pray to your Father ... (6:6)[27]
- Rising, take your up bed ... (9:6)
- And going, learn what this means ... (9:13)
- But coming, lay your hand on her ... (9:18)
- And going, preach ... (10:7)
- Going, report to John what you hear and see ... (11:4)
- Going unto the sea, cast the hook ... (17:27)
- Taking that [coin], give it to them ... (17:27)
- Untying, bring [the donkey and colt] to me ... (21:2)
- And going quickly, tell his disciples ... (28:7)
- Going therefore, make disciples ... (28:19)

Again, due to limitations in English, translations usually render all these participles with an English imperative. Most are aorist participles (except in 10:7), but the imperatives can be aorist or present in tense.[28] Although similar formulations occur in New Testament narratives outside of Matthew,[29] the participle/imperative pairing appears to be a standard Matthean narrative technique.

Observing this list, we see that the force of the participle does not merely concern the circumstance in which the imperative occurs. Rather, each participle establishes some motion that inevitably precedes the accomplishment of the imperative.[30] Nonetheless, the imperative itself is clearly what is most important in each instance.

When the magi are told, "Going, make a careful search for the child," they are being instructed fundamentally to find the child, not merely to "go." When Joseph is instructed, "Arising, take the child and his mother, and flee to

Egypt," the central import rests on his need to take them and flee, not on his "arising." Similar observations could be made throughout the examples given above. Thus, I would suggest that these participles convey something we can call the "necessary antecedent motion." By this we allow that the motion is a prerequisite to the command, but the command clearly is the stressed point of the sentence.

This whole discussion reminds us that the Great Commission is not fundamentally about "going"; rather, Jesus' central command is to "make disciples."[31] It was admittedly necessary for the eleven disciples, sitting at Jesus' feet on the mountain, to get up and go in order to recruit others to follow Jesus. However, their commission was principally a charge to disciple-making.

Make Disciples

The focus of the Commission, then, is to "make disciples of all the nations." Certainly, the commentators have commonly observed this; yet, this fact needs to be continuously brought before the English reader, since our translations often place "go" on a par with "make disciples." The command is not merely (or even fundamentally) to "go." Rather, Jesus' commission to his disciples was for them to continue his task of discipleship.

The discerning reader must then ask, in the context of Matthew's Gospel, what it means to make disciples. Here a single Greek verb conveys the imperative (μαθητεύω); this verb occurs only two other times in Matthew (13:52; 27:57).[32] It describes favorably the scribe "who has become a disciple of the kingdom of heaven" (13:52), and it depicts Joseph of Arimathea as one "who himself also was a disciple of Jesus" (27:57). In both of these cases, the verb is used to designate the person as a disciple.[33] Matthew's Gospel more often designates disciples with the cognate noun μαθητής; hence, we can further our study of discipleship by examining the nominal cognate.

The noun "disciple" (μαθητής) occurs seventy-two times in this Gospel. Most often it designates Jesus' disciples, though occasionally it indicates disciples of John the Baptist (Matt. 11:2; 14:12) or even disciples of the Pharisees (22:16). When referring to disciples of Jesus, the noun can broadly signify all those who are committed to following Jesus, or it can speak specifically of the twelve disciples (e.g. Matt. 10:1; 11:1; cf. 28:16) – often it is difficult to tell if only the twelve are intended. This widespread use of "disciple" throughout Matthew, especially as a common term for the more committed followers of Jesus, demonstrates that discipleship provides an undergirding theme to the whole Gospel.[34] The theme is so broad that it properly cannot be limited to just those many verses/passages that use discipleship terminology.[35] Rather, the whole of Matthew's Gospel informs us what it means to be a disciple of Jesus.

Hence, we need to see the concept of "making disciples" against the broad backdrop of Jesus' relationships to his followers throughout the book. Jesus often calls people to be his disciples, and he is almost constantly instructing those who have taken on such a commitment. Thus, when we wish to ask how one "makes disciples," Jesus himself becomes our best tutor for what this means in Matthew. This broad understanding of discipleship, encompassing as it does the whole range of Jesus' teachings and life, must be maintained, though it admittedly has also allowed for many different contemporary views as to all that discipleship entails.

What, then, are some essentials to making disciples?[36] Jesus' principal concern throughout the Gospel is instruction, but this must be understood in terms of both what he did and what he said. He intentionally brought the disciples with him almost everywhere, whether he was teaching the masses, healing the sick, comforting the bereaved, confronting authorities, or simply praying; and thus they learned by his example. Jesus also took opportunities to provide specific verbal instruction principally for his disciples (at times even for the twelve alone).[37] Furthermore, Jesus called his disciples themselves to minister to others after they had received his instruction; and often the successes and failures of the disciples' own ministry experiences became opportunities for additional teaching or rebuke.[38] Thus, there is a strong educational component to the concept of "making disciples," a fact that will be significant later in this essay.

The scope of Jesus' instruction should also be noted. It is not limited to a basic knowledge of the entrance requirements into the kingdom of God, though it certainly includes such. Jesus discusses all aspects of life *coram Deo*. In contemporary terms, Jesus' approach to making disciples involved not simply evangelism (even including what we would call "follow up"), but also instruction in the whole of the Christian life.

Therefore, we see that Jesus' Great Commission to "make disciples" summarizes a major theme throughout the book. As Jesus made the twelve (and others) into his disciples, so the eleven are now called to make disciples of all nations. The scope of Jesus' ministry of education by example and instruction thus becomes the model for fulfilling this commission. Two further points should be noted: (1) The disciples are not told to make "their own disciples," but simply to "make disciples." Thus, the reader is left to assume that, as elsewhere in the book, these new disciples will be designated as disciples *of Jesus* and *of his kingdom*. (2) This discipleship now involves "all nations."

ALL NATIONS

Even though the central command in the Great Commission is to "make disciples" rather than to "go," this ought not diminish the church's missionary zeal. Yet, the breadth of Christian mission is not principally to be located in the participle "going"; rather, the extent of the church's duty is given in the command to make disciples of "*all nations*." This phrase provides the church with the directive to approach people of every language and tribe. Nevertheless, we should discuss what this phrase means in Matthew.

Some have argued that "all nations" in Matthew 28:19 intends a continuing Jewish missionary mandate, with the "nations" indicating all the places in the Jewish diaspora to which the eleven are sent to call back the Jewish people to their Messiah.[39] Conversely, others have claimed that the term "nations" is best translated as "Gentiles," and thus the mission here is actually virtually devoid of witness to Jews (the focus having shifted entirely to the Gentiles).[40] Neither of these two views adequately explains the evidence.

The word translated "nations" (ἔθνη) most often refers in Matthew to the "Gentiles."[41] Therefore, the most natural reading of Matthew 28:19 ("make disciples of all nations") demands that the nations themselves are to be discipled – not merely Jews among the nations. Does this term for "nation/ Gentile" then rule out the Jewish people? Are they to be excluded from among the targeted future disciples? It should be admitted that dire warnings do occur in Matthew of the rejection of at least some Jewish individuals (e.g. Matt. 8:11-12; 11:20-24; 12:42; 15:7-9; 21:42-46). However, when one examines the broader phrase "*all* nations" (πάντα τὰ ἔθνη) in Matthew, we see that, among its four uses, the other three likely include Jews and Gentiles alike. The judgment of the sheep and goats concerns "all nations" (Matt. 25:32), and there is no indication in the Gospel that Jewish people will escape this judgment by the Son of Man. It is also possible that, when Jesus refers in the eschatological Olivet discourse to the hatred the disciples are to receive and the proclamation they are to make, his comments would include Jewish individuals among all the nations (24:9, 14).[42] Thus, Matthew 28:19 likely embraces Jew and Gentile alike.

The broader question concerns whether Matthew has signaled to the reader earlier in the gospel this mission to "all nations." Here note that the first mission of the disciples was only to the lost sheep from the house of Israel (Matt. 10:5-6). So the Great Commission represents a broadening of the earlier mission mandate. However, such an expansion is not unanticipated, for even in that same chapter mention is made of the disciples' testimony "to the Gentiles" (Matt. 10:18).

Jesus himself focused his mission on Jewish people, as he cautions the Canaanite woman; but that very encounter also displays his willingness to minister to Gentiles (Matt. 15:21-28), as does Jesus' reaction to the centurion (Matt. 8:5-13). Moreover, Jesus affirms that his ministry fulfills the Isaianic promise (Isa. 42:1-4), including its assurance that justice will be proclaimed to the "nations" (ἔθνεσιν) and that those "nations" will put their hope in his name (Matt. 12:18, 21).[43]

Jesus actually lays the framework for the Gentile mission in his teachings. He indicates that the Pharisees will witness the kingdom of God being taken from them and being "given to a nation producing the fruit of it" (21:43).

The intent of this verse is quite complex, but it does broaden the scope of the kingdom. More importantly, the Olivet discourse indicates that the end will not come until the Gospel has been "preached in the whole world for a witness to all the nations" (24:14). And the judgment of the sheep and the goats includes members of "all nations" in both eschatological destinations (25:32).

Hence, the Gospel of Matthew evidences a tension between the teaching of Jesus (which can imply a universal ministry to all nations) and the focus of Jesus' earthly ministry (which concentrates on his Jewish brethren). The tension is resolved at the end of the Gospel when Jesus commissions the universal mission to all nations.

BAPTIZING AND TEACHING

Returning to participial syntax in the Commission, recall that "baptizing" and "teaching," since they appear after the imperative "make disciples," may have a different function in the sentence than "going," which occurs before the imperative. How do "baptizing" and "teaching" function?

There are several options. Because "baptizing" and "teaching" follow an imperative verb, they themselves could take on that imperatival force as well (thus translated as "make disciples ... baptize ... teach"). Or they could represent the means of accomplishing the command ("make disciples ... by baptizing ... and by teaching..."). Or they could convey the result or purpose of the activity of disciple-making ("make disciples ... so that you may baptize ... and teach ..."). Commentators are divided over which meaning is intended.[44]

A helpful approach to this issue begins with the last participle ("teaching"). Earlier it was noted that the principal way by which Jesus himself "made disciples" was *by* his teaching (construed both as action and as verbal instruction). This would argue that the *means* or *instrument* of making disciples is teaching. Thus, one could rightly translate: "make disciples ... by teaching."

The phrase continues, "... by teaching them to observe all that I commanded you." The disciples, who themselves received the instruction (command) of the Lord, must disciple others in those commands (cf. Matt. 5:19). This provides further support for the idea that "teaching" is to be construed as an instrumental participle – disciples are made (at least in part) by teaching the observance of commands. Moreover, this passage illustrates the breadth of the commission to "make disciples." The means of making disciples requires instruction in all Jesus taught. As noted earlier, the whole of Matthew's Gospel thus becomes the source material for future discipleship.[45] Further, this instruction intends that the new disciples "observe" (τηρεῖν) all the commands of Jesus; that is, the instruction must be lived out.[46] The church dare not consider her job of discipling new Christians to be accomplished until those converts have fully comprehended and committed to the breadth of instruction necessary to be disciples of Christ.

If the participle "teaching" is properly understood instrumentally ("by teaching"), then the parallel participle "baptizing" also conveys a central means of making disciples ("by baptizing").[47] On two accounts this is surprising. The first shock is that "baptizing" is part of the mission of the church at all, for Jesus himself did not baptize in Matthew. Nonetheless, the early church did recall Jesus as initiating baptism alongside his disciples (cf. John 3:22, 26; though see 4:1-2), and Jesus is remembered as the one who baptizes with the Holy Spirit (Matt. 3:11; cf. Luke 3:16; Acts 1:5). Yet, in Matthew it is John "the Baptist" (Matt. 3:1; 11:11-12; 14:2, 8; 16:14; 17:13) who baptizes with water (Matt. 3:5-7, 11; 21:25). Of course, in Matthew Jesus submits to John's baptism, in order "to fulfill all righteousness" (Matt. 3:15; cf. 3:13-17), and this likely serves as a model for those later disciples of Jesus who must likewise be baptized. Perhaps it is this brief episode, alongside Matthew's assumption that his audience was already acquainted with the widespread practice of Christian baptism, which allowed Matthew to assume that his audience would understand the intent of Jesus' command in 28:19.[48]

The second shock in the "baptizing" phrase concerns the way it is to be done in the Trinitarian name – "in the name of the Father and the Son and the Holy Spirit."[49] Commentators spend significant space discussing what exactly Jesus' words must have been, and at what stage such ante-Nicene Trinitarian theology must have existed in the early church.[50] Certainly, the more common expression elsewhere in the New Testament calls for baptism to be performed "in the name of Jesus Christ," although the exact phraseology varies (see Acts 2:38; 8:12, 16; 10:48; 19:5; cf. Luke 24:47; Rom. 6:3; Gal. 3:27). Space precludes our entering into the debated question of original form. However, note that Matthew's Gospel frequently brings together God the Father alongside God's Son.[51] Although Jesus' special sonship is more exalted than the disciples can claim for themselves, Jesus also instructs his disciples to recognize God as their heavenly "Father."[52] Furthermore, Jesus is so related to the Holy Spirit that to reject Jesus' works is to blaspheme the Holy Spirit (12:28-32). Jesus is the offspring of the Holy Spirit (1:18, 20). He is led by the Spirit (4:1). He will baptize in the Holy Spirit (3:11). Additionally, Jesus refers to the Holy Spirit as "the Spirit of your Father" (10:20). The Trinitarian notion in Matthew is especially evident in the baptism of Jesus, when the Holy Spirit descends on him, and God (the Father) proclaims Jesus to be the "Son" (Matt. 3:16-17).[53] Thus, although the Trinitarian formula for baptism in the Commission heightens the unity of these relationships, the careful student of Matthew is prepared in part for the theology that is implied.

JESUS' PRESENCE AND THE ESCHATON

Jesus proclaims, "Behold, I am with you always." This continuing presence of Jesus with his disciples is not new in the gospel of Matthew. Jesus announces a similar notion in his earlier ecclesial instructions: "For where two or three have gathered together in my name, there I am in their midst" (18:20). However, the earlier promise creates a dramatic tension in the gospel, because Jesus also warns of a time when the bridegroom will no longer be present (9:15; also cf. 17:17), and he cautions that his disciples will not always "have" him (26:11).[54] The resurrection of Jesus resolves this tension. Jesus' presence was removed for a while, yet now abides again with his people. And one can already look to the consummation of the kingdom when Jesus once again will drink of the fruit of the vine with his disciples (26:29).

The theme of presence also can be linked to the title Jesus bears as the Immanuel, "God with us" (Matt. 1:23).[55] Indeed, the phrase "behold, I am with you" in the Great Commission likely echoes the Old Testament refrain "'I am with you,' declares the LORD."[56] The presence of Jesus is as the presence of God himself – both are with his people.[57]

This eschatological presence will be "with you all the day, even to the end of the age" (Matt. 28:20). Matthew's Gospel frequently references the "end of the age." The "tares" will be burned at the harvest at the end of the age (13:39-40). Angels shall remove the righteous at the end of the age (13:49). And the disciples ask, "What will be the sign of your coming, and of the end of the age?" (24:3). The answer to that question draws us into the eschatology of the Olivet discourse and beyond what can be accomplished in these pages. Suffice it to note here that waiting for the "end" requires perseverance (24:13), and that such an end comes only after the Gospel is preached to "all the nations" (24:14) – note the parallel phraseology in the Great Commission. Thus, the concluding commissioning of the disciples summarizes another thematic element within Matthew's Gospel.

CONCLUSION

The Great Commission, far from being a contextless utterance of Jesus, provides a fitting finale to Matthew's Gospel. Indeed, any understanding of the Commission that fails to account fully for these important themes has missed some of the riches of Matthew's conclusion.

Matthew challenges his reader to worship the risen Lord (in all Jesus' royalty and deity) rather than exhibit a doubtful little faith. The worshiper of Christ is assured of Jesus' supreme authority as he now sits enthroned with the Father in heaven. This also vouchsafes Jesus' authority manifested throughout the Gospel, as evidenced in Jesus' right to teach; his power to rule over disease, death and demons; and his prerogative to forgive sins.

The risen Jesus, instructing his disciples to depart, principally commands them to make other disciples. The scope of discipleship encompasses all that Jesus did in action and word to instruct his followers. The destination of discipleship involves all the nations, exemplifying a missionary mandate for the whole church. The means of accomplishing discipleship are through Trinitarian baptism and instruction in keeping all Jesus' commands. The promise given in this commission to discipleship concerns the presence of the risen Lord until the end of the age. All readers of Matthew are thus challenged and encouraged to spread their Lord's worshipful discipleship.

1. Biblical translations in this essay follow the NASB or are my own.

2. E.g. Morna Hooker, *Endings: Invitations to Discipleship* (Peabody, Mass.: Hendrickson, 2003); for Matthew 28, see pp. 31-47.

3. Not all important themes reappear in just these five verses (e.g. there is no mention of "son of David" or of the crucifixion), and thus Ellis somewhat overplays the centrality of the Commission; see Peter F. Ellis, *Matthew: His Mind and His Message* (Collegeville, Minn.: Liturgical Press, 1974), esp. pp. 19-25. Nevertheless, many key emphases in the Gospel are made more prominent by their inclusion at this terminus.

4. For example, this essay does not draw on first-century context to understand this passage better, nor does it extensively note parallels with the Old Testament and with early Christianity. Not every element of the passage receives comment. Also, issues of textual criticism, of Matthew's sources, and of structure and form have been passed over (along with the extensive literature on these matters).

5. Other thematic connections could also be observed beyond those upon which we will focus here. For a brief list, see W. D. Davies and Dale C. Allison, *A Critical and Exegetical Commentary on the Gospel According to Saint Matthew*, 3 vols., ICC (Edinburgh: T & T Clark, 1988–97), 3:687–9; Benjamin J. Hubbard, *The Matthean Redaction of a Primitive Apostolic Commissioning: An Exegesis of Matthew 28:16-20*, SBLDS 19 (Missoula, Montana: Society of Biblical Literature, 1974), 98. Famously, Michel called this section the "key to the understanding of the whole book"; see Otto Michel, "The Conclusion of Matthew's Gospel: A Contribution to the History of the Easter Message," in *The Interpretation of Matthew*, ed. Graham Stanton, trans. Robert Morgan, 2nd ed. (Edinburgh: T&T Clark, 1995), 45. Other authors have also observed aspects of the thematic import of the Great Commission; for example: Oscar S. Brooks, Sr., "Matthew xxviii 16-20 and the Design of the First Gospel," *Journal for the Society of the New Testament (JSNT)* 10 (1981): 2–18 (emphasizing Jesus' authority and teaching); David R. Bauer, *The Structure of Matthew's Gospel: A Study in Literary Design*, JSNT Sup 31 (Sheffield: Almond, 1988), esp. pp. 109–28 (focusing on Jesus' authority, universal mandate, and presence); David P. Scaer, "The Relation of Matthew 28:16-20 to the Rest of the Gospel," *CTQ* 55 (1991): 245–66 (esp. pp. 252–7 on Jesus, discipleship, baptism, and teaching); Pheme Perkins, "Matthew 28:16-20, Resurrection, Ecclesiology and Mission," *Society for Biblical Literature Seminar Papers* (1993): 574–88 (esp. 583–6 on vv. 18-20 as Matthew's own composition). As will be apparent upon comparison, the core text of this article was composed before consulting these works.

6. This point is argued in Grant R. Osborne, "Redaction Criticism and the Great Commission: A Case Study Toward a Biblical Understanding of Inerrancy," *Journal of the Evangelical Theological Society* 19 (1976): 73–85; also Gerhard Maier, *Matthäus-Evangelium*, 2nd ed., 2 vols. (Stuttgart: Hänssler-Verlag, 1983), 2: 494.

7. The following section largely traces the use of προσκυνέω in Matthew. While other words for worship appear in Matthew, the worship theme is largely carried by προσκυνέω. For example, λατρεύω does not appear by itself, but in collocation with προσκυνέω in the Deut. 6:13 citation in Matt. 4:10. And the one mention of σέβομαι (in the citation of Isa. 29:13 in Matt. 15:9) might be set in contrast with the later worshipful response (employing προσκυνέω) of the Canaanite woman to Jesus in Matt. 15:25.

8. In Greek, the second "Him" is implied from context; see discussion in Donald Hagner, *Matthew 14–28*, WBC 33b (Dallas: Word, 1995), 880n. Luke 24:52 also represents worship of the risen (and likely ascended) Lord.

9. The connection is clear in Greek (all these episodes employ the term προσκυνέω) and in some ancient and modern translations (e.g. Vulgate [though not in 18:26], Peshitta, KJV), although it is obscured in many modern translations by their varying of translational vocabulary (e.g. ESV, LB, NASB, NEB, NIV, NRSV, RSV, TNIV). The theme is briefly observed in Davies and Allison, *Matthew*, 1: 236–7.

10. It is striking here that, while the Hebrew text and the Septuagint of Deuteronomy 6:13 command that the Lord is to be feared and worshiped (φοβέομαι and λατρεύω in the LXX), Matthew's Jesus collocates two words for worship (προσκυνέω and λατρεύω). Although this understanding of Deuteronomy 6:13 may have been common in early Christianity (note the parallel in Luke 4:8), nevertheless this Greek rendering helps tie the Deuteronomy citation to the προσκυνέω (worship) theme throughout the Gospel.

11. See Heinrich Greeven, "προσκυνέω προσκυνητής" in *Theological Dictionary of the New Testament* 6: 758–66 (esp. pp. 76364); contrast C. F. D. Moule, *The Origin of Christology* (Cambridge: Cambridge University Press, 1977), 175–6. Moule's comments on this Matthean theme do not sufficiently attend to Matthew's highly controlled use of προσκυνέω to refer only to Jesus, God, or to a royal figure in a parable about God. Parkhurst goes too far, however, in suggesting that the "doubt" in Matt. 28:17 concerns doubt over the propriety of such worship (after all, why was this not "doubted" in Matt. 14:33?); see L. G. Parkhurst, Jr., "Matthew 28:16-20 Reconsidered," *Expository Times* 90 (1979): 179–80.

12. Many commentators suggest a weaker sense to the verb "hesitated"; e.g. Leon Morris, *The Gospel according to Matthew*, PNTC (Grand Rapids, Mich.: Eerdmans, 1992), 744–5; Hagner, *Matthew*, 2: 885.

13. Observed as early as Chrysostom (*Homilies on Matthew*, 90); see *Nicene and Post-Nicene Fathers* I 10: 531, also cited in Manlio Simonetti, *Matthew 14-28* (Downers Grove, Ill.: InterVarsity Press, 2002). Affirmed in Alan Hugh M'Neile, *The Gospel According to St. Matthew* (London/New York: MacMillan, 1915), 434.

14. Morris (*Matthew*, 745) claims the eleven are not (since the disciples would have seen the risen Lord earlier; cf. John 20:24-25). Carson also indicates that the doubters could not be the same as the worshiping disciples, for such doubt "does not seem appropriate for true worship"; see D. A. Carson, *The Expositor's Bible Commentary: Matthew*, 2 vols. (Grand Rapids, Mich.: Zondervan, 1995), 2:593. M'Neile contends that the Greek expression does not allow for the eleven to be included (M'Neile, *Matthew*, 434). However, Hagner (*Matthew*, 2: 884–5) argues that the οἱ δέ construction implies that all the eleven simultaneously "doubted" (or, better, "hesitated"). Others contend that οἱ δέ implies that some of the eleven doubted; see Davies and Allison, *Matthew*, 3: 681–2; Joachim Gnilka, *Das Matthäusevangelium*, 2 vols., NTKNT (Freiburg: Herder, 1988), 506. On this construction, witness the interchange in *Journal for the Society of the New Testament* (*JSNT*): K. Grayston, "The Translation of Matthew 28:17," *JSNT* 21 (1984): 105–109; K. L. McKay, "The Use of *hoi de* in Matthew 28:17: A Response to K. Grayston," *JSNT* 24 (1985): 71–72; P.W. van der Horst, "Once More: The Translation of οἱ δέ in Matthew 28:17," *JSNT* 27 (1986): 27–30.

15. Ellis distinguishes διακρίνω from διστάζω (the former implying an absence of faith, the latter conveying uncertainty or hesitation); see I. P. Ellis, "'But Some Doubted'," *New Testament Studies* 14 (1967-8): 575–77. With little NT evidence for διστάζω (and no LXX instances), and with some NT evidence that διακρίνω can convey uncertainty (cf. James 1:6-8), Ellis perhaps too precisely draws such a nuanced distinction.

16. Discipleship failure is more often associated with Mark, but Matthew has a similar, if more muted, theme.

17. Richard A. Edwards, *Matthew's Narrative Portrait of Disciples: How the Text-Connoted Reader is Informed* (Harrisburg, Penn.: Trinity Press International, 1997), 139–40, 142–3. To some extent, see Ellis, "Some Doubted," 578–80. Contrast Gnilka, *Matthäusevangelium*, 2: 507.

18. A point emphasized by Charles H. Giblin, "A Note on Doubt and Reassurance in Matt. 28:16-20," *Catholic Biblical Quarterly* 37 (1975): 68–75. Also see Hagner, *Matthew*, 2:885–6.

19. See further Brooks, "Matthew xxviii 16-20," 2–18; Bauer, *Structure*, 115–21.

20. In a fine monograph, Darrell Bock locates the cause for the charge of blasphemy in Jesus' Danielic pronouncement to be the Son of Man with the authority to sit on the right hand of God. See Darrell L. Bock, *Blasphemy and Exaltation in Judaism and the Final Examination of Jesus: A Philological-Historical Study of the Key Jewish Themes Impacting Mark 14:61-64*, WUNT II/106 (Tübingen: Mohr Siebeck, 1998). Commentators frequently acknowledge an allusion to Dan. 7:13-14 in the Great Commission; e.g. Davies and Allison, *Matthew*, 3: 682–3.

21. In a more indirect fashion, the Gentile governor Pilate also sarcastically rejects Jesus' authority via the *titulus* reading "King of the Jews" (Matt. 27:37; cf. 27:11, 29 and contrast 2:2).

22. The collocation "heaven and earth" also appears in Matt. 5:18; 11:25; 24:35 (cf. 6:10). It is perhaps reminiscent of Gen. 1:1 (as per Maier, *Matthäus-Evangelium*, 2: 496), encapsulating all created order (Gnilka, *Matthäusevangelium*, 2: 507). Notably, earlier in Matthew God is said to be "Lord of heaven and earth" (Matt. 11:25); thus, Jesus' authority in Matt. 28:18 equals that of God himself.

23. So Morris, *Matthew*, 746n (though admitting the emphasis resides on "make disciples"). Hagner (*Matthew*, 2: 882, 886) calls all three participles imperatival.

24. Some, understanding the verb to be "simply an auxiliary reinforcing the action of the main verb," see it as "secondary and unemphasized"; so Peter O'Brien, "The Great Commission of Matthew 28:18-20: A Missionary Mandate or Not?" *Reformed Theological Review* 35 (1976): 72–3.

25. Daniel B. Wallace, *Greek Grammar Beyond the Basics: An Exegetical Syntax of the New Testament* (Grand Rapids, Mich.: Zondervan, 1996), 645; see also Carson, *Matthew*, 2: 595.

26. This derives from an *Accordance* (version 5.2) search of all participles in Matthew followed by at least one imperative (the verbal forms agreeing in number and within six words of one another). I have not reported those participles that are adverbial to other verbs; nor do I list any participles that are clearly genitive absolutes, pleonastic, substantival, or adjectival. The only exceptions that remain are Matt. 6:17 and 10:12. In 6:17 ("but you, fasting, anoint your head"), the participle is clearly adverbial ("when you fast"); note structurally also how the subject pronoun precedes the participle. Matt. 10:12 is more complex ("and entering into the house, greet it"), with the present participle either functioning adverbially ("when you enter") or following the "necessary antecedent motion" pattern noted in this essay.

27. Because Matt. 6:6 consists of a participle sandwiched between two imperatives, it is structurally different than the other examples cited here (since their participles are not generally also preceded by an imperative). However, even then one could make a good case that the participle conveys "necessary antecedent motion" in order to accomplish the following imperative to pray in private.

28. The imperatives are aorist in Matt. 2:8, 13, 20; 9:6, 13, 18; 17:27 (2x); 21:2; 28:7, 19. They are present in Matt. 5:24; 10:7; 11:4.

29. See Mark 16:15; Luke 5:14; 7:22; 9:60; 13:14, 32; 14:10; 17:7, 14, 19; 19:5, 30; 22:8, 46; Acts 9:11; 10:13, 20; 11:7; 16:15, 36, 37; 21:24; 22:10, 16. Possibly also see Luke 16:6; 17:8; 22:32; Acts 5:20. Doubtful is Mark 6:11.

30. Hence, "attendant circumstance" or "circumstantial participle" may not be the most descriptive label for this phenomenon.

31. Had Matthew wished to stress the command to "go" he could, of course, have chosen to render it with an imperative as he does in Matt. 2:20; 8:9; 10:6; 21:2; 22:9; 25:9, 41. It should also be noted that there are other occasions when Matthew emphasizes the motion more by placing it as an imperative alongside another imperative (e.g. Matt. 5:24; 8:4, 13; 9:5, 6; 17:7; 18:15; 19:21; 20:14; 26:18, 46; 27:65; 28:10). Some of these instances of commanded motion may be due to Matthew's stylistic preferences, since most involve ὑπάγω, which Matthew does not ever employ in its participial form.

32. Outside Matthew the verb μαθητεύω occurs in the NT only in Acts 14:21 (where its meaning closely resembles that in Matthew 28:19).

33. Via the adjectival participle in 13:52, and via the relative clause in 27:57.

34. For a helpful survey of the term μαθητής and its meaning, along with a redactional study of its use in Matthew, see Michael J. Wilkins, *The Concept of Disciple in Matthew's Gospel*, NovTSup (Leiden: E. J. Brill, 1988). Wilkins interacts thoroughly with Karl H. Rengstorf, "μαθητής," in *Theological Dictionary of the New Testament* 4: 415–61.

35. Other terms indicating discipleship are noted in O'Brien, "Great Commission," 75.

36. A useful article here, though ranging more broadly than Matthew, is Hans Kvalbein, "'Go Therefore and Make Disciples ...': The Concept of Discipleship in the New Testament," *Themelios* 13 (1988): 48–53.

37. E.g. Matt. 10:1–11:1.

38. For example, note some ὀλιγόπιστος verses mentioned above (Matt. 8:26; 14:31; 16:8; 17:20).

39. So D. W. B. Robinson according to O'Brien, "Great Commission," 73.

40. See especially: Douglas R. A. Hare and Daniel J. Harrington, "'Make Disciples of All the Gentiles' (Matt. 28:19)," *Catholic Biblical Quarterly* 37 (1975): 359–69; Stephen Hre Kio, "Understanding and Translating 'Nations' in Mattew 28:19," *The Bible Translator* 41 (1990): 230–8. Slightly less assertively stated in Ulrich Luz, *The Theology of the Gospel of Matthew* (Cambridge: Cambridge University Press, 1995), 139–40; and in Scaer, "Relation," 250–2.

41. See Matt. 4:15; 6:32; 10:5, 18; 12:18, 21; 20:19, 25; 24:7, 9, 14; 25:32; possibly cf. 21:43.

42. Note the careful argumentation in: John P. Meier, "Nations or Gentile in Matthew 28:19?" *Catholic Biblical Quarterly* 39 (1977): 94–102. Supplement with Carson, *Matthew*, 2: 596; Davies and Allison, *Matthew*, 3: 684; and Robert H. Gundry, *Matthew: A Commentary on His Handbook for a Mixed Church under Persecution*, 2nd ed. (Grand Rapids, Mich.: Eerdmans, 1994), 596. Also note Luke 24:47; Acts 17:26.

43. The magi also may represent Gentile worship of Jesus (Matt. 2:1–12). And the thematic importance of "Galilee of the Gentiles" (4:15) in Matthew may connect the Great Commission to this larger mission (cf. 28:16; so Scaer, "Relation," 250–2). See further, Bauer, *Structure*, 121–4.

44. Carson, noting a single instance in Luke, argues for some imperatival force, with baptizing and teaching "characterizing" disciple making, though he recognizes that the structure of the sentence makes imperatival less likely (*Matthew*, 2: 597).

45. So also Davies and Allison, *Matthew*, 3: 686.

46. The ethical component of this Commission is astutely observed, if over-emphasized, in Robert Harry Smith, "Matthew 28:16-20, Anticlimax of Key to the Gospel?" *Society for Biblical Literature Seminar Papers* (1993): 589–603.

47. Hill's interesting observations about the concentric structure of Matt. 28:18–20, by stressing the centrality of the baptismal formula, overlook that the participle "baptizing" is syntactically subordinate to the imperative "make disciples"; see David Hill, "The Conclusion of Matthew's Gospel: Some Literary-Critical Observations," *Irish Biblical Studies* 8 (1986): 54–63.

48. Apart from a specific command from Jesus for his disciples to baptize, it is quite difficult to explain the widespread employment of baptism in the earliest church (see Morris, *Matthew*, 747; M'Neile, *Matthew*, 435).

49. That the Greek word for "name" (ὄνομα) is singular and articular leads to the conclusion that the three persons (Father, Son, Holy Spirit) are united in a Trinitarian whole. A shorter text, found only in citations in the early Eusebius, has been put forward as original by Conybeare and Kosmala; see Hans Kosmala, "The Conclusion of Matthew," *Annual of the Swedish Theological Institute* 4 (1965): 132–47. Commentators, noting that no NT manuscript supports this reading, typically reject the Eusebius text; see especially Hubbard, *Matthean Redaction*, 151–75.

50. So Hagner doubts that this represents Jesus' *ipsissima verba* (Hagner, *Matthew*, 888). However, note that in the mid-first century, passages bringing together the three persons of the Trinity are found throughout Paul's letters: see especially 2 Cor. 13:14; also note: Rom. 8:11; 1 Cor. 12:4-6; Gal. 4:6; Eph. 4:4-6; 2 Thess. 2:13. See further Carson, *Matthew*, 2: 598; Maier, *Matthäus-Evangelium*, 2: 498–9. Patristic texts

noted in Craig S. Keener, *A Commentary on the Gospel of Matthew* (Grand Rapids, Mich.: Eerdmans, 1999), 717.

51. Matt. 2:15; 3:17; 4:3, 6; 8:29; 10:32; 11:25–27; 12:50; 14:33; 15:13; 16:17, 27; 17:5; 18:10, 19, 35; 20:23; 21:37ff.; 24:36; 25:34; 26:29, 39, 42, 53, 63–64; 27:43, 54.

52. Matt. 5:16, 45, 48; 6:1, 4, 6, 8–9, 14–15, 18, 26, 32; 7:11, 21; 10:20, 29; 13:43; 23:9.

53. Compare the Isaianic promise in Matt. 12:18; see also the transfiguration in 17:5.

54. Similar themes are evident in John 7:33; 13:33; 16:4ff.

55. Emphasized in Bauer, *Structure*, 124–7.

56. Hag. 1:13 (the Greek is virtually identical between the LXX and Matt. 28:20). Hagner also observes this connection (*Matthew*, 2: 888). Similar phrases occur in, e.g. Gen. 26:3; 31:3, 5; Ex. 3:12; Deut. 31:23; Josh. 1:5; 3:7; Judg. 6:16; 1 Sam. 20:13; 2 Sam. 7:9; 14:17; 1 Kings 1:37; 8:57; 11:38; 1 Chron. 17:8; 22:11; cf. Num. 14:23 (LXX). Further concepts connected to this could be witnessed in, e.g. Deut. 29:14; Ezek. 37:26. Contrast Deut. 1:42; Josh. 7:12.

57. The presence of God being "with you" can also be seen elsewhere in early Christianity (e.g. Luke 1:28; Rom. 15:33; 2 Cor. 13:11; Phil. 4:9; Acts 18:10; 2 Thess. 3:16; 2 Tim. 4:22); at times such expressions refer to "the Lord" being present and could be ambiguous whether the Father or Jesus are intended. A strong Pauline theme concerns the grace of the Lord being "with you" (Rom. 16:20; 1 Cor. 16:23–24; Gal. 6:18; Phil. 4:23; Col. 4:18; 1 Thess. 5:28; 2 Thess. 3:18; 1 Tim. 6:21; 2 Tim. 4:22; Titus 3:15; Philem. 25; cf. Heb. 13:25).

7

CHRIST-CENTERED ESCHATOLOGY
IN ACTS 3:12B-26

HANS F. BAYER[1]

Associate Professor of New Testament

$\mathfrak{C}$ onsidering the importance which has been attributed in recent decades to questions of Lucan Christology,[2] eschatology,[3] and the relationship between them,[4] it is useful to investigate the significant contribution of Peter's temple speech in Acts 3:12b-26 to this area of study.[5] In this speech, the interplay of Christology and eschatology is addressed in a telling way and simultaneously serves as a fundamental motivating factor in Peter's call to repentance. Furthermore, it will become apparent that the interplay between eschatology and Christology studied in Acts 3:12b-26 serves as a significant framework for the entire book of Acts.

I. THE MACRO-TEXT AND LUCAN ESCHATOLOGY AS BACKGROUND

The Macro-Text of Luke–Acts

The clarification of the interrelationship between Christology and eschatology must be attempted against the background of the purpose and perspective of Luke–Acts. Only this larger context can provide guidelines along which we may interpret successfully this interrelationship in Peter's temple speech.

According to the focus of Luke 1:1-4 and Acts 1:1–5:8, eschatology is *not* a central theme in Luke's account. Rather, the carefully researched and reliable reports[6] of the words and saving deeds of Jesus and the outlook upon the Spirit-led expansion of the Gospel as *the confirming work of Jesus after his exaltation*[7] are in the foreground.

On the other hand, Jesus' death and resurrection, and especially the continuing deeds of the exalted Christ in Acts (cf. esp. Acts 2:33), are presented in a framework of seemingly competing future expectations (near- and far-expectation), which has led in the past decades to a wide range of positions.[8]

In his extensive study, Carroll questions with good reason whether Luke really instrumentalized the problem of a disappointed near-expectation[9] by ways of paraenetically emphasizing the present (Luke 17:20ff.; Acts 3:22ff.).[10] He states against Conzelmann's position: "Delay, therefore, serves for Luke the opposite function to that identified by Conzelmann. Delay does not oppose but undergirds expectation of an imminent end in Luke's own situation."[11] Both the "today" of repentance, faith, and proclamation of salvation, and the expectation of a real, sudden, and near parousia, are, according to Carroll, fully present and intended in Luke's report. Only in the light of a lively near-expectation does Lucan paraenesis retain its urgency.[12]

According to Carroll, Luke is in this regard far less innovative than Grässer[13] and Conzelmann (among others) assume. Rather, Luke concurs basically with known early Christian views of the future. Contrary to Grässer and Conzelmann, Carroll again emphasizes those expressions in Luke– Acts which testify to continued near-expectation (see, e.g. Luke 21:29-36; Acts 2:16-21)[14] while upholding salvation-historical events (with a potential delay motif) expected before the end.[15] Furthermore, Carroll reaffirms the view that Luke was much more concerned about *causes* and the *interrelationships of events* than with time frames (see, e.g. Luke 12:35-48 and Acts 1:6-8).[16] The *certainty* of the sudden coming of Christ (Luke 21:34ff.) constitutes the foundation of Luke's portrayed future expectation.[17]

In the macro-text of Luke–Acts, we thus observe a coexistence of salvation-historical sequences (with a potential delay motif) as well as an expectation of the near end (cf., e.g. Luke 21:5-9 with 21:32). If we can explain the compatibility of this coexistence from the viewpoint of Luke,[18] we may have accomplished historically more than what tradition-historical hypotheses have produced by way of separating at the scholar's desk one strand from the other to produce a "Lucan" (salvation-historical) and a "traditional" (near-expectation) line of transmission. The latter line of argumentation short-circuits the *real* question of *explaining* the stated phenomenon by immediately building hypotheses upon this unresolved problem. Luke, for his part, was able to live with these seemingly incompatible factors and views. In this regard, we should take Luke's theological outlook, and the historical foundation upon which it builds, more seriously. Before we attempt to give an answer to this question, however, the macro-text of Acts must briefly be brought to attention.

The Macro-Text of Acts

Narrative criticism convincingly claims that a speech such as the temple speech in Acts 3:12b-26 must be studied in its narrative context[19] in order to clarify its function within a wider framework. A few observations must suffice regarding the larger context of Acts 3.

It is instructive to recognize that the theme of future expectations in Acts breaks off more or less after chapter three. The outpouring of the Holy Spirit[20] and the mission among the Gentiles[21] are viewed in Acts as fulfilled (or in the process of being fulfilled) eschatological prophecy. Merely the expectation of the parousia with its related events remains.[22] As surely as the outpouring of the Holy Spirit and the mission among the Gentiles in the process of occurring, the parousia is to be expected.

A brief glance at the first two speeches of Peter shows that the relationship between near-expectation (displayed, e.g. by Peter's Pentecost speech) and salvation-historical future events (e.g. Acts 1:6ff.; 3:19–21) is addressed here in a uniquely concentrated fashion.

On the basis of the first three chapters of Acts it becomes clear that the entire description of ensuing events (until Paul reaches Rome) is seen within this highly end-time oriented framework. While the Pentecost speech focuses on the *presently realized aspects* of end-time expectations,[23] the temple speech focuses on *present and future* events. Even if Luke does not frequently return to this eschatological perspective in the course of the unfolding narrative after chapter three,[24] it is clear that *this perspective nevertheless determines the setting in which the ensuing events take place.*[25] The context (thematic continuity with chapter two, thematic discontinuity after chapter three with regard to eschatology) thus underlines the fundamental eschatological significance of Peter's temple speech for the book of Acts.

The Context and Emphasis of the Temple Speech

The surrounding context displays the fact that the temple speech not only functions as a response to the healing of the lame but also *interprets* the healing as a manifestation of the present work of the risen Lord. Hamm goes even further and claims that the narrative of the healing *explains* the speech to a certain degree.[26]

Similar to the Pentecost speech, the temple speech looks back and, especially, forward.[27] As a review, the speech fulfills the purpose of confirming the death and resurrection of Jesus as God's act. As a glance into the present and future, the speech serves as a parameter for the connection between repentance and anticipated, eschatological events.

The Immediate Context (Acts 3:12b-26) of Acts 3:17-21

As mentioned above, the close interconnection between christology and eschatology in the temple speech aims at a clear call to repentance. Far from being sterile orthodoxy, we find a lively assurance that Christ is the divinely confirmed leader for all times. In this light alone, the call to repentance is already appropriate and necessary. The eschatological prospect with the call to repentance (Acts 3:17-21) is further embedded in a preceding "Jesus-kerygma" and a following confirmation by Scripture.

Conclusion

The results of our observations in section one may be summarized as follows:

(a) The temple speech is highly significant for the Lucan sub-domain of eschatology, despite the fact that the overall purpose of Luke–Acts focuses on Christ's eminence and deeds. Acts 1–3 does, however, set the "eschatological tone" for the entire book of Acts.

(b) In Acts 2 and 3 we find an apparent tension between near-expectation (Pentecost speech) and salvation-historical far-expectation (temple speech). This tension is repeatedly observable in Luke–Acts as a whole.

We shall now attempt to demonstrate that in Acts 3:12b–26 a highly Christ-centered eschatology, commencing with the present healing of the lame and the "Jesus-kerygma," explains the principal compatibility between far- and near-expectation of the parousia and simultaneously assigns eschatology its Christ-dependent place.

II. Characteristic Elements of Christ-Centered Eschatology

Christ Is Completely Affirmed by the "God of Our Fathers"

In the attempt to formulate a clearer definition of Christ-centered eschatology in this particular context, we stress above all the initiating agency of the "God of our fathers." Obviously, this is particularly significant for Peter's predominantly Jewish hearers. It is precisely the "God of our fathers" who affirms the past, present, and future deeds of Christ as well as his exalted identity and function.

The fact that God is the *initiator* can be traced as a red thread throughout the entire speech:

> 3:13 – *ho theos ... edoxasen ton paida autou* ("the God ... of our
> fathers glorified")[28]
> 3:15 – *ho theos ēgeiren* ("God raised")
> 3:18 – *ho ... theos ... eplērōsen* ("God. .. fulfilled")
> 3:20 – *apo prosōpon tou kyriou* ("from the presence of the Lord"; because
> of *aposteilē ton Christon* ["that he may send the Christ"], this is
> undoubtedly a reference to God)
> 3:21 – divine *dei* and *elalēsen ho theos* ("about which God spoke")
> 3:22 – *anastēsei kyrios ho theos* ("the Lord God will raise up")
> 3:25 – *dietheto ho theos* ("that God made")
> 3:26 – *anastēsas ho theos ... apesteilen auton* ("God, having raised ... sent")

Against the solid background of this recurrent emphasis on their fathers' God as the affirmer of Christ, Peter builds his Christ-testimony in a rhetorically fitting manner: he refers initially to the present deeds of Christ (vv. 12, 13a, 16), then reviews past events (vv. 13b-18), before outlining future deeds of Christ (vv.19-21).

Christ's Functional and Ontological Eminence

Verse 13 identifies the present deed of Christ in healing the lame as *one* consequence of the raising of the Righteous One from death. This signals that Christ's influence is by no means only a matter of past concerns. Exaltation and *holoklēria* (v. 16) mark the *commencement* of a new thrust of deeds of Christ.

A single outstanding event is the key and *conditio sine qua non* to this new thrust: the resurrection. Peter bridges the two known factors of present healing and past death with the hitherto unknown or rejected fact of Jesus' resurrection (v. 15) as the "missing link." Without the witness (*martus*,[29] v. 15b) to the resurrection of Christ, the present healing and past rejection[30] and death of Christ remain virtually unrelated events. Suddenly, the known factors of past death and present healing are related to the same *person*.

Already here we encounter a markedly Christ-centered connection of events which remains characteristic of yet unfulfilled salvation-historical occurrences mentioned in this speech. Only by acknowledging the witness regarding the person and work of Christ can seemingly unrelated events become plausible. This will also hold true in understanding time sequences as Christ-dependent occurrences.

While there is predominantly *functional* Christology in verse 13, we encounter in verses 14-15 predominantly *ontological* descriptions of the one in whom all this holds together: He is the "Holy" and "Righteous one" (v. 14; cf. Luke 23:47; Acts 7:52; 22:14). The attributive terms "the Holy one"[31] and "the Righteous one"[32] could take up a variety of OT concepts.[33] At least they attribute to Jesus a particular purity and availability to God, perhaps as his special Son (cf. Luke 1:35) and messianic Servant (cf. Acts 4:27.30; Isa. 53:11b), all of which stands in stark contrast to his being rejected by men (v. 14). Jesus' exalted position is further disclosed by the term *archēgos* (v. 15). The question of the true identity of Christ is thus brought to the point by the paradoxical juxtaposition of *ton archēgon tēs zōēs* and *apokteinō*. No greater extremes may be imagined: The head[34] of *life* has been put to *death*. The hearers might already be indirectly challenged to ponder (see 3:20-21) whether they too will reject the vindicated Righteous One.

The bold and, for Jewish ears, problematic reference to Jesus as the *object* of faith (v. 16) further emphasizes that the one through whom seemingly unrelated past and present events are connected stands as the exalted one in very close proximity to the "God of our fathers."

The relevance of these observations to our question of the interrelationship between Christology and eschatology is that these functional and ontological references to Jesus disclose the broadly established *eminence* of him who has suffered in the past, who has been vindicated, and who acts presently. Because of this eminence, sealed by the fact that the "God of our fathers" fully underwrites his identity and function, future salvation-historical events are fundamentally shaped in terms of content and time frame by Christ himself. The certainty of future events is thus also secured.

With verse 16, the subject of the present event of healing is taken up again. Simultaneously, Peter *prepares* the appeal (see vv. 17-26) to his hearers to repent and to trust this affirmed, eminent leader. The faith of the healed one,[35] more precisely his faith in Christ, demonstrates the fact that he was included in God's exceptional work. The God-given faith of the formerly lame provides *by example* a first link between the objective message of Peter and the hearers. They too may receive the gift of this faith.

Beginning with the event of the healing of the lame, verses 12-16 thus develop and communicate the functional and ontological eminence of Christ. Christ's capability of intervening in the present is made possible through the fact that he has been raised from the dead. The divinely vindicated, eminent Christ is thus presented to the hearers in a most actualizing manner. The present eminence of Christ dynamically influences the call to repentance, coupled with the eschatological glance into the future.

Christ Shapes Eschatology

It is no accident that the call to repentance marks the rhetorical center of the speech. As Peter's central concern and the aim of the speech, repentance[36] is surrounded by "supportive motivations"[37] (including the promise of further salvation-historical blessings) which are used as appeals to the hearers.[38] A partial motivation for repentance is thus derived from the fact that the divinely affirmed and eminent Christ will also act in the future. This demonstrates that the question of time frames is clearly secondary. Rather, repentance prior to future *deeds* of Christ is the real concern, coupled with the assurance that Christ as the divine executive will *act* as surely as he has in the past and present.

The two major traditional views on Luke's eschatology often lack this Christ-centered emphasis: position (a) would merely maintain a process-oriented "already/not yet" tension in which some scholars emphasize the "already" (Hamm, Mattill), others the "not yet" (Ridderbos[39]) aspect; position (b) maintains that the supposed delay of the parousia gave rise to a deep disillusionment and led to the pneumatological and kerygmatic "substitute theology" generated by Luke.[40] This supposedly occurred in such a way that a real expectation of the dynamic of "already/not yet" was replaced by a de-eschatologized concern for the cares of the growing church[41] (Conzelmann, Vielhauer,[42] Käsemann, Haenchen,[43] Lohfink[44]).

As far as it goes, position (a) appears to be much closer to the known facts from the viewpoint of the temple speech, for the following reasons: The "now" in 3:18 is the present time of Peter's preaching.[45] The "not yet" in 3:21 sets out the time of the restoration of all that has been prophesied. Luke does not as much as hint at a different realm of reality between the past event of the crucifixion and future events. References to OT prophecy underline this: verse 18 emphasizes the proclamation of the prophesied suffering of the Messiah; verse 21 refers to the prophesied expectation of future restoration.

However, on the basis of our above-mentioned observations, it is even necessary to correct position (a) by stating that concentration lies not on a set of *time sequences* (within the "already/not yet" spectrum) but on the *deeds* of the eminent Christ. Questions of time are simply less crucial than turning to Christ as the divinely affirmed, eminent leader, who also shapes future events.[46]

It may, however, be argued that "times of refreshment" and, to a certain degree, even "restoration" may not be so much Christ-centered as they are God-centered events (see, e.g. v. 20, *prosōpou*). As we have noted above, the *initiator* of everything mentioned in this speech is the "God of our fathers." Jesus is predominantly the one who *receives* glory from God, the father (v. 13), who *has been established* and *sent* to his people for the remission of sins (v. 19 and esp. v. 26), who is *being rejected* (vv. 14, 15a), who is *being raised* from the dead (v. 15b), who is *witnessed* to (v. 15c),[47] who is the *object* of faith (v. 16), who has *been prophesied* (vv. 18, 22-24), who *must be received* into heaven (v. 21) and who is *being sent* again (v. 20). Christ is thus presented as the one *through* whom the counsel of God, the Father, becomes visible and manifest.

Nevertheless, Peter does not explicitly state who will bring "times of refreshment" (*anapsyxis*, v. 20) and "restoration of all that has been prophesied" (v. 21).

Before we attempt to clarify in which way Christ is involved in these events, we must briefly identify the meaning and message of these two opalescent concepts in order to determine their material proximity to Christ's known future work.

kairoi anapsyxeôs (Acts 3:20)

Taking various analyses of the phrase into account,[48] we interpret *kairoi anapsyxeôs* as any divine intervention which would relieve and refresh from this world's bonds and burdens (e.g. bring occasional release from suppression and establish justice and righteousness, Isa. 32:15ff.), closely associated with repentance and forgiveness of sins.

achri chronōn apokatastaseōs pantōn hōn elalēsen ho theos (Acts 3:21)

It is noteworthy that, similar to *kairoi anapsyxeōs*, this phrase also speaks of further events (in the plural). It is thus likely that a *period of time* and *a cluster of events* are in view. This is supported by Luke's use of *achri*.[49] The diachronic spectrum of *apokatastasis* includes "restoration,"[50] "return," and "healing." An eschatological context is possible, but the term is not limited to it. Although there are no occurrences of the noun in the LXX, the term is used by Philo and Josephus in the Jewish, salvation-historical sense of "deliverance" and "return."[51] The term is used in Attic and Koine Greek in the sense of "bringing back to an original state."[52] Greek inscriptions convey the sense of "repair" (of a temple or path).[53] Later rabbinic evidence[54] mentions the Messiah Ben Perez,[55] who is supposed to restore six items which man has lost since the fall of Adam.

For a more specific determination of the phrase in our context, it is important to note that restoration refers to *as yet unfulfilled prophecy*. It is therefore legitimate and necessary to consider the broad spectrum of prophecies of and references to restoration (both in the OT and NT) which do not exclusively focus on Israel as a nation (cf., e.g. the *progression* from Acts 1:6 to 1:8). While Hamm lists important OT allusions (such as Isa. 61:1-5; Amos 9:11-15[56] and Isa. 1:26[57]), he quickly concludes that the phrase in Acts 3:21 merely refers to the restoration of the Jewish people under God and the restoration of the land[58] to its people.[59] However, already some relevant OT references point to a *universal restoration*, which the NT reinforces.

Among various OT passages, Ezekiel 37:21-28,[60] Isaiah 49:6-7,[61] Isaiah 66:18-22, and Daniel 7:13-27[62] convey the end-time expectation of a *general* and *universal* restoration[63] whereby Jews and Gentiles are being reconciled with God through a redeemer (in the NT constituting the *one* people of God, Eph. 2:11-19) and, at a future point in time, inherit the earth (cf. Rom. 4:13: Abraham as "heir of the world," fulfilling Deut. 1:8 and esp. Gen. 17:7; see Matt. 5:5).[64]

Acts 2:25-36 marks one of the pivotal turning points in the understanding of the connection between the throne of David and Jesus (cf. Mark 12:35-37), whereby Jesus, the Messiah, is now indeed the eternal and exalted ruler *on the throne of David* (Acts 2:30; as anticipated in 2 Sam. 7:13-16 and already in the promise to Abraham in Gen. 22:18).[65] The exalted Christ thus constitutes the fulfillment of Abrahamic and Davidic promises regarding an eternal, messianic rule (and possession of land).

Parallel to this, we note Luke's emphasis upon a *general* resurrection of the dead (Acts 4:2; 17:32; 24:15; 26:3) and a *general* last judgment (Acts 4:23; 10:42; 13:41; 17:31; 24:25). The *general* reference to restoration of all unfulfilled prophecy thus points well beyond Israel (now that the Messiah of God is enthroned and establishes his eternal rule).

The "small wave" of expected fulfillment of delimited promises regarding Israel and its land will thus be overtaken by the "greater wave" of God's future fulfillment of *global* promises regarding repentant Jews,[66] Gentiles, and the entire earth. Old Testament Israel thus serves as a preliminary blueprint of God's global purposes concerning his rule (cf. Acts 1:3[67]) and realm (cf. Acts 1:8: "the ends of the earth"), inaugurated with the coming and enthronement of the Son of God (Acts 2:36), culminating in their full establishment (Rev. 21:2, 10, 22, 24, 27; cf. Heb. 12:22).

While this ultimate restoration is more clearly connected with the parousia,[68] it is probable that it includes events prior to the parousia. An interpretive rendering of the phrase would thus be: "He must be received into heaven until all will have been restored of which God spoke through his holy prophets (from the beginning of the world)."[69]

The sequence of events leading to the parousia can thus be identified as events commencing with the present healing of the lame and the proclamation of repentance leading up to repentance with remission of sins. This will lead to times of divine relief from suppressing burdens. Furthermore, a worldwide restoration of repentant Jews and Gentiles (culminating in their inheriting the earth) is in view.

Summary

We now submit that the above identified "times of divine relief and refreshment," as well as the "restoration of all that has been prophesied," constitute indeed integral elements of Christ's future work. We list the following reasons:

(a) The close parallelism in verse 20 between times of *refreshment* and the sending of Christ Jesus suggests that refreshment likewise is being *administered* by Jesus.

(b) In the same way as the healing of the lame (see v. 13) and forgiveness of sins (vv. 19 and 26) are Christ's "refreshing" deeds (see v. 13), further refreshment will follow.

(c) Divine release and refreshment may be connected with the work of the Holy Spirit and, according to Acts 2:33, it is Christ who sent the Holy Spirit as his agent.

(d) Just as Christ's death has been prophesied, likewise prophesied *restoration* is bound up with him, since universal restoration is a uniquely messianic act and connotes reinstating justice and proper ownership.[70]

(e) In line with the consistent emphasis on the "God of our fathers" as the initiator and Christ as the one who administers and mediates, it is most plausible that here too Christ *executes* the fulfillment of this prophecy.

III. CONCLUSIONS AND CONSEQUENCES

We note a convergence of the various strands of Lucan themes, namely: (a) the relationship of eschatology to Christology within the context of the purpose of Luke–Acts, and (b) the question regarding the compatibility between far- and near-expectation in Luke-Acts.

In Acts 3:12b–26 these strands find their focus in Christ as the divinely affirmed and eminent leader. As prominent as eschatology might seem in Acts 1–3, and as problematic as differences between far- and near-expectation might appear, Christ-centered eschatology in Acts 3:12b-26 is the explanatory key to the latter and the determining factor of the former.[71] Furthermore, this particular emphasis concurs with the purpose of Luke–Acts in so far as the central concern of the temple speech is not eschatology but the call to turn to this eminent and alive leader. The Christology we encounter here is characterized by the "God of our fathers" who *causes and initiates*, and as such affirms Christ as the eminent leader who *conveys and administers* the counsel of God. Christ, in turn, is the one who sends the Holy Spirit (Acts 2:33) as the divine facilitator (Acts 1:8) of the witnessing believers.

Without Christ, *nothing* of the Father's counsel occurs, in the past, now, or in the future. Christ's eminence dynamically permeates present and future events as well as time frames of future expectations. Without (acknowledging) Christ's powerful eminence, events again disintegrate into unrelated occasions, expectations of future events revert into uncertainty, and dynamic time frames freeze into static (apparently incompatible) concepts.

The *eminence* of Christ thus claims primary attention and shapes events and time frames. His (salvific) *deeds* follow next in importance. *Time frames* take third place. Therefore, near-expectation can coexist in a dynamic tension with far-expectation, because it is enveloped in the eminence and work of the person of Christ.

We thus submit (at least regarding Acts 3:12b–26) that Lucan eschatology is not as much shaped by a system of salvation-historical periods (*Heilsgeschichte*) as it is characterized by its Christ-centered foundation. Time frames are clearly derivatives of this vital expectation of end-time *acts* of Christ. Contrary to a position such as that of Conzelmann, a form of near-expectation is, however, fully intact. The end *could* be near. There are not many salvation-historical conditions mentioned before the end may come. A delaying time-period may be in view only regarding the possible lack of repentance on the part of the hearers (understanding "delay" as God's active mercy). There is thus a dynamic tension between repentance and eschatological events.

The effective work of Christ and his eminent presence is, according to our view, the historically plausible and theologically meaningful "missing link" between the unfolding of salvation-history and a maintained, active near-expectation.[72] Primary structures of thinking thus follow personal and relational – "Christ-centered" – rather than conceptual or temporal lines.

Even if the anticipated temporal framework may turn out to be different than expected, *the fundamentals of future expectation remain unshaken*. Near-expectation continues to exist but only in the context of the certainty of Christ-centered events, which must take place before the end. As long as there is faith in Christ, no significant event may be missed and no disappointment (including a possible "delay of the parousia") may be unbearable. He is alive and, together with the Father and the Holy Spirit, in control (see, e.g. the divine *dei* in v. 21). Whoever turns to him may rest assured regarding the future.

The historical question of *when* this deeper Christ-centered link between seemingly competing time-expectations arose remains to be investigated. Surely the rise of the confession of the eminence of Christ to which this speech witnesses would also be the "*Sitz im Leben*" of an understanding of the future as documented in this speech. In other words: as soon as Christ was confessed and preached (see, e.g. Phil. 2:4-11 and Mark 12:35-37; 14:62) as eminently as in Acts 3:17ff., Christ- and event-centered eschatology, as outlined here, must already have existed.

Kurz[73] claims that "Acts 3:19-26 confirms that Luke's christology is heavily influenced by his eschatology." Our investigation has shown that the inverse is true: Luke's (and the early Christians') eschatology (derived from Jesus himself) is heavily influenced and shaped by a vital christology. Is not the parousia itself the *Christ-centered* eschatological event *par excellence*?

---

1. This essay is an abbreviated and revised version of Hans F. Bayer, "Christ-Centered Eschatology in Acts 3:17–26," FS I. H. Marshall, in Joel Green and M. Turner, eds., *Jesus of Nazareth: Lord and Christ* (Grand Rapids, Mich.: Eerdmans/Carlisle, U.K.: Paternoster, 1994), 236–50. Reprinted with kind permission of both W. B. Eerdmans Publishing Company and The Paternoster Press.

2. We merely note some of the important works, particularly on Acts: C. K. Barrett, "Submerged Christology in Acts," in *Anfänge der Christologie*, ed. C. Breytenbach et al., (Göttingen: Vandenhoeck & Ruprecht, 1991), 237–44; O. Cullmann, *Heil als Geschichte. Heilsgeschichtliche Existenz im Neuen Testament*, 2nd. ed. (Tübingen: Mohr, 1967); G. Delling, "Die Jesusgeschichte in der Verkündigung nach Acta," *New Testament Studies* 19, no. 4 (1972–3): 373–89; R. J. Dillon, "The Prophecy of Christ and his Witnesses According to the Discourses of Acts," *New Testament Studies* 32, no. 4, (1986): 544–56; E. Franklin, *Christ the Lord: A Study in the Purpose and Theology of Luke–Acts* (Philadelphia: Fortress, 1975); F. Hahn, "Das Problem alter christologischer Überlieferungen in der Apostelgeschichte unter besonderer Berücksichtigung von Act 3,19-21," in J. Kremer, ed., *Les Actes des Apôtres: Tradition, rédaction, théologie* (Gembloux/Leuven: Université, 1979), 129–54; M. Hengel, "Christology and New Testament Chronology," in *Between Jesus and Paul* (London: SCM, 1983), 30–47, orig. pub. as "Christologie und neutestamentliche Chronologie," in *Geschichte und Urchristentum*, ed. H. Baltensweiler and B. Reicke (Zürich/Tübingen, 1972), 43–67; G. Lohfink, "Christologie und Geschichtsbild in Apg 3,19-21," *Beihefte Zur Zeitschrift für die neutestamentliche Weissenschaft* 13, no. 2 (1969): 223–41, now in idem, *Studien zum Neuen Testament* (Stuttgart: Kath. Bibelwerk, 1989), 223–43; I. H. Marshall, *Luke: Historian and Theologian*, 2nd. ed. (Grand Rapids, Mich.: Zondervan, 1989; orig. Exeter: The Paternoster Press, 1970); J. A. T. Robinson, "The Most Primitive Christology of All?" *Journal of Theological Studies* (New Series) 7 (1956): 177–89.

3. C. K. Barrett, "Faith and Eschatology in Acts 3," in *Glaube und Eschatologie*, ed. E. Grässer and O. Merk (Tübingen: Mohr, 1985), 1–17; J. T. Carroll, *Response to the End of History: Eschatology and Situation in Luke–Acts* (Atlanta, Ga.: Scholars Press, 1988); H. Conzelmann, *Die Mitte der Zeit. Studien zur Theologie des Lukas*, ed. G. Ebeling, 17, 6th ed. (Tübingen: Mohr, 1977); E. E. Ellis, *Eschatology in Luke* (Philadelphia: Fortress, 1972); B. R. Gaventa, "The Eschatology of Luke–Acts Revisited," *Encounter* 43, no. 1 (1982): 27–42; K. Giles, "Present–Future Eschatology in the Book of Acts (I)/(II)," *Reformed Theological Review*, 40, no. 3 (1981): 65–71, and 41, no. 1 (1982): 11–18; W. H. Gloer, ed., *Eschatology and the New Testament*,

(Peabody, Mass.: Hendrickson, 1988; also contains essays by F. F. Bruce, "Eschatology in Acts," and C. K. Barrett, "Gentile mission as Eschatological Phenomenon"); J. Ernst, *Herr der Geschichte. Perspektiven der lukanischen Eschatologie* (Stuttgart: Kath. Bibelwerk, 1987); E. Grässer, *Das Problem der Parusieverzögerung in den synoptischen Evangelien und in der Apostelgeschichte* 3rd ed. (Berlin: Walter de Gruyter, 1977); R. H. Hiers, "The Problem of the Delay of the Parousia in Luke–Acts," *New Testament Studies* 20 (1974): 145–55; A. J. Mattill, *Luke and the Last Things: A Perspective for the Understanding of Lucan Thought* (Dillsboro, N.C.: Western North Carolina, 1979); W. Thüsing, "Erhöhungsvorstellung und Parusieerwartung in der ältesten nachösterlichen Christologie," *Beihefte Zur Zeitschrift für die neutestamentliche Weissenschaft* (NF) 11 (1967): 95–108, 205–22, and 12 (1968): 54–80, 223–40; J. W. Thompson, "The Gentile Mission as an Eschatological Necessity," *Restoration Quarterly* 14 (1971): 18–27; S. G. Wilson, "Lukan Eschatology," *New Testament Studies* 15 (1969/70): 330–47.

4. W. Kurz, "Acts 3:19-26 as a Test of the Role of Eschatology in Lukan Christology," in *Society for Biblical Literature Seminar Papers*, ed. P. J. Achtemeier (Missoula, Miss.: Scholars Press, 1977), 309–23; G. W. MacRae, "'Whom Heaven Must Receive Until the Time': Reflections on the Christology of Acts," *Interpretation* 27 (1973): 151–65, now in *Studies in the New Testament and Gnosticism*, ed. D. J. Harrington et al. (Wilmington, Del.: Glazier, 1987), 47–64.

5. Works listed in footnotes 2–4 will henceforth be cited only in abbreviated form. Other works will be identified completely the first time they are cited.

6. See I. H. Marshall, *The Gospel of Luke* (Grand Rapids, Mich.: Eerdmans, 1979), 35, 43ff.

7. Regarding the "deeds of Christ" in Acts, see especially Acts 1:1ff.; 2:33; 3:16, 26. Regarding Acts as confirmation of the Gospel, see W. C. van Unnik, "The 'Book of Acts' – the Confirmation of the Gospel," *Novum Testamentum* 4, no. 1 (1960): 26–59.

8. Gaventa, "Eschatology," 27ff., presents a well-informed overview of current positions concerning future expectations in Luke. Gaventa identifies the following positions: (1) Because of an unexpected and persistent delay of the parousia, Luke develops his salvation–historical concept as a "solution" (Conzelmann); (2) Luke writes in the expectation of the imminent event of the parousia (Mattill); (3.1) The parousia is expected by Luke rather soon – there is, however, no imminent expectation (Ellis, Marshall); (3.2) Luke reflects both a near and far expectation of the parousia (S. G. Wilson); (3.3) The delay of the parousia is merely a problem of the community Luke addresses; Luke himself attempts to offset this by maintaining a sure near expectation (Franklin). See also Giles, "Present–Future 1," 65ff.

9. See the carefully argued study by D. E. Aune, "The Significance of the Delay of the Parousia for Early Christianity," in *Current Issues in Biblical and Patristic Interpretation*, ed. G. F. Hawthorne (Grand Rapids, Mich.: Eerdmans, 1975), 87–109. Aune reaches the following conclusion: "We found no evidence to suggest that the so-called problem of the delay of the Parousia was in fact perceived as a problem by early Christians" (109).

10. Carroll, *Response*, 166, denies that Luke did this (against J. A. Fitzmyer, *The Gospel According to Luke*, 2 vols. [Garden City, N.Y.: Doubleday and Co., 1981 and 1985], 1: 234, who is here influenced by Conzelmann) and remarks: "... Luke's paraenetic interest shifts the center of gravity away from the eschaton toward the *sêmeron* ... Nevertheless, Luke has not, as Fitzmyer claims, dulled the edge of eschatology to make of it a paraenetic device. The eschaton is not 'swallowed up' in the sêmeron" (166ff.).

11. Carroll, *Response*, 166. Marshall, *Luke: Historian and Theologian*, 110n1, prefers to speak on good grounds of "interval" instead of "delay."

12. Carroll, *Response*, 167.

13. Grässer, *Problem*, passim.

14. See also Marshall, *Gospel of Luke*, 781.

15. See Carroll, *Response*, 166ff. See also Marshall, *Gospel of Luke*, who rightly considers it to be a false "... assumption that Jesus did not expect an interval before the parousia" (783). Cf. also my study *Jesus' Predictions of Vindication and Resurrection* (Tübingen: Mohr, 1986), 244–9.

16. See Carroll, *Response*, 165.

17. See Luke 17:22-37; 21:24ff.;,34-36; Acts 1:6ff.; 3:19-26; see further Acts 10:42 and 17:31. Regarding near expectation, see Luke 18:1-8; 21:32.

18. See the important contribution to this topic by Cullmann, *Heil*, passim.

19. See especially R. C. Tannehill, "The Functions of Peter's Mission Speeches in the Narrative of Acts," *New Testament Studies* 37, no. 3 (1991): 400–14, particularly 400–1 and note 4.

20. See Ezek. 36:25ff.; Isa. 31:31-34; LXX Joel 2:28-32; cf. Luke 3:16; Acts 1:5ff.; 2:1ff. and 1QS 55:20ff. See Giles, "Present–Future 2," 12, who points to the general outpouring of the Holy Spirit as prophesied for the end times: Joel 2:28ff.; Zech. 1:3-6; Mal. 4:5-6; T. Levi. 8:14; T. Benj. 9:2.

21. Isa. 49:6. Cf. Matt. 24:14; Luke 21:24; 24:47; Acts 11:18; see further Mark 13:10; Matt. 24:14; 28:19ff.; Luke 1:32; 3:6; 4:25-28; Acts 8:4ff.; 10:10-34.

22. Acts 1:11; 2:17; 3:20 and possibly 7:55f. Cf. Giles, "Present–Future 1," 67. The expectations of restoration (see below), as well as the resurrection of the dead (Luke 14:11-14; 20:35f; Acts 4:2; 17:32; 24:15; 26:3), and the final judgment (Acts 4:23; 10:42; 13:41; 17:31; 24:25) are essentially related to the parousia (see below).

23. Giles, "Present–Future 2," remarks: "... the death and resurrection of Christ has made future realities present possibilities" (18).

24. Nevertheless, Gaventa, "Eschatology," 34, and note 28, mentions correctly references to future judgment in Acts 10:42; 17:30ff. and 24:25.

25. Exactly this observation points (among other factors) against the positions of Conzelmann, Vielhauer (S. P. Vielhauer, "Zum 'Paulinismus' der Apostelgeschichte," Evangelische Theologie 10 (1950/51): 1–15, now in Aufsätze zum Neuen Testament [München: Chr. Kaiser, 1965], 9–27), Haenchen (E. Haenchen, Die Apostelgeschichte, 7th ed. [Göttingen: 1977]), Wilckens (U. Wilckens, Die Missionsreden der Apostelgeschichte, 3rd. ed. [Neukirchen–Vluyn: Neukirchener Verlag, 3 1974]), and others, who claim that a lively expectation of the parousia is not significant for Luke.

26. D. Hamm, "Acts 3:12–26: Peter's Speech and the Healing of the Man Born Lame," Perspectives on Religious Studies 11, no. 3 (1984): 199–217, 205.

27. Carroll, Response, 137ff.

28. English translations are taken from the English Standard Version (ESV).

29. This term is particularly important in Luke. Of a total of thirty-five occurrences in the NT, thirteen appear in Acts, two in his Gospel.

30. The severity of arneomai is emphasized by double reference (vv. 13 and 14).

31. As a reference to God: Ps. 71:22; 78:41; Isa. 1:4; 5:24; 6:3; 10:20; 12:6; 17:7; 31:1; 55:5; 60:9; Jer. 2:3; Hos. 11:9; 12:1; Amos 4:2; Hab. 1:12; Dan. 4:19; 3 Macc. 2:13; as a reference to the king of Israel: Ps. 89:19; Isa 43:15; as a reference to the redeemer: Isa. 47:4; 54:5; as a reference to Elisha, the prophet: 2 Kings 4:9; as a reference to Aaron, the priest: Ps. 106:16, ton hagion kuriou. Cf. Sir. 45:6; Mark 1:24; Luke 4:34; John 6:69. The connection of "Servant" and "Holy one" is documented in LXX Dan. 3:35: "Abraham, your friend; Isaac, your servant; Israel, your Holy one."

32. As a reference to God: Ps. 129:4; cf. Zeph. 3:5; LXX Dan. 9:14; 1 Enoch 38:2; 53:6; as a reference to the Son of Man: 1 Enoch 46:3 ("the righteous Son of Man"). The righteousness of the Messiah is mentioned in Isa. 32:1 (cf. 2 Sam. 23:3). The righteousness of the Servant is mentioned in Isa. 53:11b.

33. The connection between the terms "the Holy one" and "the Righteous" is found in Isa. 5:16 with reference to God. Cf. also Isa. 33:5ff. and Deut. 32:4 (dikaios kai hosios theos); cf. hosiōs kai dikaiōs in 1 Thess. 2:10.

34. Cf. LXX Isa. 55:4: David as archōn over the Gentiles; cf. (MT)/LXX hēgoumenos in 1 Chron. 17:7; cf. 2 Chron. 6:5. While archēgos can mean "source" or "origin," it is probable that "leader" or "head" is implied here. See the material proximity of this usage to Acts 5:31 (the functional context of 5:31 suggests there the meaning of "leader/prince" in conjunction with "savior," pace Delling, "Jesusgeschichte," 381) and the fact that the context of Acts 3:15 permits both semantic domains.

35. See the emphatic repetition of the name (v. 16) and of faith (v. 16). Grammatically, Peter's faith could also be in view, but the faith of the one administering the healing is never emphasized in Luke (cf. Hamm, "Acts 3:12–26," 204).

36. The call to repentance consists of two imperatives: metanoēsate (see Acts 2:38; cf. Acts 26:18ff.) and epistrepsate. This pair of terms hints at the fact that repentance is not only turning away from the old ways but also towards Christ. The consequence is the forgiveness of sins (see 2:38). See Delling, "Jesusgeschichte," 374, who notes that repentance (2:38; 3:19; 5:31; 17:30) and forgiveness of sins (2:38; 5:31; 10:43; 13:38) are being mentioned "in fast jeder Missionspredigt."

37. See Tannehill, "Functions," 405. The reference to "ignorance" (v. 17) as one "supportive motivation" is not a general excuse and dismissal of guilt but rather an expression of hope in the context of the possibility and necessity of repentance. Thus far their ignorance paradoxically furthered God's unsearchable ways regarding Christ. It is part of God's council (Acts 2:23; cf. Delling, "Jesusgeschichte," 382). But now they must turn. Regarding the motif of ignorance, Hamm ("Acts 3:12–26," 207) refers to Acts 17:30 and Luke 9:45; 18:34; 24:16.31.

38. Tannehill ("Functions," 406) rightly calls this speech a "repentance speech par excellence."

39. H. N. Ridderbos, The Speeches of Peter in the Acts of the Apostles (London: Tyndale Press, 1962), 14.

40. Conzelmann, Mitte, 127.

41. Theoretically, this position also concedes a "'not yet" aspect (cf. Conzelmann, Mitte, 10), which is, however, de facto irrelevant. Conzelmann (Mitte, 87–92; 123ff.) presupposes as historical fact an acute disillusionment concerning the imminent parousia in Luke's and his hearers' thought. Conzelmann gives the impression that Luke maintains the expectation of the parousia merely as a dry "article of orthodox faith."

42. Regarding Vielhauer and Käsemann, cf. Ridderbos, Speeches, 15n2.

43. Haenchen, Acts, 96.

44. Lohfink, "Christologie," 223ff.

45. See the Joel citation in Peter's first speech: at least the eschatological "now" has begun in the known space-time continuum.

46. This also holds true for the Pentecost speech where the event of the outpouring of the Spirit marks the inauguration of end times.

47. Cf. K. Haacker, "Verwendung und Vermeidung des Apostelbegriffs im lukanischen Werk," *Novum Testamentum* 30, no. 1 (1988): 9–38. Haacker convincingly emphasizes the generally limited Lucan use of *apostolos* (cf. Acts 1:21-22) as referring to the twelve.

48. See the more extensive analysis in Hans F. Bayer, "Christ-Centered Eschatology in Acts 3:17–26," in Joel Green and M. Turner, eds., *Jesus of Nazareth: Lord and Christ* (Grand Rapids, Mich.: Eerdmans/Carlisle, U.K.: Paternoster, 1994), 236–50.

49. See Acts 20:6, where *achri hêmerôn pente* covers the time-span necessary to sail from Philippi to Troas, with the emphasis upon the arrival occurring after five days. See Kurz, "Acts 3:19-26," 311, and note 12.13.

50. Heb. 13:19 contains a specialized use of "restoring" Christian fellowship.

51. Philo uses the term with reference to the liberation from Egypt (*Rer. Div. Her.*, 293) and to the return of property rights in the year of Jubilee connected with a mystical understanding of the restoration of the soul. Josephus refers to the restoration of the temple after the Babylonian exile (*Ant.*, 11.63). For more evidence, cf. A. Oepke, "apokatastasis," *Theological Dictionary of the New Testament*, vol. I, 389ff.

52. Cf. the various references in Oepke, "apokatastasis," 390: in the medical realm as "healing" (cf. Mark 3:5); in the legal realm as "returning possessions" (and freeing prisoners; Polybius, *Hist.* 3.99.6); in the political arena in the sense of "restoring public order" (Polybius, *Hist.* 4.23.1); in the realm of astronomy as the "return of the astronomic cycle to the original position."

53. Oepke, A., "apokatastasis," 389.

54 Gn. Rab. 12; cf. Strack/Billerbeck, *Kommentar*, vol. I, 19.

55. The one who "breaks out"; Mic. 2:13.

56. Rebuilding of the fallen tent of David; turning of events for the people of Israel. We note that this passage contains a *particular* (Amos 9:11.13-15) and a *universal* (Amos 9:12; see esp. LXX) thrust.

57. *Epistæmi* (restoration of the judges): "Justice shall redeem Zion, and righteousness her repentant people." Note the remnant theme in Isa. 1:27-28.

58. Cf. Jer. 16:15; 24:6; 50:19. Cf. Sir. 48:10.

59. Cf. Tannehill, "Functions," 406.

60. Ezek. 37:25: an eternal covenant and messianic rule; Ezek. 37:26: an eternal sanctuary (cf. the argument of Hebrews and Revelation 21); Ezek. 37:27: God dwells among them; Ezek. 37:28: the Gentiles/nations will know God, who dwells among sanctified Israel/Jews.

61. The chosen Servant of YHWH as: (a) the restorer of Israel *and* (b) a saving light to the *nations/Gentiles* ("to the ends of the earth"; cf. the terminological proximity to Acts 1:8), as well as c) the highly exalted servant–ruler; cf. Luke 2:32; Acts 13:47 and 26:23.

62. People from all nations will worship the messianic Son of Man, who receives an everlasting kingdom (Dan. 7:14); the people of God (Jews and Gentiles) will co-reign with the exalted Son of Man (Dan. 7:27).

63. See, e.g. Jer. 31:31-38: in Jeremiah, Israel receives a new covenant, forgiveness, and the restoration of Jerusalem. However, Heb. 8:8-10 and 10:16 apply Jer. 31:31-34 to all those who are cleansed in the atoning blood of Jesus (Jews and Gentiles alike).

64. See *palin genesia* in Matt. 9:28 and Rev. 21:1ff. See Rom. 8:20ff. and the rabbinic reference to creation in Gen. Rab. 12.

65. I am indebted for this point to Rev. Ron Lutjens.

66. See Rom. 11:5, 14, 21, 23, 26: God has not rejected Israel, or broken his promises, because he (always) preserves a remnant.

67. Cf. further Acts 8:12; 14:22; 19:8; 20:25; 28:23–31.

68. Against Hamm ("Acts 3:12-26," 214). Hamm fails to convince by pressing the entire speech into a corset of realized eschatology.

69. Literally: "until the completion (*achri*) of the times of restoration of all that which God spoke through his holy prophets."

70. See e.g. Luke 4:18-19 (Isa. 61:1ff.).

71. Hengel ("Christology," 43) speaks of the "christological consistency" with regard to the boldness of the Greek-speaking, Jewish-Christian communities to break with the "ritual regulations of the Torah."

72. See Hengel ("Christology," 41), who states that the personal relationship to the exalted Lord is expressed in the *kyrios* and the *maranatha* acclamation, especially in the Greek-speaking part of the earliest Palestinian Jewish-Christian church.

73. Kurz, "Acts 3:19-23," 318.

8

"*WHAT IS THE NATURE OF TRUE RELIGION?*":
Religious Affections *and Its American Puritan Context*

SEAN MICHAEL LUCAS

Assistant Professor of Church History
Dean of Faculty

ld Light polemicist Charles Chauncy, responding to Jonathan Edwards' apology for the Great Awakening, opened his *Seasonable Thoughts on the State of Religion in New England* with a thirty-page historical preface that referenced the "antinomians, familists and libertines, who infected these churches, above a hundred years ago." Why was Chauncy so eager to review an event that had occurred more than a century earlier? Aside from the fact that he was attempting to implement the effective debating technique of creating "guilt by association," the charge he raised – that "the like spirit and errors, prevailing now as they did then" – provided a clue to the larger American Puritan context in which the battle over the meaning of the Great Awakening took place.[1]

This battle, aimed at determining whether or not the Great Awakening was a "work of God," focused on two chief questions. The first was, "Are you 'saved'?" This question looked at the situation from the "third person" point of view – how one person perceived another's spiritual state. Bound up with this was the propriety of even asking such a question – particularly of ministers – and the resultant decrying of those who did not have an "experimental Christ." The second question – "Am I 'saved'?" – was that of the "first person," of introspection. It focused the individual upon one's own salvation, the assurance of one's own faith. How these two questions were answered, and the evidence used to support the answers, determined whether one stood with the Old Lights or the New.[2]

Even more, Chauncy's historical reference highlighted the fact that New England divines had debated questions related to salvation and assurance for over a hundred years. With their emphasis on "experimental" religion, the Puritans were well-known for their writings in the area of casuistry, or cases of conscience, wherein they sought to discern pastorally whether one had truly experienced salvation. It was fitting that the last great representative of the Puritan mind, Jonathan Edwards, struggled to determine for himself and for other New Lights what true religion was, and how it could be found in oneself and in others. The crown jewel of Edwards' thought on this issue was his book *Religious Affections* (1746).

Many historians, led by Perry Miller, misread *Religious Affections* by forcing it into the context of the eighteenth-century empiricism of John Locke and Isaac Newton and by claiming that the *Affections* represented Edwards' contribution to the psychology of religion and the modern American "mind." I would suggest, however, that Locke and Newton do not provide the correct intellectual context for *Affections*. To interpret the work solely in terms of Lockean empiricism is to interpret Edwards' argument wrongly. The proper context for *Affections* was not Lockean, but rather, Puritan. I would argue, therefore, that Jonathan Edwards' *Religious Affections* must be interpreted in its American Puritan context.[3]

In order to recognize that this is the proper intellectual context for *Affections*, we must return to Chauncy and his historical preface. Chauncy tried to connect Edwards with the Antinomians, who had captured the attention of the Massachusetts Bay Colony from 1636 to 1638. This was a pivotal point in the religious history of New England; from that time on, by the mere mention of the word "antinomianism," one minister could blacklist another, sullying his reputation by associating him with the extremist Anne Hutchinson. Moreover, Chauncy's reference reopened the theological fissures first brought to light by the Antinomian Controversy. As historian Janice Knight demonstrated, the Antinomian Controversy was a fracture in the Puritan coalition at the Massachusetts Bay Colony. This coalition was made up, on one side, of the "Intellectual Fathers"; their party included John Winthrop, Thomas Shepard, Peter Bulkeley, and Thomas Hooker. The Intellectual Fathers stood, according to Knight, in the line of William Ames; in particular, they "insisted on the usefulness of Christian works as an evidence of salvation." In the Antinomian Controversy, their champion was Shepard, who, from his Newtown (later renamed Cambridge) parish, preached a series of sermons over four years entitled *The Parable of the Ten Virgins*, in which he sought to refute the claims of the opposition.

That opposing party, whom Knight dubbed "Spiritual Brothers," were in the intellectual line of Richard Sibbes and John Preston (and, they would claim, John Calvin) and included John Cotton, John Wheelwright, and Henry Vane. This party "presented a vibrant alternative within the mainstream of Puritan religious culture." In the Antinomian Controversy, the Spiritual Brothers, led by Cotton, believed that "the transformation of the soul was neither incremental nor dependent on exercises of spiritual discipline. In this piety there are no steps to the altar."[4] The coalition that had been maintained between the Spiritual Brothers and the Intellectual Fathers was shattered with the arrival of Anne Hutchinson. The crisis which resulted shook New England to its very core. The tradition that became the dominant theological position, both in Boston and in the history that followed, emphasized the primacy of sanctification in assurance. Significantly, though Cotton agreed to keep the peace, he did not change his position; he maintained that assurance must come first without any evidence of sanctification. This led Shepard to fume, "Mr. Cotton repents not, but is hid only ... He doth stiffly hold the revelation of our good estate still, without any sight of word or work."[5]

Further, the political aspects of the theological debate – both in 1636 and in 1742 – should not be missed. As historian Louise Breen recently argued, the Antinomian Controversy of 1636 was about politics and economics as much as theology. The Antinomian party, coalescing around the leadership of Henry Vane, challenged the standing political authority of John Winthrop and other "original" Massachusetts Bay founders. Importantly, ministers such as John Wheelwright were not charged with heresy alone; they were also charged with sedition, a political charge that struck at the disordering nature of this theological division. The party headed by Winthrop and Thomas Shepard was the party of order as well as orthodoxy. The situation had changed little by 1742; the danger of disorder in the colonies brought by the New Lights threatened the disintegration of British culture in the new land. Added to this threat of internal disorder was the threat of the French and Native Americans on the western edge of the Atlantic seaboard, a threat that would be realized in the Seven Years' War. By making reference to the Antinomian Controversy and attempting to group the New Lights with the earlier Antinomians, Chauncy claimed the position of Shepard and Winthrop for himself and to pose as the restorer of order and good sense.[6]

Edwards would not choose between Cotton and Shepard, the Spiritual Brothers and the Intellectual Fathers. Rather, in *Affections*, Edwards held the two Puritan positions in tension – the new sense of the heart and the holy walk of the life. Even though quotations from Shepard account for over half of all the footnotes in *Affections*, there is clearly a Sibbes Cotton influence, particularly in the development of Edwards' new spiritual sense.[7] Though not to be argued in this essay, it could be suggested that after Edwards' death, the synthesis that he developed fragmented. In response to the Separate Congregationalists, the New Divinity men – Joseph Bellamy, Samuel Hopkins, and Jonathan Edwards, Jr. – emphasized the *evidentialist* stream in the Edwardsian synthesis; their appropriation of Edwards' dissertation *The Nature of True Virtue* contributed to his disciples' sometimes rationalistic neonomianism. In response to the Old Calvinists and the Unitarians, the Revivalists (primarily made up of Separate Congregationalists and Baptists) emphasized the *experiential* stream in the Edwardsian synthesis; this stream tended to be subjective and somewhat antinomian. Sadly, the synthesis which Edwards struggled to develop collapsed quickly in the years after his death.[8]

The American Puritan Context: The Antinomian Controversy

In order to understand the American Puritan context for Edwards' *Affections*, it is imperative to gain an understanding of the historical and theological issues in play during the Antinomian Controversy.[9] The word *antinomian* literally meant "against law"; the position described the exaltation of internal and subjective elements of Christianity, particularly the inner "witness of the Spirit," over external elements, such as obedience to the moral law. This position first appeared in the American colonies around the time of Anne Hutchinson's immigration in May 1634. By November, her husband, William Hutchinson, was elected deputy from Boston to the Massachusetts General Court. Anne occupied herself in visiting neighbors, particularly during times of childbirth. Soon she began to hold meetings in her home for the purpose of discussing the previous Sunday's sermon. In her opinion, many ministers preached a "legal" religion, because they argued for a necessary connection between sanctification and justification, between a believer's works and salvation.[10]

As a result of these opinions, some area ministers wondered if John Cotton, teacher at Boston's First Church, had anything to do with the spreading "heresy." On October 25, 1636, the ministers of the Massachusetts Bay met with Cotton, Hutchinson, and her brother-in-law, John Wheelwright. John Winthrop reported that

> Mr. Cotton was present and gave satisfaction to them, so as he agreed with them in the point of sanctification, and so did Mr. Wheelwright; so as they all did hold that sanctification did help to evidence justification. The same he had delivered plainly in public, divers times; but for the indwelling of the person of the Holy Ghost, he held that still, as some others of the ministers did, but no union with person of the Holy Ghost, (as Mrs. Hutchinson and others did,) so as to amount to a personal union.[11]

The New England clergy believed that the situation was under control; on the key point of sanctification evidencing justification, Cotton was in agreement with them. However, the Hutchinsonians were not quieted. In December 1636, another meeting was held with the ministers of New England. At this meeting, Cotton received a list of sixteen questions to answer in writing to the satisfaction of the ministers. His answers engendered several exchanges, as the keepers of orthodoxy sought to pin him down theologically.

On January 17, 1637, John Wheelwright preached the fast-day sermon. Wheelwright, described by a contemporary as "a man of bold and stiff conceit of his own worth and light," preached what this observer deemed "a seditious sermon." In warning his hearers of the dangers of falling into a "covenant of works" by linking evidences of salvation too closely to salvation itself, Wheelwright's sermon created a firestorm. He was called before the court, "and his sermon being produced, he justified it, and confessed he did mean all that walk in such a way ... After much debate, the court adjudged him guilty of sedition, and also of contempt, for that the court had appointed the fast as a means of reconciliation of differences, etc., and he purposely set himself to kindle and increase them." Though Wheelwright was convicted of sedition, the court deferred his sentencing in order to allow him to repent. He did not and was banished from the colony.[12]

After a riotous election time, during which Henry Vane, a Hutchinson supporter, was voted out of the governor's office and replaced by John Winthrop, all of New England gathered at the end of August 1637 for a general synod, the first in New England's brief history. The New England elders listed eighty-two errors of the Antinomian faction, but only five points stood in the way of a full agreement between Cotton and the other ministers. After a series of negotiations, the number was reduced to three; Cotton then agreed on those three points and reconciliation was effected. However, there was no reconciliation available for Anne Hutchinson and her followers. In November 1637, Anne Hutchinson was placed on trial for countenancing those who were seditious and rebellious against the authorities. During the trial she appeared to hold her own, until she claimed that she had immediate revelations from God's Spirit. This became the charge against the Hutchinsonians. Winthrop said as much: "We have been hearkening about the trial of this thing and now the mercy of God by a providence hath answered our desires and made her lay open herself and the ground of all these disturbances to be by revelations ... The groundwork of her revelations is the immediate revelation of the spirit and not by the ministry of the word." Hutchinson and her followers were banished from the Massachusetts Bay Colony and left to help establish Rhode Island.[13]

This historical survey shows that one of the key figures of the Antinomian Controversy was John Cotton. The Antinomian teaching developed in his church and he was charged with maintaining these teachings "too obscurely." At the trial of Anne Hutchinson, it seemed at times that Cotton was the focus of attention rather than Hutchinson; though he agreed with his clergy brothers in principle, he was forced to go through a public purgatory.

The other representative theological mind in the debate was Thomas Shepard, minister at Cambridge. As noted earlier, in June 1636 Shepard began preaching a series of sermons that was eventually published as *The Parable of the Ten Virgins*. The preface reported that these messages sought to combat the "leaven of Antinomian and Familistical opinions stirring in the country" and which were being "spread elsewhere by the new lights of these times." Not only did Shepard preach against Cotton and the Hutchinsonians, but he also engaged in correspondence with Cotton, seeking to understand his views. As a result, an investigation of Cotton's and Shepard's thought on the nature of true religion is vital to understanding the later development of Edwards' thinking on the subject.[14]

John Cotton: Union with Christ and the Spirit's Divine Light

John Cotton, the teaching elder in Boston's First Church, was the sole theological mind (until John Davenport's arrival in New England) to whom the Antinomians claimed allegiance.[15] However, he was not antinomian himself; rather, his theological viewpoints were misunderstood and misrepresented by both friends and enemies so that they became caricatured.[16] His theological statements on the issue of the believer's assurance of salvation revealed that he was Christocentric; his emphasis was on union with Christ as the first basis of assurance. Next, he emphasized a testamental view of federal (or covenant) theology, placing great emphasis upon the "absolute" promises, almost to the denigrating of "conditional" promises. Finally, he did have a place for Christian practice in assurance of faith; however, works were assigned a confirmatory, or secondary, role in the assurance of a believer.

At the height of the Antinomian Controversy, in response to the "Elders Reply," a short response to his answers of sixteen doctrinal questions posed by the New England clergy, Cotton issued a lengthy rebuttal, now called "Mr. Cotton's Rejoynder." One historian called his tract "the most important exposition of Cotton's theology at the time of the Controversy." In it, he developed union with Christ as the first basis of assurance by stating that all the promises of justification and sanctification are made directly to Christ; saints participate in these promises only as they are united to Christ: "Indeed all the promises are made first and immediately to Christ, and by right of our union with him they come to be communicated to us in a way of faith and Sanctification."[17]

For Cotton, this was the difference between the Mosaic law (which he identified with the Covenant of Works) and the Gospel (which he called the Covenant of Grace). In the law, "the promise is made to the Condition or qualification of the creature." If there were perfect obedience to the law, satisfying the divine demand, then the individual could claim the promise of God. However, in the gospel, "the promise is made to Christ, so that give me Christ and I claime my right to the promise and to all the comforts and blessings thereof." That is why the promises of the gospel were truly gracious "because all the promises are given to Christ, and all the conditions fulfilled in Christ, and the revealing of both is by the revealing of Christ given of grace freely to the Soul."[18]

Gospel promises form the first and primary basis of the individual's assurance of salvation. Since these promises belonged to Christ first and to the believer as he was in union with Christ, Cotton taught that the believer should attempt to discern whether or not he was actually united to Christ. If there were union with Christ, then the conditional promises, such as faith or obedience, belonged automatically to that individual by virtue of union.

The entire discussion of conditional promises pointed to a second facet of Cotton's understanding of the nature of true religion: namely, the entire milieu of covenant, or federal, theology. While some historians, led by Perry Miller, presented a Puritan New England that was univocal in its development of federal theology, recent studies have suggested a multivocal, or at least a bivocal, aspect to the theological discussion. The lines were generally drawn between those who emphasized the conditional promises of the covenant (the Intellectual Fathers) and those who clung to the absolute promises (the Spiritual Brothers).[19]

Cotton stood in the theological tradition that emphasized the absolute promises of the covenant. He viewed salvation in terms of a testamental bequest, in which Christ as testator died, securing the benefits of God for his passive benefactors. Because salvation was "a free gift and confirmed by the death of the giver, it was more properly called a testament, not a covenant."[20] Since salvation was a free gift, granted by the one who died to secure it, the receiver was completely passive upon reception. "Before regeneration we are not active at all," Cotton claimed, "no, nor in *proxima potentia* passive, to receive help from God to do it. But after Regeneration *Acti agimus*."[21] For Cotton, the covenantal promises were absolute; only God in Christ could fulfill them. God made these absolute promises to Christ, just as he made conditional promises in the New Covenant to Christ. Since all these promises were made to Christ, then it was incumbent on Christ to fulfill them; and because Christ did in fact fulfill these promises, only by virtue of union with him could the believer partake of them. Cotton believed that union with Christ was required in order for human beings to gain salvific blessings. Not even assurance of the blessings of Christ's grace could be "challenged" from God, except on the basis of union with Christ. As a result, it was incumbent upon Christians to ascertain that they were in fact united with Christ and then "plead [that] assured union" with Christ. Unless one had this prior assurance of union, no other evidence or sign – whether it was sanctification, works, or prayers – would be able to satisfy the anxious mind.

Although Cotton claimed that union with Christ was the basis of true religion and genuine assurance, he left room for Christian practice, albeit in a secondary role. In answering the elders' claim that he held "that we can see neither Sanctification nor faith no nor Justification, before the witness of the Spirit; but all at once by it,"[22] he summarized his position on the role of Christian practice in the evidencing of salvation:

> When the Spirit of God doth shed abroad his light into the Soul and giveth him a clear sight of his estate in a free promise of grace in Christ, such an one

clearly discerneth both his Justification and his Sanctification the one of them giving good evidence to the other, the blood to the water and the water to the blood and the Spirit to them both, 1 John 5.6, 8. And thus in evidencing his Justification by his Sanctification he doth not build his justification upon his Sanctification nor hereby go in a Covenant of Works nor go aside to it.[23]

He related Christian practice to justification in two ways. First, he argued that the Spirit's regenerating action occurred before practice; he illustrated this point using the striking image of divine light. The Spirit opened "the eyes of the understanding" so that the individual apprehended "the mysteries of Gods kingdome" through a new understanding of "the Scriptures, and works of God in us." Cotton held that "only by Spiritual light and by Spiritual understanding and by comparing Spirituall things with Spirituall things" could the believer understand the spiritual truth contained in the gospel. The light that the Spirit gave to the soul was called "a gracious sight of him [Christ] wrought by the Spirit of Grace," which caused the soul "to mourn after Christ or for him." This gracious sight was given as the Spirit breathed into the Word of God, giving it "Divine force" and making it "a divine testimony." In this manner, "the same word that calleth them to Christ, giveth them in a renewed measure his Spirit of faith, by which they do come to Christ, and do drink in the satisfaction of their Souls in the full Assurance of his grace and righteousness freely given to them of God." Thus, the condition to right appropriation of works' evidence was fulfilled in the "divine and supernatural light" of the Spirit.[24]

Second, Cotton believed that works provided evidence to assure the soul. However, it was only in the context of this new spiritual sight that sanctification could be discerned correctly. For within this context, the believer understood that he did not perform these works in his own strength and power, and in this manner evidenced salvation. Rather, the Spirit "himself [who] setteth faith awork and stirreth it up to look forth to Christ and to wait on him, who being waited on, quickeneth by his Spirit all our gifts in his name to bring forth fruits of righteousness unto God." The indwelling spirit of Christ was "the root of this tree"; by the "power of the Spirit" the tree bore fruit in active holiness. When the elders accused Cotton of denigrating works of sanctification, such as prayer, he replied, "My meaning therefore was not to beat men off the use of holy duties or from seeking the face of God and sight of Justification by Christ in the use of them, it being part of that way wherein himself hath appointed us to seek him in Christ."[25]

Cotton saw two potential dangers that could spring from the use of works in assurance of faith, dangers he sought to safeguard against by emphasizing the Spirit's prior work. The first danger was that works had no promised blessing; rather, promised blessings belonged solely to Christ and to believers by virtue of union with Christ. The second danger was the abuse of works as an evidence of salvation. Cotton feared that the believer could become complacent in his Christian practice. He observed that "such an use of them [works] whereby I either seek to attaine right of the promised blessing by doing the duty which the promise calleth for, or else do satisfie myself in the comforts and enlargements I find in the duties" was not simply a use, but an abuse of sanctifying works. Christian practice should be done in a disinterested manner, not out of desired benefit, but rather for the glory of Christ.[26] He was also concerned that works might become the sole evidence for salvation. In responding to the elders, he claimed that "if a man neither give nor can give any other ground (as having indeed no other ground to give) of his justification but only the evidence of his Sanctification ... their [*sic*] faith is not builded nor grounded at all upon the righteousness of Christ nor upon the free promise of grace wherein that righteousness is applied to us, but only upon their works." To Cotton, practice must match a profession of spiritual life in the soul. Practice alone was a spiritual relation that was "either counterfeit or very suspicious" and much more likely "to be legal than Evangelical."[27]

Thus, there were several connections between Cotton and Jonathan Edwards' later development of similar themes in *Affections*. Although Edwards does not quote from Cotton at all, ideas held by Cotton were represented in *Affections,* through the mediation of theologians such as Richard Sibbes and John Calvin. There was a parallel between Cotton's "light" and Edwards' "new sense" (which Edwards represented elsewhere as a "divine and supernatural light immediately imparted to the soul by God"). There was also a parallel in the linking of divine light and practice. However, Cotton's connection with Edwards was overshadowed by the fact that his opponent, Shepard, was quoted extensively by the Northampton divine, while he was not quoted at all.[28]

Thomas Shepard: Emphasis upon Conditional and Gradual Growth

Thomas Shepard was the leader of the majority party throughout the Antinomian Controversy. Shepard first wrote to John Cotton, querying him regarding his views and warning him that he "may meet in time with some such members (though I know none nor judge any) as may doe your people and ministry hurt, before you know it." Shepard's church in Cambridge hosted the 1637 elections, synod, and trial of Anne Hutchinson. Further, at the beginning of the Controversy, Shepard began his sermon series *The Parable of the Ten Virgins*, in which he repeatedly interacted with the claims of the Antinomians. These sermons evinced a tension within Shepard himself, as Janice Knight noted: "Shepard is the most complex of the preachers in this group – a man whose experiences bound him to both the Intellectual Fathers and to the Spiritual Brothers, and whose temperament remained divided throughout his lifetime." Shepard "quite literally embodied in nearly equal measure the competing affections marking the two fellowships." As a result, Shepard "serves as an important reminder that the issue of difference does not involve binary oppositions, even though the act of description sometimes presses in that direction."[29] During the controversy, Shepard resolved his tension in favor of order and against Cotton. While Cotton's emphasis was upon the end – Christ and his benefits – Shepard's emphasis was upon the means to that end – Christian practice. Whereas Cotton wooed the sinner and the hypocrite by reminding of Christ's love, Shepard persuaded the hypocrite by showing the deceitfulness of the heart. Cotton believed assurance came when the light of God's Spirit caused the saint to see his soul's union with Christ; Shepard held that assurance was a gradual and arduous process, gained through the consistent application of the means of grace and the regular inspection of the soul.

Shepard's aim in his sermon series on the ten virgins was to enable his audience to discover whether or not they were "wise virgins" or "foolish," whether they were saved or lost. Two themes were apparent: first, assurance developed gradually; second, assurance was gained through the use of means and consistent Christian practice. Against the Antinomians' suggestion that assurance comes through the immediate revelation of the Spirit, Shepard labored to prove that assurance was a gradual process. He believed that "the Spirit, when it comes, clears all doubts, not fully, but gradually." The Spirit provided assurance, but it came slowly, as the saint labored to be cleansed of sin. "The Lord reveals not all of himself at once; the day dawns before the sun riseth, and there is a further manifestation of the Lord in this life to his people, not for, but when they, indeed, maintain such works before him," he argued. "Sin does and will grieve God's Spirit, that he will only accuse, not speak peace to you, till all is mended."[30] Gradual growth in assurance meant that sin had to be rooted out. Shepard's searching sermons spent a great deal of time exposing the conscience's hiding places as a means of promoting assurance.

Not only was assurance a gradual process for Shepard, but it also came through the diligent use of means. In a key statement, he argued that "it is true the Spirit only can do it; but yet the same Spirit that seals the elect, the same Spirit commands the elect not to sit idle and dream of the Spirit, but *to use all diligence to make it sure*; and you shall never have it (unless you lay hold on a fancy for it) on those terms. Though there is an immediate witness of the Spirit of the love of Christ, yet *it doth most usually and* firstly *witness by means*."[31] This was in stark contrast to Cotton's emphasis upon the Spirit's illumination of the believer's union with Christ as the basis of assurance for the believer. Instead, Shepard declaimed that the Spirit generally granted assurance to the soul by the use of means. And so, he placed a strong emphasis on attendance at preaching services, prayer, Scripture reading, and, most importantly, the sacraments. If the saint did not make use of these means, he was characterized as slothful and as a potential hypocrite. "The gospel yields the fairest colors for a man's sloth, and the strongest props for that. Hence you see them walking in this garden; for the last sin God conquers in a man is his sloth," Shepard preached. "The gospel shows all fullness in Christ, and that he must do all; a slothful, false heart, therefore, closeth with Christ as the end, but neglects him in the means." The gospel provided the promise of freedom from sin's power and guilt; yet the slothful soul used that promise to excuse itself from the demands of the law.[32]

Those who were not diligent in the use of means, those who were slothful and used the gospel to excuse sin, Shepard denominated "evangelical hypocrites." Evangelical hypocrites were those who did not "rest in the law, or in a covenant of works"; rather, "they had escaped those entanglements." Now these hypocrites "pleade their interest in, and their communion, and fellowship, and love-knot with Christ"; yet, in truth, "these are your carnal gospelers, that cry down their own righteousness, and cry up Christ, and see nothing in themselves, as there is good cause so to think, and look for all from Christ." These, who were not diligent in Christian practice, would be "found false" at that time "when the Lord comes to search" because they were simply "denying [their] own righteousness, to establish [their] sin." These hypocrites were "advancing Christ to advance their lust." In order for the saint to be approved by himself and the larger community, he must use the means of grace diligently, for looking to one's practice was the way to gain assurance.[33]

Shepard claimed that the use of means applied the conditional promises to the soul in order to gain assurance of one's spiritual standing. Unlike Cotton, whose testamental view of the covenant held that the soul was passive in the reception of salvation and that the reception of assurance was based on Christ's absolute promises, Shepard argued for the efficacy of conditional promises to evidence the absolute ones; the individual's spiritual actions evidenced the spiritual root from which those actions spring. In refuting the claim that Christians should take no assurance from conditional promises, he proclaimed, "For those that have to do with them [conditional promises] as their inheritance not to apply and make use of them for their comfort, it is to trample under foot Christ's blood, that has purchased them for that end, and it is to raze out in our practice the greatest part almost of the covenant of grace." He believed that the witness of the Spirit meant that the Spirit evidenced a work that was already present in the soul of the individual through practice. If the individual "looks to no work, nor no condition promises, nor to find the condition in you, (which yet Christ must and doth work) Lord, what abundance of sweet peace do you lose!" It was "plain hypocrisy" not to "bring works to the light."[34] Like Cotton, Shepard collapsed the distinction between conditional and absolute promises; however, whereas Cotton collapsed all promises into the category of *absolute*, Shepard collapsed all promises into the category of the *conditional*.

In Shepard's *Parable* sermons, then, he put forth the idea that a believer's sense of assurance developed gradually. Indeed, it must have come gradually for it was dependent upon the second idea: that assurance resulted from the application of the means of grace in consistent Christian practice. The individual who cried down the use of means was an evangelical hypocrite, seeking to remain in sloth in order to cover up his true problem, an inordinate love for sin. Therefore, the basis for assurance must be Christian practice; the Spirit used this to give the soul the assurance of peace with God.

RELIGIOUS AFFECTIONS: A NEW SYNTHESIS OF COTTON AND SHEPARD

This American Puritan context shaped Edwards' moves in *Affections*. What Edwards developed in *Affections* was a new synthesis, one which united the emphases of Cotton's sense of union with Christ and Shepard's Christian practice as ways to assurance. Edwards wedded the two emphases – his argument in *Affections* was that the new spiritual sense infused by the Holy Spirit infallibly produces Christian practice. As unnatural as it would be to divorce body and soul, so, in Edwards' thinking, would it be unnatural to divorce the new sense – the "divine and supernatural light" – from new practice.[35]

Affections was originally a sermon series, preached to Edwards' Northampton congregation during the winter of 1742–3. He was not responding directly to Chauncy in the sermons on *Affections* (although it seems that he did respond to the Boston minister in the published version).[36] Rather, in the sermons, he dealt with spiritual pride and apathy within his own congregation, trying to defeat both Northampton Antinomians and Arminians with one blow. He gave a hint of his congregation's difficulties in a letter to Thomas Gillespie of Scotland. Gillespie, in a previous letter, had expressed shock at Edwards' dismissal from his Northampton congregation. Edwards' reply, written July 1, 1751, explained to his far-away correspondent that his dismissal was tied to two major spiritual problems within the congregation. First, he charged his congregation with spiritual pride: "The people ... are become more extensively famous in the world, as a people that have excelled in gifts and grace, and had God extraordinarily among them: which has insensibly engendered and nourished spiritual pride, that grand inlet of the Devil into the hearts of men, and avenue of all manner of mischief among a professing people. Spiritual pride is a monstrous thing." In fact, he blamed the spiritual pride of the people upon his own *Faithful Narrative,* which described the awakening of 1734–5: "There is this inconvenience attends the publishing of narratives of a work of God among a people: such is the corruption that is in the hearts of men, and even of good men, that there is great danger of their making it an occasion of spiritual pride." And so, when he spent the entirety of the sixth positive sign in *Affections* on the proposition that "gracious affections are attended with evangelical humiliation," Edwards was pointedly rebuking his people's spiritual hubris.[37]

The second spiritual issue was the congregation's misunderstanding of the workings of salvation. Edwards claimed that "another thing that evidently has contributed to our calamities is, that the people had got so established in certain wrong notions and ways in religion, which I found them in and never could beat them out of." In particular, he cited two areas where the people had a wrong understanding. First, the congregation had as "their method to lay almost all the stress of their hopes on the particular steps and method of their first work, i.e. the first work of the Spirit of God on their hearts in their convictions and conversion, and to look by little at the abiding sense and temper of their hearts, and the course of their exercises, and fruits of grace, for evidences of their good estates." Some people thought that unless their "preparation" and "closing" with Christ went according to steps that had served as the pattern for generations, they were not truly regenerated. The second area of misunderstanding was their inability "to distinguish between impressions on the imagination, and truly spiritual experiences." When Edwards had come to Northampton in 1727, he had found the people ready "to declare and publish their own experience; and oftentimes to do it in a light manner, without any air of solemnity."[38] Throughout *Affections*, he dealt repeatedly with impressions, immediate revelation, and like experiences, trying to assist his people to distinguish between their own daydreams and genuine spiritual experience. And so, in *Affections*, Edwards responded to issues within his own congregation, issues that demanded a pastoral response from the pulpit. In reaction to the spiritual pride and confusion of his people, Edwards developed the thesis that "true religion, in great part, consists in holy affections" and could be traced along two lines of thought: first, holy affections arose from a new spiritual sense in the heart; second, the new sense produced holy actions.

The New Sense of the Heart

Many Edwards interpreters considered his development of the new sense of the heart to be the height of his creative powers.[39] Though the idea of the "new sense" had precedence in earlier Puritan theology, he took the idea in new directions, demonstrating that the Holy Spirit caused the individual to feel, perceive, and think in different ways than had been possible before conversion. Edwards believed that "in those gracious exercises and affections which are wrought in the minds of the saints, through the saving influences of the Spirit of God, there is a new inward perception or sensation of their minds, entirely different in its nature and kind, from anything that ever their minds were the subjects of before they were sanctified." He called this new sense "a new principle" that produced "an entirely new kind of exercises." While he stressed that "this new spiritual sense, and the new dispositions that attend it, are no new faculties, but are new principles of nature," yet the new sense was infused into the individual so that it became "a natural habit or foundation for action."[40]

This new principle became the basis for other internal changes that developed in the believer. It enabled the saint to love God in a disinterested manner. There was a change in the person so that he could "apprehend a beauty, glory, and supreme good, in God's nature, as it is in itself." Edwards insisted that the new spiritual sense would provide "the first foundation of a true love to God" that was found in "the supreme loveliness of his nature." Saints would "first see that God is lovely, and that Christ is excellent and glorious, and their hearts are first captivated with this view." Afterwards, they would understand that God loved them and had shown them great favor in the gospel.[41]

Edwards developed this further by summarizing the supreme character of God in the word *excellency*: "A love to divine things for the beauty and sweetness of their moral excellency, is the first beginning and spring of all holy affections."[42] This moral excellency, within the argument of *Affections*, was holiness: "Holiness comprehends all the true moral excellency of intelligent beings; there is no other true virtue, but real holiness." All internal moral virtues were comprehended in the idea of holiness. He believed that "this kind of beauty is the quality that is the immediate object of this spiritual sense: this is the sweetness that is the proper object of this spiritual sense. The Scripture often represents the beauty and sweetness of holiness as the grand object of a spiritual taste and spiritual appetite."[43] By virtue of the new sense of the heart, the believer saw God's holiness and loved God because of the beauty of that divine holiness.

The new spiritual sense resulted in a new understanding. Edwards reminded his readers that "holy affections are not heat without light; but evermore arise from some information of the understanding, some spiritual instruction that the mind receives, some light or actual knowledge. The child of God is graciously affected, because he sees and understands something more of divine things than he did before."[44] First, spiritual understanding produced a new appreciation for divine holiness. Edwards argued that this new spiritual understanding "consists in a sense of the heart, of the supreme beauty and sweetness of the holiness or moral perfection of divine things, together with all that discerning and knowledge of things of religion, which depends upon and flows from such a sense. Spiritual understanding consists primarily in a sense of heart of that spiritual beauty."[45] Second, spiritual understanding "opens a new world to its view" as the Christian understood the doctrines of God's Word in a way never before contemplated.[46] Third, spiritual understanding produced spiritual conviction concerning the reality and certainty of divine things. Because there was a new principle operative within believers that enabled them to apprehend the beauty of God's holiness, saints in turn had a real conviction regarding unseen realities.

As a result, spiritual understanding produced evangelical humility in the believer. This humility "is from a sense of the transcendent beauty of divine things in their moral qualities" and from "a discovery of the beauty of God's holiness and moral perfection." A sense of God's perfections rebuked all pride in spiritual discoveries or experiences; the rule that Edwards set forth was that "we must take our measure from that height to which the rule of our duty extends: the whole of the distance we are at from that height is sin." The standard was divine perfection; Christians, recognizing that perfect standard, understood the greatness of their remaining corruption, humbling their overweening pride.[47] This movement from spiritual pride, which marked the unregenerate, to humility demonstrated an essential change of nature. The change occurred because "all spiritual discoveries are transforming; and not only make an alteration of the present exercise, sensation and frame of the soul; but such power and efficacy have they, that they make an alteration in the very nature of the soul."[48]

For Edwards, this was an important observation because nature (or disposition) was abiding. With a change in nature, though the Christian may fall into sin, yet he hated sin; and by the transforming power of the Spirit, he would conquer sin. This change in nature was the transformation of the individual from the character of the devil to the character of his new master, Christ. As a result, the individual's character "will be attended with the lamblike, dovelike spirit and temper of Jesus Christ; or in other words, [he will] naturally beget and promote such a spirit of love, meekness, quietness, forgiveness and mercy, as appeared in Christ." The soul took on the tenderness and meekness of Christ as its very character. Moreover, the character of the saint was balanced; it had "beautiful symmetry and proportion." And so, not only was there a hope of heaven, but also a fear of displeasing the King of heaven. There was love for Christ and for his excellencies, coupled with a hatred of sin. This interworking of opposing affections caused the saint to pursue Christlikeness. The saint would never be satisfied with current spiritual attainments, but rather would press on to be more like Christ.[49]

There were, then, parallels between the new sense, as described by Edwards, and Cotton's discussion of the spiritual light that the Holy Spirit gave, causing the regenerate to see the free promise via union with Christ. Just as Cotton was concerned with gaining Christ for Christ's own sake and not for any benefit found in Christ, so with Edwards there was a major concern for a disinterested love for Christ, a love for Christ on his own terms. Even more, there was a parallel between Edwards and the "party" that Cotton represented in America: the Spiritual Brothers. For example, Puritan Richard Sibbes had observed that "there is a sweet relish in all divine truths, and suitable to the sweetness in them, there is a spiritual taste, which the Spirit of God puts into the soul of his children." One can find echoes of this emphasis upon the infusion of a new spiritual taste in Cotton, John Owen, and John Davenport as well. Therefore, in developing the new sense of the heart, Edwards was developing an essentially Puritan theme, one which used the language of sensation long before John Locke.[50]

The New Resultant Actions of the Soul

Edwards did not simply base Christian assurance upon internal evidence –
not even internal evidence as strong as the new sense. Rather, he coupled the
new sense inseparably with new action. In *Affections'* first positive sign, in the
midst of the introduction of the new sense, he pointed to his greater design:
"if grace be, in the sense above described, an entirely new kind of principle;
then the exercises of it are also entirely a new kind of exercises."[51] But it was
in the twelfth positive sign that Edwards developed the new action in its
fullness and depth. "Gracious and holy affections have their exercise and fruit
in Christian practice. I mean, they have that influence and power upon him
who is the subject of 'em, that they cause that practice, which is universally
conformed to, and directed by Christian rules should be the practice and
business of his life," he observed.[52] Edwards then related the previous eleven
signs of gracious affections to this last. Most importantly, he argued that

> the power of godliness is exerted in the first place within the soul, in the
> sensible, lively exercise of gracious affections there. Yet the principal evidence
> of this power of godliness, is in those exercises of holy affections that are
> practical, and in their being practical; in conquering the will, and conquering
> the lusts and corruptions of men, and carrying men on in the way of holiness,
> through all temptation, difficulty and opposition.[53]

Hence, the individual had his first assurance from an internal working of the
Spirit, preserving Cotton's argument. But the principal, the most important,
the "chief" evidence was the consistent practice of godliness, preserving
Shepard's argument. Christian practice assured both the individual and the
community about the person's gracious state.[54]

Regeneration had "a direct relation to practice; for 'tis the very end
of it, with a view to which the whole work is wrought." Every gracious
experience had its end in practice. This connection between profession and
practice, experience and evidence, was one that Edwards called "constant and
dissoluble." In true saints, "their good profession and their good fruit, do
constantly accompany one another: the fruit they bring forth in life, evermore
answers the pleasant sound of their profession."[55] He was careful not to
collapse the "root" of faith and the "fruit" of faith, but rather maintained the
distinction. If there was a holy action, it indicated that there was a holy root
that produced it. In this way, Edwards supported Shepard's contention that
one evidenced justification by sanctification. If there truly were fruit, there
must have been some life principle producing that fruit.[56] He called Christian
practice the "sign of signs," in that "it is the great evidence, which confirms
and crowns all other signs of godliness. There is no one grace of the Spirit of
God, but that Christian practice is the most proper evidence of the truth of
it." Practice evidenced saving faith, repentance, saving knowledge of Christ,
thankfulness, and holy joy.[57] Edwards, however, also reminded his readers

that "no external manifestations and outward appearances whatsoever, that are visible to the world, are infallible evidences of grace." No one could see another person's heart; evidences could not be an infallible rule in judging someone else's profession.[58]

Edwards also supported a theme that Shepard took up in *The Parable of the Ten Virgins*: the necessity of Christian practice as an evidence of justification. It was no accident that Edwards quoted Shepard over seventy times in the footnotes of *Affections*. He used Shepard's cultural authority to ward off Chauncy's charge of Antinomianism. He used Shepard to attack the true Antinomians of his own day. A careful analysis of the way Edwards quoted Shepard would demonstrate that the incantation of Shepard occurred with greatest frequency when Edwards was attacking his Antinomian opponents.

Conclusion

In *Religious Affections*, Edwards synthesized the two American Puritan positions, forged during the Antinomian Controversy, reconciling the Spiritual Brothers and Intellectual Fathers in his own creative position. With Cotton and the Spiritual Brothers, Edwards held the primacy of the new sense of the heart. This new principle that the Spirit infused into the regenerate's heart was properly the first internal evidence or assurance through which the soul gained an ideal apprehension of Christ. The soul gazed upon the excellencies of Christ, which consisted in his holiness; in doing so, the soul gained genuine understanding of spiritual truth and new spiritual conviction concerning the reality of divine things. This conviction, born of an ideal apprehension of the divine, produced a new sense of innate corruption. Hence, the gracious soul was not proud, but rather experienced further evangelical humiliation that in turn produced the character of Christ, especially the meekness and gentleness of the Savior. There was beautiful symmetry and proportion in the character regulated by the new sense. Christians loved Christ and hated sin in perfect proportion, in excellency; yet, they were not satisfied with their current state, but continued on with a changed nature, desiring to be more like Christ.

However, picking up the emphases of Shepard and the Intellectual Fathers, Edwards affirmed that holy practice was the chief evidence of one's regenerate state. New practice evidenced that one had the new sense of the heart. He was careful not to collapse the distinction between the new sense and Christian practice. Yet the bond between them was "constant and indissoluble"; it was not possible to divorce practice and profession, experience and evidence. Although Edwards may have used some Lockean terminology, such as the "new simple idea," his starting point was not Lockean, but rather Puritan. Understanding *Affections* requires an appreciation of its American Puritan context and the theological battles of the earlier Antinomian Controversy.

1. Charles Chauncy, *Seasonable Thoughts on the State of Religion in New England* (Boston: Rogers and Fowle, 1743), i–xxx; Mary Ava Chamberlain, "Jonathan Edwards Against the Antinomians and Arminians," (Ph.D. diss., Columbia University, 1990), 55–93. See also Amy Schranger Lang, "'A Flood of Errors': Chauncy and Edwards in the Great Awakening," in *Jonathan Edwards and the American Experience*, ed. Nathan Hatch and Harry Stout (New York: Oxford University Press, 1988), 160–73.

2. On the Great Awakening as a category of meaning, see Timothy D. Hall, *Contested Boundaries: Itinerancy and the Reshaping of the Colonial American Religious World* (Durham: Duke University Press, 1994). On the use of "first" and "third" person as categories of understanding, see Wayne Proudfoot, "From Theology to a Science of Religions: Jonathan Edwards and William James on Religious Affections," *Harvard Theological Review* 82 (1989): 149–68.

3. For *Affections* as "the most profound exploration of religious psychology in all American literature," see Perry Miller, *Jonathan Edwards* (1949; repr. Amherst: University of Massachusetts Press, 1981), 177–95.

4. Janice Knight, *Orthodoxies in Massachusetts: Rereading American Puritanism* (Cambridge: Harvard University Press, 1994), 3. Knight adopted the terminology from William Haller (*Rise of Puritanism* [New York: Harper, 1938]). Although I agree substantially with Knight's provocative thesis, I would suggest substituting William Perkins for William Ames as the forefather of the Intellectual Fathers (see Michael Schuldiner, *Gifts and Works: The Post-Conversion Paradigm and Spiritual Controversy in Seventeenth-Century Massachusetts* [Macon: Mercer University Press, 1991] and Michael McGiffert, "The Perkinsian Moment of Federal Theology," *Calvin Theological Journal* 29 [1994]: 117–48).

5. Thomas Shepard, "Autobiography," in *God's Plot: Puritan Spirituality in Thomas Shepard's Cambridge* (Amherst: University of Massachusetts Press, 1994), 76 (hereafter: Shepard, "Autobiography").

6. Louise A. Breen, *Transgressing the Bounds: Subversive Enterprises among the Puritan Elite in Massachusetts, 1630–1692* (New York: Oxford University Press, 2001), 17–56.

7. John E. Smith, "Editor's introduction," *The Works of Jonathan Edwards*, vol. 2: *Religious Affections* (New Haven: Yale University Press, 1959), 69–70 (hereafter: Yale, *RA*, 2).

8. Studies that support my conjecture here would include Mark Valeri, *Law and Providence in Joseph Bellamy's New England* (New York: Oxford University Press, 1994); Joseph A. Conforti, *Samuel Hopkins and the New Divinity Movement* (Grand Rapids, Mich.: Christian University Press, 1981); and C. C. Goen, *Revivalism and Separatism in New England, 1740–1800: Strict Congregationalist and Separate Baptists in New England* (New Haven: Yale University Press, 1962).

9. For a convenient overview of many of the theological issues, see William K. B. Stoever, *'A Faire and Easie Way to Heaven': Covenant Theology and Antinomianism in Early Massachusetts* (Middleton: Wesleyan University Press, 1978), 34–70.

10. David D. Hall, *The Antinomian Controversy, 1636–1638: A Documentary History*, 2nd. ed. (Durham: Duke University Press, 1990), 4–10 (hereafter: *AC*).

11. John Winthrop, "Journal," in *The Puritans: A Sourcebook of their Writings*, ed. Perry Miller and Thomas H. Johnson, 2 vols. (1938; rev. and repr., New York: Harper and Row, 1963), 1:129 (hereafter: *MJ*).

12. Shepard, "Autobiography," 68; *MJ*, 132.

13. *AC*, 173; Alan Heimert and Andrew Delbanco, *The Puritans in America: A Narrative Anthology* (Cambridge: Harvard University Press, 1985), 161; *AC*, 311–48.

14. Shepard, "Autobiography," 67; Perry Miller, *The New England Mind: From Colony to Province* (Cambridge: Harvard University Press, 1953) 62; Thomas Shepard, *The Works of Thomas Shepard*, 3 vols. (1853; repr., New York: Georg Olms Verlag, 1971), 2: 8–9 (hereafter: *PTV*; *AC*, 24–33.

15. For Cotton in New England studies generally, see Miller, *New England Mind: From Colony to Province*; Knight, *Orthodoxies in Massachusetts*; Norman Petit, *The Heart Prepared: Grace and Conversion in Puritan Spiritual Life*, 2nd. ed. (Middletown: Wesleyan University Press, 1989); Philip F. Gura, *A Glimpse of Sion's Glory: Puritan Radicalism in New England, 1620–1660* (Middletown: Wesleyan University Press, 1984); Theodore Bozeman, *To Live Ancient Lives: The Primitivist Dimension in Puritanism* (Chapel Hill: University of North Carolina Press, 1988); Edmund S. Morgan, *Visible Saints: The History of a Puritan Idea* (1963; reprint, Ithaca: Cornell University Press, 1987). For studies of Cotton specifically, see Larzer Ziff, *The Career of John Cotton: Puritanism and the American Experience* (Princeton: Princeton University Press, 1962); Everett Emerson, *John Cotton*, rev. ed. (New York: Twayne, 1990); and Sargent Bush, Jr., ed., *The Correspondence of John Cotton* (Chapel Hill: University of North Carolina Press, 2001).

16. Cotton vehemently complains of this: "But by this I discern, whence it cometh to pass, that I am thought to speak so obscurely; for if men that hear me, do instead of my words take up words of their own, and carry them to infer other conclusions than I aime at; I do not wonder if they cannot well understand, how that which I speak at one time, and that which they take me to speak at another can agree together. Words uttered in the Pulpit are transient, and may easily be mistaken and forgotten, when I see even words written and extant, and abiding extant and obvious to the sight are so much mistaken and by mistake turned upside down" (*AC*, 119).

Amazingly, Cotton has been misunderstood by modern historians as well. The majority see Cotton's theological position as the seed-bed of Antinomianism (for example, see Stoever, *'A Faire and Easie Way to*

Heaven', 35–7). Upon examination of the court records, however, it appeared that Hutchinson advocated positions at variance from Cotton's, such as the immortality of the regenerate soul (with the presumed mortality of the unregenerate soul), direct divine communication by means of revelation, and the possibility of apostasy for those united to Christ (*AC*, 349–88; see also Patricia Caldwell, "The Antinomian Language Controversy," *Harvard Theological Review* 69 [1976]: 345–67). One must not collapse distinctions between Cotton and Hutchinson, but rather preserve them by stating, as the New England ministers eventually did, that Cotton was orthodox and within the stream of Reformed thought, while Hutchinson was not.

17. *AC*, 108.

18. Ibid., 98–9. One can discern Cottonian echoes in Anne Hutchinson's now famous plea at her trial (as reported by John Winthrop):"Here is a great stirre about graces and looking to hearts, but give me Christ, I seeke not for graces, but for Christ, I seeke not for promises, but for Christ, I seeke not for sanctification, but for Christ, tell me not of meditation and duties, but tell me of Christ" (*AC*, "A Short Story," 246).

19. Knight, *Orthodoxies*, 88–129.

20. William Ames, *The Marrow of Theology*, trans. John D. Eusden (1968; repr., Durham: Labyrinth Press, 1983), 150 [1.24.12]. The one area in which Knight's study is to be faulted is in her consistent characterization of Ames as the founder of the preparationist school – those who would seek to uphold a covenant in which, upon the fulfillment of the conditions of faith and obedience, God would be obliged to grant salvation. A careful reading of Ames does not yield these conclusions; rather, Cotton and Ames are very close, particularly in the notion of faith not being antecedent to but a result of union (Knight, *Orthodoxies*, 75–81; Ames, *Marrow*, 150–2, particularly 1.24.19: "But the present covenant requires no properly called or prior condition, but only a following or intermediate condition [and that to be given by grace as a means to grace], which is the proper nature of faith"; cf. with Cotton, *AC*, 91-92).

21. *AC*, 143.

22. Ibid., 75.

23. Ibid., 57, 138–9.

24. Ibid., 96, 139–41.

25. Ibid., 103.

26. Ibid., 121, 123.

27. Ibid., 116, 120.

28. "A Divine and Supernatural Light," in Jonathan Edwards, *The Works of Jonathan Edwards, vol. 17: Sermons and Addresses, 1730–1733*, ed. Mark Valeri (New Haven: Yale University Press, 1999), 410; on Shepard's influence on Edwards, see Hall, "Introduction," *AC*, 20; Smith, "Editor's Introduction," Yale, *RA*, 2:52–7.

29. *AC*, 29; Knight, *Orthodoxies*, 55–6.

30. *PTV*, 220–1.

31. Ibid., 78–9.

32. Ibid., 194, 205–6. Elsewhere, Shepard wrote concerning "that spirit of sloth and slumber which the Lord ever leaves the best hypocrite unto, which is the dearest lust and last enemy that the Lord destroys in all his, but never destroys in these. Which so mightily oppresseth all their senses, that they cannot use effectually all means to accomplish their ends" (Ibid., 241). And again, "O, be not slothful, then; neglect no means, but use all means; get oil in your vessels, that you may get your desired end" (Ibid., 254).

33. Ibid., 191–2, 223–5.

34. Ibid., 205, 220-1.

35. Chamberlain, "Jonathan Edwards Against Antinomians and Arminians," 168–204.

36. Miller, *Jonathan Edwards*, 196.

37. "Letter to the Rev. Thomas Gillespie of Scotland," in *The Works of Jonathan Edwards, vol. 4: Great Awakening*, ed. C. C. Goen (New Haven: Yale University Press, 1972), 563; Yale, *RA*, 2, 311–40.

38. Yale, *Great Awakening*, 4:564; Chamberlain, "Jonathan Edwards Against Antinomians and Arminians," 94–158.

39. Perry Miller, perhaps more than anyone else, alerted interpreters to the idea of the new sense of the heart. However, he found Edwards' source for the new sense in Locke, not in scholastic or Puritan Calvinism. He claimed that the idea of the new sense "reveals how complete was his conversion to the empirical, sensational psychology of John Locke, whom he read with ecstasy – the word is not too strong – when an undergraduate at Yale. Though there were other intellectual influences in his life – Calvin, the traditional body of Puritan science, Cudworth, and Hutcheson – yet, Locke and Newton were far and away the dominating sources, and from them he acquired almost all his theoretical starting points ... The peculiar and fascinating character of his achievement is entirely lost if he be not seen as the first and most radical, even though the most tragically misunderstood, of American empiricists" ("Jonathan Edwards on the Sense of the Heart," *Harvard Theological Review* 41 [1948]: 124; hereafter: Miller, "Sense").

While I would not deny that Edwards used Lockean terminology as new "categories of meaning," yet I would deny that he acquired his theoretical starting points from Locke and Newton. Even his most interesting development in Miscellany 782, a section which parallels modern semiotics, had precedence in previous Puritan theologians (cf. Miller, "Sense," 135; *PTV*, 144; and Stephen H. Daniel, *The Philosophy of Jonathan Edwards* [Bloomington: Indiana University Press, 1994], 6, 65, 187–8). Moreover, in the body of *Affections*, Edwards mentioned Locke once and footnoted him not at all (though, of course, he alluded to Locke's "new simple idea"); by contrast, there were over 120 footnotes to Reformed and Puritan theologians. Therefore, it is best to place the emphasis where Edwards sought to place it, upon his Puritan influences.

40. Yale, *RA*, 2: 205–6.

41. Ibid., 241, 242, 246. Further on, Edwards wrote, "The first foundation of the delight a true saint has in God, is his own perfection; and the first foundation of the delight he has in Christ, is his own beauty; he appears in himself the chief among ten thousand, and altogether lovely ... They first have their hearts filled with sweetness, from the view of Christ's excellency, and the excellency of his grace, and the beauty of the way of salvation by him; and then they have a secondary joy, in that so excellent a Savior, and such excellent grace as theirs" (Ibid., 250).

42. Ibid., 253–4. In another connection, Edwards defined excellency: "Excellency consists in the similarness of one being to another – not merely equality and proportion, but any kind of similarness. Thus similarness of direction: supposing many globes moving in right lines, it is more beautiful that they should move all the same way and according to the same direction, than if they moved disorderly, one one way and another another. *This is an universal definition of excellency: The consent of being to being, or being's consent to entity.* The more the consent is, and the more extensive, the greater is the excellency" ("The Mind," in *The Works of Jonathan Edwards*, vol. 6: *Scientific and Philosophical Writings*, ed. Wallace Anderson [New Haven: Yale University Press, 1980], 336; emphasis added).

Edwards reversed this definition in *The Nature of True Virtue*: "That loving a being on this ground necessarily arises from pure benevolence to Being in general, and comes to the same thing. For he that has a simple and pure good will to general entity or existence must love that temper in others that agrees and conspires with itself. A spirit of consent to Being must agree with consent to Being" (*The Nature of True Virtue*, in *The Works of Jonathan Edwards*, vol. 8: *Ethical Writings*, ed. Paul Ramsey [New Haven: Yale University Press, 1989], 547–8). Thus, for Edwards, the nature of true virtue, or the nature of excellency, was consent to Being; this true virtue could only be produced by the infusion of a new principle that was different in kind from that which the unregenerate possess; therefore, one ought not to expect the unregenerate to posses true virtue, for only the regenerate had a new spiritual sense.

43. Yale, *RA*, 2: 255, 256, 260.

44. Ibid., 266.

45. Ibid., 272. In another context, Edwards wrote, "An ideal and sensible apprehension of the spiritual excellency of divine things is the proper source of all spiritual conviction of the truth of divine things, or that belief of the truth that there is in saving faith ... All saving conviction of divine truth does most essentially arise from the spiritual sense of the excellency of divine things; yet this sense of spiritual excellency is not the only kind of ideal apprehension or sense of divine things that is concerned in such a conviction, but it also partly depends on a sensible knowledge of what is natural in religion; as this may be needful to prepare the mind for a sense of its spiritual excellency" (Misc. 782, in Miller, "Sense," 143).

46. Yale, *RA*, 2: 273.

47. Ibid., 311, 325.

48. Ibid., 340. For more on Edwards' reflections on pride and humility, see Sean Michael Lucas, "'A Man Just Like Us': Jonathan Edwards and the Spiritual Formation of Ministerial Candidates," *Presbyterion* 30 (2004): 1–10.

49. Ibid., 345, 365.

50. *The Complete Works of Richard Sibbes*, 7 vols., ed. A. Grosart (Edinburgh: James Nicol, 1862–4), 6:541, as quoted in Knight, *Orthodoxies*, 118. For further similar quotations from Sibbes, see Ibid., 261n46.

51. Yale, *RA*, 2: 205.

52. Ibid., 383.

53. Ibid., 393.

54. Edwards wrote, "Christian practice or a holy life is a great and distinguishing sign of true and saving grace. But I may go further and assert, that it is the chief of all the signs of grace, both as an evidence of the sincerity of professors unto others, and also to their own consciences" (Ibid., 406).

55. Ibid., 398, 400, 401.

56. Ibid., 422.

57. Ibid., 444–9.

58. Ibid., 420.

PART THREE:

CHRIST-CENTERED DISCIPLINES

9

GOSPEL-CENTERED WORSHIP
AND THE REGULATIVE PRINCIPLE

MARK L. DALBEY
Assistant Professor of Practical Theology
Dean of Students

ecause of a misspelled name on my electronic ticket, I was spending an unknown number of extra days in Ghana, West Africa, following a two-week mission trip in 2003. I had been there with four others on Covenant Theological Seminary's January mission trip leading a workshop on worship for pastors and worship leaders in the Evangelical Presbyterian Church of Ghana, West Africa (now known as the Global Evangelical Church). It was my third visit to Ghana and my second time leading worship workshops there. I spent what ended up being four extra days in the home of pastor Seth Gbewonyo, enjoying warm hospitality and gaining deeper insight into family and church life for Presbyterians in Ghana. Seth had been a student at Covenant Theological Seminary and had taken the class I teach on Christian worship. Because of my delay, Seth and I were able to continue our ongoing discussion of the kind of worship that is pleasing to God and what that might look like in Ghana as compared to the United States.

My trips to Ghana stretched and challenged my understanding of what is known as the Regulative Principle of Worship (RPW). I grew up in a family of German ethnicity and Scottish Presbyterian ecclesiology and worship. My father was an ordained pastor in the former United Presbyterian Church of North America, which had its roots in the Scottish Presbyterian history of worship practice based on a strict adherence to the RPW. For seven years after seminary, I also served as a chaplain and Bible instructor at Geneva College in Pennsylvania, where that same Scottish Presbyterian tradition continues to the present day in the practice of the Reformed Presbyterian Church of North America of singing only the psalms without instrumental accompaniment in corporate public worship. The RPW is based on the teaching of the Westminster Confession of Faith XXI.1, which states that "the acceptable way of worshiping the true God is instituted by himself, and so limited by his own revealed will, that he may not be worshiped according to the imaginations and devices of men, or the suggestions of Satan, under any visible representation, or any other way not prescribed in the holy Scripture."[1] Yet the confession also states in I.6 that "we acknowledge the inward illumination of the Spirit of God to be necessary for the saving understanding of such things as are revealed in the word; and that there are some circumstances concerning the worship of God, and government of the Church, common to human actions and societies, which are to be ordered by the light of nature and Christian prudence, according to the general rules of the word, which are always to be observed."[2] As I reflected on the very different contexts of Presbyterian worship in my Scottish Presbyterian heritage and in Ghana, West Africa, I found myself wondering how these two sections of the Confession fit together. This was especially intriguing to me because the primary influence on the development of the ecclesiology and worship of the Evangelical Presbyterian Church of Ghana came from the Scottish Presbyterian missionaries who helped establish the church.

During my two mission trips to Ghana, I had the opportunity to worship in ten churches and to attend a four-day prayer gathering. Some of the features of Presbyterian worship in Ghana were different than those from my own background and experience as a Presbyterian in the United States. The Presbyterian churches in Ghana make use of a common lectionary in which each week's Scripture readings from the Old Testament, the Gospels, and the Epistles are the same throughout the denomination. This, along with the weekly praying of the Lord's Prayer and professing of the Apostles' Creed, reflects a more ordered and fixed liturgy than some North American Presbyterian churches. Other expressions of the biblical elements of worship were more indigenously African. All of the churches gave a prominent place to the use of drums and other percussion instruments, including one church that used only percussion instruments for the accompaniment of congregational singing. The polyphonic rhythms, together with the vocal harmonies, were expressions of a musical language rooted in the Ghanaian culture.

During times of congregational prayer, the people worshiping together would pray out loud all at once. In one church of approximately 500 people, the pastor asked the members of the congregation to stretch out their hands toward the brothers and sisters from the United States and ask for the Lord's blessings and traveling mercies for us. So, 500 people stretched their hands toward us and prayed aloud simultaneously in a very moving expression of corporate prayer. During the receiving of the offering, the members of the congregation sang songs of joy while moving rhythmically down the aisles to present their offerings to God. In another congregation, approximately

1500 people sang and danced joyfully to the front with their offerings, giving obvious expression to their cheerfulness of heart. This was all done in a very orderly way that took less than five minutes. At some point in each of the services, usually during the congregational songs of praise, many of the people danced down to the front – first the men, then later the women. At one church, the people sang a song praising God for his saving grace and asking him to bless their children with the same gracious gift of salvation. This story-song celebrating God's covenantal blessing was then acted out: the men and women formed a circle and danced in front of the worship area, into which the children were invited, as the people cried out to God to pass on his blessing to their children.

How do these African Presbyterian expressions of worship fit into a proper understanding of the Regulative Principle of Worship? To what level of detail should we expect the RPW to shape a worship service? Is the RPW tied to a particular historical expression, or is it applicable across time and geography? How should the RPW be applied as the gospel goes out geographically to the nations and across time to future generations? Is the goal in worship to be faithful to the RPW, or is the RPW a God-given tool for achieving the greater gospel purposes of corporate public worship?

THE REGULATIVE PRINCIPLE OF LIFE

A biblical understanding of the RPW is rooted in the nature of God. He has all authority as the sovereign omnipotent ruler of the universe. He is the One who reveals what he wants his creatures to know and how he wants them to live. He made people in his image for fellowship with himself and established the parameters of that fellowship. A desire to know and follow what God has revealed concerning how we are to live life before him is the proper posture of creatures. In every area of life, we are to live for God's glory; this includes corporate public worship.

God speaks with authority and clarity in his inspired, infallible, and inerrant word. He is the One who makes known what pleases him in all areas of life. This could be called the "regulative principle of life." God's will for such matters as marriage (Eph. 5), ruling over and caring for the creation (Gen. 1–2), the role of governing authorities (Rom. 13), and the utilization of spiritual gifts in the church (1 Cor. 12–14) – to name a few – is communicated in the Bible. God gives specific commands, examples, and principles that apply to various areas of life in his creation and kingdom. In some areas, he may give more specific instruction than in others. That is his prerogative as the Sovereign One. All of life is to be lived before the face of God and offered up as a living sacrifice to him (Rom. 12:1-2). This life outside of corporate public worship could be called "all of life as worship."

All of life as worship and corporate public worship on the Lord's Day are sometimes put at odds with one another as though one must be chosen over the other. The Bible does not confirm this attitude, but rather presents more of a fluid motion throughout the seven-day week. One day in seven is set apart for corporate public worship, where God's appointed means of grace converge to strengthen and equip God's people for the other six days that are to be lived to the glory of God in families, workplaces, neighborhoods, and in every area of life as wide as God's creation. The worshipful living of those six days then overflows into corporate public worship on the Lord's Day as God's people gather to celebrate the triumphs of his grace, confess their shortcomings and sin, and be renewed in covenant fellowship with God.

God's Regulating of Worship: Doing Worship the Way God Wants

When we consider corporate public worship, therefore, it is vital that we study God's Word to discover what is pleasing to him when we gather on the Lord's Day. As we approach the Bible to find instruction on corporate public worship, we must bring a proper biblical hermeneutic to the search. Obviously, we do not treat the Bible as if it were a dictionary and turn to the letter "W" to read all we need to know about worship. The Bible is an organic, progressive, unfolding, dramatic story of God creating and then redeeming a people who have intimate fellowship with him and with one another. While the offering of sacrificial animals was at one time the right way for God's people to approach him in worship, Christians agree that, at this point in the story – that is, after the life, death, and resurrection of Jesus Christ, who was the perfect sacrifice – this is no longer the case. We must remember our place in the overall story and worship God accordingly.

Once Adam and Eve fell into rebellion and sin and were driven from the garden of Eden, sinful people could only approach a holy God through an atoning sacrifice that made provision for the forgiveness of sin by this same gracious God. This principle is at the heart of what we often call gospel-centered worship – that is, worship that gives central place to the good news that, through God's gracious provision of an atoning sacrifice, sinners are forgiven and restored to fellowship with the true and living God. Jesus makes clear to his disciples (Luke 24) that Moses, the Psalms, and the Prophets all spoke concerning himself. God's regulating of corporate public worship is for the purpose of gospel-centered worship fulfilled in Jesus Christ.

In the Old Testament sacrificial system under Moses, God gave detailed instructions and requirements concerning the way sinful worshipers were to approach him in his holiness. These instructions are the core of gospel-centered worship. They involve specific descriptions in Exodus and Leviticus of the place and arrangements of worship in the tabernacle, the people offering the sacrifices through the priesthood, and the kinds and varieties of sacrifices and the ways in which they were offered. Nothing was to be added or subtracted from God's regulating of worship without the potential of severe consequences, as seen in the deaths of Nadab and Abihu in Leviticus 10:1-3 when they offered "strange fire" containing unauthorized incense. The three main sacrifices included the sin offering for the removal of guilt, the burnt offering for the consecration of the whole of life to God, and the peace offering for restoring fellowship with God. All of these, together with Passover, find their fulfillment in the sacrificial death of Christ on the cross and are therefore serving gospel purposes in the Old Testament. It is interesting to note that we do not find the same level of detail with regard to other aspects of Old Testament worship – such as prayer, singing, and instruction in the Word – as we find for the sacrificial system.[3]

As we turn to the New Testament, we see the detailed regulation of the sacrificial system under Moses now applied to a right understanding and preaching of the full biblical doctrine of the person and work of Christ. The apostle Paul in Galatians 1:6-9 states that, if anyone preaches another gospel than the one he has preached, that person is to be eternally condemned. The apostle John states that, if anyone denies that Jesus is the Christ, that person is of the antichrist (1 John 2:22); John later indicates that if anyone does not acknowledge that Jesus Christ has come in the flesh, then that person, too, is of the antichrist (1 John 4:3). The most impassioned concern about detail in both the Old and New Testaments seems to relate to the person and work of Christ as either foreshadowed in the sacrificial system or fulfilled in his incarnation, life, death, and resurrection. In other words, the strict regulation of worship and the insistence upon correct doctrine in worship is for the purpose of serving the centrality of the gospel. The other elements of worship – including prayer, song, and teaching and preaching – have greater freedom of expression and are less regulated so long as they faithfully present the gospel as centered in the person and work of Christ.

In the New Covenant, Christ is presented as the perfect sacrifice and Passover lamb (Heb. 10:10-14; 1 Cor. 5:7); the new tabernacle and temple (John 1:14, 2:18-22); the great High Priest (Heb. 4:14-16); and the one who opens the way and leads his people into the New Jerusalem (Heb. 12:22-24). Christ's sacrificial death and work as mediator restore fellowship with God and true worship of him. The teaching of Jesus himself in John 4:19-26 reveals the heart of worship that pleases God. In a discussion of the proper place of worship, Jesus communicates to the Samaritan woman that the Father is seeking true worshipers – those who will worship him in spirit and in truth. Worshipers in spirit are those who worship from the depths of their hearts, with all of their affections completely set upon God. Worshipers in truth are those who follow all that God has revealed about how he desires to be worshiped.

Who worships this way? Only the God-man Jesus Christ worships the Father fully in spirit and in truth. True worship is, therefore, about the gospel of Christ. The question of *where* one is to worship is no longer relevant. Even the question of *how* one is to worship is secondary. The primary question in worship is *through whom*? Only those who are joined to Christ by grace through faith can worship in spirit and truth and be the kind of worshipers whom the Father is seeking. Once again, true worship is about the gospel of Christ; all of the details concerning how we worship are to serve the overarching and primary goal of worship – a holy God coming near to his sinful people with the all-sufficient grace of his Son's redemptive work to restore those people into intimate fellowship with himself as true worshipers.

The RPW, then, serves the gospel purposes of corporate public worship by keeping the focus on the proper understanding of and biblical instruction regarding the sacrificial work of Jesus Christ, and by revealing the absolute necessity of our union with him by grace through faith in order to worship God in the way that he desires. Additionally, the RPW serves the gospel by revealing that God also regulates worship in his insistence that his Son be intimately and personally connected to every aspect of a corporate public worship service. Hebrews 2:10-12 makes clear that Jesus Christ is the one who stands in the midst of the worshiping congregation declaring God's name and singing God's praise. As the uniquely qualified and now ascended God-man, Jesus is to be at the center of every element in every worship service in every local church where God, in a glorious dialogue, meets his redeemed and adopted children, of whom he is not ashamed. It is Jesus who declares everything in the service that comes from God and is spoken to his people. That includes the call to worship, the declaration of forgiveness, the reading of the Word, the preaching of the Word, the invitation to the Lord's Table, and the benediction of blessing on the people. Jesus also connects himself to everything that the congregation does in response to the glorious declaration of the Gospel in worship. He stands in the midst of the worshiping congregation and sings the Father's praises, leads the people in prayer, sits with them at the table of the Lord, gives testimony to the grace of God in his people, and, as the One who became sin for us, he is even able to lead the corporate confession of sin. Christ-centered worship, then, is essentially about: (1) the correct expression of doctrinal truth regarding the person and work of Christ, and (2) true worshipers being in vital union with Christ. Undergirding both of these, however, and giving power to the proceedings, is the fact that the Lord Jesus Christ himself is present in worship through the Holy Spirit declaring God's name and singing God's praise!

Gospel-centered worship at its best is saturated with the biblical doctrine of Christ our sacrifice and priest, our vital union with him by grace through faith, and his personal presence in every aspect and element of the worship service in each local church. This Christ-centered, gospel-centered focus is foundational to worship that is pleasing to God. Only once we understand this are we then able to begin the discussion of how the RPW relates to the actual structure and elements of a service of corporate public worship. All too often, we want to apply the RPW immediately to the elements, style, and arrangement of the service before considering the Christ-centered and gospel-centered nature of what God requires and regulates in worship. The structure, style, and arrangement of the elements he commands are to serve the Christ-centered and gospel-centered goal of corporate public worship. This is the heart of worship that pleases him.

With that foundation established, we can now discuss what God desires with regard to the specifics of a worship service. While most everyone agrees that the Bible does not give us an inspired account that reveals the detailed structure of a worship service for all times and all places, some have argued that the Mosaic sacrificial system itself serves as such a structure for New Covenant worship services.[4] While rightly emphasizing that the three main sacrifices of the Old Covenant have ongoing relevance to gospel-centered worship, using the details of these sacrifices as the precise pattern for New Covenant worship seems to be an overextension of their primary purpose, which is to point to the sacrificial work of Jesus Christ. And while there is a kind of "gospel flow" in moving from the cleansing of the sin offering to the consecration of the burnt offering to the communion of the peace offering, there is also a distinctly New Covenant freedom in the expression of the various elements of worship presented in the New Testament.

The best approach to planning worship services that make proper use of the RPW is to discover the commanded elements for New Covenant worship and then structure them in such a way that they serve the Gospel by: (1) being centered in the sacrificial work of Christ, who brings sinners into fellowship with a holy God; (2) nurturing the faith of the worshipers, who are in vital union with Christ; and (3) facilitating the present work of the ascended Christ, who personally meets with his people as he declares God's glorious name and sings praise to God. What, then, are the commanded elements for New Covenant worship?

While there is no comprehensive list found in the New Testament, there are places where the foundational elements are given by direct biblical command, through apostolic example, or derived from biblical principles. The commands to pray (1 Tim. 2:1); to read and preach the Word of God (2 Tim. 4:2); to sing psalms, hymns, and spiritual songs (Col. 3:16 and Eph. 5:19); and the celebration of the sacrament of the Lord's Supper (1 Cor. 11:23-26) seem quite clear and obvious as the foundational commanded elements of New Covenant worship. In a simple yet profound way, the synagogue elements of prayer, Scripture reading and explanation, and song, coupled with the temple focus on sacrifice and covenant renewal, are combined in New Covenant church worship through prayer, Scripture reading and explanation, song, and the celebration of the Lord's Supper. What was anticipated in the Old Covenant is now fulfilled in the gospel-centered, Christ-centered worship of the New Covenant. Through apostolic example, we add the element of the offering (1 Cor. 16:2). Additionally, through biblical principle, we might also include professions of faith (such as the Apostles' Creed), oaths and vows (such as baptismal vows), and personal testimonies, all of which serve as windows into the lives of people being transformed by the grace of the gospel of Christ.

What overarching principle does God desire us to follow as we use these commanded elements in the structuring, arranging, and planning of a worship service on any given Lord's Day? Once again, the guiding light is the Christ-centered, gospel-centered goal of corporate worship. This can be expressed through the concept of a gospel "storyline," in which the inherent drama of the gospel unfolds throughout the movement and flow of the service, from the call to worship through the benediction. In worship, we are invited into God's holy presence as adopted sons and daughters of whom he is not ashamed because of Christ's work on our behalf. We come adoring and praising him for his goodness, greatness, and grace. We come confessing our sins and looking to him for forgiveness and strength. We come making requests on behalf of ourselves and others in prayer. We praise and admonish and pray through song. We rejoice in the work of God's grace in one another as we hear the gospel story expressed through the lives of fellow believers. We profess enthusiastically together what we believe. We listen to God's Word read, proclaimed, and applied. We offer our lives and our substance to him. We baptize new converts and children of believers as he adds to our number. We gather in table fellowship remembering what Christ has done in his atoning, sacrificial death in our place. We receive his good word in the benediction as he sends us forth to live as salt and light for his glory in every area of life. We are captured and transformed into greater Christlikeness by the gospel drama represented in a carefully planned worship service that proclaims that gospel story afresh each week.

Each local church's worship service has a unique gospel storyline for a particular Lord's Day as songs, prayers, Scripture readings, sermons, testimonies, and other elements are selected and arranged. Worship planners should be able to show and explain how each aspect of the service serves the unique gospel story of that service. It is also important to root the storyline of each church service in the gospel storyline of the Bible. Our worship services must be faithful to the story of God's Word. Additionally, it is a mark of a well-crafted service of worship to build bridges from the biblical storyline through the specific worship service into the gospel storyline that God is writing in the life of every believer. The dramatic movement of worship does not simply go from the call to worship to the benediction of a particular worship service. Rather, the flow is from God's unfolding drama in the Bible into the everyday lives of the gathered worshipers with an eye toward the eternal city where the story finds its ultimate fulfillment. The biblical-theological flow of Scripture roots our weekly worship services in the redemptive work of God in the historical past, as well as in the anticipated and promised eschatological work of the future – a work which is already present in some sense even now as the Holy Spirit brings both past and future together in the present gathering of God's people in local church worship services. This is the kind of worship God desires. Any discussion of the RPW that separates the detailed particulars of a worship service from this dynamic gospel drama is incomplete and shortsighted.

A Suggested Fivefold Approach to the RPW

As I have thought about and studied these topics in detail over the past ten years, I have been developing the following fivefold approach to understanding and applying the RPW. It is still a work in progress, but does, I believe, provide a useful starting point for thinking about and planning corporate public worship services.

1. Commanded Elements

Worship should be pleasing to God and according to his regulations; therefore, we must make use of the biblically commanded elements of worship. These are the basic building blocks of corporate public worship, and, as discussed above, include prayer; reading and preaching of Scripture; singing of psalms, hymns, and spiritual songs; the sacraments of baptism and the Lord's Supper; offerings; professions of faith; oaths and vows; and testimonies of God's grace.

2. Biblical Content

The commanded elements must be filled with content that is faithful to biblically revealed truth. A commanded element is not pleasing to God and according to his regulations if it lacks true biblical content. We must not only use the elements God requires, but we must also fill them with his revealed truth.

3. Gospel Shape

Biblically commanded elements filled with biblically faithful content must also be arranged in a gospel-centered fashion. Commanded elements that are not arranged in a way that serves the gospel storyline of the particular worship service can be confusing and incomplete. To simply "plug in" new content to the various "slots" in the program (such as hymns, responsive readings, unison prayers, and creeds) without giving them any gospel-shaped flow does not serve the overall goal of worship that is gospel-centered and Christ-centered.

4. Variety of Valid Expressions

These commanded elements filled with biblical content and arranged with gospel shaping can be expressed a variety of valid ways. Pre-written or spontaneous prayers are both valid expressions of prayer. The singing of the Lord's Prayer, the unison praying of the Lord's Prayer, or the structuring of directed prayers around the various petitions of the Lord's Prayer are all valid expressions of the Lord's Prayer. Psalms read in unison, responsively, or sung are all proper expressions of the Psalms in corporate public worship. The singing of historic hymns filled with biblical content can be properly done with musical tunes centuries old or with tunes written in the past month. They can be sung without musical instrumentation or with a combination of winds, strings, and percussive instruments. One sermon could be preached in a one-hour service or three sermons could be preached in a three-hour service. The Lord's Supper could be served to the congregation as they sit in rows or at tables, or it could be served as people come to the front of the worship area to receive it from the elders.

5. Unique Local Church Contexts

As the gospel has gone out to the nations and from one generation to the next, the corporate worship of God's people has never been monolithic in style or practice. The reality is that each local church has a unique context in which biblical worship regulated by God is carried out. Each has a unique spoken language, characteristic styles of dress, particular places where people gather for corporate worship, distinct kinds of musical instrumentation and style, particular education levels, specific numbers of children present, characteristic body movements, and many other qualities that make every local church different from every other local church to a greater or lesser degree. While each of these unique contexts must use the commanded elements of worship – giving them biblical content and gospel shape – the unique historical and geographical place in which worship happens must also be taken into account in any evaluation of worship that is pleasing to God.

A Sixteenth-Century Case Study: Geneva, Switzerland

John Calvin's approach to worship in the sixteenth century provides a good case study of a Reformer who was passionate about facilitating corporate public worship according to the patterns God requires in his Word. Calvin insisted on using all of the commanded elements (including singing) with biblical content (mostly psalms) in ways that took gospel shape (praise and regular celebration of the Lord's Supper), with his own variation on valid expressions (new tunes for versified psalms) in his own unique local church context (Geneva, Switzerland).

The Reformation arrived in Geneva by way of the cities of Berne and Zurich. The liturgy inherited from this process was without music. As part of their own program of reform in Geneva, Farel and Calvin co-authored the "Articles of 1537," in which they tried to institute psalm-singing:

> It is a thing very expedient for the edification of the church to sing some psalms in the form of public prayers through which one may pray to God or

sing his praise so that the hearts of all might be moved and incited to form like prayers and to render like praises and thanks to God with similar affection.[5]

The proposal was rejected, and, for a variety of reasons, Calvin was banished from Geneva in 1538.[6] He went to Strasbourg and there came under the influence of Martin Bucer, whose view of the reformation of worship was much more balanced than that of Zwingli, which held considerable sway throughout Switzerland. Bucer advocated the weekly observance of the Lord's Supper, as opposed to the more infrequent observances held by others, and placed an emphasis on the sharing of a meal rather than a mass of sacrifice, as practiced by Roman Catholics. He placed a communion table before the people and on their level, rather than having an altar elevated beyond the people.[7] He also came to quite different conclusions on the use of music in public worship than those of Zwingli. At numerous points in the service of worship, there was congregational singing not only of psalms and hymns of praise, but also of the Ten Commandments.[8] As a result of Bucer's influence, Calvin came to believe wholeheartedly that the reform of worship was central to the reform of the church and that, with the arrival of the Reformation and the gospel of grace, there was every reason to sing – and to sing enthusiastically.[9]

After three years in Strasbourg, Calvin returned to Geneva in 1541 with his views on music in worship even more firmly established. Upon his return, he instituted psalm singing. The Geneva Psalter included metrical psalms, the Ten Commandments, the Apostles' Creed, and the Song of Simeon. As he developed the Psalter from 1542 to 1562, Calvin employed the services of Clement Marot, Theodore Beza, and Louis Bourgeois. These men were gifted in poetry and music and worked to versify the psalms into Western meter and put them to singable tunes.[10] In doing this, Calvin was drawing on the greatness of past expressions of biblical worship – the Psalms – while looking for fresh expressions and applications of biblical worship that connected well with the contemporary culture of his day. The Hebrew meter of the psalms did not easily lend itself to Western meter that was singable. Therefore, Calvin had the words arranged in a way that reflected the essence of the Psalms while also adapting them to music that could be sung by the congregation he served in Geneva. He urged his composers to capture the emotion of the Psalms in their musical compositions. He also stood against the current of his time in Switzerland by insisting that congregational singing be a vital part of the worship of God's people. Many of the tunes used were of a very lively character.[11] His passion for the singing of the psalms is reflected in the following statement from Calvin as quoted by Ross Miller:

> The psalms could incite us to raise our hearts to God and to move us with such ardor that we exalt through praises the glory of his name ... And truly, we know through experience that song has great force and vigor to move and enflame hearts to invoke and to praise God with a more lively and ardent zeal.[12]

Calvin showed great creativity and innovation by using children to teach the new versification of the Psalms to the worshiping congregation. Miller again quotes Calvin:

> If some children, whom someone has practiced beforehand in some modest church song, sing in a loud and distinct voice, the people listening with complete attention and following in their hearts what is sung by mouth, little by little each one will become accustomed to sing with the others.[13]

Additionally, Calvin was not cold and stern in his approach to worship. William Maxwell gives insight into this aspect of his character as he quotes a biographer of Calvin named Doumergue:

> Finally, after these acts of adoration, these prayers said kneeling, this quickening instruction, the worship culminates in the supreme ceremony of holy communion. Calvin has been very greatly misunderstood. For him the complete act of Christian worship is that at which the Lord's Supper is celebrated, and the complete Sunday morning office is that which includes the celebration of the Lord's Supper. Have men said that this worship, the true Calvinian cult, was in its nature poor and cold? Those who were present at it have told us that often they could not keep back tears of emotion and joy. Singings and prayers, adoration and edification, confession and forgiveness of sins, acts ritualistic and spontaneous – all the essential elements of worship were there; and what is not less important, they were combined into an organism that though very simple, was yet both supple and strong.[14]

Here we also see Calvin's desire to celebrate the Lord's Supper on a weekly basis. He even included the singing of psalms during the celebration of the Lord's Supper itself.[15] He designed his order of worship to be a unity of Word and Table.[16] Though Calvin's position was never fully adopted in Geneva, he ordered his worship services to end with prayer and praise that set the stage for the Lord's Supper – even when it was not celebrated.[17]

To follow in the worship heritage of Calvin, we too must be willing to go where the Scripture directs us. We must have the same desire to be deeply rooted in historical expressions of biblical worship while finding creative and relevant ways to make that gospel-centered worship glorifying to God and edifying to his people in our time and place.

THE CONVERGENCE OF THE MEANS OF GRACE IN CORPORATE PUBLIC WORSHIP

God has established corporate public worship in the way that he has for the purpose of his own glory. He receives glory in the praise of his people for his goodness, greatness, and grace. He also receives glory as his people are transformed into greater Christlikeness through the convergence of the means of grace, which he commands to be brought together and regulated in corporate public worship. Prayer, the reading and preaching of Scripture, and the administration of the sacraments, when combined in gospel-centered worship, have the power to form and transform the people of God and bring them into greater conformity with the likeness of his Son. God's glory and our edification are also greatly enhanced when the local congregation comes together in the fellowship of gospel-centered worship in a spirit of unity with one mouth and one heart (Rom. 15:5-6).

Conclusion

Let us now return full circle to my experiences in Ghana. How am I to respond to the manner of Scripture reading, praying, receiving offerings, and use of drums in that worship context? When the Presbyterians in Ghana brought their tithes and offerings forward while singing songs of joy and dancing with rhythmic body movements, were they using commanded elements filled with biblical content and given gospel shape in a valid expression consistent within their own unique local church context? I am convinced that the answer to that question is a resounding yes! Does that mean that all Presbyterian churches – or even all Presbyterian Church in America (PCA) churches – must receive offerings in precisely the same manner? I am convinced that the answer to that is a resounding no!

In the PCA and other denominations, churches must consider the element of offering within the overall gospel storyline of the worship service in their unique local church context. The commanded element of offering is to be filled with the biblical content of joy as it takes gospel shape through various valid expressions in each local church. That might mean that the offering is placed after the sermon as a response to the indescribable gift of grace in God's Son, and it might be expressed through the singing of a congregational song of joy while remaining seated in the pew or chairs. But the offering might also look quite different than this in a different context.

As one who teaches classes on worship at Covenant Theological Seminary, I have a deep passion for gospel-centered worship that is served well by the RPW. I long to see our graduates have a vision for corporate public worship that includes an understanding of gospel-centered worship as presented in this essay – a vision that enables them to plan and lead services of corporate public worship with great wisdom, discernment, and skill. As the gospel goes to the nations and to future generations, I pray that an appreciation for the depth and beauty of the Christ-centered and gospel-centered worship that God desires and regulates by his Word and Spirit will spread as well. In so doing, may it glorify God, edify his people, and draw many others to the joyful task of worshiping him in spirit and in truth.

---

1. *The Westminster Standards* (Suwanee, Ga.: Great Commission Publications, 2005), 22.
2. Ibid., 4–5.

3. John M. Frame, *Worship in Spirit and Truth: A Refreshing Study of the Principles and Practice of Biblical Worship* (Phillipsburg, N. J.: P&R Publishing, 1996), 22–3.

4. Jeffrey J. Meyers, *The Lord's Service: The Grace of Covenant Renewal Worship* (Moscow, Idaho: Canon Press, 2003), 85.

5. "Articles Concernant L'Organization de l'eglise et du cultea Geneve, proposes au conseil par les ministres, le 16, Janvier 1537," in *Ionnis Calvini Opera Quae Supersunt Omnia*, ed. Guillaume Baum, Eduard Cunitz, and Eduard ReussRoss (Brunsvigae: C. A. Schwetschke et Filium, 1863–1900), X.6. Quoted in Ross J. Miller, "Calvin's Understanding of Psalm-Singing as a Means of Grace," in *Calvin Studies VI: A Colloquium on Calvin Studies at Davidson College*, ed. John H. Leith (Davidson, N.C.: Davidson College, January 1992), 35–6. Hereafter referred to as Miller, "Calvin's Understanding of Psalm-Singing."

6. Miller, "Calvin's Understanding of Psalm-Singing," 35.

7. Hughes Oliphant Old, *The Patristic Roots of Reformed Worship* (Zurich: Theologischer Verlag, 1976), 26.

8. Charles Garside, *The Origins of Calvin's Theology of Music: 1536–1543*, Transactions of the American Philosophical Society, vol. 69, part 4 (Philadelphia, Pa.: The American Philosophical Society, 1979), 11.

9. Lawrence C. Roff, *Let Us Sing* (Norcross , Ga.: Great Commission Publications, 1991), 47.

10. Miller, "Calvin's Understanding of Psalm-Singing," 35–6.

11. Roff, *Let Us Sing*, 59.

12. Miller, "Calvin's Understanding of Psalm-Singing," 39.

13. Ibid., 36.

14. E. Doumergue, *Jean Calvin: Les hommes et les choses de son temps*, 2 vols. (Lausanne: Georges Bridel, 1902), 2: 504. Quoted in William D. Maxwell, *Concerning Worship* (London: Oxford University Press, 1948), 27.

15. Maxwell, *Concerning Worship*, 72.

16. D. H. Hislop, *Our Heritage in Public Worship* (Edinburgh: T & T Clark, 1935), 188.

17. Maxwell, *Concerning Worship*, 26.

10

GOD SPEAKS AS A SAGE SOMETIMES:

Moving Beyond the Merely Prophetic in Preaching

ZACHARY W. ESWINE

Assistant Professor of Homiletics
Director, Doctor of Ministry Program

Conduct yourselves wisely toward outsiders, making the best use of the time. Let your speech always be gracious, seasoned with salt, so that you may know how you ought to answer each person. (Col. 4:5-6)[1]

C hristians have an important speaking role to play as they relate to the world. According to the apostle Paul, the Christian life is filled with dialogue with "outsiders" – those who are not followers of Christ. When Paul spoke of "outsiders," he meant nothing pejorative or demeaning; rather, he referred to the spiritual status of these dear ones as they relate to God and his people. Paul's concern that such spiritual outsiders be reached by the Christian community indicates his longing that they not remain "outside" of God. In other words, those "inside" are meant to grow as a community that welcomes and cares for these "outside" neighbors. Notice that Paul assumes that Christians are to speak to others from a context of wisdom. In other words, Christians are, by nature and calling, a people who must speak graciously and with an earthy weightiness, according to the questions of each individual they encounter. The Christian community is meant to live in and speak wisely to the world.

THE HEROES OF PREACHING

Traditionally, as the Christian community has considered its approach to communicating in the world, we have come to recognize that it is the prophets, not the sages, who are the undisputed heroes of our preaching

153

and testifying. In his *The Message and the Messengers*, Fleming James well represents this universal conviction when he says that preaching "in its most glorified form" is demonstrated in "Hebrew prophecy."[2] John Broadus, the nineteenth-century father of expository preaching, also captures the reason for this recurring sentiment: "The prophets reminded the people of their sins, exhorted them to repent, and instructed them in religious and moral, in social and personal duties." Furthermore, "when they predicted the future, it was almost always in the way of warning or encouragement, as a motive to forsake their sins and serve God."[3] In short, Broadus points out, "The prophets were preachers." The implication of Broadus' statement is that students of preaching can look to the biblical prophets as mentors divinely given for their instruction in proclamation. The apostle Paul establishes this prophetic approach to communicating Christ when he calls Timothy "the man of God," and urges him to rightly handle "the word of God." Paul continues the prophetic imagery by charging Timothy to preach that word "in the presence of God" with a readiness to "reprove, rebuke and exhort, with complete patience and teaching" (2 Tim. 3:16–4:2). Preachers regularly and rightly assume a prophetic posture.

At times, however, gospel communicators have seen fit to remind us that the sage can also be a potential and even credible mentor for preachers. For example, in *The Art of Preaching,* Edwin Dargan briefly notes that Proverbs and Ecclesiastes both offer "hints" regarding "the preparation of ... religious teachers."[4] Likewise, in his *Lectures on Preaching*, Broadus mentions Solomon as an exemplary preacher and states that the book of Ecclesiastes exposes us to a "certain class of sermons." But in typical fashion, like Dargan and others, Broadus explicitly prefers the prophetic model for the student of preaching.[5] The point is this: There is little denying that Christians through the generations (myself included) have usually approached the communicative task by letting the prophetic framework of the Bible undergird and inform our message giving.

And why not? It is from the prophets that we learn to steward the Word of God, to submit to its authority, and to rely on the attending power of the Holy Spirit. The voice of the lone prophet crying in the wilderness harnesses our imagination and arouses our courage to preach with passion and conviction. From these mighty men, we learn that preaching is ordained by God, directed by God, and meant for God's glory. Therefore, preaching is a declarative and authoritative event. In addition, God's judgment upon sin and his mercy for sinners form the heart of the prophet's authoritative call to repentance, giving a rationale for direct, plain, and heart-searching speech. Likewise, it is from the prophets that we learn that a preacher is, in practice and in reputation, "a man of God." Our Lord Christ preached as a prophet and fulfilled the Old Testament office. Consequently, the prophetic paradigm for preaching is foundational to a theology of gospel communication and should remain so.

Preachers are right to maintain a prophetic paradigm for their calling and for their Christ-given task in the world.

What, then, does Paul have in mind when he pictures the Christian community in a sage-like posture when speaking to outsiders? With this question before us, I would like to suggest that if the church relies on preaching and testifying *solely* from a prophetic posture, her mission to nonbelievers may be significantly hindered. I use the word "solely" because I want to maintain the importance of a prophetic paradigm for Christian proclamation. However, the Bible shows us that God intends his people to communicate not only prophetically, but also wisely – that is, sagely – to their neighbors. This concern forms the heart of this essay. My assumption is that a prophetic paradigm must be accompanied, in the power of the Holy Spirit, by a wisdom paradigm[6] in order to strengthen our gospel effectiveness for our times.

GOD'S VOICE AS A SAGE

As J. I. Packer once said, "The Bible is God preaching."[7] Evangelical and Reformed affirmations of the infallibility of the Bible do not exclude the books of Job, Proverbs, Ecclesiastes, and the Song of Solomon. The Bible forms the collected sermons of God, and the Wisdom Books form a part of that collection; therefore, we see that when God "preaches" to humanity, he does not limit himself to prophetic forms of speech. Strange as it may sound to many of us, the Wisdom Literature reminds us that God has not hesitated to speak to his people with riddles, maxims, metaphors, or poetry.[8] He has not been afraid of transparency, mystery, emotion, appeals to nature, or an intimate familiarity with the beauties and messes of people and things. "The voice of the Old Testament has many accents," Derek Kidner reminds us, including "a whole world of poetry, law, storytelling, psalmody and vision."[9] Consequently, because the Bible presents wisdom paradigms to us as God's speech, preachers and gospel testifiers also must learn to concern themselves with such paradigms for communication.

In addition, the varying speech patterns of the Bible reveal another biblical rationale for a more-than-prophetic approach to biblical proclamation. As Leon Morris points out, "God's messengers are not all alike."[10] The Bible presents at least three paradigms for communicating the Word of God in the world – the prophetic, the priestly, and the sagacious. Consider, for example, the following three texts from Scripture. Two come from the prophets – Jeremiah and Ezekiel – and one is from our Lord Jesus. Each text expresses the idea that the word-ministry of the prophet is accompanied by two other kinds of biblical word-ministry among the people of God in their communities.

> For the law shall not perish from the priest, nor counsel from the wise, nor the word from the prophet (Jer. 18:18).

> They seek a vision from the prophet, while the law perishes from the priest
> and counsel from the elders (Ezek. 7:26).

> Therefore I send you prophets and wise men and scribes, some of whom you
> will kill and crucify, and some you will flog in your synagogues and persecute
> from town to town ... (Matt. 23:34).

Notice how each text reveals to us the importance and necessity of the prophet, the priest/scribe, and the wise man/elder. Throughout the history of God's people, a priest or scribe such as Ezra would study, practice, and instruct the people in the Word of God (Ezra 7:10). He might also lead God's people in the pursuit of reconciliation with God (Ezra 10:1). God gave his people this priestly provision for learning his Word in the context of offering sacrifice for the forgiveness of sin. The sage, on the other hand, is sometimes associated with the elders and sometimes not. Solomon, for example, is the sage *par excellence*. Throughout the covenant community, God's people could seek practical advice and God's leaders could seek political insight from these men of wisdom. Furthermore, as established above, God also spoke to his people by the prophets. These men brought a local and immediate revelation to God's people with God's authority. Through them, the followers of God were meant to encounter God directly as he applied the implications of his character to the people's trends of thought and life.

Though the priest and the sage did not have an immediate revelation from God, as did the prophet, they nevertheless meditated on and studied God's written Word. By these three avenues of Word-ministry, God led and communicated to his people. In sum, the first reason that we ought to be concerned about the absence of a wisdom paradigm for Word-proclamation is simply that the Bible assumes such an approach from God among and for his people. In other words, God speaks as a sage sometimes.

TITANIC SHIFTS IN WESTERN CULTURE

The second reason that a prophetic paradigm alone is insufficient to equip God's people for preaching and testifying is cultural. Preachers and other Christian communicators can tend to caricature the prophetic paradigm. Caricatures come by way of family experience or theological tradition as preachers assume that certain tones of voice, a particular animation of expression, an attitude of harshness on sin, or a loudness of manner which reflects their own experiences with preachers, are prerequisites for true prophetic preaching. Caricatures also arise as these cultural lenses overlook the wisdom aspects of the prophets, such as their appeals to nature or their use of maxims, or by forgetting that Habakkuk, for example, is a song (3:19).

Moreover, the church in the West finds itself increasingly called to minister the Word in contexts that are socially broken, ethnically diverse, visually saturated, postmodern in worldview, and biblically uninformed. Some in the church respond to this complexity by denying the viability of preaching in such contexts. As every generation seems to do, many people today are calling for the cessation of preaching altogether. Others are calling for a strong return to preaching on the basis of what Scripture dictates. The appeal to what Scripture dictates, however, often means only an emboldened return to what is commonly understood as the prophetic approach to preaching. While this approach may be good in itself, it usually means that the avenues of wisdom and priestly biblical communication remain largely unexplored. Still others are shaping their preaching according to "relevant" sociological or cultural concerns and seeking to supplement traditional preaching (by which they often mean the caricature of the prophetic approach) with styles "more appealing" to modern culture.

I would certainly agree with those who advocate a return to a biblical view that rightly maintains the centrality of preaching. But I would also suggest that there is no need to reshape our preaching to "fit" the times. God has already provided in his Word the communication resources we need for the culturally challenging situations we may encounter. The Wisdom Literature, along with the prophetic and priestly paradigms, comprises a significant portion of these God-given resources. In other words, we who submit to Scripture can learn to say what God says with the resources that God himself has provided in his Word. Let us now look briefly at what I mean by this as we examine some aspects of postmodernism in light of the Wisdom Literature.

SKEPTICISM

Postmodern people are often *skeptical.* In their eyes, claims of exhaustive knowledge, the possession of – or even the existence of – absolute truth, and the unbounded capacity of human reason are simply not credible positions to hold. Often a preacher's imitation of the authoritative certainty of the prophets leads him to present himself in the pulpit as if he is exhaustively correct and always without error. This is, of course, antithetical to the whole postmodern mindset. The Wisdom Literature, however, assumes and values the existence of mystery. In fact, according to the Bible, the wise must uphold skepticism of a certain kind. "The one who states his case first seems right," says the sage, "until the other comes and examines him" (Prov. 18:17). Therefore, the wise will wait, listen, and ponder before making assertions. They are skeptical, not of God, but of men. Whereas a preacher's interpretation of the prophet's dogmatics will often not tolerate questions, the sage's approach reminds preachers that God also communicates in ways that give room for challenge and further dialogue. Truth is not settled by one sermon or one preacher, unless that sermon is delivered by a preacher named Jesus. Therefore, questions and dialogue which resist a face-value acceptance of our biblical assertions may actually indicate a wise response among our "outside" neighbors as they first encounter the claims of Scripture.

Likewise, reason is also valued by the sage, though it is assumed to be faulty to some degree. "There is a way that seems right to a man, but its end is the way to death" (Prov. 16:25). Only God has exhaustive knowledge. Consequently, Solomon testified, "I said, 'I will be wise,' but it was far from me" (Eccl. 7:23). For all that we know of God, we must confess along with Job that we are still only "at the outskirts" of God's ways (Job 26:14).

Furthermore, the Wisdom Literature assumes that what one can know of God requires more than the action of man's reason. Revelation from God is necessary for our knowledge. Therefore, we find knowledge by "calling out" for it and "raising our voice" to God (Prov. 2:4-6) rather than by human effort alone.

The wise man, therefore, reminds the preacher and the testifier that he does not have to fear admitting that there are things he does not know. Nor does he have to make it appear as if what he does know is exhaustive or completely correct in all of its parts. With the apostle Paul, we may readily acknowledge that we know only as in a mirror dimly. Yet, we may also acknowledge that what we know is substantially true. As finite creatures, we can know truth truly, even if not exhaustively. The Wisdom Literature poignantly assumes that it is the foolish and not the wise who claim exhaustive knowledge and leave no room for the mysteries of God (Prov. 18:2).

Spirituality

In addition to their skepticism, postmodern people also value the supernatural, the use of metaphor, the validity of personal experience, and the recognition that nature is not a machine. The Wisdom Literature helps us here, since it also assumes supernatural realities (Job 1:6-7). To borrow a phrase from poet Wendell Berry, the sage possesses no "indoor piety." Birds and flowers, spiders and creeks beckon for the sage's attention, and he has no sense of guilt about this, nor any sense of time being wasted. Moreover, words are understood to be powerful and to actually affect the soul. Joy and wisdom are the provision of God, and the Spirit of God is given in the wisdom context of repentance (Prov. 1:23). The sage believes that something can actually happen between God and a person so that the person becomes supernaturally something – or rather, someone – that he or she was not before.

The sage does not avoid or devalue personal experience. The inward thoughts and feelings of Job and of the "preacher" of Ecclesiastes are made transparent to any who read those Scriptures, as are the hopes and convictions of the father for his son in the book of Proverbs. In a similar way, the Song of Solomon transparently pursues the love that leads to marriage. The intensely personal nature of Solomon's revelation here may make many modern readers blush, yet such a reaction would, in many ways, have seemed foreign to him. This kind of redemptive transparency is often missing in prophetic approaches to preaching, in which the preacher seeks rightly to avoid "preaching oneself" and desires to speak objectively as God's herald. The sage reminds us, however, that speaking objectively does not negate or invalidate one's personal experience of the truth. Moreover, when preachers are tempted to interpret a prophetic paradigm in a dualistic way, they emphasize issues of the soul and eternity to the detriment of the body and nature. The sage reminds the preacher that he must take general revelation into account and recognize the proper delight and instruction that God gives in and through his creatures.

COMMUNITY

Postmodern people also value relationships, incarnation, and shared space and time. The wise man likewise assumes the value of community. "Whoever isolates himself seeks his own desire; he breaks out against all sound judgment," says the sage (Prov. 18:1). Proverbs, for example, assumes the necessity of the daily impact of extended family, marriage, siblings, friends, and counselors. Significantly in this regard, the sage assumes that doctrine is learned in relationship to others – not in isolation from them. "Whoever walks with the wise becomes wise," the sage says, "but the companion of fools will suffer harm" (Prov. 13:20; see also 22:24-25). Preachers therefore need not fear coming out of their studies and away from their programs to learn of God.

This assumption of the vital relationship between community and doctrine supplements and at times corrects an interpretation of prophetic preaching that isolates and elevates the preacher to the role of sole dispenser of truth. In this model, he becomes a kind of doctrinal "lone ranger" within the community. But doctrinal discussion devoid of proper relational contexts is foreign to the wise. Piety is both an individual and a corporate endeavor. If the prophet is like the voice of one crying out with authority in the wilderness, the sage is like the voice of one actively teaching and learning in a relational community. The authority of either one is never in doubt, but for the sage, that authority is put in relational rather than declamatory terms, much like the way in which the father or mother teaches the son wisdom in the book of Proverbs.

ICONIC FAMILIARITY

Visual media – technology for the physical eyes – are another underlying "given" for today's postmodern contexts. The iconic media of the wise man, however, do not require expensive equipment or access to electricity or the Internet. The wise man teaches "us to use our eyes as well as our ears to learn the ways of God and man."[11] The wise man is constantly watching people and places, observing and bringing human ways to our attention. His urgings to pay careful attention to the world around us can inspire us to lift our media-saturated eyes from the television or the computer screen and focus them on the community of people who are so important for the well-being of our souls. This sage-like engagement with the world through observation and reflection gives balance to more prophetic approaches that often assume the necessity of a physical separation from the world or a disinclination toward noticing or caring about the daily moments and issues of our neighbors who are "outside."

FELT BROKENNESS

Furthermore, postmodernism distrusts slogans or formulaic answers to life's complexities. Relevant for this realistic approach to life is the fact that the biblical sage does not "use texts as a substitute for dealing with life."[12] The sage is not entertained by folly, but he does learn from it, so that he can wisely deconstruct it, with its various costumes, for our health. To see that this is true, simply take a brief excursion through the Wisdom Literature and observe the questions it asks. These questions are real and complex, engaging the full range of human life and longing in a fallen world. The sage unmasks the things that tempts us. He takes human pain and desire seriously because he knows that we are creatures who need our Creator's conversation. In this vein, Job and Ecclesiastes address truth without minimizing pain, discomfort, or disorder. Such a sage perspective refuses to supply merely formulaic answers and denials of pain in the name of faith. This is a far cry from some of the posturing that too often characterizes preachers who rely solely on caricatures of prophetic paradigms.

BIBLICAL IGNORANCE

Post-Christian conversations also find help in the Wisdom Literature. People in the communities in which we preach increasingly live their lives with no church, no Sunday school, and no biblical frame of reference. For example, I once had the opportunity to preach to a group of young people to whom I mentioned that "Stephen was stoned to death." In response, there was a general murmuring in the group and some surprise. They did not realize that the Bible was so relevant as to talk about a guy named Stephen who overdosed on drugs and died!

As with the prophetic and priestly paradigms, God's Word for the wise is true and absolute. But, unlike the literature related to the prophetic and priestly paradigms, in the Wisdom Literature the exodus and covenant repentance play only implicit roles. Wisdom has a "generic" ethos that is not dependent upon an "upfront" understanding of God as Savior in order for one to learn meaningfully about God.[13] Whereas the normative audience for the prophet is the covenant people of God – especially as they are stubborn and straying – the Wisdom Literature is generally more universal in its assumptions. Whereas the prophetic call to repentance normally involves a straying people who know the stories of their history, the laws of their God, and the covenant of God, the Wisdom Literature makes these assumptions only sparingly. In this way, the Wisdom Literature may help preachers talk to people about God and life without assuming a shared knowledge of the biblical history.

One aspect of this is that the sage offers the preacher another tone. Often, the prophets confront the hard-heartedness of those who claim to follow God, and they do so with speech that is very direct, commands that are much defined, and a requirement for immediate change. The reason for this plain and direct challenge is that judgment is coming upon "the insider." The tone of the prophet therefore is often harsh in its descriptions and implications, which exposes the prophetic assumption that God's people know his laws and know the stories of his redemption and promises. In other words, those whom the prophets normally address should know better. This pattern is reflected in John the Baptist and in our Lord Jesus. The harshest words of "woe" – such as "white-washed tombs," "brood of vipers," and "hypocrites" – are given to those who claim to follow God with their words but refuse him with their lives. The book of James follows this pattern when it refers to believers who are coveting, quarreling, and fighting as "adulterers and adulteresses." The imagery of a spiritual adultery is prophetic and denotes the fracture of the most intimate covenant relationship.

The prophetic caricatures which sometimes adorn our preaching – dressing in black, yelling and shouting with red-faced anger, calling "outsiders" names, and bellowing the judgment to come – bear witness to the insufficiency of the prophetic paradigm when untempered by other approaches. Preachers have to come to terms with the fact that Jesus did not speak to the woman at the well in the same way that he spoke to the hardened religious teachers. Yet, in contrast to Jesus, preachers and other Christian communicators often give the harshest words to those who are not aware of God or of his ways. We must remember, however, that when shared knowledge of God's being and Word is eroded, our hearers do not know of what they are supposed to repent, to whom they are to repent, or why such repentance should matter. The issues for the biblically unaware person are different from those for a recalcitrant covenant people; they do not primarily concern a malicious hard-heartedness. Only after proper instruction has been given to one who is uninformed can defiant stubbornness be confidently detected and confronted.

In this regard, the apostle Paul's teaching is of some help to us. He says, "We urge you, brothers, admonish the idle, encourage the fainthearted, help the weak, be patient with them all" (1 Thess. 5:14). Paul informs us that we are not to admonish the fainthearted and the weak but to encourage and to help them. Likewise, we are not to encourage the idle but to admonish them. In a biblically uninformed climate, God's preachers and people must learn to communicate with the ignorant as well as with the stubbornly hard-hearted – and we must grow in being able to tell the difference.

As an example of how this might work, the following exercise helps compare and contrast the differing tones that the prophet and the sage might use to confront the sin of drunkenness (see the diagram below).

THE PROPHET	THE SAGE
Isaiah 5:11-12, 22-23	**Proverbs 23:29-35**
Woe to those who rise early in the morning, that they may run after strong drink, who tarry late into the evening as wine inflames them! They have lyre and harp, tambourine and flute and wine at their feasts, but they do not regard the deeds of the Lord, or see the work of his hands…Woe to those who are heroes at drinking wine, and valiant men in mixing strong drink, who acquit the guilty for a bribe, and deprive the innocent of his right!	Who has woe? Who has sorrow? Who has strife? Who has complaining? Who has wounds without cause? Who has redness of eyes? Those who tarry long over wine, those who go to try mixed wine. Do not look at wine when it is red, when it sparkles in the cup and goes down smoothly. In the end it bites like a serpent and stings like an adder. Your eyes will see strange things, and your heart utter perverse things. You will be like one who lies down in the midst of the sea, like one who lies on the top of a mast. "They struck me," you will say, "but I was not hurt; they beat me, but I did not feel it. When shall I awake? I must have another drink."
Isaiah 28:1-3, 7-8	**Proverbs 31:4**
Ah, the proud crown of the drunkards of Ephraim, and the fading flower of its glorious beauty, which is on the head of the rich valley of those overcome with wine! Behold the Lord has one who is mighty and strong; like a storm of hail, a destroying tempest, like a storm of mighty, overflowing waters, he casts down to the earth with his hand. The proud crown of the drunkards of Ephraim will be trodden underfoot ... These also reel with wine and stagger with strong drink; the priest and the prophet reel with strong drink, they are swallowed by wine, they stagger with strong drink, they reel in vision, they stumble in giving judgment. For all tables are full of filthy vomit, with no space left.	It is not for kings, O Lemuel, it is not for kings to drink wine, or rulers to take strong drink, lest they drink and forget what has been decreed and pervert the rights of all the afflicted. Give strong drink to the one who is perishing, and wine to those in bitter distress; let them drink and forget their poverty and remember their misery no more.

Notice that both ministers of the Word identify and confront drunkenness as a sin. Both also describe the effects of the drink on the person, although the prophet is more graphic and less concerned with the social niceties of description. The prophet is also denouncing abuses and declaring woe and judgment. There is no dialogue, no discussion. He does so in the explicit context of God's erring people.

The sage, on the other hand, speaks without exclamation points and without the condemning "woe." Rather, he asks his hearers to consider if "woe" forms the heart of their personal experience. His is a description of the alluring reasons for temptation and the devastating consequences of giving in to it. Like the prophet, the sage gets to the heart, but his is a more personal and dialogical appeal that leaves room for the hearer to consider his ways and respond. The sage also speaks more universally, without any explicit reference that might limit the force of his comments only to Israelites.

Consequently, the sage offers an approach to dealing with sin that does not supplant, but rather, complements the prophetic ministry of the Word. The sage, as it were, draws from a well deep with resources for gospel communication – resources rich and varied enough to meet the many challenges that modern preachers will face.

THE TRIUNE SAGACITY

The third reason that a prophetic paradigm alone is insufficient to equip God's pastors and people for gospel communication has to do with the nature of the Trinity itself. God the Father, God the Son, and God the Spirit are the source of the sage's wisdom: "For the Lord gives wisdom; from his mouth come knowledge and understanding" (Prov. 2:6). In light of this fact, perhaps the greatest incentive for preachers to develop their ministries through a perspective that is not only prophetic and priestly,[14] but also sagacious, is the centrality of Jesus as the one who fulfills each of these roles perfectly.

The New Testament assumes, among other things, that Jesus is the Sage of sages.[15] Christ is our wisdom and in him "one greater than Solomon is here" (Matt. 12:42 NIV) In him "are hidden all the treasures of wisdom and knowledge" (Col. 2:3). Therefore, not only does the preacher learn from Christ to preach prophetically, but he also learns to preach sagaciously. Robert Stein notes the frequent neglect of this point: "The teachings of Jesus possess qualities in common with the teachings of both the wise men and the prophets of the Old Testament. But, whereas the prophetic aspect of the teachings of Jesus usually receives its due recognition, there is a tendency to overlook and underestimate the role of Jesus as a sage."[16] This tendency is avoided when the student of preaching begins to recognize that it is the Lord who teaches by pointing to lilies and birds. It is the Lord who can tell a story of two houses built disparately on sand and rock and then contrast the wisdom of the one builder with the folly of the other. What would it look like for us as preachers and gospel communicators if we learned again how to see the triune sagacity and to follow the lead of God's wisdom into the world?

Conclusion

Christians are meant to engage their "outside" neighbors with a sage communication that is gracious, earthy, weighty, and practically applied. Hughes Oliphant Old, in his important series on the history of preaching, notably observes the influence of such wisdom on preaching. He concludes, "If there is a covenantal theology of preaching, and if it is complemented by a prophetic theology of preaching, then we must add to this a sapiential[17] theology of preaching."[18]

In light of the biblical, cultural, and Trinitarian reasons for complementing a prophetic approach to preaching with a wisdom paradigm, the findings of this essay affirm what Old suggests. Christian preachers require and are helped by a fuller reliance upon more than a prophetic form of preaching. God preaches like a sage sometimes. In so doing, he gives us resources for engaging the changing contexts of the twenty-first century with the power and authority of his unchanging Word.

1. Unless otherwise indicated, Bible quotations used in this essay are taken from the English Standard Version (esv).

2. Fleming James, The Message and the Messengers: Lessons from the History of Preaching (New York: Thomas Whittaker, 1897), 7.

3. John Broadus, Lectures on the History of Preaching (New York: A. C. Armstrong and Son, 1901), 11–12.

4. Edwin Charles Dargan, The Art of Preaching in the Light of its History (New York: George H. Doran Co., 1922), 20.

5. Broadus, History of Preaching, 10.

6. Though focusing primarily on the wisdom aspects of preaching, I assume that preachers also require a fuller consideration of the priestly/scribal implications for our theology and practice – a task that is beyond the scope of this essay. This need has been sorely neglected in the history of preaching. Some of this neglect has been intentional. See Broadus, History of Preaching, 10: "You are no doubt all aware that the New Testament minister corresponds not at all to the Old Testament priest, but in important respects to the Old Testament prophet." See also, John Ker, Lectures on the History of Preaching (London: Hodder and Stoughton, 1889), 16.

7. Quoted in John Stott, Between Two Worlds: The Art of Preaching in the Twentieth Century (Grand Rapids, Mich.: Eerdmans, 1982), 103.

8. For explorations of wisdom for ministry, see Walter Brueggemann, In Man We Trust (Richmond, Va.: John Knox, 1972).

9. Derek Kidner, The Message of Ecclesiastes: A Time to Mourn, and a Time to Dance, The Bible Speaks Today (Downers Grove, Ill.: Intervarsity, 1976), 13.

10. Leon Morris, The Gospel According to Matthew, The Pillar New Testament Commentary, ed. D. A. Carson (Grand Rapids, Mich.: Eerdmans, 1992), 588.

11. Kidner, The Message of Ecclesiastes, 13.

12. Charles F. Melchert, Wise Teaching: Biblical Wisdom and Educational Ministry (Harrisburg, Pa.: Trinity Press International, 1998), 273.

13. See for example, Daniel J. Estes, Hear, My Son: Teaching and Learning in Proverbs 1–9 (Grand Rapids, Mich.: Eerdmans, 1997), 88. Estes notes: "The Wisdom Literature ... nearly always views life in generic terms. Unlike the legal, historical, prophetic and hymnic literature of the Old Testament, the wisdom texts contain no explicit references to events in the history of Israel."

14. Davison assumes that the connection between Old Testament sages and contemporary pastor-teachers is explicit. W. T. Davison, The Wisdom Literature of the Old Testament (London: Charles H. Kelly, 1894), 4.

15. See, for example, Matt. 12:42ff.; 1 Cor. 1:22-25; Col. 2:3.

16. Robert Stein, The Method and Message of Jesus' Teachings (Philadelphia: The Westminster Press, 1978), 2.

17. "Sapiential" means "wise or deep with discernment."

18. Hughes Oliphant Old, *The Reading and Preaching of the Scriptures,* Vol. 1: *The Biblical Period* (Grand Rapids, Mich.: Eerdmans, 1998), 92. Old's important contribution describes the sage in scribal terms. Some distinctions between the wise man of the Wisdom Literature and the Scribe are therefore underestimated.

11

SYSTEMATIC THEOLOGY AS A BIBLICAL DISCIPLINE

MICHAEL WILLIAMS
Professor of Systematic Theology

I n *Between Two Horizons: Spanning New Testament Studies and Systematic Theology*, a group of biblical theologians and systematic theologians came together to discuss and write on the relationship between Scripture, hermeneutics, and systematic theology. The contributors to the project – perhaps somewhat to their own dismay, but not surprisingly at all – quickly located the disciplinary Moloch that seems to haunt all discussions of the relationship between biblical theology and systematics: what are we to make of systematic theology? The participants could reach no consensus on the question. "Our disagreement on this score," write the editors, "had to do with ongoing controversies among systematicians regarding definitions of their task as theologians and with some of our own caricatures of 'theology' as attempts merely to organize the core, historic doctrines of Christian faith."[1]

While there has been a spate of attempts to offer some definition of the discipline in recent years,[2] these attempts have usually come through the elucidation of theological hermeneutics. Theologians describe what systematic theology does (or should do) and set down some guidelines for the doing of it, but never quite define just what it is that is done. When definitions are proffered, they have tended toward either the banal – such as the organization of doctrines – or the outright dismissive and demeaning. Systematic theology, we are told, is the product of a Greek philosophical mind, and as such is foreign to and subversive of the Christian faith's actual substance and shape. It is argued that the emphasis upon topics rather than story, rationality rather than action, and ideas rather than persons suggests that systematic theology is simply the wrong tool for the job. In the doing of systematic theology, the particularity of the biblical story is absorbed into the abstract, the relational into the cognitive, the historical into timeless truth. In contrast, it is said that the Christian faith invites us to accept the biblical story as our story, to know and live within an encompassing drama that produces Christian identity and calls us to live within a transformed and transforming community for the sake of God's kingdom mission over all things. In short, its critics say that systematics makes no claims upon us and nurtures no relationships, but merely encourages us to bend the Word of God to questions not of its own asking.

I have cited no examples of these criticisms of systematic theology. I have said them all myself. And I am a systematic theologian. My goal in this essay is to present a defense of systematic theology, a discipline that suffers from decidedly poor reviews within present Christian academia and some sectors of the church. Along the way, I will offer my own definition of systematic theology, one that is humbler and more circumspect than some would like, but one that is defensible in light of the sources and calling of the theologian. My thesis is simple, but, I believe, profound and provocative.[3] I will argue that systematic theology, within the evangelical and Reformed tradition,[4] is properly bound by the Reformation principle of *sola scriptura*, and thus should be regulated by the scriptural message and by sound biblical hermeneutics.

Systematics is, first of all, a biblical discipline, and not a speculative one. Far too often, the Bible has functioned merely as a limiting principle within systematic theology, a negative stricture: if Scripture does not disallow an idea, we are free to employ it. Thus, the Bible is more of a constraining authority than a positive guide to theology. My thesis, however, is that Scripture must be allowed to lead our theological reflection rather than merely test it. While those who take the approach toward systematics just described may, and often do, appeal to the authority and even the inerrancy of Scripture, the Bible often fails to function for them as a constructive guide. I want to argue this precise point: the biblical narrative structure, the story of God's relationship with his creation – from Adam to Christ crucified and resurrected to Christ triumphant in the restoration of all things in the kingdom of God – forms the regulative principle and interpretative key for systematic theology no less than it does for biblical theology. This suggests that a systematic theology that is oriented to the biblical narrative and scriptural ways of knowing ought to be redemptive-historically grounded rather than ordered to a cultural convention of rationality or an extra-biblical conception of system.

TRADITIONAL SYSTEMATIC THEOLOGY

The Movement from Task-Driven Reflection to Systematic Discipline

The discipline of systematic theology did not simply come with the revelation of Scripture. Broadly speaking, theology may be defined as a disciplined reflection upon divine revelation,[5] and systematic theology is a particular approach toward theological reflection. While Christians have always sought to make sense of their faith and understand its implications and applications to life – and thus it may be said that there has been a theological enterprise as long as there have been believers – the earliest theology of the church could not really be called systematic theology. Thinkers such as Irenaeus and Tertullian were engaged in theological reflection for the purpose of polemical engagement with teaching that they took as contrary to Scripture (e.g. the Marcionite denigration of creation and rejection of the Old Testament as Scripture), doctrinal exposition of problematic issues (e.g. the relationship between Jesus Christ and God), and the exposition and summation of Scripture for catechetical purposes in the life of the church. In other words, for these early Christian writers, theology was an occasional and task-driven enterprise.[6]

As a disciplined approach toward doctrinal reflection which seeks to create a summary of what the Bible teaches, systematic theology had its beginnings in the medieval church, in the work of such thinkers as Thomas Aquinas and Peter Lombard.[7] The first real textbook of what would become systematic theology, and what would set the model for theological reflection for centuries to come, was Peter Lombard's *Sentences* in the twelfth century. Following John of Damascus' topical division of doctrine, Lombard gathered into his book statements from church fathers and theologians throughout the history of the church and organized them under six topics (*loci*).

In this model, theology became a topical and synthetic discipline, the goal of which was the creation of a system – an integrated, coherent and comprehensive statement of Christian doctrinal teaching. That sounds innocent enough, and there was nothing inherently pernicious about it. But problems did attend the approach. Over the next several centuries, theological study became increasingly abstract and distanced from the text of Scripture. One primary principle would inform both the move toward abstraction and the relativization of Scripture: the goal of theology came to be understood as a declaration of timeless truth – eternally true doctrinal statements. This goal itself seems to have been influenced by the Greek suspicion of history (think Pythagoras, not Heraclitus). Theology was not oriented toward historical knowing, but ahistorical knowing, toward definitions rather than relationships, toward things rather than persons or processes.[8]

The Impulse Toward Abstraction

I have just mentioned the suspicion of history that came from Greek philosophy and informed so much of the Western mind. As that is a very vague broadside sort of statement, let me offer a particular example. From Aristotelian metaphysics, medieval theology inherited the distinction between essences and accidents. According to this way of thinking, an essential attribute is necessary to a thing such that the loss or diminution of that attribute would constitute a loss of being. When applied to God, a divine attribute is a property that God could not lose and continue to be God. Indeed, knowing these attributes constitutes a kind of knowledge of God, for they define what God is; they define his essence. But things also possess nonessential properties. Aristotle called them "accidents." A table, for example, could be painted, varnished, or left unfinished. One could cut its legs shorter, move it to another room, use it as a surface upon which to serve the evening meal or perform open heart surgery, but in all these cases, the thing would still be a table. Its essence would not be changed. The only changes effected by carrying out any of these proposed actions would be to the nonessential characteristics of the table (the accidents).

Many of the predicates ascribed to God in Scripture denote not attributes or essential properties but nonessential properties – accidents. These nonessential properties, according to Thomas Aquinas, do not define what God is but relate God to his creatures. Relational predicates such as personhood, emotional states, character traits, and actions do not denote essential divine attributes. They are relations that are extraneous (accidental) to the divine being. To say that God is the Creator, or that God is the covenant Lord of Israel, is to make nonessential statements. It is rationally possible that God may never have chosen to create in the first place or to enter into a covenant relationship with Abraham. And if he had not done those things he would still be what he is. Historical actions and relationships are of negligible import philosophically since they are voluntary, nonessential, accidental. They are, then, irrelevant to knowing God's essence (the accumulation of his attributes).[9]

With this construction, high medieval theology (what may be called *scholasticism*) would move toward a distinction between nature and works. Nature (essences) became the subject of natural theology and was thought of as prior to and determinative for the study of works and relationships, which are known through biblical revelation. God, and what is most important to know about God, can be known apart from his actions and relationships in history. Theology came to be a defining of the divine, an abstractive and metaphysical knowledge of God apart from the plane of history.[10]

The Metaphysical Orientation

We might think of the scholastic relativization of history as an attempt to position human knowing on the transcendent side of the Creator–creation boundary. To use Karl Barth's memorable phrase, the scholastics sought "to lighten heaven with earth's searchlights," rather than "let the light of heaven be seen and understood on earth."[11] Curiously, the ahistorical impulse of scholastic theology even extended to the divine acts within history. According to the datum that whatever God does in history he has already determined in eternity, scholastic theology thought of creation, sin, redemption, and glorification as categories in the mind of God rather than as historical events.

Once these things have been abstracted from the temporal sequence of Scripture and turned into divine ideas or free-floating theological constructs, they are free to be ordered according to the preferences of the theological system. And, of course, this would give birth in seventeenth-century Reformed thought to complex systems of decrees in which the theologian speculates upon a pre-creational moment in the mind of God rather than attending to the biblical and temporal order. What we have, then, is theology as a virtual dissection of the divine mind and an assumed familiarity with that mind. Notice that in this move away from history and toward metaphysics, actual, living, breathing human beings and actual history become irrelevant to the theological agenda. And that was intentional within the scholastic theological scheme. Persons, relationships, and events are messy things, hard to fit into the unilateral views of agency favored by the canons of logic and rationality that emerged with the Western academy. Unfortunately, the kind of unilinear, rational neatness prized by the scholastic theologians is not much in evidence in the Bible.

Scripture Under the Assumption of an Extra-Biblical System

Under the theological method I have just described, the Bible came to be understood not as a story but as a data dump, a collection of timelessly true propositions that were somewhat haphazardly thrown together. As one modern evangelical theologian who follows this traditional method of theology put it: the Bible is a huge jigsaw puzzle that the theologian must put together.[12] The analogy of mining a hillside for precious jewels has also been employed. Criticizing rather than affirming the proof-text approach toward theology, Kevin Vanhoozer writes that "for large swaths of the Western tradition, the task of theology consisted in mining propositional nuggets from the biblical deposit of truth."[13]

What is the Bible in such a system? It is a depository for proof-texts. A proof-text is a biblical statement or citation that does not require a context in order to be coherent and meaningful. Its function has nothing to do with the over arching biblical story in which it is embedded or the specific genre in which it is found. Also, the function of a proof-text is assigned by an extra-biblical structure: the system of doctrine. The Bible exists primarily to support the system, in the same way that bricks provide building material for a building. As the bricks are but raw material for the builder, with the building itself being his goal, so here the goal is the system of doctrine, not the knowing of Scripture. God is known not through Scripture so much as through the system.

What of events? At best, biblical events and relationships became instantiations of eternal truths. And according to this way of thinking, that is the real purpose of Scripture: to provide declarations and examples of eternal truths. The historical drama that stands behind the text is but the delivery mechanism for the collection of eternal verities. Vanhoozer suggests that the traditional systematic tendency of focusing on the propositional content of proof-texts "leads one to *dedramatize* the Scriptures, and in so doing misrepresenting the Bible."[14] Trevor Hart has added the helpful insight that the traditional habit of thinking of the Bible merely as a collection of doctrinal propositions undermines the integrity of the Bible as canon and its unity as revelation, or at least redefines canon and biblical unity in unfortunate ways. As bits of text are "torn away from their textual, let alone their canonical, contexts and reassembled within some framework of interpretation," we implicitly declare that the canon of Scripture is merely "'these particular texts and no others' rather than 'these texts as a whole'," because the whole, the unifying principle, or what Hart calls "the essential logic behind proof-texting" lies within the theologian's system rather than within Scripture.[15]

BIBLICAL THEOLOGY

Beginnings: The Reaction Against Scholasticism

The beginnings of biblical theology are hard to trace, if by *beginnings* we mean the identification of that one person or point in time as the genesis. We might better speak of contributors to the phenomenon. Luther's principle of *sola scriptura* – the Bible as the *norming norm* for all theological reflection – and Calvin's use of the humanist dictum *ad fontes* ("back to sources") must both be counted as early igniters of the movement toward biblical theology. Johannes Cocceius (1603–69) anticipated later developments in biblical theology through his emphasis on the biblical covenants and God's dealing with his people in the history of salvation. The first uses of the term *biblical theology* appear to have come from the Pietist tradition of Spener and Franke (ca. 1700). And the rise throughout the Enlightenment period – with its emphasis upon historical interpretation – of what might be called the *historical consciousness* and new tools for critical and historical research also played an important role in the maturation of biblical theology.[16]

What all of the persons and movements mentioned here had in common was that they were all reacting against the scholastic tradition in theology. All noticed the disconnect between the Bible and the theological habits of scholasticism: *this* does not look like *that*. The Bible does not read like a scholastic textbook; to find the conclusions of a lot of scholastic theology in Scripture, one must begin by presupposing them in the first place. And if that is the case, the question arises: are we reading those conclusions out of Scripture, or reading them into it?

Some recent definitions of biblical theology have concentrated merely upon the idea of order. Thus, Scott Hafemann writes that "biblical theology attempts to ascertain the inner points of coherence and development within the biblical narrative and exposition. It does its work inductively from within the Bible in an attempt to bring out the Bible's own message."[17] Likewise, Trevor

Hart suggests that biblical theology seeks to unfold unifying patterns within the biblical canon, "thereby to offer some more organized interpretation of the faith which vibrates through what is intrinsically an 'unsystematic' body of literature, and so to offer an account of Scripture's own theological priorities and emphases."[18] Yet, as Hart notes, if this is all biblical theology is or does, what truly distinguishes it from systematic theology? If biblical theology's concern is to trace patterns and find connections within the biblical text, is it not "already involved in a 'systematic' enterprise, and ... therefore a form of systematic theology"?[19]

Well, not in the sense of traditional systematic theology. The question is: what is being ordered and what is being traced? Biblical theology begins with the insight that the Bible is a referential revelation.[20] I. Howard Marshall makes the point most elegantly when he proclaims that "evangelicals would want to insist that if the text does not witness to a genuine saving and judging intervention of God in human history, 'we are of all men most miserable.'"[21] In other words, the Bible is about – refers to – God's mighty deeds in history. The biblical revelation is about something other than the mere words of the text.

"Christianity is not in the last resort about relations between texts, but about events in the real world: the Word of God did not for us become incarnate in a book, but in a life."[22] This means, as Hart is quick to point out, that "the real point of Scripture, what it is 'about,' is God's dealings with humankind in history, and its meaning is bound up, therefore, with *the meaning of events* in which this history unfolds, events in the life of Israel and the life of Jesus through which God in some sense reveals himself and his purposes for us."[23] This is not to denigrate or marginalize Scripture in any way, for "our access to the referent of the text is *through the text*."[24] Within the Reformed and evangelical understanding, the Bible belongs to the organism of God's special or particular revelation, but the biblical text does not exhaust that revelation. Richard Gaffin has depicted the relationship between Scripture and historical referent this way:

> Scripture is a record of revelation. It witnesses to the special revelation of God which consists in his ongoing covenant faithfulness in word and deed and which has its consummation in the person and work of Christ. In an important respect inscripturation as a mode of revelation is not an end in itself but the (necessary and sufficient) means to an end. And the proper focus of interpretation is the subject matter of the text, that is, the history with Christ at its center that lies in back of the text.[25]

Looking for the Story:
Affirmation of the Bible as a Historical Document

Biblical theology seeks to read the Bible as a historical document. In this it is almost the opposite of scholastic theology. The biblical theologian is looking for the story, what Geerhardus Vos called "the history of redemption." Why look for the story? Vos' answer is: that's what the Bible is. "God has embodied the contents of revelation, not in a dogmatic system, but in a book of history ... The Bible is not a dogmatic textbook but a historical book full of dramatic interest."[26] The Bible's subject matter is not abstract ideas or context-free truth-claims; rather, Scripture is oriented toward and is meant to be a disclosure of God's action in history. Richard Gaffin, using words that sound amazingly like those of Calvin, describes Vos' understanding of the nature of Scripture: "Revelation is not so much divinely given *gnosis* to provide us with knowledge concerning the nature of God, man, and the world as it is divinely inspired interpretation of God's activity of redeeming men so that they might worship and serve him in the world."[27] Gaffin summarizes the Vosian notion this way: "The deepest motive controlling the flow of the history of revelation is not instruction but incarnation." He then quotes Vos himself: "The circle of revelation is not a school, but a 'covenant.'"[28]

What is Vos doing? If he is right that salvation depends on what God has done in history, especially in the work of Christ, then the fact that biblical revelation comes to us as an organically unfolding historical drama bears theological import. That fact should set the theological agenda. It should structure the theological mind. Vos wants to allow the structure of biblical religion to set the structure of theological reflection.

The Relation Between Biblical Theology and Systematic Theology

Systematics and Rationalism

We should note that, even if we subtract the more speculative aspects of traditional systematic theology – that which we typified as the scholastic interest in the metaphysical at the expense of the creational and the temporal – the discipline is still oriented to the rational more than to the relational, and to the pursuit of a timeless statement of the *facts* more than to the historical unfolding of God's Word. In the words of D. A. Carson, the traditional and still prevailing model of systematic theology is oriented to the rational and hierarchical rather than to the temporal, and thus does not "encourage the exploration of the Bible's plot-line, except incidentally."[29]

Wayne Grudem's *Systematic Theology* makes Carson's point. Grudem sees systematic theology as a topically driven, synthetic presentation of Christian doctrine in which all the facts of revelation "fit together in a consistent way" within the revelational jigsaw puzzle. The goal of rational consistency is an organized, internally coherent, non-contradictory system of truth.[30] Grudem's own system is seen in his stated methodology:

1. Select all the "verses" that speak to a topic.
2. Summarize the teaching of each verse.
3. Synthesize them into a coherent doctrinal statement.[31]

Under this scheme, the doctrine of God is a rational explication of the facts about God, the doctrine of Christ is a rational presentation of the facts about Christ, and so on. Theology is a systematization of revelatory facts, collected into a rationally organized encyclopedia. We should note the *disembodiment of proposition* in this approach toward theology. It assumes that the truth statements of Scripture are so sufficiently self-contained that they are separable not only from the literary genres and contexts (both literary and historical) that bear them (making the exegete cry "foul"), but also from the historical relationships and acts which are their intended biblical referents (driving the biblical theologian crazy). What is the assumed hermeneutic here? The assumption that the Bible is a loose collection of disembodied propositions produces its own way of reading God's Word.[32]

Focusing upon Scripture as doctrinal propositions, traditional systematics tends to flatten out the biblical text. The complexity and ambiguity of reality is lost in the press toward univocal neatness and rational fit, and the dynamic of events and relationships is reduced to broad generalities. Noting the bloodless and impoverished world depicted in many systematics texts, Rainer Albertz commented that "they often have an effect that is remarkably static, lifeless, and at times boring."[33] Applying and developing J. L. Austin's speech-act theory, Kevin Vanhoozer has located the failure of systematics to capture the vitality and depth of Scripture not simply in its sacrifice of the historical but also in the way systematics has tended to treat all biblical expression as if it were ontological and conceptual. In handling all biblical statements as if they were the same sort of statement – didactic declaration – systematics treats the Bible as if it were nothing more than a collection of lecture notes.[34]

Vos' Criticism of Systematics

Working more than half a century ago, Geerhardus Vos was critical of traditional systematic theology. But to what was Vos opposed? Did he reject the very idea of systematic theology, in which case biblical theology is presented as an alternative theological approach? Many people see the relationship between biblical theology and systematic theology as antithetical. If biblical theology is good, then systematics must be bad. And, of course, within this dichotomous construct, if systematic theology is good, then biblical theology must be bad.[35] Characterizing systematic theology as the elevation of ideas over history, the abstract over the relational, the biblical theologian John Goldingay writes that "if systematic theology did not exist, it might seem unwise to invent it."[36]

Vos was not so eager to dismiss systematics. Take note of the way in which Gaffin couches Vos' criticism. Gaffin notes that because Vos understood the Bible as itself possessing a unified structure – the history of redemption – Vos was opposed to "the ever-present tendency to view the Bible as a mass of ambiguously related particulars for which some extra-biblical prolegomena or systematics supplies the necessary structuring principle."[37] Gaffin continues: "There is little question that Vos is countering what he considers a tendency in Protestant orthodoxy to deal with Scripture largely in terms of the *loci* or topical structure of dogmatics and in so doing to treat its statements as more or less isolated proof-texts."[38]

Summarizing the Vosian biblical theological criticism of systematics, Gaffin writes:

> The notion has to be avoided that the historical character of the Bible must somehow be overcome before we have the truth for today. It is no more the case that the Bible is true in spite of or apart from its historical qualification than it is the case that the death of Christ is efficacious in spite of its historicity. In fact, to remove the negatives and disjunctives from the preceding sentence will disclose the integral tie between truth and history from a biblical point of view: the Bible is true in view of its historical qualification, just as the death of Christ is efficacious in view of its historicity.[39]

Neither Vos nor Gaffin are suggesting that systematics is automatically wrong-headed. But they are asking us to rethink what we mean by systematic theology and how we go about practicing it.

The Call to Reform Systematic Theology

Let us begin by affirming that there is nothing wrong with asking topical questions of the biblical text. We all do it. And, after all, synthesis is unavoidable. All human beings seek coherence of thought. We add this to that, and, if need be, order the two in some way. Thus, if we do theology, the impulse toward systematic coherence will be present.

I am making the assumption that such a practice is not inherently foolhardy or contrary to the spirit of Scripture. Yet, two immediate objections arise to the impulse to systematize. First, it might be pointed out that all attempts to ask questions of the Bible as a single book assume that it speaks with one voice and presents a unified, lucid perspective on reality. To object to this assumes that the biblical materials are just too diverse to bear the weight of the synthetic enterprise. Rather than get a single answer to a question – say, "what is the nature of sin?" – a survey of Scripture will produce a multitude of answers. One answer (or perhaps three) will come from Isaiah, another from the Psalms, another from John, another from Paul. And there is no reason to expect (insist?) that these different answers will gibe with one another. Indeed, one may end up with a series of answers that defy synthesis, even answers that contradict one another (or, in some cases, with no answers at all).

Although this objection might strike the evangelical as the product of liberal assumptions about the nature of Scripture, we should at least appreciate that it wants to do justice to the diversity within the Bible. Evangelicals confess that the Bible is the Word of God, by which we mean that ultimately

God is the author – and the authority – who stands behind the text. While there is one speaker – God in the written revelation of his ways to his people – Scripture is mediated to us by means of many voices, voices that have their own specific historical and cultural circumstances, needs, and interests. The multiplicity of voices within the canon of Scripture presents the theologian with challenges, but they are actually allies rather than impediments.

Second, even if we confess Scripture as a faithful and reliable revelation of God, and even if we affirm a principle of analogy that will allow the synthesis that the topical agenda requires, it might still be asked whether the systematic impulse arises from and complements the biblical message, or in fact obscures or even loses that message in the forest of systematic *loci*. Reminiscent of the biblical theology movement of the post-World War II era, John Goldingay goes so far as to allege that systematic theology emerged from within a Greek philosophical framework in which ideas replace stories as the bearers of truth and meaning. And thus, systematic theology, he says, is an alien branch grafted onto the vine of Christian faith. From this perspective, the systematic project is foreign in heritage and contrary in method – the wrong tool for the job of faithful reflection upon biblical faith.[40] Although I do not wish to gloss over the issues raised in Goldingay's fine essay, I find his assertions relative to the heritage and essential nature of systematics too broad and somewhat ill-defined. Regardless, we will seek to keep a number of his challenges to systematics in mind as we proceed.

What Is Systematic Theology?

Defining systematic theology is both as easy as pie and as vexing as trying to understand one's spouse. First, the easy part. Systematic theology is oriented to this question: What does the entirety of God's revelation tell us about X? And that question itself tells us two things. First, systematic theology is a topically driven discipline.[41] Second, systematic theology is synthetic in nature; it is an integrative, interdisciplinary activity. Systematic theology is dependent upon the exegesis of Scripture; dependent upon the entirety of Scripture; and dependent upon the insights of biblical theology, two millennia of the church's theological reflection, the church's confessional heritage, and whatever else from human experience and academic study that can help us to answer the question.

Now for the hard part: What does the word *system* mean? We might begin by hazarding the notion that *system* refers to that which holds together all the different parts and dependencies just noted. But what might this system be? The truth is, *system* is a vague term, so vague in fact that people often throw up their hands and fall silent here. In an essay devoted to the nature of systematic theology, John Murray offers a number of warnings about the discipline – such as "there is an ever-present tendency toward abstraction in systematic theology,"[42] – but beyond that he spends most of the essay talking about biblical theology. John Frame also struggles with the word *system*. He explicitly asks, "What does the word 'systematic' mean in the phrase 'systematic theology'?" Does it mean logical consistency and orderliness? Yes, but should not all theological disciplines be consistent and orderly, and be sensitive to the rules of valid inference and inductive generalization? Does it mean coherence? Yes, but does that mean that other approaches to theology are then to be seen as incoherent? It seems that most of the adjectives used to distinguish systematic theology from other approaches to theology fail to distinguish it at all, for they name general, even expected, reflective virtues. And just where *is* this system, whatever it is? If the system is something other than Scripture itself, then we have set up some extra-biblical grid through which we access God's Word, and that is dangerous. We have created a new *norming norm*, the very thing from which the Reformers were seeking to escape. When we talk about a *system of doctrine,* we had better be talking about Scripture itself, or we have violated the principle of *sola scriptura.*[43]

Some years ago, Richard Gaffin wrote an article for the *Westminster Theological Journal* on the relationship between biblical theology and systematics. Spending the lion's share of his efforts on defining and defending biblical theology, Gaffin really had little to say about systematic theology. In this, he was simply following Vos and Murray before him. Comparing biblical theology and systematics, Gaffin wrote:

> The approach of biblical theology is historical, while that of systematic theology is logical. The former deals with revelation as an activity or process, the latter deals with it as a finished product. Vos uses the difference between drawing a line (biblical theology) and a circle (systematics) to illustrate how they differ.[44]

Footnoting his comment, Gaffin elaborates on systematic theology by saying that the use of the terms "logical" and "systematic" as descriptors are, of course, "conventional."[45] This is not much help, although I am convinced that Gaffin is right. Frame too gives up on trying to define systematic theology. After speaking of the scope or calling of the discipline (what does the whole Bible teach us about X?), Frame says simply, "I cannot make any positive sense of the term 'system' in the phrase 'systematic theology'."[46] But one phrase in Frame is helpful. While admitting defeat in trying to define "systematic," he does go on to speak of a "systematic perspective."

I would like to suggest that the idea of a *system* comes from the ancient Christian notion of *the analogy of faith.* As the Word of God, the Bible constitutes a harmonious whole. This means that all the parts – that is, those beliefs generated by the reading of Scripture and our familiarity with the historical discussion of the church – will cohere with one another. The systematic impulse perceives that coherence from the standpoint of the whole (Frame's "systematic perspective" or Vos' circle). Systematic theology is thus a holistic discipline. By itself, that suggests that the key to systematic theology is its accumulative and integrative character. It seeks to synthesize all the elements from the standpoint of the whole.

But a bit more needs to be said. D. A. Carson argues that systematic theology is characterized by cultural engagement, a bridging of the original horizon of the text with the present cultural horizon of the people of God. While exegesis and biblical theology cannot escape cultural influence, their focus is the biblical text. One can legitimately argue, as has Harvie Conn, that all theology is "historically contextual" in that the theologian functions within a particular cultural moment, a moment that invariably informs and shapes his or her reflection.[47] Systematic theology, however, takes cultural engagement as part of its explicit focus. The systematic theologian asks his questions from the historical-cultural standpoint of the church, and seeks to speak to the church. But Carson takes this a step further. Not only does systematic theology emanate from within a cultural moment as the church asks: What does it all add up to?, but the culturally embedded systematic impulse also shapes the questions that are asked. As an integrative, holistic, culturally engaged enterprise, systematic theology is also the most worldview-forming of all the theological disciplines.[48] It seeks to shape the theological reflection and the cultural engagement of the church from the vantage point of the big picture (Carson), or the systematic perspective (Frame). Pursuing a "large-scale, worldview-forming synthesis," systematic theology stands one step further away from Scripture than does biblical theology, and one step closer to culture.[49] While I do not much like the characterization of systematic theology as relatively distant from Scripture, I appreciate Carson's point that systematics not only arises from within a particular historical-cultural location – as does all theological reflection – but is also conscious of the fact that it speaks to a particular historical moment.

Reforming the Method: How Do We Do It?
Biblical truth is neither ahistorical nor acultural. Contrary to Carson and Conn, evangelicals have traditionally tended to think of theology in acultural and decontextual terms, that is, as the pursuit of timeless and universal truth. Accordingly, systematic theology seeks to emancipate theological reflection from any historical-cultural context. But this is exactly the problem: it represents a right insight gone wrong. The right insight is that God's character and ways are universally true and universally relevant to human life. Where it goes wrong is that traditional systematics seeks to find the universality of theological assertions through an ahistorical, rationalist method. As the rational construct comes to dominate theological discourse, the biblical story fades into comparative irrelevance. What is missed here is that the Bible refuses to function this way. The truth about God, about sin, about angels, about Christ, about the Holy Spirit, is transcultural, but it is never acultural. It is transhistorical rather than ahistorical. The biblical message – doctrine –

arises within historical-cultural context in the sense that it is revealed within, is always applicable to, and is inseparable from human cultural and historical existence. Curiously, the very historicity of the story is crucial to the biblical message, to doctrine. As the biblical materials begin with creation and refuse to end before the promise of recreation is fulfilled, all history – and thus all people within their particular historical contexts – are addressed by the biblical message.

William Edgar suggests that the movement toward abstraction in which the biblical materials are transformed into ahistorical, universal themes, is both unnecessary and, ultimately, less than helpful:

> The second person of the Trinity became not humanity in general, but a man, a unique person from a unique place. Jesus Christ and his teachings, as William Temple once put it, were a "scandal of particularity." In S. Mark Heim's felicitous expression, "If God were to be as human as we are, Jesus must have a fingerprint as unique as each one of ours." Only from this extraordinary particularity can Jesus then be universal. He did not look down from heaven and proclaim timeless truths with no application to culture. Rather, he became a real human being, a particular Semitic male, at a particular time of history, because such concreteness is the only way to be human. Because Jesus is a particular man, his message is then truly applicable to all of humanity, to women and to men from every tribe and group.
>
> And so, the message has a shape. It has contours. It is particular in order to be universal. Just as God brought about the redemption of every kind of person through the one man, the God-man Jesus Christ, so his revelation, though encapsulated in words from the Hebrew, Aramaic, and Greek languages, is universal, valid across all boundaries of time and space and culture.[50]

One of the reasons that systematic theology is forced to fight the battle of relevance is because of its own abstraction away from the historical-cultural concreteness of the biblical drama. By choosing a philosophical frame of reference for talking about God – a language which speaks in universal, abstract, and often impersonal categories – classical systematics spoke about God in ways that were less than biblically relevant to the realities of our historical life in the world.

An example or two might help us to make the point. It has long been the tradition within dogmatics to speak of God's power under the term *omnipotence*. I have to admit that there is something about the classical "*omnis*" (i.e. the entire method of thinking about the divine attributes by classical theism) that leaves me cold. They may be correct in a technical sense, in the sense that a schematic or a diagram or a flowchart is correct, but they are also somewhat lifeless. Does God possess all power? Yes, of course. As Yahweh himself says to Abraham when Sarah laughed at God's promise of a child for them, "Is anything too hard for the LORD?" (Gen. 18:14).[51] He is the maker of worlds. Isaiah 40 speaks of God measuring out the waters in the palm of his hand and marking off the heavens by his mere fingertip. Truly, his power is incomparable and inconceivably great.

My problem with the notion of omnipotence – and I admit that it may be at least partly linguistic – is that the language of the classical *omnis* is too diffuse, too general, too abstract. When Scripture speaks of God's power, it is always directed power, personal power, righteous power. It is not power in the abstract, but *his* power. The classical approach, however, was concerned to articulate God's power, knowledge, and presence in universal, undifferentiated, and extensive terms. Thus God is *omnipotent, omniscient, omnipresent*. But God's particularity, his person, suffered in the equation. Yes, God's lordship is universal, but it is as a particular God that he is also the universal LORD. Furthermore, and terminally adding to the abstraction, classical theism has often developed the divine attributes such that they become mere ideas, separated from any hint of particularity; omnipotence, for example, is not *God's power* so much as it is the raw *idea of unlimited power*. Thus the discussion becomes a philosophical analysis of omnipotence *per se*.

The Apostles' Creed might help us here. The first article of our English translation describes God as *the Father Almighty*. The word *almighty* is a translation of the Greek παντοκράτωρ (all-governing one). Latin versions of the Creed employed the word *omnipotens*. The Latin *omnipotens* speaks of unqualified, universal, impersonal, extensive power. Παντοκράτωρ, however, is directed, purposeful, particular, personal power. After all, a ruler presupposes a subject or a realm that is ruled, and thus relationship, a context in which power is exercised. Further, a particular kind of rule is implicit within the Creed, namely, a morally righteous rule.

From a biblical perspective, παντοκράτωρ (all-governing) is closer to the biblical reality than is *omnipotens* (omnipotent). The term *omnipotence* represents power within itself, without reference to anything else. And this was a real problem in medieval theology. For many theologians in the middle ages, God was *potentia absoluta* (absolute possibility). By definition, God can do anything. Thus, he might do anything (this was the conclusion of medieval nominalism). This caused real anxiety of soul for Martin Luther as a young monk. Perhaps, thought Luther, God will change his mind about me, for as absolute power, God is arbitrary power. Biblically, however, we must say that God's power is bound to his covenant word. There are, after all, things God *cannot* do. He cannot, for example, fail to keep his promises. Simply put, God's covenant promises limit the range of things he can do. God binds himself to his promises.

What of omniscience and omnipresence? Psalm 147:5 says that there is no limit to God's understanding. We would, then, be right to conclude that God knows everything there is to know. And I want to affirm that. Yet the biblical focus usually lies upon an intensive knowing on God's part. The existential relevance of God's knowledge is that God knows each one of us inside and out. We see this quite clearly in Psalm 139, a classic text relative to God's knowledge and presence. In that text, divine knowing and presence are functions of God's covenantal lordship. Nothing is hidden from his gaze. There are no secrets in his universe:

> O LORD, you have searched me and known me! You know when I sit down and when I rise up; you discern my thoughts from afar. You search out my path and my lying down and are acquainted with all my ways. Even before a word is on my tongue, behold, O LORD, you know it altogether. You hem me in, behind and before, and lay your hand upon me. (vv.1-5)

In verse 7 and following, David focuses his attention on the presence of God:

> Where shall I go from your Spirit? Or where shall I flee from your presence? If I ascend to heaven, you are there! If I make my bed in Sheol, you are there! (vv.7-8)

This is no diffuse presence that exists everywhere like oxygen. Rather, it is personal, intensive, and purposeful presence. There is nowhere for the sinner to hide. There is nowhere where God cannot help his covenant people. God may be present everywhere, but he is intensively so, covenantally so. In Jeremiah 23:23-24, Yahweh himself warns us against limiting his presence to the parochial as well as making his presence so vague and universal that it is of no practical good.

> Am I a God at hand, declares the LORD, and not a God afar off? Can a man hide himself in secret places so that I cannot see him? declares the LORD. Do I not fill heaven and earth? declares the LORD.

In a sense, the classical emphasis upon divine attributes as the key to knowing God is a bit misplaced. More often than not, Scripture reveals God by way of his actions and relationships rather than by a discussion of the divine nature. God's identity and character, rather than his nature, seem to be the fundamental biblical concern. As depiction is more central than definition, the operative question for theological reflection is not so much *what* is God? as it is *who* is God?[52] Creating, judging sin, calling a people to himself through acts of redemption, making promises, walking with his people: these are the ways that God is known in the biblical story. The *little credo* of Deuteronomy 26:5-9 identifies and confesses God through a recitation of his mighty deeds on behalf of Israel: his calling of Abraham to walk in his ways, his rescuing of the seed of Abraham from the Egyptian brick pits, and his bringing of them into the land he had promised to the patriarchs. In effect, the *credo* answers the question, *who* is God? Its answer is that he is the One who calls, redeems, and walks with us. This story was, if you will, Israel's gospel, the story she was called to live within and declare to the nations. Further, as Goldingay notes, "New Testament faith sees itself as the continuing of that story. Like the Old Testament, the New Testament takes predominantly narrative form, and the form corresponds to the nature of the faith. Its gospel is not essentially or distinctively a statement that takes the form of 'God is love,' but one that takes the form 'God so loved that he gave ....'"[53]

Elsewhere Goldingay has written:

> Christian theology has not regularly talked about God in narrative terms. The creeds, for instance, are structured around the persons of the Father, Son and Spirit, and systematic theology has often taken God's trinitarian nature as its structural principle. Before the revival of trinitarian thinking in the late twentieth century, systematic theology often emphasized the fundamental significance of attributes of God such as omnipotence, omniscience and perfection. The Old Testament narrative does incorporate equivalent statements about God's character, such as God's self-description in Exodus 34:6–7. But the kinds of statements about God that emerge more directly from the narrative itself are not those one typically sees in a systematic theological treatment of divine attributes. It is narrative that nuances who the Father is, for example, or what omnipotence is, or what grace is.[54]

That Scripture primarily reveals God's identity and character by his active involvement in the life and history of his people does not mean that it cannot also speak in more discursive, even metaphysical, ways in its depiction of God. Next to the *little credo* stood the *Shema* of Deuteronomy 6:4-5 as a fundamental Old Testament confession of faith: "Hear, O Israel, The LORD our God, the LORD is one. You shall love the LORD your God with all your heart and with all your soul and with all your might." Certainly this text is making an ontological assertion about God. Yet this statement is itself grounded in the story of Israel's deliverance, in which narrative declarations such as Deuteronomy 5:6-7 ("I am the LORD your God, who brought you out of the land of Egypt, out of the house of slavery. You shall have no other gods before me") give not only the context of the ontological assertion, but also, it seems to me, the essential clues for the correct interpretation of the meaning of the assertion. Referring both to Deuteronomy 6:4 and Exodus 34:6-7 (in which Yahweh himself proclaims his identity to his people, and does so in relational and contextually significant ways seemingly less compatible with the classical systematic approach to divine attributes), Goldingay writes that "the statements are inextricably linked to narrative; they gain their meaning from the narrative contexts in which they are set. But they are open to being reflected on as statements offering insight on God's nature that hold beyond their narrative context."[55] Does the Word speak "beyond" its "narrative context?" Yes. But always in terms of and through that context.

The Centrality of Biblical Theology. Does the criticism of the abstractive tendency of systematics necessarily mean the death of systematic theology? Some undoubtedly have said that it does. Others have tried different routes. Although writing from a decidedly postmodern context, Stanley Grenz has helpfully asked the question: What would systematic theology look like if we were to step out of the traditional model and cast a systematic along narrative lines? He answers his own question by saying that "we must view theology in terms of its proper context within the narrative of God's action in history."[56]

Taking his commitment to story from the biblical drama of redemption rather than postmodern notions about the sociology of knowledge, Richard Lints provides us with both a description of the rationalist loci method and a challenge to traditional notions of system:

> It is important to ask whether the conception of doing theology by stringing together Christian doctrines like pearls in a necklace might not be undermining the essential unity of the biblical message. As it stands, evangelical theology tends to deal with each component part individually, at best stitching things together after the fashion of a patchwork quilt. There may be interesting patterns evident in each of the individual pieces, but there is no pattern that holds the quilt together overall, other than its diversity.[57]

Henry Vander Goot offers the same criticism of classical systematic theology, but in even more pointed language:

> When we fail to notice the character of Scripture as dramatic narrative, we reduce the text of Scripture to abstractions of the mind. We tap the conflict out of the text and subsequently out of our view of human life as well .... Rationalism and the narrative form of Scripture are incompatible.[58]

Following in the redemptive-historical tradition of Geerhardus Vos, both Vander Goot and Lints argue that there may be better ways to "package theology" (Lints' phrase) than the rationalist method of traditional systematics. In the pursuit of timeless truth, classical systematics obscured both the biblical storyline and the unitary interrelatedness of Scripture that the story provides. The historical referents of the biblical Word – the mighty acts of God in creation, preservation, and redemption – if not annulled, are rendered theologically less relevant. Thus, Lints appropriately comments:

> Evangelicals have traditionally emphasized the *speech* of God by encapsulating it in doctrinal formulations. In doing so, they have neglected the *acts* of God. They have ably defended the historicity of these acts, but they have virtually ignored the centrality of their theological character.[59]

The diminution of historical reference sidelines the dramatic movement of story, and the Bible is – at the very least and at its most fundamental level – a story, the telling of God's historical relationship with mankind and creation. The Bible does not present itself as a theological dictionary or doctrinal treatise, and the content of scriptural revelation does not exist in isolated compartments, awaiting an external theological framework to provide some sort of order. The Bible has an order – the redemptive-historical story it tells. Lints contends, and I agree, that the framework of the theological enterprise "ought to be linked to the actual *structure* of the biblical text and not merely to the *content* of the Bible."[60] While the topical question, What does the Bible teach?, is legitimate, the answer is always regulated and mediated by the redemptive-historical story. The biblical way is the way of the story. The metanarrative of creation, fall, redemption, and new creation, along with the embeddedness of that grand drama in covenantally particular episodes, constitutes the subject of the divine accommodation that is biblical revelation. As such, the biblical story itself – and not some rational structure extraneous to Scripture – ought to regulate the framework by which we theologize about God and his ways. I believe that Goldingay is right when he argues that the overall narrative structure of Scripture is not accidental to the Christian faith and our theological reflection upon the faith, but rather corresponds to the very nature of the biblical faith, and as such should inform and drive our reflection.[61] "The biblical gospel is not a collection of timeless statements such as God is love. It is a narrative about things God has done."[62]

This is no less true of the New Testament. While the Gospels clearly have a narrative feel, Christians have often been tempted to think of the New Testament epistles, especially Paul's writings, as strictly discursive in character. Paul wrote doctrinal treatises, not narrative.[63] What is missed, however, is what Bruce Longenecker calls the "narrative bedrock,"[64] or what N. T. Wright has characterized as the "narrative world" that undergirds all of Paul's writings.[65] Herman Ridderbos was on to the same insight when he observed that Paul was more interested in the history of salvation (*historia salutis*) than an order of salvation (*ordo salutis*).[66] The Old Testament story of God calling a people who will be his mediators in the undoing of the Adamic fall – a story that finds its acme and fulfillment in Jesus the Messiah – is not only a recurrent theme but also a controlling heuristic of Paul's thought. This is displayed with special vividness in the Epistle to the Romans.[67]

What I am arguing for here is a redemptive-historical approach toward theological reflection, one that seeks to respect not only the content of Scripture, but also the methodologies and pedagogies of the biblical text. I. Howard Marshall has recently called for the same thing:

> My intuition is that if we are directed by Scripture as our authority in *what* we are to believe and do, then we are also directed in our investigation of *how* we are to interpret Scripture by Scripture itself rather than by any overriding external authority. What we need, then, is some kind of *scriptural* approach to the problem of development and interpretation.[68]

What we see, both within the pages of Scripture itself and in the early development of Christian theology, is that the telling of the story (ultimately the story of Jesus as the fulfillment and goal of Israel's story) in contextually relevant ways and for the sake of contemporary Christian practice was fundamental both to the identity of the people of God and their understanding of the faith. Although often ignored, this is implicit in the New Testament language of "doctrine" and "tradition." Doctrine (διδαχζ), as it was understood by the writers of the New Testament,[69] included the gospel story of Jesus, for doctrine was the teaching of God's redemptive Word and deed.[70] We might think of doctrine as both the declaration of the redemptive drama and its application to the faith and life of the people of God. It seems to me that Vanhoozer is certainly in the ballpark when he comments that "my view is that doctrine is direction for the church's fitting participation in the ongoing drama of redemption."[71] Tradition, that which is handed down, is often a virtual synonym for doctrine in Paul, so much so that the editors of the NIV rendered παράδοιζ ("tradition") as "teaching" in 1 Corinthians 11:2 and 2 Thessalonians 2:15 and 3:6. What was it that was handed down or taught? What was the doctrine that Paul was so careful to teach and protect throughout his epistles? It was the gospel, the story of the fulfillment of Old Testament messianic promise in Jesus Christ.

Is it possible that our theological reflection is tied to the biblical story in such a way that the "eventedness" and particularity of the drama of redemption are theologically crucial ("if Christ has not been raised, then our preaching is in vain and your faith is in vain" [1 Cor. 15:14])? Is it also possible that, if our theologies do not take stock of the historical and organic nature of Scripture and the Christian faith, they risk the very loss of the biblical truth? And is it possible that – to borrow the phrase from Dorothy Sayers – the dogma is the drama? If this is so, it will mean that systematics needs to take a step closer to biblical theology and at least a step or two away from philosophical theology. Systematic theology is about the contextualization of the faith, not an exercise in abstraction. It must be bounded by the biblical story – in method as well as in content.

We need to carefully think through the relationships between systematic theology and biblical theology and between systematic theology and biblical hermeneutics. The academic discipline of biblical theology originally arose in the eighteenth century as an alternative to systematic theology. It was a descriptive discipline that sought to recover the beliefs of the biblical authors, and therein saw no rationale for dogmatics. Yet, the integration of biblical theology into the curriculum of Princeton Seminary under the leadership of B. B. Warfield and Geerhardus Vos did not pit the two disciplines against one another. Indeed, from the beginning of Vos' tenure as professor of biblical theology, systematics was understood as being dependent upon biblical theology. One might well expect Vos to think of all theological reflection as being dependent upon Scripture. He held that systematics is as much a biblical reflection as is biblical theology. The two disciplines differ not in content but merely in mode of organization, biblical theology being organized according to the history of redemption and systematics according to a thematic or topical framework.[72] Warfield argued along similar lines. He envisioned a process of dependence in which exegesis forms the foundation for biblical theology, and biblical theology in turn funds systematics.[73]

> Biblical Theology is not, then, a rival of Systematics; it is not even a parallel product of the same body of facts provided by exegesis; it is the basis and source of Systematics. Systematic Theology is not a concatenation[74] of a scattered theological data furnished by the exegetic process; it is a combination of the already concatenated data given it by Biblical Theology.[75]

Why can the theologian not move straight from exegesis to systematics? Warfield recognized that such a move lends itself to a simplistic proof-text approach to Scripture. The biblical materials exist within an organic-historical unity from which they can never be truly abstracted. Even though systematics focuses upon topical concerns and views Scripture as a completed whole – a canon – the theologian "must recognize the organic unity of the data of Scripture and in this must see the facts not in inductive isolation from one another but in organic relation to one another."[76] While systematic theology presents the biblical materials topically, and hence in a fashion that is not identical to the narrative pattern of Scripture, it must be careful to respect and, whenever possible, work from the historical structure of the text.[77] No contemporary theologian has argued this point as consistently or for so long as Richard Gaffin. The tendency toward abstraction is so strong in the Western theological tradition, the habit of treating the Bible as the servant of a system – as a collection of disconnected proof-texts – is so second-nature to us, the practice of viewing the Bible "as a manual of 'timeless' first principles or static truths" is so common, that the systematician needs to be ever reminded that these are biblical vices, not theological virtues.[78] And that is achieved by anchoring systematics in biblical theology, which focuses upon the very historical and covenantal dynamics that systematics is apt to ignore. If it is true that the biblical message is not merely *situated* within a narrative structure – the progressively unfolding story of creation, fall, Israel, and Jesus – but that the overall theme and point of Scripture *is* that epic story itself, then a systematic theology that fails to think historically and narratively as it thinks topically will not only miss the vitality of Scripture, but also be in danger of sacrificing the integrity and meaning of the text.

Systematics and Hermeneutics. Both Warfield and Murray[79] insisted that systematic theology is dependent upon the proper exegesis of Scripture. The tasks of the exegetical and biblical theologian precede the synthetic and integrative calling of the systematic theologian. A reasonable correlate of this contention is that systematics also bears a dependent relationship to biblical hermeneutics. Where biblical theology is naturally organized textually and historically, systematic theology has tended to access the Bible without reference to the historical nature of biblical revelation and without much attention to contextual issues – that is to say, without respect to sound biblical hermeneutics. But if systematics asks the question, what does the whole Bible teach about X?, then it is inherently connected to *what the Bible teaches* – that is, what Scripture intends to teach, or even what the text demands. Does not the principle "do not go beyond what is written" hold for our theologizing? The single most important principle of hermeneutics – figuring out the meaning of a communication – is *authorial intent*. Just as we expect people to interpret our words according to our intention, so too do the authors of Scripture.[80]

Remember the analogy of faith? There is a closely related traditional principle of biblical hermeneutics called *the analogy of Scripture*. All this means is that Scripture interprets Scripture. But the principle itself has been interpreted in two different ways. Systematic theologians have taken it to mean that different texts which speak to the same topic can be brought together, and the clearer text sheds light on the less clear text. Thus, Scripture interprets Scripture. In biblical theology, however, the analogy of Scripture is understood a bit differently. Richard Gaffin explains the principle this way:

> To say that Scripture interprets itself means that it has one pervasive sense – a unified meaning. Because it is God's word, the Bible is a unity, so that any one part has its place within the unified teaching of the whole. A particular passage is located within a pattern of God-given contexts which can only serve to clarify. The pervasive meaning of Scripture should be brought to bear on any single portion. Biblical revelation is self-elucidating because it has an organic, unified structure.[81]

In short, the principle is simply *follow the story*. Interpret the text as it gives itself to be read. Read the text as it was intended to be read. Do not read the text contrary to the author's intention or contrary to its character. Carl Armerding suggests that the dogmatic approach toward Scripture – reading it by looking for timeless doctrinal verities rather than seeing it as an unfolding story of God's redemptive ways with his creatures – dictates to the text how we will allow it to speak to us. We stop being listeners and become speakers. We become dictators rather than cooperators. Being a listener, however, is a matter of submitting to the text, allowing the biblical authors to speak, and "seeking within the story itself the guidelines for its exegesis."[82]

While not every biblical text is narrative in genre, the ultimate context that controls any text is the overarching story that the Bible tells. "In the final analysis the analogy of Scripture is the analogy of parts in an historically unfolding and differentiating organism."[83] The unity of Scripture – or the Christian faith – is not found within an extra-biblical system or rational principle; it is in the biblical story of the divine purpose for our world. This suggests that the unfolding drama of God's redemptive ways ought to be both the fundamental control upon exegesis and the informing principle of theological reflection.

This is not a new idea in any way. The second-century Rule of Faith (which would become what we call the Apostles' Creed) delineated the faith for believers. To counter heretical interpretations of the faith, Irenaeus and Tertullian used the Rule to declare that the Bible is about the creative and redemptive work of the Triune God.[84] Yet, the Rule was not so much a summary of the content of the Christian faith as it was a direction for the proper interpretation of Scripture. Its broadly narrative form identifies what the Bible is about. Biblical religion is a declaration of the works of the triune God in the progressively historical work of creation, fall, redemption, and new creation. That which Christians are to believe, that which they are to proclaim to the world, is not a collection of static concepts, but a story. And that story is the fundamental principle for the true interpretation of Scripture.[85] Thus, the Rule of Faith provided something of a regulative principle for biblical interpretation: Read the Word according to the story. Look for the declaration of the great things God has done.[86]

Does the emphasis upon authorial intention, the narrative analogy of Scripture, and the early church's use of the Rule of Faith as a hermeneutical guide declare the systematic use of the analogy of Scripture illegitimate? No, but it does set limits upon it. John Murray put it this way: "Texts will not thus be forced to bear a meaning they do not possess nor forced into a service they cannot perform."[87] In other words, the systematic use of the analogy of Scripture should not violate the authorial intention of the text. But this can be stated more positively and concretely. Echoing Vos, Lints aphoristically writes that "theology, in its content and form, ought to be what the Scripture irresistibly demands."[88]

Although Christian theologians have always seen the Bible as authoritative for their reflection, it is often difficult to discern just how the Bible relates to a lot of systematic theology, even within evangelical and Reformed circles. The way Scripture is often employed implies that "whatever is not forbidden is permitted." If we can make something fit with all the statements of the Bible – read as decontextual propositions – we may employ any idea within our theology. But just because we *can* do so does not mean that we *should*. This is the great limitation of thinking of systematic theology as a fundamentally rational enterprise. The law of non-contradiction does not include – nor does it suggest – any positive or constructive ethic for understanding historical or personal dynamics, or for reading texts for that matter. What is needed is a regulative principle for theological construction. Whatever is not demanded by the Word of God is forbidden. Our theologies must tell the story.[89] Simply because an idea might seem justified by a biblical statement, it does not follow that the text should be so understood. Romans 4:17 says that God "gives life to the dead and calls into existence the things that do not exist." This text has often been used as a proof-text for the doctrine of creation out of nothing. Taken as a refrigerator-magnet sort of declaration, one can see how the text might be so used. God calls into being what does not exist. *Creatio ex nihilo*. But, of course, that is not what Paul is saying in Romans 4:17 at all. It is not a reference to the original act of creation, but to God's call of Abraham to faith and fatherhood. To use the text as a proof-text for the doctrine of creation out of nothing is illegitimate, for this ignores the communicative intention of the text, the purpose of the statement within its context in the book of Romans, and its context within the unfolding biblical story. As Christopher J. H. Wright has stated the point, "the text must govern the framework, and not the other way round."[90] What is the framework of which Wright speaks? The biblical drama of redemption – the story that comes from the biblical text – which is the special focus of biblical theology.

THE CHALLENGE OF BIBLICAL THEOLOGY

I have spoken of Scripture as a regulative principle or informing story for the theological enterprise – both in terms of its communicative intent for any particular text and as the cosmic narrative of God's unfolding work of the restoration of all things. However, I have not sought to produce a rule book or a how-to for doing theology. My concern is to apply the Reformation principle of *sola scriptura* for the sake of theological reflection. I feel quite comfortable in this enterprise, for if our theological labors do not take place for the sake of bringing the Word of God home to the contemporary church, then those efforts are in vain. Anchoring systematic theology in biblical theology, with its attendant emphases in the biblical story and authorial intention, does not dictate how systematics must be done. But biblical theology does offer some positive challenges to systematics.

First, biblical theology challenges systematic theology to do justice to the historical character of Scripture. The tendency to abstraction which moves theological reflection toward ahistorical formulations of timeless truths and thus obscures the historical-covenantal dynamic of Scripture must be resisted. As we move away from the historical dynamic and toward the reductively thematic, we will also experience a commensurate loss of biblical meaning. Stated as a positive prescription, persons and events take precedence over ideas and rational neatness in biblical reflection. While inferential relationships are not to be ignored in our systematic endeavors, personal relationships take priority and are the ultimate referents of systematic analysis. Historicity, beginnings and endings, events, development and growth, continuity and discontinuity, and the character of persons must all be part of, or at least accounted for by, the theologian's *system*.[91] The systematic theologian must always respect the nature of Scripture as a *history* of redemption. Put in simplest terms, the narrative structure of Scripture encourages the systematic theologian to think in historical and storied ways, even as he pursues the topical agenda. At the very least, systematic theology needs to reflect on matters that have not often appeared within the traditional *loci* of the discipline. What is the nature of history? Why is story the most foundational form of biblical communication? Why are events so crucial to the gospel story? I suspect that if systematicians were to take up such questions, we would be weaned away from the traditional trajectory of seeing natural religion as the foundation for revealed religion, and in so doing discover greater depths – scandalous depths! – in the personal particularity of the God declared in the biblical story.

Second, biblical theology reminds the systematician that the Bible is more than a repository of things to know. If our theological labors are to provide direction for walking in the way of truth, they need to do more than merely describe the world. They must also generate an identity for those who are called to live the life of faith within the world. This is one of the particular advantages of story over other forms of discourse. Story seeks to depict not merely a way of *seeing* the world, but also a way of *being* within it. As Kevin Vanhoozer aptly notes, "To become a Christian is not to become a subscriber to a philosophy; it is to become an active participant in God's triune mission to the world."[92] And the only way to become such a "participant" is by entering into the story, to take it as our own. The biblical story is not a tale told about strangers, people to whom we have no relation. It is the story of the heirs to the faith of Abraham. It is *our* story, and as such invites us to indwell it. As God's identity is known only by way of the story – his ongoing involvement in his creation with his people – so our true identity can only be known in the same way. This is precisely what Christian faith is all about: the formation of Christian identity as the world of Scripture becomes our world as well. Vanhoozer has recently made the same point:

> As C. S. Lewis knew, stories too are truth bearers that enable us both to "taste" and to "see," or better, to experience as concrete what can otherwise be understood only as an abstraction. What gets conveyed through stories, then, is not simply a proposition but something of reality itself. For example, the biblical narrative does not simply convey information about God but displays God's triune identity itself as this is manifest through the creative and redemptive work of his two hands. One can state "that God is good" in a proposition, but it takes a narrative to "taste and see that the Lord is good."[93]

Third, biblical theology reminds us that our systems are just that – *our* creations. Trevor Hart's comment is a sober relativization of the systematic agenda: "Christian Scripture offers no neat system, and ambitious attempts to systematize it ought to attract suspicion rather than assent in the first instance from those whose concern is faithfulness to the text, and acknowledgment of its authority in the integrally related tasks of theological reflection and Christian discipleship."[94] Scripture does not exist to serve our systems. Just the reverse. Theological reflection takes place for one reason: to help us think through the biblical faith in our moment in history. As such, theology is the servant of the Word of God and faith. Systematics is not the goal of Scripture, but a means for our application of the biblical world to our own.

Finally, as biblical theology is oriented to the historical unfolding of God's redemptive ways, it reminds us of the grand purpose of Scripture – a purpose that all else serves – namely, that biblical religion is not firstly or ultimately about contacting a cognitive deposit of ideas or facts, but coming into a living and vital relationship with the Savior and King who is revealed to us in the biblical Word. When the people of God read the Bible, we are not simply attending words on a piece of paper, or even a story found in a book. We are attending, through the medium of the written word, Jesus Christ our Lord, who is first a person, not an idea or a proper noun. The Bible is referential to the acts of God in history – his *covenantal relationship* with his people. This principle must inform the theologian as he uses this Word and must regulate how he reads it.

1. Max Turner and Joel B. Green, "New Testament Commentary and Systematic Theology: Strangers or Friends?" in Max Turner and Joel B. Green, eds., *Between Two Horizons: Spanning New Testament Studies and Systematic Theology* (Grand Rapids, Mich.: Eerdmans, 2000), 12.

2. E.g. Robert K. Johnston, ed., *The Use of the Bible in Theology: Evangelical Options* (Atlanta, Ga.: John Knox, 1985); Trevor Hart, *Faith Thinking: The Dynamics of Christian Theology* (Downers Grove, Ill.: InterVarsity Press, 1995); Charles J. Scalise, *From Scripture to Theology: A Canonical Journey into Hermeneutics* (Downers Grove, Ill.: InterVarsity Press, 1996); David K. Clark, *To Know and Love God: Method for Theology* (Wheaton, Ill.: Crossway, 2003). Aside from these evangelical contributions, see David H. Kelsey, *The Use of Scripture in Recent Theology* (Philadelphia, Pa.: Fortress, 1975) for a liberal treatment of theological hermeneutics, and Gerald O'Collins and Daniel Kendall, *The Bible for Theology: Ten Principles for the Theological Use of Scripture* (New York: Paulist Press, 1997) for a Roman Catholic treatment.

3. Profound in the sense that I wish I had been exposed to it somewhere during my theological studies (I was not), and provocative in the sense that it will produce a measure of discomfort among many of my peers.

4. By limiting myself to the evangelical and Reformed tradition, I acknowledge the possibility of other ways of envisioning and doing systematic theology. As theological reflection is oriented to the resources for thinking about God and his ways that a tradition accepts as legitimate, the discipline of theology will take on quite different contours.

5. I am here making a distinction between revelation and theology. Revelation is a divine activity; theology is a human activity undertaken in reflective response to revelation. See John Jefferson Davis, *Foundations of Evangelical Theology* (Grand Rapids, Mich.: Baker, 1984), 44; John Feinberg, "Introduction," in David K. Clark, *To Know and Love God* (Wheaton, Ill.: Crossway, 2003), xv; Stanley J. Grenz and Roger E. Olson, *20th-Century Theology: God and the World in a Transitional Age* (Downers Grove, Ill: InterVarsity Press, 1992), 9.

6. See Yves M. J. Congar, *A History of Theology* (New York: Doubleday, 1968), 37ff.

7. Origen's *De Principiis* and Augustine's *Enchiridion* may stand as pre-medieval forays into systematics, as both men sought to produce a sort of compendium of Christian doctrine.

8. G. R. Evans, *Old Arts and New Theology: The Beginnings of Theology as an Academic Discipline* (New York: Oxford, 1980), 137ff.

9. See Thomas Aquinas, *Summa Theologica*, part 1, for a discussion of the divine attributes.

10. Addressing the medieval habit to engage in "ontologizing thought," and thus the development of theology as a "metaphysical science of speculation," Harvie M. Conn notes that "the danger of this abstractionist thinking has always been that things are viewed as existing in themselves without taking into

consideration the relationships in which they stand to other things." (Harvie M. Conn, *Eternal Word and Changing Worlds: Theology, Anthropology, and Mission in Trialogue* [Grand Rapids, Mich.: Baker, 1984], 217–18).

11. Quoted in G. C. Berkouwer, *A Half Century of Theology* (Grand Rapids, Mich.: Eerdmans, 1977), 38.

12. Wayne Grudem, *Systematic Theology: An Introduction to Biblical Doctrine* (Grand Rapids, Mich.: Zondervan, 1994), 29.

13. Kevin J. Vanhoozer, "Lost in Interpretation? Truth, Scripture, and Hermeneutics," *Journal of the Evangelical Theological Society* 48, no. 1 (March 2005): 94.

14. Ibid., 102. Vanhoozer has also employed the metaphor of fishing to describe the proof-text approach toward systematics: "Much systematic theology that passes as 'biblical' enjoys only a casual acquaintance with the biblical texts. The method of proving doctrines by adducing multiple proof-texts leaves much to be desired. One typically begins with a doctrinal confession and then sets off trawling through the Scriptures. One's exegetical 'catch' is then dumped indiscriminately into parentheses irrespective of where the parts are found" (Kevin J. Vanhoozer, "From Canon to Concept: 'Same' and 'Other' in the Relation Between Biblical and Systematic Theology," *Scottish Bulletin of Evangelical Theology* 12, no. 2 [1994]: 104).

15. Trevor Hart, "Tradition, Authority, and a Christian Approach to the Bible as Scripture," in *Between Two Horizons*, 200.

16. For a useful survey of the emergence and history of biblical theology as an academic discipline, see Craig Bartholomew, "Biblical Theology and Biblical Interpretation: Introduction," in Craig Bartholomew, et al., *Out of Egypt: Biblical Theology and Biblical Interpretation* (Grand Rapids, Mich.: Zondervan, 2004), 1–10. For a more detailed exposition, see Charles H. H. Scobie, *The Ways of Our God: An Approach to Biblical Theology* (Grand Rapids, Mich.: Eerdmans, 2003), 9–28.

17. Scott J. Hafemann, ed., *Biblical Theology: Retrospect and Prospect* (Downers Grove, Ill.: InterVarsity Press, 2002), 16.

18. Trevor Hart, "Systematic – In What Sense?" in *Out of Egypt*, 345.

19. Ibid.

20. The debate surrounding historical reference and the Bible is far more complex than we can entertain here. See Scalise, *From Scripture to Theology*, 27–41, and the contributions in Hafemann, *Biblical Theology*. For a recent defense of historical referentiality, see Craig Bartholomew and Michael Goheen, "Story in Biblical Theology," in *Out of Egypt*, 144–71.

21. I. Howard Marshall, *Beyond the Bible: Moving from Scripture to Theology* (Grand Rapids, Mich.: Baker, 2004), 22.

22. John Barton, *People of the Book?* (London: SPCK, 1988), 34, quoted in Trevor Hart, *Faith Thinking*, 114.

23. Hart, *Faith Thinking*, 114.

24. Vanhoozer, "Lost in Interpretation?" 105.

25. Richard B. Gaffin, Jr., "Systematic Theology and Biblical Theology," *Westminster Theological Journal* 38 (1976): 293–4.

26. Quoted in Richard Gaffin, "Introduction," in Geerhardus Vos, *Redemptive History and Biblical Interpretation: The Shorter Writings of Geerhardus Vos*, ed. Richard B. Gaffin, Jr. (Phillipsburg, N.J.: P&R Publishing, 2001 [1980]), xv. The focus of the written biblical word is the redemptive history, which is declared and interpreted by the written word. Vos wrote: "Revelation is so interwoven with redemption [God's redemptive action in history] that, unless allowed to consider the latter, it would be suspended in the air" (Geerhardus Vos, *Biblical Theology* [Grand Rapids, Mich.: Eerdmans, 1948], 24).

27. Gaffin, "Introduction," xvii.

28. Ibid.

29. D. A. Carson, "Systematic Theology and Biblical Theology," in *New Dictionary of Biblical Theology*, (Downers Grove, Ill.: InterVarsity Press, 1988), 102.

30. Grudem, *Systematic Theology*, 21–4.

31. Ibid., 36.

32. For a provocative reflection on the point that our assumptions about the nature of Scripture and how the believer accesses revelation affect what we actually find in the reading of the Bible, see Calvin G. Seerveld, *How to Read the Bible to Hear God Speak: A Study of Numbers 22–24* (Sioux Center, Ia.: Dordt, 2003).

33. Quoted in John Goldingay, *Old Testament Theology*, vol. 1: *Israel's Gospel* (Downers Grove, Ill.: InterVasity Press, 2003), 38.

34. For a helpful summary of speech-act theory, see Kevin Vanhoozer, "The Semantics of Biblical Literature: Truth and Scripture's Diverse Literary Forms," in D. A. Carson and John D. Woodbridge, eds., *Hermeneutics, Authority, and Canon* (Grand Rapids, Mich.: Zondervan, 1986), 85–92.

35. Richard Gaffin has recently noted the phenomenon that some "question the value of biblical theology, if they have already concluded that it has introduced novelties detrimental to the well-being of the church," or that they believe that biblical theology undermines "doctrinal stability by diminishing interest and confidence in the formulations of classical Reformed theology." Yet Gaffin is quick to point

out that biblical theology is no modernist innovation. Centering our faith and our theological reflection upon the history of redemption can be traced to the second century and the church's battle against the Gnostic heresy. Irenaeus of Lyons championed the insight that "salvation resides ultimately not in who God is or what he has said, but in what he has done in history, once for all, in Christ." (Richard B. Gaffin Jr., "Biblical Theology and the Westminster Standards," *Westminster Theological Journal* 65 [2003]: 165.)

36. John Goldingay, "Biblical Narrative and Systematic Theology," in *Between Two Horizons*, 138.

37. Gaffin, "Introduction," xviii.

38. Ibid., xix–xx.

39. Ibid., xx–xxi.

40. "Perhaps it is indeed the case that humanity's rationality necessitates analytic reflection on the nature of the faith; at least, the importance of rationality for intellectuals necessitates our analytic reflection on the nature of the faith as one of the less important aspects of the life of Christ's body. Yet such rational and disciplined reflection need not take the form of systematic theology … We need to distinguish between the possible necessity that the church reflects deeply, sharply, coherently, and critically on its faith, and the culture-relative fact that this has generally been done in a world of thought decisively influenced by Greek thinking in general as well as in particular (e.g. Platonic or Aristotelian)" (John Goldingay, "Biblical Narrative and Systematic Theology," 129).

41. I agree with Richard Gaffin that the topical nature of systematics does not make it an inherently abstract and rationalistic endeavor. While the so-called *loci* method may be easily bent to a dehistorical and decontextual understanding the faith, there is no reason that it must do so. See Richard B. Gaffin, Jr., "The Vitality of Reformed Dogmatics," in J. M. Batteau, et al., *The Vitality of Reformed Theology* (Kampen: Kok, 1994), 28–9.

42. John Murray, "Systematic Theology," in *Collected Writings of John Murray*, vol. 4: *Studies in Theology* (Edinburgh, Scotland/Carlisle, Pa.: Banner of Truth, 1982), 17.

43. John Frame, *The Doctrine of the Knowledge of God* (Phillipsburg, N.J.: P&R Publishing, 1987), 212–14.

44. Richard Gaffin, "Systematic Theology and Biblical Theology," 290.

45. Gaffin cannot seem to make up his mind whether the terms "logical" and "systematic" have any real meaning at all. In one footnote he says that "while the appropriateness of these adjectives for distinguishing the discipline in view is subject to question, surely the intention is to identify its *topical* or loci structure" ("Systematic Theology and Biblical Theology," 290n24). A bit later he writes that "'systematic' or 'logical' hardly serve to identify the topical approach that distinguishes it" (ibid., 295n29).

46. Frame, *The Doctrine of the Knowledge of God*, 214.

47. Harvie Conn, *Eternal Word and Changing Worlds*, 241–2.

48. D.A. Carson, "Biblical Theology and Systematic Theology," 102.

49. Ibid., 103.

50. Willam Edgar, *Truth in All Its Glory: Commending the Reformed Faith* (Phillipsburg, N.J.: P&R Publishing, 2004), 2–3.

51. Unless otherwise noted, Bible quotations in this essay are taken from the English Standard Version (ESV).

52. See Vanhoozer, "From Canon to Concept," 108.

53. Goldingay, "Biblical Narrative and Systematic Theology," 130. Goldingay's comment betrays a false dichotomy, one that can be allowed to stand only as a relative statement identifying a general trajectory, and not an absolute. After all, Scripture does tell us that "God is love" (1 John 4:16).

54. Goldingay, *Old Testament Theology*, 32.

55. Goldingay, "Biblical Narrative and Systematic Theology," 134.

56. Stanley Grenz, *Theology for the Community of God* (Nashville, Tenn.: Broadman and Holman, 1994), 72.

57. Richard Lints, *The Fabric of Theology: A Prolegomenon to Evangelical Theology* (Grand Rapids, Mich.: Eerdmans, 1993), 261.

58. Henry Vander Goot, *Interpreting the Bible in the Church and Theology* (Toronto: Edwin Mellen, 1984), 69.

59. Lints, *The Fabric of Theology*, 264n8.

60. Ibid., 271.

61. Goldingay, "Biblical Narrative and Systematic Theology," 130; *Old Testament Theology*, 28–9, 40–1.

62. Goldingay, *Old Testament Theology*, 31.

63. It is still common within evangelical and Reformed circles to hear the book of Romans described as Paul's systematic theology, by which is meant that Paul is developing doctrine rather than telling or engaging in story.

64. Bruce W. Longenecker, "The Narrative Approach to Paul," *Currents in Biblical Research* 1, no.1 (2002): 88–111.

65. N. T. Wright, *The New Testament and the People of God* (Minneapolis, Minn.: Fortress, 1992), 403–8.

66. Herman Ridderbos, *Paul: An Outline of His Theology* (Grand Rapids, Mich.: Eerdmans, 1975), e.g. 14, 205–6, 214ff, 221–2.

67. Notice Paul's description of the gospel in 1:1–3 as the fulfillment of God's redemptive purposes in Jesus Christ, the covenant indictment against all sin, including the presumptions of God's Old Testament people (1:18–3:20), Abraham as the father of all believers (chapter 4), Christ as the second Adam (5:12-21), the law and sin (2:12-29; 7:7-25), the groaning of creation for the consummation (8:18-30), the future of the Jewish nation (chapters 9–11), the restoration of the law as love (chapters 12–14), Christ the hope of Jews and Gentiles alike (chapter 15). All of these constitute what is essentially a reflection upon the significance of the Old Testament story of Israel in light of the coming of Christ.

68. I. Howard Marshall, *Beyond the Bible*, 48. David Wells was heading in the same direction when he wrote that "the biblical revelation is worked out within a *historical framework* comprised of God's redemptive acts. It is a framework within which meaning is given by God ... Systematic theologians make a great mistake if they allow their systematic interests to carry them away too far from the kind of framework for understanding which Geerhardus Vos provided for us so well" (David F. Wells, "On Being Framed," *Westminster Theological Journal* 59 [1997]: 299).

69. Vos, *Biblical Theology*, 6–7. The New Testament occurrences of διδαχζ are not in and of themselves transparent as to the meaning of the term (Rom. 16:17; Eph. 4:14; 1 Tim. 1:3, 10; 4:6; 6:3; Tit. 1:9; 2:1, 10; Heb. 6:1). The meaning must be inferred from the texts. The same holds for διδχσκαλύα, "the teaching," or "that which is taught" (e.g. Mark 7:7; Col. 2:22; 1 Tim. 1:10).

70. So Vos could say that "without God's acts the words would be empty, without His words the acts would be blind" (Geerhardus Vos, "The Idea of Biblical Theology," 10, quoted in Richard Lints, "Two Theologies or One? Warfield and Vos on the Nature of Theology," *Westminster Theological Journal* 54 [1992]: 247).

71. Kevin Vanhoozer, "Into the Great 'Beyond': A Theologian's Response to the Marshall Plan," in Marshall, *Beyond the Bible*, 87. A bit later in his essay, Vanhoozer helpfully expands upon this definition: "To exposit the Scriptures is to participate in the canonical practices – practices that form, inform, and transform our speaking, thinking, and living. To interpret the Bible in this manner is to make the church itself into an exposition, or what Paul calls a 'spectacle' (*theatron*) to the world (1 Cor. 4:9). This theatrical metaphor highlights the pastoral, and practical, function of doctrine. Doctrine, I submit, is an aid in understanding the *theodrama* – which God has done in Jesus Christ. As such, doctrine provides direction for our fitting participation in the ongoing drama of redemption. It is the canonical script that guides the church's performance of the way, the truth, and the life" (ibid., 94).

72. Vos, *Biblical Theology*, 4-5.

73. Lints notes that "Warfield suggested that biblical theology provides the soil out of which systematic theology grows. To use another metaphor, exegesis is not the proper parent of systematic theology but rather its grandparent. Biblical theology is the proper parent. The data for systematic theology is not individual texts or individual results of exegesis of individual texts but rather the completed conception of revealed truth offered by biblical theology" (Lints, "Two Theologies or One?" 237).

74. *Concatenation*: that which is linked or united into a sequence or system.

75. B. B. Warfield, "The Idea of Systematic Theology," *Presbyterian and Reformed Review* 7 (1896); quoted in Lints, "Two Theologies or One?" 238.

76. Lints, "Two Theologies or One?" 239.

77. Lints notes that the theological method in which systematics is dependent upon biblical theology put forth by Warfield and Vos was an innovative departure from the proof-text method of Charles Hodge (Lints, "Two Theologies or One?" 244n35). He poignantly comments that "it is unfortunate that they have not exercised the influence on later evangelical theological method which their work merits" (ibid., 243n34). Perhaps this was due, at least in part, to the fact that Warfield himself was not very successful in integrating the historicity of the biblical text into his own systematic endeavors. "It is as if he is standing on the edge of the promised land convinced that it must be entered and yet not sure of how to embark on the journey" (ibid., 250).

78. Gaffin, "Systematic Theology and Biblical Theology," 292; "The Validity of Reformed Dogmatics," 22.

79. Murray, "Systematic Theology," 1–2.

80. Stephen Fowl has well defended the notion of authorial intention for hermeneutics, not as an ideal subjective moment in the author's mind but as the "communicative intent" revealed within the text (Stephen Fowl, "The Role of Authorial Intention in the Theological Interpretation of Scripture," in *Between Two Worlds*, 71–87).

81. Richard Gaffin, "Introduction," xvii.

82. Carl Armerding, "Faith and Method in Old Testament Study: Story Exegesis," in P. E. Satterthwaite and D. F. Wright, eds., *A Pathway Into the Holy Scripture* (Grand Rapids, Mich.: Eerdmans, 1994), 46.

83. Gaffin, "Systematic Theology and Biblical Theology," 294.

84. Irenaeus, *Against Heresies*, 1.9.3; 1.10.1, 3; Tertullian, *Prescription*, 1.19.

85. See Paul M. Blowers, "The *Regula Fidei* and the Narrative Character of Early Christian Faith," *Pro Ecclesia* 6 (1997): 199–228; Henri Blocher, "The 'Analogy of Faith' in the Study of Scripture: In Search of Justification and Guide-lines," *Scottish Bulletin of Evangelical Theology* 5 (Spring 1987): 17–38.

86. Robert Wall writes that "there is a sense in which biblical interpretation that is truly Christian in content and result is the by-product of the interpreter whose theological convictions conform to the Rule of Faith" (Robert Wall, "Reading the Bible from within Our Traditions: The 'Rule of Faith' in Theological Hermeneutics," in *Between Two Horizons*, 101).

87. Murray, "Systematic Theology," 21.

88. Lints, "Two Theologies or One?" 247.

89. See John Frame, "Crucial Questions About the Regulative Principle," *Christian Counterculture Newsletter*, May 23, 2005: 1–7, for an appeal for expanding the regulative principle beyond Reformed worship.

90. Christopher J. H. Wright, "Mission as a Matrix for Hermeneutics and Biblical Theology," in *Out of Egypt*, 138.

91. I argue this point at length in a number of essays: "God: Idea or Person? The Necessity of Historical Revelation to a Personal Knowledge of God," *In Covenant* 12, no. 2 (April/May 1997); "Scripture and Theology: Doctrinal Facts, a Community's Narrative, or Redemptive-Historical Fabric?" *Pro Rege* 24, no. 3 (March 1996); "Climbing Out of Lessing's Ditch: History and the Christian Faith," in Michael Bauman, ed., *God and Man: Perspectives on Christianity in the 20th Century* (Hillsdale, Mich.: Hillsdale College Press, 1995).

92. Vanhoozer, "Lost in Interpretation?" 102.

93. Ibid., 109. Some years ago, Harvie Conn put it this way: "From a redemptive-historical perspective the interpreter affirms not only that he or she stands in the same continuum of the presence of the kingdom as, for example, the apostle Paul; the interpreter also affirms that, just as biblical theology demands fullest justice to the cultural context of redemptive history, so the commentator too must look at his or her own situational context with care. Our contemporary setting is part of that flow of redemptive history that is addressed by the Scriptures" (Harvie Conn, *Eternal Word, Changing Worlds*, 228).

94. Hart, "Systematic – In What Sense?" 342.

12
CHRIST-CENTERED ETHICS

DAVID CLYDE JONES
Professor of Theology and Ethics

Show me thy ways, O Lord, and teach me thy paths.
Lead me forth in thy truth, and learn me:
for thou art the God of my salvation;
in thee hath been my hope all the day long.
– Psalm 25:4-5 (Coverdale)

WHAT IS ETHICS?

To comprehend the distinctiveness of Christian ethics, it is useful to begin by asking, What is ethics? The question sounds ungrammatical, but there is a reason for it. Critical reflection on the principles that should guide human conduct was first undertaken by the ancient Greeks, who called such principles *ta ēthika*, "the ethical things." These were originally "customs," but, under critical scrutiny, they became normative principles. The branch of philosophy that studied *ta ēthika* and moved beyond the merely descriptive eventually took its title from the subject matter, and the name "ethics" stuck.[1] So, ethics as a discipline is the study of the principles of human conduct, or "morality," to use the Latin-based synonym. Three types of questions are typically addressed under the rubric of ethics: (1) What is the purpose of human life, that is, its chief end or *summum bonum*? (2) What is moral excellence (virtue) and how is it acquired? (3) What is the standard by which human conduct is measured as right or wrong?

The questions of ethics receive different emphases according to the framework or worldview in which the ethical system is grounded. Classical

Greek ethics was primarily concerned with purpose and virtue questions, to which it sought rational rather than strictly moral answers. The focus was on personal fulfillment rather than obligations to others. The advent of Christianity, with its roots in the earlier biblical covenantal revelation, directed concerns to the question of right and wrong in interpersonal relations, which included man's relationship to God as well as to other human beings and civil society. As the Scripture says, "The one who loves another [lit., "the other"] has fulfilled the law" (Rom. 13:8).[2]

With the secularization of Western culture, a tension has developed in philosophical ethics. Rejecting the ground for moral law in the nature and will of God, many moral philosophers advocate a return to the virtue ethics of the pre-Christian era. The original impetus for the change in direction may be traced to an article by Elizabeth Anscombe, in which she argued that neither of the main contenders in post-Enlightenment philosophical ethics, Kantianism and utilitarianism, makes sense in the context of the collapse of belief in a divine lawgiver.[3] Anscombe proposed a return to Aristotelian ethics, understood as a system of conditional rather than categorical imperatives. As one writer has summed up the point: "Unless we take God to be the authority, we ought to give up talk about moral obligations, and just talk, as Aristotle does, about the virtues – about, that is, the kinds of actions characteristic of a fully developed specimen of humanity."[4] On this view, what are called "moral wrongs" are more properly mistakes in judgment, not failures in duty. Behavior that does not measure up to the standard is deemed "inappropriate" rather than immoral, because for an action to be immoral implies that there is a universal law – and a universal law entails a Lawgiver.

Whether or not the moral law ultimately requires the biblical doctrine of creation to be coherent is a significant talking-point for Christian apologetics. Anscombe was surely correct in her analysis of the unperceived anomaly of arguing over moral law absent a Lawgiver. But her understanding of classical virtue ethics needs to be qualified. Alasdair MacIntyre, himself an advocate of a type of neo-Aristotelian ethics, acknowledges that "it is a crucial part of Aristotle's view that certain types of action are absolutely prohibited or enjoined irrespective of circumstances or consequences."[5] Granted, Aristotle's account of duty is brief – indeed, "so brief as to be cryptic" – but it is there all the same, bearing muted but significant testimony to the truth of Romans 2:15. The witness is more pronounced in Cicero in the century before Christ. There is a natural as well as a scriptural knowledge of the moral law, to which human beings deep down know they are accountable.

Given the biblical revelation of the Triune God as the one and only Lawgiver and Judge (James 4:12), it might seem that biblical ethics should concern itself exclusively with the standard of right and wrong by which human conduct is measured according to the will of God. Such a reduction would seriously undermine the genius of biblical ethics, which never presents the *what* apart from the *how* and the *why*. It is deadly to attempt to expound the precepts apart from grace – "For the letter kills, but the Spirit gives life" (2 Cor. 3:6). The God who commands is also the God who molds human beings into the image of Christ in order to prepare them to share in his kingdom and glory. That dynamic and that vision provide the necessary context for living the Christian life.

Unity of faith and practice is the hallmark of biblical religion. The history of redemption follows this pattern: God reveals his covenant to his chosen friends, who embrace the promise in (divinely engendered) faith, and a distinctive way of life ensues, leading to fulfillment of God's glorious purpose (Gen. 12:1-3, 15:6, 18:17-19). This pattern comes to expression in the prologue and stipulations of the national covenant with Israel (Ex. 20:1-17), and most compactly and eloquently in the Scripture known from its opening word in Hebrew as the *Shema*: "Hear, O Israel: The LORD our God, the LORD is one. You shall love the LORD your God with all your heart and with all your soul and with all your might" (Deut. 6:4-5). A comprehensive and corporate way of life (vv. 6-9) flows from the theological affirmation of the oneness of Israel's God, who has revealed himself as the LORD (Yahweh). In effect, the *Shema* calls God's people to practice the truth they have received, "living the truth in love," as the apostle says (Eph. 4:15).[6]

Goal, motive, and standard are inextricably linked in biblical ethics. The threefold structure characterizes Christian ethics as well as some other systems, but in Christianity it is transformed by becoming radically Christ-centered.

CHRIST-CENTERED PURPOSE

Deep within the human spirit is a longing for meaning, for purpose, for authentic fulfillment, for lasting satisfaction. Everyone has a hungry heart, everyone has a thirsty soul. As the Preacher says, "He has made everything beautiful in its time. Also, he has put eternity into man's heart, yet so that he cannot find out what God has done from beginning to end" (Eccl. 3:11). This "restlessness" and its cure, which Augustine so eloquently articulated in the first book of his *Confessions,* is the centerpiece of St. Paul's evangelistic outreach before the Athenian Areopagus. God, the creator of the world and everything in it, made human beings to live on all the face of the earth "that they should seek God, in the hope that they might feel their way toward him" (Acts 17:27). When he comes to the altar call, the great apostle to the Gentiles points to God's purpose in Christ now fully assured by his resurrection from the dead. Some mocked, others demurred; but some believed, among them two whose names are recorded: Dionysius and Damaris, a subtle reminder, perhaps, that the gospel does not discriminate between male and female. Whatever yearnings human beings have for truth, beauty, and goodness, they have by virtue of their creation in the image of God and preservation by his common grace. These yearnings are intended to lead us back to him in penitent trust. The gospel fits human nature, particularly its aspirations for meaning and significance.

Psalm 25 happens to be the first psalm to contain an explicit reference to God's covenant. Of particular interest is verse 14: "The friendship [mg., "secret counsel"] of the Lord is for those who fear him, and he makes known to them his covenant." The verse is redolent with the intimacy that exists between the Lord and his people. Not for nothing was Abraham called God's friend (Isa. 41:8; 2 Chron. 20:7; James 2:23). But the ultimate expression of this covenant language is reserved for the upper room, on the evening of the Last Supper, where Jesus says to his disciples, "No longer do I call you servants, for the servant does not know what his master is doing; but I have called you friends, for all that I have heard from my Father I have made known to you" (John 15:15). These words prepare us for the full revelation of God's purpose in Christ given through the apostles for the encouragement and edification of believers.

In contrast to the wisdom and rulers of this age, Paul says, "We impart a secret and hidden wisdom of God, which God decreed before the ages for our glory" (1 Cor. 2:7). One expects the words "for his glory," which Paul uses quite often; but here the focus is on the destiny of believers – "what God has prepared for those who love him" – unimaginable things that God has revealed to the apostles through the Spirit (vv. 9-13). God's purpose in Christ for the new humanity that he has redeemed is breathtaking in scope:

> In him we have redemption through his blood, the forgiveness of our trespasses, according to the riches of his grace, which he lavished on us, in all wisdom and insight making known to us the mystery of his will, according to his purpose, which he set forth in Christ as a plan for the fullness of time, to unite all things in him, things in heaven and on earth. (Eph. 1:7-10)

In a parallel text (Col. 1:13-20), mention of redemption and forgiveness of sins again leads Paul to the thought of God's cosmic purpose in Christ, as all things were created through him and for him. "For in him all the fullness of God was pleased to dwell, and through him to reconcile to himself all things, whether on earth or in heaven, making peace by the blood of his cross" (Col. 1:19-20). Paul goes on to reflect on his stewardship "to make the word of God fully known, the mystery hidden for ages and generations but now revealed to his saints ... which is *Christ in you* [plural], *the hope of glory*" (Col. 1:25-27).[7] To the application of verse 28 we will return in due course.

The letter to the Hebrews understands Psalm 8 to be referring to Christ as the one to whom God subjected the world to come. We do not see that world yet, but we do see Jesus, the divine–human Son, "crowned with glory and honor because of the suffering of death, so that by the grace of God he might taste death for everyone" (Heb. 2:5-9). The suffering of death is a jarring note, so the writer goes on to explain, "For it was fitting that he, for whom and by whom all things exist, in bringing many sons to glory, should make the founder of their salvation perfect through suffering" (Heb. 2:10). Later in the epistle, there is this further reflection, highly relevant to ethics that would be Christ-centered: "Although he was a son, he learned obedience through what he suffered. And being made perfect, he became the source of eternal salvation to all who obey him" (Heb. 5:8-9).

This dovetails nicely with Romans 8. The adopted sons of God through faith in Christ are assured that they are destined to inherit, being heirs of God and fellow heirs with Christ, "provided we suffer with him in order that we may also be glorified with him" (Rom. 8:16-17). Lest the thought of suffering take the wind out of anyone's sails, Paul immediately adds, "For I consider that the sufferings of this present time are not worth comparing with the glory that is to be revealed in us" (Rom. 8:18). After pursuing the theme of the redemption of the whole creation and the hope of the resurrection, Paul returns to his exposition of the Christ-centered purpose of God: "And we know that for those who love God all things work together for good, for those who are called according to his purpose." This purpose, expressed in terms very like those in Hebrews, is that God's elect might be "conformed to the image of his Son, in order that he might be the firstborn among many brothers." In pursuit of this purpose, God calls, justifies, and glorifies the people he has chosen and redeemed by his grace. Though called to share in Christ's sufferings as well as his glory, they may be assured that nothing in all creation will be able to separate them from the love of Christ (Rom. 8:35-39).

Paul draws out some of the implications of the Christian hope in a benediction he pens later in the epistle: "May the God of hope fill you with all joy and peace in believing, so that by the power of the Holy Spirit you may abound in hope" (Rom. 15:13). Jesus also struck the note of joy in the upper room when he said to his disciples, "These things I have spoken to you, that my joy may be in you, and that your joy may be full" (John 15:11). The reciprocal joy of Redeemer and redeemed picks up a significant Old Testament theme. The Lord promises those who return to him in response to his gracious gospel invitation, "For you shall go out in joy and be led forth in peace; the mountains and the hills before you shall break forth into singing, and all the trees of the field shall clap their hands" (Isa. 55:12). But mountains and hills singing as an expression of joy pale in comparison to the vision of Zephaniah: "The Lord your God is in your midst, a mighty one who will save; he will rejoice over you with gladness; he will quiet you by his love; he will exult over you with loud singing" (Zeph. 3:17).

Whichever way the question is put – What is the purpose of human life? What is the chief end of man? What is the *summum bonum*? – the New Testament revelation of the will of God in Christ leads to this conclusion: The goal of the new humanity is to share the glory and joy of Christ, and to reign with him in his peaceable kingdom forever.[8] "For the kingdom of God is not a matter of eating and drinking but of righteousness and peace and joy in the Holy Spirit" (Rom. 14:17). The most glorious stage of the kingdom is future, yet it is already present in grace.

CHRIST-CENTERED VIRTUE

The divine purpose for human beings in Christ manifestly requires union with Christ for its fulfillment. Only such persons as share his nature are prepared to share his glory. The central truth of the doctrine of salvation is thus union with Christ. As the Gospel says, "And from his fullness we have all received, grace upon grace. For the law was given through Moses; grace and truth came through Jesus Christ" (John 1:17). So how do we become united to Christ? In the familiar words of the Westminster Shorter Catechism, "The Spirit applies to us the redemption purchased by Christ by working faith in us and thereby uniting us to Christ in our effectual calling" (Q. 30). Effectual calling, I would suggest, is that mighty act of God whereby we are summoned into union with Christ to become partakers of his grace and virtue. The Shorter Catechism is profoundly accurate in its treatment of faith as the graciously bestowed pivot on which the process of salvation turns. Since the word *cardinal* conveys the idea of a hinge, if faith in Jesus Christ is a virtue, it is *the* cardinal virtue. But it is more accurately a saving *grace*, and a virtuous person, on biblical principles, is a *gracious* person whose heart has been regenerated by the Holy Spirit.

Peter calls this initial work of the Holy Spirit in the conversion of sinners "cleansing their hearts by faith" (Acts 15:9) as the word of the gospel goes forth to Jew and Gentile alike. For, Peter says, "we believe that we will be saved through the grace of the Lord Jesus, just as they will" (Acts 15:11). The Christian community is thus later described as "those who call on [i.e. worship] the Lord from a pure heart" (2 Tim. 2:22, with implications for Christian living spelled out in context). In his first epistle, Peter uses an expression that echoes his apology in Acts. He writes to those who have become believers in God through Christ crucified, resurrected, and glorified – believers whose faith and hope are in God, "Having purified your souls by your obedience to the truth for a sincere brotherly love, love one another earnestly from a pure heart, since you have been born again ... through the living and abiding word of God" (1 Peter 1:22-23). As in the salutation to this letter (1 Peter 1:2), *obedience* is the believing response to the gospel, the initial reception and submission to God's gracious word, and commitment to Christ as Savior and Lord. The context of this obedience is the cleansing of the heart through sanctification of the Spirit and sprinkling with the blood of Christ. It is the *obedience of faith* understood as a subjective genitive (the obedience that consists of faith) rather than an objective genitive (the obedience that flows from faith). Both are certainly true, but here the context points to the "hinge" event. Those who have purified their souls by obeying (i.e. responding in faith to) the gospel, are reminded that faith works itself out in love, particularly, though certainly not exclusively, for the Christian community.[9]

The concept of virtue is thus radically altered by the introduction of God's grace. The classical understanding took virtue to be something self-developed, acquired by repetition of good acts until they became second nature or habitual. On this construction, the virtuous person would be necessarily proud, which prompted Augustine to label the virtues on classical principles "splendid vices." On the biblical principle of grace, virtue is not human achievement but divine gift. It begins in faith – itself a posture of humility – and expresses itself in love because it has experienced the love of God. Its hallmark is gratitude rather than pride. The moral life does not consist of virtues to be acquired by human effort, but of fruit to be cultivated by the means of grace under the leading of the Holy Spirit.[10]

Might it not be better, then, for Christian ethics to abandon the term "virtue" altogether? I do not think so. Although the New Testament uses the Greek equivalent *aretē* sparingly (Phil. 4:8; 1 Peter 2:9; 2 Peter 1:3, 5), the thought of moral excellence occurs in many places without the term (e.g. Phil. 1:9-11), and Peter's use of *aretê* in the opening section of his second epistle seems to me to be highly instructive. Here are the relevant verses (slightly abbreviated):

> May grace be multiplied to you in the knowledge of God and of Jesus our Lord. His divine power has granted to us all things that pertain to life and godliness, through the knowledge of him who called us to his own glory and excellence [*aretē*], by which he has granted to us his precious and very great promises, so that through them you may become partakers of the divine nature ... (2 Peter 1:2-4)

> For this very reason, make every effort to supplement your faith with virtue [*aretē*; better, "in your faith supply virtue" (ASV)], and virtue [*aretē*] with knowledge, and knowledge with self-control, and self-control with steadfastness, and steadfastness with godliness, and godliness with brotherly affection, and brotherly affection with love. For if these qualities (*tauta*) are yours and increasing, they keep you from being ineffective or unfruitful in the knowledge of our Lord Jesus Christ. (2 Peter 1:5-8)

I take it that "the knowledge of him who called us to his own glory and excellence," in which the referent is somewhat ambiguous, is specifically "the knowledge of our Lord Jesus Christ," as the last phrase makes clear. The ESV understands "his own glory and excellence" to be a locative rather than an instrumental dative. Hence, the translation is "called to" rather than "called by," which to me makes more sense in this context, where the goal rather than the means of salvation is the paramount concern. Furthermore, it coheres well with what we have already observed from other scriptures about the purpose of God and the glory of Christ. What this verse brings out is the coordination of the glory and moral excellence (*aretē*) of Christ that believers are called to, which carries the thought of the promises by which they become sharers (*koinōnoi*) of the holy nature of God. Union with Christ by faith is the fundamental fact of salvation; conformity to Christ by the enablement of the Spirit is the progressively realized goal of salvation. Peter calls for responsible activity on the part of believers ("make every effort") to richly furnish (*epichorēgeō*) their faith, and to make lavish provision for moral excellence (*aretē* in v. 5), which is equivalent to Christlikeness (cf. *aretē* in v. 3).[11]

Virtue in Christian ethics is thus radically Christ-centered. Paul follows the disclosure of God's rich mystery – "Christ in you, the hope of glory" – with his pastoral concern "that we may present everyone mature in Christ" (Col. 1:28). And he is near exasperation with the Galatians over their misguided attraction to a religion of self-effort: "my little children, for whom I am again in the anguish of childbirth until Christ is formed in you!" (Gal. 4:19). Glorification consists in being made like Christ, the perfect image of God in human nature. The goal is finally attained in the age to come, but even now those whom God calls are being transformed into the Lord's likeness with ever-increasing glory (2 Cor. 3:18; cf. Eph. 4:24, Col. 3:10). As Luther pertinently remarks:

> This life is not righteousness, but growth in righteousness; not health, but healing; not being, but becoming; not rest, but exercise. We are not yet what we shall be, but we are growing toward it; the process is not yet finished, but it is going on; this is not the end, but it is the goal; all does not yet gleam with glory, but all is being purified.[12]

Most intriguing is the observation, "this is not the end, but it is the goal." God's purpose for the people he has redeemed is being realized in the present. What moves them toward that end is the love of Christ. Peter writes to believers undergoing the test of the genuineness of their faith so as to result in praise and glory and honor at the revelation of Jesus Christ: "Though you have not seen him, you love him.[13] Though you do not see him, you believe in him and rejoice with joy that is inexpressible and filled with glory, obtaining the outcome of your faith, the salvation of your souls" (1 Peter 1:8-9). So also Paul: "The love of Christ compels us [lit., "holds us in its grip"] ... He died that [we] might live for him" (2 Cor. 5:14-15; cf. Phil 1:21: "to me to live is Christ"). Paul's meaning in this text is likely Christ's love for us (objective genitive), but there is an inevitable connection with our love for Christ as the supreme motive of the Christian life. As Paul writes elsewhere, "And walk in love, as Christ loved us and gave himself up for us, a fragrant offering and sacrifice to God" (Eph. 5:2). The objective and subjective loves are joined in Paul's benediction at the end of the epistle: "Peace be to the brothers, and love with faith, from God the Father and the Lord Jesus Christ. Grace be with all who love our Lord Jesus Christ with love incorruptible" (Eph. 6:23-24).

CHRIST-CENTERED PRACTICE

The same Lord who, on Mount Sinai, above the thunder and the ear-splitting trumpet, spoke his word of grace — "showing steadfast love to thousands of those who love me and keep my commandments" — in the quietness of the upper room tells his disciples, "If you love me, you will keep my commandments" (John 14:15). Love cleaves to the Savior and is loyal in carrying out his commands, obeying his precepts, practicing his principles. The opposite is also true: "Whoever does not love me does not keep my words" (John 14:24). The principle of obedient love has its origin in nothing short of the inner life of the Holy Trinity, as Jesus repeatedly emphasizes in this context: "I do as the Father has commanded me, so that the world may know that I love the Father" (John 14:31); "If you keep my commandments you will abide in my love, just as I have kept my Father's commandments and abide in his love" (John 15:10). This "abiding in love" is perhaps the most arresting feature of the passage. Jesus says not only, "He who has my commandments and keeps them, he it is who loves me," but strikingly adds, "And he who loves me will be loved by my Father, and I will love him and manifest myself to him" (John 14:21). Again, "If anyone loves me, he will keep my word, and my Father will love him, and we will come to him and make our home with him" (John 14:23). Although now rare in discussions of love in the Bible, the earlier theological distinction between *benevolentia* and *complacentia* is serviceable here. God's antecedent love, by which he chooses and redeems and calls his people to himself, is *pure benevolence*, sovereignly bestowed quite apart from any qualities in the redeemed. God's consequent love, however, does have a reciprocal quality, being the love of *complacence* or *delight*. God's enemies have now through grace become his friends. "The Father himself loves you, because you have loved me and have believed that I came from God" (John 16:17). This is the means by which the joy of Christ is communicated to his people that their joy may be full (John 15:11).

The centerpiece of Christ-centered practice is the new commandment: "A new commandment I give to you, that you love one another: just as I have loved you, you also are to love one another. By this all people will know that you are my disciples, if you have love for one another" (John 13:34-35); "This is my commandment, that you love one another as I have loved you" (John 15:12); "These things I command you, so that you will love one another" (John 15:17). What makes the new commandment new (*kairos*, new in respect to form or quality, fresh) is its concrete demonstration in the life of Christ: "as I have loved you." To walk in God's ways is always in the Scriptures to walk not simply in the ways that God prescribes, but to walk in the paths he has himself marked out by example. This reaches its pinnacle in the incarnate life of the Son of God, who gave ultimate expression to the meaning of obedient love in relation to carrying out the will of the Father.

"As I have loved you" sets before us the complete open-endedness of any discipleship worthy of the name. Jesus not only taught the perfection and spirituality of the moral law in the Sermon on the Mount; he also fulfilled it in his own life of obedience, culminating in the sacrifice of himself on Mount Calvary. The whole Old Testament revelation finds in Jesus "its completion, its fulfillment, its confirmation, its validation."[14] Raised from the dead and given all authority in heaven and on earth as a result of his redemptive accomplishment, Jesus gives to his apostles – and to the whole church through them – the Great Commission to disciple the nations, "baptizing them into the name of the Father and of the Son and of the Holy Spirit, teaching them to observe all that I have commanded you. And behold, I am with you always, to the end of the age" (Matt. 28:20; note the parallel in Josh. 1:8-9).

Sometimes "commandment" (*entolē*) is used in the New Testament (e.g. 1 Tim. 6:14; 2 Peter 3:2) with reference to the whole Christian religion – i.e. the "new law," or better, the New Covenant, the new administration of the covenant of grace, the dynamic of which is the Holy Spirit of promise (Heb. 8:8-12, citing Jer. 31:31-34), who enlightens and moves believers in their new obedience. The Holy Spirit enables believers to yield loving obedience to the Person and precepts of Christ, to which the apostle Paul refers explicitly in two places as the law (*nomos*) of Christ (1 Cor. 9:21; Gal 6:2).

Writing to the Corinthians, Paul feels a need to defend the integrity of his stewardship of the gospel. To some it might appear that he has no core values, that he is as sensitive as anyone else to peer-pressure and thus adjusts his behavior to conform to other people's standards. In response, Paul points out that, in the first place, he is not financially dependent on anyone (1 Cor. 9:15-18), which would be the most plausible reason one might have for trimming one's sails. In this important sense, Paul is "free from all," and his accommodation to various groups is motivated exclusively out of concern for the progress of the gospel among all (1 Cor. 9:19-23). Paul explains: "To the Jews I became as a Jew, in order to win Jews. To those under the law [the Mosaic administration of the Covenant of Grace] I became as one under the law (though not being myself under the law) [because of the change in administration]. To those outside the law I became as one outside the law [*anomos*] (not being outside the law of God but under the law of Christ [*ennomos Christou*]) that I might win those outside the law." In the Corinthian context, the practices that Paul adjusts according to circumstances are clear. As a Christian, he is no longer bound to the dietary restrictions of the Old Covenant, though he is perfectly free to "keep kosher" when among Jews. And he is also perfectly free to change his practice when among Gentiles – though he does not want *anomos* to be misunderstood. He does not mean it to be taken in the *moral* sense ("lawless" is equivalent to "godless" in 1 Tim. 1:9). Paul says he is not lawless toward God; rather he is "inlawed" to Christ, subject to the law of God as incarnated in Christ – which was the goal of the Old Covenant all along (Rom. 10:4). Paul distinguishes between "keeping the law" in the sense of maintaining Jewish distinctives – which had served their (temporary) purpose in the history of redemption – and following the principles and precepts of Christ – which of course overlap with the previously promulgated moral commandments of God (1 Cor. 7:19), now written on the heart by the promised Spirit of God (Ezek. 36:26-27).

In Galatians, the ministry of the Holy Spirit is even more pronounced. Paul has one overriding concern: that "Christ is formed in you" (Gal. 4:19). But the way in which the Galatian Christians are going about it, relying on the law rather than the Spirit and thus compromising the gospel of grace with an anti-gospel of self-effort, will in the end be their undoing. "For," Paul says pointedly, "if a law had been given that could give life, then righteousness would indeed be by the law" (Gal. 3:21). The law is worse than useless if it is thought to have inherent power to subdue the self-centeredness of human nature and to produce the fruit of righteousness. Read the psalms (particularly Ps. 119) that speak highly of the law of the Lord, and notice how often praise for the divinely revealed way of life is accompanied with prayer for divine illumination and enablement. "Lead me forth in thy truth and learn me," runs the Coverdale translation of Psalm 25:5, capturing in now archaic English the causative force of the Hebrew. The whole of Galatians 5 takes up the role of the Spirit in the life lived in the freedom of the gospel, epitomized as "faith working through love" (Gal. 5:6) – love being above all the fruit of the Spirit (Gal. 5:22). In contrast to the community-destroying works of the flesh, the fruit of the Spirit, being the qualities of Christ himself, are eminently community-building.

The first application of Christlikeness is the gentle restoration of those caught in some transgression, a restoration founded in the humility of recognizing one's own dependence on the means of grace. "Bear one another's burdens," Paul adds – which surely includes the ministry of restoration he has just highlighted – "and so fulfill the law of Christ" (Gal. 6:2). Burden-bearing essentially characterized the life of Christ (cf. Isa. 53:4), and believers are called to love as he loved. To fulfill the law of Christ is to follow Jesus' teaching and example. All the great example texts in which believers are called to imitate Christ' love (Eph. 5:1-2), humility (Phil. 2:1-11), obedience (Heb. 5:8-9), service (Mark 10:45), and endurance (1 Peter 2:21) have this in common: *the cross*. So the apostle John draws out the implication: "By this we know love, that he laid down his life for us, and we ought to lay down our lives for the brothers" (1 John 3:16). The first application, however, is not martyrdom, but the sharing of economic resources: "But if anyone has the world's goods and sees his brother in need, yet closes his heart against him, how does God's love abide in him? Little children, let us not love in word or talk but in deed and in truth" (1 John 3:17-18).

Conclusion

The goal of the new humanity is to share the glory and joy of Christ. What impels believers to seek this end is the love of Christ. The means to fulfillment is to practice the law of Christ, to walk in his ways, to follow his example. Paul completes the circle of Christ-centered goal and Christ-centered practice when he says, "The Spirit himself bears witness with our spirit that we are children of God, and if children, then heirs – heirs of God and fellow heirs with Christ, provided we suffer with him in order that we may also be glorified with him" (Rom. 8:16-17). The joy that is the fruit of the Spirit is the joy that is born of the pursuit of excellence in fulfilling the law of Christ, "looking to Jesus, the founder and perfecter of our faith, who for the joy that was set before him endured the cross, despising the shame, and is seated at the right hand of the throne of God" (Heb. 12:2).

1. And we seem to be stuck with it, despite the fact that it is not the language of the NT, which, following the pervasive OT usage, speaks of "the way (*hodos*) of the Lord" or "the way of God" or "the way of salvation" or "the way of truth" (Acts 18:25-26, 16:17; 2 Pet 2:2). In light of this, and the NT preference for *anastrophē* (manner of life, behavior), I have previously offered the following definition: "Christian ethics is the study of the way of life that conforms to the will of God as revealed in Christ and the holy Scriptures and illuminated by the Holy Spirit" (David Clyde Jones, *Biblical Christian Ethics* [Grand Rapids, Mich.: Baker, 1994], 16).

2. Unless otherwise indicated, Bible quotations used in this essay are taken from the English Standard Version (ESV).

3. G. E. M. Anscombe, "Modern Moral Philosophy," *Philosophy* 33 (1958): 1–19.

4. Robert B. Kruschwitz and Robert C. Roberts, eds., *The Virtues: Contemporary Essays on Moral Character* (Belmont, Calif.: Wadsworth, 1987), 4.

5. Alasdair MacIntyre, *After Virtue: A Study in Moral Theory*, 2nd ed. (Notre Dame, Ind.: University of Notre Dame Press, 1984), 150.

6. Most translations render this phrase "speaking the truth in love," but the Greek is literally "truthing in love" (*alētheuontes en agapē*). In Gal. 4:16 the meaning of the participle is clearly "speaking the truth," but in this context a broader perspective is likely in view of such expressions as "the body ... builds itself up in love" (v. 16), "the truth is in Jesus" (v. 21), and "walk in love" (5:2).

7. See also 2 Thess. 2:14: "To this he called you through our gospel, so that you may obtain the glory of our Lord Jesus Christ."

8. One of Augustine's formulations of the *summum bonum* appears to capture something of this: "The happy life is joy born of the truth (gaudium de veritate)." Cited in Servais Pinckaers, *Morality: The Catholic View* (South Bend, Ind.: St. Augustine's Press, 2001), 77.

9. It should perhaps be noted that, whereas the law (or Covenant of Works) imposes real conditions, the gospel (or Covenant of Grace) is wholly gratuitous, so that faith and repentance are simply the means by which God applies to the sinner life and salvation; they are not legal requirements but gracious endowments.

10. NT virtues are consistently described as fruit: of faith, of righteousness, of the gospel, of the vine, of the Holy Spirit.

11. Cf. John W. Sanderson, "We are tempted therefore to say that the 'moral excellence' of 2 Peter 1:5 is Christlikeness" (*The Fruit of the Spirit* [Phillipsburg, N.J.: P&R, 1985], 147).

12. Cited in John Theodore Mueller, *Christian Dogmatics* (St. Louis, Mo.: Concordia Publishing House, 1934), 389.

13. The epigraph to Jonathan Edwards' *Religious Affections*.

14. John Murray, *Principles of Conduct* (Grand Rapids, Mich.: Eerdmans, 1956), 150. For a full presentation, see Edmund P. Clowney's final book, completed shortly before he departed this life: *How Christ Transforms the Ten Commandments* (tentative title, forthcoming from P&R).

13

CHRIST-CENTERED EDUCATIONAL MINISTRY:

An Overview of Frameworks and Practices

DONALD C. GUTHRIE
Associate Professor of Christian Education
Vice President for Academics

BUILDING A FRAMEWORK FOR EDUCATIONAL MINISTRY

One of the favorite pastimes of the beloved comic strip characters Calvin and Hobbes is playing a game they call Calvinball. It's a simple game – it usually includes a ball and some rules. Humorously, the game is fun at first as the ball takes different shapes and sizes, and so do the rules. As the game goes on, both contestants seek to gain an advantage by habitually reinterpreting the rules just uttered by the other player. Neither side ever wins and both characters eventually end up feeling manipulated. Calvinball is what you get when you make up the rules as you go. It is also what happens when educational ministries have no center or grounding. It is what happens when one does not employ a framework. Perhaps too many of us are playing Calvinball in our educational ministries.

An educational framework is a theoretical structure that accounts for an author or thinker's assumptions, worldview, and practices. In a real sense, Jesus provided his "framework" for living when he uttered the greatest commandment. As Christian educators, we respond to that framework of loving God and neighbor and thus place Jesus' norm in the center of our ministries. Using this foundational framework allows us to understand and act in God's world by asking and answering the crucial question: What must we account for as we plan, conduct, and evaluate our ministry in light of the lordship of Jesus Christ and his framework? Our response follows his initiative. Therefore, I strongly encourage all educators to reflect carefully about the frameworks we employ, whether tacitly or explicitly, even as he is the center of our service. If you have not yet named your framework, give it a try. Work at it. Test it. Discuss it with others. Modify it. Whatever you do with it, do it to the glory of God.

Contemporary Christian educators who have proposed helpful frameworks include Habermas (reconciliation), Kuhl (kingdom of God), Anthony (spiritual formation), and Pazmino (foundational integrative).[1] We educators would do ourselves and our participants a service by examining any or all of these works as we plan and pray for our educational ministries. Common themes from these four frameworks include: grounding all concepts and practices in Scripture, embracing the cooperative nature of the sanctification process that goes on between God and Christians, recognizing that all of life is to be lived in response to and under the lordship of Jesus Christ, and harnessing the insights from a wide variety of theologians and theorists for the good of God's people.

My ongoing reflection on the question of what we must account for as we plan, conduct, and evaluate our ministries has led me to a working outline that includes the following framework factors: Participants, Context, Curriculum, Process, Accountability, and Authority. It should be noted that any framework is constructed from a particular perspective. There is no such thing as a view from nowhere. We must account for our own assumptions, biases, and perspectives. The Lord regularly overcomes such human limitations to provide potentially helpful tools to his people through human means. It is fruitful to examine each element of the framework separately, although each is closely bound to the others. Thus, we could link them together by completing a "catechetical" question and response: *Q: What must we account for as we plan, conduct, and evaluate our educational ministry? A: The Participants in a Context through a Process with a Curriculum towards Accountability under Authority.*

Although these elements could easily be examined at length, for the purposes of this overview, I will offer only a brief description of each.

Element 1: The Participants

Broadly speaking, the participants in educational ministry include teachers, learners, pastors, staff members, curriculum writers, volunteer leaders, the churched and non-churched, and God himself. These participants may be thought of as stakeholders with both articulated and unspoken interests. They express their interests directly and indirectly by planning, approving, funding, leading, attending, ignoring, and evaluating educational programs. Obviously, without participants, there is no educational ministry. By accounting for the interests of the participants, the educational planner goes a long way toward assuring the active, engaged presence of the participants. The educator should ask questions such as:

- What are God's interests for the teachers and learners (Phil. 2:21)?
- What do the participants already know?
- What are they ready to learn?
- What kinds of learning styles do the learners possess?
- Who makes decisions?
- What is learned at what rate in what contexts?
- Who will teach?
- Who will learn?

Element 2: In a Context

The context for educational ministry includes its history, culture, practices, learning climate, and environment. Accounting for the context of ministry may be the most overlooked factor in this framework among evangelical ministries. I do not believe this is a malicious oversight, just a critical one. We should take our cue from the Lord Jesus Christ himself, for the incarnation is the beginning point of all discussion regarding context for ministry. He is the Word made flesh who has dwelt among us, as John describes him in John 1:14. God declares in Jesus Christ that the creation is neither beyond the scope of his redemptive gaze nor beyond the grasp of his redemptive hand. In light of his gospel, we could ask questions such as:

- What has gone on here before us in God's providence?
- What are we inheriting from previous participants and programs?
- What are the participants' current cultural practices?
- What has God built into the physical world that might be used in the learning process?
- What needs to be and can be changed?
- Where will the learning take place?
- How will the teachers and learners facilitate a healthy psychological and physical learning climate?

Element 3: With a Curriculum

There is nothing more exciting than playing a role in God's plan to reconcile someone to him. Participating in the grand story of creation, fall, redemption, and consummation is a truly humbling and exhilarating experience. We are perhaps most human when we hear and tell and live the gospel, because it is in the gospel that we enjoy the full benefits of God's redemptive actions this side of eternity. It is this activity of teaching and learning how to respond to the gospel that forms the core of our curriculum.

Curriculum is often thought of as the content, with a particular scope and sequence, that is to be delivered to learners. For Christian educators, the Bible is at the center of this content, along with church history, systematic theology, and contemporary Christian perspectives. Bible-based curriculum is scoped and sequenced in such a way that the teacher and student know how much there is to learn, in what order, and in what increments. Often produced by publishing houses, this type of curriculum has a dependable feel and look to it. To be sure, in a confessionally grounded church or denomination, this is a large and necessary part of the element we call curriculum. It is especially useful for instructing children or new believers in the rich foundations of the faith. However, curriculum also includes more than text-based lessons that assume a didactic delivery methodology.

More broadly understood, curriculum reflects an outlook similar to that expressed in Deuteronomy 6 – an "as you walk along the way" approach to teaching and learning. Its scope is the whole of God's creation and its sequence is informed by daily living. Incorporating this approach into our educational ministries can be a significant challenge. It requires creaturely creativity involving the creation. Christians in other contexts may more easily approach teaching and learning as an integrated daily process. However, we North Americans generally find the Deuteronomy 6 perspective quite a challenge given our individualistic, fast-paced, consumer-driven culture. Briefly stated, as educators, we must explore ways in which to wed our traditional dependence on church-located, text-based approaches with approaches that account for personal and technological availability at home, play, and work – and everywhere in between.

This Deuteronomy 6 perspective is why I place methodology under Element 3 in the framework. If learning to love God and neighbor in all of life is our curricular goal, then educators must exploit every redemptive method available. For example, educators can promote general critical thinking with all age groups whether the specific curricular material includes Scripture, films, music, or literature. Building the skill of critical thinking promotes a way of seeing and thinking among Christians that helps them own their faith even as they model the mind of Christ. As we account for our learners' needs, styles, and interests, may God grant us wisdom to choose appropriate methods to match the wideness of his redemptive intentions.

Element 4: Through a Process

The process element in this framework includes both the planning and learning processes. As stated above in Element 1: Participants, planning goals, and processes must account for the participants' interests and decision-making capacities. But how? Once the participants' interests have been identified through multiple feedback systems, they must be negotiated within the relationships of power present on the planning team. Since power is the capacity to act or influence, everyone has power, however much or little. Christian educational planning teams constantly face the challenge of stewarding their own power and interests even as they seek to represent the interests of participants who are not physically present at the planning table, including God.

Planning teams should ask themselves questions that will help draw their attention to appropriate relational, representational, and stewardship issues, questions such as:

- Who has an interest in the program, issue, or meeting?
- What are the interests?
- How do these interests relate to one another?
- What is the relative merit and importance of each interest?
- What are the power relationships among the interested parties?
- Which negotiation strategies would be most appropriate given the interests and power relationships among the stakeholders?
- How do our biblical, theological, and ethical convictions inform our choices and decisions about such things as budget and funding priorities, evaluation strategies, teaching methods, teacher selection, safety, and dispute resolution?

Educational goals and processes are not new concepts for the Christian educator. What might be new, however, is to understand that for Christians, the goal of conforming to the image of Christ is the conforming process itself. In other words, the goal is the process and the process is the goal. This is perhaps how best to understand the core of what it means to conduct "Christ-centered educational ministry." It is to participate in the wonderful eschatological mystery of Christ in us, the hope of glory – the "already/not yet" aspect of our sanctification. As Paul writes in Philippians 1:6, "He who began a good work in you will carry it on to completion."

This wedding of goal and process is especially crucial as Christians follow Christ in our increasingly postmodern contexts. The more Christians mature, the more they realize how dependent they are on God and how interdependent they are as members of the body of Christ (John 14, 16; 1 Cor. 12; Eph. 4). A maturing Christian is one who, through the ministry of the Holy Spirit, moves from resisting God's discipline to accepting God's discipline to seeking God's discipline. The core of educational ministry lies in this mysterious interplay between goals and processes. Superintended by the Holy Spirit, the goal and process of educational ministry may be summarized as: The iterative critical evaluation of participant assumptions, under the authority of Scripture, moving toward maturity in Christ, among the church, in God's world, for the sake of others.

This multi-pronged description requires some explanation in addition to the previous discussion about maturity. First, the sanctification or discipleship process is iterative – and that is a good thing! We hardly become fully mature in a lifetime, let alone a day. This reality awaits us in glory. However, we do grow and develop as whole people created in God's image. This creational truth extended to Jesus himself as Luke reports that Jesus "grew in wisdom and stature and in favor with God and man" (Luke 2:52). Imagine! The second person of the Trinity accumulated wisdom as well as height, reputation as well as skills. Jesus' human development should encourage us to pay close attention to factors such as what developmental psychologists call teachable moments, age-appropriate learning materials, and age/stage and phase/transition theory. We can harness insights from the social and psychological fields knowing that God built progressive and iterative holistic growth into the very fabric of our image-bearing being.

Secondly, following the normative pattern of Jesus, educators should employ the critical evaluation of assumptions in ministry. Jesus was the great assumption checker. His very presence caused human beings to ponder a response to the reality of God incarnate. Jesus' questions pierced the hearts and minds of his hearers. Effective use of critical thinking, skill building, disequilibration theory, and Bloom's taxonomy, for example, can harness the powerful notion that people learn best when their deepest convictions are challenged, reconsidered, and reformulated. This fact should cause us to polish our question-asking skills for use with all age groups.

In addition to challenging our learners to evaluate their assumptions critically, we should also provide structure and support for them throughout the learning process. This trio of challenge, structure, and support must be kept in healthy tension. Too much of one or two of these factors will skew our ministry with growing believers. By maintaining all three in healthy tension, we can more effectively meet emerging needs and address God-designed personalities and patterns.

Element 5: Towards Accountability

The final three factors of the goal and process of educational ministry (see Element 4) might be considered under this element because all educational activity takes place among the church, in God's world, and for the sake of others. These three factors remind us that we are members of a dynamic, organic body in our Father's world, working as his ambassadors for others' sake (Matt. 25:31-46, 1 Cor. 10:23–11:1; 2 Cor. 5:17-21). They also remind us that God does not overlook his intentions for appropriate responses from his creation. The patterns he set forth are for our benefit. When we go against his good will, it is truly no good for us, either in this life or throughout eternity. Such accountability is sobering as well as freeing. In his revealed Word, God has let us know who he is, who we are, where we stand, what is required, and where we are going.

The general evaluation of program goals and processes fits well under the accountability element. We must do more than sending our "hired" volunteer teachers into the classroom with such assurance as "Thank you for teaching Sunday school for the rest of your life. Call me if you need me." In addition to many off-the-shelf evaluation methods that would strengthen our programs and teaching, one simple tool is CATs, or Classroom Assessment Techniques. CATs provide immediate feedback for the teacher and reflection-on-learning for the learner. Following a lecture or discussion, learners articulate major themes and remaining questions. Teachers are then able to capitalize on learner response to fine-tune delivery, and learners benefit from increased attention to reflection-on-learning – which has been demonstrated to increase learning depth significantly.

Element 6: Under Authority

God's loving initiative toward his people includes gracious provision for all we need. Thus, his authority over us is not a suffocating, crimping rule, but rather, a freeing, liberating emancipation from the grip of sin. Just as he made all things, he has also established what the appropriate responses toward him and toward our fellow creatures should be. Figure 1 (see below) depicts God's intended relational responses from his creation. God created all things good, and, even though all good things are marred by the Fall, God's comprehensive restoration includes the ability to respond appropriately to him, to one another, and to the wider creation as he originally intended. He is redeeming each relationship and will ultimately bring each relationship to its intended harmonious end through Jesus Christ by the power of the Holy Spirit. In light of the good Creator, Redeemer, and Sustainer's wonderful plan, how fitting it is for Christians to celebrate God's authority in their lives.

FIGURE 1

God's Intended Relational Responses from His Creation

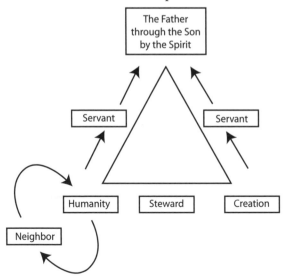

This delight in God extends, of course, to a delight in his Word. In Paul's excellent summary from 2 Timothy 3:16, we are told that Scripture is God-breathed and useful for teaching, rebuking, correcting, and training for righteousness. Paul explains that the goal of the Word's usefulness is the thorough equipping of young Timothy for every good work. Questions we should ask ourselves are:

- How do we delightfully steward the treasure of God's Word so that it bears fruit in God's season?
- How do we nurture learner responses that account for God's intention for us as servants, neighbors, and stewards?
- How could Christians encourage one another to yield joyfully to God's good will in the face of trials and triumphs?
- How might we advance this culturally subversive ethic of willful submission in our ministry, work, and family contexts – contexts in which this is a strange activity indeed?

CURRENT TRENDS AND PRACTICES

Many current trends and opportunities in educational ministry may be noted to help us answer the questions raised above. These include the increased use of case-study teaching; the combining of mercy and teaching ministries; a decreased dependence on lecture-only teaching methodologies; a growing ability to engage and discern media influence and technology; and a broadened use of manuscript Bible study, book and movie discussion clubs, and pre-evangelistic home studies.

Finally, one trend that requires particular attention is the move toward more intergenerational teaching and learning programming. Christian educators should enthusiastically embrace such opportunities, for it is long past time to consider the implications of our over-reliance on affinity- and age-based strategies. In the final section of this essay, we will consider briefly the topic of intergenerational teaching and learning issues as a case study. In this way, we can observe how the framework might be applied in practice to a specific ministry area.

INTERGENERATIONAL OPPORTUNITIES

I will utter hidden things, things from of old –
what we have heard and known,
what our fathers have told us.

We will not hide them from their children;
we will tell the next generation
the praiseworthy deeds of the Lord ...
and they in turn would tell their children. (Psalm 78:2b-4, 6 NIV)

A generation is often understood as a group of people born within the same general time period who share collective interests and who experience common societal events. The time-span between one generation and the succeeding generation is usually estimated at twenty-five to thirty-five years. While it is often difficult to determine exactly when one generation ends and another begins, we can get some sense of the scope of a particular generation by looking at the important societal and/or global events that shape it. Thus, we refer to those who were at least in their young adult years during the Great Depression and World War II as the "Builder Generation." We characterize the "Boomer Generation" as those born in the large cohort following World War II until the early 1960s. The generation after that, often called Generation X, we might also refer to as the "Busters" because of their relatively small birth cohort from roughly the early 1960s through the early 1980s. Finally, the current generation of young people has been labeled the "Millennials" because they span the second and third millennia and were born from the early 1980s through today.

Before going any further, we should affirm the notion that generational analysis is a productive but necessarily broad approach. A person may or may not find himself identifying with all of his generation's characteristics, but he nevertheless is influenced by the sociological and historical realities in which he has participated. Thus, we can safely, though carefully, discuss generational and intergenerational ministry.

Many resources exist that discuss the similarities and differences among all four current generations and their significance in various contexts. For example, a business management text may look at generational realities in order to train "Boomer" managers in the fine art of managing part-time "Millennial" hires. Another example might find a volunteer agency researching how to recruit "Builders" because that generation is known for its dependability and battle-tested wisdom. Whatever the desired end, it is clear that generational study is a hot topic in many fields, businesses, agencies, and institutions, including the church.

It is appropriate for the church to explore generational ministry because the Bible itself depicts God's redemptive ministry throughout all generations. Amazingly, God guarantees the generational transmission of the gospel by entrusting it to forgetful people whom he empowers to pass it on to equally forgetful offspring. How does he overcome such forgetfulness? By wisely grounding the gospel's core in his own character, by wisely rooting the gospel's security in the finished work of Jesus Christ, and by wisely ensuring the gospel's fruitfulness in the ministry of the Holy Spirit. Out of this sure foundation, he gifts his people to communicate his message in their own generation even as he assures that every generation hears the gospel.

Thus, in addition to the *trans*generational nature of the gospel, the Bible robustly assumes an *inter*generational stance throughout its pages. Whether it is genealogies in Numbers, Moses' exhortations in Deuteronomy, Asaph's declaration in Psalm 78, remnant pledges in the prophets, Jesus' promises in the gospels, or Paul's instructions to Timothy in the Epistles, Scripture situates the gospel's proclamation in the midst of multiple generations serving God together.

Given this brief biblical apologetic, how can God's people nurture such intergenerational contexts and relationships as they seek to serve God's kingdom purposes today? How might God's people maximize the strengths of one generation to serve the needs of other generations? The literature on and practice of intergenerational ministry has grown slowly but steadily over the years. Educational ministry leaders in local churches continue to wrestle with the tension between offerings that categorize participants by age or stage of life and those that encourage a mix according to affinities or life transition events. According to practitioners and the literature, the wisest course continues to be some blending of the two approaches.

Suppose a local church wants to experiment with intergenerational ministry options. What should the leaders account for as they pray and plan? What questions could they ask in light of the framework? Here are some possibilities:

1. *Participants*
- Who has an interest in the program?
- What are the interests of the potential participants?
- How might the planners find answers to these questions?
- Should they conduct surveys or interviews?
- Who has the power or needs to be empowered to make decisions regarding the information-gathering findings?
- Who are potential internal or external partners with whom the planners might consult?

2. *Context for Ministry*
- Where is the church located?
- What have been or are local ministry opportunities in which an intergenerational approach may be appropriate?
- What is the church's history with intergenerational initiatives?
- What has already been done?
- What is currently being planned?
- Where has the Lord brought about fruitful ministry in the life of the congregation?

3. *Curriculum*
- What kinds of programs will be offered?
- How will the group decide the ratio of young-to-old, old-to-young, and combined offerings?

- Does the church desire an inward, edifying program purpose, an outward, service program purpose, or a combination of the two?
- Are there existing best-practice sites the leaders might visit in order to gain insight about their own planning and materials?
- Will leader training be needed?

4. *Process*
- What needs to be done first?
- What kind of step-back plan needs to be devised in order to identify goals, program options, event timing, advertising, etc.?
- Can the existing budget carry intergenerational initiatives or will special funding need to be secured? Who will need to sign off either way?

5. *Accountability and Authority*
- How will the initiatives be evaluated and by whom?
- What rubric exists or needs to be developed in order to accurately evaluate our program goals?
- How will the participants know to what extent learner needs are met and God is glorified?

While intergenerational ministry is difficult to measure, it would appear that such ministry is an occasional reality in the North American church. As is the case with most new ventures, it is highly advisable to begin a ministry of this sort with small practices and build momentum toward more comprehensive offerings.

Whether focusing on intergenerational ministry or some other educational area, Christian educators should seek to cultivate a robust, Christ-centered and Christ-honoring framework for ministry and avoid the pitfalls of Calvinball. Read widely. Reflect carefully on your practice. Experiment with methods and curriculum. Seek feedback. Pray for wisdom. Follow the Holy Spirit's lead as you respond to his conviction and guidance. Make the judgment call: What do you need to account for as you plan, conduct, and evaluate your ministry in light of the lordship of Jesus Christ and in response to his foundational framework of love for God and love for neighbor?

RECOMMENDED RESOURCES FOR FURTHER INVESTIGATION

Anthony, Michael, ed. *Introducing Christian Education: Foundations for the Twenty-First Century*. Grand Rapids, Mich.: Baker Book House, 2001.

Cross, Patricia, and Thomas Angelo. *Classroom Assessment Techniques*, 2nd ed. San Francisco: Jossey-Bass Publishers, 1993.

Epstein, Ann S., and Christine Boisvert. *Let's Do Something Together: Identifying the Effective Components of Intergenerational Programs*. Ypsilanti, Mich.: The High/Scope Educational Research Foundation, 2003.

Generations United (a national membership organization focused on promoting intergenerational strategies, programs, and public policies) Web Site: http://www.gu.org.

Habermas, Ronald T. *Teaching for Reconciliation: Foundations and Practice of Christian Educational Ministry*, rev. 10th ed. Eugene, Ore.: Wipf and Stock Publishers, 2001.

Harkness, Allan G. "Intergenerational Christian Education: An Imperative for Effective Education in Local Churches, Parts 1 and 2." *Journal of Christian Education* 41, no. 2 (July 1998): 5–14, and 42, no. 1 (May 1999): 37–50.

Kuhl, Roland G. "The Reign of God: Implications for Christian Education." *Christian Education Journal* NS 1, no. 2 (Fall 1997): 73–88.

Pazmino, Robert W. *Foundational Issues in Christian Education: An Introduction in Evangelical Perspective*. Grand Rapids, Mich.: Baker Book House, 1988.

Rosebrook, Vicki, and Elizabeth Larkin. "Introducing standards and guidelines: A Rationale for Defining the Knowledge, Skills, and Dispositions of Intergenerational Practice." *Journal of Intergenerational Relationships: Program, Policy, and Research* 1, no. 1 (2003): 133–44.

---

1. See the list of Recommended Resources at the end of this essay for further reading on these and other topics related to Christian education.

14

THE SEARCH FOR TRUTH
IN PSYCHOLOGY AND COUNSELING

RICHARD WINTER[1]
Professor of Practical Theology

𝕴n the early years of the twenty-first century we find our Western world inundated with many different systems of counseling and psychotherapy. Most therapists use a pragmatic mixture of theories and techniques. This is characteristic of the postmodern era where no one theory or school dominates the field. To understand where we are today, it is helpful to reflect on the roots of twentieth-century psychology.

Since around 1900, there have been an increasing number of schools of psychology and psychiatry from which most of the contemporary therapeutic practices have sprung. From its earliest days as a scientific discipline, psychology wanted to establish itself on an equal footing with the other sciences. Prior to that time, there had been no lack of psychology, counseling, and psychotherapy in all cultures, but it was not established as a systematic, scientific body of knowledge and practice. Through the centuries there has always been much practical wisdom, often mixed with ignorance and superstition, in the secular therapies of each age. The early church fathers, the Reformers, and the Puritans left a treasure of pastoral counseling literature.[2] One issue of the *Journal of Psychology and Christianity* looked at the contributions of Augustine, Thomas Aquinas, and Richard Baxter, among others.[3] Eric Johnson and Stanton Jones have a helpful overview of "A History of Christians in Psychology" in their book *Psychology and Christianity: Four Views*.[4]

In the late nineteenth and twentieth centuries, the church was strongly influenced by revivalism, pietism, and early liberalism, and seemed to have lost sight of the depths of the depravity of the human heart, understood so well by the early Puritans. It thus gave relatively simple and superficial solutions to the problem of human sin and brokenness. Powlison writes of evangelical fundamentalism in the last generation offering simplistic formulae and truisms. "The church was weak where psychology was strong."[5] This sad vacuum in the evangelical church meant that secular psychology, laden with humanistic assumptions, was taken into the church carelessly and uncritically by those who, albeit with good intentions, were eager to minister more effectively to hurting people. Only now, as a new century begins (excepting a spurt of papers in the 1970s and 1980s), are Christians beginning to reclaim the ground that was lost by formulating an adequate anthropology and psychology based on a biblical understanding of people.

There is a great need for mental health professionals with a good knowledge of both theology and psychology in order to develop the skills of discernment necessary to sort out the truth and error found in secular psychology. The last decade has seen a revival of interest in the relationship between the disciplines of psychology and theology in the *Journal of Psychology and Theology*, the *Journal of Psychology and Christianity*, and the *Journal of Biblical Counseling*.[6] The American Association of Christian Counselors has sponsored the Geneva Conferences, described as "a clinical and theological symposium for academicians, counselors and pastors," to foster dialogue on the interface of theology and therapy.

THE SEARCH FOR TRUTH ABOUT HUMAN NATURE

At least seven dominant schools of counseling, psychotherapy, and psychiatry have developed since the turn of the last century and are represented as overlapping circles in Figure 1. The three lower left circles, Psychoanalysis, Behaviorism (traditionally known as the First and Second Forces in psychology) and the Organic/Medical approach, grew out of the scientific-materialistic philosophy of the day, which believed that all of reality could be defined and described by the scientific method. These schools developed a view of human nature and its problems that was largely deterministic, mechanistic, naturalistic, and reductionist. From a Christian perspective, in their original form, these schools tended to dehumanize people, defining us as less than we really are and seeing us as complex machines or animals with little responsibility or significance.

In the 1950s and 1960s Carl Rogers and Abraham Maslow developed Humanistic Psychology (the Third Force), with its much less deterministic view of human nature, as a reaction to the prevailing mechanistic and deterministic models of human nature. Rogers and Maslow wanted to reclaim human significance, dignity, responsibility, and freedom, but, certainly initially, without any reference to God or the supernatural. Carl Rogers wrote,

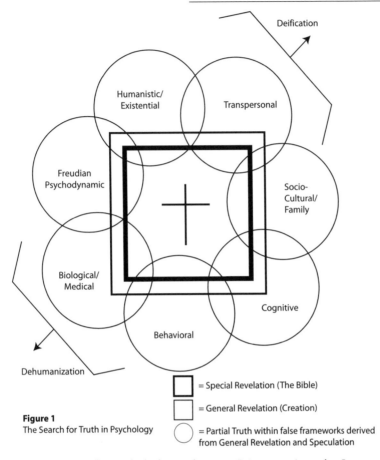

Figure 1
The Search for Truth in Psychology

□ = Special Revelation (The Bible)

□ = General Revelation (Creation)

○ = Partial Truth within false frameworks derived from General Revelation and Speculation

> Experience is for me the highest authority .... It is to experience that I must return again and again to discover a closer approximation to the truth as it is becoming in me. Neither the Bible nor the prophets, neither Freud nor research, neither the revelations of God or man, can take precedence over my own direct experience.[7]

Philosophically this view has humanist and existential roots. There is a separate and distinct Existential school of psychotherapy, which identifies with Victor Frankl, Rollo May, and others, and emphasizes the importance of a sense of meaning and purpose. In the 1970s, Transpersonal Psychology (the Fourth Force), with its open interest in spirituality and eastern mysticism, gathered momentum. Key names here were Maslow, Assagioli, and Wilber. Maslow wrote:

> Without the transcendent and transpersonal we get sick.... We need something "bigger than we are" to be awed by and to commit ourselves to in a new, naturalistic, empirical, non-churchly sense ....[8]

Transpersonal Psychology is now a powerful and increasingly popular influence. Carl Jung, with his interest in religion, acted as a bridge from the older Psychoanalytical psychology to the Humanistic and Transpersonal schools. From a Christian perspective, these movements, in contrast to the earlier schools, tend to deify human nature by saying that we have all that we need within us to become godlike through our own efforts, or that we are already God if we could only realize it.

The Cognitive and later Cognitive Behavioral schools focus on identifying and correcting irrational and maladaptive thinking patterns and habitual behaviors and are, at the level of philosophical assumptions, an offshoot of the humanist philosophical system. The Sociocultural and Family Systems schools also emerged at about the same time from a similar humanistic root and shifted the focus from individuals with pathology to the dysfunctional family or society that surrounded and influenced them.

Each of the circles in Figure 1 represents a philosophy of life and a world-view. None of them is neutral. All are trying to find the answers to the big questions of life: Where have we come from? Why do we have the problems we do? How do we know what is right and wrong? What is the purpose of life? How should we live? What is our destiny?

If Christianity is true and depends on God's revelation in the Bible, then the other views are, at best, partial truths, and at worst, misleading and false. All men and women, whether they acknowledge it or not, are made in the image of God and, in their scientific work, will describe parts of God's creation. In their daily lives, as we will see, they cannot escape the boundaries of reality which God has created, although they may not believe in God.

REVELATION AND SPECULATION IN THE SEARCH FOR TRUTH

In Figure 1 the central, darker square represents the Christian worldview, given by "special revelation" in the Scriptures. The outer, lighter square represents "general revelation" in creation, including people. The Christian view rests on observation and revelation, while the non-Christian view rests on observation and speculation. Non-Christian views are based on the study of natural revelation, though conceptualized simply as nature, and interpreted through alternative worldviews. The circles here represent partial truths within false frameworks. The area of overlap of the circles and rectangles represents common ground between Christian and non-Christian worldviews. Calvin expressed this view of general revelation in his *Institutes*:

> Therefore, in reading profane [non-Christian] authors, the admirable light of truth displayed in them should remind us, that the human mind, however much fallen and perverted from its original integrity, is still adorned and invested with admirable gifts from its Creator. If we reflect that the Spirit of God is the only fountain of truth, we will be careful, as we would avoid

offering insult to him, not to reject or condemn truth wherever it appears ... But if the Lord has been pleased to assist us by the work and ministry of the ungodly in physics, dialectics, mathematics and other similar sciences, let us avail ourselves of it lest, by neglecting the gifts of God spontaneously offered to us, we be justly punished for our sloth.[9]

The theologian Van Til expresses a similar idea:

The actual situation is therefore always a mixture of truth with error. Being "without God in the world" the natural man yet knows God, and, in spite of himself, to some extent recognizes God. By virtue of their creation in God's image, by virtue of the ineradicable sense of deity within them and by virtue of God's restraining general grace, those who hate God, yet in a restricted sense know God, and do good.[10]

MIXTURE OF TRUTH AND ERROR

Some examples will help to clarify this mixture of truth and error. Freud was profoundly atheistic, seeing religion as the ultimate neurosis, but he accurately highlighted the depths of the inner alienation and disintegration that we experience in our hearts. His description of the split between the superego and the id, the "oughts" and the "wants" of life, relates to Paul's agonized cry in Romans 7:14: "For what I want to do I do not do, but what I hate I do." Post-Freudian analysts were less reductionist than Freud and have given us insight into the complexities of early parent child relationships. To take a very practical example, the fact that parents are now allowed to stay in the hospital with young children was largely due to research by John Bowlby on attachment and loss.[11]

B. F. Skinner and other Behaviorists describe the ways in which we are like animals and are conditioned by our environment. There is truth in the fact that we are shaped to some degree by our upbringing and culture, but, unlike the strict Behaviorists, we do not believe that we are completely determined by our circumstances.

And then the psychiatrist who espouses the Organic/Medical model as the primary explanation tends to reduce all emotions to the function of neurotransmitters in the brain. Again, it is true that we are affected by our brain chemistry. Antipsychotics can be dramatically effective and lifesaving in schizophrenia, and antidepressants are helpful in relieving severe clinical depression. But we are far more than mere biochemistry.

The Humanistic psychologist is right to stress our dignity and responsibility, but dismisses the need for God or an external framework of values. He believes that all we need is within us. The Cognitive therapist rightly emphasizes the role of our thinking in shaping our emotions, but tends to reduce nearly all problems to faulty thinking. The Family therapist rightly stresses the importance of the system of relationships in which the person lives, but sometimes at the expense of the significance of individual choices. The Transpersonal psychologist recognizes the need for something greater than ourselves and rightly reintroduces the importance of the supernatural, but often sees the way of salvation as realizing our essential divinity by means of psycho-spiritual exercises.

The circles in Figure 1 overlap the central squares to represent the areas of common ground with Christian truth. The circles also lie partially outside the squares, thus representing the areas of difference from a Christian view of reality. Each of these circles can be seen as a lens through which we see and interpret reality.

The Search for the Right Lens

In Figure 2 the circles have, for the sake of simplicity and clarity, been moved out to show a highly distilled summary of the main working points of each system under the headings of Cause of Dysfunction, Technique of Counseling, and Therapy Goals, as most are described by Comer in his textbook *Abnormal Psychology*.[12] Each circle represents a theoretical formulation and systematic categorization of psychological and sociological data. Each, we might say, is one lens of contemporary science and should be evaluated through the lens of Scripture. Calvin spoke of the Scriptures as "spectacles":

> For as persons who are old, or whose eyes are by any means become dim, if you show them the most beautiful book, though they perceive something written, but can scarcely read two words together, yet, by the assistance of spectacles, will begin to read distinctly, so the Scripture ... dispels the darkness and gives us a clear view....[13]

It is apparent that the lens through which we choose to view reality will certainly affect what we see, how we understand what we see, and how we will respond to it. The philosophers Kuhn[14] and Polanyi[15] have highlighted the effects of presuppositions and assumptions on the scientific observer, demonstrating that nobody can be objectively neutral. Everybody has his or her own lens for seeing and making sense of the world. The Christian claim is that there is one true lens that enables us to see most clearly and accurately. Only when this lens is used do we realize how blurred and distorted our previous vision was. And even this lens may sometimes be slightly out of focus, as our understanding of Scripture may not be completely accurate. Our theology may also need correction.

The softer sciences of psychology and sociology – compared with the harder sciences of, for example, anatomy and physiology – are much more open to distortion because they are so much more dependent on the worldview (lens) of the observer who is doing the describing, interpreting and prescribing. This does not mean that there is no value in them, but as we use the lens of Scripture to test their accuracy we will be careful to discern the areas of

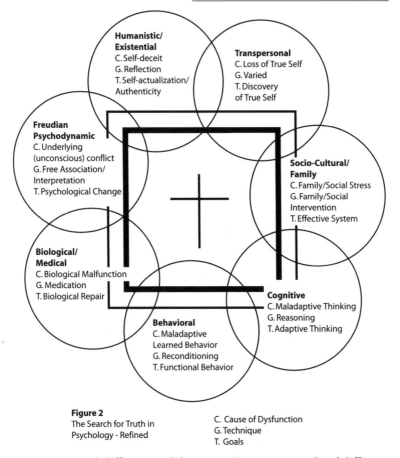

Figure 2
The Search for Truth in
Psychology - Refined

C. Cause of Dysfunction
G. Technique
T. Goals

common ground, difference and distortion. Common ground and difference will be seen in philosophical assumptions and values, aims and goals, and methods and techniques. Others have already done work on this detailed task, and this article is intended only as an overview and summary.[16]

POSTMODERNISM AND MULTIPLE THERAPIES

From each of the circles in Figure 1 has sprung a veritable smorgasbord of therapies. Some are pure derivatives of one circle only; others arise from a combination of circles. The majority of therapists today would probably call themselves eclectics or pragmatists, taking from each of the circles what seems to fit their personality, worldview, mood and the client's need on any given day! This postmodern pragmatism is popular in many disciplines and reflects a deep and fairly recent philosophical shift. Hurding, for example, has addressed this debate in relation to the interplay between pastoral theology and pastoral psychology.[17]

Since the Enlightenment, there has been a general faith and belief that some universal truth can be found in either objective, rational, and logical science and reason, or in subjective, intuitive, non-rational experience. This has been the faith of modernity for the last 200 years. Today, in the post-positivist, postmodern world, there is no faith that any universal truth exists or can be discovered or known. So each person has his own subjective view of reality. This is, of course, profoundly different from a Christian view, which claims that God has revealed truth that is true for all people and for all time – truth about himself, about our origins, about our present state, about a framework for ethics in day-to-day life and about our destiny. This Christian view does not exclude the fact that there is some subjectivity in each person's view of reality, but it holds that there is objective truth toward which we can move and which can be increasingly known both scientifically and experientially. Of course, our knowledge is limited by our finiteness and, on this side of glory, by our fallenness.

The influence of postmodernism in psychology is particularly seen in Solution Focused and Narrative Therapies. (This could be another circle in the diagram.) The emphasis is on the power of language to construct reality and to create different meanings to clients' problems. Relationships are interpreted as power struggles where there are victims to be protected and victimizers to be blamed. No one can claim to have a core identity because of the arbitrary nature of the social construction of identity. It is assumed that the therapist has no better view of reality than the client. Ultimately, some therapists are forced into an inconsistency. Fidelibus writes, "They work for achieving a better state of affairs for their clients, while denying that such value judgments are valid."[18] There are obvious problems for the Christian with this philosophical framework, but in therapy, narrative therapists are often rightly sensitive to the oppressive aspects of many clients' stories. They deeply respect human dignity and creativity, ask great questions and give hope that change is possible. Again, we find partial truths within a false framework.

I have spent many summers learning to sail in the fog off the coast of Maine. Even though I may have a compass and sophisticated electronic navigational instruments, without a chart I can only make limited sense of the information and thus will have no idea where I am! It seems as if those who have rejected the possibility of revelation from God in the Scriptures have thrown the chart overboard and are sailing in a cultural fog of relativism and subjectivity and are in danger of hitting some nasty rocks. Assuming that there are no "given" rules in God's universe and that we can create our own gives no solid basis for science, morality, meaning or hope. For a Christian the chart, or map, is the Bible, and it is with this map that we make sense of the information gathered from the world around us.

GENERAL AND SPECIAL REVELATION

A clear understanding of general revelation encourages us to see value in the science of psychology. It is part of the God-given task of dominion to explore and develop his world. The Bible itself tells us that from the creation alone, without Scripture, we can deduce the existence of God and something about his character (Rom. 1:19-20; Ps. 19:1-4). There are, says Shakespeare, "tongues in trees, books in the running brooks, / Sermons in stones, and good in everything."[19] Romans 2:14-15 tells us that God's law is written on our hearts, and although it may be twisted and hardened by sin, conscience gives some reminder of the law of God to all. It is significant that the Mosaic law finds parallels in the ancient pagan legal codes of Babylon and Assyria. The latter were codified about half a century before the law was given to Moses.[20] The Bible also draws attention to the fact that it was through the creativity of the descendants of the rebellious Cain that farming, music and metal work were developed (Gen. 4:20-22). This scientific knowledge and craft were later taken up and used by the people of God in their worship.

The Bible also tells us that we can learn lessons for life from nature, specifically from the ants and their hard-working habits (Prov. 6:6-8). The farmer does not get his knowledge of when and how to sow particular seeds directly from the Scriptures or by a voice from God, but learns by patient observation and passes on his wisdom to the next generation. But through his experience, the Scriptures say, "God instructs him and teaches him the right way" (Isa. 28:23-29). We are also to learn from the wisdom and experience of our parents and elders (Prov. 1:8). The wise men of Ecclesiastes and Proverbs obviously learned much from their observations of life and from the existing Wisdom Literature of the day. "Let the wise listen and add to their learning, let the discerning get guidance – for understanding proverbs and parables, the sayings and riddles of the wise" (Prov. 1:5-6). They were able to discern what was true and useful because of their commitment to God and his revelation to them in Scripture. The wise teacher "pondered, searched out and arranged many proverbs" (Eccl. 12:9, 10). The people turned for advice to the wise men, the prophets and the priests (Jer. 18:18).

The Bible is not a textbook of biology, physiology, geology, or medicine, and we do not expect it to be so. However, the Bible *is* partially a textbook of psychology and sociology. It deals with relationships, attitudes, thoughts, emotions, and behavior, by direct command and also in many stories of people from whom we can learn, by their example, to do good and to avoid evil and folly. In this sense the Bible gives comprehensive principles that cover the whole of life, and thus it is, as Nouthetic counselors are fond of reminding us, sufficient. But this sufficiency is comprehensive, not exhaustive. The behavioral sciences can add to our understanding of life in a fashion similar to that of the other sciences. They give a systematic description of the effects of sin and righteousness, although, of course, not calling them that. For example, the predisposing causes and the aftereffects of alcoholism, divorce, and family problems are being mapped out in ever-increasing and sobering detail. Research is demonstrating the different dimensions and effects of perfectionism. Genetic and biochemical research is gradually helping us to understand the complex intricacies of the relationship between mind and body. The relative contribution of genes, biochemistry, environment, and the individual's thoughts, feelings, and choices in depression, anorexia nervosa, phobias, schizophrenia, and homosexuality are gradually being unraveled. This is part of exploring the complexities of the fallen world in which we live. Just as in medicine we have explored different diseases and brought untold benefit to millions, so in the psychological realm there is a place for such observation, research and therapy.

But a large caution is in order. We need to remember that scientists are not neutral. As we have seen, each of us brings a worldview and perspective to our descriptions, interpretations and prescriptions. Distortion is present at all levels and therefore we need much discernment and wisdom in the search for truth. All claims to interpret general revelation are to be tested by the principles of Scripture. The Bible is the lens through which we must view the world. And finally, as we have already noted, we must remember that psychology and sociology are relatively soft sciences and are therefore much more vulnerable to distortion than the harder sciences (e.g. physiology and anatomy), which depend far more on accurate observation than on interpretation.

The model of careful, creative and Christocentric integration that has been presented here requires knowledge of theology and psychology and a desire to allow Scripture to be the ultimate reference point and lens by which all else is tested.

> Scripture is senior because it is propositional and direct ... creation is subordinate because it is non-verbal and distorted since the fall. Creation must be interpreted by Scripture ... theology and psychology are "sciences" organizing human thoughts about God's revelation. As human products they both may contain human errors. They may challenge one another and are both subordinate to Scripture and creation.[21]

Some years ago, Larry Crabb wrote in *Understanding People*,

> Studying the thinking of other people, whether Christian or not, can be legitimately provocative. The data and theories of psychology can serve as catalysts, stimulating us to consider new directions in our thinking. Both our power of reason and our intuition must be permitted a role in our efforts to build a counseling model. But in all that we do the Bible must provide the *framework* within which we work and the *premises* from which we draw our conclusions.[22]

CONFRONTATION WITH REALITY

Evidence of the truth of God's revelation in Scripture is found in a confrontation with empirical reality. If the world was created with certain built-in physical and psychological structures and laws, then it should not be surprising to find that living by the Maker's instructions is profoundly practical and healthy. We see this in several areas where we find that contemporary behavioral science has, for pragmatic reasons, as a result of research and experience, embraced a Christian view of certain parts of reality without openly acknowledging them as such. In the last ten years there have been some challenging voices and significant shifts of opinion in the secular therapeutic culture. Some brief examples may help to illustrate this point.

Religion, long seen as neurotic and immature by many therapists, has now been demonstrated to be beneficial to both mental and physical health.[23] Forgiveness, for many years hardly mentioned among secular therapists and remarkably absent from the literature, is now increasingly recognized as pragmatically helpful in restoring relationships.[24] Forgiveness is, of course, at the heart of the gospel, and Christian therapists have always emphasized the destructiveness of bitterness and lack of forgiveness. Raising self-esteem has been seen for years as the answer to many problems in life. This view is now being challenged as it is realized that low self-esteem may often be a result of other problems rather than a cause, and that unqualified affirmation may create false self-confidence and narcissism.[25] Honesty about an individual's strengths and weaknesses will help him to develop a more realistic view of himself. The Bible is clear that we need to develop a realistic sense of both our dignity and our depravity, resting fundamentally on God's view of us rather than on our view of ourselves or on other people's view of us. In recent years, the flood of research on the damaging effects of divorce has restrained many therapists from encouraging easy divorce when marriages run into problems.[26] Frank Pittman, psychiatrist, author, and well-known speaker, is a self-proclaimed atheist, but he is very critical of humanistic counseling that has encouraged narcissism, easy divorce, and preoccupation with victimization. He emphasizes the importance of faithfulness in marriage, honesty, responsibility, and forgiveness for health and happiness.[27] The harsh reality and devastation of sexually transmitted diseases and broken relationships has allowed once-scorned abstinence programs to be taught in the school system.[28]

Finally, a recent interesting development is found in what is called "positive psychology." This is a corrective balance to a hundred years of "negative psychology" which has focused on abuse, trauma, illness and pathology. Martin Seligman, following Maslow and others, is promoting research on positive qualities that "promote happiness and well-being, as well as character strengths such as optimism, kindness, resilience, persistence and gratitude … what used to be called 'the virtues.'"[29]

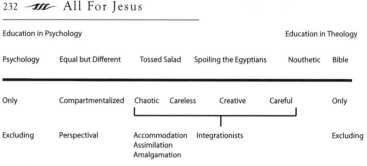

Figure 3
A Christian Counseling Spectrum: Psychology and Scripture

THE CHRISTIAN SPECTRUM

When we look at the spectrum of views on the relation between theology and psychology among Christians, we find an enormous range (see Figure 3 above). To describe these views, I have used words that have been used consistently in the integrationist literature and added a few of my own.

Those at the "psychology only" end of the spectrum tend to compartmentalize their lives into the sacred and the secular. Larry Crabb calls this the "equal but different" model, in which psychological and spiritual languages are different ways of talking about life that are essentially unrelated.[30] To caricature, those at this end of the spectrum may use biblical concepts on Sunday but Freudian or Jungian concepts the rest of the week at work, without any understanding of how the two worlds relate.

A far more sophisticated "equal but different" view is expressed by David Myers in the "levels-of-explanation" or "perspectival" model. He says that psychology and theology are different ways of examining and talking about reality.[31] The many legitimate findings of the science of psychology may cause us to correct our understanding of theology.

At the other end of the spectrum, "Bible only" counselors are those who believe that any attempt at "integration" is wrong. James Beck calls this the anti-psychology approach, in which practitioners are "convinced that the use of any psychology by the church is a travesty on the gospel and poses a substantial threat to the life and health of the church at large."[32] Books such as *Psychoheresy* by Martin and Deidre Bobgan, *Christian Psychology's War on God's Word* by Jim Owen, and *Why Christians Can't Trust Psychology* by Ed Bulkley all attack as unbiblical any attempt to see any good in the integration of psychology and theology.[33] Jim Craddock writes of

> a desperate orgy of syncretism that welded together the so-called truths of psychology with the precious truths of the word of God, which gave birth to an illegitimate child that is neither Christian nor psychology. Rather it is a new religion that I call "Psycho-ianity," and it is rapidly replacing Evangelical faith today.[34]

Nouthetic counseling was named by its founder, Jay Adams, who in the early 1970s reacted to the pervasiveness of the medical and psychological models, calling Christians back to the Word of God and to a moral model that is not afraid of responsibility and "sin." Nouthetic counseling has, in recent years, taken the name "Biblical Counseling," although there are many other types of Christian counselors who would claim that their work is worthy of the same label. Traditional Nouthetic counselors claim that Scripture is comprehensive and sufficient, containing all the principles and information that we need for living. To these counselors, mental illness and psychopathology are not useful or true categories. Problems of living are divided into organic medical problems and problems of sin – either personal sin or the results of being sinned against. A spectrum of views has emerged within the Nouthetic camp. Some, represented by the National Association of Nouthetic Counselors (NANC), strongly resist any attempt at integration. Others, represented by the Christian Counseling and Education Foundation (CCEF), while wanting to reframe everything in biblical categories, recognize some value in secular psychology and are more open to thoughtful and respectful dialogue. In contrast to many integrationists, many Nouthetic counselors do not believe that the exploration of general revelation is an important God-given task. They claim that special revelation in Scripture is adequate to give us the principles we need to help any counseling problem.[35]

In the middle of the spectrum are a variety of so-called Christian Integrationists or Eclectics who range from the "Chaotic and Careless" – Crabb's "Tossed Salad" category – in their ability and approach to relating theology and psychology, to the "Careful and Creative" – what Crabb calls "Spoiling the Egyptians."[36] Some, writes Soverson, "believe that faith has no relevance for clinical work except for its influence on external issues of personal piety and ethics."[37] He calls this "uncorrelated" integration. Some add a biblical text to their secular psychological wisdom to make it sound more Christian ("accommodating, amalgamating, and assimilating"), while others carefully try to appreciate what is true in secular psychology and work hard to use discernment in recognizing areas of common ground and difference. The classic integrationist position is described very succinctly by Gary Collins, the founder and past president of the huge and rapidly expanding American Association of Christian Counselors, in his contribution to Johnson and Jones' *Psychology and Christianity: Four Views*.[38]

Another view, described in *Four Views* as "Christian Psychology," has been developed by Robert Roberts, professor of ethics at Baylor University. While not rejecting secular psychology, Roberts encourages us to focus on the wealth of insights and interventions from the Christian tradition through the ages. He claims that

> Our task as Christian psychologists, as I see it, is in large part to retrieve
> the Christian psychology of the past, understand what these writers have to

say, sift it for what has enduring Christian importance and present it to our contemporaries in a form that can be understood and used.[39]

There are also a number of popular Christian counseling ministries, each with psychological and theological strengths and weaknesses. Beck mentions Neil Anderson's Christ-Centered Therapy and Ed Smith's Theophostic Counseling as contemporary examples.[40] Many American cities have significant Christian counseling ministries working in or alongside the local churches. Each has had to develop its own philosophy and statement on the relationship of psychology and theology.

Each of us can place ourselves somewhere on the spectrum of Christian counseling. I would be delighted to find a better term than the rather clumsy mouthful of "Careful Christian Integrationist." The word "integration" carries the political connotation of racial integration, of bringing together equals. "Eclectic" is no better as it implies picking and choosing without an overarching framework of belief to inform those choices. "Christian" or "Biblical Eclecticism" sounds too weak. Hurding puts forward "circumspect eclecticism,"[41] and Powlison and Welch have suggested "recasting, recycling, reformatting, interpreting, and reinterpreting."[42] Hurley and Berry recognize the "severe liabilities of the term 'integration.'" They prefer to "talk about 'relating' psychology and theology, rather than 'integrating' them."[43] We are attempting to "reclaim" what is rightfully ours as part of God's general revelation and to "reframe" it in its original biblical framework.

In recent years, especially among those who are strongly influenced by Reformed theology, I have seen the emergence of much common ground in foundational biblical teaching on: (1) the great overarching themes of Creation, Fall, Redemption, and Future Glory; (2) the healing power of friendship, lay counseling, spiritual direction, and community in the church; and (3) the relevance and practicality of scriptural teaching on sanctification for helping people to grow and change. These three areas are at the heart of the current ministries of Larry Crabb (New Way Ministries)[44] and David Powlison and Paul Tripp (Changing Hearts, Changing Lives Seminars). While agreeing strongly with such foundational issues, Dan Allender (Mars Hill Graduate School), Diane Langberg (AACC), and many others also emphasize the need for well-trained professional counselors to minister to those whose lives are particularly broken or confused, and who may need extra experience, time and help.

There is another spectrum as well (no diagram) on which counselors must find their place in relation to the role of the demonic and "spiritual warfare." There are those who understand every psychological problem to be the result of direct demonic activity and for whom healing involves the exorcism of, for example, spirits of lust, depression, and addiction. At the other end of this spectrum are those who believe that such demonic activity was only seen in biblical times and that deliverance ministries are not relevant or helpful today. Most people hold positions somewhere between these two extremes. Two examples would be Neil Anderson's *The Bondage Breaker* and David Powlison's *Power Encounters*.[45] Unfortunately, I lack space to develop this theme further in this essay.

CONCLUSION

In this postmodern world where the very concept of truth is being undermined, Christians have a vital contribution to make to the field of psychology. Postmodernism has two sides: On the one hand it is open to new ideas and recognizes the limits of science, but on the other hand, it is closed to the possibility of any overarching truth about the human condition. As the old "faith" in science crumbles we may meet a new resistance which is less open to rational persuasion, but at the same time we may find that we have new opportunities for the gospel as people experience the consequences of trying to live outside God's reality by abandoning any concept of truth.

There is a need for men and women, committed to the Lordship of Christ over the whole of life, who take delight in the God-given tasks of discerning truth and error in the field of psychology. We can struggle together to "reclaim" whatever is true in psychology as part of God's revelation in the world, and to relate psychological and biblical categories to each other, attempting to apply the Truth appropriately to each detail of day-to-day life.

Beck wisely notes the dangers of lack of balance in this endeavor. Most professionals in this field are trained in one of the two disciplines, psychology or theology, far more than in the other. Beck points out that the ratio of undergraduate degrees in psychology to degrees in religious studies in 1997–8 was 12:1. At the postgraduate level it is better, at 3:1. He writes: "The size of both fields is enormous, and any scholar who tries to master not just one but both disciplines faces a monumental challenge."[46] For my part, that is the reason why I cherish the opportunity to train counselors in a seminary setting where they can receive excellent teaching in both fields.

The "fear of the Lord" is indeed the beginning of wisdom (Prov. 1:1). Exploring general revelation is part of our obedience to the call to dominion (Gen. 1:28). There is potential for healthy dialogue and "iron sharpening iron" among those who wish to be faithful to the One who has given us the Scriptures through which, like a lens, we discern and test all psychological and sociological "truth." God's special revelation in the Bible, and a relationship with him, are crucial for keeping us from error and idolatry.

1. This essay was originally published in *Presbyterion: Covenant Seminary Review* 31, no. 1 (Spring 2005): 18–36.

2. See, for example, D. Benner, *Psychotherapy and the Spiritual Quest* (Grand Rapids, Mich.: Baker Books, 1988); W. A. Clebsch and C. R. Jaekle, *Pastoral Care in Historical Perspective* (Engle-wood Cliffs, N.J.: Prentice-Hall, 1964); E. Brooks Holifield, *A History of Pastoral Care in America: From Salvation to Self-Realization* (Nashville, Tenn.: Abingdon, 1983); J. McNeil, *A History of the Cure of Souls* (New York: Harper and Brothers, 1951); T. Oden, *Classical Pastoral Care* (Grand Rapids, Mich.: Baker Books, 1994).

3. *Journal of Psychology and Christianity* 17, no. 4 (Winter, 1998).

4. E. L. Johnson and S. L. Jones, *Psychology and Christianity: Four Views* (Downers Grove, Ill.: InterVarsity Press, 2000).

5. D. Powlison, "Integration or Inundation," in M. Horton, ed., *Power Religion: The Selling Out of the Evangelical Church?* (Chicago: Moody Press, 1992), 205.

6. For an overview of this debate on integration within modern and postmodern contexts, see R. Hurding, *Pathways to Wholeness: Pastoral Care in a Postmodern Age* (London: Hodder and Stoughton, 1998), 186–200.

7. C. Rogers, *On Becoming a Person* (New York: Houghton Mifflin Co., 1961), 23–4.

8. A. Maslow, *Toward a Psychology of Being* (New York: Van Nostrand, 1968), iv.

9. J. Calvin, *Institutes of the Christian Religion*, ed. and trans. Henry Beveridge (London: James Clarke and Co., 1962; c1559), II.15.16 (pp. 236–7).

10. C. Van Til, *An Introduction to Systematic Theology* (Phillipsburg, N.J.: P&R Publishing, 1974), 27; quoted in J. Frame, "Van Til on Antithesis," *Westminster Theological Journal* 57 (1995): 86.

11. J. Bowlby, *Attachment and Loss* (London: Hogarth, 1969).

12. R. J. Comer, *Abnormal Psychology* (New York: Worth Publishers, 2004).

13. J. Calvin, *Institutes of the Christian Religion*, vol. 1, ed. and trans. J. Allen (Philadelphia, Pa.: Presbyterian Board of Christian Education, 1936), 80.

14. T. Kuhn, *The Structure of Scientific Revolutions* (Chicago: University of Chicago Press, 1962).

15. M. Polanyi, *Personal Knowledge: Towards a Post-Critical Philosophy* (Chicago: University of Chicago Press, 1958).

16. See, for example, R. Hurding, *Roots and Shoots: A Guide to Counseling and Psychotherapy* (London: Hodder and Stoughton, 1985, 2003); and S. Jones and R. Butman, *Modern Psychotherapies* (Downers Grove, Ill.: InterVarsity Press, 1991).

17. Hurding, *Pathways to Wholeness* (1998).

18. J. Fidelibus, "Being of Many Minds: The Post-Modern Impact on Psychotherapy," in *The Death of Truth*, ed. Dennis McCallum (Minneapolis, Minn.: Bethany House Publishers, 1996), 160.

19. W. Shakespeare, *As You Like It*, act 2, sc. 1, lines 16–17; in *The Riverside Shakespeare* (New York: Houghton Mifflin Co., 1974).

20. J. B. Hurley and J. T. Berry, "The Relation of Scripture and Psychology in Counseling from a Pro-Integrative Position and Response to Powlison and Welch." *Journal of Psychology and Christianity* 16 (1997): 4.

21. Hurley and Berry, "The Relation of Scripture and Psychology in Counseling," 342.

22. L. Crabb, *Understanding People* (Grand Rapids, Mich.: Zondervan, 1987), 44.

23. See C. G. Ellison, "Symposium on Religion, Health, and Well-Being: Introduction to the Symposium." *Journal for the Scientific Study of Religion* 37 (1998): 4; D. B. Larson and A. Ellis, "On Religion and Mental Health." *Insight on the News* 11 (1995): 10; H. G. Koenig, *Handbook of Religion and Mental Health* (San Diego, Calif.: Academic Press, 1998).

24. Radhi H. Al-Mabuk, C. V. L. Dedrick, and K. M. Vanderah, "Attribution Training in Forgiveness Therapy." *Journal of Family Psychotherapy* 9, no. 1 (1998); J. P. Pingleton, "Why We Don't Forgive: Biblical and Object Relations Theoretical Model for Understanding Failure in the Forgiveness Process." *Journal of Psychology and Theology* 24, no. 4 (1997): 403; "Religion: The Power of Forgiveness." *Time Magazine*, April 5, 1999: 54.

25. California Task Force to Promote Self-Esteem, *Towards a State of Self-Esteem* (Sacramento: California State Department of Education, 1990); R. A. Eder, "The Overemphasis on Self-Esteem." *St. Louis Post-Dispatch*, April 17, 1997; R. A. Eder and S. C. Mangelsdorf, "The Empirical Basis of Early Personality: Implications for the Emergent Self-Concept," in R. Hogan, J. Johnson, and S. Briggs, eds., *Handbook of Personality Psychology* (New York: Academic Press, 1997); A. M. Mecca, N. J. Smelser, and J. Vasconcellos, *The Social Importance of Self-Esteem* (Berkeley: University of California Press, 1989); A. Sullivan, "Lacking in Self-Esteem? Good for You!" *Time Magazine*, October 14, 2002: 102.

26. E. M. Hetherington, "Parents, Children and Siblings Six Years After Divorce," in R. Hinde and J. Stevenson-Hinde, eds., *Relationships Within Families* (Oxford: Clarendon Press, 1988), 311–31; J. Wallerstein, "Children of Divorce: Ten Years After," in Bryan Strong and Christian DeVault, eds., *The Marriage and Family Experience* (St. Paul, Minn.: West Publishing Co., 1992); J. Wallerstein, J. Lewis, and S. Blakeslee, *The Unexpected Legacy of Divorce: A 25-Year Landmark Study* (New York: Hyperion, 2000).

27. F. Pittman, *Grow Up* (New York: Golden Books, 1998); this information also comes from seminars and personal conversations with Dr. Pittman.

28. L. Kay, "Adolescent Sexual Intercourse: Strategies for Promoting Abstinence in Teens." *Postgraduate Medicine* 97, no. 6 (1995): 121; H. R. Khouzam, "Promotion of Sexual Abstinence: Reducing Adolescent Sexual Activity and Pregnancies." *Southern Medical Journal* 88, no. 7 (1995): 709; A. Shin, "Just Don't Do It! – It didn't get much notice then, but last year's welfare overhaul gave a high priority to sexual abstinence instruction." *National Journal* 29, no. 43 (1997): 2161.

29. P. Vitz, "Psychology in Recovery." *First Things* 151 (2005): 19.

30. L. Crabb, *Effective Biblical Counseling* (Grand Rapids, Mich.: Zondervan, 1977).

31. D. Myers, "A Levels of Explanation View," in E. L. Johnson and S. L. Jones, eds., *Psychology and Christianity: Four Views* (Downers Grove, Ill.: InterVarsity Press, 2000), 54–83.

32. J. R. Beck, "The Integration of Psychology and Theology: An Enterprise Out of Balance." *Journal of Psychology and Christianity* 22 (2003): 23.

33. M. and D. Bobgan, *Psychoheresy: The Psychological Seduction of Christianity* (Santa Barbara, Calif.: EastGate Publishers, 1987); J. Owen, *Christian Psychology's War on God's Word* (Santa Barbara, Calif.: EastGate Publishers, 1993); and E. Bulkley, *Why Christians Can't Trust Psychology* (Eugene, Ore.: Harvest House, 1994).

34. J. Craddock, "The Shrinking of the Church," *1ˢᵗ Monday* 2 (1993): 6.

35. E. Welsh and D. Powlison, "'Every Common Bush Afire with God': The Scripture's Constitutive Role for Counseling, and Response to Hurley and Berry." *Journal of Psychology and Christianity* 16 (1997): 303–22; D. Powlison, "A Biblical Counseling View," in E. L. Johnson and S. L. Jones, eds., *Psychology and Christianity: Four Views* (Downers Grove, Ill.: InterVarsity Press, 2000), 196–225.

My differences with Nouthetic counseling have to do with the relative emphasis that we place on certain issues. From my perspective, some Nouthetic counselors underemphasize: (1) the importance of general revelation; (2) the importance of common grace; (3) psychological factors, especially the damaging effects of others' sins; and (4) the time it takes to change deeply rooted patterns of sin.

36. Crabb, *Effective Biblical Counseling*, 35–52; D. Powlison, "Critiquing Modern Integrationists." *The Journal of Biblical Counseling* 11 (1993): 3.

37. R. Soverson, "The Faces of Integration." *Christian Counseling Today* (Winter 1996): 27.

38. G. Collins, "An Integration View," in E. L. Johnson and S. L. Jones, eds., *Psychology and Christianity: Four Views* (Downers Grove, Ill.: InterVarsity Press, 2000), 102–29.

39. R. Roberts, "A Christian Psychology View," in E. L. Johnson and S. L. Jones, eds., *Psychology and Christianity: Four Views* (Downers Grove, Ill.: InterVarsity Press, 2000), 153.

40. Beck, "The Integration of Psychology and Theology," 153.

41. Hurding, *Roots and Shoots*, 269.

42. Welch and Powlison, "'Every Common Bush Afire with God,'" 316.

43. Hurley and Berry, "The Relation of Scripture and Psychology in Counseling," 328.

44. A. Tennant, "A Shrink Gets Stretched: Why Psychologist Larry Crabb Believes That Spiritual Direction Should Replace Therapy." *Christianity Today* (May 2003): 52–9.

45. N. Anderson, *The Bondage Breaker* (Eugene, Ore.: Harvest House, 1990); D. Powlison, *Power Encounters: Reclaiming Spiritual Warfare* (Grand Rapids, Mich.: Baker Books, 1995).

46. Beck, "The Integration of Psychology and Theology," 27.

15

GRACE-SHAPED COUNSELING

DANIEL W. ZINK
Assistant Professor of Practical Theology

For more than four decades, Christian counseling has been wrestling with itself in an attempt to define its identity. The place and relationship of the Bible, psychology, theology, counseling theory, and practice techniques have been widely discussed and debated. Biblical, psychological, and integrative methods have been proposed and reacted to with great interest and intensity. While there has been growth as a result of this wrestling, the discussion has not led to a unified Christian counseling approach or to a group of approaches that are similar in scope, method, sequence, or process. Rather, Christian counselors have settled into their respective camps, apparently content to work from their own particular counseling viewpoints while leaving others to work from their own as well.

In the development of Christian counseling, many biblical and theological truths have been incorporated into current approaches. However, the process of debate in the field has accentuated differences, rather than finding common ground upon which to build. As a result, truths that should be common to the various approaches to Christian counseling have not been consistently articulated. Fundamental truths, whose presence would best distinguish counseling done by Christians from counseling done by others, are missing from many Christian approaches. One such truth that is commonly missing is a clear and deep understanding of grace. Therefore, much Christian counseling is less shaped by grace than one would hope.

Grace, well understood, can significantly shape our assumptions, assessments, understanding of change, and choices of methods in helping others. For Christian counselors to move toward a more fully grace-shaped approach to their work, they must be clear on the foundational aspects of grace and the nature of change in light of God's grace, and how these together should shape the helping process.

GRACE-SHAPED FOUNDATIONS

Christian counseling is less shaped by grace than is desirable. Why is this? To answer this question, we must remember the pattern of God's gracious work in our lives and our own natural tendencies as we move through life.

The Pattern of God's Gracious Work

God's work in people's lives follows a common pattern. Theologians talk of facets of God's redemptive work – such as regeneration, justification, sanctification, and adoption – as being parts of a single pattern that all believers experience as God works to bring them to himself. While this is true, we also know that God's work in individual lives is experienced in ways that are unique to each person. We all have a story to tell of God's gracious work in our lives. Some stories lead to a climactic crisis point resulting in a clear, marked-in-time decision. Others have no clear crisis or decision point in their stories. The beginning of their walk with the Lord takes place over an extended period of time with no clear point of commitment. Regardless of these differences, one thing is clear: everyone who has come to Christ came to realize that he or she was a sinner. In light of this knowledge of their own sin and their inability to overcome their sin on their own, they knew they needed a Savior. As they came to understand the gospel in light of their need, they took hold of their Savior by faith as God enabled them to do so. God's gracious work was comprehended and apprehended at the point at which they became clear about their own need. Awareness of need is crucial in the process of God's gracious work in our lives.

The Natural Life Patterns of Men and Women

The natural life patterns of men and women living under the impact of Adam's sin run contrary to the pattern of God's supernatural work. Deeply rooted in the hearts of men and women is the tendency to try to handle life on their own. Ignoring limits inherent in their brokenness and neediness, people strive to handle life in their own power. The first hint of this is seen in the early accounts of Scripture. In Genesis 3, as Satan tempts Eve, the enemy says, "You will not surely die ... For God knows that when you eat of it your eyes will be opened, and you will be like God knowing good and evil" (Gen. 3:5).[1] Clearly this is deception flowing from the mouth of the deceiver. But it is more than that. It is also descriptive of the bent of the heart of man once Adam and Eve sinned. "You will be like God." You are sufficient. You are able. You do not need another. You are independent. Work it out on your own. Human persons live out these and many more manifestations of this lie of Satan every day. Living under the effects of Adam's fall, all of us tend to try to take control of life and its circumstances.

This bent of our hearts leads us to assume that when we are confronted with difficulty, we need to do something. We need to solve the situation. It depends on us. When the difficulty is more than we can hope to handle, our efforts shift. We distort our view through the blindness of denial, or by avoiding the pain through numbing activities, or by filling our days and nights with distracting experiences. How can we experience afresh the gracious work of God at such times? We once again need to be clear about our inability to solve our problems or cure the sin in our lives, just as we were when we received Christ as our Savior. This is a fundamental point – the apprehension of grace is grounded in the apprehension of our need, particularly our need for the work of another on our behalf.

Maintenance of These Natural Life Patterns

How are these patterns sustained in the lives of believing men and women who have been transformed by God's grace? Several significant factors could be identified as contributing to this process, but it will suffice here to discuss three.

First, the brokenness that results from Adam's fall extends not only to the external world, but also to the human heart. A remnant of this brokenness continues to impact believers. We live in a time that is in between the work of Christ on the cross and the full completion of his work at the end of the age. This "in-betweenness" shapes God's sanctifying work. The Westminster Confession of Faith tells us that sanctification is "throughout, in the whole man; yet imperfect in this life, there abiding still some remnants of corruption in every part; whence ariseth a continual and irreconcilable war, the flesh lusting against the Spirit, and the Sprit against the flesh" (WCF XIII.2). This "remnant of corruption in every part" continues to have influence. We know that Christ will complete his work in us, but this completion will not be until "the day of Jesus Christ" (Phil. 1:6). Until then, the battle will continue. This battle is deeper and more subtle than merely the behavior that flows from moral choice. The battle includes the inclinations of our hearts. This "continual and irreconcilable war" includes the struggle between those transformed aspects of our heart that are directed toward God in attitude and affections, and those remnants that are directed toward self. These remnants influence believers to maintain the life pattern of trying to handle life and its circumstances independently. This is especially true in areas of life that are less obvious to us, such as the inner life of the heart.

Another influence that encourages the maintenance of this pattern is the current culture. We live in a technological age. Solutions to problems of technical difficulties are often found easily. When my computer will not work properly, I have grown accustomed to calling a service technician who will give me the information I need to get my computer working again. She tells me what files to throw away so I can restart the computer and get back to functioning normally. The solution is relatively easy. I do not need to know exactly what was wrong. I only need to know what to do to get it restarted on a fresh course. We may come to expect that all change will be like this. We may expect that a counselor will be like a service technician for the problems of life. The counselor will aid us by telling us what adjustments to make, enabling us to start afresh while avoiding having to figure out what was wrong. Such expectations prevent us from looking more deeply at what is stirring within us, so that we do not understand the depth and nature of our problems. As a result, we continue to assume that we are strong enough to fix what needs to be solved. We continue to try to handle life and its circumstances on our own.

A final influence in the maintenance of these patterns in the lives of believers is self-deception. Often the Enemy, the great deceiver, is at work in this process of deception. But we are involved as well, enough so that self-deception is an appropriate description. This self-deception manifests itself in at least two forms. First, we deceive ourselves by not noticing what we are thinking and feeling in a specific situation, especially if that situation is painful. R. D. Laing said, "The range of what we think and do is limited by what we fail to notice. And because we fail to notice that we fail to notice, there is little we can do to change; until we notice how failing to notice shapes our thoughts and deeds."[2] We are especially prone to the failure to attend to the area of emotions, the inner life of the heart.

A second aspect of self-deception compounds our failure to notice. We strive to keep ourselves convinced that whatever we might be concerned about is of no real importance. We try to convince ourselves that it does not really matter. A clear example of this occurred in my own life. My father died when I was five years old. In that experience of loss, I faced a very painful circumstance. Even though I was a young child, I was able to distort the story and largely avoid the pain, convincing myself that my loss did not matter. In the process, I became blind to the realities and numb to the pain attached to the death of my father. With quiet conviction, I subsequently tried to keep others convinced that my loss did not matter. For example, when my little league baseball teammate asked why my dad did not come to games, I calmly explained that he had died. "Oh, I'm sorry," my teammate would say. My reply? "Oh, it's all right. I was little. It was a long time ago. Don't worry about it." This self-deception was the easy way out, but it did not – and could not – work. The truth is that my father's death mattered very much, but I was doing whatever I could to handle this circumstance in my own strength. The self-deception of not noticing and of reducing the importance of life's events contributes to people maintaining the pattern of independent management of life.

Returning to Foundations of Grace

Comprehending God's gracious work requires us to continually comprehend our inability to solve life's issues without connection to God and without his help. This understanding is only the beginning. We must also take hold of this truth. We must apprehend this work of God's grace by embracing our personal need – that need that flows from our sinfulness and which includes our deep, heartfelt inclinations to control our lives without God. We must work against those things that prevent us from embracing our brokenness, for in embracing it, we begin to lean on him as he works and enables us to be effective in his strength. We begin to act dependently in our life situations.

GRACE-SHAPED CHANGE

Change is hard. Anyone who has tried to eat less, exercise more, be less impatient, be more kind, or love better knows that change is hard. Why is this? Change that is genuine and lasting must derive from a wholehearted transformation. Merely modifying behavior or thinking or feeling is not likely to produce change that endures in the face of life's challenges. Lasting change addresses the whole person. We are people with complex hearts. The Bible teaches that from our hearts flow our thoughts, feelings, will, words, actions, and everything else that comprises who we are.[3] To address the whole person, we must deal with the heart. This is difficult, as people do not know their own hearts well.[4] The work to understand our hearts is hard, slow, and never complete.

Emotions and Change

We fear the pain entailed in knowing our hearts. Therefore, we try to control life so we do not have to experience the intensity of the pain head on. Rather than being honest about that pain, and finding the perspective and comfort that such a truthful look brings, we turn and run to other things. As I write this sentence, I am sitting on a bench outside a Ben and Jerry's Ice Cream store. The poster in the window caught my eye. It says, "Waffle Cone Sundaes: Your Emotional Rescue." Something in me believes this. I know that to eat that Waffle Cone Sundae would do something to my emotions that I want done. And if I do eat it, I never have to be very aware of what it is that stirs inside me, driving me toward "emotional rescue." So I am tempted to use the delightful experience of eating that ice cream to cover over those unnamed, little-recognized stirrings. That is the way our sinfulness works. If we can find something that will cover over our pain, or numb us, or distract us, we are likely to use it to do so. If we do not, we are left to face the true stirrings, and often that is very painful indeed. It is this pain that we are trying to avoid. It is the hurt or fear or shame or guilt that we would prefer not to face as we pursue our chosen emotional rescue.

The area of the heart that people have the most difficulty recognizing and understanding is the area of feelings. Thoughts, words, and behavior are more obvious to us. Some feelings may seem obvious to us, since they are right there on the surface. A feeling may seem to be consistent with our thoughts and clearly connected to our words and behavior, but this is usually not the case. The difficulty comes from the fact that feelings seldom occur alone. Usually, feelings come in constellations.[5] Teyber explains that "a sequence of interrelated feelings will often occur together in a predictable way."[6] We usually do not recognize the constellation, only the single feeling, the one we are most comfortable expressing. For example, we may experience and express our anger, but in doing so we avoid identifying the hurt that lies beneath that anger. Deeper still, we may feel shame for being so weak that we get hurt in this circumstance. If we could recognize our hurt, and the shame connected to it, a different conversation could occur. Confessing our hurt and shame leads to a much more productive relational moment, more positive than only expressing our anger.

Affective constellations can come in a variety of combinations. We each have our own preferences. But whether we are most comfortable experiencing and expressing anger, hurt, fear, or some other feeling, we all find it hard to recognize the other parts of the constellation. Change, if it is to be wholehearted, must include change in the area of emotions. For this emotional change to occur, we must recognize the whole affective constellation we are experiencing, so that we may begin to own and use the whole range of our emotions in our relationships. To do so requires a new level of honesty with ourselves about ourselves. This high level of self-awareness has been described as a keystone of emotional intelligence.[7]

Perspective and Change

Honesty with ourselves produces a context where we understand the inner workings of our hearts more accurately. In doing so, we are able to name these inner stirrings. A maturing toddler uses his or her growing vocabulary to name objects in the surrounding environment in order to relate more fully to those objects. In the same way, the maturing adult names the feelings stirring in his or her heart in order to better relate to those emotions. In the process, a new perspective is often obtained. This perspective contributes to change by the correction of long-held assumptions. All of us have been impacted negatively in past relationships. Relationships with parents and siblings are especially powerful. Usually, we take on ourselves negative messages in response to the difficult aspects of these relationships. "There is something terribly wrong with me that caused my father to abuse me," one might say. Another concludes, "I am not capable of anything worthwhile because I was not as good, and was not loved as much, as my sister." Still another is sure that her parents divorced because she got sick with cancer. Whatever the case may be, most feel these assumptions deeply, and seldom can easily name or state them. These assumptions are often part of an affective emotional constellation that occurs regularly, and are a driving force to patterns in relationships. Naming these assumptions and relating to them often allows people to see them more accurately: "I was abused because there was something wrong with my father, not me." "I am different from my sister, not worse than her." "My parents' divorce was their responsibility, not mine." Armed with this new perspective, individuals are better able to see when they are likely to behave out of the old assumptions, and seeing this, have the opportunity to act differently.

Responsibility and Change

This new perspective that grows from honesty leads to a second important characteristic. People who live more honestly can be clearer about responsibility. An important part of maturity is to be clear on those things for which we must bear responsibility and the things for which we must not. Most of us have taken too much responsibility for what happened to us in the past. We are often unaware of this, as there are strong feelings attached to these events, and these feelings are kept at the lower levels of our emotions. Striving to be more honest about our emotions and paying attention to the parts of our affective constellations can bring clarity on responsibility.

Grief and Change

The correction of assumptions and the clarity on responsibility that come from the honesty of a growing self-awareness create the context for another important aspect of change: grieving. Grief is central to the process of change in people; it is a letting-go process whereby we come to accept life as it is. We normally associate grieving with death, but it is an important facet of all change. Losses of many kinds are built into life. Too often our defenses against the pain of these losses have hindered our self-awareness. If these losses have not been properly grieved, we look for villains we can blame for the misfortune in our lives; parents, children, spouses, God, pastors, and friends are all likely candidates. Taking an honest look at our emotions can aid us in the grieving process, helping us move through the various phases to acceptance of life as it is.

Forgiveness and Change

Finding new perspective and grieving losses in the context of a more honest self-awareness leads to another important aspect of change: forgiveness. We often rush to forgive because we know that we should. In these premature efforts, we struggle to forgive, mostly because we have not taken the time or received the help we need from God and his people to be clear about what it is that we are forgiving. So we forgive, only to be haunted by anger because we did not know how truly angry we were. We try to forgive again, but still wrestle with the hurt of the betrayal we experienced. We wonder what is wrong with us. Eventually we forgive, but this forgiveness is based on a deeper understanding of the hurt we experienced. Knowing more clearly the damage done to us, we can, with God's help, let go of the revenge we desire. Such forgiveness is necessary for healing present hurts and betrayals and for relieving us of the lingering damage of previous events.

A Way of Escape

A crucial aspect of change that is enhanced by increased awareness of what stirs in us is a recognition of our efforts to handle life on our own. Seeing this process more clearly helps us see that the context for choices and behavior stretches further back than we often know. The apostle Paul tells us that we have not been tempted beyond what we can endure, but that God provides a way of escape (1 Cor. 10:13). We often do not recognize this way of escape because we assume that the path to temptation has been short. So the alcoholic looking for God's rescue as he sits at the bar has missed the fact that the process started much earlier in his life and at a moment that may not seem to him to be related to alcohol at all. With a more careful look, he can see that thoughts and feelings about needing to numb the pain of rejection at home, or stress at work, or some other challenge are closer to the beginning of his process. His way of escape will be here, and will include facing the truth and pain, and seeking God's help to keep an accurate perspective as he moves through these situations. Our way of escape will not be the running away we are tempted to do. It will include staying in the battle – the battle between flesh and spirit – as it is waged in its specific ways in our lives.

We must remember the pattern of God's gracious work at this point. Anything we do, not to be based on our own works, must be prefaced and encompassed by a practical, lived-out awareness of our fundamental inability and need. Then there is the opportunity to experience grace as God works, and we respond dependently in our actions. We are not inclined to recognize the ignored parts of our affective constellations. Reading paragraphs like the ones above may inform us of the need to take certain actions, but this knowledge does not give us sufficient means to change. We need God's work in us to help us pause and look, to tolerate the discomfort from experiencing the ignored feelings, to make sense of those feelings, and to act differently in light of this more honest appraisal of ourselves. In remembering that we cannot do this ourselves, we can call for God's help and proceed to depend on him as we act.

Change as Process

Change is a process. It may take an entire lifetime for the Holy Spirit to work changes in our lives that he wants to effect. We need to live with a moment-by-moment awareness of what is stirring in us and what it is that drives our choices and our decisions. In noticing these things, we are enabled to be more honest with ourselves. In this honesty, we are better able to see how our own self-reliance and our sinfulness have been lived out. In seeing this neediness, we are better able to cry out to the Father for help. And in this attitude of dependence, we are then enabled, by his grace, to make better choices. We will not be able to do this, however, if we fail to recognize our own pain and our desperate need for God's work in us.

The path of change is unique for each person, as God superintends the various events of life to encourage change. Counseling is one piece of the puzzle of how God works in people's lives; it can be an extremely effective tool if we remember the nature of change in light of God's grace. When we do, we can help people to be more honest, teach them to face painful emotions while they examine their thinking and behavior, and assist them in knowing that we all need to depend on God's work and not our own as we seek to change.

GRACE-SHAPED COUNSELING

It is common for counselors to match the natural tendencies of the people with whom they are working. Most clients have the unspoken expectation that the counselor is going to tell them what is wrong and what they need to do to fix the problem. Clients, whether they realize it or not, usually assume they have what it takes to work through their problems if they can just be redirected or better informed in how to approach their issues. These expectations and assumptions are powerful; they have great influence on how counselors go about their work. As a result, many approaches to Christian counseling pursue remedy by strengthening strengths, attempting to grow the client in his or her ability to work against the problem. Christian counselors must clearly understand grace, and change in light of grace, so that they can resist these influential expectations and assumptions. Then, they can pursue the helping process in a way that is consistent with God's patterns of grace.

The Attitudes of Grace-Shaped Counseling

The counselor whose work is shaped by grace understands the challenges of living and how mysterious it can be to pursue change. Knowing that change will require more than filling in gaps in the counselee's knowledge, the counselor resists the role of expert. Rather, the counselor takes a collaborative approach, coming alongside the client in order to help in the walk forward.

The counselor also knows that the prospect of change often results in the person being afraid. On the one hand, the client may understand that change will require getting closer to painful things than he or she has been willing to get for a long time. This realization results in fear. On the other hand, the counselee may not know what is ahead. This factor of the unknown also results in fear. Whatever the cause, the counselee will experience some apprehension. The counselor knows that this fear is likely to result in resistance to change. Therefore, the counselor will need to be compassionate toward the person and demonstrate this compassion sufficiently to help the client enter into a more intense phase of the process of change.

The Focus of Grace-Shaped Counseling

Grace-shaped helping focuses on the whole person. This wholehearted approach will address thoughts, feelings, will, behavior – all aspects of the heart that seem appropriate to the situation. Since we know that people's self-generated, self-protective patterns distort their story and its impact, we know we must include looking at the painful events and emotions from the past. What meaning has the person made of these events? Does the person take them seriously? Does the person avoid thinking about them? What did the person feel about the events at the time? Does the person take too much responsibility for what happened? Has the person seen these things for what they are, grieved the losses involved, and forgiven those he needs to forgive? These and other questions will help us explore the counselee's heart, especially that area that is least accessible to the person – his or her emotions.

The Goal of Grace-Shaped Counseling

The goal of helping that is shaped by grace is to assist counselees in being more honest with themselves about the nature of their struggles. This honesty includes growth in self-awareness so that they can see more clearly the truth about past and present hurtful events and situations in their lives. Such honesty leads counselees to recognize their self-protective attempts to control life and its circumstances. It also creates opportunities for them to see more clearly, with the counselor's help, the truth: the depth of God's love for them, the nature of his work in their lives, and his continuing presence and the resources of his Spirit as they wrestle with life's issues.

The Method of Grace-Shaped Counseling

The method of the counselor whose helping is shaped by grace will be relational. It is through relationship with the client that the counselor builds an atmosphere of safety and support that will temper the discomfort of the hard work of change. Counselees need to experience high levels of acceptance, care, and support from the counselor. As a result of this kind of care, counselees will be encouraged to explore with the counselor issues that might never be faced otherwise. The counselor should strive to provide a relationship that is different than most other relationships people may have experienced. The counselor gets to know each client deeply, yet accepts each one as he or she is and does not use this knowledge to exploit counselees.

Balanced Relationship

The counseling relationship will be a balanced relationship. Not only must the counselor exhibit the gentle, caring attributes and provide the safe atmosphere described above, but also must expect change from clients. At times, the counselor will push clients to go further than they want to go in examining certain issues. The counselor may cause a client to be uncomfortable by stating clearly the distortions the counselor sees in that person's view of his or her story. The client may feel some pressure from the counselor to keep working at the needed change. This expectation of change is part of the counselor's responsibility to love his or her clients well. This push for change can only be done effectively if the gentler, caring aspects of the relationship are in place and are experienced by clients as genuine.

Loving Relationship

The counselor whose method is grace-based will love people well. This can be more difficult than it might seem. Much of our training as pastors and counselors focuses on learning what to teach those who need to be taught.[8] We can lose sight of the fact that these people need to be loved first, and then taught within this context. We can fail to see that most individuals need a relationship within which they are loved well. We can misunderstand and set out to "enter people's world only enough to change them, not necessarily to love."[9] Are we willing to "simply delight in them as created beings made in the image of God?"[10]

Empathy

The counselor whose work is shaped by grace will empathize with clients. He or she will strive to understand what it is like to experience life as his or her clients do. This must not be a mere exercise in helping to facilitate change. It must be sincere and birthed from compassion for clients. Empathy requires imagination on the part of counselors. Without imagination, counselors cannot envision themselves in the situations of their clients. Such empathy is required to be able to assess clients' deeper heart issues; without it, we will be hard-pressed to go beyond the cognitive level of our clients' lives.

Listening

The counselor whose helping is shaped by grace will listen well. Listening is more difficult than we usually recognize. Again, because we live in a world that wants quick answers, the importance of listening is diminished. Also, training programs for pastors usually equip them more for the "telling" role associated with teaching and preaching than they do for the "asking" role involved in listening.

Listening requires patience – and more of it than most of us possess. To listen well, especially to the painful feelings clients find difficult to share, we need to slow down and search for the meaning underneath and behind clients' statements. Our listening should lead us to hypotheses about the makeup of clients' affective constellations, and should include sharing our hypotheses for clients to affirm or correct. We need to listen for the level of intensity in counselees' feelings about events, people, and God. We need to listen attentively enough that we can lead them to bring into the open their unasked questions, their painful assumptions, and their deeper hurts, fears, shame, and guilt. In such a context, clients experience grace as the darkest parts of their psyches are drawn out, heard, and accepted as reasonable without being judged. To listen in this way is to love well, which is a powerful force for change.

Use of Questions

Lastly, counselors reflect grace in their method through wise use of questions. Counseling sessions in which more questions are asked than statements made will be more effective than those in which statements are the main approach. Questions can be less threatening than statements of fact. Using questions is more likely to aid counselees in drawing their own conclusions, leading them to take greater responsibility for the needed change.

Questions are most effective for exposing the underlying thoughts and feelings of clients. These thoughts and feelings are often obvious to the observer, but usually are not self-evident to clients. If the counselor attempts to tell clients what he or she has observed, resistance is very likely. Asking clients questions that lead them to the same conclusion that the counselor has seen can circumvent resistance. Counselees are much more likely to accept conclusions they have come to "on their own" than those given to them by the counselor.

Questions can be used effectively to draw clients into reconnection with God and others. Questions such as, "What do you think God is up to?" or "Do you see God's care for you in this moment?" or "What would you like to ask God about this?" encourage thoughtful connection with God. Questions can also be used to help clients gain perspective on others in their lives. Asking a question such as, "If we assume your father loved you, what do you think kept him from showing his love more?" encourages a client to use his imagination to put himself in another position. From this place, he may be able to see for the first time that, for example, his father was not the evil one he had always assumed. "What keeps you from being able to forgive your mother?" is another example of the kind of question that can confront and draw clients into reconnection with others.

Conclusion

The counselor who strives to work in a way consistent with God's patterns of grace will set out to have loving relationships with his or her clients. Within those relationships, clients will experience deep and genuine empathy from one who listens well and uses questions as his or her primary tool for encouraging change. The counseling experience will be marked by a sense of collaboration, as counselor and counselee work together to address the issues of the heart, leading to a more honest self-awareness. Resting dependently on God and his work, clients can stay in the battle as they work toward desired changes.

1. Bible quotations in this essay are taken from the New International Version (NIV).

2. R. D. Laing, quoted in Stephen R. Covey, *The Eighth Habit: From Effectiveness to Greatness* (New York: Free Press, 2004), 43.

3. See, for example, Ex. 25:2; Deut. 30:2; 1 Kings 3:9; Ps. 19:14; Ps. 44:21; Ps. 112:8; Prov. 27:19; Matt. 12:34; Matt. 15:19; Luke 6:45; 1 Cor. 4:5, Eph. 1:18; 1 Tim. 3:1; Heb. 4:12.

4. See Jer. 17:9.

5. Edward Teyber, *Interpersonal Process in Therapy: An Integrative Model*, 5th ed. (Belmont, Calif.: Thomson Brooks/Cole, 2006), 172.

6. Ibid.

7. Daniel Goleman, *Emotional Intelligence: Why It Can Matter More Than IQ* (New York: Bantam Books, 1995), 43.

8. Peter Scazzero, *The Emotionally Healthy Church: A Strategy for Discipleship That Actually Changes Lives* (Grand Rapids, Mich.: Zondervan, 2003), 177.

9. Ibid.

10. Ibid.

PART FOUR:

CHRIST-CENTERED MISSION

16

CHRIST-CENTERED MISSIONS

J. NELSON JENNINGS
Associate Professor of World Mission

---

esus is going to complete his mission. He has already gone to hell and back to prove it.

God's Spirit by his Word assures our hearts that these and many other things about Jesus and his mission are true. God promised for centuries that his unique chosen Servant would come and make things right in this broken world: Jesus of Nazareth was that very man. Jesus' life, death, resurrection, and enthronement essentially accomplished the mission of restoring the world to the way God made it. His Holy Spirit is empowering the hazardous cleanup operation as he uses Jesus' servants throughout the world. Jesus, the combined Chief-Servant and Commander-in-Chief, will return to earth for the ultimate completion of not only the restoration but even the re-creation of his world into the indescribably wonderful place he intended it to be.

This is the basic framework of Christ-centered missions. God in Christ will guide and empower the whole Church's organized activities – Christian "missions" – to spread the whole gospel into the whole world. The Triune God has initiated his overarching single "mission," he has accomplished it in Jesus Christ, and he will fully complete it through the continuing work of the Holy Spirit and Jesus' second coming. Christ-centered missions recognize this divine initiative, divine empowerment, divine guidance, and divine commitment.

JESUS SPEAKS ENGLISH, TOO

One assuring piece of evidence that Jesus is continuing his mission is the fact that human beings can talk in English (and countless other languages) about him and his mission. There was no English language when Jesus told his disciples that they would spread out from Jerusalem to Judea, Samaria, and the ends of the earth – which included the eventual English-speaking pagan Britons. More than a command directing believers to spread outward in concentric circles from our own local or regional "Jerusalems," Jesus' words recorded in Acts 1:8 predicted what began to unfold at Pentecost (Acts 2), then continued by the scattering of the early disciples through persecution "throughout the regions of Judea and Samaria" (Acts 8:1), through Philip's evangelistic ministry in Samaria and to the Ethiopian eunuch (Acts 8), and through the church-planting ministry of Paul (Acts 13ff.) and other apostles. Throughout that process, either by the miraculous display of the Spirit's power or through Spirit-guided human translation, people have been hearing "in our own tongues the mighty works of God" (Acts 2:11) – including Greek-speaking Gentiles (Acts 11:20). Eventually, in the fourteenth century AD, God's Word was translated even into English. The omnilingual Jesus does indeed speak English, too! He is relentless in his mission to redeem the whole earth, including people from every tribe, tongue, and nation.

This universal Jesus Christ keeps shouldering his way into particular situations and languages all over the world through the Spirit-guided translation of the Bible. In so doing, he speaks afresh to, and is trusted by, first-generation and subsequent-generation believers alike. How he is in fact understood by those believers amid their various situations and in their various languages is manifested in quite distinct ways. First-generation Christians are aware that they are on the frontiers of Christianity's engagement with the world. Battle lines are clear, confrontations with evil spirits are overt, and new expressions of Christian living must be forged in the crucible of fresh Bible translations and worship forms. Christians in succeeding generations then face the challenge of staying on the cutting edge of God's ongoing redeeming work. In fact, what inevitably seems to occur as the generations go by is a consolidation and protection of systems (including theological ones), structures (including organizations), and monuments (buildings, statues, and otherwise) that are constructed. "We've always done it this way" and "My, what a beautiful, but practically empty, cathedral" can become all too common remarks. Apart from the fresh winds of Spirit-induced awareness of the need to be continually engaging the world, a hazy entropy can begin to envelop Christians and cloud their view of their mission. This engagement takes place both in one's local situation and in other contexts with which one is organically connected through various local expressions of the global Christian community.

An institution such as Covenant Theological Seminary, which is engaged in training people to carry out the Christian mission, is a perfect case in point. Located in the Midwestern United States, Covenant Seminary has, throughout its half-century of existence, seen its faculty, administration, and student body made up primarily of middle-class, English-speaking U.S.-Americans of northwest European ancestry. The Christian gospel entered this general stream of humanity centuries earlier, and the Protestant churches that have been nurturing most members of the Covenant Seminary community have heritages that stretch back over several generations. Part of the inheritance of these church traditions has been a European Christendom, settled church society, whereby the church has tended to maintain both its own structures and the surrounding societal status quo. (This became true of most Protestant churches that developed out of the Reformation, along with the established Roman Church.) Furthermore, "missions was thought of as something distinct from the mainstream of the church's life," an activity of a select few that took place in faraway and exotic lands. Similarly, theological disciplines had become fixed – biblical, systematic, historical, and practical – and it was unclear where mission studies, if they were even seen as necessary or thought of as legitimate, were supposed to fit in relation to the other disciplines.[1] With such an inheritance, it has been a great challenge to Covenant Seminary to train ministers who understand that they are on the frontier of theological and gospel-driven service in the world. Thankfully, God has not left those of us at Covenant Seminary to our own devices, nor has he left us to sink into the black hole of monocultural myopia. While no doubt bearing marks of an inheritance that had ceased to see itself as being on a frontier mission into its own context, Covenant Seminary has had a steady and passionate involvement with various settings around the world, both through graduates (U.S.-American and international) and through its various faculty, staff, and board members. Along with the prodding of such stalwarts as former missions professor Addison Soltau (quoted above), these international involvements have kept the Seminary's eyes searching far and wide. And while "missions" has thus been understood to pertain to people and places "out there," nevertheless these wider connections have helped to cultivate the Seminary's perspective of being on a God-given mission to "train servants of the triune God" for a lifetime of ministry. This well-articulated statement of the Seminary's mission springs out of an understanding of and vision for God's worldwide redemptive mission.

God has indeed acted decisively in Jesus Christ to redeem the entire cosmos – including those Midwestern U.S.-Americans of northwest European descent. No aspect of creation has been left untouched, whether visible or invisible, macro or micro, corporate or individual, public or private. In his redemptive work, Jesus grants faith to people: those who were dead in their sins have been awakened to new life by the Spirit of Jesus calling them to belief in him. Jesus never gives up on maturing his church: that includes adding new members as well as growing the Spirit's fruit in and through his people. Jesus' ongoing mission includes giving glimpses or foretastes of the just and peaceful world to come. God's people are thus interested and involved in social and public issues, both local and international. All of these aspects make up the full-orbed mission that Jesus will complete upon his second coming.

Jesus is often disruptive, gripping, and challenging in his ongoing mission of maturing his people. His work can have a topsy-turvy effect among those who assume they know him well – such as those of us at Covenant Theological Seminary. Take, for example, the English designation "Lord" that we use for Jesus. On the one hand, it might seem silly to ask whether or not the term is a biblical one. After all, it is right there in the Bible for anyone to see, plain as day. However, the New Testament originally called Jesus *Kurios*. This was a radical, confrontational confession that had public, religio-political connotations within the Roman Empire. The question then arises (as Jesus somewhat uncomfortably shoulders his way into our contemporary, U.S.-American religio-socio-economic-political setting): what is the best equivalent confessional term to use for him? "Lord" may have been the best word several centuries ago in England. But we do not have "lords" in the United States of today, apart from apartment "land*lords*" or fictitious "lords" in video games and movies. Jesus will not be relegated to such sideline, esoteric positions as he presses in on us as our Sole Owner, President, Master, Boss, CEO, King, Commander-in-Chief, Hero, and whatever other designation best approximates – in live, up-to-date, all-encompassing terms – all that he is as *Kurios*. He will complete his mission among us, even when it is disruptive, messy, and disconcerting.

JESUS' COMPREHENSIVE MISSION

Christ-centered missions have as their aim to contribute to God's "plan for the fullness of time, to unite all things in him, things in heaven and things on earth" (Eph. 1:10). Only God's gracious heart would want to orchestrate such a plan to save the world he created, a world that has thumbed its rebellious nose at him. Christ-centered missions embody that grace and love, as God sends his people into his world – whether across cultural boundaries or within their own contexts – to serve and reclaim the earth for its rightful and caring owner.

Once again, "missions" are organized, intentional Christian efforts to bring the whole gospel to the whole world. Normally the term "missions" connotes cross-cultural or international (in a geopolitical sense) ministry. In considering here "*Christ-centered* missions," we are focusing first and foremost on Christ's gracious initiative. We also therefore must remember that Christian missions efforts are to be ever looking to Jesus for his leading, his enablement, and ultimately, for his glory. Therefore, we must also expand our notion of Christian missions. In addition to the simple idea of our going across cultures to proclaim the gospel, we must include the notion of our being sent by Jesus into our own cultural settings. Qualifications are needed here and will come later. The point is this: one does not have to go across the world to be involved in missions.

Just as important is the notion that, as we are sent as servants into both our own and others' settings, we are molded and matured by Jesus within those settings. God shapes and changes his people as he uses them for gospel ministry. What happens to Peter as he follows God's call to minister to the house of Cornelius is a classic example (Acts 10:1–11:17). This *coram Deo*-type of self-awareness is an essential aspect of Christian missions.

One more crucial note is needed here before we continue. Insofar as Christ's church is inherently international and, today, more worldwide than ever, the "we" who are sent into our own and others' cultures consists of all types of nationalities, languages, races, and ethnicities, living all over the world. Christ-centered missions is initiated and empowered by Christ, not by any single sector of his international people.[2] *The latent assumption that we know what "missions" means, and that, namely, it involves "my" kind of people – U.S.-Americans, in this case – going elsewhere, must be checked and critically examined.* The importance of this point cannot be over-exaggerated, and it will emerge at various places throughout our discussion.

Whatever meaning we give to the word, "missions" spring from God's singular "mission" in Christ, which is all-encompassing and as such permeates the entire world, and indeed the whole created order. We will use these two overarching constructs of the world and the created order to organize the remainder of our discussion of how God's single, comprehensive mission works itself out throughout all that he has made.

A Mission Throughout the World

"The whole church taking the whole gospel to the whole world" has been a watchword of the modern missions movement.[3] There is little debate among Christians about the validity of such an overarching statement of Christian missions (although non-evangelicals might be uneasy with the imperialistic sound of "taking" any religious truth to other people). The worldwide church is to minister the entirety of Christ's gospel to everyone.

In speaking of Jesus carrying out his mission through his church and throughout the world, it helps first to clarify both the spiritual and extensive-geographic meanings of "the world."[4] That is, God's "world" mission concerns, on the one hand, "the realm that does not yet acknowledge the rule of God." This meaning is the more theological one used on occasion by the apostle John – for example, when he records Jesus saying, "In the world you will have tribulation. But take heart; I have overcome the world" (John 16:33b); and when he himself says, "Do not love the world or the things in the world. If anyone loves the world, the love of the Father is not in him" (1 John 2:15). Indeed, "The whole world lies in the power of the evil one" (1 John 5:19) and as such is the object of God's mission to reclaim it through Christ's salvation (and, sadly, but to God's glory, through its destruction by God's judgment).

The other side of the same coin is that the "world" refers to all of creation in its entirety, and in particular the entire human race spread throughout the global expanse. Paul thus writes of the gospel that "in the whole world it is bearing fruit and growing" (Col. 1:6). Similarly, Jesus says, "For God so loved the world, that he gave his only Son, that whoever believes in him should not perish but have eternal life" (John 3:16). Because of God's love in Jesus for the entire world, "Whoever believes in him is not condemned" (John 3:18), no matter who they are.

Peoples

The full scope of the "world" God loves thus includes all kinds of people, or all "nations." These are *panta ta ethne*, "all nations" or "all the peoples," of whom Jesus speaks to his disciples in the Great Commission (Matt. 28:19). It is to "all nations" that "repentance and forgiveness of sins should be proclaimed in his name ... beginning from Jerusalem" (Luke 24:47). Because God is the universal Creator of all peoples and is not some local tribal deity, "everyone who calls on the name of the Lord will be saved" (Rom. 10:13), irrespective of nationality or ethnicity.

Some interpreters stress that the Bible's frequent references to "the nations" have a primarily religious meaning: "mankind in its separation from the Creator and Redeemer God."[5] They would caution against the sociological or anthropological understanding of "the nations" as "people groups" which is quite common today in evangelical circles. Thankfully, we do not face an either-or choice here. "The nations" of the world are all sinful bearers of God's image. They/we manifest unique cultural characteristics within their/our various socio-political groupings, from language to educational structures to inheritance customs to goods-production systems. Using both religious and sociological lenses to view the world's peoples helps in determining how Jesus would use us to speak and live out the gospel most pointedly in all of our particular situations – including to people groups still "unreached" by the Christian gospel.[6]

The Christ-centered character of Christian missions is summed up well in Jesus' post-resurrection declaration to his disciples: "Peace be with you. As the Father has sent me, even so I am sending you" (John 20:21). Jesus has sent his disciples out among the peoples of the world. Sometimes he has led his church to organize itself to send missionaries to different kinds of people, as when the Christian community in Antioch sent out Paul and Barnabas (Acts 13:1–3). Today, God has given Covenant Theological Seminary specific organizational relationships with various international missions organizations. In particular, Mission to the World (MTW) is the international missions sending agency of the Presbyterian Church in America; several Covenant Seminary graduates serve in various parts of the world as MTW missionaries doing church planting, street children ministry, theological education, and other ministries. Presbyterian Mission International (PMI) is a network of support relationships involving certain international Covenant Seminary graduates who are engaged in strategic ministries all over the world. These and other structures are examples of the myriad of organized Christian missions efforts being carried out among the nations.

At the same time, Jesus has sent all of his people into the world. All of us live among imperfect and unredeemed peoples/nations. We all are "sojourners and exiles," living in societies, workplaces, and families (1 Peter 2:11–3:7). In that sense, all graduates (as well as present students, faculty, board, and staff) of Covenant Theological Seminary, along with all other Christians, are missionaries whom Jesus has sent into his world. Some serve as missionaries in the organized sense, while others lead God's people in various types of pastoral service in North America.

Places

In the same "unorganized" sense that God has sent all Covenant Seminary graduates into the world as his ambassadors and missionaries, all of them also serve on the mission field. There is no geographical location, no geopolitical entity exempt from God's redemptive, missional concern. Moreover, there is no locale that once did but at some point ceased to lie within that same redemptive, missional concern. The gospel has had its effect in some areas of the world earlier and longer than in others, but no area of the world is as yet fully redeemed. *Every locale, culture, people, and socio-political setting throughout the earth – whether "reached" or "unreached" by the gospel message – remains an object of God's worldwide mission.*

To think otherwise is to slip into unbiblical and destructive alternatives. One alternative would be racist or nationalistic, wherein "my kind of people" or "my country" alone is blessed of "god." Such a deity is tribal, not the universal God of the Bible. Another alternative, which can be both racist and nationalistic, would be an Islamic or European Christendom-type of territorial religious faith. Islam separates the world into *dar al-Islam* ("house of submission" or "house of God") and *dar al-Harb* ("house of war"), where infidels and unbelievers live.[7] Roughly speaking, the former lands are ruled by Muslim governments, and the latter have non-Muslim governments. Similarly, European Christendom – which was carried over into the North American colonies and still has its lingering effects – saw Europe as Christian and the rest of the world as inhabited by heathens in darkness. Such simplistic, black-and-white views of the world neglect the sin and injustice present in all settings, as well as the worldwide presence of God's image-bearing human beings, not to mention the practically global Christian community scattered among the nations of the world.

Christ-centered missions see *Kurios* Jesus as too dangerous and unmanageable for any hint of racist, nationalistic, or territorial notions of

God's kingdom or of missions. Thus, even such a useful construct as the well-known and widely appreciated "10/40 Window"[8] needs to be scrutinized to ensure that it is not abused. All people are susceptible to deeply intertwined geopolitical and religious allegiances, which often lie under the radar of our conscious examinations. Without great care and insight, Christians from a U.S. setting, such as that of Covenant Theological Seminary, can allow racial or national interests to overshadow their biblically informed views of people living in such missiologically defined areas as the 10/40 Window – as well as of ourselves as people living in supposedly Christian territory. All of us, in Adam, are marred bearers of God's image. All of our settings are marred by injustice and sin. And all of us in the international body of Christ have the privilege and responsibility of communicating to others the gospel of grace.

God's mission, and hence Christian missions, is directed throughout his world, to all peoples and places. In the earliest Christian generations, the gospel spread into India, northeast Africa, southern Europe, Syria, and China. After settling in Europe and going through fits and starts elsewhere, the gospel has now spread into all regions of the world in recent generations. God's all-encompassing missional concern is for all nations and locales, not just those defined by certain theological, missiological, sociological, national, or other categories. Jesus has sent his people throughout the world.

A Mission Throughout the Created Order

Insofar as God's world mission is his redemption of the cosmos, that mission extends in one way or another to all levels of his creation. While we could employ various organizing schemes to describe this whole aspect of Jesus' mission (for example, the biblical cosmology of creatures in the heavens, on the earth, and under the earth; or, things seen and unseen), here we will consider his mission throughout the created order, vis-à-vis spiritual beings, human beings, and social structures.

Spiritual Beings

Luke records how the seventy-two disciples whom Jesus sent out on a short-term missions trip returned and reported, "Lord, even the demons are subject to us in your name!" Jesus' immediate response to them is striking: "I saw Satan fall like lightning from heaven" (Luke 10:1-18). This is an important glimpse into the macrocosmic, unseen drama described by John: "The reason the Son of God appeared was to destroy the works of the devil" (1 John 3:8b). Paul, too, notes that God's "manifold wisdom," exercised in Christ's gospel, is being "made known to the rulers and authorities in the heavenly places," wherein God points to his international people and mocks Satan's foiled attempt to deceive the world's peoples (Eph. 3:10; Rev. 20:3). In other words, a central part of Jesus' mission to redeem his Father's created order has been to taunt and destroy Satan and his legions. God's obedient angels have also been active in an ongoing way as "ministering spirits sent out to serve for the sake of those who are to inherit salvation" (Heb. 1:14).

Those of us who have inherited a scientific worldview tend to snicker at any mention of angels and demons. Even if those of us at a Bible-believing institution such as Covenant Theological Seminary acknowledge – at least, intellectually – such spiritual realities, operatively we have a hard time recognizing their existence. However, both the Bible and other cultures that have been influenced only minimally by scientific rationalism testify clearly to the continuing reality and activity of spiritual beings, whether those beings are good or evil, and whether they are understood as ancestors or various types of intermediaries. Moreover, dealing with these real and often powerful beings is a crucial part of living in these settings: Christ's work – and thus that of Christian missions – does in fact deal with them.

To explain the disparity between scientifically oriented (particularly Western) and other cultures' experiences of spiritual realities, Christian anthropologist and missiologist Paul Hiebert developed what is now a well-used category of analysis: "the flaw of the excluded middle."[9] By this scheme, Western worldviews include a top tier of a supreme being and a bottom tier of nature, but the middle tier of spiritual realities, commonly recognized in other three-level worldviews, is absent. But as Covenant Seminary Master of Divinity graduates Natee Tanchanpongs (PMI missionary), Dave Veldhorst, and Graham Waterhouse (both as MTW missionaries) know from serving in Bangkok, the most pressing issue Thai Christians face is how to deal with spiritual forces.[10] Unseen beings are seemingly more overt in their activity in places where people acknowledge their existence than they are in contexts where they have allegedly been explained away.

Jesus came to destroy Satan's work. Part of his plan for accomplishing that is to send his people – armed with the gospel – out into the world, the whole of which (as we have already noted) "lies in the power of the evil one." Carrying out Jesus' mission with respect to spiritual beings is not everything to Christian ministry, despite what those who blame all ills on demonic activity and possession would have us believe. At the same time, Christ-centered missions will necessarily deal with these realities – realities with which Jesus himself certainly dealt and which he continues to subdue – overtly or covertly – in his redemptive mission.

Human Beings

Christians whose missions are Christ-centered will, of course, also co-labor with Jesus in his mission to redeem people throughout all of creation. Human beings are the apex of God's creation. Through the original sin of Adam, creation's representative, the covenant curse rightly fell on the entire cosmic order. The second Adam's finished work will save God's creation – with a present focus on people who, by grace, receive the free gift of right standing with their

Creator, from whom they have been previously estranged: "If, because of one man's trespass, death reigned through that one man, much more will those who receive the abundance of grace and the free gift of righteousness reign in life through the one man Jesus Christ" (Rom. 5:17). One day "the creation itself will be set free from its bondage to decay and obtain the freedom of the glory of the children of God" (Rom. 8:21). Human beings rightly are the central focus of Christ-centered missions – and that means human beings not only in the individual sense, but also in the corporate senses of the church and the larger social structures within which those individuals live their lives.

Individuals. Evangelical missions, with their eighteenth-century pietist beginnings, have always had a basic, and often pervasive, concern for individuals hearing and believing the gospel of God's love for them as shown in the crucifixion and resurrection of Jesus. The Bible's teaching of individual responsibility before God,[11] intertwined with Western individualism, has cultivated the bedrock conviction of modern missions that its central (if not only) goal is the salvation of individual souls.

But Christ-centered missions also mean that all types of individuals, particularly with respect to cultural context, hear the gospel in an appropriate, understandable fashion. The modern Western legacy of Descartes' "I think, therefore I am" connotes an ultimate human identity of an acultural, disembodied, individual soul-mind. Unfortunately, such a notion, without self-critical examination, informs foundational evangelical assumptions about who people are. The African proverb "We are, therefore I am" jives better with the biblical notion of personhood located in concrete contexts of language and culture. Thus, when Paul writes in Romans 10:10 that "with the heart one believes and is justified, and with the mouth one confesses and is saved," he means a concrete individual who speaks a particular language, wears a particular type of clothing, and eats particular types of foods. Indeed, at the core of the gospel of grace is the liberating message that all kinds of people, without distinction, are welcome to come to God in Jesus Christ. As Paul continues, "For the Scripture says, 'Everyone who believes in him will not be put to shame.' For there is no distinction between Jew and Greek; the same Lord is Lord of all, bestowing his riches on all who call on him. For 'everyone who calls on the name of the Lord will be saved'" (Rom. 10:11-13). "Everyone" here refers not just to every single individual per se, but to "all kinds of people."

Christ-centered missions thus focus on individuals throughout the world, people who identify with all sorts of contexts, traditions, and languages. That is one reason why Covenant Theological Seminary teaches the original biblical languages of Hebrew, Aramaic, and Greek. Faithful interpreters of God's Word must be familiar with God's message as it was originally given. They must then translate that message responsibly in order to convey it to their contemporaries (including, of course, twenty-first-century U.S.-Americans), who speak languages and live in situations quite different than those of the people who first received the biblical revelations. The Protestant instinct to translate the Scriptures into every human language recognizes the basic contextual and linguistic location of the very people to whom Jesus is carrying out his worldwide mission.

The Church. While extending to individuals throughout all nations, Jesus' mission also is focused on gathering a corporate people: Christ's body, the Church. Evangelicals' individualistic notions have always predisposed them towards individuals in their missions efforts. Even so, church planting has been at the forefront of Reformed missions (as well as more recent evangelical missions) because of the recognition that God's covenant is with his corporate people, not just with individuals. God's basic covenantal promise – "I will be your God, and you will be my people" – involves both the Old and New Covenant people of God in the collective sense. The early Reformed missiologist Gisbertus Voetius (1589–1676) thus had as the second point of his three-pronged goal for missions the planting of churches.[12]

Jesus' mission to gather his church has many facets; and so, therefore, must Christian missions. One obvious matter is to bring in people "from every tribe and language and people and nation" for whom Christ died (Rev. 5:9). Christ-centered missions will focus on unreached people groups, having as their goal an indigenous Christian movement that is able to communicate the gospel message effectively in its own cultural context. The determination of Jesus to bring in all types of people – as shown in his declaration that "I have other sheep that are not of this fold. I must bring them also, and they will listen to my voice. So there will be one flock, one shepherd" (John 10:16) – ought to inspire Christian missions to be ever pushing to see that the unreached hear the voice of the Good Shepherd who lived, died, rose, reigns, and is coming again.

Another crucial aspect of Jesus' gathering of his people is the calling of his church to be inclusive of all kinds of people. This often means bringing together into one local congregation a variety of people from widely different economic, cultural, or ethnic backgrounds. The apostle Paul was intent on helping the Christians in Rome, Galatia, Ephesus, and elsewhere to understand and flesh out the reality that, as Christians, "There is neither Jew nor Greek, there is neither slave nor free, there is neither male nor female, for you are all one in Christ Jesus" (Gal. 3:28). Paul did not mean, of course, that such human traits disappear when people become Christians. Nor did he mean, I believe, that every local congregation has to be what we would call a multicultural or international church. A congregation's context helps to determine its makeup, so a relatively monocultural context will naturally give rise to a relatively monocultural church. Moreover, Donald MacGavran's well-known and oft-criticized Homogenous Unit Principle (HUP) is powerfully accurate and quite constructive for understanding how and why churches grow within particular sociological boundaries.[13] For convincing examples of the HUP in operation, Covenant Theological Seminary and its parent denomination, the Presbyterian Church in America (PCA), need look no further than their own constituencies. What a Christ-centered missions focus does require us to remember, however, is that the universal Savior of the world will not be confined to any one kind of people – and thus, neither should his church.

Related to this facet of Jesus' mission is the understanding that the church itself never ceases to be an object of Jesus' missional concern. Christ-centered missions originate with Christ, and he remains ever concerned about the maturing of his people. We his people will never be perfect until the eschaton. Moreover, the contexts into which Jesus sends us are ever-changing; we can never hope to "nail everything down" and have final answers for all the many issues – theological or otherwise – that we face in any given situation (e.g. what is an alleged final, orthodox, meaningful, faithful English-language description of who Jesus is?). Furthermore, each Christian church's own marred, sinful, and imperfect context is always militating against its people's godliness, faithfulness, and effectiveness. Churches are always at odds with their settings, even while they are at home there and care deeply about the welfare of those settings. For all of these reasons and more,[14] the church – both at large and in particular – is always the object of Jesus' missional goal to mature his people, even while he uses it as his instrument in Christ-centered missions.

Social Structures. Jesus' creation-wide mission is concerned with spiritual beings, human beings, and, indeed, with matters of public justice and mercy. Only in the new heavens and new earth will God's kingdom be fully realized. For now, Jesus gives glimpses and foretastes of that perfect kingdom – shafts of light, as it were, breaking into the darkness of a still broken and unredeemed world.

Evangelicals (especially in the West) have not always been comfortable with a "social justice" focus. After all, it was in the wake of the post-World War II formation of the World Council of Churches (WCC) that evangelicals intentionally organized themselves into the separate Lausanne Movement – a movement whose watchword was "world evangelization," in distinction from the socio-political interests prevalent in many WCC circles.

Even so, there have always been evangelical voices (Carl Henry in the West, for example, as well as many more outside the West) that have stood for the biblical fullness of God's mission to redeem the entirety of his world. Such artificial distinctions as the eternality of God's Word and people's souls versus the temporality of everything else that will be burned up – thus justifying some evangelicals' exclusive interest in evangelism (and possibly church planting) at the expense of any ultimate interest in this world – arise out of unexamined philosophical dualisms and neglect the Bible's overarching emphasis on God's more seamless kingdom priorities. Thankfully, the more holistic world-and-life-view of a Reformed theological perspective aids our understanding of Christ-centered missions as rightly focusing on all matters of God's created order – including the wide variety of complex, context-dependent human social structures such as family, economics, government, education, medicine and healing, laws and their enforcement, and work.

We should note that cities, whether big or small, form a unique and crucial locus of interrelated social structures. Surely it is no accident that ever-accelerating rates of urbanization on a worldwide scale are bringing all kinds of people from all over the world together into international conglomerates. The twin sweeps of Scripture and history show that God's redemptive providence is moving from a garden-centered creation to a New Jerusalem. As a particular and even central focus of following Christ's mission, Christian churches have unprecedented challenges and opportunities to serve people and the cause of social justice in today's cities.

At least four qualifications are appropriate at this point. First, any number of different Bible passages could be cited concerning this particular topic of social structures. Within recent missiological discussions, Luke 4:18-19 has been used to counter an allegedly truncated view of the Great Commission that focuses exclusively on evangelism and church planting. A rejoinder points to Paul's allegedly exclusively evangelistic and church-planting interests. And on the arguments go. For our purposes, the overarching covenantal interest of Jesus' mission is an adequate redemptive-historical and biblical-theological theme to constrain social and public focus.

Second, Jesus' mission to reclaim social structures and bring his kingdom to bear in contemporary settings is not dependent on our millennial positions. While various views may lend themselves more or less to active social engagement in connection with Christ-centered missions, premillennialism, amillennialism, postmillennialism, and the increasingly popular pan-millennialism ("it'll all pan out in the end") are all compatible with a vital interest in what happens in matters of justice and mercy.

Third, whatever degree of social interest or type of millennial view we might have, we must caution ourselves against expecting to usher in the kingdom of God prematurely. The new heavens and new earth will be realized after Jesus returns, not before. For now, we and the whole creation groan "in the pains of childbirth" as we wait eagerly in hope (Rom. 8:22-24).

Finally, much of the rub comes when the discussion enters the realm of social service versus social action. This is particularly true concerning the involvement of expatriate missionaries in their host environment's social issues. On the one hand, few evangelicals disagree with the importance of social concern (even if some are reluctant to give it much emphasis for fear of de-emphasizing evangelism and church planting). "Word and deed" ministry (i.e. social service) has become an important rallying cry in recent evangelical missions circles, with a corresponding rise in ministries focused on street children, AIDS, medical care, and economic development, to name a few. Many evangelicals balk at the suggestion of social action which involves organized, intentional efforts at addressing socio-economic-political matters.

Different contexts alone contribute to varying evangelical attitudes: churches in the U.S. and Iran, for example, have extremely different heritages and political environments with which to deal. Even within the New Testament period we see different approaches and effects in various situations. Jesus was at times confrontational (e.g. driving out money changers from the temple), at times compliant (e.g. submitting to his arrest and execution), but always disconcerting and challenging (e.g. "The poor you always have with you," "You have no authority over me at all unless it had been given you from above"). Paul could use his Roman citizenship as leverage (e.g. in Philippi; Acts 16:35-40)), and his ministry sometimes caused social-economic-political upheaval (e.g. in Ephesus; Acts 19:23-41).

Moreover, contemporary interpretations of biblical incidents and teaching can vary considerably based on the interpreters' contexts. U.S. conservative evangelicals living in relative peace and affluence – most members of the Covenant Seminary and PCA communities, for example – understand Jesus' "render unto Caesar and to God" retort to the religio-political leaders of his day as advocating a political philosophy of church–state separation. We would also understand Paul's Romans 13:1-7 instructions as teaching obedience to political authorities (aside from blatant cases requiring civil disobedience, such as in Acts 4:19-20). However, Jesus' answer to the Pharisees and Herodians could just as easily (and, I believe, more faithfully to Jesus' intention) imply a broadside attack against the leaders' charade of outward religiosity; their "piety" actually serves as a means of preserving an unjust and oppressive status quo. And less advantaged readers of Romans can interpret Paul's instructions there as anything from a scheme for resistance to a type of coping strategy, particularly when 13:1-7 is put into the larger context of the entire letter.[15]

Different strategies, issues, socio-economic-political status, and a myriad of other factors make the particulars of social involvement a complicated matter (albeit an essential one) requiring much Christian forbearance, liberty, and mutual understanding. What is most important for us to note is the full scope of Christ-centered missions in light of Jesus' comprehensive mission for his entire created order. He cares about spiritual beings, about people, and about the corporate structures within his world. His mission is to work throughout his creation, including the elimination of the scandals of poverty, disease, and wars. Christian missions must cooperate and follow accordingly.

SUMMING UP THE UNMANAGEABLE

In his mission, Jesus orchestrates both organized Christian missions and unorganized Christian witness throughout the various sectors of his world into which he sends his people to live and to serve. Christ-centered missions thus focus on Jesus: his service, his initiative, his enablement, his leading, and his glory.

Jesus the *Kurios* is untamed and unmanageable; his mission is thus difficult if not impossible to encapsulate. Here we have sought to describe how he disruptively shoulders his way into our various linguistic (and, indeed, total) contexts. We have considered how he works out his comprehensive mission among all peoples and places, as well as among all levels of his creation. In so doing, we have seen how Jesus leaves no area of individual or corporate life untouched. My ethnicity, my mother tongue, my nationality and patriotism, my socio-economic standing, my intimate relationships – my everything – are subject to Jesus' penetrating gaze, refinement, and use. Moreover, our human academic categories (including our theological disciplines), our macro-economic systems, our geopolitical maneuverings, our family arrangements – everything about our societies – are also objects of Jesus' redemptive mission.

Thus, while remembering that any tidy summation of Jesus' mission would be inadequate, here is the working definition of "God's world mission" that we use at Covenant Theological Seminary: "the triune God's redemption of the cosmos, wherein he grants, among all the world's peoples, faith in Jesus Christ, maturing of the church, and foretastes of the heavenly city." Christ-centered missions humbly seek to carry out God's gracious initiative throughout his world. He *will* complete his mission. We know that heaven and hell are subject to him. Jesus is *Kurios*.

Maranatha and *amen*!

1. Addison P. Soltau, "Mobilizing the Seminaries," in Harvie M. Conn, ed., *Reaching the Unreached: The Old-New Challenge* (Phillipsburg, New Jersey: P&R Publishing Company, 1984), 153.

2. The worldwide presence of the Christian church, due to a global southward shift resulting in the undeniable demographic reality that the majority of Christians now live outside the West, is increasingly well known. Perhaps the single most comprehensive analysis of this dramatic change is Philip Jenkins, *The Next Christendom: The Coming of Global Christianity* (New York: Oxford University Press, 2002). Related to this remarkable shift is the increasing number of non-Western missionaries, who serve cross-culturally both within and outside their own countries. Missionaries within and from South Korea, Nigeria, Brazil, and India are among the many examples.

3. This phrase is taken from the Lausanne Covenant, drawn up in 1974 as an evangelical alternative to the ecumenical documents of the World Council of Churches. Even so, the understanding of the church as worldwide, as well as of the gospel as holistic, characterizes both the evangelical and ecumenical expressions of the twentieth-century missions movement – even if there are some crucial differences in nuance as to what constitutes "the gospel." Lausanne Committee for World Evangelization, *The Lausanne Story: The Whole Church Taking the Whole Gospel to the Whole World* (Charlotte, N.C.: Lausanne Committee for World Evangelization, 1987), 29.

4. This framework and the following quotation are from Wilbert R. Shenk, *Changing Frontiers of Mission*, American Society of Missiology Series, No. 28 (Maryknoll, NY: Orbis Books, 1999), 184. Earlier (17), Shenk notes five connotations of the Bible's use of the word "world": (1) the physical universe, (2) the

earth's human habitants, (3) the scene of human activity, (4) forces arrayed against God, and (5) the object of God's mission. Shenk's fine historico-theological analysis is required reading for the core curriculum course "God's World Mission" at Covenant Theological Seminary.

5. Richard De Ridder, *Discipling the Nations* (Grand Rapids, Mich.: Baker Book House, 1971), 189. Cf. Pieter Tuit's further explanatory comments in his "The Relationship Between Church and Kingdom Within the Missionary Theology of Johan H. Bavinck," *REC FOCUS*, Vol. 1, No. 4, December 2001, note 15. Available online at http://community.gospelcom.net/Brix?pageID=3799; accessed July 20, 2005.

6. The capacity of an indigenous Christian community to reach its own people with the gospel has been the central criterion in the evolving definition of an "unreached" people group which seems to have settled on approximately 2 percent of the general population. Cf. "Joshua Project," available online at http://www.joshuaproject.net/definitions.php#unreached; accessed July 20, 2005.

7. "Dar al-Islam," in *Wikipedia: The Free Encyclopedia*, available at http://en.wikipedia.org/wiki/Dar_al-Islam; accessed July 20, 2005. As pointed out in this article, there is a third category of *dar al-Ahd*, meaning the "house of treaty," invented to describe the Ottoman Empire's relationship with its Christian tributary states.

8. "The rectangular area of North Africa, the Middle East and Asia between 10 degrees north and 40 degrees north latitude where 95 percent of the world's least-evangelized poor are found." From "Joshua Project," available online at http://www.joshuaproject.net/definitions.php#1040window; accessed July 20, 2005.

9. Paul G. Hiebert, "The Flaw of the Excluded Middle," *Missiology* 10, no. 1 (January, 1982): 35–47.

10. Part of the missions training that Covenant Seminary offers is regular international trips. One of those trips was in January, 2003. Previous graduates Natee and Dave helped to plan the trip; Graham was one of the student participants. Dave requested that I provide some training to the unprepared missionaries on this important but sorely neglected topic of spiritual beings and warfare – something I, too, was very ill-equipped to do.

11. See, for example, Ezekiel 18:20: "The soul who sins shall die. The son shall not suffer for the iniquity of the father, nor the father suffer for the iniquity of the son. The righteousness of the righteous shall be upon himself, and the wickedness of the wicked shall be upon himself."

12. The conversion of the heathen was the first point; the glory of God was the third. Cf., for example, J. H. Bavinck, *An Introduction to the Science of Missions* (Phillipsburg, N.J.: P&R Publishing, 1960), 155; Johannes Verkuyl, *Contemporary Missiology: An Introduction* (Grand Rapids, Mich.: Eerdmans, 1978), 21.

13. Working in the 1920s and 1930s as a third-generation missionary in India, MacGavran observed that people came to Christ, and local churches grew, in culturally uniform groups. The sociological explanation of that pattern, supported by biblical examples, is the Homogenous Unit Principle. Based on that principle, MacGavran formulated a model of church growth that accepted and even encouraged the development of culturally homogenous churches. MacGavran's writings and his teaching at Fuller Theological Seminary thus gave rise to the Church Growth School.

14. For example, Christians always have much to learn from venturing cross-culturally in ministry. Part of missions involvement is the maturing process through which Jesus takes his missionary agents. On a larger scale, one can say that the modern Western missions movement of the past half-millennium has brought great changes to the Western churches, just as it has effected great changes throughout the non-Western world.

15. One thought-provoking and challenging non-evangelical example of a relatively radical interpretation is Monya A. Stubbs, "Subjection, Reflection, Resistance: An African American Reading of the Three-Dimensional Process of Empowerment in Romans 13 and the Free-Market Economy," in Yeo Khiok-khng, ed., *Navigating Romans Through Cultures: Challenging Readings by Charting a New Course*, Romans Through History and Culture Series, ed. by Cristina Grenholm and Daniel Patte (New York: T&T Clark International, 2004), 171–97. An interpretation utilizing an exegetical methodology more agreeable to most evangelicals (and written within a "First World" context) would be Johannes Nissen, "Conformity, Non-Conformity, and Critical Solidarity: The Church-State Issue and the Use of the Bible," *Mission Studies* XVII–1/2, 33/34 (2000): 240–62.

17
PASTORAL LEARNING AFTER SEMINARY

ROBERT W. BURNS

Director, Center for Ministry Leadership
Adjunct Professor of Practical Theology

Covenant Theological Seminary has always had a passion for pastors. The Seminary was established, first and foremost, as a place to prepare leaders for the local church. This should not come as a surprise, since its founding president, Dr. Robert G. Rayburn, was a pastor. Though known primarily for his work in academia, Dr. Rayburn remained vitally involved in the work of the local church throughout his life. His legacy remains a hallmark of the seminary.

The pastors who have graduated from Covenant Theological Seminary highly value the formal education they received as students. They consider the three or more years of pre-professional academic training at the seminary as an investment in their ministry. But neither these pastors nor the seminary faculty expect the granting of a degree to be the end of such education. Most of these pastors continue in varied forms of formal and informal educational pursuits, such as personal reading, attendance at conferences or retreats, dialogue with others in ministry, and advanced degree programs.

PROFESSIONAL LEARNING

When pastors think of education, they tend to overlook their professional experience of ministry practice in favor of procedural and theoretical elements of knowledge.[1] For example, I recently invited a Covenant Seminary graduate, who has spent years successfully planting a city church, to come to the seminary and share his experience with students. His response was sad, but typical: "What would I have to share with them?" He was unaware of the practical wisdom he had gained on the job.

Since a primary goal for pastors is to maintain an educated ministry, it is important for them – and for those charged with educating them – to understand how pastors acquire knowledge in daily practice. Donald A. Schön argues that the prevailing theory of professional knowledge separates knowing from doing and research from practice.[2] This theory, which he calls Technical Rationality, assumes that "professional activity consists of instrumental problem-solving made rigorous by the application of scientific theory and technique."[3]

In order to promote an informed ministry and to equip pre-professional and continuing pastoral education, it is important to identify how pastors learn on the job. Popular wisdom suggests that they acquire knowledge in the day-to-day struggles of the ministry. There is a body of adult education literature that coheres with this assumption, thus indicating that knowledge of the ministry is learned, but not necessarily taught. Schön believes that the knowledge of professionals develops through reflective practice.[4] The practical knowledge they draw on, built from a repertoire of examples, images, understanding, and actions, is called "knowing-in-action."[5] Schön calls the process of professionals applying this knowing-in-action to solve particular problems "reflection-in-action." As professionals, pastors are not fully aware of the knowledge they have in their professional repertoire.[6] Therefore, it is vital to help pastors make their practical knowledge explicit.[7]

At the same time, continuing pastoral education has focused primarily on updating technical knowledge and discussing special issues of practice.[8] One need only review the core courses of most Doctor of Ministry programs to verify this truth. This reflects the professionalization of ministry practice as a whole, which, Carroll states, is dominated by technical rationality.[9] There is a significant need for continuing pastoral education to be informed by and directly linked to the context of professional practice. [10]

METHODOLOGY OF THE STUDY

During 2000–1, I completed a qualitative research study with eleven pastors and church staff members. One purpose of this study was to identify the non-formal ways in which pastors learn after their time in seminary. Participants in the study were selected from two Presbyterian denominations in which a significant majority of Covenant Seminary graduates serve: the Presbyterian Church in America (PCA) and the Evangelical Presbyterian Church (EPC). In order to be included in the study, participants had to meet the following criteria: they had to be currently serving in a local church with over 200 members, have a minimum of ten years' experience in ministry, and at least five years of service in their current church. Seven different states spanning the entire continental United States were represented, including the West Coast, Midwest, and Southeast.

Since a significant number of churches in the two target denominations have fewer than 200 members, it is valid to ask why this criterion was used in the selection process. There is nothing intrinsically better or worse in a large congregation. However, there can be unique social differences between churches of more than 200 members and those with fewer than that number.[11] While "attendance figures, staff size, operating budget and the like are simplistic, sometimes misleading measures,"[12] for the purposes of this study it was felt that larger congregations would provide a wider variety of experiences and learning contexts.

Why was a qualitative research design selected to explore how pastors learn after seminary? Quantitative research focuses on a large, representative sample and seeks to test a prediction that can be generalized across a large population. Qualitative research, however, seeks to learn the meaning embedded in people's experiences, focusing on developing understanding gained through the stories of the participants. It is the task of qualitative research to define a specific group of interest and do an intensive study of that sample. The qualitative method was chosen for this study because it provides the appropriate means for accessing the personal life-worlds of participating individuals.[13] Furthermore, the study used a particular form of qualitative research called the critical incidents technique. This technique highlights particular, concrete, and contextually specific aspects of the participants' lives.[14] As interviews were conducted and transcribed, highlighted data was constantly compared to other data within the same transcript and across different transcripts.[15] By working back and forth between the data and emerging themes, categories were developed that, as much as possible, captured the participants' understanding of each incident.

THE LEARNING EXPERIENCE OF PASTORS

This study confirmed that pastors are trained both through *formal learning* (i.e. seminary education) and *learning in practice*. As the participating pastors reflected on their seminary education, they viewed it with sincere appreciation, but saw it as limited in providing an understanding of what they would truly experience in ministry. Their learning in practice involved a knowledge that developed on the job.

Formal Learning

Pastors often reflect on the relevance of their seminary education. The pastors involved in this study did not criticize their pre-professional training through traditional theological education. Those who commented on it reflected the statement of Karla, a staff member in a large midwestern church, who said, "Seminary was, to me, very satisfying."[16] At the same time, a constant refrain among the participants was that, upon entering the ministry, they were naïve about what they might face. For example, while Don, the pastor of a mid-sized church in the Midwest, deeply appreciated his formal seminary training, he said he learned everything about being an elder from mentors in his congregation. And, although he graduated with honors and received the highest award for preaching in his class, he confessed that when he began his ministry, "I did not know what I was doing. All I had was head knowledge." Brian, the pastor of a mid-sized southern church, agreed, saying, "I was prepared academically, but in terms of people skills and church dynamics, no. It was a baptism of fire for me."

For most participants, the aspect of their ministry preparation in seminary that stood out most in their memories was not the technical information that they received, but the personal sharing from professors about their own ministry experiences. Don and James (an African-American pastor of a multiracial church in a major city) both expressed how much the transparent lifestyles and honest sharing of seminary professors meant to them. This sharing took place in the classroom and in chapel sermons, where professors related their own ministry backgrounds. Don remembered, "One professor had little case studies from his pastoral ministry. He would give those to us and say, 'Now, how would you deal with those things?' And listening to how he actually dealt with them in his church was an eye-opener to me."

Learning in Practice

Learning in practice refers to the growth in knowledge that takes place as pastors gain experience and reflect on that experience. Participants in this study shared critical incidents from their own ministries, from which four ways of learning in practice were identified: reflection-in-action, reflection-on-action, mentors and models, and negative experiences.

Reflection-in-Action

The pastors shared how, in pastoral ministry, they face indeterminate situations and have to draw on whatever experience or information they have to make the best decisions under particular circumstances. This trial-and-error method does not imply random attempts to seek solutions. Rather, as the pastors face new challenges, they form the best solution possible, take steps of implementation, and adjust their plan in process as they evaluate the results. Reflection takes place "on the go" as they, like boxers in a ring, "bob and weave" through the multifaceted issues encountered in daily ministry.

For example, after Arthur began a new church, he and the elders decided to begin multiple congregations of the same church. He shared,

> When I started, I had no idea how to start a church. So it certainly was not in my mind to know how to start a second or a third. So it was all experimental as we went. We very much thought of it as one church. It was a bizarre situation. It was so novel. No one had ever done it. So what does this look like? How would it work? And we made some real mistakes in how we organized this thing.

Similarly, when the senior pastor was forced to resign after Brian had been on his staff for only two months, Brian related,

> I was flying by the seat of my pants and trying to hang on for dear life. I was trying to evaluate in my own mind, "What can I do to salvage this pastorate? What can I do to help the senior pastor, so that he doesn't get what I think is the shaft?" Then in the board meeting when he resigned, there were no negative votes, no real questions raised at the meeting. And I said to myself, "If the board's not going to support this guy, my leading a charge is not going to do any good." Then I had to go to the first congregational meeting I ever attended and serve as moderator, dealing with the senior pastor's resignation. I didn't know what I was doing. I was just absolutely a nervous wreck.

Even experienced pastors continued to learn through reflection-in-action. When his associate left to start a new congregation with a contemporary worship format in the same community, Ray – the pastor of a large church in a southern city – responded by initiating a similar worship service in his church.

> However ... our music guy couldn't do it. And we were hurt by what we were doing. It started off well, but in the long term, it was deadly. It tore up our Sunday school. So we finally decided – the elders decided – that we had to just axe that contemporary service because it was doing more harm than good. Well, when that happened, the people who liked the contemporary service left the church. Not all of them, but a lot of them. And I learned at that time you've got to be real careful, when you're in a difficult or crisis time, with the decisions you make. You can make decisions that have a short-term solution, but have a long-term problem.

As pastors use reflection-in-action, they build their repertoire of experience.

Reflection-on-Action
The pastors learned by thinking through a situation after it happened. They deepened their understanding of ministry practice by reflecting on their experience.

Joseph, a pastor in the Midwest, shared that, when he was a campus pastor, he would take time to compare his approach with other campus ministries. He would ask himself where and how the ministries were similar and different. "I would ask, 'How does this ministry compare with what other ministries do that I don't do? How are we different?'"

Sometimes reflection came in response to a crisis. When Brian shared his critical incident about the resignation of the senior pastor, he commented, "Most of the reflection took place after the fact." When he discussed a different experience, this time with a critical elder who fomented dissension toward him, he said, "I'm still learning lessons from that."

Sometimes the reflection of participants took place over an extended period of time. For example, Felix shared the lessons he learned from the disaster he went through in his first church:

> I went straight from that situation into working with one of the most effective leaders in the American church today. That one-two punch left me with – it's very hard to describe: a desire to learn from that pastor, even though we have quite different personalities and leadership styles, and the realization that I did make mistakes in that first church, and not to make them again.

Few pastors in this study reported that they ever consciously took time to reflect. Their learning seemed to be an unconscious process of accumulated experience. In fact, a number of the pastors expressed sincere thanks for the opportunity to sit down and talk about their experiences in such depth. "This has been good," they would say. "I've never taken the time to really think about what I've gone through." When asked how they had learned what they learned over the years, a number responded by saying either "I don't know" or "hard knocks."

Mentors and Models

In this study, a mentor was considered a wise and trusted person who acted as a guide on the educational journey.[17] A model was an individual or church that served as an example for imitation or comparison. Mentors and models had an important place in the learning of the participating pastors. This was evident in one of Don's critical incidents, where older elders served as mentors in helping him learn how to do ministry. He shared, "The grasp they had of what it meant to lead people was overwhelming to me. I would say the majority of what I've learned about being a pastor has come from that experience of working with those elders."

When Felix was trying to make sense of his trauma in the process of losing his first pastorate, he called older, experienced pastors for insight and advice. We have already seen that, when he left his church, he went "straight from that into working very closely with one of the most effective leaders in the American church today." That individual had an indelible impact on Felix: "I took everything I could from that leader, and by watching him I contrasted what he did with the mistakes I had made in my previous church."

Joseph experienced a unique model of ministry when he visited a particularly effective church in a different part of the country.

> That weekend blew me away. I mean, just completely blew me away. It was just amazing. Overwhelming. I realized that I wanted to be part of a ministry that is able to take people from coming to faith, to growing, and then to have all of their relationships affected. That church – it almost ruined me. It raised the bar to what we should be. I wasn't trying to duplicate them, but it was the intensity, the way in which they expected God to see something happen.

James was also impacted by a number of church models.

> While attending [his first seminary], I went to a black, inner-city church. And while I was at [his second seminary], I'd moved from going to an inner city black church to a very upper-class white church. My wife and I were probably the only black people in the whole place. And it was a huge church. At the same time, I was working in an inner-city ministry. This whole time it was building in me a kind of cross-cultural, crazy, mixed-up involvement in all kinds of stuff – from the poorest of the poor to the most wealthy; from folks that were white and black. I mean the whole experience really shaped the way I think about people in ministry.

Negative Experiences

Every participant in the study told stories of learning ministry practice through pain and disillusionment. The mantra, expressed one way or another by almost every pastor, was, "I learned the hard way." James experienced weeks of pain after some of his elders disagreed with the extent of his cross-cultural worship service.

> I was a defeated man. I went home, stood in front of my refrigerator in my kitchen, and broke down crying. I was messed up. And for two weeks, I started to quit, started to shut down. Then three elders came to me and said, "We are behind you 100 percent." When the fourth elder returned from a business trip, he'd moved to wanting a cross-cultural church. Now I have a session that is committed. It was all settled. And something in that crisis period did this.

Arthur, the pastor who had tried to start multiple congregations of the same church, shared that, in the process of growing one of these church plants, he was blindsided by Tom, the associate pastor who was leading the new congregation. The two men had been close friends in seminary, and Arthur had invited Tom to be part of his team based on the trust built in their past relationship. The deepest pain came when Arthur confronted Tom in a session meeting: "I asked him [if he had done a certain divisive thing]. He said, 'Yup, that's what happened.' And when he did, I broke out crying; I just started sobbing. I felt so betrayed. And I had been defending him."

This idea of learning through difficult experiences was stated most dramatically by Henry, an African-American pastor. He said he felt raped when leaders of his ministry did not trust him and colluded behind his back. "I didn't understand," he shared. "I never wanted the train to go down that track. But they didn't trust my integrity. They didn't know me."

According to Ray, learning through difficult experiences is even more poignant because the majority of pastors have an idealistic perspective when they enter into church ministry. Brian confirmed this:

> [The experience of the senior pastor being asked to resign the day after Brian's ordination] was sort of a wake-up call. I had never personally experienced any negative stuff in church. My assumption was rather naïve, that church life was more pleasant, more idyllic, that people more or less loved each other, after a fashion, anyway ... It made me less trusting. It scared me to death.

Henry also affirmed this initial idealism about the ministry. He said, "I was naïve. Here I came into this Christian environment and I thought, 'I can trust all these people.' Now, I'm still very trusting, but when I don't get that trust in return, I'll say to myself, 'They're going to get me. They're going to burn me. It's just a matter of time.'"

The Developmental Nature of Learning

As previously noted, this study identified learning in practice as cumulative in nature for pastors; they mature through levels of proficiency. Pastors generally enter the ministry with a great deal of technical knowledge, but little understanding of ministry practice. As Brian noted above, he was equipped academically, but ill prepared for the people skills he would need and the relational dynamics he would face in the church. Felix illustrates this undeveloped condition. When asked why, in his first church, he had selected people for eldership who turned on him immediately after their ordinations, Felix stated, "I was not experienced enough in leadership to realize where they were coming from." And when Henry shared his experience within a black parachurch organization, he noted, "I was young. I was just out of seminary. I just didn't know anything about how things worked."

Although Felix didn't know what to do early in his ministry, today his years of experience help him understand things differently. When asked how he would use what he learned in his first church to teach young church planters, he said:

> Well, it's hard for me to just look at that one experience, because there are more lenses I am looking through today. There is the lens of that first experience. And then there is the lens of the experience of working with a great pastoral leader while on the staff of his church. And finally, there is the lens of things going well in this church now for six years.

Joseph also emphasized the development of his knowledge. As he shared his critical incidents, he explained how his ministry philosophy grew through three different phases. Each new phase built on lessons learned in the previous phase, expanding and developing the maturity and complexity of knowledge.

New phases of ministry practice require new learning. Brian is now serving in his fifth pastorate and has been in the ministry for twenty-three years. However, he explained that every new ministry creates a new learning experience. To put it in his words, "You never know the full story [about ministry in a particular church] until you're swimming in the pond."

The wisdom of the oldest pastor in the sample puts this developmental nature of learning into perspective. He shared that it takes time and patience to grow and learn. This is hard when young pastors receive a seminary degree and believe they are ready to fulfill their dreams. When asked what he would say to a group of seminary graduates going into the ministry, Ray said:

> I think you need to make peace with reality. I think a lot of people just can't do that. They can't make peace with what is, and what should be. That just frustrates a lot of young people. I find they come out of seminary and have got this very idealistic idea of how people in a church should be, how officers should be, and so forth. And when things don't measure up to that ideal, they start hammering at them. And that really causes problems. Make peace with reality, where you look at what is and what you want to have happen. Then figure out, "How am I going to get what is to become what I think should happen?" And do it without pounding on the people, because that won't work.

IMPLICATIONS OF THE STUDY

As mentioned above, Covenant Theological Seminary was founded as a place to prepare leaders – especially pastoral leaders – for the church. At the same time, like all seminaries, Covenant must be attuned to its calling as an academic institution. This study reflects the tension found in this dual challenge. The participants shared their experience that seminaries usually do not link their teaching to the realities encountered in ministry life. And, while there were notable exceptions, even these exceptions took place in "practical theology" courses. This lack of connection between theoretical content and real-world practice is also consistent with the available literature on this topic.[18] Though fighting uphill against the tradition of technical rationality, seminaries that are truly interested in preparing candidates for the ministry should take steps to link the education of ministers to the realities facing clergy. This is particularly true for theoretical classes, where ways must be found to enable teacher-learners to test the relationship of the class content to their own existing store of practical knowledge.[19] While this is not news for seminary administrators, faculty members, or graduates, it should be a matter of great concern and extensive exploration given that the primary objective of these institutions is to equip leaders for the church.

Covenant Seminary faculty is exploring a number of methods for establishing this connection between class content and ministry practice. These methods include:

- process groups for theoretical classes;
- the use of case studies relating theoretical information to practice;

- the requirement of field education with mentoring oversight;
- the involvement of faculty from theoretical departments in people-centered ministry (not just teaching classes in church);
- providing teaching methodology seminars for faculty;
- assigning exercises of reflective practice for theoretical courses;
- developing a "pastor in residence" program where the visiting pastors are involved in classes, small groups, and ministry luncheons;
- using pastoral focus groups and online surveys to glean insights on practice; and
- developing a practice-based Center for Ministry Leadership (funded by a grant from Lilly Endowment) that speaks to the life and work of the Seminary.

Learning ministry practice involves knowledge that is developed on the job. In this study, as we have seen, four ways of learning emerged out of the pastoral context: reflection-in-action, reflection-on-action, mentors and models, and negative experiences.

Pastoral Reflection

This research affirms Kuhne's finding that very few pastors take time to reflect consciously on their actions.[20] In addition, Schön's comments about managers can also be applied to pastors:

> Managers do reflect-in-action, but they seldom reflect on their reflection-in-action. Hence this crucially important dimension of their art tends to remain private and inaccessible to others. Moreover, because awareness of one's intuitive thinking usually grows out of practice in articulating it to others, managers often have little access to their own reflection-in-action.[21]

While some examples of reflection-on-action were identified, few of the pastors in this study reported that they ever consciously took time to reflect. Preliminary findings in a new study being conducted by Covenant Seminary's Center for Ministry Leadership show that there is a great need among pastors to make time for such reflection. This study shows that pastors grow in their knowledge over time and should be given permission to develop in this way rather than be expected to acquire instantaneous understanding as a result of their formal education and ordination.

Furthermore, it seems that the professional learning of pastors, as well as the need to care for their long-term emotional health, should include both planned and spontaneous opportunities for reflection. A church's elders, in their role of providing oversight for their pastoral staff, need to take such findings into consideration. An example of such care is seen in the Pastors Summit program sponsored by Covenant Seminary's Center for Ministry Leadership. This program brings pastors together in small groups for periodic times of discussion and focused reflection on their ministry experiences. In order to participate in this program, pastors must have the approval of their elder boards. These elder boards have recognized the real needs of their pastors for reflection and renewal, and have strongly affirmed the pastors' participation in the Pastors Summit activities. Yet another encouraging recognition of the need for reflection and renewal is a movement in some Reformed and evangelical denominations to promote pastoral sabbaticals. This is a longstanding practice in denominations such as the United Church of Christ, the Lutheran Church – Missouri Synod, the Presbyterian Church (United States of America), the Reformed Church of America, and the United Methodist Church. The Center for Ministry Leadership is beginning to take steps to promote the consideration of sabbaticals in presbyteries of the PCA.

Negative Experiences as a Learning Context

Negative incidents provided rich descriptive material on the learning experiences of the pastors involved in this study. Every one of the interviews included stories of learning through pain and disillusionment. While for most of the pastors a positive, growth-oriented outcome seemed to be the result, a number of them carried significant scars that produced defensiveness and a level of cynicism about the ministry and the people with whom they worked. Regarding growth through negative experiences, Merriam and colleagues suggest the need to establish supportive environments where learners can feel safe and be given time to get beyond the experience, and to grapple with it in healthy ways.[22] These elements were identified in a number of interviews in this study.

An important additional finding from the study is that the first church in which a pastor serves becomes an integral part of that pastor's learning experience. Fifteen of the twenty-six critical incidents shared in the study came from circumstances encountered in the pastor's first church experience. The literature confirms this finding. Mills and Koval discovered that nearly half of all the highest stress periods experienced by pastors occurred in the first five years of ministry; and half of those periods occurred in years one to three.[23] This is confirmed by Oswald, who also cites the first five years as critical in pattern-setting experiences.[24]

The Pastors Summit program directly addresses this issue of learning from negative experiences. In this program, cohorts of ten pastors meet together three times a year to develop supportive relationships, explore their mutual callings, and equip one another through reflection and shared experiences. The initial sessions of the Pastors Summit show that honest discussion about negative experiences has provided some of the most fruitful learning. To be effective, however, this sharing must be done in a safe environment where the pastors do not feel they are competing to prove their competence or that their present or future job opportunities may be threatened.

Models and Mentors

Model churches also had a vital role in the continuing education of pastors. Joseph was "blown away" by a brief exposure to a model congregation. And James was also impacted by a number of church models. Daley points out that the learning process involves looking at both past experiences and new experiences, and reflecting on these for the purpose of finding meaning in these events.[25] Exposure to model churches moves pastors through a process of thinking about the information, comparing and contrasting their new experience with their existing knowledge, and determining how this knowledge is relevant to their practice.

For the past few decades, a number of larger churches in the evangelical tradition – such as the Crystal Cathedral, Willow Creek Community Church, Fellowship Bible Church (Little Rock, Arkansas), and Saddleback Community Church – and within the evangelical Presbyterian community – such as Coral Ridge Presbyterian Church, Briarwood Presbyterian Church, and Perimeter Church – have presented seminars and conferences sharing their experiences as ministry models. For many years, Covenant Seminary has promoted the use of models through the sponsorship of "ministry lunches" during which seasoned pastors share their experiences and challenges with the seminary community. The seminary has also made a regular practice of offering opportunities for students to visit churches that reflect "best practice" characteristics. Recently, the seminary instituted the *Connect* Conference, where pastors and others involved in ministry can hear from seasoned leaders and network with others facing similar issues in ministry practice.

It is vital to promote this activity of churches sharing what they have learned through years of practical ministry. However, in doing so, we should be aware of the temptation to assume that ministry solutions may be found merely in the reproduction of programs. This mindset ignores the unique contextual issues facing each individual congregation and fails to address the specific needs of a local church body. At the same time, rich lessons learned from the ministry practice of other churches could promote healthy evaluation and enlightened program planning for any church willing to assume the stance of a learning organization. In this study, Joseph provided an example of healthy modeling when he said, "That church raised the bar to what we should be. I wasn't trying to duplicate them, but it was the way in which they expected God to see something happen."

Such modeling could have a strategic role in the ongoing education of pastors. For example, churches with pastoral staff could look beyond their immediate needs to see themselves as learning organizations.[26] The staff hired by churches usually leave after a period of time, often to start a new church or to become senior pastors. Hiring and staff development practices should view staff pastors as employed not only to do a job, but also to be trained for future ministry responsibilities. In thinking this way, these churches would be equipping pastors for success in their current staff roles as well as preparing them for serving the broader church in the future.

Few of the pastors in this study are consciously involved in mentoring others. All of the mentoring that took place for these pastors came as a by-product of work commitments. Don was mentored by elders he was fortunate enough to inherit when he became pastor of their church. Felix viewed the senior pastor with whom he worked as a mentor, but this was not a reciprocal understanding. And while Joseph described the pastor with whom he first worked as a mentor, this was a relationship that grew as a result of being called to work together. It was fortunate – even providential – that such a rapport developed, but it was not consciously planned.

If pastors are going to pass on their knowledge, then it would seem that mentoring relationships should be consciously established and purposefully nurtured. Models for mentoring need to be explored in order to help ministry practitioners pass on the explicit knowledge gained through years of experience and to promote pastoral excellence over a lifetime of ministry. The Center for Ministry Leadership is exploring a number of methods of creating mentoring models. One idea is to invite veteran pastors to the Seminary campus as Pastors in Residence. These pastors would be available on campus to share in both formal and informal ways the wisdom gained from their years of ministry experience. Another idea is to create a Pastors Summit cohort made up of five seasoned pastors, each of whom would invite another pastor who is in his first five years of ministry to join the group.

Conclusion

The results of this study show that the participants' pastoral learning after seminary was cumulative in nature; that is, the pastors matured through various levels of proficiency. These pastors considered their formal seminary education to be helpful, but limited in providing an understanding of what they would face in practice. Popular wisdom among pastors is that they develop practice knowledge in the day-to-day struggles of the ministry. They conduct their ministries in the "swamp" of the church that presents messy, confusing problems that defy technical solutions. Through learning in practice – by reflection-in-action, reflection-on-action, negative experiences, and exposure to mentors and models – these pastors have demonstrated learning characteristics that need to be better understood if seminary graduates are to develop an informed practice.

Covenant Theological Seminary is seeking to do just that. Through an ongoing dialogue among faculty, administration, and graduate pastors, the Seminary is exploring the nature of pastoral learning, reviewing and adapting curriculum, and attempting to provide enriching learning experiences that, the Lord willing, will continue to bear fruit in practice well beyond the time of graduation and throughout a pastor's life in ministry.

1. Ronald M. Cervero, *Effective Continuing Education for Professionals* (San Francisco: Jossey-Bass, 1988); Gary Kuhne, "Needs Assessment in Continuing Professional Education: Applying the Word Context Triad Approach with Evangelical Protestant Clergy," (Ph.D. diss., The Pennsylvania State University, 1991); Donald A. Schön, *Educating the Reflective Practitioner: Toward a New Design for Teaching and Learning in the Professions* (San Francisco: Jossey-Bass, 1987); Donald A. Schön, *The Reflective Practitioner* (New York: Basic Books, 1983).

2. Schön, *Educating the Reflective Practitioner*; Donald A. Schön, "Professional Knowledge and Reflective Practice," in *Schooling for Tomorrow*, ed. T. J. Sergiovanni and J. H. Moore (Boston: Allyn and Bacon, 1989); Schön, *The Reflective Practitioner*.

3. Schön, *The Reflective Practitioner*, 21.

4. Schön, *Educating the Reflective Practitioner*; Schön, "Professional Knowledge and Reflective Practice"; Schön, *The Reflective Practitioner*, 49, 50-3.

5. Schön, *Educating the Reflective Practitioner*; Schön, *The Reflective Practitioner*, 54–69.

6. Cervero, *Effective Continuing Education for Professionals*; Ronald M. Cervero, "A Model of Professionals as Learners," in *Visions for the Future of Continuing Professional Education*, ed. Ronald M. Cervero, John F. Azzaretto, and Associates (Athens, Ga.: Georgia Center for Continuing Education, 1990); Michael Eraut, *Developing Professional Knowledge and Competence* (London: The Falmer Press, 1994); Michael Eraut, "Knowledge Creation and Knowledge Use in Professional Contexts," *Studies in Higher Education* 10, no. 2 (1985); Victoria J. Marsick and Karen E. Watkins, *Informal and Incidental Learning in the Workplace*, International Perspectives on Adult and Continuing Education (London: Routledge, 1990); Schön, *Educating the Reflective Practitioner*; Schön, *The Reflective Practitioner*.

7. Cervero, *Effective Continuing Education for Professionals*.

8. Monroe Brewer, "The Lifelong Learning Link: Twelve Reasons for Continuous Education for Missionaries," *Missiology: An International Review* 14, no. 2 (1991); Michael Combermere, "Religious Studies in Adult and Continuing Education," in *Turning Points in Religious Studies*, ed. Ursula King (Edinburgh: T. & T. Clark, 1990); Cynthia Crowner, "Program Planning, Development, and Evaluation," in *A Lifelong Call to Learn*, ed. Robert E. Reber and D. Bruce Roberts (Nashville, Tenn.: Abingdon, 2000); Fred R. Wilson, "Continuing Education and the Religious Professional: 1960–1985," *Lifelong Learning* 9, no. 2 (1985); Douglas E. Wingeier, "Assessing Needs and Interests: Individual, Church, and Society," in *A Lifelong Call to Learn*, ed. Robert E. Reber and D. Bruce Roberts (Nashville, Tenn.: Abingdon Press, 2000).

9. Jackson W. Carroll, "The Professional Model of Ministry – Is It Worth Saving?" *Theological Education* 21, no. 2 (1985): 29–32.

10. D. Bruce Roberts, "Motivated Learning and Practice: A Peer Group Model," in *A Lifelong Call to Learn*, ed. Robert E. Reber and D. Bruce Roberts (Nashville, Tenn.: Abingdon Press, 2000).

11. Bill M. Sullivan, *Ten Steps to Breaking the 200 Barrier* (Kansas City, Mo.: Beacon Hill Press, 1988), 11–16.

12. George Barna, *The Habits of Highly Effective Churches* (Ventura, Calif.: Issachar Resources, 1998), 9.

13. Sharan B. Merriam, *Qualitative Research and Case Study Applications in Education* (San Francisco: Jossey-Bass, 1998), 6.

14. Stephen D. Brookfield, "Using Critical Incidents to Explore Learners' Assumptions," in *Fostering Critical Reflection in Adulthood: A Guide to Transformative and Emancipatory Learning*, ed. Jack Mezirow and Associates (San Francisco: Jossey-Bass, 1990), 80.

15. Sharan B. Merriam, Vivian W. Mott, and Ming-Yeh Lee, "Learning That Comes from the Negative Interpretation of Life Experience," *Studies in Continuing Education* 18, no. 1 (1996): 10.

16. Quotations from participants in this study are taken from transcripts of interviews with them conducted during the years 2000-1.

17. Laurent A. Daloz, *Mentor* (San Francisco: Jossey-Bass, 1999), xvii, 15.

18. Samuel W. Blizzard, "The Minister's Dilemma," *The Christian Century* 73, no. 17 (1956); Elizabeth A. Dreyer, "Excellence in the Professions: What Theological Schools Can Learn from Law, Business, and Medical Schools," *Theological Education* 33, no. 1 (1996); Edward Farley, *Theologia* (Philadelphia: Fortress Press, 1983); Robert W. Ferris, *Renewal in Theological Education* (Wheaton, Ill.: The Billy Graham Center, 1990); Peter Jarvis, "The Parish Ministry as a Semi-Profession," *The Sociological Review* 23 (November 1975); H. Richard Niebuhr, *The Purpose of the Church and Its Ministry* (New York: Harper and Brothers, 1956); James E. Plueddemann, "The Challenge of Excellence in Theological Education," in *Excellence and Renewal*, ed. Robert L. Youngblood (Australia: The Paternoster Press, 1989).

19. Cervero, *Effective Continuing Education for Professionals*, 42, 56, 159.

20. Kuhne, "Needs Assessment in Continuing Professional Education: Applying the Word Context Triad Approach with Evangelical Protestant Clergy," 162.

21. Schön, *The Reflective Practitioner*, 243.

22. Merriam, Mott, and Lee, "Learning That Comes from the Negative Interpretation of Life Experience," 20.

23. Edgar W. Mills and John P. Koval, *Stress in the Ministry* (Washington, D.C.: Ministry Studies Board, 1971).

24. Roy M. Oswald, *Crossing the Boundary between Seminary and Parish* (Washington, D.C.: The Alban Institute, 1980).

25. Barbara J. Daley, "Creating Mosaics: The Interrelationships of Knowledge and Context," *The Journal of Continuing Education in Nursing* 28, no. 3 (1997): 108–9.

26. Karen E. Watkins and Ronald M. Cervero, "Organizations as Contexts for Learning: Differentiating Opportunities and Experiences of a Certified Public Accountant," *Journal of Workplace Learning* 12 (2000): 187–194.

18
CHRISTIANITY AND THE ARTS

JERRAM BARRS
Professor of Christian Studies and Contemporary Culture
Resident Scholar, Francis A. Schaeffer Institute

GOD AND MAN AS CREATIVE ARTISTS

My desire in this essay is to help us to think scripturally about the arts as Christian believers, for this is one of those areas where, at this present time, there appears to be great confusion in our churches. On the one hand, many Christians seem to think that we ought only to listen to music, read books, or watch films that have been produced by fellow believers. On the other hand, almost all Christians will read newspapers and books, watch television shows and movies, go to plays and musicals, listen to music, and buy art cards and pictures for our walls simply because we *like* these things – and we will do this without much reflection unless we encounter something that is obviously blasphemous, gratuitously violent, or clearly pornographic. Even those who suggest most passionately that Christians should only enjoy art by other Christians will take delight in buildings, bridges, roads, interior decoration, clothes, or beautifully prepared and presented meals, and they will take this delight without asking whether the architect, builder, designer, or chef is a committed believer in the Lord Jesus Christ. So, how are we as Christians to think about the arts? To approach this subject, we begin with the biblical doctrine of creation.

God, the Creator of All Things, Visible and Invisible
Every orthodox creed and every believing theologian throughout the history of the Church has affirmed the Christian's faith in God, who is the Creator of heaven and earth and of all things visible and invisible. We all have our

favorite scriptural passages that affirm this doctrine, that express our hope in the Lord who made all things, and that communicate this faith and hope with words of marvelous beauty – such as Psalm 8:1: "O LORD, our Lord, how majestic is your name in all the earth"; or Psalm 19:1: "The heavens declare the glory of God and the sky above proclaims his handiwork."[1] We praise God now for the wonder of his creation and we will praise him for this for all eternity: "Worthy are you, our LORD and God, to receive glory and honor and power, for you created all things, and by your will they existed and were created" (Rev. 4:11). Many other Scriptures also explore this conviction – sometimes at great length as well in glorious poetry; see, for instance, Job 38–41, Psalm 148, and Psalm 19 (a psalm that C. S. Lewis called one of the greatest lyric poems ever written).

John Calvin, in exquisitely beautiful French prose, writes of the wonder of God's creation in words that retain their remarkable power even in our English translations and are worth quoting at length:

> Since the perfection of blessedness consists in the knowledge of God, he has been pleased, in order that none might be excluded from the means of obtaining felicity, not only to deposit in our minds that seed of religion of which we have already spoken, but so to manifest his perfections in the whole structure of the universe, and daily place himself in our view, that we cannot open our eyes without being compelled to behold him. His essence, indeed, is incomprehensible, utterly transcending all human thought; but on each of his works his glory is engraven in characters so bright, so distinct, and so illustrious, that none, however dull and illiterate, can plead ignorance as their excuse... And because the glory of his power and wisdom is more refulgent in the firmament, it is frequently designated as his palace. And, first, wherever you turn your eyes, there is no portion of the world, however minute, that does not exhibit at least some sparks of beauty; while it is impossible to contemplate the vast and beautiful fabric as it extends around, without being overwhelmed by the immense weight of glory. Hence, the author of the Epistle to the Hebrews elegantly describes the visible worlds as images of the invisible (Heb. 11:3), the elegant structure of the world serving us as a kind of mirror, in which we may behold God, though otherwise invisible ...
>
> In attestation of his wondrous wisdom, both the heavens and the earth present us with innumerable proofs, not only those more recondite proofs which astronomy, medicine, and all the natural sciences, are designed to illustrate, but proofs which force themselves on the notice of the most illiterate peasant, who cannot open his eyes without beholding them. It is true, indeed, that those who are more or less intimately acquainted with those liberal studies are thereby assisted and enabled to obtain a deeper insight into the secret workings of divine wisdom. No man, however, though he be ignorant of these, is incapacitated for discerning such proofs of creative wisdom as may well cause him to break forth in admiration of the Creator ... Still, none who have the use of their eyes can be ignorant of the divine skill manifested so conspicuously in the endless variety, yet distinct and well ordered array, of the

heavenly host; and, therefore, it is plain that the Lord has furnished every man with abundant proofs of his wisdom.[2]

The English poet Gerard Manley Hopkins delights us with his poetic paean of praise in one of his best known works, "God's Grandeur":

> The world is charged with the grandeur of God.
> It will flame out, like shining from shook foil;[3]

In another of Hopkins' poems, "Pied Beauty," we find that he holds up for our pleasure the amazing diversity of color, texture, taste, and action in creation:

> Glory be to God for dappled things –
> For skies of couple-color as a brinded cow;
> For rose-moles in all stipple upon trout that swim;
> Fresh-firecoal chestnut-falls; finches' wings;
> Landscape plotted and pieced – fold, fallow, and plough;
> And all trades, their gear and tackle and trim.
>
> All things counter, original, spare, strange;
> Whatever is fickle, freckled (who knows how?)
> With swift, slow; sweet, sour; adazzle, dim;
> He fathers-forth whose beauty is past change:
> Praise him.[4]

Daniel Loizeaux considers God's creativity under four headings. He writes: "How God's imagination daily loads us with benefits. Contemplate this embarrassment of riches from a four-fold aspect: their perfection, diversity, profusion, inventiveness."[5] I am indebted to Loizeaux's discussion in my own exploration of these four aspects of God's creative genius.

Perfection
If we look at anything God has made under a microscope to see it in all its detail, we will discover that the more we see, the more amazing is his creative genius. A closer view enables us to see new and unimagined beauties and infinitesimally tiny wonders. Look at the structure of a leaf, a diamond, a snowflake, or a human cell. If we compare any product of human technology to any work of God – for example, try looking at an object made of polished steel, copper, or bronze – and try the same experiment, we very soon will observe the difference. It is lovely to our eyes, but if we look at our own works under a microscope, we will soon see the flaws.

Diversity
Think of the many different varieties of birds, insects, trees, and flowers; or, for an even more extraordinary example, the infinite variety of snowflakes,

sunrises, sunsets, or, more importantly, human beings: no two are exactly the same.

Profusion

God loves abundance: think of the flowers in a meadow, or the stars in the night sky – if you can get away from bright city lighting to see them, such as out in a deep forest, in a desert, or high up on a mountain. In such a setting, the sky seems to be nothing but stars. Indeed, astronomers tell us that there are 60 billion galaxies in the universe.

Inventiveness

We admire men and women who come up with new designs – and rightly so. But just think how this activity is only a miniscule copy of the inventiveness of the Lord, who delights in making all things new – not just at the beginning of the creation, but every day.

No Asceticism – Rather, the Glad Receiving and Enjoyment of the Gifts of God's Creativity

It is evident as we read Genesis 1 that God believed that all he had made was good. Repeatedly during the account of the creation, this refrain occurs: "God saw that it was good" (Gen. 1:4, 10, 12, 18, 21, 25). At the high point, when he has created man, we find this expression of the Lord's delight in his work: "And God saw everything that he had made, and behold, it was very good" (1:31). Some Christians believe that this world and the created order are no longer good after the Fall and have concluded, therefore, that the enjoyment of life and of God's daily gifts is no longer genuinely spiritual; they see this as somehow suspect. Calvin responded to this view with a resounding affirmation of the beauty of this world and the appropriateness of delight: "Should the Lord have attracted our eyes to the beauty of the flowers, and our sense of smell to pleasant odors, and should it then be sin to drink them in? Has he not even made the colors so that the one is more wonderful than the other?"[6]

Scripture itself insists that delight in creation and the enjoyment of God's gifts is not only right and good, but that asceticism – the insistence that taking pleasure in our creaturely life is somehow unspiritual or even sinful – is in fact a heretical teaching. See Paul's passionate words in 1 Timothy 4:1-5 as an example of this:

> Now the Spirit expressly says that in later times some will depart from the faith by devoting themselves to deceitful spirits and teachings of demons, through the insincerity of liars whose consciences are seared, who forbid marriage and require abstinence from foods that God created to be received with thanksgiving by those who believe and know the truth. For everything created by God is good, and nothing is to be rejected if it is received with thanksgiving, for it is made holy by the word of God and prayer.

In these words, Paul insists that food, sex, marriage – indeed all the gifts of creation – are good and holy, for God himself has declared them to be so in his word. Paul demands that we see that asceticism, even if it comes under the guise of spirituality, is heretical, even demonic. Why does he speak with such strong language? The simple answer is that the teaching that it is sinful to enjoy the gifts of creation is blasphemous because it is a rejection of God's own valuation of creation.

Repeatedly in the history of the church, Christians have been tempted to devalue the richness of creation and therefore to devalue also the arts, as if it would be somehow more "spiritual" to live a life devoid of beauty, of good things, of music, of literature, of painting, of color, etc. It is as if bare simplicity, barrenness, and even ugliness were somehow considered to be more pleasing to God. Behind this idea is the conviction that it is only what is "spiritual" that matters, and that the physical, therefore, is only of secondary value at best. In this view, the arts are thought of as an optional, rather extravagant, and unnecessary extra in life. But this belief is nonsense, and is, according to Paul, a heresy of the most serious kind, for in the end it is a denial of the goodness of creation. George Herbert, in his poem "Teach Me, My God and King," captured this obligation of the Christian to value as good all that God has made. This poem may be found in many hymnals; I include here stanzas one, three, and four:

> Teach me, my God and King,
> In all things thee to see,
> And what I do in anything
> To do it as for thee.
>
> All may of thee partake:
> Nothing can be so mean
> Which with this motive, "For thy sake,"
> Will not grow bright and clean.
>
> This is the famous stone
> That turneth all to gold;
> For that which God doth touch and own
> Cannot for less be told.

Reflecting further on this theme, we may point to five foundational doctrines that affirm the value of the richness of life here in this world:

Creation
See Genesis 1 with God's repeated "it is good," and Paul's words in 1 Timothy 4:1-5 (noted above).

Common Grace – or, God's Providential Care for All Creation
See Genesis 9:8-17 and the everlasting covenant that God makes with all creatures after the Flood. God cares for *all* creation, as evidenced in Psalms 103 and 145, and also by Jesus' words in Matthew 6:26-29 and 10:29-31, where he speaks of God watching over and providing for the flowers and the birds, and, even more, for all people.

The Incarnation
The eternal Son of God, the second person of the Trinity, became flesh; he became a man; he became a part of this physical universe – not merely for the thirty years of his earthly life, but for all eternity to come.

Bodily Resurrection
See Paul's joyful words about our physical resurrection in 1 Corinthians 15 and 2 Corinthians 5:1-5. Nothing expresses with greater clarity that our physical life in this world is precious than this conviction of God's commitment not "to unclothe us, but to further clothe us, so that what is mortal may be swallowed up by life."

The New Creation
There will be a renewed earth, with the curse removed (see Rom. 8:18-25; 2 Peter 3:13; Rev. 21:1-4). This promise of the glory of the earth to come underlines the significance and value of all that God has made for our enjoyment here and now. Redemption will not be complete until our human life is restored to its full delight in the wonder of God's good creation.

Man and Woman, God's Image Bearers,
Are Made to Be Sub-Creators Following After Their Creator

The God who made all things made us to exercise dominion under him over this good creation (Gen. 1:26-28). In Psalm 8, David declares that it is this likeness to God as we rule over this earth and its creatures that constitutes our glory as human persons. He asks:

> When I look at your heavens, the work of your fingers,
> the moon and the stars, which you have set in place,
> what is man that you are mindful of him?

He replies to his own question:

> You have made him a little lower than the heavenly beings
> and crowned him with glory and honor.
> You have given him dominion over the works of your hands;
> you have put all things under his feet.

In exercising dominion over God's good creation we are not creators in an absolute sense, like God, but, rather, sub-creators at best. We never create *ex nihilo* (out of nothing) like God, for we are always working with some aspect of what he has already made. We might say that our dominion over this earth means that we "till the garden" of color, words, form and texture, sound and harmony, stone and clay, imagination, God's works in creation, and human works in history and in society. Sir Isaac Newton likened our ruling the earth with the arts and sciences to the playing of a child:

> I do not know what I may appear to the world, but to myself I seem to have been only like a boy playing on the seashore, and diverting myself in now and then finding a smoother pebble or a prettier shell than ordinary, whilst the great ocean of truth lay all undiscovered before me.[7]

C. S. Lewis recognized that all great artists acknowledge there is something outside themselves that is greater than they are, and that is greater than the works that they make: "The greatest poems (*indeed all of the greatest artistic works*) have been made by men who valued something else much more than poetry."[8] For the Christian, there needs to be the humble bowing before God the Creator and the glad acceptance of the gift of his created order with which we all do our work.

We exercise dominion now by "making things" with our hands, minds, and imaginations. This task will be ours forever, for on the renewed earth all the creative glory of all the nations will be brought into the kingdom of God to honor Christ (Rev. 21:24-26).

Sometimes, Christians will insist that the only work that is truly worthwhile, pleasing to God and spiritual is the work of serving the proclamation of the gospel across the world. This view suggests that, if we were all truly earnest Christians, we would leave our "secular" jobs, in which we are simply making a living and ruling the world, and we would all join the "sacred" work of mission. But if we stop and think about Jesus' life, we see that he was doing so-called "secular" work as a carpenter or a fisherman for many more years than he was a preacher and teacher. It is impossible to suppose that during these years Jesus was living in a manner that was not fully godly and completely pleasing to his Father in heaven.

The import of this reflection on our human calling to "till the garden" of this world with body, mind, and imagination is that the arts need no justification; they are good gifts of God, a basic part of the creation order. Our calling is simply to be thankful for these gifts of sub-creativity.

We may say, however, that there are five aspects of our God-given creativity, or, rather, five "callings," as we engage in the work of creating:

- We are to seek to *glorify God* in all we do.

- We are designed to *find fulfillment for ourselves* in using, developing, and expressing the gifts God has so richly given us.

- We are to seek to *be of benefit to others*, so that they may be able to look at what we create and say of it: "It is good." The Christian artist always lives in community and is called to serve others in the development and expression of the gifts God has given to each one for the blessing of all.

- In being creative, we fulfill our human design by *exercising dominion* over the earth.

- We are called, in all we do, including in our creative work, to *set back the boundaries of the Fall* – to restrain the abnormality of our present human life in its brokenness and sorrow, and of our present world that is under the curse and that resists our dominion.

The Heart of the Christian's Approach to Creativity Will Be Imitation

In acknowledging that we live in God's world and that we are his creatures, the Christian ought to have a rather more humble approach to the work of art than is sometimes found in the reflections of those who see themselves at the center of reality. Shakespeare had this humility about his work, though if we consider both the dramas and the poetry that poured out from him, we might justly call him a creator. The poet Dryden said of Shakespeare: "After God, he has created most." Yet Shakespeare said of himself that he simply held "a mirror up to nature." George Herbert, a Christian like Shakespeare, wrote: "True beauty lives on high. Ours is but a flame borrowed thence."

Lewis comments on this understanding of the artist as being an imitator rather than an original creator, and in the process he challenges much contemporary reflection about the work of the artist:

> What are the key-words of modern criticism? *Creative*, with its opposite *derivative*; *spontaneity*, with its opposite *convention*; *freedom*, contrasted with *rules*. Great authors are innovators, pioneers, explorers; bad authors bunch in schools and follow models. Or again, great authors are always "breaking fetters" and "bursting bonds." They have personality, they "are themselves." I do not know whether we often think out the implication of such language into a consistent philosophy; but we certainly have a general picture of bad work flowing from conformity and discipleship, and of good work bursting out from certain centres of explosive force – apparently self-originating force – which we call men of genius.[9]

Lewis then draws our attention to the way in which the New Testament speaks about the Christian life in very different terms:

Thus in Gal. iv. 19 Christ is to be "formed" inside each believer – the verb here used meaning to shape, to figure, or even to draw a sketch. In First Thessalonians (i. 6) Christians are told to imitate St. Paul and the Lord, and elsewhere (1 Cor. x. 33) to imitate St. Paul as he in his turn imitates Christ – thus giving us another stage of progressive imitation. Changing the metaphor we find that believers are to acquire the fragrance of Christ, *redolere Christum* (2 Cor. ii. 16); that the glory of God has appeared in the face of Christ as, at the creation, light appeared in the universe (2 Cor. iv. 6); and, finally, if my reading of a much disputed passage is correct, that a Christian is to Christ as a mirror to an object (2 Cor. iii. 18).[10]

Lewis points out that thinking of oneself as "original" and as a "creator" is very close to summing up the reality of the Fall, where humans turned from what is better and greater than themselves – God, who is the Originator – to what is lesser and derived – themselves. He then applies this biblical insight to the work of the writer and the artist:

> Applying this principle to literature, in its greatest generality, we should get as the basis of all critical theory the maxim that an author should never conceive of himself as bringing into existence beauty or wisdom that did not exist before, but simply and solely as trying to embody in terms of his own art some reflection of eternal Beauty and Wisdom.[11]

He comments on the difference between the Christian and the man who sees himself at the center of reality:

> St. Augustine and Rousseau both write *Confessions*; but to the one his own temperament is a kind of absolute (*au moins je suis autre*), to the other it is "a narrow house, too narrow for thee to enter – oh make it wide. It is in ruins – oh rebuild it."[12]

Lewis explicitly acknowledges the similarities between a Christian and a Platonic view in seeing the arts as imitative of something transcendent. For the Platonist and Neo-Platonist, this world is a copy, a shadow of the divine world above. The arts will not be satisfied with exploring what is found here – the copies – but will seek to enter into heaven itself to imitate the true origin of all that we see here on earth. Lewis quotes Plotinus: "The arts do not simply imitate what they see but re-ascend to those principles from which Nature herself is derived."[13] Art and Nature thus become rival copies of the same supersensual original, and there is no reason why Art should not be the better of the two.

Using Sir Philip Sidney as an example, Lewis further notes that:

> The poet, unlike the historian, is not "captived to the truth of a foolish world," but can "deliver a golden." Sidney ... inherited, in a Christianized form, the Platonic dualism. Nature was not the whole. Above earth was heaven; behind

the phenomenal, the metaphysical. To that higher region the human soul belonged. The natural world, as Bacon said, was "in proportion inferior to the soul." The man who ... improved on Nature, and painted what might be or ought to be, did not feel that he was retreating from reality into a merely subjective refuge; he was reascending from a world which he had a right to call "foolish" and asserting his divine origin.[14]

We may describe a Christian understanding of the arts in the following way: Our work in any field of the arts will be imitative. We will be thinking God's thoughts after him – painting with his colors; speaking with his gift of language; exploring and expressing his sounds and harmonies; working with his creation in all its glory, diversity, and in-built inventiveness. In addition, we will find ourselves longing to make known the beauty of life as it once was in Paradise, the tragedy of its present marring, and the hope of our final redemption. All great art will contain this element of being an echo of Eden: Eden in its original glory, Eden that is lost to us, and Eden restored.

I do not mean to suggest that there is no room for creativity or originality in a Christian understanding of the arts. Lewis thought it appropriate to use the term "sub-creation" for J. R. R. Tolkien's work *The Lord of the Rings*. We may use the terms "creative" and "original" as long as we understand that we do not mean them in an absolute sense, for everything we do we do as those who are created and as those who are working within the boundaries of this created universe.

In this secondary sense of "sub-creation," we delight in the work of a Christian poet who designs new forms (as did John Donne or T. S. Eliot); or the compositions of a Christian musician who writes music in styles that are original (as did Bach); or the canvases of the Christian painter who paints in a manner that breaks with tradition (as did Rembrandt or Van Gogh). However, a Christian will just as gladly use forms already in existence if those forms fit the purposes and passions of one's work.

Another way to express this recognition of the secondary nature of all our art would be to understand that all creative work is a form of praise and worship: by creating we declare the glory of God, who made us in his likeness.

The Arts Should Not Be Simply an Expression of the Self

Since the Romantic period, the arts have become increasingly a matter of mere self-expression. The artist is seen as having a special sensibility that gives him a higher understanding of and insight into the human condition and which therefore elevates him above the average person as one to be admired. The Christian who works in the arts will not see himself as the great revealer, as another god, as the prophet or priest of the age, a special mentor breaking new barriers. To do so is to become the priest in a smaller and smaller cult. The more inward and purely self-expressive art becomes, the more inaccessible it is to others. For artistic communication to occur, art cannot be simply an expression of the self. True art must have some contact with life, with reality, with other people who exist alongside the artist. Lewis puts it this way: "Great writing (and all great art) exists because there is a world not created by the writer."[15]

In contrast to the Romantic view, the artist needs to see himself as a creature of God, using gifts given by God, to the glory of God, for the enrichment of the lives of others.

The Creativity of Others Helps Us Enter into God's Creativity

We are finite, and that is good, for this is the way God made us; yet, God's world surrounds us with all its extraordinary variety, beauty, order, and richness. Lewis reflects on how we may experience more of the wonder of God's world as we read and so enter into someone else's perspective on this world. This is true of all the arts – each painter, sculptor, writer, composer, musician, or designer sees something of the world that we do not see, and so, as we look or listen or read, we are enriched by each artist's vision. Lewis asks why we enjoy reading (and we may apply this to all the arts). He answers:

> The nearest I have yet got to an answer is that we seek an enlargement of our being. We want to be more than ourselves. Each of us by nature sees the whole world from one point of view with a perspective and a selectiveness peculiar to himself. And even when we build disinterested fantasies, they are saturated with, and limited by, our own psychology. To acquiesce in this particularity on the sensuous level – in other words, not to discount perspective – would be lunacy. We should then believe that the railway line really grew narrower as it receded into the distance. But we want to escape the illusions of perspective on higher levels too. We want to see with other eyes, to imagine with other imaginations, to feel with other hearts, as well as with our own. We are not content to be Leibnitzian monads. We demand windows. Literature as Logos is a series of windows, even of doors. One of the things we feel after reading a great work is "I have got out." Or from another point of view, "I have got in"; pierced the shell of some other monad and discovered what it is like inside.[16]

Lewis points out how reading (or the enjoyment of any artwork) is similar to love, moral activity, and the exercise of the mind, for in each of these activities we are called out of ourselves into the life of another. This would be a joy and an enlargement of us even if we were not fallen creatures, for even before the Fall it was "not good for the man to be alone" (Gen. 2:18). We need others to complement us in every aspect of our lives.

God has not made us to be isolated individuals who find fulfillment simply by ourselves, or even – and I say this carefully – only in relationship with him. He has made us for others so that, together as finite persons, we can reflect the unity and diversity within the godhead, and so that, together, we can take delight in the gifts, wisdom, and insight of our fellow men and women.

When we add to this the fact that we are fallen and that the essence of the Fall is to worship and serve oneself, we begin to see how important are the arts, for they give us a wider and fuller view of God's good world. The arts enable us to look beyond ourselves and the horizons of our own experience. They help us to stop being so self-centered. Lewis writes:

> Good reading, therefore, though it is not essentially an affectional or moral or intellectual activity, has something in common with all three. In love we escape from our self into one other. In the moral sphere, every act of justice or charity involves putting ourselves in the other person's place and thus transcending our own competitive particularity. In coming to understand anything we are rejecting the facts as they are for us in favour of the facts as they are. The primary impulse of each is to maintain and aggrandize himself. The secondary impulse is to go out of the self, to correct its provincialism and heal its loneliness. In love, in virtue, in the pursuit of knowledge, and in the reception of the arts, we are doing this. Obviously this process can be described either as an enlargement or as a temporary annihilation of the self. But that is an old paradox; "he that loseth his life shall save it"...
>
> This, so far as I can see, is the specific value or good of literature considered as Logos; it admits us to experiences other than our own. They are not, any more than our personal experiences, all equally worth having. Some, as we say, "interest" us more than others. The causes of this interest are naturally extremely various and differ from one man to another; it may be the typical (and we say "How true!") or the abnormal (and we say "How strange!"); it may be the beautiful, the terrible, the awe-inspiring, the exhilarating, the pathetic, the comic, or the merely piquant. Literature gives the entrée to them all...
>
> Literary experience heals the wound, without undermining the privilege, of individuality. There are mass emotions which heal the wound; but they destroy the privilege. In them our separate selves are pooled and we sink back into sub-individuality. But in reading great literature I become a thousand men and yet remain myself. Like the night sky in the Greek poem, I see with a myriad eyes, but it is still I who see. Here, as in worship, in love, in moral action, and in knowing, I transcend myself; and am never more myself than when I do.[17]

De Quincey expressed this same thought very simply. He said that "Literature makes us feel more about things, and feel about more things." Again, what is true of literature is true of all the arts. In the enjoyment of others' creativity, I enter into a vision and richness beyond my own: "Familiar things made new; new things made familiar." Chesterton understood this and sums it up for us: "Fiction is common things seen by uncommon people." T. S. Eliot also writes of this as he thinks about the nature of poetry. The poet, he suggests, leads us into a new level of consciousness,

> ... making people more aware of what they feel already, and therefore teaching them something about themselves. But he is not merely a more conscious

individual than the others; he is also individually different from other people, and from other poets too, and can make his readers share consciously in new feelings which they had not experienced before.[18]

In this expansion of the self, the arts are indeed like love or moral action. One gives oneself to another, yet is never more fully oneself.

Art by Christians and by Non-Christians

An important question arises here that takes us back to an idea brought up at the beginning of this essay: Are Christians better artists than non-Christians? Put this way, the question seems absurd! But many believers speak as if it is impossible for the Christian to enjoy or to be edified by the creative works of unbelievers. As I pointed out earlier, the truth is that there is not a single Christian in the world who does not daily benefit from the creative gifts and hard work of the unbelievers around him. Our clothes, our food, our homes, our public buildings, our transport, our furnishings, our machinery, our technology – the greater part of all of this has been designed and made by people who are not Christians.

On even the briefest reflection, it is obvious that God has given his creative gifts to believers and unbelievers alike. Scripture acknowledges this in many ways, and we should need no other evidence than the insistence of God's Word that all human persons are made in his image (see Ps. 8 once more, or James 3:9-10).

In Acts 14:17, we see Paul talking to the idolatrous pagans in the city of Lystra about God's generosity. He says, "God has not left himself without a testimony; but has shown kindness by giving you gifts from heaven." Jesus calls us to be like our heavenly Father, who gives his good gifts to the believer and the unbeliever, the righteous and the wicked (Matthew 5:43-48). The writer of Proverbs declares that God's wisdom raises her voice not just to the people of Israel but to the whole human race so that there can be good laws and just rule in every nation (Prov. 8:1-4, 15-16). In 1 Kings 5, we read how God is pleased that Solomon is hiring the finest craftsmen of the day, unbelievers from Hiram, king of Tyre, to build the temple and to work on its interior design.

This is a particularly interesting example, for it teaches us that it is perfectly appropriate for us to use the gifts of non-Christians to help us build our houses of worship or to aid our worship in other ways (we will return to this issue later). On this subject of what is generally called the "common grace" of God, John Calvin writes with great passion about the folly and blasphemy of denying that God has given his gifts liberally to unbelievers:

> Therefore, in reading profane authors, the admirable light of truth displayed in them should remind us, that the human mind, however much fallen and perverted from its original integrity, is still adorned and invested with

admirable gifts from its Creator. If we reflect that the Spirit of God is the only fountain of truth, we will be careful, as we would avoid offering insult to him, not to reject or condemn truth wherever it appears. In despising the gifts, we insult the Giver.[19]

And again:

The sum of the whole is this: From a general survey of the human race, it appears that one of the essential properties of our nature is reason, which distinguishes us from the lower animals, just as these by means of sense are distinguished from inanimate objects. For although some individuals are born without reason, that defect does not impair the general kindness of God [*the Battles translation here has "general grace"; the French is "la grace generale de Dieu"*], but rather serves to remind us, that whatever we retain ought justly to be ascribed to the Divine indulgence. Had God not so spared us, our revolt would have carried along with it the entire destruction of nature. In that some excel in acuteness, and some in judgment, while others have greater readiness in learning some peculiar art, God, by this variety commends his favour toward us, lest any one should presume to arrogate to himself that which flows from His mere liberality. For whence is it that one is more excellent than another, but that in a common nature the grace of God is specially displayed [*Battles translates here "Why is one person more excellent than another? Is it not to display in common nature God's special grace?" The French is "la grace special de Dieu"*] in passing by many and thus proclaiming that it is under obligation to none. We may add, that each individual is brought under particular influences according to his calling.[20]

Calvin in this passage speaks of "general grace" and also of "special grace" as he reflects on the generous giving of gifts by God to the whole human race. He is quite happy to acknowledge that in many areas of human activity unbelievers may be more gifted and have more wisdom than believers. If in reading this statement you are troubled by it, just think of the planes in which you fly, the buildings that you admire, the technology or medical care from which you benefit – almost certainly the majority of these have been designed and made by non-Christians. This truth should not trouble us at all, but rather cause us to magnify the grace of God, who gives to all so generously. The question we need to ask about any human artifact is not "Is this made by a Christian or a non-Christian?" Rather, we should ask the question that Genesis 1 prompts us to ask: "Is this good?"

Arts and Crafts

In this section, we will briefly address the issue of the unity between what tend to be called "arts" (such as music, literature, painting, etc.) and "crafts" (such as the making of household furnishings, clothes, buildings, etc.). Hans Rookmaaker, who was for many years professor of art history at the Free University of Amsterdam, and also a director of the L'Abri Fellowship in

Holland, wrote very helpfully on this subject. Rookmaaker points out that at one time – through the Middle Ages and on beyond the Reformation – what we now refer to as the arts were all considered crafts; artists were workmen and women like any other laborers. Young people were apprenticed in painting or music just as they were in furniture making or metalwork or dyeing. "Art" was simply the beauty that one expected to find in things made by skilled craftsmen and artisans. Christians were a part of this cultural way of seeing, recognizing their abilities in these areas as gifts and callings from God. The result was a great wealth of music, literature, painting, sculpture, architecture, furniture, and many other things which people still flock to see, hear, and enjoy. Consider the examples of Bach, Rembrandt, and Shakespeare – each of them is an outstanding artisan in his particular craft.

A change began to take place in this perception about the arts during the Romantic period. Art came to be seen as ART – , that is, as "fine art" or "high culture"; the crafts came to be considered inferior. The arts became disconnected from life; the artist began to be thought of as a kind of noble genius. What were some of the results of this shift in thinking about the nature of the arts? Here we will summarize some of the points that Rookmaaker makes in his writing on this subject (see, in particular, his essay *Art Needs no Justification*).[21]

One result of this shift was that art became museum art. Instead of artistically made objects that were part of the everyday life of the ordinary person, we now go to museums to see the works of "great artists" – works which may be beautiful and meaningful in many ways, but which have been set apart from the "ordinary" by the fact that they are ART. Think in comparison of the great outpouring of paintings that decorated the churches and public buildings in the late medieval period or at the time of the Renaissance. These works were part of people's lives; wherever they went in the course of a day or a week, they met with artistic works created to beautify everyday existence. With the rise of ART, this became less and less the case.

Along with this shift in thinking and the divorce of artistic endeavors from the everyday, ART also became very expensive. Unlike at the time of Michelangelo or Leonardo da Vinci, the common man and woman had very little access to the works of the great artists until the rise of public museums.

In addition, there developed a separation of ART from "commercial art" or "entertainment art," though in every field, a few artists managed to bridge the gap: Toulouse-Lautrec, Johann Strauss, Duke Ellington. Nowadays we are able to enjoy at a popular level some of the works of the great artists of a previous time – artists who did not think of themselves as working away at some "higher calling," but who saw themselves as serving the men and women of their day with the gifts God had given them. Think here of some of the excellent recent films made of the plays of William Shakespeare or of the novels of Jane Austen, which are fine examples of how great ART and commercial art can come together.

Another consequence of this separation of arts and crafts is the alienation of most ordinary people from the arts (again, consider the contrast with the plays of Shakespeare, which, in his day, were enjoyed by king and commoner alike). Along with this alienation of ordinary people there has arisen the development of a special class of "art interpreters" – reviewers and critics whose job it is to educate the rest of us so that we are able to understand the ARTS. Romantic notions of ART create practical difficulties for the artist and art student who are sensible enough to see the problems of this approach. Indeed, we currently see a crisis in the arts, a crisis that leads to the question: "Why am I working at this?" By the Romantic vision of art, the artist is driven inward to find his identity in and through his work. But a problem arises here: what if one finds only emptiness inside?

The Romantic conception of the artist as a tortured genius expressing his inmost being creates particular difficulty for Christians, for "the arts are the epitome and very clear expression of the non-Christian Spirit of the age." This generates a reaction among the vast majority of Christians and raises two problems that have constantly to be faced by the believer who senses that God is calling him or her to be an artist:

First, art is considered by many in our churches to be unnecessary and unspiritual, even worldly. Therefore, Christians who desire to be artists are told, "Leave art to the pagans. Our Christian calling is to be spiritual and to bear witness to Christ." But, even if we take this negative attitude towards the arts, we still find that art is inescapably part of our lives.

Second, the Christian who perseveres and enters the arts has to face all sorts of criticisms: the charge of hedonism, of worldliness, of being sinful or carnal. Artists are considered by many people to be lazy, for art is not "real work." The artist is in danger from the world. If a young believer persists in following his calling he is told, "If you have to be an artist, then at least use your art for evangelistic purposes. This can be your only justification for pursuing such a life."

How are we as Christians to respond to such charges, criticisms, and challenges? We do need to make a response for the sake of Christians who have been gifted by God and who wish to pursue this calling. And our response will have to be:

- *Art needs no justification.* It is simply a gift of God, part of his created reality, to be received like any other gift – with gratitude.

- *We must not say that "art is for art's sake," for this is the Romantic heresy.* Art is to be tied to the reality of God's creation and to our human calling to live as his image bearers.

- *The Christian artist will regard himself or herself as a craftsman.* The artist will not see himself as a self-serving visionary, but as an ordinary human (that is glorious enough!) with a particular calling from God to serve him and one's fellows by working with words, music, color, stone, metal, etc.

- *Most importantly, the Christian in the arts will commit himself or herself to humility.* The true artist does *not* say, "I will be an ARTIST, an "inspired voice of the gods" (this is too religious a claim); or the "revealer of truth," as if I were a prophet or a "self-revealing genius" (these suggest that only the artist can truly see reality). Rather, the true artist sees his or her work within the context of and as a sub-set of God's own larger and infinitely more creative work. The true artist values something more than self.

BUILDING A CHRISTIAN UNDERSTANDING OF THE CALLING OF THE ARTIST

Now that we have explored various attitudes toward the arts and seen how human artistic endeavors are actually echoes of the greater creative activity of God, we are prepared to ask several questions that will help us develop a truly Christian understanding of the calling of the artist.

Are There "Christian Subjects" for Art and Is There Any Such Thing as "Christian Art"?

The expressions – "Christian subjects" and "Christian art" – are often used, and we need to ask ourselves, what is intended by such language? Do we mean that there are particular subjects, and only those subjects, that are appropriate for a Christian artist to explore in painting, music, writing, or any other area of the arts? Do we believe that only some particular kinds of work should be called "Christian art"?

I suppose we might mean by these expressions that "Christian art" is art that is designed for use in worship or devotion, such as: hymns, sacred music, devotional literature, meditations, prayers, paintings and banners for churches, stained glass windows, and the like. There is, of course, a need for such art, but rather than lumping it into a separate category called "Christian," we must learn that this kind of art will have to be judged by the same criteria as all other art. C. S. Lewis is once again a great help to us here:

> The rules for writing a good passion play or a good devotional lyric are simply the rules for writing tragedy or lyric in general: success in sacred literature depends on the same qualities of structure, suspense, variety, diction, and the like which secure success in secular literature. And if we enlarge the idea of Christian Literature to include not only literature on sacred themes but all that is written by Christians for Christians to read, then, I think, Christian Literature can exist only in the same sense in which Christian cookery might exist. It would be possible, and it might be edifying, to write a Christian cookery book. Such a book would exclude dishes whose preparation involves

unnecessary human labour or animal suffering, and dishes excessively luxuri-
ous. That is to say, its choice of dishes would be Christian. But there could be
nothing specifically Christian about the actual cooking of the dishes included.
Boiling an egg is the same process whether you are a Christian or a Pagan. In
the same way, literature written by Christians for Christians would have to
avoid mendacity, cruelty, blasphemy, pornography, and the like, and it would
aim at edification in so far as edification was proper to the kind of work in
hand. But whatever it chose to do would have to be done by the means common to all literature; it could succeed or fail only by the same excellences and
the same faults as all literature; and its literary success or failure would never
be the same thing as its obedience or disobedience to Christian principles.[22]

A second possible use of such terms as "Christian art" is to describe art with
what we might call "Christian content." By this is usually meant art containing
depictions of biblical scenes, or scenes from church history. However, people
generally have a narrow view of this type of art and usually mean "sacred,"
"holy," "edifying," or even "nice" works of art. Yet, consider in contrast to
this some of the not-so-edifying scenes to be found in the Bible. Read the
rape of Tamar (2 Sam. 13), for instance; or the gang rape unto death of the
Levite's concubine, whose body is cut up, and the subsequent war (Judg. 19);
or the Song of Solomon, with its explicit sex and graphic nudity; or the book
of Ecclesiastes, with its pessimistic themes. In other words, there are sections
of the Bible that would seem to fail this test for "Christian art" or "Christian
subjects."

A third way to use this language is to refer to art that is didactic, teaching
us spiritual or evangelistic lessons. But, again, many scenes in the Bible
itself would fail this test (see again the passages mentioned above). There
are no spiritual lessons in the Song of Solomon, though many Christians,
uncomfortable with the idea that God might have included in his infallible
Word a book that appears to be mainly about sex, have tried to make the
book be about the marriage of the soul to Christ or the union of the church
to her Lord. Of course, some art will be "spiritual" in this sense, but some will
not. Art does not need this justification for it to be considered good art, or art
that a Christian can produce or enjoy.

A fourth manner in which this language is used is to refer to art produced
by Christians. But this is also problematic. Some of the best-loved hymn
tunes, for example, were borrowed from folk melodies rather than being
composed specially for the purpose of worship; think of the tunes we use for
"Fairest Lord Jesus," "Amazing Grace," "What Wondrous Love Is This?" and
"I Cannot Tell." In addition, some of the greatest composers of sacred music
were not believers (Vaughan Williams is an example here), and many great
hymn tunes were taken from the music of composers who were not believers,
or from contexts that were not "Christian" (such as Beethoven's rousing "Ode
to Joy" or Sibelius' beautiful "Finlandia," both of which are used for dearly
loved hymns).

This is also true within the Bible itself. The book of Proverbs contains many sayings from ancient Egypt. The poetic form of the psalms, and many of the metaphors used – even for God – are part of the poetic language of the surrounding culture and are not unique to the Old Testament. We find some of those metaphors used of Baal and of other gods, one common one being the description of God as the one who rides on the clouds and on the wings of the wind. This should not bother us any more than it would if we discovered that the most beautiful and acoustically perfect church building in our city was designed by a non-Christian architect.

At the most basic level, when it comes to the arts, we must hold Christians to the same standards of judgment as we would any other artist – just as we hold Christians in medicine, or teaching, or business, or any other calling to an objective set of standards. We might do well to speak of Christian artists, or of Christians who are called to be artists, in the same way that we speak of Christians who are doctors, lawyers, teachers, homemakers, or cooks, rather than speaking of Christian medicine or Christian cooking. Then, once we learn to speak this way, our challenge to all believers will be to pursue their callings with heart, soul, mind, and strength to the glory of God.

What Will This Mean for Topics?

The above conclusion will also help us as we think about appropriate topics for the Christian who is an artist. There are no "secular" topics. All creation is God's and therefore is proper material for artistic expression. The world and human life in all its fallenness and brokenness is appropriate subject matter. The hope for redemption from this state of brokenness is also appropriate.

The themes of all great art – whether produced by Christians or non-Christians – are the world and human life as they came from the hand of God; the world and human life as they now are subject to sorrow, sin, and death; and the world and human life as they will be when restored. Which theme predominates will vary from piece to piece in the work of any particular artist, and will vary from artist to artist depending on his or her belief system and experience of life. It is hard to imagine Tamar in her desolation after her rape, for instance, writing upbeat songs of joy. Indeed, it would be false if she were to write and sing such songs. Her life in this world was ruined by the wicked act of her half brother.

This means, too, that there will be no room for sentimentality in a Christian approach to the arts. Hagiographies, for example, which many Christian biographies are, have no place here. The Bible itself does not glorify human beings in this way. Rather, it speaks with deep and sometimes brutal honesty about the failures of the people of God. This, of course, is why we find reading the Bible to be such a comfort, for God's Word is about people like us, not plaster saints. Related to this issue are the many paintings of Christ in which his humanity is diminished to make him appear "sweet."

Simple integrity constrains us to communicate faithfully and truthfully, not only about people in the Bible, but about our current human condition as well. Honest art will delineate human shame as well as human glory, not because we wish to wallow in that shame, but because it represents the truth about who we sometimes are.

Of course, the Christian artist should also be ready at all times to say simply and plainly, "My God and King!" We have many glorious examples of this in the poetry of George Herbert, John Donne, Gerard Manley Hopkins, and T. S. Eliot.

Is Representational Art Forbidden by the Second Commandment?

Is representation forbidden in the visual arts? We all are familiar with the commandment that we are not to make a graven image, but if we read the whole commandment, we see that what is forbidden is idolatry, not representation in and of itself. This is simple to demonstrate by considering some of the examples of artwork that God commissioned specifically for his houses of worship. There were to be representations of cherubim (things in heaven above) in both the tabernacle and the temple; representations of pomegranates, almond blossoms, bells (things created by God and by man on the earth beneath) in the tabernacle; and lions, bulls, lilies, gourds, palm trees, wreaths, wheels, and other things in the Temple. These were designed at God's command, some according to exact instructions given by him, others with considerable artistic freedom.

Some Christians attempt to resolve this issue of representational art by insisting that we no longer need such art now; they see it as "carnal," "unspiritual," or given specifically "for a time of spiritual immaturity or infancy." This view, however, is foolish, for the Bible tells us that both the tabernacle and the Temple were patterned after a heavenly design, and the basic requisitioning was given by God himself.

Nor will it do to declare that we only need the spoken and written Word now that Christ is come, for when we see him face to face heaven itself will contain the cherubim and all the other realities that the tabernacle and temple decorations represented. And, most probably, we will find other representations in heaven as well, even though we will be in the presence of the realities. In fact, we might say that all sacraments, representations, and symbols we have been given will find fulfillment in the kingdom to come; they will not disappear, but rather, they will be fully present in all their glory. We will partake of the marriage supper of the Lamb, and the Lord's Supper will then find its consummation, for Christ himself will serve us at his table. The tree of life will also be present for the healing of the nations.

The key here, of course, is that we ourselves will still be physical beings in the new heavens and the new earth, rather than being disembodied spirits. Therefore, we may conclude that physical representations of heavenly and spiritual things can be appropriate, for God created us to be eternally bodied.

This leads to a second area of consideration: what about representations of the Godhead in the visual arts and in literature? Are these necessarily blasphemous and idolatrous? What, exactly, is forbidden by the second commandment? Consider all the paintings people have made of Jesus, all the Christmas cards with manger scenes and the infant Christ, all the crèches, all the literary presentations of Christ (such as Aslan the lion in C. S. Lewis' Narnia stories) – are all of these idolatry? Are all of these blasphemous? Again, the answer here is not quite as obvious as some suggest.

Think of the many images and metaphors used for God in Scripture. God is a shepherd, he is a physician, he is the owner of a vineyard, he is one who rides his chariot in the clouds. Christ is vine, door, bridegroom, lion, lamb. The Spirit broods over the waters in metaphorical language that suggests a bird; and the Spirit also appears in the form of a dove. When we read such images, is it possible for us to read them and reflect on them without imagining a form in our minds? I do not think so, for feeding the imagination is the very purpose and intent of this language.

Look at Ezekiel 1 or Revelation 1 and ask yourself if it is possible to read these chapters without imagining pictures in your mind of what Ezekiel and John are describing. In both cases, the writers struggle with words to represent to us something of what they have seen in their prophetic visions. If it were truly illegitimate to represent the Lord to us, then these descriptions would not be in Scripture. In fact, we may go further and suggest that, because these word pictures are given to us in Scripture, it is appropriate for us to have paintings or sculptures that include representations of Jesus, and also to have acted representations of Jesus in plays and movies. What is inappropriate is to use any of these representations as an object of worship. That which signifies should never be confused with what it actually represents. A representation of God is never to be worshiped as God himself.

Thinking about this issue at an even deeper level, we have to acknowledge that the incarnation itself does, of course, give the second person of the Godhead a particular physical form. The Son of God was incarnate in the likeness of man – and not a generic man, but rather, an actual individual person, a specific man, just like any other man we meet every day – apart, of course, from his moral perfection and his full conformity to the likeness of God.

Jesus the God-man could be seen, heard, and touched. People met Jesus and went away with a visual image in their minds and hearts of who he was and what he looked like. This was not a problem; it is impossible to suppose that his mother was disobeying the commandment against images when she cradled her infant son in her lap and looked at him with love, or that later she was sinning whenever she pictured Jesus in her mind. In the same way, who can doubt that the disciples and all those whom Jesus healed kept glad memories of his face and form in their minds?

Seeing Jesus, the Son of God, very God of very God, and remembering him cannot have been, then, for his contemporaries, a violation of the second commandment, nor will it be for us when we shall see him face to face one day. Surely we cannot imagine that having seen him in his glory we will ever forget his appearance!

If Jesus had become incarnate in our own time, photographs could have been taken of him. We have to suppose that some of the children he played with as a young boy would have had artistic gifts and might have made sketches of him; or that later in his life a few of the many thousands who heard him speak might have made pictures of scenes of his teaching, just as our children's story Bibles have such pictures. In other words, we are saying that it is acceptable to visualize Christ.

We all have pictures of Jesus in our minds, first of all because he was fully human, and second, because of the vivid word pictures in Scripture. Indeed, I think that much of the time when we think about Jesus and events in his life, we picture him, and we do this because it is completely natural for us to think this way. This means that all that is happening when we see a painting, sculpture, or acted portrayal of Jesus is that we get to see someone else's picture of Jesus. As long as it is faithful to Scripture, and as long as the intention of the artist is not to encourage worship of the image, surely this can only enrich our understanding of our Lord.

What about representation in drama? Again, this subject cannot be dismissed as lightly as it often is. God himself uses dramatic signs to communicate to us. Consider the rainbow, or the whole sacrificial system, or the Passover. The Lord's Supper and baptism are simple dramas displaying for us the nature of our redemption through Christ. The Old Testament is full of stories that are enactments in history of what God himself has done and will one day do. See the story of Abraham sacrificing Isaac; the life of David; the life of Joseph – each of these historical records pictures dramatically for us what God would do one day when Christ would come into the world. The incarnation itself is the greatest drama ever imagined or told, and whenever a preacher speaks about the incarnation, death, and resurrection of Jesus, he is rehearsing this drama for those who are listening.

We also have several examples in Scripture of the prophets using drama to aid their spoken words. See the examples of Isaiah (8:1-4; 20:1-6), Jeremiah (13:1-11; 16:1-9; 18:1-11; 19:1-13), and Ezekiel (4:1-17; 5:1-4). Given these biblical illustrations of God commanding the use of dramatic actions and signs to go with the spoken word, how can we possibly argue that the use of drama is always an unspiritual accompaniment to the proclaimed Word? While drama can be abused by being a mere show designed only for human appeal or entertainment, there is not a biblical justification for frowning upon or condemning an *appropriate* use of drama within the context of the preaching of God's Word.

What about Abstract Art?

How should we think about abstract painting, sculpture, tapestry, and other visual forms of artistic expression? Some Christians think that all abstract art is somehow dishonoring to God and is necessarily uncreative. However, just think about some of the art in the tabernacle and temple; it is not all strictly representational. Consider as examples the seven-branched candelabra (almond branches and blossoms, but clearly not an exact likeness) or the pomegranates in various unrealistic colors on the garments of the high priest. Think also of every sunrise or sunset you have ever seen – each one is different and changes every second, producing a constantly shifting series of abstract designs made by the greatest master of all abstract painters! Think of moving sand dunes, or waves on the sea, or branches against the sky, or fall colors – everywhere we look, if we have eyes to see, we can begin to understand a little of where the abstract artist finds inspiration.

How Do We Judge the Arts?

We now come to another area about which Christians express a variety of passionate views. Often in magazine articles and on the radio, we can find preachers and commentators condemning all sorts of literature, music, and visual art. Certainly it is appropriate for us to test everything, to hold fast to that which is good, and to abstain from every form of evil, for Scripture commands us to do this. (In the context of 1 Thessalonians 5:20-22, the words of Paul are written about the discernment of prophecy, but we may quite appropriately apply them to the way we think about the arts as well).

There are objective standards by which we can judge any work of art, whether in music, literature, film making, painting, sculpture, or dance. Our knowledge of the existence of such standards is partly a matter of giftedness and intuition, but perhaps even more a result of training and practice. In this the arts are like any other field of human endeavor, for the arts are not above judgment, nor is the artist. So, how do we judge the arts? Following are the beginnings of a list of appropriate criteria.

First, we need to ask whether giftedness from God is evident in the work of a particular composer or performer of music, poet or novelist, painter, sculptor, or film maker. We should ask this question whether the artist is a Christian or not. We have already seen Calvin's thoughts about God giving gifts of grace to those who are not Christians. Now let us see how Abraham Kuyper applied Calvin's words in his own time:

> Calvinism, on the contrary, has taught that all liberal arts are gifts which God imparts promiscuously to believers and to unbelievers. "These radiations of divine light," he wrote, "shone more brilliantly among unbelieving people than

among God's saints." ... The highest art instincts are natural gifts, and hence belong to those excellent graces which, in spite of sin, by virtue of common grace, have continued to shine in human nature; it plainly follows that art can inspire both believers and unbelievers, and that God remains sovereign to impart it, in His good pleasure, alike to heathen and to Christian ... This applies not only to art, but to all the natural utterances of human life.[23]

Flannery O'Connor, the great novelist, wrote about art as a divine calling, and clearly believed that this calling is given by God to both believers and unbelievers:

This is first of all a matter of vocation, and a vocation is a limiting factor which extends even to the kind of material that the writer is able to apprehend imaginatively. The writer can choose what he writes about, but he cannot choose what he is able to make live, and so far as he is concerned, a living deformed character is acceptable and a dead whole one is not.[24]

We have no space to develop this theme further here, but we should be able, I think, to express how we determine where we observe this gift for each area of the arts and in each particular form within that area.

Second, we should look for the dedicated development of the artist's gift through humble learning from others, through practice, and through faithful application – in other words, through hard work as the artist lives as a good steward of the gift God has given.

Third, we should find a commitment by artists to use their gifts for others as well as for their own fulfillment. For the Christian who is an artist, the most significant other to serve will be the Lord. For a Christian working in the arts, just as for a Christian working at anything else, there should be a commitment first to offer one's gift for the glory and delight of God (think of the movie *Chariots of Fire,* in which the Scottish racer Eric Liddell says, "When I run I feel God's pleasure"). There should also be the desire to use one's gift for the pleasure and enrichment of others. If either the creation of art or its performance is purely self-centered, even a great artist will not reach full potential, for God has made us to be other-centered. A Christian will also understand that every artist, both believer and unbeliever, will be seeking to express dominion over creation and to set back the consequences of the Fall.

Fourth, there will be humble submission to the rules of one's discipline, respect for its traditions, and a readiness to find freedom of expression within these forms and within the forms of God's created order. No artist ever starts from an absolutely new beginning – except for the Lord himself at the original creation. Any human artist is a sub-creator working within these creational and historical forms. Once more, remember that I am not suggesting that the development of new forms to express one's message and one's gifts is inappropriate, but rather, I am recognizing that all artists work within artistic traditions.

Fifth, we must ask ourselves: Is this work of art true? Is it in accord with reality? People cannot create their own universe. Rather, both Christians and non-Christians live, reflect, and work within the universe that God has made. This is true whether they acknowledge and worship him or not. The artist is bound by the reality of what God has created and cannot inhabit any other universe, for there is no other universe. Even when a person refuses to bow before the Lord, he or she must live in the Lord's world, and so, that person's art will have to be in touch with reality at some level, no matter what he or she may claim to believe. Only rarely will we find art that attempts to be completely consistent to some system of unbelief; but art that becomes pure propaganda for a totally false universe of the artist's making ultimately ceases to be art (consider the example of John Cage, with his chance music, which is no longer music, but merely noise).

All truly great art will appeal universally because of this element of truthfulness to the world as God made it and to the world of our human existence. Think of the worldwide appreciation of Shakespeare's tragedies *Hamlet* and *Macbeth.* Consider also Jane Austen's appeal in a postmodern age; she is so evidently dealing with human relationships and moral questions that exist in all times and all places that, though her deeply held Christian convictions are thoroughly out of step with the beliefs and practices of our postmodern society, her novels have become increasingly popular, both in print form, and in the many movie versions of them. Austen's work touches deep chords in the human soul because she wrote truth.

Sixth, we need to bring any work of art before the bar of moral criteria. We must ask questions about the moral intention of the artist. Is the purpose of a work to deprave or corrupt? If a work contains immoral behavior or evil, what is the context? It should be evident to us that the Bible contains many accounts of wicked behavior, sometimes very graphically portrayed. Works of art must not necessarily be condemned because they contain such violence, but context and intention have to be considered.

The same is true with issues of cursing or blasphemy. It is not enough for Christians to say, "This movie or literature is full of blasphemy, therefore it is immoral and we are not to see or read such works." Think about the book of Job. It is full of blasphemy, for the trite comments about God and the easy answers to the problem of suffering that Job's comforters offer to him are false and ultimately dishonoring to God's name.

Christians can easily judge foul language and obvious blasphemy; I have no wish to defend such abuse of language or the dishonoring of God. But before we make such judgments about the way unbelievers curse and swear, we need to take the planks out of our own eyes. Think about the misuse of God's name by Christians – for example, saying, "God bless you!" when we do not really mean it; or, when we say, "I will pray for you," with no intention of actually doing so; or, when we pretend a devotion to the Lord and a deep spirituality that is far from genuine. Such misuse of God's name and such hypocrisy are as blasphemous as the open cursing in many movies or in some rap music.

So, we need to ask: What is the moral impact of reading or viewing this piece of work? There are, of course, "artistic" works that need to be judged and found wanting – such as the novels about the cannibalistic murderer Hannibal Lecter, where the intention clearly seems to be to create interest in appalling wickedness for its own sake. (Interestingly, the movies made from these novels have not been as bad in this regard as the books, for the actor who plays Lecter, Anthony Hopkins, is quite good and is able to invest the character with a humanity that is absent from the novels.)

Seventh, we must ask questions about appropriate continuity between the form and the content of a given work of art. Is the form the artist has chosen one that works with or against the message of the piece the artist is creating? Consider Eliot's fragmented form in *The Waste Land,* a poem of disconnected pieces, disparate images, constant variations in poetic form, and a lack of rational or linear progression. This structure (or, it might be better to say, lack of structure) is completely appropriate for Eliot's prophetic vision of a doomed postmodern world.

Eighth, in art as in any other area of human endeavor, we need to look for technical excellence. For the Christian especially, good work faithfully done is honoring to God.

Ninth, we should have a concern for how well a work of art reflects the integrity of the artist. Is the work true to who the artist is? Or is the work merely fashionable or commercial, or is it even false to the artist's own convictions and understanding? (We are not suggesting here that there is a problem with an artist getting appropriate pay for hard work; there is nothing inherently wrong with writing, making music, or painting in order to earn a living.)

Tenth, we should expect to see integrity in the work itself. For example, we all know that there is a difference between genuine sentiment and sentimentality. Does the artist seek to manipulate our emotional response by cheap tricks, or seek to generate genuine emotional response by the power of the work? Preaching is a helpful example here. Any experienced preacher knows how to make people cry or laugh, or how to produce many other responses through the power of the preached words; but, as the apostle Paul tells us in 2 Corinthians 4:2, God calls us to "renounce such disgraceful, underhanded ways and by the open statement of the truth commend ourselves to everyone's conscience in the sight of God." A preacher knows when he is manipulating people, and he also knows that such manipulation will not bring about deep repentance or genuine spiritual transformation in people's lives. What is true of the preacher is also true for the composer, hymn writer, film maker, poet, painter, and every other artist.

Eleventh, we must be aware that simple entertainment is fine in any of the art forms, for God created us to enjoy his gifts and one another's gifts. When we watch the sun going down or pick a rose for the table, we do not need to look for any thing other than the pleasure of the act itself. Human art, just like God's art, does not need to have a "higher" purpose. We may watch a movie, listen to music, read a book, or hang a painting simply because we like to do so. What matters here is the purpose or kind of the particular piece of art. The question is: Does this piece of art succeed at what it sets out to do?

There are additional factors we should take into consideration, as well as thinking about the matter of objective aesthetic criteria. Christians – and all others, for that matter – need to recognize that it is not appropriate to be elitist or snobbish about other people's likes and dislikes with regard to the arts. Of course, it is fine that we all enjoy books, films, and music that are not particularly good when judged by objective aesthetic criteria. Till the end of his life, C. S. Lewis enjoyed the stories of H. Rider Haggard, even though he did not regard them as great literature. Everyone has different tastes. My wife does not pretend to like fantasy literature, so she has never read *The Lord of the Rings,* even though it is a very great piece of literature. I do not think less of her because of this, though I myself have read the book at least twenty times. Another way to express this is to say that we must not regard artistic taste or pleasure as a moral issue or a matter of spiritual superiority; we should simply delight in the diversity of taste.

This is an important issue. It means that we must speak with great care about the pleasures of others. We do not want to make people feel inferior because they may like a work that is not great, or even good, by objective standards of quality. But, though we must respect people's likes and tastes, it is also essential to remember and to teach that there are objective standards by which books, films, or music, or any other art, should be judged. We ought to resist the "equalizing heresy" (about which Lewis wrote so well) that tells us that we must never regard some works as better than others, and that any mention of standards is necessarily elitist and snobbish.

It is important to teach that there are standards for judging the arts, no matter how popular a given work or artist may be, just as it is important to teach that we must judge theology, no matter how popular a given work may be. In some cases theological weaknesses and other problems must be pointed out, and appropriate questions about the quality of the writing (or filmmaking, or whatever) must be raised. No matter how carefully we speak, some people will be offended and will think we are being judgmental, or elitist, or snobbish; but this does not mean that we should be silent.

We also recognize that there is the matter of the heart. It may be that Aunt Jane, or Mr. Jones, or young Henry loves to play the piano and enjoys tapping out the music of hymns and songs of worship. Their hearts may be full of praise for the Lord as they do this, praise that he delights in, but this does not mean that it would be right and good to ask these persons to accompany the singing for our Sunday worship, if, objectively speaking, they are not skilled or trained musicians. King David appointed leaders for music and singing who were good at their work, and so must we.

In the same way, many of us love to sing, and even though we may be greatly out of tune as we do so, our heart devotion is most certainly pleasing to the Lord. But, we may be tone deaf, and therefore, out of love for our neighbors in worship, we need to restrain ourselves from singing loudly when we are in church so as not to distress their tuneful ears and make it difficult for them to sing their praises to the Lord. We must have skilled and competent musicians and song-leaders, but we also seek to encourage these musicians to serve the Lord in their hearts in the same way that Aunt Jane, Mr. Jones, or young Henry serve him with love.

We need also to affirm that a person's artistic giftedness, even when it is great, does not make that person a better, greater, more virtuous, or more godly human being. Tolkien is a wonderful example here. He was, without doubt, the greatest scholar of the past century in his field. He was also a gifted writer of stories and a thoroughly competent poet. However, he understood that this did not, in and of itself, make him a better person or a more important man in the kingdom of God. He realized that God had given him these gifts and that he was a servant who had an obligation to God to use his gifts faithfully. He knew that how God chose to use those gifts for the glory of his kingdom was God's business. He also knew that how he loved God (including the way in which he used his gifts), how he loved his wife and children, and how he behaved to students, neighbors, colleagues, and tradesmen were the fundamental measures of his growth as a Christian – not the greatness of his gifts.

C. S. Lewis had this quality about him as well. He was a great scholar, teacher, and writer, yet he never became puffed up by the marvelous gifts God had given him. Both Lewis and Tolkien understood that they were stewards called to use their gifts wisely and well. But they also understood that it was their desire to please God by living a life of justice, mercy, and faithfulness in *all* they did that was important to the Lord. For Christians involved in the arts – or in anything else – there can be no higher calling than this.

---

1. Unless otherwise indicated, Bible verses quoted in this essay are taken from the English Standard Version (ESV).

2. John Calvin, *Institutes of the Christian Religion*, 2 vols., ed. John T. McNeill, trans. Ford Lewis Battles (Philadelphia, Pa.: Westminster, 1960), I.v.1–2.

3. Gerard Manley Hopkins, "God's Granudeur," in *The Poems of Gerard Manley Hopkins*, ed. W. H. Gardner and N. H. MacKenzie, 4th ed., rev. and enlarged (New York: Oxford University Press, 1970), 66.

4. Hopkins, "Pied Beauty," in Ibid., 69–70.

5. Daniel Loizeaux, "The Imagination of God," *Genesis: Journal of the Society of Christians in the Arts*, Inc. 1, no. 2 (1975): 72.

6. John Calvin, *On the Life of the Christian Man* (Grand Rapids, Mich.: Baker Book House, 1952), 88.

7. Quoted in Loizeaux, "The Imagination of God," 74.

8. C. S. Lewis, "Christianity and Literature," *Genesis: Journal of the Society of Christians in the Arts*, Inc. 1, no. 2 (1975): 22.

9. This and the next several quotes are taken from Lewis, "Christianity and Literature," 18–20.

10. Ibid.

11. Ibid.

12. Ibid.

13. Plotinus, *Ennead*, V.viii, 320. Quoted in C. S. Lewis, "English Literature in the Sixteenth Century, Excluding Drama," *Oxford History of English Literature* (London: Oxford University Press, 1954), 320.

14. Lewis, "English Literature in the Sixteenth Century," 320–1.

15. Ibid.

16. This and the following quotation are excerpts from C. S. Lewis, *An Experiment in Criticism* (Cambridge: Cambridge University Press, 1965), 137–41.

17. Ibid.

18. T.S. Eliot, "On Poetry and Poets," quoted in *Reading Literature: Some Christian Approaches*, ed. David Barratt and Roger Pooley (Leicester, UK: UCCF Literary Studies Group, 1985), 8.

19. Calvin, *Institutes* II.ii.15.

20 Ibid., II.ii.17.

21. Hans Rookmaaker, *Art Needs No Justification* (Downers Grove, Ill.: Intervarsity, 1978).

22. Lewis, "Christianity and Literature," 14.

23. Abraham Kuyper, *Lectures on Calvinism* (Grand Rapids, Mich.: Eerdmans, 1931), 160–1.

24. Flannery O'Connor, *Mystery and Manners: Occasional Prose*, ed. Sally and Robert Fitzgerald (New York: Farrar, Strauss, and Giroux, 1969), 27.

19
GRACE-CENTERED CHURCH PLANTING

PHILIP D. DOUGLASS
Associate Professor of Practical Theology

And they sang a new song, saying,

> "Worthy are you to take the scroll
>   and to open its seals,
> for you were slain, and by your blood you ransomed people for God
>   from every tribe and language and people and nation,
> and you have made them a kingdom and priests to our God,
> and they shall reign on the earth." (Rev. 5:9-10)[1]

JOHN CALVIN: TRAINER OF CHURCH PLANTERS

In Geneva, during the last ten years of his life, John Calvin committed himself to training men for evangelism and church planting – especially in France but also throughout Europe. The Venerable Company of Pastors, as the presbytery of Geneva called itself, became a powerful church-planting agency under Calvin's leadership. His church planters slipped across the border into France after midnight, making use of back roads and alleyways. They preached the gospel clandestinely in sheds, gathered new converts, and discipled them in the Scriptures just as they themselves had been discipled by Calvin. When these church planters were captured by the king's soldiers, put on trial, and sentenced to death, Calvin wrote sympathetic, affectionate notes of support, reminding them from the Scriptures to persevere in their faithfulness to the Lord. Over that ten year period, thousands of churches were planted by men such as these.[2] Most of the trainees had come to Geneva as refugees, fleeing from the persecution in France. Yet, after Calvin had equipped them in the study of the Scriptures, godliness of character, and proclamation of the gospel, they went back to plant churches in the same hostile country from which they had recently fled. These efforts by Calvin led to a rapid expansion of the kingdom of God. In 1555, there were five Reformed churches in France (in Paris, Meaux, Angers, Poitiers, and Loudon). In 1559, there were almost 100. By 1562, the number had reached 2,150. The total membership of these churches in 1562 has been estimated at three million (out of a total population in France of approximately 20 million).[3] By any historical comparison, these reports indicate astounding evangelistic and church-planting effort.[4]

Planters also were sent from Geneva to Italy, the Netherlands, Scotland, Hungary, Poland, the city-states in the Rhineland, and Brazil. New Testament scholar Philip Hughes concluded that Calvin's Geneva was "a dynamic centre of missionary concern and activity ... an axis from which the light of the Good News radiated forth through the testimony of those who, after thorough preparation in this school, were sent forth in the service of Jesus Christ."[5]

So fruitful was this church planting endeavor that it stirred up the wrath of the king of France. In 1561, Charles IX sent a letter to the Council of Geneva, accusing the church planters sent from that city of instigating "seditions and dissensions which had been disturbing his reign."[6] The king demanded that the Council order these evangelists to return to Geneva in order to restore his nation to its former state of peacefulness. Calvin refused to recall his soldiers of the gospel.

The result of Calvin's extraordinary efforts to evangelize France was that Reformed churches were established all over that nation. Williston Walker writes that "a great national Church, for the first time in Reformation history, was created independent of a hostile State; and the work was one for which Calvin had given the model, the inspiration, and the training."[7]

Throughout All of Europe

Calvin's church planting training center in Geneva became a focal point for equipping men for the propagation of the gospel and the establishment of Reformed churches throughout Europe. People came from all over Europe to be trained as missionaries and went back out as ministers of the gospel. Gordon Laman writes that,

> through the coming and going of these refugees, and through the evangelical writings from the printing presses of Geneva and elsewhere in Latin, French, English, and Dutch, the Reformed faith was exported widely, even to Poland and Hungary. By correspondence, Calvin encouraged, guided, and dialogued with this diaspora of evangelical Christians witnessing under persecution.[8]

New Testament scholar Philip E. Hughes notes that

Calvin's Geneva ... was not a theological ivory tower that lived to itself and for itself, oblivious of its responsibility in the gospel to the needs of others. Human vessels were equipped and refitted in this haven, not to be status symbols like painted yachts safely moored at a fashionable marina, but that they might launch out into the surrounding ocean of the world's need, bravely facing every storm and peril that awaited them in order to bring the light of Christ's gospel to those who were in the ignorance and darkness from which they themselves had originally come. They were taught in this school in order that they in turn might teach others the truth that had set them free.[9]

Such explosive church planting compels us to ask the question: What is the nature of the beliefs held by the Venerable Company of Pastors of Geneva in the mid-1500s – and which flourish today under the name of Reformed theology – that fostered then as well as now such a zeal for evangelism and church planting?

GRACE-CENTERED, REFORMED THEOLOGICAL CONVICTIONS THAT EMPOWER CHURCH PLANTING

Conviction 1: The Indicatives Empower Us, the Imperatives Direct Us

At the heart of the grace-centeredness of Reformed theology are what we call the "indicatives" and the "imperatives." Reflecting the Greek grammatical moods, the indicatives are a declaration of who God is, what he has done in Christ, and whom he has made us to be in union with Christ as a result. The indicatives empower the second grammatical mood – the imperatives, which challenge and guide us in responding to who God is in Christ and how he relates to us. The indicatives are the basic truths of a biblical passage; the imperatives are declaratives, the "therefores" which command us to do thus and so in response to the preceding truths. The indicatives are the roots and vine – the imperatives are the branches (John 15). The indicatives are the sources of power; the imperatives are the communicators of direction.

There are innumerable examples in Scripture of the indicatives empowering the imperatives. Perhaps the most famous is Romans 12:1: "I appeal to you therefore, brothers, by the mercies of God [i.e. the indicative statements presented by Paul in the previous eleven chapters of his epistle] to present your bodies as a living sacrifice, holy and acceptable to God, which is your spiritual worship [i.e. the imperative statements presented in the subsequent five chapters]."

The imperatives are the law or commandments of God. As J. I. Packer says, "God's law expresses his character. It reflects his own behavior."[10] And especially, it reflects his behavior towards us as his people. This understanding leads us to what we might call the Platinum Rule: "Do unto God and one another even has he has so graciously and lovingly done unto us in Christ." And the corollary to this Rule is: "To the degree that our hearts are gripped by the Lord's gracious and loving work done on our behalf, to that same degree we will be motivated and empowered by the Holy Spirit to go and do likewise to one another by keeping his commandments."

This is why the apostle John tells us, "And by this we know that we have come to know him, if we keep his commandments" (1 John 2:3). In other words, if we know him in the ways he relates to us, then we will relate in the same way to him and to one another by keeping his commandments.

John Murray states in *Principles of Conduct* that, "We must not forget that the fountain from which our love of God flows is the love of God to us (cf. 1 John 4:19)." And furthermore, "Our love is always ignited by the flame of Christ's love."[11]

John Owen, the great Puritan, understood this principle as well:

> We need to keep our heart full of a sense of the love of God. This is the greatest perspective available to us against the power of temptation in the world ... Fill your heart with a sense of the love of God in Christ, and apply the eternal design of grace and shed blood to yourselves. Accept all the privileges of adoption, justification, and acceptance with God.[12]

Moralism: Reversing the Order

Moralism, which stifles evangelism, occurs when we place the imperatives ahead of the indicatives. Powerlessness and deep spiritual weariness result. Moralism reverses the order of 1 John 3:16, which says: "By this we know love [the love of God for us], that he laid down his life for us, and we ought to lay down our lives for the brothers." In the moralistic frame of mind, this becomes, "We ought to lay down our lives for the brethren in order to have God love us or love us more."

As Richard Lovelace notes in his *Dynamics of Spiritual Life,*

> Moralism, whether it takes the form of denunciation or pep talks, can ultimately only create awareness of sin and guilt or manufactured virtues built on will power. A ministry which leads to genuine sanctification and growth, on the other hand, avoids moralism, first by making clear the deep rootage of sin-problems in the flesh so that the congregation is not battling these in the dark, and then by showing that every victory over the flesh is won by faith in Christ, laying hold of union with him in death and resurrection and relying on his Spirit for power over sin ... Ministries which attack only the surface of sin and fail to ground spiritual growth in the believer's union with Christ produce either self-righteousness or despair, and both of these conditions are inimical to spiritual life.[13]

Theologian Geerhardus Vos says, "To take God as source and end of all that exists and happens, and to hold such a view suffused with warmth of genuine devotion, stands not only related to theology as the fruit stands to the tree: it is by reason of its essence a veritable theological tree of life."[14] And Tim Keller of Redeemer Presbyterian Church of Manhattan, New York, points out, "... it [the gospel] tells us that we are more wicked than we ever dared believe, but more loved and accepted in Christ than we ever dared to hope – at the same time. In fact, if the gospel is true, the more you see your sin, the more certain you are that you were saved by sheer grace and the more precious and electrifying that grace is to you."[15]

Edward Fisher, in his classic *The Marrow of Modern Divinity* (1646), states that "God the Father ... cheers the hearts of poor sinners, and greatly delights them with singular comfort and heavenly sweetness, assuring them that whosoever is married unto Christ, and so is in Him by faith, he is as acceptable to God the Father as Christ himself ... and so shall the love and favor of God be as deeply insinuated in you as it is into Christ himself."[16]

There is nothing we can do to make ourselves more acceptable to God than we are now in Christ because the issue of our complete approval with God was accomplished and finished 2,000 years ago in the loving sacrifice of Jesus, "... wherein He has made us accepted in the Beloved" (Eph. 1:6, 7 KJV).

Sinclair Ferguson writes in *Children of the Living God*, "Christ is giving us access to the presence of his Father, and saying to us: 'You may now speak to Him as I speak to Him; with the same right of access, with the same sense of intimacy, with the same assurance that He loves you.'"[17]

The Opposite of Moralism

The opposite of moralism is cheap grace. Whereas moralism kills, cheap grace deludes and eventually destroys. We have to avoid both traps. In *The Cost of Discipleship*, Dietrich Bonhoeffer makes this statement (the brackets are mine):

> Cheap grace is the deadly enemy of our church. We are fighting today for costly grace. Cheap grace means grace sold on the market like the cheapjack's wares. Cheap grace is the preaching of forgiveness [indicative] without requiring repentance [imperative], baptism [indicative] without church discipline [imperative], Communion [indicative] without confession [imperative], absolution [indicative] without personal confession [imperative]. Cheap grace is grace without discipleship, grace without the cross, grace without Jesus Christ, living and incarnate.[18]

Indicatives and Imperatives in Various Expressions of the Great Commission

Let us see how the indicatives and imperatives are illustrated in Scripture by looking at several passages that express the theme of the Great Commission in various ways.

For example, Matthew 10:5-8 says:

> These twelve Jesus sent out, instructing them, "Go nowhere among the Gentiles and enter no town of the Samaritans, but go rather to the lost sheep

of the house of Israel. And proclaim as you go, saying, 'The kingdom of heaven
is at hand.' Heal the sick, raise the dead, cleanse lepers, cast out demons. You
received without paying [indicative]; give without pay [imperative]."

A basic understanding of the gospel is that we have done nothing to earn or
deserve this free gift of salvation. To the degree that our hearts are gripped by
the realization that our salvation is all of God from beginning to end, we will
be compelled to freely offer this gospel of grace to others.

In Matthew 16:16-19, we are told:

> Simon Peter replied, "You are the Christ, the Son of the living God." And
> Jesus answered him, "Blessed are you, Simon Bar-Jonah! For flesh and blood
> has not revealed this to you, but my Father who is in heaven. And I tell you,
> you are Peter, and on this rock I will build my church, and the gates of hell
> shall not prevail against it. I will give you the keys of the kingdom of heaven
> [indicative], and whatever you bind on earth shall be bound in heaven, and
> whatever you loose on earth shall be loosed in heaven [imperative]."

The illumination of the Spirit of the Father enabled Simon Peter to see with
eyes of faith that Christ is the Son of the living God. This is a basic truth
of the gospel: Jesus will build his church and death cannot stop its advance
because of the power of his resurrection that raises his followers from the
dead. This great gospel message forms the keys to the kingdom of heaven;
no one can enter into heaven apart from the Spirit of the Father opening the
eyes of his heart to this truth. Peter and the apostles had the opportunity to
proclaim this gospel as the means to open up the gates of Hades for those who
were dead in their sins and trespasses and to allow them to walk into heaven.
The apostles had the opportunity – as do we as followers of Christ – to do
unto others, through the proclamation of the gospel, as had been done so
graciously unto them.

John 20:21-23 says, "Jesus said to them again, 'Peace be with you. As
the Father has sent me [indicative], even so I am sending you [imperative].'"
Again, the principle is that we are empowered to do unto others that which
we recognize that God in Christ has graciously done unto us. The corollary
is this: the deeper our faith recognition of that gracious work of God in our
lives, then the deeper our commitment to go and do likewise.

Conviction 2: Covenant Framework of the Great Commission
The Great Commission itself is given to us in Matthew 28:16-20:

> Now the eleven disciples went to Galilee, to the mountain to which Jesus
> had directed them. And when they saw him they worshiped him, but some
> doubted. And Jesus came and said to them, "*All authority* [εξουσια] *in heaven
> and on earth has been given to me.* Go therefore and make disciples of all
> nations, baptizing them in the name of the Father and of the Son and of the

Holy Spirit, teaching them to observe all that I have commanded you. And behold, I am with you always, to the end of the age" (emphasis added).

As this and other Scriptures tell us, Jesus Christ remains with the church (Matt. 28:20), lives in the church (Col. 1:27), and works through the church (Mark 16:20). Our mission as disciples is simply a continuation of his. Our authority derives from his. Thus, we must now explore the question: What is the nature of the authority Jesus received that he uses to empower us to proclaim the gospel to the end of the age? To answer this question, we will need to look briefly at covenant theology.

In Genesis 15, God reaffirms his covenant promise to give Abraham "offspring." This promise will be fulfilled in three ways. First, "your offspring will be sojourners" (Gen. 15:13) – that is, Abraham will be given many blood descendants. Second, "... your 'Offspring,' who is Christ" (Gal. 3:16) – that is, Abraham's descendant will be the Messiah. Third, "... Abraham's offspring, heirs according to promise" (Gal. 3:29) – that is, Abraham will be given many descendants who will be in union with his Offspring. The scene in which this reaffirmation takes place is worth revisiting:

> And he [the Lord] brought him [Abram] outside and said, "Look toward heaven, and number the stars, if you are able to number them." Then he said to him, "So shall your offspring be." And he believed the Lord, and he counted it to him as righteousness.
>
> And he said to him, "I am the LORD who brought you out from Ur of the Chaldeans to give you this land to possess." But he said, "O LORD God, how am I to know that I shall possess it?" He said to him, "Bring me a heifer three years old, a female goat three years old, a ram three years old, a turtledove, and a young pigeon." And he brought him all these, cut them in half, and laid each half over against the other. But he did not cut the birds in half. And when birds of prey came down on the carcasses, Abram drove them away.
>
> As the sun was going down, a deep sleep fell on Abram. And behold, dreadful and great darkness fell upon him. Then the Lord said to Abram, "Know for certain that your offspring will be sojourners in a land that is not theirs and will be servants there, and they will be afflicted for four hundred years. But I will bring judgment on the nation that they serve, and afterward they shall come out with great possessions. As for yourself, you shall go to your fathers in peace; you shall be buried in a good old age. And they shall come back here in the fourth generation, for the iniquity of the Amorites is not yet complete."
>
> When the sun had gone down and it was dark, behold, a smoking fire pot and a flaming torch passed between these pieces. On that day the Lord made a covenant with Abram ... (Gen. 15:5-18)

In the Old Testament, covenant בְּרִית was at the foundation of all relationships. A covenant could represent a treaty between nations that was to be faithfully honored, or it could be a contract between two businessmen. A variety of agreements between parties were given binding status by the making of a covenant. The most binding was the "covenant of blood." Animals were killed and divided (hence the term "cutting" a covenant), and both parties to the treaty passed between the pieces, binding themselves to its provisions with a self-maledictory oath. If one party failed to keep the stipulations of the covenant, then, according to the stipulations of the oath, he could be cut in two or slain in punishment. Old Testament commentators Keil and Delitzsch note, "Thus God condescended to follow the custom of the Chaldeans, that he might in the most solemn manner confirm his oath to Abram the Chaldean."[19]

God's oath to Abraham is described in Hebrews 6:12-15: "... so that you may not be sluggish, but imitators of those who through faith and patience inherit the promises. For when God made a promise to Abraham, since he had no one greater by whom to swear, he swore by himself, saying, 'Surely I will bless you and multiply you.'"

In this way, God made (literally, "cut") a formal treaty (a covenant) with Abram, even though Abram was in "a deep sleep" at the time and did not enter into the covenant himself. However, Abram's Offspring – Abram's Mediator, the second member of the Trinity – entered into covenant with the Holy God for him. The Westminster Larger Catechism Question 31 asks: "With whom was the covenant of grace made?" Answer: "The covenant of grace was made with Christ as the second Adam, and in him with all the elect as his seed." Question 32 asks: "How is the grace of God manifested in the second covenant?" Answer: "The grace of God is manifested in the second covenant, in that he freely provideth and offereth to sinners a Mediator, and life and salvation by him." Christ is our Mediator, our Intermediary, our Representative, and Substitute, who walks the blood covenant path with the Holy Righteous God in our place.

In John 8:56, Jesus makes the connection between the Genesis 15 covenant ceremony and himself: "Your father Abraham rejoiced that he would see my day. He saw it and was glad." Jesus is referring to the covenant ceremony in Genesis 15 in which God the Son participated. Abraham was given faith to look forward 2,000 years through the covenant ceremony to see Christ's "day" (i.e. his crucifixion).

There must be punishment for those of us who transgress the covenant with God by breaking God's covenant requirements for all mankind. Either we must take the punishment – which is eternal hell – or our Substitute must take it for us in our place and we are set free. Through the grace of God, it is this second circumstance which pertains, as we read in Galatians 3:27, "For as many of you who were baptized into Christ have put on Christ ..." We were baptized by the Spirit into Christ's "cutting," or punishment, in our place. Galatians 3:29 says, "If you are Christ's, then you are Abraham's offspring, and heirs according to the promise." Christ bestows his merit or inheritance upon us as "clothing."

Luther called this the Great Exchange:

> Christ, the rich, noble, and holy bridegroom, takes in marriage this poor,
> contemptible, and sinful little prostitute, takes away all her evil, and bestows
> all his goodness upon her! ... This means that what Christ possesses belongs to
> the believing soul, and what the soul possesses belongs to Christ. Thus Christ
> possesses all good things and holiness; these now belong to the soul. The soul
> possesses lots of vices and sin; these now belong to Christ.[20]

Those who have been granted the gift of salvation from punishment for
covenant violation have been given to Christ by the Father. John 17:6 tells us,
"I have manifested your name to the people whom you gave me out of the
world. Yours they were, and you gave them to me." And in Revelation 21:27
we learn with regard to the New Jerusalem that "nothing unclean will ever
enter it ... only those who are written in the Lamb's book of life" – that is,
believers who have eternal life with Christ.

In order that the grace of God should deliver us out of the first Adam
and place us into union with Christ as the second Adam (Rom. 5:15), it
was necessary that a Mediator act as our Substitute in order to fulfill the
requirements of God's justice. The Father thus gave the elect to his Son in
accordance with the stipulations of the covenant. The Son accepted the elect,
recorded their names in his book, became the Mediator for all of them, and
promised to accomplish the Father's purpose by leading them to salvation.

This answers our question: What is the nature of the authority Jesus
received that he uses to empower us to proclaim the gospel to the end of
the age? That authority comes to him by virtue of his role and status as the
covenantal Mediator and Substitute, and is given to those who follow him by
virtue of their covenantal union with him through faith.

As John Stott notes:

> The concept of substitution may be said to lie at the heart of both sin and
> salvation. For the essence of sin is man substituting himself for God, while the
> essence of salvation is God substituting himself for man. Man asserts himself
> against God and puts himself where only God deserves to be; God sacrifices
> himself for man and puts himself where only man deserves to be. Man claims
> prerogatives which belong to God alone; God accepts penalties which belong
> to man alone.[21]

Scriptural Support for the Covenant between the Father and the Son
That there was such a covenant made between God the Father and the Lord
Jesus on our behalf can be seen in many passages of Scripture.

In Psalm 89:19-37, we read:

> Of old you spoke in a vision to your godly one, and said:
> "I have granted help to one who is mighty;

> I have exalted one chosen from the people.
> I have found David, my servant;
> > with my holy oil I have anointed him,
> so that my hand shall be established with him;
> > my arm also shall strengthen him.
> The enemy shall not outwit him;
> > the wicked shall not humble him.
> I will crush his foes before him
> > and strike down those who hate him.
> My faithfulness and my steadfast love shall be with him,
> > and in my name shall his horn be exalted
> I will set his hand on the sea
> > and his right hand on the rivers.
> He shall cry to me, 'You are my Father,
> > my God, and the Rock of my salvation.'
> And I will make him the firstborn,
> > the highest of the kings of the earth.
> My steadfast love I will keep for him forever,
> > and my covenant will stand firm for him.
> I will establish his offspring forever
> > and his throne as the days of the heavens.
> If his children forsake my law
> > and do not walk according to my rules,
> if they violate my statutes
> > and do not keep my commandments,
> then I will punish their transgression with the rod
> > and their iniquity with stripes,
> but I will not remove from him my steadfast love
> > or be false to my faithfulness.
> I will not violate my covenant
> > or alter the word that went forth from my lips.
> Once for all I have sworn by my holiness;
> > I will not lie to David.
> His offspring shall endure forever,
> > his throne as long as the sun before me.
> Like the moon it shall be established forever,
> > a faithful witness in the skies."

In this psalm, statements are made about David and about Christ as he is foreshadowed in David. Specifically, verses 19 to 37 refer to Christ. He is spoken of as "your godly one" (v. 19; cf. Luke 1:35); one "who is mighty" (v. 19; cf. Ps. 45:3); "my servant; with my holy oil I have anointed him" (v. 20; cf. Ps. 45:8); "the firstborn, the highest of the kings of the earth" (v. 27; cf. Heb. 1:6; Rev. 19:16); and "his throne shall endure as long as the sun before me. Like the moon it shall be established forever, a faithful witness in the skies" (vv. 36-37; cf. Ps. 72:5).

The Father, in sending the Lord Jesus to be Mediator and Savior, presents him to the elect and gives them to him so that he may earn and achieve salvation for them. For this reason, the Father gave several covenant requirements to the Mediator and mandated that he fulfill them: "… but the Father who sent me has himself given me a commandment – what to say and what to speak. And I know that his commandment is eternal life" (John 12:49-50a); "This charge I have received from my Father" (John 10:18). These covenant requirements include the following:

- He would be Immanuel, God and man: "'Behold, the virgin shall conceive and bear a son, and they shall call his name Immanuel' (which means, God with us)" (Matt. 1:23).

- He would take on our nature as sinners: "… one who in every respect has been tempted as we are, yet without sin" (Heb. 4:15).

- He would place himself under the law: "God sent forth his Son, born of woman, born under the law, to redeem those who were under the law" (Gal. 4:4–5), which demanded perfect obedience to merit eternal life (Matt. 6:48: "You therefore must be perfect, as your heavenly Father is perfect") and judgment for transgression of that perfection (Gal. 6:7: "Do not be deceived: God is not mocked, for whatever one sows, that will he also reap").

- On our behalf, he would bear all the wrath which our sins have deserved, and would be crucified (1 Peter 2:24, "He himself bore our sins in his body on the tree"), as if he himself had transgressed.

- He would be buried and then resurrected from the dead: "I lay it [my life] down of my own accord. I have authority to lay it down, and I have authority to take it up again. This charge I have received from my Father" (John 10:18). These events would occur in accordance with the plan of God: "… this Jesus, delivered up according to the definite plan and foreknowledge of God, you crucified and killed" (Acts 2:23).

- On our behalf, he would have to "to fulfill all righteousness" in order to bestow his righteousness on us. "For as by the one man's disobedience the many were made sinners, so by the one man's obedience the many will be made righteous" (Rom. 5:19); "In Christ God was reconciling the world to himself, not counting their trespasses against them … For our sake he made him to be sin who knew no sin, so that in him we might become the righteousness of God (Rom. 5:19, 21). In this way, Christ would fulfill the prophecy of Isaiah 42:6: "I will keep you and will make you to be a covenant for the people and a light for the Gentiles."

- He would grant to us the salvation that he merited by proclaiming himself as the gospel, causing us to be born of the Spirit, blessing us with faith, persevering with us, raising us from the dead, and leading us to heaven. Thus, the fulfillment of this great salvation would rest entirely on him.

"And this is the will of him who sent me, that I should lose nothing of all that he has given me, but raise it up on the last day" (John 6:39).

To these stipulations, the Father attached magnificent promises to Christ and to those who are in union with Christ. These blessings enable us to understand the nature of the authority of Christ, about which he speaks in Matthew 28:19. The promises include:

- The Father promised that his will would prosper through Christ. "When his soul makes an offering for sin he shall see his offspring; he shall prolong his days; the will of the LORD shall prosper in his hand" (Isa. 53:10).

- The Father promised that Christ would be king over "the nations" – not merely over the Jews, but over the Gentiles as well. "As for me, I have set my King on Zion, my holy hill ... Ask of me, and I will make the nations your heritage, and the ends of the earth your possession" (Ps. 2:6, 8); "May he have dominion from sea to sea, and from the River to the ends of the earth ... all nations serve him" (Ps. 72:8, 11).

- The Father promised that Christ would have power over all creatures in order to govern them to the benefit of his elect. "For 'God has put all things in subjection under his feet'" (1 Cor. 15:27).

- The Father promised that Christ would be honored in a glorious way that would be recognized by the entire creation. "You are my Son ... I will make the nations your inheritance" (Ps. 2:7-10). "All the nations are your inheritance" (Ps. 82:8). "... after making purification for sins, he sat down at the right hand of the Majesty on high" (Heb. 1:3).

- In Daniel 7:13-14, the prophet foresaw sovereign authority being given to Christ: "I saw in the night visions, and behold, with the clouds of heaven there came one like a son of man, and he came to the Ancient of Days and was presented before him. And to him was given dominion and glory and a kingdom, that all peoples, nations, and languages should serve him; his dominion is an everlasting dominion, which shall not pass away, and his kingdom one that shall not be destroyed."

- The Father promised to Christ that we would receive all the blessings of the covenant through our union with him: forgiveness of sin, reconciliation, newness of life, peace, joy in his presence, and eternal glory. "He that spared not his own Son, but delivered him up for us all, how shall he not with him also freely give us all things?" (Rom. 8:32).

Since the Lord Jesus has perfectly fulfilled the covenant conditions, he has also fully deserved the fulfillment of all the promises that have been made to him by the Father and to us in Christ. The granting of these promises is a just payment that Christ has deserved on the basis of his achievements.

This means that Christ has earned "all things" for us as his compensation for keeping the covenant stipulations perfectly.

Calvin's famous statement in the *Institutes* speaks to the point of our being made partners with Christ in receiving the gifts he has merited:

> ... I acknowledge that we are devoid of this incomparable gift until Christ become ours. Therefore, to that union of the head and members, the residence of Christ in our hearts, in fine, the mystical union, we assign the highest rank, Christ when he becomes ours making us partners with him in the gifts with which he was endued. Hence we do not view him as at a distance and without us, but as we have put him on, and been engrafted into his body, he deigns to make us one with himself, and, therefore, we glory in having a fellowship of righteousness with him.[22]

This covenant exemplifies the love between the two covenant keepers that is revealed in the Father giving us as a reward to the Son. We are eternally blessed to have been included in this covenant of love and therefore are moved to proclaim, "We love him, because he first loved us" (1 John 4:19). This is the message of Jonathan Edwards' great unpublished treatise "Discourse on the Trinity":

> ... there proceeds a most pure act, and an infinitely holy and sweet energy arises between the Father and Son: for their love and joy is mutual, in mutually loving and delighting in each other. Prov. 8:30, "I was daily his delight rejoicing always before [him]." This is the eternal and most perfect and essential act of the divine nature, wherein the Godhead acts to an infinite degree and in the most perfect manner possible. The Deity becomes all act, the Divine essence itself flows out and is as it were breathed forth in love and joy. So that the Godhead therein stands forth in yet another manner of subsistence, and there proceeds the third person in the Trinity, the Holy Spirit, viz., the Deity in act, for there is no other act but the act of the will.[23]

All Authority Given to Christ

Because he has kept this covenant perfectly, the Lord Jesus has the right to say to us, "All authority in heaven and on earth has been given to me. Go therefore and make disciples of all nations, baptizing them in the name of the Father and of the Son and of the Holy Spirit, teaching them to observe all that I have commanded you. And behold, I am with you always, to the end of the age" (Matt. 28:18-19). And we can go forth with the full confidence that Christ is worthy: for the people of God join the angels in singing, "Worthy are you to take the scroll and to open its seals, for you were slain, and with your blood you ransomed people for God from every tribe and language and people and nation" (Rev. 5:9).

With the apostle Paul during his first church-planting effort at Antioch of Pisidia, we can have confidence that "all who were appointed unto eternal life believed" (Acts 13:48), and that, as the Lord later told Paul, "'I have many in this city who are my people.' So Paul stayed a year and six months, teaching the word of God among them" (Acts 18:9-11). We proclaim the gospel in a community with the confidence that God has "many people" there. When we communicate the gospel of grace clearly and in terms they can understand, then "those appointed unto eternal life" will believe.

CONCLUSION

These were the beliefs held by Calvin's Venerable Company of Pastors that fostered such a grace-centered zeal for church planting. These truths continue to flourish today as central tenets of Reformed theology. Through the faith granted us by the illumination of the Holy Spirit, we are empowered by these indicatives to be obedient to the imperatives of Christ. We can "go therefore and make disciples of all nations" and enfold those disciples into new churches because "all authority in heaven and on earth has been given to" him and to us as those in union with Christ.

1. Unless otherwise indicated, Bible verses quoted in this essay are taken from the English Standard Version (ESV).

2. Frank James, "Calvin the Evangelist," *Reformed Quarterly* (Fall 2001): no page given; available online at http://www.rts.edu/quarterly/fall01/james.html.

3. Robert M. Kingdon, *Geneva and the Coming of the Wars of Religion in France* (Genève: Librairie E. Droz, 1956), 59, 79.

4. This phenomenal growth was recorded in letters written by the pastors of some of these churches to Calvin and the leaders of Geneva. The church in Montpelier "rejoiced, 'Our church, thanks to the Lord, has so grown and so continues to grow every day that we are obliged to preach three sermons on Sundays to a total of five- to six-thousand people' ... A pastor in Toulouse wrote to the Genevan Consistory: 'Our church has grown to the astonishing number of about eight- to nine-thousand souls" (James, "Calvin the Evangelist," no page given).

5. Philip Hughes, ed. and trans., *The Register of the Company of Pastors of Geneva in the Time of Calvin* (Grand Rapids: Wm. B. Eerdmans, 1966), 25.

6. Kingdon, *Geneva and the Coming of the Wars of Religion in France*, 34.

7. Williston Walker, *John Calvin: The Organizer of Reformed Protestantism, 1509–1564* (New York: Knickerbocker Press, 1906), 385.

8. Gordon D. Laman, "The Origin of Protestant Missions," *Reformed Review* 43 (Autumn 1989): 52–67.

9. Philip E. Hughes, "John Calvin: Director of Missions," in *The Heritage of John Calvin*, ed. John H. Bratt (Grand Rapids, Mich.: Eerdmans, 1973), 44–5.

10. J. I. Packer, *Growing in Christ* (Wheaton, Ill.: Crossway, 1994), 232.

11. John Murray, *Principles of Conduct: Aspects of Biblical Ethics* (Grand Rapids, Mich.: Eerdmans, 1957), 226.

12. John Owen, *Sin and Temptation: The Challenge to Personal Godliness* (Minneapolis, Minn.: Bethany House Press, 1996), 132.

13. Richard Lovelace, *Dynamics of Spiritual Life: An Evangelical Theology of Renewal* (Downers Grove, Ill.: InterVarsity Press, 1979), 214.

14. Geerhardus Vos, *The Pauline Eschatology* (Grand Rapids, Mich.: Eerdmans, 1953), 61.

15. "The Redeemer Vision: Core Values and Beliefs," section 2: "The Gospel's Power for Change," available online at the Redeemer Web site: http://www.redeemindy.org/vision.htm.

16. Edward Fisher, *The Marrow of Modern Divinity*, chapter 2, section 3. 3; available online at http://www.mountzion.org/text/marrow/c2s33.html.

17. Sinclair B. Ferguson, *Children of the Living God* (Edinburgh and Carlisle, Pa.: Banner of Truth Trust, 1989), 33.

18. Dietrich Bonhoeffer, *The Cost of Discipleship* (New York: Touchstone, 1959), 43.

19. C. F. Keil and F. Delitzsch, *Commentary on the Old Testament*, 10 vols. (Grand Rapids, Mich., Eerdmans, 1949), 1.214.

20. Martin Luther, "Two Kinds of Righteousness," quoted in *The Christian Theology Reader*, ed. Alister E. McGrath (Oxford: Oxford University Press, 1995), 229ff.

21. John Stott, *The Cross of Christ* (Downers Grove, Ill.: InterVarsity Press, 1986), 160.

22. John Calvin, *Institutes of the Christian Religion*, trans. Henry Beveridge (Edinburgh: Calvin Translation Society, 1997), III.xi.10.

23. Jonathan Edwards, "Discourse on the Trinity" in *The Works of Jonathan Edwards, vol. 21: Writings on the Trinity, Grace, and Faith*, ed. Sang Hyun Lee (New Haven, Conn.: Yale University Press, 2003), 121.

20

WHAT THE READER WANTS
AND THE TRANSLATOR CAN GIVE:

1 John as a Test Case

C. JOHN COLLINS[1]
Professor of Old Testament

---

everal English Bible translations have appeared in the last ten years, including the Contemporary English Version (CEV) in 1995, the New Living Translation (NLT) in 1996, the English Standard Version (ESV) in 2001, Today's New International Version (TNIV: New Testament, 2001; complete Bible, 2005), and the Holman Christian Standard Bible (HCSB) in 2004. The translation philosophies behind these versions differ in important ways, and these differences have precipitated vigorous discussion. Of course, a "hot topic" has been the approach to translating gender language, but the perceptive have seen that this question is closely tied to the wider question of what constitutes translation.

I called the discussion "vigorous," and that is what it *should* be. The issues reach far beyond the linguistic and theological academy, right to the kind of Bible ordinary people will read, study, and use in church. When we add to that the sense of desperation at the decreasing Bible literacy of English-speaking culture, and the seemingly enormous task of reaching our fellows, we can see that too much is at stake to leave the matter solely in the hands of the specialists. On the other hand, we need the specialist for his or her advanced insight into the problems. But even here we have trouble: the specialists do not all say the same things.

While the discussions have been vigorous, I am not sure that they have always been productive; it seems at times that the various sides talk past each other, and even focus on caricatures of their opponents in order to win an easy victory. I think that much of this misunderstanding comes from the differing assumptions and definitions that each party brings to the discussion (and possibly some of these are not even explicit). As Greenstein put it,

> I can get somewhere when I challenge the deductions you make from your fundamental assumptions. But I can get nowhere if I think I am challenging your deductions when in fact I am differing from your assumptions, your presuppositions, your premises, your beliefs.[2]

Further, it is easy to score points against an opponent by selecting out particular Bible passages, and this is what many reviews have done; but this fails, whether because the translation under review may or may not reflect its stated philosophy well in that particular place, or because the reviewer may or may not understand how the translators applied their philosophy, or because we have to see how the version performs on a whole body of text.

In view of this, here is what I aim to do: first, I will consider what an ordinary person might think of as "translation"; second, I will aim to make this more rigorous by considering the dynamics of communication;[3] third, I will compare how the various approaches to translation perform on a continuous text, namely, 1 John.

ORDINARY NOTIONS OF TRANSLATION

A. J. Krailsheimer was a teacher of French at Oxford, and translated a few French works into English. He was certainly, therefore, familiar with the task of translation, without himself being a theorist of the endeavor. Here is how he explained his goal in translating Pascal's *Pensées*:

> The purpose of any translation is to enable those who have little or no knowledge of the original language to read with reasonable confidence works which would otherwise have been inaccessible to them. It does not help if the translator introduces variants of his own, instead of following as faithfully as possible the chosen original, ultimate criterion of accuracy and authenticity... .[4]

Krailsheimer mentions one specific way in which he aimed at a "faithful" translation, which will be pertinent to our discussion below:

> As regards the actual translation I have tried to follow one cardinal principle apparently rejected by most previous translators of Pascal: I know of no other author who repeats the same word with such almost obsessive frequency as Pascal, and failure to render this essential feature of his style makes a translation not only inadequate but positively misleading. Wherever possible, and especially within the same fragment or section, I have used one English word for the same keyword recurring in French.[5]

(Krailsheimer acknowledges that "some keywords ... cannot be treated with absolute consistency.")

That Krailsheimer's goal is what the ordinary person thinks of as translation becomes clear if we consider something where we have no emotional investment. I teach Latin to my children, so my sister gave me a Latin *Daily Phrase and Culture Calendar* for 2000.[6] In this calendar, most days have a Latin phrase and a suggested translation, and sometimes a "literal" translation in brackets. Consider the entry for May 10:

> **Mutatis mutandis.**
> After making the necessary changes.
> (lit.: Things having been changed that had to be changed.)

The "literal" version offered is a fairly straight rendering of the Latin, even following the word order, but does not sound very good in English. We could rework it as *the things that had to be changed having been changed*, and from there to *the necessary changes having been changed*; here we see that the repetition of *change* is the offender. So we would end up with *the necessary changes having been made*, and we can see that the proffered translation simply gives us the active version of that. We would have no difficulty in calling *the necessary changes having been changed* a "literal but rough" translation, and *the necessary changes having been made* a "smoothed literal" translation (or "essentially literal" or "transparent," as we shall see below).

Consider what we get for July 1:

> **Ubi leges valent, ibi populus potest valere. (Publilius Syrus)**
> Where the laws are good, there the people are flourishing.

This translation might be "literal" after a fashion, but it is a failure, because it does not capture the repetition of *valere*.[7] It would be better to render, *where the laws are healthy, there the people can be healthy*. This shows that a mere word-for-word translation does not fulfill Krailsheimer's aim; it must also let you see something of the literary effect of the original.

Here is one that works reasonably well (April 16):

> **Quod cibus est aliis, aliis est venenum.**
> One man's meat is another man's poison.
> (lit.: That which is food to some is poison to others.)

Actually, the "literal" version here is not quite literal enough, since it does not capture the chiasmus: *What is food to some, to others is poison*. The proffered translation aims to convey the aphoristic quality of the Latin by giving us an English proverb of virtually identical import.[8] We might call this translation an "almost literal" one.

But aphoristic sayings are asking for trouble, as my two final examples show. For August 27 we get:

> *Pares cum paribus facillime congregantur. (Cicero)*
> Birds of a feather flock together.
> (lit.: Equals most easily congregate with equals.)

The sense of the Latin words has exercised virtually no control over that of the English (unless we count *flock* and *congregate* as being semantic kin). But when we turn to June 20, we find something that is off the charts:

> *Mundus vult decipi.*
> There's a sucker born every minute.
> (lit.: The world wants to be deceived.)

Few lay people would call these last two "accurate" translations, because the words of the original have exercised no control over the renderings.

TRANSLATION AND THE COMMUNICATION SITUATION

It is common to find translations put on a continuum between two poles, the "literal" and the "idiomatic," or the "formal equivalent" and the "dynamic (or functional) equivalent." Usually you can tell where a person's sympathies lie by the way he describes the two. For example, consider:

> There are two general theories or methods of Bible translation. The first has been called "formal equivalence." According to this theory, the translator attempts to render each word of the original language into the receptor language and seeks to preserve the original word order and sentence structure as much as possible. The second has been called "dynamic equivalence" or "functional equivalence." The goal of this translation theory is to produce in the receptor language the closest natural equivalent of the message expressed by the original-language text – both in meaning and in style. Such a translation attempts to have the same impact on modern readers as the original had on its own audience.

This comes from the introduction to the NLT, which is a dynamic equivalence version.[9]

Although the NLT presents formal versus dynamic equivalence as an antithesis, most recognize it as a continuum:[10]

literal	dynamic

Under this scheme, the publicity for the NIV and TNIV can represent that translation as having found the sweet spot between the poles, calling itself a "balanced, mediating version – one that would fall about halfway between the most literal and the most free."[11] Thus we might rank Bible versions along the scale:[12]

literal		dynamic	
RV NASB KJV RSV/ESV	NIV	NLT TEV CEV	

I have argued elsewhere that this model is inadequate[13] because it does not allow for what might be called an "essentially literal" or "transparent" translation, as Van Leeuwen describes it:

> A transparent translation conveys as much as possible of what was said, and how it was said, in as near word-for-word form as the target language allows, though inevitably with some difference and imperfectly. [14]

This translation philosophy has been misunderstood, so I must amplify it a little more. The goal is for the syntax and semantics of the original text to govern the translation in such a way that such things as text genre, style (including irony and word play), register,[15] figurative language, interpretive ambiguities, and important repetitions show through.

Let me use an example: Everyone knows that pure transcription is not translation, because the syntax and lexicon of one language do not line up uniformly with those of another. Hence, the final phrase of the Tenth Commandment (Ex. 20:17), in a transcription, would be "and all which to-neighbor-of-you": this is not English, so it is not any kind of translation. A woodenly "literal" rendering would be, "and all which is to your neighbor" (this seems to be what the NLT preface means by "formal equivalence"). A transparent rendering, however (represented by ESV=RSV, compare KJV), would be, "or anything that is your neighbor's." This employs recognized linguistic operations to make smooth English: the sense "any" is part of the range of the Hebrew *kol* ("all"); translating a Hebrew verbless clause requires an English verb of being, and the datival preposition ("to") includes possession as part of its range (though this need not imply ownership).

In other words, the transparent (or essentially literal) translation philosophy agrees with everyone else that translation really does involve transferring a text from one language to another, but it aims to keep its interpretation to the level of recognized linguistic operations on the text. As this example shows, however, there is an interpretive ambiguity: since this clause finishes a list that includes a man's wife, does this imply that an Israelite man was seen as owning his wife? The Hebrew does not of itself answer the question; to give an answer would take a study of the law as a whole.[16] Other translations have not left the ambiguity intact: "or anything that belongs to your neighbor" (NIV); "or anything else your neighbor owns"

(NLT, compare TEV, CEV). These imply the interpretation that the man does indeed own his wife, and make it difficult for the English reader to consider another option.[17]

This means that the single line continuum does not give enough insight into the translation situation; a better diagram might be:

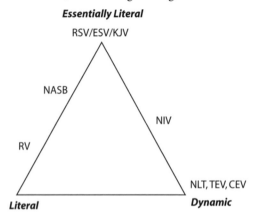

(I will justify later, as needed, the places I have assigned to the versions.)

This is an improvement, but it still does not capture the complexity of translation. Consider what place a text has in an act of communication. It is far too simple to say that we have a speaker, an audience, and a message that connects them. Rather, we should see that the speaker and audience have a picture of the world that to some extent they share between them: that picture includes, for example, knowledge, beliefs, values, experiences, language, and rhetorical conventions. For example, I am writing this essay in English, and I assume that you know what I mean by "the Hebrew Bible." A text is a means by which the speaker (or author) operates on that shared picture of the world to produce some effect (the message) in the audience: perhaps by adding new things for them to know, or by correcting things that they thought they knew; or by drawing on some part of it (such as their experience of God's love) in order for them to act upon it; or by evoking some aspect of it for celebration or mourning; or even by radically revising their orientation to the world (their worldview). The authors and their audiences also share linguistic and literary conventions, which indicate how to interpret the text; for example, everyone who is competent in American English knows what to expect when a narrative begins with "once upon a time." For an audience to interpret a text properly, they must cooperate with the author as he has expressed himself in his text. (In terms used by the linguists, the "message" includes such things as illocutionary force, implicatures, and so on.)

The diagram would look like this:

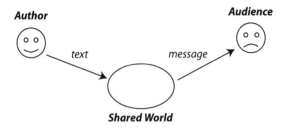

Since we are discussing Bible translating here, we must of course add another aspect, namely, that of *appropriation* or *application*: by this we designate those in following times who read the text as part of their Bibles. The world of these later readers overlaps with that of the original communication, though only partially. This is actually a challenge for a translation that aims to be interdenominational, since there are no agreed-upon principles by which to appropriate the text.

This diagram allows us to bring some of the translation issues into focus: to what degree is translation based on the text alone, and to what degree should the translator supply information from the shared world, and how explicit should he make the "message"? Before we look at Bible translation, let us consider some examples from other kinds of text.

My first example is William Blake's poem "A Poison Tree":

> I was angry with my friend:
> I told my wrath, my wrath did end.
> I was angry with my foe:
> I told it not, my wrath did grow.[18]

No doubt the poem uses a past incident to illustrate what always happens; in other words, the poem is equivalent in force to the poem with present tenses:

> If I am angry with my friend,
> I tell my wrath, my wrath does end.
> If I am angry with my foe,
> I tell it not, my wrath does grow.

But of course we should not stop there: the poet wants also to affect our behavior – that is his "message." Hence, the poem is pragmatically equivalent to a translation with imperatives, purpose clauses, and second-person reference:

> When you're angry with your friend,
> tell your wrath, that your wrath may end.
> If you're angry with your foe,
> don't tell it not, lest your wrath do grow.

Although these are pragmatically equivalent, they are not rhetorically equivalent. Blake's poem makes its impact precisely because of its concreteness (found in the past tenses) and its indirection (it leaves you to draw the conclusion).

Should a translation make the pragmatic force explicit? Not if the purpose of the translation is to allow the reader to listen in on the English poem.[19]

My second example is from C. S. Lewis' *The Voyage of the Dawn Treader*.[20] In the first chapter, the return of the Pevensie children to Narnia for their second visit (recounted in *Prince Caspian*) is likened to King Arthur coming back to Britain. The translation into Modern Hebrew transposes this to King David coming back to the land of Israel.[21] This replaces something in the shared world of Lewis' audience with something in the world of the translator's audience, presumably for equivalent effect: but the result does not take the reader on a trip to England. A further move of this translator is to render the word "Lamb" (in the final chapter) with the Hebrew *taleh* rather than *seh*.[22] Lewis surely meant us to see here a reference to Christ, the sacrificed lamb, and the Hebrew New Testaments use *seh* for that. The Hebrew translation does not allow the reader even to consider the reference. I do not know whether ideological factors played a part here; but in any case, the translator has not shown the reader Lewis' world.

Now we can move on to look at Bible translation in the light of this improved communication model.

For example, if we explain that the chaff of Psalm 1:4 is "worthless" (as does NLT), we are bringing in factors from the shared world; we can go even further if we replace the imagery found in Psalm 1:3-4, based on the climate and agriculture of Palestine, with something with which the translator's audience is more familiar.[23] Since the literary conventions, such as poetic parallelism, are part of the shared world, then any operation we perform on that is likewise an effort to explicate or alter the appearance of that world.[24]

Some translators have thought that they must guide the reader in drawing out implications and interpreting figures – in other words, they go beyond the linguistic requirements of the text in order to convey the message. Consider, for example, three versions of Proverbs 5:15-19:

ESV	NLT	TEV
[15] Drink water from your own cistern, flowing water from your own well.	Drink water from your own well – share your love only with your wife.	Be faithful to your own wife and give your love to her alone.
[16] Should your springs be scattered abroad, streams of water in the streets?	Why spill the water of your springs in public, having sex with just anyone?	Children that you have by other women will do you no good.

ESV	NLT	TEV
[17] Let them be for yourself alone, and not for strangers with you.	You should reserve it for yourself. Don't share it with strangers.	Your children should grow up to help you, not strangers.
[18] Let your fountain be blessed, and rejoice in the wife of your youth,	Let your wife be a fountain of blessing for you. Rejoice in the wife of your youth.	So be happy with your wife and find your joy with the girl you married –
[19] a lovely deer, a graceful doe. Let her breasts fill you at all times with delight; be intoxicated always in her love.	She is a loving doe, a graceful deer. Let her breasts satisfy you always. May you always be captivated by her love.	pretty and graceful as a deer. Let her charms keep you happy; let her surround you with her love.

The fully dynamic versions, NLT and TEV, have abandoned the poetic format of the Hebrew, and printed their material as prose paragraphs. They have also aimed to spell out what they see as the implied behavioral force of the text, though they differ on the consequences of unfaithfulness: the NLT sees it as focused on the husband and wife relationship, while the TEV sees it as including children (both illegitimate and one's own).[25] As a matter of fact, I think they are both wrong: surely verses 16-17 push a man to ask himself the question, "How would I feel if my wife were promiscuous?" in order to foster his commitment to avoiding adultery on his own part.[26]

It has become conventional in translation literature to separate *form* from *meaning*, with the implication that it is *meaning* that translation conveys. Although there is a sense in which this is obvious – see the discussion of Exodus 20:17 above – the statement as it is normally made leads to some difficulties. To begin with, just what is the meaning of *meaning*? Is it a feature of the syntax (including discourse, paragraph, and sentence levels) and lexical sense of the text, or does it include the referential world (and if so, how much?), or does it even extend to the pragmatics? This is, of course, a well-known problem; but it is rarely spelled out – a situation that leads easily to equivocation on terms. Another difficulty is similar, namely, the fact that *form* might have more than one level as well. The literary form of Proverbs 5:15-19, with its poetry and imagery, requires that the reader exercise his imagination in order to cooperate. The dynamic versions have tended to emphasize the cognitive content – which itself implies a particular notion of what communication (and possibly even human wholeness) is.[27] Further, the effort to make the *message* explicit interposes the translator between the text and the reader, and, as we can see in the case of Proverbs 5:16-17, translators do not always agree.

Another matter, into which I do not intend to delve, is that of gender language. For example, the address of Proverbs 6:1, "my son," is certainly to a male child – that is the sense of the Hebrew. It is part of the literary convention of Hebrew wisdom to be concrete, allowing the reader to apply it, *mutatis mutandis*. Consider, however, how the NLT translation handles this:

> The Hebrew term my son (or my sons) is used twenty-seven times in the book of Proverbs. In most instances, as in this verse, the message applies equally to sons or daughters, so the NLT translates it "my child." Note, however, that the literal translation is retained in 5:1, 7, since the message of that entire chapter is clearly addressed to young men. [28]

This conflates matters of sense (in the text) and reference (in the shared world) with what may – or may not – be the legitimate range of application.[29]

Everyone acknowledges that differences of judgment concerning the approach to translation will depend on the purpose for which the translation is to be used; but there is something even deeper, namely, the very definition of "translation." Consider how Nida defines translation:

> To translate is to try to stimulate in the new reader in the new language the same reaction to the text as the one the original author wished to stimulate in his first and immediate readers.[30]

If we *define* translation this way, then of course we must embrace the functional equivalence approach; we must even include the part I have called the *message* in our rendering. But if we think of translation the way that Krailsheimer did in rendering Pascal, we might define translation more generally as something like, "allowing the reader to listen in on the foreign language communication." Then we can go on to speak of different kinds of "listening in."

This allows us to address the question of whether a translation should "sound like" a translation. The difficulty with this is in being clear on what we might mean. On the one hand, as we saw in the Exodus 20:17 example, we want the product to be grammatical and intelligible in the target language. On the other hand, the shared world between the author and his audience is inherently *foreign*, whether it be in regard to the things they share knowledge about, or in regard to genres, or to rhetorical conventions, or to ideology. A translation whose goal is to allow us to listen in on the original act of communication ought to display some of the "local color" of that act. Some dynamic versions reduce idioms and even major metaphors (such as "walking" for one's moral conduct) to more prosaic renderings, and thus lose some of that local color.[31]

As Anthony Nichols put it,

> A translation of the Bible, in principle, should aim to retain as far as possible the exegetical potential of the source text. This would mean in practice that a good translation of the NT will preserve a sense of historical and cultural distance ... It will take the modern reader back into the alien milieu of first-century Judaism where the Christian movement began. It will show him how the gospel of Jesus appeared to a Jew, and not how that Jew would have thought had he been an Australian or an American.[32]

Considering Different Kinds of Translations

This leads us to consider what kind of Bible translation might be suited to a particular context. Nida and Taber argued for this, distinguishing the contexts by the social stratum of the intended audience:

> For languages with a long literary tradition and a well-established traditional text of the Bible, it is usually necessary to have three types of Scriptures: (1) a translation which will reflect the traditional usage and be used in the churches, largely for liturgical purposes (this may be called an "ecclesiastical translation"), (2) a translation in the present-day literary language, so as to communicate to the well-educated constituency, and (3) a translation in the "common" or "popular" language, which is known to and used by the common people, and which is at the same time acceptable as a standard for published materials.[33]

The criteria we might use to distinguish the different contexts are – or should be – controversial. I might have divided the pie differently, based on characteristic uses rather than audiences: (1) a Bible for church; (2) a Bible for family reading, which includes children and personal study; and (3) a Bible for outreach to the uninitiated. But the point remains: these different contexts might be best served by different translation philosophies. What kind of translation might suit these various contexts for the English reader?

The King James Version (KJV) held the field for at least the first two categories – whichever way we slice the pie – for about three centuries; and when it was first issued, it also supplied the third category of translation. At present, it cannot supply any of these categories, because too much of it reflects obsolete English.[34] But it has certainly set the pace for what the English Bible should "sound like," and an ecclesiastical translation should respect that.

Can we say what else we would ask for from an ecclesiastical translation? I do not intend here to venture into any kind of liturgical theology, specifying norms for anyone else. You can find a wide range of worship styles in the English-speaking world, from formal and structured to informal and free-flowing.[35] However, I do not believe that we must have liturgical uniformity to be able to say what features the Bible version should have.

I will simply list a few important features that I imagine most people will agree with (given enough supporting argument).[36] To begin with, the Bible version should be *intelligible*: that is, its English should be grammatical and broadly current without being too local either in time or place.[37]

Second, it should be *ecumenical*: that is, it should serve Anglicans, Baptists, Calvary Chapelites, Dispensationalists, and so on throughout the alphabet soup of Christian bodies. Indeed, how good it would be if Eastern Orthodox, Protestants, and Roman Catholics had a common Bible (at least for the books on whose canonicity and textual basis they agree)! How else can we express our unity with other churches?

Third, a church Bible should be *orally rhythmic*: it should sound good even after countless readings aloud. Christian people have the Bible read aloud, not simply in the text before the sermon, but also in unison readings and Bible songs.

Fourth, this Bible should be *preachable*: it should allow the preacher to preach from the text without having to wrestle with or correct the translation. The translators must be careful that they not limit the preacher's options beyond linguistic necessity. Please note: I am not here insisting that all preaching must be expository, after the model of Chrysostom; rather, I am simply saying that an adequate translation will not get in the way of those who wish to preach in this way.

And finally, its English style should be *poetic* and *dignified* (where the original is), without being stuffy. This last feature does not depend on whether the particular worship service itself is dignified or casual; I have attended, for example, a very lively and contemporary Calvary Chapel that used the NASB for the sermon because of their commitment to expository preaching.

A translation that echoes the language use and essentially literal philosophy of the KJV best suits this context.

Now consider the other categories of audience or use, as mentioned above. I prefer to think of the other categories by way of characteristic use rather than audience, because I hold that the question of which criteria we should use is not strictly a linguistic or sociological one – in which case, a specialist in sociolinguistics does not necessarily have the advantage in discussing this. That is, I cannot accept theologically that the well-educated and the popular audiences should use different Bibles. It was not so in ancient Israel, nor in the early Christian church; and to make it so today would be to institutionalize (or even to baptize) distinctions of class and race that the apostles declared to be of no account (Col. 3:11).[38]

The characteristic use of the second category of translation, then, would be Bible reading and study in the home. As long as the ecclesiastical translation is intelligible, I see no reason for the home version to be different from the one used in church, except for the sake of variety from time to time. One might object, however, that the higher level of the language in this version excludes children; but in my own experience I have not found this to be a viable objection. Children – mine, at least – live up to what is expected of them, and aim to expand their language capacity anyhow; I do not find them to be embarrassed to admit that they do not understand something, and the exercise of explaining a passage to young children has done me good. I admit that this puts more weight on parents' shoulders, but then our churches ought to welcome this, and equip their families for the task.

The third category of translation is the one for outreach. Here we might indeed prefer a Bible version simpler than the ecclesiastical one; but if we do use such a version, we should explain to people that its purpose is to be introductory. We need not apologize for the discipleship of the mind that Christian faithfulness calls us to; as C. S. Lewis observed in a work addressed to those outside the faith,

> [Christ] wants a child's heart, but a grown-up's head. He wants us to be simple, single-minded, affectionate, and teachable, as good children are; but He also wants every bit of intelligence we have to be alert at its job, and in first-class fighting trim ... If you are thinking of becoming a Christian, I warn you that you are embarking on something which is going to take the whole of you, brains and all.[39]

THE GREEK OF 1 JOHN

Let us see how different translation philosophies perform on a body of text, namely, 1 John. Then we can say what philosophy is best suited to the various characteristic uses we discussed above.

I was sitting in church one day in the spring of 2004, listening to a sermon series on 1 John, where the sermon text was the NIV (I had a Greek New Testament on one knee, and my son on the other). It struck me that this translation made it hard for the English reader to see the key features of the Greek text, and hard for the preacher to draw attention to these features.

As I sat, I drew up a list of those features that the translator ought to allow the English reader to see. Here is what I came up with (slightly revised after further reflection):

(1) The author repeats key terms throughout the book.
(2) He uses generally simple vocabulary, syntax, and sentence conjunctions to express profound thoughts (one reason why many Greek teachers use this book for beginning students).
(3) Within this general simplicity, there are some puzzling ambiguities (which is why I no longer use this book for beginners).
(4) The author makes careful use of verbal aspect.
(5) There are expressions of tender affection toward readers.

(6) Even though there are no direct Old Testament citations, there are plenty
  of evocations.

(7) There are important parallels with the Gospel of John.[40]

I then made a table with parallel texts of the Greek and several English
translations. I chose the ESV as a representative of the "transparent" strategy;
the NLT as a "functional [or dynamic] equivalence" version, and the NIV as a
"partly dynamic" version. I can justify these classifications from the translators'
prefaces, but I will go further to show why the NIV is partly dynamic (since
this may be controversial).

Robert Bratcher lists the basic tenets of the dynamic equivalence approach,
based on its focus on equivalent response in the receptor: *contextual consistency
over verbal consistency* ("no attempt is made to translate a given Greek word by
the same word in English"), *naturalness* ("express the meaning of the original
as naturally as possible in English"), *making implicit information explicit*, and
ready *intelligibility* ("the meaning of idioms and figures of speech must be set
forth plainly so that today's readers will understand them as did the readers
of the original").[41] I will use these features in classifying the translations
compared.

I have quoted the NLT preface already, noting its claim to be dynamic. The
ESV preface claims,

> The ESV is an "essentially literal" translation that seeks as far as possible to
> capture the precise wording of the original text and the personal style of each
> Bible writer. As such, its emphasis is on "word-for-word" correspondence, at
> the same time taking into account differences of grammar, syntax, and idiom
> between current literary English and the original languages. Thus it seeks to
> be transparent to the original text, letting the reader see as directly as possible
> the structure and meaning of the original.

The translators recognize that there are always trade-offs between "literal
precision and readability," and thus they have not aimed to be woodenly
literal. They further have set themselves deliberately in the KJV stream of
language use, which gives the version a traditional feel.

The NIV preface says,

> Because thought patterns and syntax differ from language to language,
> faithful communication of the meaning of the writers demands frequent
> modifications in sentence structure and constant regard for the contextual
> meanings of words.

There seem to be echoes of the form – meaning distinction here, as well
as the priority of contextual consistency over verbal consistency, which are
mainstays of dynamic equivalence theory. Our study of 1 John will verify that

such considerations do in fact lie behind the NIV strategy, but not to the same extent as with the NLT.

Let us see how the different philosophies handle selected features of the Greek.[42] It might or might not be possible to convey all of these, but the degree to which we do determines how clear a window we provide into the original act of communication.

Repetition of Key Words

The author of 1 John repeats a number of words throughout his letter, such as μένω ("remain, abide"), especially in the combination μένω ἐν ("to abide in");[43] τηρέω ("to keep"), especially with objects such as "word" and "commands"; κόσμος ("world"); words related to ἀλήθεια ("truth"), ἀγάπη ("love"), ψεῦδος ("lie"). We might add some minor ones such as γεννάω ("to beget"); παρρησία ("confidence"); λέγω/εἶπον ("to say"); and τελειόω/τέλειος ("to perfect," "perfect").

The verb μένω ("abide") appears 24 times in 18 verses in 1 John (2:6, 10, 14, 17, 19, 24, 27, 28; 3:6, 9, 14, 15, 17, 24; 4:12, 13, 15, 16); all but two of those (2:17, 19) use the combination μένω ἐν ("abide in").[44] Believers *abide in* Christ, in the light, in the Son, and in the Father, and not in death; while God, or the word of God, or God's anointing, or eternal life, or the love of God *abides in* the believer. These two kinds of abiding – the believer's in God and God's in the believer – are two sides of the same coin, alternate ways of describing genuine spiritual life. A good illustration of the connection is 2:24 (compare also 2:27; 3:14-15, 24; 4:16):

Let what you heard from the beginning *abide in* you. If what you heard from the beginning *abides in* you, then you too will *abide in* the Son and in the Father.

This repetition is so prevalent that it must be part of the author's intended literary effect.[45] The "essentially literal" tradition in English (KJV, RSV, ESV) has successfully conveyed this repetition.[46]

How do the more dynamic versions perform? Consider first the fully dynamic NLT. This version renders our verb with quite a variety of terms: "live" (2:6, 10, 14, 17; 3:24b; 4:12, 13, 15, 16; "continue to live," 2:27b; 3:6; "live with," 2:27a);[47] "live in fellowship with" (3:24a; "continue to live in fellowship with," 2:24c, 28); "remain faithful" (2:24a); "be" (3:9, 17; "be still," 3:14); a dummy "do" (2:24b); and even no rendering at all (3:15). (The unusual 2:19 has "stay.") The explanation for such variation seems to be the translators' adherence to the tenets of dynamic equivalence, especially contextual consistency, naturalness, and ready intelligibility.

Consider what happens in 2:24:

So you must *remain faithful* to what you have been taught from the beginning. If you *do*, you will *continue to live in fellowship with* the Son and with the Father.

The connection that the Greek repetition establishes does not come through at all.

The NIV renders our term with "live" (2:6, 10, 14, 17; 3:6, 24ab; 4:12, 13, 15, 16ab); "remain" (2:24ac, 27ab; 3:9, 14); "continue" (2:28); "be" (3:17); a dummy "do" (2:24b), and no rendering at all (3:15; 4:16c). (It uses "remain" in 2:19.) Although the variation is not as much as we found in the NLT, it still appears that the NIV has also followed the principles of contextual consistency, naturalness, and ready intelligibility.

Consider 2:24:

> See that what you have heard from the beginning *remains in* you. If it does, you also will *remain in* the Son and in the Father.

At least here the repetition comes through; but just a few verses later (2:27-28) we find:

> As for you, the anointing you received from him *remains in* you, and you do not need anyone to teach you. But as his anointing teaches you about all things and as that anointing is real, not counterfeit – just as it has taught you, *remain in* him. And now, dear children, *continue in* him, so that when he appears we may be confident and unashamed before him at his coming.

This shows that displaying the repetition over a long stretch of the text was not a goal for the NIV.

We might criticize the dynamic versions further by asking whether "live" and "live in fellowship with" are semantically accurate, when the Greek verb is used for the nuance of remaining or enduring. This would certainly give difficulty to a reader or preacher who wanted to point out the repetition and its implications. Indeed, one recent commentary on 1 John (which uses the NIV as its running English text), expounding 2:17 (NIV "lives forever"), cites passages from John's Gospel where "Jesus stresses that those who believe in him ... shall never perish but shall live and remain forever" (the passages are John 6:51, 58; 8:51; 10:28; 11:26), and none of them uses μένω.[48] I believe the commentator was seriously hampered by the NIV translation strategy.

We could pursue this kind of study for the other repeated words, but space does not permit that – though we shall return to τηρέω and τελειόω/τέλειος in later discussions.

Puzzling Ambiguities

Anyone who reads 1 John carefully will be fascinated by the ambiguities we find there – that is, by the expressions that have more than one possible grammatical analysis, and it is not immediately clear which one the author intended. The tenets of dynamic equivalence push the translator to decide between the options on behalf of the reader (except in those cases where the translator recognizes the literary effect of the ambiguity), since too much ambiguity is taken as a blemish.[49]

If, on the other hand, the Greek expressions themselves are ambiguous, it is quite possible that the extra effort it takes to decode them is part of the communicative act. It is also true that different expositors will analyze these differently; and a translation that resolves them ties the expositor's hands.[50]

One of these ambiguities in 1 John is the expression ἡ ἀγάπη τοῦ θεοῦ/ τοῦ πατρός/αὐτοῦ – "the love of God/of the Father/of him" (2:5, 15; 3:17; 4:9, 12; 5:3): is this "love for God," or "God's love," or "love that comes from God," or something else?[51]

We could argue that, since the cognate verb ἀγαπάω appears in phrases of the type "believers love God" (4:20, 21; 5:1, 2), then the genitive is objective ("love for God"). However, phrases of the type "God loves people" also appear (4:11, 19), so we cannot rule out "God's love" or "love from God." (In 4:10 they appear together!) Westcott concluded that the expression describes "the love that God has made known," while Bruce concluded just the opposite: it is "our love for God."[52] I do not need to adjudicate at this point; it is enough to make the difficulty clear.

The essentially literal approach will be to pass the responsibility on to the reader to decide, just as the readers of the Greek had to decide. Hence, the ESV renders these as "the love of God" (2:5; 4:9; 5:3) and "the love of the Father" (2:15). In two places the rendering probably steers away from the objective genitive: "God's love" (3:17) and "his love" (4:12) – although an expositor who wanted to do so could describe it as "the love that is due to God from us."

The dynamic NLT decides in favor of the objective genitive some times, "really do love [God]" (2:5), "loving God" (5:3); and the subjective genitive at others, "he loved us" (4:9). Though 4:12 in the NLT has "his love" like the ESV, the sentence "his love has been brought to full expression" leaves little room for anything other than the subjective genitive. In 2:15 and 3:17, the rendering is open like the ESV.

The NIV leaves the expression ambiguous in 2:15 and 3:17; and, if we include "God's/his love," the ambiguity appears also in 2:5 and 4:12. In 4:9 it is taken as a subjective genitive ("God showed his love"), while in 5:3 it is objective ("love for God").

Each of these versions has been true to its principles. Now, it may be that one should take all of these genitives the same way, or that we should find a mixture. Only the essentially literal approach consistently leaves the decision to the reader and expositor, however.

The ambiguous genitive appears in 2:5; 4:12, 17, 18, in a phrase that is itself ambiguous, involving the repetition of the verb τελειόω ("to make perfect or complete," 2:5; 4:12, 17, 18) and its cognate adjective τέλειος ("perfect or complete," 4:18). Consider 2:5 (Greek and ESV):

ἀληθῶς ἐν τούτῳ / ἡ ἀγάπη τοῦ θεοῦ τετελείωται	in him truly the love of God is perfected

Does this mean that the person perfectly loves God,[53] or that God's saving love has reached its perfect goal – and if it has done so, how?[54] And how does this connect to "perfect love" and being "perfected in love" (4:18)?

To convey the force of the Greek, a translation should display the repetition and allow the reader to puzzle it out. Consider how the three versions perform:

ESV	NIV	NLT
[2:5] but whoever keeps his word, in him truly *the love of God is perfected.*	But if anyone obeys his word, *God's love is truly made complete* in him.	But those who obey God's word *really do love him.*
[4:12] No one has ever seen God; if we love one another, God abides in us and *his love is perfected in us.*	No one has ever seen God; but if we love one another, God lives in us and *his love is made complete in us.*	No one has ever seen God. But if we love each other, God lives in us, and *his love has been brought to full expression through us.*
[4:17] By this *is love perfected with us*, so that we may have confidence for the day of judgment, because as he is so also are we in this world.	In this way, *love is made complete among us* so that we will have confidence on the day of judgment, because in this world we are like him.	And as we live in God, *our love grows more perfect.* So we will not be afraid on the day of judgment, but we can face him with confidence because we are like Christ here in this world.
[4:18] There is no fear in love, but *perfect love* casts out fear. For fear has to do with punishment, and whoever fears *has not been perfected in love.*	There is no fear in love. But *perfect love* drives out fear, because fear has to do with punishment. The one who fears *is not made perfect in love.*	Such love has no fear because *perfect love* expels all fear. If we are afraid, it is for fear of judgment, and this shows that *his love has not been perfected in us.*

As before, I have not set out to resolve the interpretive difficulties, only to evaluate how well the translation allows the English reader to see the issues and decide for himself. The ESV has shown both the repetition and the ambiguity in the kind of love. The NIV – which, as we saw above, tends to resolve the ambiguities – has almost shown the repetition with "made complete" (2:5, 4:12, 17), though it inexplicably veers off to "made perfect" in 4:18. The NLT, true to its dynamic principles, has no interest in this kind of repetition: instead it has sought "contextual consistency" and ready intelligibility.

Old Testament Evocations

The use of the Old Testament in 1 John is a fascinating study in its own right, and I will only be able to make a few observations here. The author does not cite an Old Testament text, and when he refers to one, as in 3:12 (Cain and Abel, Gen. 4:8), his key Greek term (σφάζω, "slay, murder") differs from that of the LXX (ἀποκτείνω, a less colorful term for "kill").[55]

On the other hand, there are plenty of evocations of the Old Testament, using the language of the LXX. For example, the notion of sacrificial blood "cleansing" or "purifying" from sin (1:7) comes from the Old Testament, as in Leviticus 16:19: "And he shall sprinkle some of the *blood* on it with his finger seven times, and *cleanse* (καθαρίζω, Heb. *tihar*) it and consecrate it from the uncleannesses of the people of Israel" (compare also Heb. 9:14) – an evocation that all three versions allow their readers to see.

Similarly, the term ἱλασμός (2:2; 4:10) comes from sacrificial language: in Leviticus 25:9 and Numbers 5:8 it represents Hebrew *kippurim*.[56] The Hebrew term is rendered as "atonement" in all three versions, while the Greek term in 1 John is "propitiation" (ESV), "atoning sacrifice" (NIV), and "sacrifice" (NLT). The NLT has under-translated, while the NIV has made the effort to show the connection with the Old Testament. The ESV is based on the conviction that the Greek term properly designates "propitiation," and follows that over the Old Testament connection.[57] Either the NIV or the ESV can be justified as reasonable attempts to convey the Greek, whereas the NLT is due, apparently, more to the requirements of ready intelligibility.

Another important evocation of the Old Testament is the repeated use of τηρέω ("keep") with objects such as "word" and "commands" (2:3, 4, 5; 3:22, 24; 5:3).[58] The analogous expressions in Hebrew use the verbs *shamar* and *natsar*,[59] both of which, when a command is the object, convey the notion of "keep, carefully attend to," and even "treasure."[60] The LXX renders these verbs mostly with φυλάσσω and τηρέω, with φυλάσσω predominating. In the New Testament both words are common and appear to be interchangeable in such a context.

Apparently, since the idea of "carefully attending to" God's commands implies obedience, the NIV and NLT have focused on that element for their translations: they have fastened on "obey" in most places, with "do" (2:4, NIV) and "keep" (5:3, NLT) appearing once each. This rendering does not allow the English reader to consider whether the term conveys more than obedience, extending into the *attitude* of the believer, and hence it does not allow him to ask the questions that a Greek reader would ask.

How do the more dynamic versions handle the relevant terms in the Old Testament? They vary, with the NIV being closer to the proper sense. (Of course, then, it is harder for the English reader to see how 1 John uses the Old Testament idea.) For example, in Psalm 105:45 we have "that they might *keep* (*shamar*) his statutes and *observe* (*natsar*) his laws" (ESV, NIV almost identical), but also "so they would *follow* his principles and obey his laws" (NLT). Consider a few verses from the first stanza of Psalm 119, a psalm that rings the changes on the attitude of delight in God's requirements:

ESV	NIV	NLT
[2] Blessed are those who keep his testimonies, Who seek him with their whole heart.	Blessed are they who keep his statutes And seek him with all their heart.	Happy are those who obey his decrees And search for him with all their hearts.
[4] You have commanded your precepts to be kept diligently.	You have laid down precepts that are to be fully obeyed.	You have charged us to keep your commandments carefully.
[5] Oh that my ways may be steadfast in keeping your statutes!	Oh, that my ways were steadfast in obeying your decrees!	Oh, that my actions would consistently reflect your principles!
[8] I will keep your statutes; do not utterly forsake me!	I will obey your decrees; do not utterly forsake me.	I will obey your principles. Please don't give up on me!

Again, the rendering "obey" is probably an under-translation.[61]

Consider the expression "the last hour" (ἐσχάτη ὥρα), found twice in 2:18. Some have taken this to show that the author thought the end of the world was quite near (either in actuality, or at least potentially).[62] However, it seems far more likely to me that this term evokes the prophetic "last/latter days" of such texts as Isaiah 2:2 and Hosea 3:5 (Hebrew *be'acharit hayyamim*; ESV "in the latter days"; LXX, ἐν ταῖς ἐσχάταις ἡμέραις/ἐπ ἐσχάτων τῶν ἡμερῶν [with other variations]).[63] In both Isaiah and Hosea the term denotes the times of the Messiah, and the New Testament uses it this way in Acts 2:17; 1 Peter 1:20; almost surely in Hebrews 1:2; James 5:3; and likely in 2 Timothy 3:1; 2 Peter 3:3; Jude 18.[64] This makes contextual sense of the "antichrist," a term unique to John's letters (1 John 2:18, 22; 4:3; 2 John 7). The antichrists oppose the Christ (or Messiah) by denying that Jesus is the Christ (come in the flesh).

As an expositor, I will take one approach or another; but as a translator it is not my task to decide on behalf of the reader. The ESV and NIV allow the reader to see the term against its Old Testament background, while the NLT renders the term "the last hour" in its first appearance (the beginning of the verse), and "the end of the world" in its second (at the end of the same verse).

When people refer to a translation as interpretive, this is just the sort of thing they have in mind: it shuts the English reader off from other options.

There are other possible Old Testament evocations,[65] but these will suffice for the point. In the terms of my communication model above, these Old Testament patterns were part of the shared world between the author and his audience. A good translation is one that allows us to listen in on this communication – which means it allows the English reader to detect the evocations. Judged by this criterion, the essentially literal ESV outperforms the partly dynamic NIV, which outperforms the fully dynamic NLT. Again, this is not an accident; it is, rather, a case of the versions being true to their stated translation principles.

CONCLUSIONS

Let us survey where we have been and what I think I have shown. First of all, we may dictate the translation philosophy by how we define "translation." Before we do that, though, we do well to stand back and consider what takes place in an act of communication. The model I have described above clarifies some of the challenges of translation, namely, to what extent we may properly explicate aspects of the shared world and the illocutionary force ("message"), and how much we should follow the sense and syntax of the text itself.

We cannot answer the simple question: which is the best approach to translation? We must instead qualify it: best for what purpose? I have argued that the essentially literal translation, carefully defined, is the kind of translation that best suits the requirements for an ecclesiastical translation and for family reading and study. This is because it allows the reader to listen in on the original act of communication, but refrains from "clarifying" based on what we think we know of the shared world and the illocutionary force; it also aims to provide a translation that preserves the full exegetical potential of the original, especially as it conveys such things as text genre, style, and register, along with figurative language, interpretive ambiguities, and important repetitions. Of course, this lays a heavier burden on the reader to learn about the shared world and its literary conventions, and we might decide not to lay this burden on the outsider to the Christian faith *in our outreach* (though we should make it clear that the burden exists).

In order to warrant this conclusion, I have examined some of the most obvious features of 1 John in the light of these considerations. Of the longer list I gave earlier, I selected three items: repetition of key terms, puzzling ambiguities, and Old Testament evocations. I tested three translations in places where they were true to their stated translation philosophies: the ESV (essentially literal), the NIV (partly dynamic), and the NLT (dynamic equivalence). The essentially literal approach does the best job of allowing the English reader to see these features, and the fully dynamic equivalent approach does the worst. This means that if a careful preacher were to use a dynamic version, he would find himself arguing with the translation – and the more dynamic, the more the argument. A family reading 1 John in a dynamic version will be severely limited in its ability to see the ways the author himself has signaled his communicative interests.

Although this study has been limited to some features of 1 John, it would not be hard to carry out a similar study, say, for Romans, or for Genesis 1–4, or Ecclesiastes, selected psalms, and so forth. My preliminary surveys of this material indicate that we will find the same conclusions.

What does the reader want, and what can the translator provide? An opportunity to listen in on the original foreign language communication, without prejudging what to do with that communication.

An irony arises from all this: the motive for the dynamic philosophy is a laudable one, namely, to let everyone in on the wonders of the Bible without allowing the experts to get in the way. Its result, however, is to interpose the translator between the reader and the text. The essentially literal philosophy, whose main interest is in doing justice to the original act of communication, opens up a new world to all manner of people, if they are willing to take the trouble to learn the customs of this foreign land.

BIBLIOGRAPHY

Barker, Kenneth L. "The Balanced Translation Philosophy of the TNIV." *Light Magazine* (2002): 18–21.

Barnwell, Katharine. *Bible Translation: An Introductory Course in Translation Principles* (Dallas, Tex.: Summer Institute of Linguistics, 1986).

Beekman, John, and John Callow. *Translating the Word of God* (Grand Rapids, Mich.: Zondervan, 1974).

Bratcher, Robert G. "The Nature and Purpose of the New Testament in Today's English Version." *The Bible Translator* 22, no. 3 (1971): 97–107.

Bratcher, Robert G., and William Reyburn. *A Translator's Handbook on the Book of Psalms* (New York: United Bible Societies, 1991).

Bruce, F. F. *The Epistles of John* (Grand Rapids, Mich.: Eerdmans, 1970).

Callow, Kathleen. *Discourse Considerations in Translating the Word of God* (Grand Rapids, Mich.: Zondervan, 1974).

Carson, D. A. "The Limits of Functional Equivalence in Bible Translation – and Other Limits, Too," in *The Challenge of Bible Translation*, ed. Glen G. Scorgie, Mark L. Strauss, and Steven M. Voth, (Grand Rapids, Mich.: Zondervan, 2003), 65–113.

Chapple, Allan. "The English Standard Version: A Review Article." *Reformed Theological Review* 62, no. 2 (2003): 61–96.

Collins, C. John. "The Eucharist as Christian Sacrifice." *Westminster Theological Journal* 66 (2004): 1–23.

_____. "Psalm 1: Structure and Rhetoric." *Presbyterion* 31 (2005): 37–48.

_____. *Science & Faith: Friends or Foes?* (Wheaton: Crossway, 2003).

_____. "When should we translate *poieô* 'to make' as 'to reckon'?" *Selected Technical Articles Related to Translation*, no. 16 (1986): 12–32.

_____. "Without Form, You Lose Meaning," in *The Word of God in English: Criteria for Excellence in Bible Translation*, ed. Leland Ryken (Wheaton: Crossway, 2002), 295–327.

Crisp, Simon. "Icon of the Ineffable? An Orthodox View of Language and its Implications for Bible Translation," in *Bible Translation on the Threshold of the Twenty-First Century*, ed. Athalya Brenner and Jan Willem van Henten (London: Sheffield Academic Press, 2002), 36–49.

Crystal, David. "Liturgical Language in a Sociolinguistic Perspective," in *Language and the Worship of the Church*, ed. David Jasper and R. C. D. Jasper (New York: St Martin's Press, 1990), 120–46. .

Davids, Peter H. "Three Recent Bible Translations: A New Testament Perspective." *Journal of the Evangelical Theological Society* 46, no. 3 (2003): 521–32.

de Regt, Lenart J. "Otherness and Equivalence in Bible Translation: A Response to Simon Crisp," in *Bible Translation on the Threshold of the Twenty-First Century*, ed. Athalya Brenner and Jan Willem van Henten

(London: Sheffield Academic Press, 2002), 50–2.

de Waard, Jan, and William A. Smalley. *A Translator's Handbook on the Book of Amos.* London: United Bible Societies, 1979.

Dryden, J. de Waal. "The Sense of *sperma* in 1 John 3:9." *Filologia Neotestamentaria* 9 (1998): 85–100.

Edwards, Ruth B. *The Johannine Epistles.* New Testament Guides (London: Sheffield Academic Press, 1996).

Eldridge, Michael D. "A New Addition to the King James Family." *Expository Times* 114, no. 7 (2003): 241–4.

Ellis, E. Earle. "Dynamic Equivalence Theory, Feminist Ideology and Three Recent Bible Translations." *Expository Times,* 115:1 (October 2003): 7–12.

Fehderau, Harold W. "The Role of Bases and Models in Bible Translations." *The Bible Translator* 30, no. 4 (1979): 401–14.

Fueter, Paul D. "The Therapeutic Language of the Bible." *International Review of Mission* 75 (1986): 211–21.

Funk, Robert, and Roy Hoover. *The Five Gospels* (New York: Macmillan, 1993).

Greenstein, E. L. "The Role of Theory in Biblical Criticism," in *Proceedings of the Ninth World Congress of Jewish Studies: Jerusalem, August 4-12, 1985* (Jerusalem: World Union of Jewish Studies, 1986), 167–74.

Griffith, Terry. "A Non-Polemical Reading of 1 John: Sin, Christology and the Limits of Johannine Christianity." *Tyndale Bulletin* 49, no. 2 (1998): 253–76.

Gutt, Ernst-August. "What is the Meaning We Translate?" *Occasional Papers in Translation and Textlinguistics* 1 (1987): 31–58.

Haas, C., M. de Jonge, and J. L. Swellengrebel. *A Translator's Handbook on the Letters of John.* Helps for Translators (London: United Bible Societies, 1972).

Hansford, Keir L. "The Underlying Poetic Structure of 1 John." *Journal of Translation and Textlinguistics* 5, no. 2 (1992): 126–74.

Holy Bible: New Living Translation, Text and Product Preview (Wheaton: Tyndale House Publishers, 1996).

Jacobs, Alan. "A Bible for Everyone." *First Things,* no. 138 (2003): 10–14.

Kruse, Colin G. *The Letters of John.* Pillar New Testament Commentary (Grand Rapids, Mich.: Eerdmans, 2000).

Larson, Mildred L. *Meaning-Based Translation: A Guide to Cross-Language Equivalence* (Lanham: University Press of America, 1984).

Lewis, C. S. *Hammassa' be-Dorek Hashshachar.* Translated by Gideon Turi (Tel Aviv: Zmora, Bitan, Modan, 1979).

_____. *Mere Christianity* (New York: Scribner, 1952).

_____. *The Voyage of the Dawn Treader* (New York: Macmillan, 1952).

Lyons, John. *Language, Meaning and Context* (London: Fontana, 1981).

Lyons, Michael, and William A. Tooman. "Three Recent Bible Translations: An Old Testament Perspective." *Journal of the Evangelical Theological Society* 46, no. 3 (2003): 497–520.

Malatesta, Edward. *Interiority and Covenant.* Analecta Biblica (Rome: Biblical Institute Press, 1978).

Moskovitz, Yechiel. *Sefer Yechezqel.* Da'at Miqra (Jerusalem: Mossad Harav Kook, 1985).

Neff, David. "Meaning-Full Translations: The world's most influential Bible translator, Eugene Nida, is weary of 'word worship.'" *Christianity Today* 46 (2002): 46–9.

Nichols, Anthony. "Dynamic Equivalence in Bible Translations." *Colloquium: The Australian and New Zealand Theological Review* 19 (1986): 43–53.

_____. "Explicitness in Translation and the Westernization of Scripture." *Reformed Theological Review* 47, no. 3 (1988): 78–88.

_____. "The Fate of 'Israel' in Recent Versions of the Bible." *In the Fullness of Time: Biblical Studies in Honour of Archbishop Donald Robinson* (Homebush West, NSW: Lancer, 1992).

Nida, Eugene A. "Formal correspondence in translation." *The Bible Translator* 21, no. 3 (1970): 105–113.

_____. *Toward a Science of Translating* (Leiden: Brill, 1964).

_____. "Translating Means Communicating: A Sociolinguistic Theory of Translation (I)." *The Bible Translator* 30, no. 1 (1979): 101–7.

_____. "Translating Means Communicating: A Sociolinguistic Theory of Translation (II)." *The Bible Translator* 30, no. 3 (1979): 318–25.

Nida, Eugene A., and Charles Taber. *The Theory and Practice of Translation* (Leiden: Brill, 1982).

Omanson, Roger. "Dynamic Equivalence Translations Reconsidered." *Theological Studies* 51 (1990): 497–505.

Pascal, Blaise. *Pensées.* Translated by A. J. Krailsheimer (London: Penguin, 1995 [1670]).

Plummer, A. *The Epistles of St John: With Notes, Introduction and Appendices.* Cambridge Greek Testament for Schools and Colleges (Cambridge: Cambridge University Press, 1916).

Porter, Stanley E. "Some Issues in Modern Translation Theory and Study of the New Testament." *Currents in Research: Biblical Studies* 9 (2001): 350–82.

Prickett, Stephen. *Words and the Word: Language, Poetics, and Biblical Interpretation* (Cambridge: Cambridge University Press, 1986).

Punt, Jeremy. "Translating the Bible in South Africa: Challenges to Responsibility and Contextuality," in *Bible Translation on the Threshold of the Twenty-First Century*, ed. Athalya Brenner and Jan Willem van Henten (London: Sheffield Academic Press, 2002), 94–131.

Ritchie, Daniel. "Three Recent Bible Translations: A Literary and Stylistic Perspective." *Journal of the Evangelical Theological Society* 46, no. 3 (2003): 533–45.

Roberts, J. H. "Dynamic Equivalence in Bible Translation." *Neotestamentica* 8 (1974): 7–20.

Ryken, Leland. *The Word of God in English: Criteria for Excellence in Bible Translation* (Wheaton: Crossway, 2002).

Schmid, Hansjorg. "How to Read the First Epistle of John Non-Polemically." *Biblica* 85, no. 1 (2004): 24–41.

Schnackenburg, Rudolph. *The Johannine Epistles* (New York: Crossroad, 1992 [German 1984]).

Scott, J. W. "Dynamic Equivalence and Some Theological Problems in the NIV." *Westminster Theological Journal* 48 (1986): 351–61.

Statham, Nigel. "Dynamic Equivalence and Functional Equivalence: How Do They Differ?" *The Bible Translator* 54, no. 1 (2003): 102–11.

Strauss, Mark L. "Review of Leland Ryken, *The Word of God in English*." *Journal of the Evangelical Theological Society* 46, no. 4 (2003): 738–40.

Thomson, Greg. "What Sort of Meaning is Preserved in Translation? (I)." *Notes on Translation* 2, no. 1 (1988): 1–24.

_____. "What Sort of Meaning is Preserved in Translation? (II: Sense)." *Notes on Translation* 3, no. 1 (1989): 26–49.

_____. "What Sort of Meaning is Preserved in Translation? (III: Pragmatic Meaning)." *Notes on Translation* 3, no. 4 (1989): 30–54.

_____. "What Sort of Meaning is Preserved in Translation? (IV: Presupposition)." *Notes on Translation* 4, no. 1 (1990): 21–32.

Turner, Nigel. *Style*. Volume IV of J. H. Moulton, W. F. Howard, and N. Turner, eds., *A Grammar of New Testament Greek* (Edinburgh: T & T Clark, 1976).

Van Leeuwen, Raymond C. "On Bible Translation and Hermeneutics," in *After Pentecost: Language and Biblical Interpretation*, ed. Craig Bartholomew, Colin Greene, and Karl Moeller (Grand Rapids, Mich.: Zondervan, 2001), 284–311.

_____. "We Really Do Need Another Bible Translation." *Christianity Today* 45, no. 13 (2001): 28–35.

Walsh, J. P. M. "Contemporary English Translations of Scripture." *Theological Studies* 50 (1989): 336–58.

_____. "Dynamic or Formal Equivalence? A Response." *Theological Studies* 51 (1990): 505–8.

Wendland, Ernst. *Comparative Discourse Analysis and the Translation of Psalm 22 in Chichewa, a Bantu Language of South-Central Africa* (Lewiston: Edwin Mellen, 1993).

Westcott, Brooke Foss. *The Epistles of St John: The Greek Text with Notes and Essays* (Cambridge: Macmillan, 1892).

Wright, Benjamin G. *No Small Difference: Sirach's Relationship to its Hebrew Parent Text*. Septuagint and Cognate Studies Series (Atlanta: Scholars, 1989).

Wright, Christopher. *God's People in God's Land* (Carlisle: Paternoster, 1997).

1. This essay was originally published as a chapter in Wayne Grudem, Leland Ryken, C. John Collins, Vern S. Poythress, Bruce Winter, and J.I. Packer, *Translating Truth: The Case for Essentially Literal Bible Translation* (Wheaton, Ill.: Crossway, 2005), 77–111. Used by permission of Crossway Books.

2. E. L. Greenstein, "The Role of Theory in Biblical Criticism," *Proceedings of the Ninth World Congress of Jewish Studies: Jerusalem, August 4-12, 1985* (Jerusalem: World Union of Jewish Studies, 1986), 167–174, at 167.

3. Compare my approach in *Science & Faith: Friends or Foes?* (Wheaton, Ill.: Crossway, 2003), chapter two: We make a mistake if we let the philosophers or scientists define what rationality is. "A good philosophy will start from everyday rationality and build on it, and refine it" (21).

4. Blaise Pascal, *Pensées*, ed. and trans. A. J. Krailsheimer (London: Penguin, 1995 [1670]), xxviii.

5. Ibid., xxix; and Krailsheimer appeals to Pascal's own principle in Pensée 515: "When words are repeated in an argument and one finds, on trying to correct them, that they are so apposite that it would spoil the work to change them, they must be left in."

6. Published by the Living Language division of Random House.

7. It also leaves out the potential *potest*, "can."

8. The proverb has archaic features that might mislead some contemporary readers, however. I assume

that the word "meat" is used in its older sense of "food"; and nowadays one must be careful about using "man" for "human person."

9. The introduction goes on to say, "A thought-for-thought translation prepared by a group of capable scholars has the potential to represent the intended meaning of the original text even more accurately than a word-for-word translation."

10. For example, E. A. Nida, *Toward a Science of Translating* (Leiden: Brill, 1964), 24; J. Beekman and J. Callow, *Translating the Word of God* (Grand Rapids, Mich.: Zondervan, 1974), 21.

11. K. L. Barker, "The Balanced Translation Philosophy of the TNIV," *Light Magazine, Special Edition: Shedding Light on the TNIV* (International Bible Society, 2002), 18–21, at 19.

12. This is similar to the diagram found in Barker, "Balanced Philosophy," 21. The main difference is that Barker (or the artist) has put the KJV in the "most literal" category, and this is contrary to, e.g. Nida, *Translating*, 17. (See discussion below.)

13. C. John Collins, "Without Form You Lose Meaning," in L. Ryken, *The Word of God in English: Criteria for Excellence in Bible Translation* (Wheaton, Ill.: Crossway, 2002), 295–327, at 296–8.

14. R. C. Van Leeuwen, "We Really Do Need Another Bible Translation," *Christianity Today* 45, no.13 (October 22, 2001): 28–35, at 30. See also Van Leeuwen, "On Bible Translation and Hermeneutics," in C. Bartholomew et al., eds., *After Pentecost: Language and Biblical Interpretation* (Grand Rapids, Mich.: Zondervan, 2001), 284–311.

15. For a jarring mismatch in register, compare the solemn "woe to you" with the sputtering "damn you" in the Jesus Seminar's *Five Gospels.*

16. For such a study, showing that the man does not own his wife, see Christopher Wright, *God's People in God's Land* (Carlisle, UK: Paternoster, 1997), 181–221, on the wife's status in Old Testament law.

17. When people refer to a translation as "interpretive," they are not usually denying that some degree of interpretation goes on at the linguistic level; they are instead saying that the interpretation has gone beyond what the linguistic details require, and that it forecloses interpretive options for the English reader. Those who defend dynamic equivalence do not often notice the distinction; perhaps a cumbersome phrase like "more interpretive than linguistically necessary" helps to convey the actual critique.

18. Text in J. M. and M. J. Cohen, *The New Penguin Dictionary of Quotations* (Harmondsworth: Penguin, 1992), 62:2.

19. There may, however, be occasions in which changing the tense from the past to the present may be necessary, if it is too difficult in the target language to infer from a specific event the normal pattern. This is the problem faced with the so-called gnomic tenses (in both Hebrew and Greek), on which see the discussion in C. John Collins, "Psalm 1: Structure and Rhetoric," *Presbyterion* 31, no. 1 (Spring 2005): 37–48, Appendix 2.

20. C. S. Lewis, *The Voyage of the Dawn Treader* (New York: Macmillan, 1952).

21. C. S. Lewis, *Hammassa' be-Dorek Hashshachar,* trans. Gideon Turi (Tel Aviv: Zmora, Bitan, Modan, 1979), 15.

22. Lewis, *Hammassa' be-Dorek Hashshachar,* 178.

23. For such a suggestion, see Robert Bratcher and William Reyburn, *A Translator's Handbook on the Book of Psalms* (New York: United Bible Societies, 1991), 19–20.

24. For advice about how to handle Old Testament poetry, see Jan de Waard and William A. Smalley, *A Translator's Handbook on the Book of Amos* (London: United Bible Societies, 1979), 11: "However, the important point to remember here is that such parallelism should come into a translation where it contributes to effective communication in the language of the translation and should not be carried over only because it is in the Hebrew or an English translation of the Hebrew. This means that quite often when something is said twice in the Hebrew in this way, it will be said only once in good translation." See further Ernst Wendland, *Comparative Discourse Analysis and the Translation of Psalm 22 in Chichewa, a Bantu Language of South-Central Africa* (Lewiston, Edwin Mellen, 1993) for the suggestion that we must seek an "equivalent" genre in the target language as well. It is often said that the translation strategy behind parts of the LXX (such as Proverbs) adapts the biblical world to that of Alexandria, even extending to the worldview.

25. We might add as well the TEV's more delicate (or prudish) "charms" for "breasts."

26. In verse 15, the wife is the water source, and verse 16 portrays this source as fouled by multiple users.

27. Compare the distinction between "digital" and "analogical" language in Paul Fueter, "The Therapeutic Language of the Bible," *International Review of Mission* 75 (July 1986): 211–21 = *The Bible Translator* 37, no. 3 (1986): 309–19.

28. *Holy Bible: New Living Translation, Text and Product Preview* (Wheaton: Tyndale House Publishers, 1996), 18.

29. Because this goes beyond the sense and syntax of the words, this would be another example of a translation that is "more interpretive than linguistically necessary."

30. Cited in Robert G. Bratcher, "The Nature and Purpose of the New Testament in Today's English Version," *The Bible Translator* 22, no. 3 (1971): 97–107, at 98. See also Eugene A. Nida and Charles R. Taber, *Theory and Practice of Translation* (Leiden: Brill, 1982), 1: "The new focus [in translating], however, has shifted

from the form of the message to the response of the receptor"; on page 28 they use the receptors' response as a criterion of accuracy.

31. Indeed, when the BBC reported that scientists think the universe is shaped like a "football," I had to remember what a British football is; and when a Briton refers to something as an "own goal" or "queering the pitch," I need to know something about soccer. But if a translator reduces these idioms, he also reduces the feel of traveling to Britain.

32. Anthony Nichols, "Dynamic Equivalence Bible Translations," *Colloquium: The Australian and New Zealand Theological Review* 19 (1986): 43–53, at 53.

33. Nida and Taber, *Theory and Practice*, 31; see also what Nida told David Neff in the interview, "Meaning-Full Tanslations: The world's most influential Bible translator, Eugene Nida, is weary of 'word worship,'" *Christianity Today* 46 (September 16, 2002): 46–9, at 49, where the third category is for "particular constituencies – children, for example."

34. Nida uses the fact that "hallowed be thy name" is mostly unintelligible today as an argument for "meaningful" translations (Neff, "Meaning-Full Translations," 46), but this hardly supports the idea of dynamic or functional equivalence; it only argues for intelligibility, which most translation philosophies endorse.

35. Even so, it is still possible to analyze the sociolinguistics of language in worship. An English Roman Catholic author, David Crystal, has provided a useful discussion that extends beyond that denomination's boundaries: "Liturgical Language in a Sociolinguistic Perspective," in David Jasper and R. C. D. Jasper, eds., *Language and the Worship of the Church* (New York: St Martin's Press, 1990), 120–46.

36. Ryken, *The Word of God in English*, elaborates on these and other desirable features in chapters 13–17.

37. Of course there are judgment calls involved regarding what is "current," and we further must allow for the variety of language levels in the Bible.

38. Compare also 1 Cor. 1:31, in the context of verses 26–9.

39. C. S. Lewis, *Mere Christianity* (New York: Scribner, 1952), book 3, chapter 2.

40. Further on the features of the letter: Alfred Plummer, *The Epistles of St. John: With Notes, Introduction and Appendices* (Cambridge Greek Testament for Schools and Colleges; Cambridge: Cambridge University Press, 1916), lvii–lxii; Brooke Foss Westcott, *The Epistles of St. John: The Greek Text with Notes and Essays* (Cambridge: Macmillan, 1892), xxxix–xliii; Rudolph Schnackenburg, *The Johannine Epistles* (New York: Crossroad, 1992 [German 1984]), 6–11; Nigel Turner, *Style* (A Grammar of New Testament Greek, vol. IV; Edinburgh: T & T Clark, 1976), 132–8; Ruth B. Edwards, *The Johannine Epistles* (New Testament Guides; Sheffield: Sheffield Academic Press, 1996), 37–8.

41. Bratcher, "The Nature and Purpose of the New Testament in TEV," 98–100.

42. In my private notes, I have examined them all in detail, and these selections are intended to be representative.

43. Compare as well ἐστίν ἐν ("to be in"). A book-length study of these terms is Edward Malatesta, *Interiority and Covenant*. Analecta Biblica (Rome: Biblical Institute Press, 1978).

44. Compare also John 5:38; 6:56; 8:31; 15:4, 5, 6, 7, 9, 10, 16.

45. Recall Krailsheimer's remark on Pascal that we noted earlier: "I know of no other author who repeats the same word with such almost obsessive frequency as Pascal, and failure to render this essential feature of his style makes a translation not only inadequate but positively misleading." But now we can see that 1 John has equaled this obsession.

46. In fact, the only occurrence of μένω that gets a different rendering in these versions is in 2:19, "they would have continued with us." In defense of the tradition, we may note that this is not μένω ἐν. Further, the past participle of English "abide" ("abode" or "abidden," or even "abided"?) has long been problematic, as the OED testifies: the contrary-to-fact expression, "they would have abode/abidden with us," sounds very awkward. Had the tradition used "remain," however, it could have captured even this instance of the verb.

47. Note that this version renders εἶναι ἐν ("to be in") as "to live in" in 2:5; 4:4: perhaps the translators decided that the "meaning" of the two is the same?

48. Colin G. Kruse, *The Letters of John*. Pillar New Testament Commentary (Grand Rapids, Mich.: Eerdmans, 2000), 96–7.

49. Compare Nida and Taber, *Theory and Practice*, 7–8.

50. Compare Anthony Nichols, "Explicitness in Translation and the Westernization of Scripture," *Reformed Theological Review* 47, no. 3 (1988): 78–88.

51. The same ambiguity exists in the English construction. We can see that such ambiguity is a property of native English (and not just translation) from the way John McKay answered a reporter's question. McKay was lured away from a successful career at USC to be the first coach of the Tampa Bay Buccaneers. After the final loss in an 0–14 season, he was asked, "What do you think of the execution of your team?" McKay replied, "I'm all for it." (Cited from Ron Cook's column in the *Pittsburgh Post-Gazette*, February 28, 2004, accessed October 28, 2004 at http://www.post-gazette.com/pg/04039/270287.stm.)

52. Westcott, *Epistles of St. John*, 48–9; F. F. Bruce, *The Epistles of John* (Grand Rapids, Mich.: Eerdmans, 1970), 51–2.

53. Compare, for example, Bruce, *Epistles of John*, 52, and Plummer, *Epistles of St. John*, 38–9.

54. Compare Malatesta, *Interiority and Covenant*, 128–32.

55. Interestingly enough, John's terms "evil" and "righteous" (πονηρό δίκαιο) do not correspond to either the LXX or to anything in the MT; but the terms do resemble the near-contemporary Josephus, who (*Antiquities*, 1.53) said that Abel "had respect for righteousness (δικαιοσύνη ἐπεμελεῖτο), while Cain was "very evil" (πονηρότατο).

56. For a brief discussion of New Testament uses of Old Testament sacrificial terminology to describe what Jesus accomplished in his dying, see C. John Collins, "The Eucharist as Christian Sacrifice," *Westminster Theological Journal* 66 (2004): 1–23, at 21–3.

57. Compare the NIV margin, "the one who turns aside God's wrath" – which leaves out the notion of the sacrifice being the means of turning aside.

58. Compare also John 8:51, 52, 55; 14:15, 21, 23, 24; 15:10, 20; 17:6.

59. Delitzsch's Hebrew New Testament uses *shamar* in these places in 1 John, while the Syriac uses *netar* (the Aramaic cognate of Hebrew *natsar*).

60. Compare Keith N. Schoville, "*shamar*," no. 9068 in W. A. VanGemeren, ed., *New International Dictionary of Old Testament Theology and Exegesis*, 5 vols. (Grand Rapids, Mich.: Zondervan, 1997), 4: 182–4.

61. See also Prov. 3:1b, where ESV has "let your heart keep my commandments." We cannot compare this with NIV and NLT, since they analyze the syntax differently (and wrongly, in my judgment): "keep my commands in your heart" (NIV) and "store my commands in your heart" (NLT). "Your heart" is surely the subject of the verb "keep" (*natsar*), as the ESV (see LXX and KJV) takes it, and this shows that attitude is in fact part of the meaning of the expression.

62. For example, Plummer, *Epistles of John*, 55–6; Bruce, *Epistles of John*, 64–5; C. Haas, M. De Jonge, and J. L. Swellengrebel, *A Translator's Handbook on the Letters of John*. Helps for Translators (London: United Bible Societies, 1972), 62; Kruse, *Letters of John*, 98.

63. For ἐπ ἐσχάτων τῶν ἡμερῶν, see Gen. 49:1; Num. 24:14; Hos. 3:5; Mic. 4:1; Jer. 30:24; 49:39; Ezek. 38:16; Dan. 2:28. For ἐπ ἐσχάτῳ τῶν ἡμερῶν, see Deut. 4:30; 31:29; Dan. 10:14. For ἐν ταῖς ἐσχάταις ἡμέραις, see Isa. 2:2. For ἐπ ἐσχάτου τῶν ἡμερῶν, see Jer. 23:20. Ezek. 38:8 has "in the latter years" (LXX, ἐπ ἐσχάτου ἐτῶν), which seems to be a variant of this term, as verse 16 shows (so Y. Moskovitz, *Sefer Yechezqel*. Da'at Miqra [Jerusalem: Mossad Harav Kook, 1985], 304 n8).

64. See Westcott, *Epistles of St. John*, 69. A similar interpretation, without appeal to the prophetic texts, appears in Theophylact, *PG* 126, column 23.

65. For example, consider 5:3, where God's commands are not βαρεῖαι (ESV/NIV "burdensome"); this rendering is far truer to the LXX usage of βαρύνω and βαρυνι than the NLT "difficult" (compare Ex. 5:9; 1 Kings. 12:4, 11, 14; Neh., 5:15, 18; Ps. 38:4; Isa. 47:6; Sir. 40:1; 1 Macc. 8:31). Compare also the Syriac at 5:3, using *yaqqir* "heavy, oppressive."

PART FIVE:

CHRIST-CENTERED SERMONS

21

THE LORD IS AGAINST ME!

A Sermon on the Book of Ruth

JAY SKLAR[1]
Assistant Professor of Old Testament
Director, Th.M. Program

So [Naomi and Ruth] went on until they came to Bethlehem. And it came about when they had come to Bethlehem, that all the city was stirred because of them, and the women [of the city] said, "Is this Naomi?" And she said to them, "Do not call me Naomi; call me Mara, for the Almighty has dealt very bitterly with me. I went out full, but the LORD has brought me back empty. Why do you call me Naomi, since the LORD has witnessed against me and the Almighty has afflicted me?" (Ruth 1:19-21)[2]

𝕴 wonder if Naomi's words make you feel uncomfortable? They are blunt; they are angry; and they are accusatory against the LORD. What would lead an ancient Israelite to be so bitter?

It all starts some ten years earlier. To begin, Naomi and her family have to leave Bethlehem and travel east to the land of Moab due to a severe famine. To make matters worse, Naomi's husband dies in Moab, leaving her a widow. Now only Naomi and her two sons remain. Things seem to brighten slightly: her sons marry, and they all continue to live in Moab for another ten years. But then Naomi's sons also die. Losing her husband was bad enough; losing her two children as well was unbelievably tragic.

NAOMI'S REBUKE

All of this leads Naomi to conclude that the LORD is against her! You can see this first in her words to her daughters-in-law. After her sons die, Naomi prepares to return to Bethlehem, where the famine has now ended. Her two daughters-in-law, Orpah and Ruth, decide to go with her. Naomi, however, cannot ask them to make that kind of sacrifice, so she tells them not to come. When her daughters-in-law protest, Naomi tells them again not to come and underscores her words by saying: "No, my daughters, for it is more bitter for me than for you, *for the hand of the* LORD *has gone out against me*" (Ruth 1:13b).[3] Naomi has concluded that the LORD is against her.

Naomi expresses the pain and distance from God that she feels even more strongly in her words to the women of Bethlehem. She has just returned home after a ten-year absence. Naturally, the entire town is abuzz! We read that the women of the town in particular were asking one another: "Is this Naomi – the 'pleasant one'?" And yet, right in the midst of all this buzz and excitement comes a rebuke from Naomi: "Do not call me Naomi ['Naomi' means 'pleasant' in Hebrew]; call me Mara ['Mara' means 'bitter' in Hebrew], *for the Almighty has dealt very bitterly with me*" (Ruth 1:20).

Naomi sees it as an insult to be called "pleasant" after all that has happened to her! And to underscore her feelings, her rebuke continues: "I went out full, *but the* LORD *has brought me back empty*. Why do you call me Naomi, *since the* LORD *has witnessed against me and the Almighty has afflicted me?*" (Ruth 1:21). Naomi feels like the LORD himself has taken the witness stand against her! More than that, she feels like the LORD has brought calamity upon her, that he has set her in his sights and has begun to embed fiery arrows of pain in her heart, one after another.

Naomi has looked at the tragedies in her life and concluded: The LORD is against me! Perhaps there are times in our own lives when painful circumstances have made us feel the same way as Naomi. But the book of Ruth as a whole comes to a different conclusion than Naomi does. The book of Ruth teaches that in a fallen world of pain and hurt, the LORD does not forget his covenant children. This book does not explain the problem of evil; it does not explain why bad things happen to good people. It assumes that we live in a fallen world and that we will feel the effects of pain, and sin, and death. But it does not conclude – as Naomi does – that these realities mean that the LORD has forsaken us. Time and again it teaches instead: in the midst of the brokenness, the LORD does not abandon his steadfast love for his covenant children.

THE LORD'S PROVISION OF RUTH

We can see this first in the LORD's provision of Ruth to Naomi. As Naomi tries to convince her daughters-in-law not to return to Bethlehem with her, a ray of the LORD's steadfast love beams down onto the field of her life. Instead of leaving Naomi, Ruth *clings* to her and says, "Do not urge me to leave you or to return from following you. For where you go I will go, and where you lodge I will lodge. Your people shall be my people, and your God my God. Where you die I will die, and there will I be buried. May the LORD do so to me and more also if anything but death parts me from you!" (Ruth 1:16-17).

Ruth is making a commitment here to love Naomi until her dying day. It is a commitment of what the Israelites would call *hesed*: steadfast love. And this is what has happened: in the midst of Naomi's hurt and pain and unspeakable grief, the LORD has provided Ruth *to* Naomi as a manifestation of his steadfast love *for* Naomi. It is a whisper of the voice of the LORD: "Naomi, my precious covenant child: please know that the presence of tragedy in your life does not mean that I am against you. Please know that even in the midst of tragedy I am still your LORD of *steadfast love*."

Naomi could not hear the whisper at this point in the story. There are times when the pain is so raw, or when we focus upon it so much, that we are oblivious to the LORD's care for us in the midst of it. Such was Naomi's situation. And yet the steadfast love of the LORD for Naomi continues as the story goes on.

The Lord's Provision Through Boaz

When Ruth and Naomi return to Bethlehem, we are introduced to a man named Boaz (Ruth 2:1). We are not told much about him, only that he is a relative of Naomi's deceased husband and a man of some standing. The story moves quickly along.

It is the beginning of the barley harvest and Ruth says to Naomi, "Let me go to the field and glean ..." (Ruth 2:2). According to Israelite law, the poor and needy were allowed to go into the farmers' fields after the harvest and pick up any of the cut grain that had not been bundled (Lev. 23:22). Ruth sets out to gather grain in this manner.

Significantly, Ruth "happened to come to the part of the field belonging to Boaz ..." (Ruth 2:3). The word "happened" may sound at first as though it was blind chance that Ruth ended up in Boaz's field. Not so! When the author of Ruth says that she "happened" upon the field of Boaz, it is his way of saying "that no *human intent* was involved. For Ruth and Boaz it was an accident, *but not for God*. The tenor of the whole story makes it clear that the narrator sees God's hand throughout."[4] In short, the LORD guides Ruth to this very field. As we will see, he does this as another demonstration of his steadfast love for Naomi and for Ruth.

No sooner do we read that Ruth has ended up in Boaz's field, then who should appear? Boaz himself! After greeting the reapers Boaz asks the foreman, "Whose young woman is this?" (Ruth 2:5). The foreman replies, "She is the young Moabite woman who came back with Naomi from the country of Moab" (Ruth 2:6). It seems that the sacrificial and steadfast love that Ruth had shown to Naomi was known throughout Bethlehem. In fact, when Boaz learns that the young lady is Ruth, he wastes no time in rewarding her with a generous provision of food and drink and a promise of physical protection while she is gleaning in his fields.

Ruth is overwhelmed; this man, whom she has never met and has never even heard of, is treating her as though she were part of his own household.

Bowing with her face to the ground, Ruth asks, "Why have I found favor in your eyes ...?" (Ruth 2:10). Some might suspect that Boaz was attracted to Ruth and was trying to win her heart with all these gifts. But the answer that Boaz gives points in another direction. He says: "All that you have done for your mother-in-law since the death of your husband has been fully told to me, and how you left your father and mother and your native land and came to a people that you did not know before" (Ruth 2:12).

Boaz recognizes fully the steadfast love that Ruth has shown for Naomi, and now wishes the same steadfast love to be shown to her. He goes on to say, "May the LORD repay you for what you have done, and a full reward be given you by the LORD, the God of Israel, under whose wings you have come to take refuge!" (Ruth 2:13). And the reward does indeed come – through Boaz himself! Not only does he let Ruth glean in his field and offer her protection, but Boaz even commands his harvesters to pull some of the grain out of the bundles so that Ruth has more than just the scraps to pick up (Ruth 2:16). In fact, when Ruth comes home at the end of the day, Naomi is amazed at the amount of food that she brings home: "Where did you glean today? And where have you worked? Blessed be the man who took notice of you!" (Ruth 2:19a). And when Ruth tells Naomi that it was Boaz, Naomi utters these words, "May he be blessed by the LORD, whose *steadfast love* (*hesed*) has not forsaken the living or the dead" (Ruth 2:20).

Naomi is not only receiving the steadfast love of the LORD through his provision of Ruth, she is now receiving the steadfast love of the LORD through his provision of Boaz. And it is as though the LORD whispers again: "Naomi, my precious covenant child: please know that the presence of tragedy in your life does not mean that I am against you. Please know that even in the midst of tragedy I am still your LORD of steadfast love."

The whisper becomes a stronger voice as the story continues ...

NAOMI MAKES A PLAN

After hearing of the kindness of Boaz, Naomi makes a plan. In chapter two, Ruth was the problem-solver, essentially saying, "We don't have food and I want to help with that; I'm going to go and glean." In chapter three, Naomi becomes the problem-solver, essentially saying, "Ruth, you don't have a husband and I want to help with that."

The prospective husband is Boaz. The basic plan is this: Ruth is to go and find Boaz and let him know that she would like to become his wife. Here are some of the specifics. It was the harvest season, and Boaz and the other harvesters would be down at the threshing floor working, and many of them would even sleep there at night. With this in mind, Naomi tells Ruth, "Wash therefore and anoint yourself, and put on your cloak and go down to the threshing floor ..." (Ruth 3:3a). Some understand Naomi to be telling Ruth to dress her best; it is just as likely that she is telling Ruth to change out of the garments that a widow wore (see Gen. 38:14, 19) in order to signal the end of her mourning and her return to regular life (see 2 Sam. 12:20).

In either case, Naomi goes on to say, "... do not make yourself known to the man until he has finished eating and drinking. But when he lies down, observe the place where he lies. Then go and uncover his feet and lie down, and he will tell you what to do" (Ruth 3:3b-4). When we read this we wonder, "What in the world is going on?" Naomi's plan seems so foreign to us, and for good reason: marriage customs, and customs surrounding marriage, are some of the most complex customs a society has. There are things in this chapter that we might not ever completely understand because the culture is so different from our own. But we can still grasp the overall point of what is going on.

Ruth carries out Naomi's plan exactly. She goes down to the threshing floor, waits until Boaz is finished eating and drinking and falls asleep, and then goes and uncovers his feet and lies down at the place of his feet. In the middle of the night Boaz suddenly realizes that there is a woman lying at his feet. He asks, "Who are you?", to which Ruth replies, "I am Ruth, your servant. Spread your wings [i.e. the corners of your garment] over your servant, for you are a redeemer" (Ruth 3:9).

There is a play on words going on in this verse. The Hebrew word for "wing" is used to describe the "wing" of a bird and it is also used to describe the "corner" of a garment. In chapter two, when Boaz first meets Ruth, he says to her, "May the LORD repay you for what you have done, and a full reward be given you by the LORD, the God of Israel, under whose *wings* you have come to take refuge!" (Ruth 2:12). Now in chapter three Ruth says to Boaz, "Please take the corners of your garment – your *wings* – and cover not only your feet, but me as well, and in this way symbolically demonstrate that you will take me under the refuge of your wings as your wife."

Boaz understands immediately that Ruth is asking to be his wife, and he is only too happy to agree! He says to her, "And now, my daughter, do not fear. I will do for you all that you ask, for all my fellow townsmen know that you are a worthy woman" (Ruth 3:11). There are a few issues that Boaz will need to iron out (4:1-12), but in the meantime, he sends Ruth home with a generous gift of barley, telling her that she "must not go back *empty-handed* to [her] mother-in-law" (v. 17).

It is at this point that the voice of the LORD becomes more than a whisper. This is the second time in the book that the word "empty" or "empty-handed" has been used. In chapter one it was spoken in anger by Naomi as an accusation against the LORD: "I went out full but the LORD has brought me back *empty*" (1:21). In chapter three, however, it is spoken by Boaz in tenderness and steadfast love, as he insists that Naomi's "emptiness" be addressed. It is as though the LORD himself is responding to Naomi's accusation and even using her own words to say tenderly to her through Boaz, "Naomi, my precious covenant child: I have not forgotten your emptiness. Please know that the presence of tragedy in your life does not mean that I am against you. Please know that even in the midst of tragedy I am still your LORD of steadfast love."

The LORD will continue to speak these words to Naomi as the story concludes.

THE LORD PROVIDES A REDEEMER

By the end of the story, Ruth and Boaz marry and Ruth gives birth to a son. The women of the city – the same women who greeted Naomi in chapter one and whom she rebuked – now bless the name of the LORD and make one thing crystal clear: the LORD is not against Naomi; he is for Naomi. Looking at the little child that Ruth has borne, these women say to Naomi, "He shall be to you a restorer of life ..." (Ruth 4:15). Their words may be translated literally: "He shall be to you *one who causes* life *to return* ..." We miss it in the English, but in the Hebrew the women use the same word that Naomi did in chapter one when she said, "The LORD *has caused me to return* empty ..." (Ruth 1:21). In chapter one, this expression was used by Naomi as an accusation against the LORD. In chapter four, these words are used as a reminder that the LORD is not against Naomi; indeed, they are one more whisper of the LORD's steadfast love.

In fact, when the women finish speaking, we read these words in verse 16: "Then Naomi took the child and laid him on her lap and became his nurse." The word used here for "child" occurs one other time in the book of Ruth. It is chapter one. We read there that Naomi lost her two "children," her two "boys" (1:5). We read here that Naomi now takes another "child" – a child that the LORD has provided – and holds him tenderly to her breast. And once more we hear the LORD's tender voice: "Naomi, my precious covenant child: please know that the presence of tragedy in your life does not mean that I am against you. Please know that even in the midst of tragedy I am still your LORD of steadfast love."

It is important to emphasize what the book of Ruth is and is not teaching. It is not teaching that the provision of this child, or the provision of Boaz, or the provision of Ruth, simply makes things all better. When Naomi's husband and children died, a piece of Naomi died with them, and not even a grandchild can fully replace that missing piece or erase that scar.

But the book of Ruth is teaching that, even when this ancient believer walks through the valley of the shadow of death – and there will be times in the lives of all believers when that valley comes – even there the LORD is still her Shepherd of steadfast love. When the LORD places another child on the lap of Naomi, he is not saying, "See, it's all better now." What he is saying is this: "I have not forgotten you. The world is often a dark place, and the effects of sin in this world are painful and real, but even when the pain of a fallen world hits you most keenly and you feel as though you are walking through the valley of the shadow of death, I am still there, by your side, ever ready to comfort and help. I am still your LORD of steadfast love."

This is the same message God gives to the believer today. If you have put your faith in the Lord Jesus Christ and have come to know God the Father through Him, then this is what the Lord says to you as a Christian: "My precious covenant child: please know that the presence of tragedy in your life does not mean that I am against you. Please know that even in the midst of tragedy I am still your LORD of steadfast love."

The book of Ruth thus becomes a call to trust in the LORD of steadfast love even in the midst of suffering and loss. It does not answer the "why" of Naomi's suffering, at least from Naomi's perspective. But throughout the book the voice of the LORD continually beckons her to trust in him even in the midst of the "whys." And his voice beckons us to do the same. When we feel like the Naomi of chapter one, we need to remember the LORD of chapters one, two, three, and four – the LORD of steadfast love who continually says to his covenant children, "I have not forgotten you; I am not against you; I am, and will ever be, your LORD of steadfast love."

---

1. A slightly different version of this sermon was originally preached in Rayburn Chapel on the campus of Covenant Theological Seminary in 2004 and published in *Covenant* 20, no. 1 (Spring 2005): 6–9, 27.

2. Unless otherwise indicated, Bible quotations used in this essay are taken from the New American Standard Bible (NASB).

3. Italics used within Bible verses indicate emphasis added.

4. Ronald M. Hals, *The Theology of the Book of Ruth* (Philadelphia: Fortress Press, 1969), 12; emphasis added.

22

To Know and Be Known:

How Christ's Love Moves Us into

Intimacy, Humility, and Risk.

A Sermon on John 13:1-17

GREG PERRY[1]
Assistant Professor of Biblical Studies

---

ave you ever visited a city when it was filled beyond capacity for an event like the Olympics? There are no hotel rooms, parking is tight, traffic is slow, and the license plates you see are mostly from out of state. Try to imagine such a crowd in first-century Jerusalem. People were packed in to celebrate Passover. The city had not doubled or tripled; it had ballooned to over twelve times its normal size. But the Passover feast we read about in John 13 was unlike any other. There was an electric current running throughout the pilgrim crowd. People were asking questions.

"Did you hear what happened in Bethany? They say he raised a man from the dead after four days in the tomb. Could it be? Could he be the Anointed One from God?" Even as they celebrated their miraculous deliverance from slavery in Egypt, the people wondered if Jesus of Nazareth was the Promised One, the One who would throw off their Roman rulers and tax burden. Could Jesus be the Messiah, who would again bring God's people into an inheritance of their own? Already, many had given him a royal welcome into the city with palm branches and shouts of "Hosanna!" It was an exhilarating time, and accordingly, John positions this story at the turning point of his Gospel.

Six times before in John's Gospel we have heard Jesus say, "My hour has not yet come." At the wedding in Cana, near the beginning of his ministry, Jesus had responded to his mother's agenda by saying, "My hour has not yet come" (John 2:4b).[2] The momentum builds throughout his public ministry until, in answer to questions from Jewish leaders, Jesus says, "A time is coming and has now come when the dead will hear the voice of the Son of God, and those who hear will live!" (John 5:25). Indeed, these words were on the minds of many who had arrived in Jerusalem from Bethany: Lazarus had heard Jesus and come to life!

In John 12 and 13, "the hour" is no longer coming. Jesus says, "The hour has come for the Son of Man to be glorified... Now, my heart is troubled, and what shall I say? 'Father, save me from this hour?' No, it was for this very reason I came to this hour. Father, glorify your name!" (John 12:23, 27, 28). Of what sort of glory does Jesus speak? Is it not the glory of the King? If so, then why is He so troubled on this night of celebration? Yes, Jesus brought Lazarus back to life, but reactions include a plot to kill him. Yes, he was anointed with oil, but by a woman with unbound hair who poured her perfume on his feet, not his head. Yes, he entered the city in triumph, but riding a donkey colt, not a chariot. Who is this King and what kind of strange glory is he to receive?

KNOWING JESUS IS PERSONAL

Jesus knew that the hour had come for him to leave this world and go to the Father. Having loved his own who were in the world, he now showed them the full extent of his love. The evening meal was being served, and the devil had already prompted Judas Iscariot, son of Simon, to betray Jesus. Jesus knew that the Father had put all things under his power, and that he had come from God and was returning to God; so he got up from the meal, took off his outer clothing, and wrapped a towel around his waist. After that, he poured water into a basin and began to wash his disciples' feet, drying them with the towel that was wrapped around him. (John 13:1a-5)

Do we really want to know this Jesus? Do we want to understand this strange glory of his? Or, do we just want to know *about* Jesus? Everyone who was anyone in Jerusalem wanted to know about Jesus. But, if we only want to know *about* Jesus, we can keep our own agendas for him. We can try to manage him much like those who had plans for him during this Passover. Yet, amidst the clamor for information, Jesus slips away from the crowds to have dinner with his disciples.

Jesus' dinners were not like those of the Pharisees. The Pharisees' dinners resembled the Greco-Roman symposia, with their rhetorical matches and honor bestowed on the greatest debater. But at his meal, the host, Jesus, takes off his outer robe to dress like a slave and do the work of a slave. Not even a Hebrew slave was to wash people's feet, yet Jesus pours water into the basin to undertake the necessary task.

We do not have any traditional parables in John's Gospel; instead we have living parables. The living parable of John 13 is like a cardiac crash cart: it is designed to shock the system. In Luke's account of this same dinner we read that a "dispute broke out among [the disciples] as to which one of them was considered to be the greatest" (Luke 22:24). Even as doctors and nurses only jolt a patient with electricity when his heart is dysfunctional, Jesus jolts the disciples by making himself their servant. Does the Lord's Supper jolt us like this? Clearly, Jesus was anticipating the cross at his meal. Do we look back on it in order to know Jesus like this, the Jesus who does this?

Yet even as a servant, Jesus is at the head of the table, not us. He sets the terms of the relationship, not us. If we are to know Jesus, he must first know us. If we are to get involved with Jesus, he must first get involved with us. That is what is happening here at this meal during this strange revelation of his glory. Jesus acts like a slave to get near his disciples in a way that involves personal knowledge, intimacy, and exposure. He "shows the full extent of his love" (John 13:1b) for them and for us. Jesus moves into those parts of our lives that we would just as soon keep covered or at a safe distance.

My son Stephen has a dog named Max. Max is a beautiful yellow Labrador and Stephen professes to love him. Yet, one day last summer, when it came time to wash Max, Stephen, with new clothes on, stood at a distance and started to spray Max down with the hose. Every dad knows the next move. I pulled off my tie, opened my collar, kicked off socks and shoes, came beside Stephen, and said, "You too, Son! Take off your shirt and shoes, and get ready to get wet. If you love Max, we're going to have to get personal."

Knowing Jesus means that he knows you. Getting involved with Jesus means he is already involved with you. By the time Stephen and I were finished washing Max, we smelled like dogs and had wet clumps of Lab hair all over us. That is what happens when Jesus gets involved with us. "He who knew no sin, became sin for us, so that in him we might be made the righteousness of God" (2 Cor. 5:21). Knowing Jesus is *personal*.

KNOWING JESUS IS HUMBLING

> He came to Simon Peter, who said to him, "Lord, are you going to wash my feet?" Jesus replied, "You do not realize now what I am doing, but later you will understand." "No," said Peter, "you shall never wash my feet." Jesus answered, "Unless I wash you, you have no part with me." "Then, Lord," Simon Peter replied, "not just my feet but my hands and my head as well!" Jesus answered, "A person who has had a bath needs only to wash his feet; his whole body is clean." (John 13:6-10a)

Knowing Jesus is not only personal, it is also very *humbling*. But Simon Peter is not buying that. He cannot imagine allowing his Lord to wash his feet. "It will never happen!" he says. Simon was a no-nonsense kind of guy, a self-made man; he could wash his own feet. But, Jesus plainly tells him, "You don't realize what I am doing for you, but later you will understand." Later, after Peter's denial, after the cross and the resurrection, after Peter's restoration, then he would understand that self-sufficiency has no place in knowing Jesus.

Knowledge comes through connection, not isolation; through relationship, not self-sufficient autonomy. Jesus says, "Unless I wash you, you have no *part* with me" (John 13:8). John's language of "part" or "portion" is the language of inheritance. Jesus is saying to Peter – and to us – unless I wash you, you cannot *share* in my kingdom.

Peter takes Jesus' rebuke, but his exuberant desire to correct his error only reveals his inability to understand this living parable. One biblical scholar guides us through the difficulties of this text by suggesting that Jesus is applying the metaphor of cleansing in three ways: as the bath that is needed for (1) conversion, (2) sanctification, and (3) example. Peter seems to be confusing the second application for the first.[3] But Jesus reminds Peter that he has already been bathed (John 13:10a). What he needs now is the regular foot washing of sanctification. Like Peter, those of us who have been bathed by Jesus need to humble ourselves daily in repentance and confession to have our feet washed again.

German pastor and theologian Dietrich Bonhoeffer diagnosed the situation of many of our churches all too well when he wrote,

> The final breakthrough to fellowship does not occur, because, though they have fellowship with one another as believers and as devout people, they do not have fellowship as the undevout, as sinners. The pious fellowship permits no one to be a sinner. So, everybody must conceal his sin from himself and the fellowship. We dare not be sinners! Many Christians are unthinkably horrified when a real sinner shows up. So we remain alone with our sin, living in lies and hypocrisy ... It is the grace of the gospel that is so hard for the pious to understand.[4]

Jesus' living parable requires humility in all three of its applications – to be converted, to repent in an ongoing manner, and to serve. Knowing Jesus is *humbling*.

KNOWING JESUS IS RISKY

> "... you are clean, though not every one of you." For he knew who was going to betray him, and that was why he said not every one was clean. When he had finished washing their feet, he put on his clothes and returned to his place. "Do you understand what I have done for you?" he asked them. "You call me, 'Teacher' and 'Lord,' and rightly so, for that is what I am. Now that I, your Lord and Teacher, have washed your feet, you also should wash one another's feet. I have set you an example that you should do as I have done for you. I tell you the truth, no servant is greater than his master, nor is a messenger greater than the one who sent him. Now that you know these things, you will be blessed if you do them." (John 3:10b-17)

For years, I missed the element of risk we embrace in knowing Jesus. Yet these verses clearly teach such risk. Jesus said, "You are clean, though not every one of you." Jesus knew who was going to betray him, and that was why he said not every one was clean. When he had finished washing their feet, Judas was still in the room! Jesus, with full knowledge of Judas' plans, washed his feet, too. Only two disciples are mentioned here, one a denier, the other a betrayer. Jesus knows them both.

We do not know people's hearts like Jesus did and does. We would like to be able to look on the outside and discern who will take advantage of us and who will be appreciative. The fact of the matter is that we do not even know our own hearts like Jesus does. The final point of Jesus' living parable is that he serves the denier and the betrayer alike, the takers and the thankful, and he calls his followers to do the same. Knowing Jesus is *risky*.

Once again, we are jolted by the enormous difference between knowing *about* Jesus and knowing him intimately enough to accompany him on his way. Jesus showed the full extent of his love to Peter the denier. Later, he would ask him three times, "Peter, do you love me?" Peter answered, "Lord, you know all things; you know that I love you" (John 21:15-19). Those who are known *by* Jesus know Jesus. Those who know Jesus follow his steps. It is a risky business. Peter himself would write to Christians enduring "all kinds of trials" (1 Peter 1:6), saying, "To this you were called, because Christ suffered for you, leaving you an example, that you should follow in his steps" (1 Peter 2:21).

Jesus' living parable in John 13 is so essential to a true knowledge of him that it is captured not only in the narrative of the upper room, it is also preserved for us in one of the earliest Christian hymns, as recorded in Philippians 2. Consider this parallel:

John 13:3a: "Jesus knew the Father had put all things under his power ..."	Philippians 2:6: "Who being in very nature God, [Jesus] did not consider equality with God something to be grasped ..."
John 13:4b: "... [Jesus] wrapped a towel around his waist."	Philippians 2:7: "[Jesus] made himself nothing, taking the very nature of a servant ..."
John 13:5b: "... [Jesus] began to wash his disciples' feet, drying them with the towel that was wrapped around him."	Philippians 2:7: "[Jesus] made himself nothing, taking the very nature of a servant ..."
John 13:12a: "[Jesus] put on his clothes and returned to his place." John 13:13: Jesus said, "You call me 'Teacher' and 'Lord,' and rightly so, for that is what I am."	Philippians 2:9–11: "... God exalted him to the highest place and gave him the name that is above every name, that at the name of Jesus every knee should bow ... and every tongue should confess that Jesus Christ is Lord ..."

Knowing Jesus means getting involved with him and his world, because he is involved with us in our world. Knowing Jesus means staying close to him as we follow where he is going, because he has already come near to us. Knowing Jesus means we cannot play it safe.

The need for risky involvement in God's world becomes all the more real to many of us as we face the aftermath of Hurricanes Katrina and Rita, which devastated the U.S. Gulf Coast recently. My brother, a Baptist pastor in New Orleans, was left with no income after the storms hit. This is not a time for me or any other person involved in his life to play it safe. Many others are in the same situation, so we must follow Jesus into risky involvement. We cannot stay at a distance if we are to be servants of our Master. Be it suffering from storms or from human injustices, Jesus' followers must get involved. It will be risky. It will be costly. But it is the only way to follow Jesus, because that is where he will be.

1. A slightly different version of this sermon was originally preached in Rayburn Chapel on the campus of Covenant Theological Seminary on September 13, 2005. The current version was published in *Covenant* 20, no. 4 (Winter 2005-6): 6–10.

2. Unless otherwise indicated, Bible verses quoted in this essay come from the New International Version (NIV).

3. D. A. Carson, *The Gospel According to John*, The Pillar New Testament Commentary Series (Grand Rapids, Mich.: Eerdmans, 1991), 465.

4. Dietrich Bonhoeffer, *Life Together*, trans. J. W. Dubertsein (London: SCM Press, 1954), 100.

APPENDICES

FACULTY BIBLIOGRAPHIES:
PROFESSORS CALHOUN, JONES, AND VASHOLZ

Compiled in Several Categories Using Inverse Chronological Order

STEPHEN G. JAMIESON
Reference and Systems Librarian, J. Oliver Buswell, Jr., Library

JAMES C. PAKALA
Director, J. Oliver Buswell, Jr., Library

DAVID B. CALHOUN

Thesis/Dissertation

"The Last Command: Princeton Theological Seminary and Missions (1812–1862)." Ph.D. diss., Princeton Theological Seminary, 1983.

"The Ceremonial Law in the Psalms." Th.M. thesis, Covenant Theological Seminary, 1963.

Books

The Splendor of Grace: The Independent Presbyterian Church of Savannah, Georgia, 1755–2005. Greenville, S.C.: A Press Printing, 2005.

Grace Abounding: The Life, Books, and Influence of John Bunyan. Fearn, Scotland: Christian Focus Publications, 2005.

Cloud of Witnesses: The Story of First Presbyterian Church Augusta, Georgia, 1804–2004. Augusta, Ga.: First Presbyterian Church, 2004.

Theology on Fire: Sermons from the Heart of J. A. Alexander. Birmingham, Ala.: Solid Ground Christian Books, 2004 (biographical sketch by Calhoun; sermons by Alexander).

A Place for Truth. Edited by Stephen R. Berry. James Henley Thornwell Lectures, February 4–5, 1995. Greenville, S.C.: Reformed Academic Press, 1996.

Princeton Seminary. 2 vols. Edinburgh; Carlisle, Pa.: Banner of Truth Trust, 1994–6.

The Glory of the Lord Risen Upon It: First Presbyterian Church, Columbia, South Carolina, 1795–1995. Columbia, S.C.: First Presbyterian Church, 1994.

Handbook for Church Growth. Coral Gables, Fla.: Ministries in Action, 1983 (with Terry L. Gyger and E. Walford Thompson).

Articles and Essays

"By His Grace, For His Glory: The Story of Covenant Theological Seminary." In *All for Jesus: A Celebration of the 50ᵗʰ Anniversary of Covenant Theological Seminary.* Fearn, Scotland: Mentor/Christian Focus Publications, 2006, Chapter 2.

Biblical and Theological Studies, by the Members of the Faculty of Princeton Theological Seminary, Published in Commemoration of the One Hundredth Anniversary of the Founding of the Seminary. New York: Charles Scribner's Sons, 1912. Reprinted with an introduction by David B. Calhoun. Birmingham, Ala.: Solid Ground Christian Books, 2003.

"Thornwell on Truth." *Presbyterion: Covenant Seminary Review* 28 (Fall 2002): 65–76.

"The Scots Confession of 1560." *Presbyterion: Covenant Seminary Review* 26 (Spring 2000): 3–12.

"Southern Presbyterian Review." *Presbyterion: Covenant Seminary Review* 24 (Fall 1998): 79–91.

"'His Bright Designs': The Doctrine of Providence." *Presbyterion: Covenant Seminary Review* 24 (Spring 1998): 3–8.

"Over the Rainbow: A Sermon Based on Revelation 4:1-3." *Presbyterion: Covenant Seminary Review* 20 (Fall 1994): 67–71.

"Climbing Rainbows: A Sermon Based on Genesis 9:8-16." *Presbyterion: Covenant Seminary Review* 20 (Spring 1994): 3–7.

"'What is the Name of That Place?'" *Presbyterion: Covenant Seminary Review* 18 (Spring 1992): 3–9.

"John Eliot: Apostle to the Indians." *Presbyterion: Covenant Seminary Review* 15 (Fall 1989): 35–8.

"David Brainerd: 'A Constant Stream.'" *Presbyterion: Covenant Seminary Review* 13 (Spring 1987): 44–50.

"Of Ships and Books: The Travel Journeys of the Early Princeton Seminary Foreign Missionaries." *Princeton Seminary Bulletin*, n.s., 8, no. 7 (1987): 34–8.

"Of Ships and Books: The Travel Journeys of the Early Princeton Seminary Foreign Missionaries." *Presbyterion: Covenant Seminary Review* 12 (Spring 1986): 33–7.

"John Calvin: Missionary Hero or Missionary Failure?" *Presbyterion: Covenant Seminary Review* 5 (Spring 1979): 16–33.

Audio-Visual

The Glory of the Lord Risen Upon It: First Presbyterian Church, Columbia, South Carolina 1795–1995. Columbia, S.C.: First Presbyterian Church, 1995 (with Bob Bailey, Steve Folks, and Elaine Cooper). Videocassette.

Job – Coming to Grips with Life the Way It Really Is. St. Louis: Covenant Theological Seminary, 1986. Set of 7 audiocassettes.

Reviews

The Reformation Theologians: An Introduction to Theology in the Early Modern Period, edited by Carter Lindberg. *Presbyterion: Covenant Seminary Review* 31 (Spring 2005): 60–2.

Biographical Dictionary of Evangelicals, edited by Timothy Larsen. *Presbyterion: Covenant Seminary Review* 30 (Fall 2004): 117–19.

The Dictionary of Historical Theology, edited by Trevor A. Hart. *Presbyterion: Covenant Seminary Review* 30 (Spring 2004): 57–8.

John Calvin: A Biography, by Bernard Cottret. *Presbyterion: Covenant Seminary Review* 27 (Spring 2001): 61–4.

A Golden Treasury of Puritan Devotion: Selections from the Writings of Thirteen Puritan Divines, edited by Mariano Di Gangi. *Presbyterion: Covenant Seminary Review* 26 (Fall 2000): 128.

The Legacy of Sovereign Joy: God's Triumphant Grace in the Lives of Augustine, Luther, and Calvin, by John Piper. *Presbyterion: Covenant Seminary Review* 26 (Fall 2000): 124–5.

Confessions and Catechisms of the Reformation, edited by Mark A. Noll. *Presbyterion: Covenant Seminary Review* 18 (Spring 1992): 69–70.

Luther the Reformer: The Story of the Man and His Career, by James M. Kittelson. *Presbyterion: Covenant Seminary Review* 18 (Spring 1992): 70.

Grace in Winter: Rutherford in Verse, by Faith Cook. *Presbyterion: Covenant Seminary Review* 16 (Fall 1990): 145–6.

Some Favourite Books, by John Macleod, and *My Life and Books: The Reminiscences of S. M. Houghton*, by S. M. Houghton. *Presbyterion: Covenant Seminary Review* 16 (Fall 1990): 139–41.

Teach Us to Pray: Prayer in the Bible and the World, edited by D. A. Carson. *Presbyterion: Covenant Seminary Review* 16 (Fall 1990): 135.

Princeton and the Republic, 1768–1822: The Search for a Christian Enlightenment in the Era of Samuel Stanhope Smith, by Mark A. Noll. *Journal of Church and State* 32 (Spring 1990): 418–20.

In Retrospect: Remembrance of Things Past, by F. F. Bruce. *Presbyterion: Covenant Seminary Review* 12 (Spring 1986): 58–62.

David C. Jones

Thesis/Dissertation

"The Doctrine of the Church in American Presbyterian Theology in the Mid-Nineteenth Century." Th.D. diss., Concordia Seminary, 1970.

"Eucharistic Sacrifice in Protestant Discussion in the Last Quarter Century." Th.M. thesis, Westminster Theological Seminary, 1963.

Books

Biblical Christian Ethics. Grand Rapids, Mich.: Baker Books, 1994.

Articles and Essays

"Christ-Centered Ethics." In *All for Jesus: A Celebration of the 50th Anniversary of Covenant Theological Seminary*. Fearn, Scotland: Mentor/Christian Focus Publications, 2006, Chapter 12.

"The Westminster Standards and the Structure of Christian Ethics." In *The Westminster Confession into the 21st Century*, edited by J. Ligon Duncan, III. Vol. 3. Fearn, Scotland: Mentor/Christian Focus Publications, forthcoming (volume one was published in 2003).

"The Posture of the Theological School." In *Aims and Purposes of Evangelical Theological Education*, ed. Paul Bassett. Grand Rapids, Mich.: Eerdmans, 2005.

"Birth Control," "Theology of Nature," "James Cone," "Mary Daly," "Elizabeth Schüssler Fiorenza." In *Evangelical Dictionary of Theology*, ed. Walter A. Elwell. 2nd ed. Grand Rapids, Mich.: Baker, 2001.

"Restless Hearts." *Covenant*, June–July 2001, 4–7.

"The Character Education Movement." *Presbyterion: Covenant Seminary Review* 26 (Fall 2000): 84–92.

"The Public Character of Theological Education: An Evangelical Perspective." *Theological Education* 37, no. 1 (Autumn 2000): 1–15 (with Jeffrey P. Greenman and Christine D. Pohl).

"Just Saying 'NO' Is Not Enough." *Christianity Today* 43, no. 11 (1999): 50–2, 54–5 (with Richard J. Mouw, Stephen Spencer, and Mary Stewart Van Leeuwen).

"The Holy Spirit and the Preaching of the Gospel." *Living Pulpit* 5, no. 1 (1996): 21.

"The Multiracial City." *Presbyterion: Covenant Seminary Review* 21 (Spring 1995): 67–72.

"Editor's Preface." *Presbyterion: Covenant Seminary Review* 18 (Fall 1992): 73–4.

"*The Only Way* of Bartolomé de Las Casas [edited by Helen Rand Parish and translated by Francis Patrick Sullivan]: A Review Article." *Presbyterion: Covenant Seminary Review* 18 (Fall 1992): 117–21.

"A Note on the LXX of Malachi 2:16." *Journal of Biblical Literature* 109 (Winter 1990): 683–5.

"The Westminster Confession on Divorce and Remarriage." *Presbyterion: Covenant Seminary Review* 16 (Spring 1990): 17–40.

"Malachi on Divorce." *Presbyterion: Covenant Seminary Review* 15 (Spring 1989): 16–22.

"Economics in Teleological Perspective." In *Biblical Principles and Economics: The Foundations*, ed. Richard C. Chewning. Colorado Springs, Co.: NavPress, 1989, 101–12.

[Heroic Measures in Medicine.] "Report of the Heroic Measures Committee, Presbyterian Church in America." In *PCA Digest, Part V, Position Papers, 1973–1993*, edited by Paul R. Gilchrist. Atlanta: Presbyterian Church in America, 1993, 378–89. This also may be found as Appendix S (pp. 509–15) in the Minutes of the 16th General Assembly of the PCA (1988). David Jones was a co-author of this report, although the authors' names do not appear with it.

"Christian Responsibility in the Nuclear Age." In *PCA Digest, Part V, Position Papers, 1973–1993*, edited by Paul R. Gilchrist. Atlanta: Presbyterian Church in America, 1993, 439–52. David Jones was the primary author. This also may be found as Appendix S (pp. 463–73) in the Minutes of the 14th General Assembly of the PCA (1986) and, owing to tabling by that

Assembly and adoption at the next, it also appears in the Minutes of the 15th General Assembly (1987) as Appendix U (pp. 517–28).

"Love: The Impelling Motive of the Christian Life." *Presbyterion: Covenant Seminary Review* 12 (Fall 1986): 65–92.

"Christian Responsibility in the Nuclear Age." In *Minutes of the Fourteenth General Assembly of the Presbyterian Church in America* (1986), 463–71. The 14th General Assembly met in Philadelphia.

"The Supreme Good." *Presbyterion: Covenant Seminary Review* 11 (Fall 1985): 124–41.

"*Diakonia.*" *Presbyterion: Covenant Seminary Review* 4 (Fall 1978): 90–4.

"Who Are the Poor?" *Evangelical Review of Theology* 2, no. 2 (October 1978): 215–35; including responses by James W. Skillen (pp. 227–9) and Harvie M. Conn (pp. 229–35). The article is the same as those cited immediately below, except that it uses Roman numerals for section numbers and lacks quotations of Isa. 3:13-15 and a few other texts. The Skillen and Conn responses are the same as those in the Reformed Ecumenical Council *Theological Forum* cited below, except that the Conn response lacks the opening paragraph that it has in *Theological Forum*. (That paragraph explains why Conn actually is not responding to David Jones, but is offering a reaction to the world Reformed community's "hidden theological curriculum.")

"Who Are the Poor?" Reformed Ecumenical Synod *Theological Forum* 6, no. 1 (February 1978): 1–24; including responses by Andrew Kuyvenhoven (pp. 12–13), Robert Recker (pp. 14–16), James W. Skillen (pp. 17–18), Harvie M. Conn (pp. 19–23), and a reply to these four by the author (p. 24). The article itself is the same as that cited immediately below.

"Who Are the Poor?" *Presbyterion: Covenant Seminary Review* 3 (Fall 1977): 62–72.

"The Gift of Prophecy Today." *Presbyterian Guardian* 43 (December 1974): 163–4.

"Machen's Ecclesiology." *Presbyterian Guardian* 32 (October 1963): 134–42.

"Abortion: The Disruption of Continuity." In *Documents of Synod: Study Papers and Actions of the Reformed Presbyterian Church, Evangelical Synod – 1965–1982*, edited by Paul R. Gilchrist. Lookout Mountain, Tenn.: Reformed Presbyterian Church, Evangelical Synod, 1982, 7–17. The report also may be found in the Minutes of the denomination's General Synod for 1975 (pp. 98–108). Co-authors were Claude DePrine, Mark Pett (chair, Study Committee on Abortion), Fredric Sloan, and Wilber Wallis.

[Divorce and Remarriage.] "Report of a Study Committee on Divorce and Remarriage" in 1973, continued and completed in 1974, contained in the 151st and 152nd (RPCES) General Synod Minutes. In *Documents of Synod: Study Papers and Actions of the Reformed Presbyterian Church, Evangelical Synod – 1965–1982*, edited by Paul R. Gilchrist. Lookout Mountain, Tenn.: Reformed Presbyterian Church, Evangelical Synod, 1982, 199–204. David Jones was the primary author. The report also may be found in the Minutes for the denomination's 1973 General Synod (pp. 52–56, 138) and 1974 (pp. 135–38).

Audio-Visual

Responding as Christians to the Global Crisis: Faculty/Pastor Panel Discussion on the Situation in Iraq. St. Louis: Covenant Theological Seminary, 2003 (with Hans Bayer, Stephen Estock, Nelson Jennings, and Donald Guthrie [moderator]). Compact Disk.

"Gender and Faith in Philipi [sic]" and "The Social and Cultural Calling of Women"; and "Q & A" (with Nancy Pearcey). In *Gender and Faith: An Examination of Women's Roles in Society*, discs 1–3. Francis A. Schaeffer Lecture Series, Spring 2001. St. Louis: Covenant Theological Seminary, [2001]. Compact Disk.

"Historical Roots of Racial Alienation." In *Racial Reconciliation*, volume [tape] 5. Francis A. Schaeffer Lecture Series, Spring 1997. St. Louis: Covenant Seminary Media Ministries, 1997. Audiocassette.

What Did Jesus Really Say?: A Forum on the Historical Jesus. Francis A. Schaeffer Lecture Series, Spring 1994. St. Louis: Francis Schaeffer Institute, Covenant Theological Seminary, 1994 (with Stephen J. Patterson, Jay Harrington, Robert Yarbrough and Jeffrey A. Gibbs). Audiocassette.

The Kingdom and the Church: The Biblical Basis for Christian Social Ethics. Summer Institute on Urban Ministries, 1976. St. Louis: Covenant Theological Seminary, 1976. Audiocassette.

Reviews

By the Renewing of Your Minds: The Pastoral Function of Christian Doctrine, by Ellen T. Charry. *Presbyterion: Covenant Seminary Review* 23 (Fall 1997): 120–2.

Not the Way It's Supposed to Be: a Breviary of Sin, by Cornelius Plantinga, Jr. *Presbyterion: Covenant Seminary Review* 23 (Fall 1997): 116–17.

The Hastening That Waits: Karl Barth's Ethics, by Nigel Biggar. *Westminster Theological Journal* 57 (Spring 1995): 270–2.

[Fall 1992 *Presbyterion* review article treating *The Only Way*, by Bartolomé de Las Casas, edited by Helen Rand Parish and translated by Francis Patrick Sullivan, is cited above under Articles.]

Theonomy: A Reformed Critique, edited by William S. Barker and W. Robert Godfrey. *Presbyterion: Covenant Seminary Review* 16 (Spring 1990): 68–9.

Ethical Writings, by Jonathan Edwards. The Works of Jonathan Edwards, vol. 8, edited by Paul Ramsey. *Presbyterion: Covenant Seminary Review* 16 (Spring 1990): 69–70.

The Westminster Dictionary of Christian Ethics, edited by James F. Childress and John Macquarrie. *Presbyterion: Covenant Seminary Review* 15 (Spring 1989): 58–9.

Evangelical Dictionary of Theology, edited by Walter A. Elwell. *Presbyterion: Covenant Seminary Review* 13 (Spring 1987): 51–5.

Dictionary of Latin and Greek Theological Terms: Drawn Principally from Protestant Scholastic Theology, by Richard A. Muller. *Presbyterion: Covenant Seminary Review* 12 (Spring 1986): 62–3.

The Bible in the Modern World, by James Barr. *Westminster Theological Journal* 38 (Winter 1976): 276–9.

Baker's Dictionary of Christian Ethics, edited by Carl F. H. Henry. *Presbyterion: Covenant Seminary Review* 1 (Spring 1975): 57–58.

Toward a Theology for the Future, edited by David F. Wells and Clark H. Pinnock. *Westminster Theological Journal* 35 (Winter 1973): 243–45.

A Framework for Faith: Lundensian Theological Methodology in the Thought of Ragner Bring, by Thor Hall. *Westminster Theological Journal* 34 (November 1971): 102–3.

Robert I. Vasholz

Thesis/Dissertation

"Philological Comparison of the Qumran Job Targum and Its Implications for the Dating of Daniel." D.Th. diss., University of Stellenbosch, 1976.

"The Quotations and Allusions to the Pentateuch within the Old Testament." Th.M. thesis, Covenant Theological Seminary, 1967.

Books

Leviticus [commentary]. Fearn, Scotland: Mentor/Christian Focus Publications, forthcoming (projected for release in the second half of 2006).

Pillars of the Kingdom: Five Features of the Kingdom of God Progressively Revealed in the Old Testament. Lanham, Md.: University Press of America, 1997.

The Old Testament Canon in the Old Testament Church: The Internal Rationale for Old Testament Canonicity. Lewiston, N.Y.: E. Mellen Press, 1990.

Data for the Sigla of the BHS. Winona Lake, Ind: Eisenbrauns, 1983.

Hebrew Exercises: A Programmed Approach. Grand Rapids, Mich.: Baker Book House, 1981.

Articles and Essays

"'But Where Sin Abounded, Grace Did Much More Abound': Lessons From the Book of Genesis." In *All for Jesus: A Celebration of the 50th Anniversary of Covenant Theological Seminary.* Fearn, Scotland: Mentor/Christian Focus Publications, 2006, Chapter 5.

"The Character of Israel's Future in Light of the Abrahamic and Mosaic Covenants." *Trinity Journal*, n.s., 25 (Spring 2004): 39–59.

"Transmission of Biblical Texts in Qumran: The Case of the Large Isaiah Scroll 1QIsa[a]." *Journal of Biblical Literature* 121 (Fall 2002): 556–9.

"Genesis 9:19–25." *Presbyterion: Covenant Seminary Review* 26 (Spring 2000): 32–3.

"Scribes and Schools: the Canonization of the Hebrew Scriptures." *Journal of the Evangelical Theological Society* 42 (December 1999): 701–4.

"A Note on Ezra 10:34." *Presbyterion: Covenant Seminary Review* 25 (Spring 1999): 54.

"'He (?) Will Rule Over You': A Thought on Genesis 3:16." *Presbyterion: Covenant Seminary Review* 20 (Spring 1994): 51–2.

"Israel's Cities of Refuge." *Presbyterion: Covenant Seminary Review* 19 (Fall 1993): 116–18.

"Gomer – Chaste or Not? A Philological Note." *Presbyterion: Covenant Seminary Review* 19 (Spring 1993): 48–9.

"Military Censuses in Numbers." *Presbyterion: Covenant Seminary Review* 18 (Fall 1992): 122–5.

"Habakkuk: Complaints or Complaint?" *Presbyterion: Covenant Seminary Review* 18 (Spring 1992): 50–2.

"A Legal 'Brief' on Deuteronomy 23:15–16." *Presbyterion: Covenant Seminary Review* 17 (Fall 1991): 127.

"A Legal 'Brief' on Deuteronomy 22:13–21." *Presbyterion: Covenant Seminary Review* 17 (Spring 1991): 62.

"Sarcasm in Malachi 1:8a." *Presbyterion: Covenant Seminary Review* 16 (Fall 1990): 129–30.

"A Legal 'Brief' on Deuteronomy 13:16–17." *Presbyterion: Covenant Seminary Review* 16 (Fall 1990): 128–9.

"Isaiah and Ahaz: A Brief History of Crisis in Isaiah 7 and 8." *Presbyterion: Covenant Seminary Review* 13 (Fall 1987): 79–84.

"You Shall Not Covet Your Neighbor's Wife." *Westminster Theological Journal* 49 (Fall 1987): 397–403.

"Amusements on the Sabbath: A Puritan Response." *Presbyterion: Covenant Seminary Review* 13 (Spring 1987): 24–8.

"Is the New Testament Anti-Semitic?" *Presbyterion: Covenant Seminary Review* 11 (Fall 1985): 118–23.

"An Additional Note on the 4QEnoch Fragments and 11QtgJob." *Maarav* 3 (January 1982): 115–18.

"4Q Targum Job versus 11Q Targum Job." *Revue de Qumran* 11, no. 1 (1982): 109.

"Isaiah versus 'the Gods': A Case for Unity." *Westminster Theological Journal* 42 (Spring 1980): 389–94.

"A Further Note on the Problem of Nasalization in Biblical Aramaic, II Q Tg Job, and I Q Genesis Apocryphon." *Revue de Qumran* 10, no. 1 (1979): 95–6.

"Two Notes on II Q Tg Job and Biblical Aramaic: Masculine Emphatic *he*; Verbs tertiae infirmae." *Revue de Qumran* 10, no. 1 (1979): 93–4.

"Qumran and the Dating of Daniel." *Journal of the Evangelical Theological Society* 21 (December 1978): 315–21.

Reviews

From Exegesis to Exposition: A Practical Guide to Using Biblical Hebrew, by Robert B. Chisholm, Jr. *Presbyterion: Covenant Seminary Review* 25 (Fall 1999): 121–2.

Textual Criticism of the Hebrew Bible, by Emanuel Tov. *Presbyterion: Covenant Seminary Review* 20 (Spring 1994): 53–7.

The Origins of Biblical Law: The Decalogues and the Book of the Covenant, by Calum M. Carmichael. *Presbyterion: Covenant Seminary Review* 19 (Fall 1993): 120–3.

Variable Spellings of the Hebrew Bible, by James Barr. *Presbyterion: Covenant Seminary Review* 17 (Spring 1991): 71–2.

The Progress of Redemption: The Story of Salvation from Creation to New Jerusalem, by Willem VanGemeren. *Presbyterion: Covenant Seminary Review* 17 (Spring 1991): 75.

From Plight to Solution: A Jewish Framework for Understanding Paul's View of the Law in Galatians and Romans, by Frank Thielman. *Presbyterion: Covenant Seminary Review* 16 (Fall 1990): 133–4.

Theodore of Mopsuestia on the Bible: A Study of His Old Testament Exegesis, by Dimitri Z. Zaharopoulos. *Presbyterion: Covenant Seminary Review* 16 (Fall 1990): 143–4.

Israel's Apostasy and Restoration: Essays in Honor of Roland K. Harrison, edited by Avraham Gileadi. *Presbyterion: Covenant Seminary Review* 16 (Spring 1990): 66–7.

Isaiah, the Eighth Century Prophet: His Times and His Preaching, by John Hayes and Stuart A. Irvine. *Presbyterion: Covenant Seminary Review* 16 (Spring 1990): 67.

The Jew and the Christian Missionary: A Jewish Response to Missionary Christianity, by Gerald Sigal. *Presbyterion: Covenant Seminary Review* 11 (Fall 1985): 142–6.

Appendix B

Succession of Presidents, Faculty, and Trustees
Covenant Theological Seminary
1956–2005

Wayne Sparkman
Director, PCA Historical Center

Presidents

Robert G. Rayburn, 1956–1977
William S. Barker II, 1977–1985
Paul D. Kooistra, 1985–1994
Bryan S. Chapell, 1994–

Faculty
(by date of election)

Rayburn, Robert G., 1956–1990
Buswell, J. Oliver, Jr., 1956–1970
Harris, R. Laird, 1956–1981
Sanderson, John W., Jr., 1956–1957; 1963–1964; 1976–1984
Smick, Elmer, 1956–1971
Wallis, Wilbur B., 1956–1982
Buswell, John W., 1963–1974
Mare, W. Harold, 1963–1994
Jones David C., 1967–
Killen, R. Allen, 1967–1968
Webber, Robert E., 1967–1968
Reymond, Robert L, 1969–1990
Hall, Joseph H., 1970–1989

Knight, George W., III, 1970–1989
Lyra, Synesio, 1971–1976
Barker, William S., II, 1972–1985
Long, V. Philips, 1985–2000
Chapell, Bryan S., 1986–
Douglass, Philip D., 1987–
Barrs, Jerram, 1988–
Peterson, Robert A., 1990–
Doriani, Daniel M., 1991–2003
Yarbrough, Robert W., 1991–1996
Winter, Richard, 1992–
Collins, C. John, 1993–
Bayer, Hans F., 1994–
Zink, Daniel W., 1995–
Williams, Michael D., 1996–
Guthrie, Donald C., 1998–
Jennings, J. Nelson, 1999–
Chapman, David W., 2001–
Eswine, Zachary W., 2001–
Sklar, Jay, 2002–
Perry, Gregory, 2005–
Lucas, Sean Michael, 2005–
Dalbey, Mark, 2005–
Bradley, Anthony, 2005–

FACULTY
(BY ALPHABETICAL ORDER)

Barker, William S., II, 1972–1985
Barrs, Jerram, 1988–
Bayer, Hans F., 1994–
Bradley, Anthony, 2005–
Buswell, J. Oliver, Jr, 1956–1970
Buswell, John W., 1963–1974
Calhoun, David B., 1978–
Chapell, Bryan S., 1986–
Chapman, David W., 2001–
Collins, C. John, 1993–
Dalbey, Mark, 2005–
Doriani, Daniel M., 1991–2003
Douglass, Philip D., 1987–
Eswine, Zachary W., 2001–
Guthrie, Donald C., 1998–
Hall, Joseph H., 1970–1989

Harris, R. Laird, 1956–1981
Jennings, J. Nelson, 1999–
Jones David C., 1967–
Killen, R. Allen, 1967–1968
Kirwan, William T., 1974–1979
Knight, George W., III, 1970–1989
Long, V. Philips, 1985–2000
Lucas, Sean Michael, 2005–
Lyra, Synesio, 1971–1976
Mare, W. Harold, 1963–1994
Palmer, P. Robert, 1979–1985
Payne, J. Barton, 1972–1979
Perry, Gregory, 2005–
Peterson, Robert A., 1990–
Rayburn, Robert G., 1956–1990
Reymond, Robert L, 1969–1990
Robertson, O. Palmer, 1980–1985
Sanderson, John W., Jr., 1956–1957; 1963–1964; 1976–1984
Sklar, Jay, 2002–
Smick, Elmer, 1956–1971
Soltau, Addison P., 1977–1989
Vasholz, Robert I., 1975–
Wallis, Wilbur B., 1956–1982
Webber, Robert E., 1967–1968
Williams, Michael D., 1996–
Winter, Richard, 1992–
Yarbrough, Robert W., 1991–1996
Zink, Daniel W., 1995–

TRUSTEES
(BY DATE OF FIRST ELECTION)

Anderson, Kenneth O., 1956–1959
Belz, Max V., 1956–1973
Dillard, E. Archer, 1956–1958
Edwards, Presley, 1956–1971
Gebb, Linwood G., 1956–1962
Jackson, Otis, 1956–1957
Johnson, Hugh, 1956–1957; 1966–1975
Juliusson, Oliver, 1956–1965
Krauss, John, 1956–1959
Lewis, Ralph, 1956–1957
MacNair, Donald J., 1956–1962; 1966–1974
Malkus, Nelson, 1956–1963

Mare, W. Harold, 1956–1963
Noé, Edward T., 1956–1974
Oakley, C. Howard, 1956–1957
Rayburn, Robert G., 1956–1965
Scott, McGregor, 1956–1964
Shepperson, Flournoy, 1956–1961
Soltau, T. Stanley, 1956–1972
Storey, George B., 1956–1964
Thurman, Kyle, 1956–1963
Veon, Ralph, 1956–1961
Williams, G. W., 1956–1961
Barnes, Marion, 1958–1978
Helms, J. L., 1958–1961
Rigdon, Clyde, 1958–1959
Chapman, Floyd, 1961–1963
Harrah, Robert, 1961–1963
Ivery, Cliff, 1961–1962
Leonard, William B., Jr., 1961–1964; 1967–1982
LeRoy, Walter H., 1961–1964; 1966–1971
Sloan, Fredric J., 1961–1964; 1973
Smith, Hugh, 1961–1965
Clifton, Fred, 1962–1964
Franks, E. Newell, 1962–1964
Hoogstrate, John P., 1962–1964
Kennedy, Nelson M., 1962–1968
Pierce, Vernon, 1962–1968; 1986–1993
Sidebotham, Thomas E., 1962–1964
Soltau, George, 1962–1964; 1967–1970
Van Kley, Harold, 1962–1984
Linder, George, 1963–1971
Smick, Frank, 1963–1965
Tilton, Richard, 1963–1965
Cross, Thomas G., 1965–1967
Finch, Harold, 1965–1967
MacGregor, John M., 1965–1967
Steele, Francis Rue, 1965–1967; 1979–1982
Alexander, Paul H., 1966–1982; 1994–1999
Freeland, Martin C., 1966–1968
Holliday, Charles B., Jr., 1966–1971; 1975–1991
Lanz, Jack, 1966–1967
Osborn, Robert R., 1966–1968
Palmer, P. Robert, 1966–1968
Stoll, Arthur C., 1966–1989; 1991–2003

Moore, T. M., 1981
Pett, Mark E., 1981–1985
Thompson, William P., 1981–1986
Wulf, Richard, 1981–1984
Robeson, Edward J., 1982–1983
Stortz, Rodney D., 1982–1991
Troup, W. Lee, 1982–1983; 1985–1988
Burrows, Robert P., III, 1983–1994
Combs, William (Bill), 1983–1990
Fiol, J. Robert, 1983–1986; 1989–1992
Neill, Robert, 1983–1984
Buswell, John W., 1984–1987
Hatch, James D., 1984–1991; 1994
Reeves, John K., 1984; 1987–1990
Struck, Robert F., 1985–1988
Taylor, Robert N., 1985–1986
Tyson, Richard W., 1985–1992
Grauley, John E., 1986–1989
Hollender, Herbert A., 1986–1989
Huisingh, Will, 1986–1989
Prentis, John, 1987–1989
Robertson, John W., 1988–1991
Barton, Whaley, 1989–1995
Caines, J. Render, 1989–1992
Carraher, Charles E., 1989–1992
Harris, Edward S., 1989–1996; 1998–
Hezlep, Robert B., Jr., 1989–1992
Knox, Allen L., Jr., 1989–1996
Mawhinney, Allen, 1989–1992
Spink, William Jr., 1989–1996; 2001–
Van Gilst, Mark, 1989–1992
Wright, John C., 1989–1992
Hay, William G., 1990–1997
Malone, Michael N., 1990–1993
Reed, John J. (Jack), 1990–1998; 2000–2003
Reynolds, James, 1990–1993
Alexander, David, 1991–1994
Armerding, Hudson T., 1991–1998
Bartholomew, G. Samuel, 1992–1995
Bostrom, Steven, 1992
Green, Charles, 1992
Schmidt, Rudolph F., 1992–1999; 2001–
Maddox, S. Fleetwood, 1993–2000; 2002–

Marcey, Michael R., 1993–2000
Dunton, Ronald W., 1994–1995
Herring, Wayne G., 1994–1997
Kitchen, Bruce G., Jr., 1994–2001
Ensio, Mark, 1995–
Turner, Walter, 1995–
Wood, John, 1995–1998
De Heer, Larry, 1996–1999
Dermeyer, Dan, 1996–2003
Novenson, Joseph, 1996–
Singleton, Robert, 1996–2003
Albritton, John N., 1997–2000
Hamby, Robert E., 1997–2004
Kramer, Jack, 1997–2004
Silman, H. Andrew, 1997–2004
Campbell, Michael A., 1998–
Doty, Stephen, 1998–
Flayhart, Robert K., 1999–
French, William B, 1999–
Sinclair, David, 1999–
Stephenson, Craig, 1999 –
Breeding, Bruce, 2000–
Furuto, Donald, 2000–
Rogers, Michael, 2000–2001
McNalley, Ron, 2002–
Suh, Jung Kon, 2002 –
Hansen, Carlo, 2003–
Parsons, C. Scott, 2004
Wood, John Halsey, 2004–
Hayward, Robert B., 2005–
Ortlund, Raymond, C., Jr., 2005–
Owens, Jean, 2005–
Wicks, Frank, 2005–

TRUSTEES
(BY ALPHABETICAL ORDER)

Albritton, John N., 1997–2000
Alexander, David, 1991–1994
Alexander, Paul H., 1966–1982; 1994–1999
Anderson, Charles W., 1974–1982
Anderson, Kenneth O., 1956–1959
Armerding, Hudson T., 1991–1998
Baldwin, Allan M., 1967–1987

Barnes, Marion, 1958–1978
Bartholomew, G. Samuel, 1992–1995
Barton, Whaley, 1989–1995
Belz, Max V., 1956–1973
Bostrom, Steven, 1992
Brake, Robert, 1975–1980
Breeding, Bruce, 2000–
Breeding, Clark, 1974–1994
Brown, Robert B., 1967–1969
Burrows, Robert P., III, 1983–1994
Buswell, John W., 1984–1987
Caines, J. Render, 1989–1992
Caldwell, P., 1967–1969
Campbell, Michael A., 1998–
Cannon, R. Daniel, 1967
Carraher, Charles E., 1989–1992
Chapman, Floyd, 1961–1963
Clark, Robert, 1968–1970
Clifton, Fred, 1962–1964
Collins, Norman S., 1967–1968
Combs, William (Bill), 1983–1990
Crews, Herbert, 1980
Cross, Thomas G., 1965–1967
De Heer, Larry, 1996–1999
Dermeyer, Dan, 1996–2003
Detlor, W. Lyall, 1968–1970
Dillard, E. Archer, 1956–1958
Donaldson, L. LaVerne, 1968–1971
Doty, Stephen, 1998–
Dunton, Ronald W., 1994–1995
Edwards, Presley, 1956–1971
Ellingsworth, Richard P. 1972–1983; 1985–1993; 1995–
Ensio, Mark, 1995–
Finch, Harold, 1965–1967
Fiol, J. Robert, 1983–1986; 1989–1992
Flayhart, Robert K., 1999–
Franks, E. Newell, 1962–1964
Freeland, Martin C., 1966–1968
French, William B, 1999–
Furuto, Donald, 2000–
Gebb, Linwood G., 1956–1962
Gorab, Edward A., 1973–1978
Grauley, John E., 1986–1989

Green, Charles, 1992
Hamby, Robert E., 1997–2004
Hansen, Carlo, 2003–
Harrah, Robert, 1961–1963
Harris, Edward S., 1989–1996; 1998–
Hatch, James D., 1984–1991; 1994
Hay, William G., 1990–1997
Hayward, Robert B., 2005–
Helms, J. L., 1958–1961
Herring, Wayne G., 1994–1997
Hezlep, Robert B., Jr., 1989–1992
Hollender, Herbert A., 1986–1989
Holliday, Charles B., Jr., 1966–1971; 1975–1991
Hoogstrate, John P., 1962–1964
Huisingh, Will, 1986–1989
Ivery, Cliff, 1961–1962
Jackson, Otis, 1956–1957
Johnson, Hugh, 1956–1957; 1966–1975
Jones, G. Paul, Jr., 1981–1992
Jones, Thomas F., 1967–1974
Juliusson, Oliver, 1956–1965
Kaufman, J., 1968–1970
Kennedy, Nelson M., 1962–1968
Kitchen, Bruce G., Jr., 1994–2001
Knox, Allen L., Jr., 1989–1996
Kramer, Jack, 1997–2004
Krauss, John, 1956–1959
Lanz, Jack, 1966–1967
Leonard, William B., Jr., 1961–1964; 1967–1982
LeRoy, Walter H., 1961–1964; 1966–1971
Lewis, John B., 1976–1985
Lewis, Ralph, 1956–1957
Linder, George, 1963–1971
Long, John C. (Jack), 1968–1972
MacGregor, John M., 1965–1967
MacNair, Donald J., 1956–1962; 1966–1974
Maddox, S. Fleetwood, 1993–2000; 2002–
Malkus, Nelson, 1956–1963
Malone, Michael N., 1990–1993
Marcey, Michael R., 1993–2000
Mare, W. Harold, 1956–1963
Martin, J. Robert, 1972–1979
Martin, Theodore W., 1969–1971

Mawhinney, Allen, 1989–1992
McColley, William D., 1970–1972
McDowell, H. Fletcher, 1971–1973
McNalley, Ron, 2002–
Miladin, George, 1972–1977
Moore, Lanny W., Sr., 1973–1986; 1992–2004
Moore, T. M., 1981
Morrison, Robert E., 1979–1989; 1991–1994
Neill, Robert, 1983–1984
Noé, Edward T., 1956–1974
Novenson, Joseph, 1996–
O'Rourke, William, 1975–1980
Oakley, C. Howard, 1956–1957
Orders, James B., Jr., 1971–1982; 1984–1988; 1990–1996
Ortlund, Raymond, C., Jr., 2005–
Osborn, Robert R., 1966–1968
Owens, Jean, 2005–
Palmer, P. Robert, 1966–1968
Parsons, C. Scott, 2004
Peace, Fred, 1970–1975
Pett, Mark E., 1981–1985
Pierce, Vernon, 1962–1968; 1986–1993
Prentis, John, 1987–1989
Ragsdale, William, 1972–1977
Rayburn, Robert G., 1956–1965
Reed, Gordon, 1977–1980
Reed, John J. (Jack), 1990–1998; 2000–2003
Reeves, John K., 1984; 1987–1990
Reynolds, James, 1990–1993
Rigdon, Clyde, 1958–1959
Roberts, Linleigh J., 1971–1972
Robertson, John W., 1988–1991
Robeson, Edward J., 1982–1983
Rogers, Michael, 2000–2001
Russell, Larry D., 1980–1982
Schmidt, Rudolph F., 1992–1999; 2001–
Scott, McGregor , 1956–1964
Shepperson, Flournoy, 1956–1961
Sherow, Donald Carl, 1979–1985
Sidebotham, Thomas E., 1962–1964
Silman, H. Andrew, 1997–2004
Simpson, Raese, 1974–1979
Sinclair, David, 1999–

Singleton, Robert, 1996–2003
Sloan, Fredric J., 1961–1964; 1973
Smallman, Stephen E., 1972–1983; 1988–1995
Smick, Frank, 1963–1965
Smith, Hugh, 1961–1965
Smith, Ted, 1973–1978
Soltau, George, 1962–1964; 1967–1970
Soltau, T. Stanley, 1956–1972
Spencer, John E., 1978–1991; 1993–2005
Spink, William Jr., 1989–1996; 2001–
Steele, Edward A., III, 1971–1976
Steele, Francis Rue, 1965–1967; 1979–1982
Stephens, John P., 1980–1982
Stephenson, Craig, 1999 –
Stoll, Arthur C., 1966–1989; 1991–2004
Storey, George B., 1956–1964
Stortz, Rodney D., 1982–1991
Stout, H. Stober, 1978–1980
Struck, Robert F., 1985–1988
Suh, Jung Kon, 2002 –
Taylor, Robert N., 1985–1986
Thompson, William P., 1981–1986
Thurman, Kyle, 1956–1963
Tilton, Richard, 1963–1965
Troup, W. Lee, 1982–1983; 1985–1988
Turner, Walter, 1995–
Tyson, Richard W., 1985–1992
Van Gilst, Mark, 1989–1992
Van Horn, Leonard, 1966–1968
Van Kley, Harold, 1962–1984
Veon, Ralph, 1956–1961
Wicks, Frank, 2005–
Wilkins, James R., Jr., 1976–1985
Williams, G. W., 1956–1961
Wood, John, 1995–1998
Wood, John Halsey, 2004–
Wright, John C., 1989–1992
Wulf, Richard, 1981–1984

SUBJECT/PERSONS INDEX

THE
PRACTICAL
CALVINIST

An introduction to the Presbyterian
and Reformed Heritage

In Honor of
D. Clair Davis'
Thirty Years at Westminster Theological Seminary

Contributors include:
• Sinclair B Ferguson • Robert Godfrey •
Edmund Clowney • Richard Gaffin
• William Barker •

Word to the World

The collected writings of William Barker

The modern church is suffering from crises in identity, belief and involvement with the State. As you read this collection of the works of William Barker you will find that they are all connected.

The reason why the church has problems interacting with government is because it doesn't understand its mission, history and authority. Barker, an internationally respected Professor of Church History, shows what the church should look for in creating proper relationships with governments, other faiths and society in general. He also explains how we should deal with divisions inside the church and what role the Bible should play in defining its faith.

"The publication of Word to the World *is a cause for rejoicing. The book is marked by both variety and constancy. ...Running through all this variety, though, are certain constants: good writing; a combination of forthrightness and fairness; prudence and much wise counsel; a reverent, even worshipful, tone; and above all, the fruitfulness of a mind and heart devoted to the Bible."*

Robert A. Peterson, Professor of Systematic Theology, Covenant Theological Seminary, St Louis, Missouri

"Ambassadorial, wise, kind, careful and brilliant, ...Dr. Barker is a first-rate church historian... His generous spirit, powerful mind and pastoral heart are productive of theological discourse that is a model, in both tone and content, for reformed ministers and scholars as we engage with a hostile postmodern culture."

J. Ligon Duncan III, President, Alliance of Confessing Evangelicals

William S. Barker was until his retirement Professor of Church History at Westminster Theological Seminary (Philadelphia). He remains Adjunct Professor of Church History at Covenant Theological Seminary, St Louis, Missouri.

ISBN 1-84550-050-4

Christian Focus Publications

publishes books for all ages

Our mission statement –

STAYING FAITHFUL

In dependence upon God we seek to help make His infallible Word, the Bible, relevant. Our aim is to ensure that the Lord Jesus Christ is presented as the only hope to obtain forgiveness of sin, live a useful life and look forward to heaven with Him.

REACHING OUT

Christ's last command requires us to reach out to our world with His gospel. We seek to help fulfill that by publishing books that point people towards Jesus and help them develop a Christ-like maturity. We aim to equip all levels of readers for life, work, ministry and mission.

Books in our adult range are published in three imprints.

Christian Focus contains popular works including biographies, commentaries, basic doctrine and Christian living. Our children's books are also published in this imprint.

Mentor focuses on books written at a level suitable for Bible College and seminary students, pastors, and other serious readers. The imprint includes commentaries, doctrinal studies, examination of current issues and church history.

Christian Heritage contains classic writings from the past.

Christian Focus Publications, Ltd
Geanies House, Fearn,
Ross-shire, IV20 1TW, Scotland, United Kingdom
info@christianfocus.com

For details of our titles visit us on our website
www.christianfocus.com